Coping with Stress

In a Changing World

Fourth Edition

Coping with Stress

In a Changing World

Richard Blonna, Ed.D., C.H.E.S.
William Paterson University
www.healthystressdoctor.com

Boston Burr Ridge, IL Dubuque, IA Madison, WI New York San Francisco St. Louis
Bangkok Bogotá Caracas Kuala Lumpur Lisbon London Madrid Mexico City
Milan Montreal New Delhi Santiago Seoul Singapore Sydney Taipei Toronto

Higher Education

COPING WITH STRESS IN A CHANGING WORLD

Published by McGraw-Hill, a business unit of The McGraw-Hill Companies, Inc., 1221 Avenue of the Americas, New York, NY, 10020.

Some ancillaries, including electronic and print components, may not be available to customers outside the United States.

This book is printed on acid-free paper.

1 2 3 4 5 6 7 8 9 0 QPD/QPD 0 9 8 7 6

ISBN-13: 978-0-07-302660-2
ISBN-10: 0-07-302660-3

Vice President and Editor-in-Chief: *Emily Barrosse*
Publisher: *William Glass*
Senior Sponsoring Editor: *Christopher C. Johnson*
Director of Development: *Kathleen Engelberg*
Developmental Editor: *Ann Kirby-Payne*
Developmental Editor for Technology: *Julia D. Ersery*
Executive Marketing Manager: *Pamela S. Cooper*
Managing Editor: *Jean Dal Porto*
Senior Project Manager: *Catherine R. Iammartino*
Art Director: *Jeanne Schreiber*
Designer: *Marianna Kinigakis*
Photo Research Coordinator: *Natalia C. Peschiera*
Senior Production Supervisor: *Carol A. Bielski*
Composition: *10/12 Times Roman, by Interactive Composition Corporation*
Printing: *45# Scholarly Matte Plus Recycled, Quebecor World*

Credits: The credits section for this book begins on page 400 and is considered an extension of the copyright page.

Library of Congress Cataloging-in-Publication Data

Blonna, Richard.
Coping with stress in a changing world / Richard Blonna. — 4th ed.
p. cm.
Includes bibliographical references and index.
ISBN-13: 978-0-07-302660-2 (softcover : alk. paper)
ISBN-10: 0-07-302660-3 (softcover : alk. paper)
1. Stress (Psychology) 2. Stress management. I. Title.
BF575.S75B57 2007
155.9'042—dc22

2006017456

The Internet addresses listed in the text were accurate at the time of publication. The inclusion of a Web site does not indicate an endorsement by the authors or McGraw-Hill, and McGraw-Hill does not guarantee the accuracy of the information presented at these sites.

www.mhhe.com

DEDICATION

This edition of *Coping with Stress in a Changing World* is dedicated to Gregg Krech, Linda Anderson Krech, and Trudy Boyle, my teachers and mentors at the ToDo Institute in Vermont. Their hard work, compassion, and understanding have introduced Naikan and Morita therapies to thousands of teachers and helpers across North America.

Contents in Brief

CONTENTS

Preface

As a stress management instructor, you are well aware of the myriad potential stressors that students face on a daily basis. As a Certified Health Education Specialist (CHES) who has been teaching stress management in the classroom and online for more than twenty years, I have written this book with both the instructor and the student in mind. *Coping with Stress in a Changing World* is designed to help students learn to cope with stress and transform potential stressors into personal challenges that will invigorate their days and enrich their lives. The book draws on real-world examples and solutions to provide a solid understanding of stress along with practical tips for managing it.

Highlights of the Fourth Edition

Like previous editions, the fourth edition of *Coping with Stress in a Changing World* empowers students to take control of their lives by recognizing stressors and implementing strategies to deal with them. The organization, flow, and pedagogical aids are designed to allow the instructor to present the material easily and in a manner that appeals to students.

This fourth edition has been thoroughly revised and reorganized. New data and examples have been added throughout, and the organization has been fine-tuned to take students even more logically through each step in identifying and dealing with potential stressors. The goal for these organizational changes is to allow students to approach new material in a simple, logical manner, while at the same time offering opportunities to integrate material across chapters to build a comprehensive, multilevel stress management plan.

A Strong Theoretical Framework

Coping with Stress in a Changing World melds together two primary models—Lazarus's Stress Appraisal and Coping Model and the National Wellness Institute's Wellness Model—to create a new theoretical framework for understanding stress.

This theoretical framework presents stress as a dynamic transaction involving a potential stressor, an individual, and the environment at a specific point in space and time. The term *potential stressor* is used throughout the text and reflects the author's beliefs about the individual nature of stress appraisal. In order for a potential stressor to become an actual stressor, individuals must appraise it as something with which they cannot cope and thus view it as capable of causing them loss or harm.

Stress transactions vary according to space and time and are influenced by an individual's overall state of wellness across the six dimensions of health. Stress and health are interconnected; one's level of health influences both the appraisal of potential stressors and the ability to cope with them.

A New Focus on Spirituality: Living Constructively

Most approaches to emotional and spiritual well-being in North America are rooted in Western psychological and religious traditions, respectively. The fourth edition of *Coping with Stress* features a new focus on stress management approaches to emotional and spiritual health rooted in Asian philosophy, psychology, and spirituality, along with their applications to life in contemporary Western society.

Introduced in chapter 2 and revisited in subsequent chapters in boxes called "Living Constructively," this feature draws from Japanese Naikan and Morita therapies. Naikan therapy represents the self-reflective or introspective element of Japanese psychology; its origins are in Pure Land Buddhist philosophical teachings that emphasize grace and a sense of interconnectedness among all things in life. Morita therapy represents the action element of Japanese psychology; an important element of Morita therapy is teaching people how to accept and co-exist with unpleasant feelings, rather than *working on* understanding and controlling them.

The Living Constructively approach borrows from the work of Krech (2000) and Reynolds (1984), who have combined Naikan and Morita in innovative ways to show us how we can use their principles to find our purpose and live meaningful lives. The activities focus on building three specific skills: (1) co-existing with unpleasant feelings, (2) paying attention, and (3) self-reflecting. Taken together, the three skills help us find direction and purpose in our lives and encourage us to appreciate the interconnectedness of all things and the role they play in our lives.

Focus on Diversity

My experience is that a diverse classroom complements the teaching of stress management, and so this text is designed to provide examples, illustrations, and activities that appeal to diverse populations, including both traditional-age and nontraditional-age students. Recurring "Diverse Perspectives" boxes, as well as a wealth of in-text examples, offer insights into the specific stresses that affect individuals of different ages, races, ethnicities, sexual orientations, and cultural backgrounds. My hope, further, is that the developmental perspective on stressors and coping will give students a deeper understanding of and appreciation for the tasks and stressors people face at various points in their development.

Organization and Content

This text is written in three parts and designed so that one part flows smoothly into the next. The three-pronged approach focuses first on the causes of stress (Part I), then moves on to practical coping methods (Part II). Finally, Part III offers a developmental approach to stress, offering coping strategies appropriate to each stage of life.

Foundations

The groundwork for the course is offered in Part I, which introduces the concept of stress and the theoretical framework for the book (chapter 1) and goes on to examine stress in all its forms over the following four chapters: The emotional and intellectual basis of stress (chapter 2), the environmental and occupational basis of stress (chapter 3), the social and spiritual basis of stress (chapter 4), and the physical basis of stress (chapter 5). A discussion of the effects of stress on the body (chapter 6) rounds out Part I.

The Five Rs of Coping with Stress

A unique approach to coping with stress is offered in Part II, which introduces the Five Rs of Coping model, an integrated, multidimensional approach. Each of the five chapters offers a different approach to coping and contains useful strategies, tips, and tools.

- Chapter 7 (Rethink: Changing the Way You View Things) challenges students to recognize and change illogical thoughts about potential stressors.
- Chapter 8 (Reduce: Finding Your Optimal Level of Stimulation) focuses on modifying potential stressors by eliminating unnecessary demands and managing limited resources like time and money.
- Chapter 9 (Relax: Using Relaxation Techniques to Offset the Effects of Stress) offers a thorough introduction to passive relaxation techniques like stretching, deep breathing, and meditation.
- Chapter 10 (Release: Using Physical Activity to Dissipate the Effects of Stress) details the benefits of physical activity, with tips on how to incorporate activity and exercise into your life and stress management routine.
- A thoroughly revised chapter 11 (Reorganize: Becoming More Stress-Resistant by Improving Your Health) offers a practical approach for building a multi-dimensional stress management plan. The author's two-pronged model for reorganizing your health offers problem-based and emotions-based coping techniques for dealing with particular stressors and applies these methods across all six dimensions of wellness.

A Developmental Look at Stress

Most stress management textbooks take a piecemeal approach to the application of coping skills to typical stressors (such as school, relationships, parenting, and career). In Part III, *Coping with Stress in a Changing World* uses Erik Erikson's model to present a systematic, developmental model of coping across the life cycle. Stressors and coping strategies appropriate to each stage of life are examined in full detail, offering students of all ages real tools that they can employ in their lives. Chapter 12 (Childhood and Adolescent Stress), for example, doesn't merely detail the basis for childhood stress—it offers parents tools for teaching stress management techniques to their children through example and skill building. Chapter 13 (Young Adulthood: Relationships, College, and Other Challenges) addresses the stresses of typical traditional-age students, including relationships, academic concerns, finances, and career. Finally, chapter 14 (Stress in Adulthood and Older Adulthood) offers insights into stress in Erikson's last two stages, with a focus on work and career, relationships, and aging.

Features and Learning Aids

The fourth edition of *Coping with Stress* offers a complete program of pedagogical aids and features designed to interest students and aid them in study and review.

Chapter Opening Objectives

Each chapter begins with a chapter outline and a list of objectives that provide students with a road map to the material ahead.

Key Definitions

All important words from the text are set in boldface type and defined on-page. The placement of the definitions within the text allows the students to find the meaning of key words without having to flip pages.

Keys to Understanding

Important concepts, boxed and labeled "Keys to Understanding," are also set apart in the body of the text. The keys provide simple explanations for important concepts and reinforce essential ideas covered in the text.

NEW! Living Constructively Boxes

As noted, these boxes offer students a unique approach to stress management that is both spiritual and pragmatic. Rooted in Japanese Naikan and Morita therapies, the skills offered are quite different from those emphasized in Western clinical psychology and yet quite complementary to Western spirituality. Living Constructively activities teach students to accept and co-exist with unpleasant feelings, to focus their attention, and to take time to reflect on positive things about themselves and their lives.

Stress in Our World Boxes

"Stress in Our World" is a boxed feature that offers a personal perspective on stress. The characters featured in "Stress in Our World" are real people drawn from the author's classes and personal experience. They are used to give a human face to the discussion of stress.

Diverse Perspectives Boxes

"Diverse Perspectives" boxes provide a look at stress as it affects people of different ages, sexual orientations, and cultural and ethnic backgrounds. These boxes reinforce the underlying message of the book—that stress is individual and that different people appraise potential stressors differently.

Stress Buster Tips

"Stress Busters Tips" are handy, application-oriented tips on coping. They are designed to help students use theoretical information presented in the chapter to manage their stress by breaking it down into useful nuggets.

Discover Our Changing World (with Critical Thinking Questions)

The end-of-chapter feature "Discover Our Changing World" focuses on a key Web site that provides in-depth information about a topic covered in the chapter. An overview of the Web site is provided, along with critical thinking questions. The questions are designed to help students analyze the information provided in the site and apply it to their own stress management plans.

Are You Thinking Clearly?

Another end-of-chapter feature, "Are You Thinking Clearly?" is geared toward getting students to think logically about the stressors they may encounter in everyday life.

Assess Yourself

The "Assess Yourself" evaluations at the ends of chapters are self-surveys designed to provide students with personal information about stress-related topics. The evaluations can be used privately by students to gain a broader understanding of stress in their lives. They can also be used in group discussions, in which students have the opportunity to share information about their personal stressors and coping strategies with their peers.

NEW! End-of-Book Glossary

This new listing of key terms and their definitions at the end of the book enhances students' ability to quickly check their understanding of important terminology and concepts.

Supplements

A comprehensive package of supplementary materials is available with the fourth edition of *Coping with Stress in a Changing World.*

Online Learning Center for *Coping with Stress in a Changing World*

(www.mhhe.com/blonna4e)
The Online Learning Center to accompany this text offers a number of resources for both instructors and students.
Resources for the instructor:

- Instructor's Manual, featuring chapter overviews, learning objectives, suggested teaching outlines with notes and recommended activities for each chapter, personal assessments, issues in the news, suggestions for guest lecturers, media resources, and Web links to professional resources.
- Test bank, containing multiple choice, true/false, matching, and essay questions. The questions are available as Word files and with EZ Test computerized testing software. EZ Test provides a powerful, easy-to-use test maker to create printed quizzes and exams. For secure online testing, exams created in EZ Test can be exported to WebCT, Blackboard, PageOut, and EZ Test Online. EZ Test comes with a Quick Start Guide; once you install the program, you have access to a User's Manual and Flash tutorials. Additional help is available online at www.mhhe.com/eztest.

- PowerPoint slides for each chapter, providing a tool that you can alter or expand to meet the needs of your course. The slides include key lecture points, making it easier for you to teach and ensuring that your students can follow your lectures point by point.

Resources for the student:

- Chapter quizzes, glossary flash cards, and other study aids
- The PowerPoint slides for each chapter
- Interactive Web activities
- Web links for further study and exploration for chapter topics

Classroom Performance System (CPS)

The Classroom Performance System (CPS) brings interactivity into the classroom or lecture hall. CPS is a wireless response system that gives instructors and students immediate feedback from the entire class. Each student uses a wireless response pad similar to a television remote to instantly respond to polling or quiz questions. CPS is the perfect tool for engaging students while gathering assessment data. For more information about using CPS with *Coping with Stress in a Changing World,* contact your McGraw-Hill sales representative.

Additional Options Available

- Fitness and Nutrition Journal
- *Letting Go of Stress* audiotape

For information about packaging these items with the text, contact your McGraw-Hill sales representative.

Mindful Thank-Yous and Formal Acknowledgments

Thank you, instructors and readers, for making the fourth edition a reality. Without loyal users and new adopters this edition would not be possible. I am very excited about this edition and feel it is the best version of the textbook yet. The fusion of Western and Eastern theory and methods is a first among stress management textbooks.

Mindful Thank-Yous

I'd like to use one of these methods I learned at the ToDo Institute in Vermont to acknowledge all of the friends and people who have contributed so much to this year and this project. Without you I would not have had the good fortune, success, fun, and fulfillment that writing this book has brought:

Thank you, Heidi, for your love, support, encouragement, and patience throughout the writing of this book. It all starts and ends with you.

Thank you, Mike and Will, for being who you are. You both make me proud, provide many moments of joy, and challenge me in ways that continue to force me to listen, think, and grow as a dad and a man.

Thank you, Mom and Dad, for reminding me of my roots and being there for the boys so they can see what family, good and bad, is all about.

Thank you, Ann, for your guidance, hard work, attention to detail, and openness to bringing Japanese psychology to the world of stress management. Our book is more like a "new first edition" than a fourth edition.

Thank you, Gregg, Linda, and Trudy, my teachers, mentors, and friends, for teaching me about Japanese psychology and helping me see what has always been right before my eyes but often missed for lack of true attention.

Thank you, Gary, for your time, caring, and help in getting my "second career" as a stress trainer under way.

Thank you, Dan, for your help and guidance as I chart the waters of professional counseling. Your caring is much appreciated.

Thank you, Christine, for managing my financial matters. Money is still my number one stressor, and your help and guidance in navigating the financial waters is much appreciated.

Formal Acknowledgments

I'd like to formally thank Kate Engelberg and Christopher Johnson at McGraw-Hill for their belief in the project. This book would not exist without their support.

I'd like to thank Pam Cooper of McGraw-Hill for understanding how the Japanese psychology material could position this book in the marketplace to gain as much exposure and market share as possible.

I've worked with enough editors to know how lucky I was to have Ann Kirby-Payne as my developmental editor for this edition. Ann's creative vision and work ethic distinguishes her from her peers. Thanks, Ann, for seeing what needed to be seen and doing what needed to be done to bring this project together.

I'd also like to thank Cathy Iammartino for her excellent editorial work on the final manuscript. Cathy is unequaled in her ability to finish a project and bring it to the market on time and in excellent shape.

I'd also like to thank Sarah B. Hill, Julia Ersery, Nancy Null, and everyone else involved at the home office who was involved in the project.

I'd like to acknowledge Dr. Jay Segal of Temple University, who got me interested in stress to begin with. Dr. Segal's help and encouragement helped me get my feet wet teaching my first classes as an adjunct faculty member as I finished my dissertation.

Even though I've never met them, I'd like to acknowledge Drs. Richard Lazarus, Susan Folkman, and Albert Ellis. Your work has inspired me and helped me shape my perspective on stress and coping. If this book seems a tome to the three of you, it is because I believe so strongly in your interpretation of the role of cognitive factors in appraising potential stressors and coping with stress. I hope some day that we get the chance to meet.

Once again, I'd like to thank Gregg Krech, Linda Anderson of the ToDo Institute in Monkton, Vermont and Trudy Boyle of the Constructive Living Learning Center on Gabriola Island, British Columbia. Thanks for having the faith in me to be able to present this material through the filter of my consciousness while staying true to your teachings.

Lastly, I'd like to thank Dr. David K. Reynolds for bringing Morita and Naikan to the United States. Dr. Reynolds, the creator of Constructive Living, has devoted his life to studying these Japanese therapies and making them available to the Western world.

I would also like to express my appreciation to the reviewers of all four editions for their excellent suggestions. Their insightful contributions helped shape every aspect of the development of *Coping with Stress in a Changing World:*

Susan Clark *Ball State University*
Kathleen Farrell *Murray State University*
Beth Gebstadt *Central Oregon Community College*
Katherine L. Haldeman *American University*
D. Randall Haley *Northwestern State University*
Loeen Irons *Baylor University*
John Janowiak *Appalachian State University*
Kandice M. Johnson *Indiana University*
Mark J. Kittleson *Southern Illinois University*
Theresa Landis *University of Michigan—Flint*
Laurie Lang *University of North Florida*
Frank S. Lemmon *University of Utah*
Chad Lewing *University of South Dakota*
Melody Madlem *Central Washington University*
Julia Malia *University of Tennessee*
Josie Metal-Corbin *University of Nebraska—Omaha*
Peggy Plato *San Jose State University*
Bruce M. Ragon *University of North Carolina—Wilmington*
Janet Sholes *Frederick Community College*
Gerald D. Sjule *Orange Coast College*
Bill Thompson *Belmont University*
James L. Toman *University of Southern California*
Patricia A. Tyra *University of Massachusetts—Lowell*
Marie Zannus *Nicholls State University*

PART

I

Stress and Wellness

Stress is everywhere. We are all familiar with the more exotic scenarios: air traffic controllers who know that a wrong move could result in the loss of a multimillion-dollar aircraft and hundreds of lives, police in urban areas who face constant danger and close public scrutiny, and the men and women who defend our allies in faraway places such as Afghanistan and Iraq. These situations represent the extremes. However, stress affects all of us regardless of our gender, age, race, or class.

Men and women are stressed. Some are stressed trying to balance the demands of husband/wife, mother/father, and homemaker/professional. Others are struggling merely to survive, doing the best they can in an economy that is recovering from the excesses of the 1990s. They are competing for jobs in a market flooded with the recently unemployed as companies downsize. Still others are caught in the cycle of unemployment, poverty, welfare, and despair.

Children are stressed. Some, such as the typical 5- or 6-year-old, are stressed adjusting to the new world of school. Others worry that their three-block walk to school may put them in the middle of cross fire between rival street gangs. Others are stressed from trying to cope with the pressures that accompany divorce, single-parent households, and blended families.

College students are stressed. Some are trying to cope with the demands of adapting to a new living environment, new peers, academic pressure, and sexual concerns. College can also put financial stress on students and their families, and it seems that there is never enough time to attend class, study, and work enough hours to pay the bills.

The elderly are stressed. Some are caught between the demands of forced retirement and the difficulty of meeting their financial needs. Others cope with the demands of frail health status and escalating health care costs. Still others are stressed by the loss of their spouses or the dissolution of their families as their adult children leave home.

Such situations can leave us with trembling hands, tense muscles, migraine headaches, and multiple other symptoms of stress. They can also contribute to a host of chronic diseases, ranging from hypertension to peptic ulcers, and can predispose us to premature disability and death.

To understand and manage our stress, we need to view it in the context of our overall level of well-being across the six dimensions of health: physical, social, emotional, intellectual, spiritual, and environmental/occupational. Our overall well-being across these domains affects both our stress level and our ability to cope. Robust health with high levels of well-being is protective, helping to reduce our overall levels of stress and provide the energy and stamina necessary to cope with daily pressures. It can also facilitate coping as we draw on resources ranging from social support to the inner strength that spiritual well-being provides.

Change is common in life, although it varies in intensity, frequency, and degree of permanency. The only real constant in life is change; however, not everyone perceives change the same way. Some people view it positively, transforming change into challenge. For them these situations are catalysts for growth and action. Others view change as a stressor and are mesmerized into inactivity.

In this book, we will answer many of the questions people have about stress and explore what it is and what it does to us. Is it a physical symptom or problem, is it something within us, or is it an outside force? Is it some combination of events that pushes us over the brink? Isn't stress supposed to be good for us? Don't we need it to succeed? What does it really mean to be stressed out?

Stress is one of the most commonly referred to but least understood health problems. We examine the differences between stress and challenge, with an emphasis on the importance of the role of perception in distinguishing between the two. We examine the many common sources of stress for most people, understanding that not everyone perceives them the same way. We also examine strategies for managing stress. We show how to find the optimal levels of challenge and describe ways to control stress instead of letting it control us.

CHAPTER

1

WHAT IS STRESS?

OUTLINE

Four Common Ways of Describing Stress

- Stress as Response
- Stress as Stimulus
- Stress as a Transaction
- Stress as a Holistic Health Phenomenon

A New Definition of Stress

OBJECTIVES

By the end of the chapter students will:

- Describe the four classical ways of describing stress.
- Explain the relationship between life events and the stress response.
- Describe the three phases of Selye's General Adaptation Syndrome (GAS).
- Describe the role of threat appraisal in the stress response.
- Describe how the stress response is related to a person's level of functioning across the six dimensions of wellness.
- Compare the author's definition of stress with the classical definitions.

Stress is different for everyone. Ten people would probably describe stress ten different ways. However, there are four basic descriptions of stress that are commonly used by people to describe the phenomenon.

Four Common Ways of Describing Stress

Some people describe stress in terms of the stimuli, constraints, situations, or outside forces that put excessive demands on them, making them feel as if they can't cope. These demands are also referred to as stressors: "Stress is bills." "Stress is having too much to do and too little time to do it." "My boss is stress." Others define stress as a response, something that goes on physically or emotionally within themselves: "Stress is a tension headache." "Stress is a knot in my stomach." "Stress is feeling anxious." "Stress is feeling afraid."

For others stress is a **transaction**—an exchange between a potential stressor, how they perceive it, and the stress response it causes: "Stress is the muscle tension I get when I think about giving a speech in front of the class and feel out of control." Still others describe stress as a **holistic** health phenomenon, an imbalance in one's physical, social, spiritual, emotional, intellectual, occupational, or environmental well-being: Stress is "being too busy to eat well and take care of myself." "Stress is being a full-time student, part-time worker, and somebody's girlfriend without having time to play any of those roles well."

Stress can cause both migraine and tension headaches.

Key to Understanding

Stress is very individualistic. What stresses one person may have no effect on another.

Each of these descriptions of stress is flawed to some extent. Some place too little emphasis on the role of **perception** in a potentially stressful transaction. Others do not take into account one's overall level of well-being and the environment in which the transaction occurs.

Although flawed, each of the four common ways of describing stress discussed above contains a valuable piece of the puzzle we call stress. In reality, stress combines elements from each of the common descriptions. In the sections that follow, we'll investigate the possibilities and theories related to each of these common descriptions of stress. At the end of the chapter, we'll complete the puzzle by assembling the pieces into a new, more comprehensive definition of stress.

In this chapter, we will examine the nature of stress, the theoretical issues and problems surrounding the different ways of describing stress, and the etiology of the author's new way of defining it.

Stress as Response

The understanding of the physiological basis of stress grew largely out of the pioneering work of three men: Claude Bernard a French physiologist, Walter B. Cannon, an American physiologist, and Hans Selye, a Canadian endocrinologist. These three pioneers of stress research laid the foundation for the identification and understanding of the stress response.

Homeostasis and the Internal Environment

Bernard, a French physiologist, spent the last half of the nineteenth century refining the concept of the **milieu interieur,** or the internal environment. Long before the

transaction an exchange involving two or more parties or events, which reciprocally affect one another during the process of the exchange

holistic related to the whole rather than to its individual parts

perception the subjective way in which information is regarded and interpreted

milieu interieur the body's internal environment

concept of stress was developed, Bernard described how living organisms attempt to maintain an internal constancy or balance and how this struggle goes on despite changes in the outside environment.[11]

An example would be the body's attempt to maintain a balance in heart rate, temperature, and respiration when exposed to a change in weather conditions. As the temperature grows colder, the body must stay in balance and not follow the environmental changes. Heart rate must continue in rhythm, internal temperature must be at an acceptable level, and breathing must be regular. If the body did not maintain its internal balance and fluctuated too greatly with the weather, it would begin to malfunction and break down.

Bernard's work was expanded upon fifty years later by Walter Cannon,[2] a Harvard physiologist. In his original work Cannon refined Bernard's concept of the *milieu interieur* and renamed the process **homeostasis,** from the Greek words *homios* (meaning "similar") and *stasis* (meaning "position"). This steady position or state of being is the normal pattern of internal functioning under which living things operate.

Cannon[2] theorized that living things seek to maintain homeostasis to prevent their various body systems from deviating too far from their normal limits of functioning. When body systems deviate from the norm too greatly, they put the entire organism in danger. To prevent this from happening, internal physiological processes are set into motion automatically, and in this way the body balances the effects of external environmental stressors.

Stress as a Nonspecific Response

Hans Selye,[10] a Canadian endocrinologist, continued Cannon's work. In 1926, as a second-year resident at the University of Montreal Medical School, Selye began his research in the area of homeostasis. Selye's laboratory experiments exposed rats to a variety of noxious chemicals and extreme environmental stressors. The environmental stressors included freezing temperatures, constant light (he actually sewed the rats' eyelids so that they could not close them), deafening noise, and nonstop exercise via motor-driven treadmills and constant swimming to avoid drowning.[8] He confirmed what Cannon had found: When an organism's normal operating systems (respiration, circulation, digestion, and temperature regulation) were thrown too far out of their normal range of functioning, the organism was in danger of dying.[10] The demands created by the need to adapt to these external stimuli were far too great for their bodies to cope with.

However, Selye went one step farther than Cannon. He found not only that his laboratory animals adjusted to these demands by initiating a complex pattern of physiological responses but that the responses were the same regardless of the source of the demand. Selye called this phenomenon the *nonspecific response to demand.* Not only was the phenomenon the same, it was replicated with mice, rabbits, dogs, cats, and other laboratory animals.[8] The nonspecificity of the response to any demand was the key factor in the development of Selye's stress theory,[10] and he later defined stress as the nonspecific response of the body to any demand.

Furthermore, Selye believed that any demand was capable of triggering this nonspecific response. He labeled negative demands as **distress** and positive demands as **eustress.** A positive demand could be an event such as getting married or inheriting a lot of money. A negative demand could be an argument with one's boss or getting involved in a traffic accident. Selye felt that both kinds of demands taxed the body's ability to stay in balance (maintain homeostasis). In order to maintain homeostasis in the face of such demands, the body mobilized energy by initiating the stress response. In a sense, the stress response can be viewed as an energy-intensive process needed to maintain homeostasis in the face of eustress or distress that threaten to throw the body out of balance.

Selye developed a model for describing this nonspecific response and the adaptations it forces the body to make. He called that model the **General Adaptation Syndrome (GAS),** and it has three distinguishable phases: **alarm, resistance,** and **exhaustion.**[10] These three phases are sequential; that is, the source of stress sounds the alarm to initiate the GAS and if the stress is not removed or coped with, the body progresses to resistance and eventual exhaustion. However, recovery is an alternative outcome to exhaustion when the source of stress is removed or coped with effectively (fig. 1-1).

In a fascinating historical account, Rosch[8] describes the etiology of Selye's use of the word *stress.* Because of

homeostasis a state of relative stability in the body's internal environment, sustained by natural adaptive responses

distress any negative demand that is capable of triggering the GAS

eustress any positive demand that is capable of triggering the GAS

General Adaptation Syndrome (GAS) the three-phase stress response identified by Selye, involving three phases: alarm, resistance, and exhaustion

alarm the first phase of GAS, in which the body mobilizes energy to meet the demands of stressors

resistance the second phase of GAS, in which the body attempts to maintain homeostasis in the face of chronic stressors

exhaustion the third phase of GAS, in which a body part or system breaks down as a result of the energy demands of chronic stressors

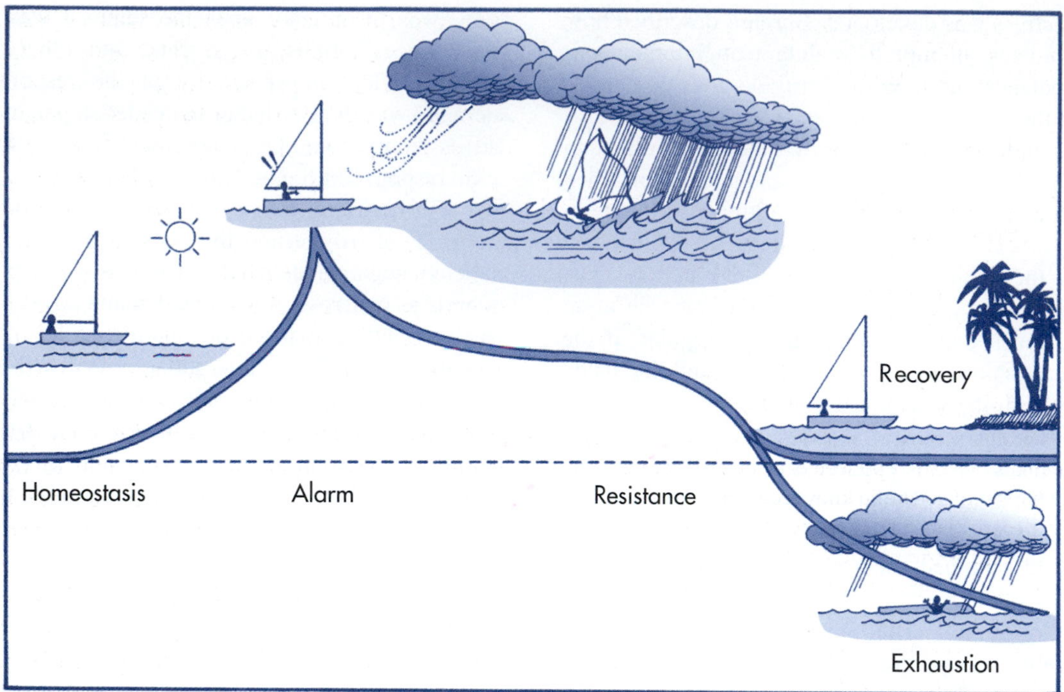

Figure 1-1
When we are not stressed, we are like a sailboat cutting a mild wake through our day. As stressors appear like clouds on the horizon, we get ready for turbulent seas and stormy weather. If we cope successfully, we resist the rough times and rechart a course through calmer seas. If we can't cope, like the sailboat, we crash and sink into exhaustion.

his lack of facility with the English language, Selye used the word *stress* instead of his preferred word **strain** to describe the nonspecific responses of the body to these demands. In Selye's view, the noxious environmental stressors he subjected his laboratory animals to placed great *strain* on their ability to maintain homeostasis. The strain on their body parts and systems caused by the physiological adaptations necessary to maintain homeostasis in the face of environmental stressors eventually resulted in exhaustion and death. In this way Selye separated the stressor (environmental stimuli) from the strain (the stress response caused by the stressor) and the resultant exhaustion.

An underlying concept in Selye's GAS model is his belief that all living organisms are equipped with a vital force he called **adaptation energy.** This adaptation energy is stored in the body and is drawn on whenever organisms have to adapt to demands from outside forces. When Selye's laboratory animals were exposed to outside stimuli, their internal *alarms* were triggered to initiate a complex set of physiological processes to mobilize energy for action.[12] **Fight-or-flight,** a phrase coined by Cannon,[2] is what Selye used to describe the state of the body at this point. The fight-or-flight response refers to the options available in coping with stressors at this point in the stress response. The body is primed to either confront the stressor or avoid it.

KEY TO UNDERSTANDING

The brain treats symbolic and real threats to our wellbeing the same way; they energize the body to fight or flee.

Selye found that when his laboratory animals couldn't fight or flee, they had to adjust to the stimuli by shifting to a lower-level but more complex stress response. This response prompted various organs and glands of the animals to produce a variety of hormones, salts, and sugars to supply the energy necessary to *resist* the demands of the stimuli and keep the body in balance. Selye believed that the effects of the resistance phase of GAS result in the gradual wearing down of what he

strain minor muscular damage due to excessive physical effort; the wear and tear on body parts and systems as they fight to maintain homeostasis in response to stressors

adaptation energy the body's finite energy reserves available for coping with stressors

fight-or-flight the state of physiological readiness for action created by the body during the alarm phase

STRESS IN OUR WORLD

Selye's World: Researching Stress in the 1930s

Sometimes it is difficult to picture what the world was like before many of the scientific breakthroughs we now take for granted were made. Think about Selye's world in the 1930s when he conducted his laboratory experiments and discovered the General Adaptation Syndrome. There were no "institutional review boards" to assess experimental protocols and protect subjects' rights. There were no People for the Ethical Treatment of Animals (PETA) and other animal rights groups serving as watchdogs to prevent cruelty to animals. Scientists policed each other regarding ethics in the pursuit of scientific knowledge. Most of Selye's early experiments on rats, mice, dogs, cats, and other animals would not be allowed today.

The level of technological sophistication was also very different. There were no X rays, ultrasound machines, or other sophisticated techniques, such as mass spectrometry and gas chromatography, to assess structural changes or the presence of minute amounts of chemicals and other substances in blood, tissue, and other specimens. Selye discovered changes such as the enlargement of the adrenal glands and the shrinkage of the thymus through autopsies. He performed countless autopsies on his experimental animal subjects to observe gross anatomical changes and crafted his theory from those observations.

characterized as **weak links,**[10] or body parts or systems that bear the brunt of adaptive attempts during the resistance phase. These weak links are the first body parts or systems to malfunction during the latter stages of resistance. When his animals were no longer able to resist the stimuli acting on them, they broke down, were *exhausted,* and died.

In studying this process of alarm, resistance, and exhaustion, Selye measured and quantified these physiological symptoms. His findings confirmed his earlier hypothesis about the nonspecificity of the response regardless of the type of stimuli.

Stress as Stimulus

Pressures associated with work, school, relationships, family life, and other environmental demands often cause people to describe themselves as "being under stress." In fact, such stressors have been found to affect physical health. Thomas Holmes and Richard Rahe,[3] pioneers in the study of life demands and their relationship to stress, noticed what seemed to be a relationship between stressful events and susceptibility to illness. As researchers at the University of Washington School of Medicine, Holmes and Rahe examined the past medical records of their subjects and discovered that major life changes were often followed by the development of serious illnesses.

They wondered if this relationship was coincidental or if instead it could be used to predict the development of illness in people who might experience such changes in the future. They used the term **life events** to refer to life-changing experiences. Some of these events are joyous—marriage, the birth of a child, a new job—and others are sad—the death of a loved one, the loss of a job. Holmes and Rahe[3] believed that these events, regardless of whether they were happy or sad, throw the body out of balance, forcing it to readjust. These **readjustments** use up energy and make demands on the body. Holmes and Rahe, like Selye, believed that the body has a finite amount of adaptation energy available to make these readjustments. If people experience too many life events in too short a period of time, they will be at increased risk for the development of disease.

To test this theory, Holmes and Rahe developed the Social Readjustment Rating Scale to measure these events. The scale consists of a variety of life events that are typically experienced by numbers of people in any given year. They assigned a score for each event; serious events (death of a spouse, divorce) were awarded the highest score values. Subjects who took the test checked the events that they had experienced in the past year, and these events were tallied and their scores were correlated with the presence or absence of disease. Holmes and Rahe's research findings supported their hypothesis that there is a relationship between life events and disease. They found that the subjects with the highest scores were most likely to develop a disease within the next year.

Critics of Holmes and Rahe's work argue that this type of stress theory ignores the role of perception in the stress response. They would argue that life events are stressful only if people perceive them to be. It is important to realize that these life events are normal occurrences and are harmful only if too many of them occur in too short a time span. These arguments will be examined in detail in chapter 2.

Stress as a Transaction

As we mentioned earlier in this chapter, viewing stress as a transaction implies that it is much more than just a stimulus or a response. It is even more than the action of a stimulus automatically resulting in a response. A

weak links susceptible body parts or systems that break down under the wear and tear of chronic stressors

life events life-changing experiences that use energy and can cause stress

readjustments the body's physiological adaptations to life events transactional way of viewing stress involves a person perceiving a stimulus as threatening, thus transforming it into a stressor. Once the stimulus becomes a stressor, it triggers the stress response.

This way of viewing stress is entirely different from that of Selye who never considered the role of perception in his nonspecific response conceptualization. And unlike Holmes and Rahe, a transactional way of viewing stress does not support the notion of life events being universal stressors for everyone. A transactional way of viewing stress is built on the belief that people respond to life events differently, depending on how they perceive them. An event such as a divorce, for instance, may be perceived as very stressful by a particular person in a particular situation, while another person in a different situation might celebrate the occasion.

Wired for Stress: The Work of A.T.W. Simeons

The history of viewing stress as a transaction begins with the work of Albert Theodore William (A.T.W.) Simeons,[11] a stress researcher and disciple of Hans Selye. Simeons believed that the brains of modern men and women are wired for stress in exactly the same way as those of their primitive ancestors. That is, when they are threatened, they mobilize a stress response to maintain homeostasis in the face of demand. In other words, whether someone is threatened by a saber-toothed tiger or stuck in freeway traffic, their brains work the same way in triggering a stress response. The trigger is a threat and the response is a life-saving mobilization of energy to fight-or-flee.

Simeons called contemporary stressors like freeway traffic jams *symbolic* threats because while they are threatening, they are more of a threat to an individual's ego than to their actual physical well-being. Simeons paved the way for a new generation of psychological stress researchers who were interested in the nature of threat and how perception of threat was related to the stress response. This new generation of psychological stress research was based on the premise that with the exception of certain environmental stimuli (extremes in temperature, pollution, noise, etc.), most of the things that cause stress are people and situations that we determine to be potential threats to our well-being.

KEY TO UNDERSTANDING

Nonspecificity means that there aren't 1,001 different responses to 1,001 types of stressors. For example, we don't have a school stress response and a family stress response. Our bodies respond the same way to each different type of stressor.

The Perception of Threat: The Basis for a Transactional Model of Stress

Richard Lazarus[4] is the psychological stress researcher credited with developing a unique model of how our minds work when perceiving potential stressors. His theory of psychological stress revolves around the belief that people or things become stressors when they pose a **threat** to our well-being in some way. The threat may be physical harm, but more often than not it is psychosocial in nature. For instance, a comment someone makes about our clothing is not a direct threat to our well-being, yet it may be enough to initiate a stress response if we interpret it as a threat. Threat implies a state of anticipating a confrontation with a harmful condition. Whether the stressor is real or imagined is immaterial. It is the perception of the stimuli as threatening that determines whether they become stressors.

Lazarus[4] called the perception of potential stressors a *transaction* and called the actual evaluation of stimuli the **threat appraisal process.** Lazarus's model involves three appraisals of the potential stressor: Primary appraisal determines if the stressor is a threat; secondary appraisal determines if the individual is capable of coping with the threat; and cognitive reappraisal draws on the information from the first two appraisals. Figure 1-2 illustrates Lazarus's perception of threat.

The primary appraisal examines both stimulus and personality factors to determine if the potential stressor is a threat. Occurring simultaneously with the primary appraisal process is the secondary appraisal process, which attempts to answer the question "Can I cope with this threat?" Belief in one's ability to cope plays a big part in the stress appraisal process. The role of coping and the secondary appraisal will be covered in detail in chapter 2.

When both questions are answered ("Is it a threat?" and "Can I cope?"), the situation is reappraised and a determination is made by the brain concerning whether this potential stressor becomes a real stressor.[5] In his most recent synthesis of stress, Lazarus[7] identifies the key "stress emotions" and the emotional narratives that accompany the stress appraisal process. We will explore these factors in detail in chapter 2.[6]

In the next section of this chapter, we will see how this transaction is influenced by our overall level of health and well-being.

threat the perception of harm

threat appraisal process the evaluation of potential stressors in terms of their threat potential and our ability to cope with them

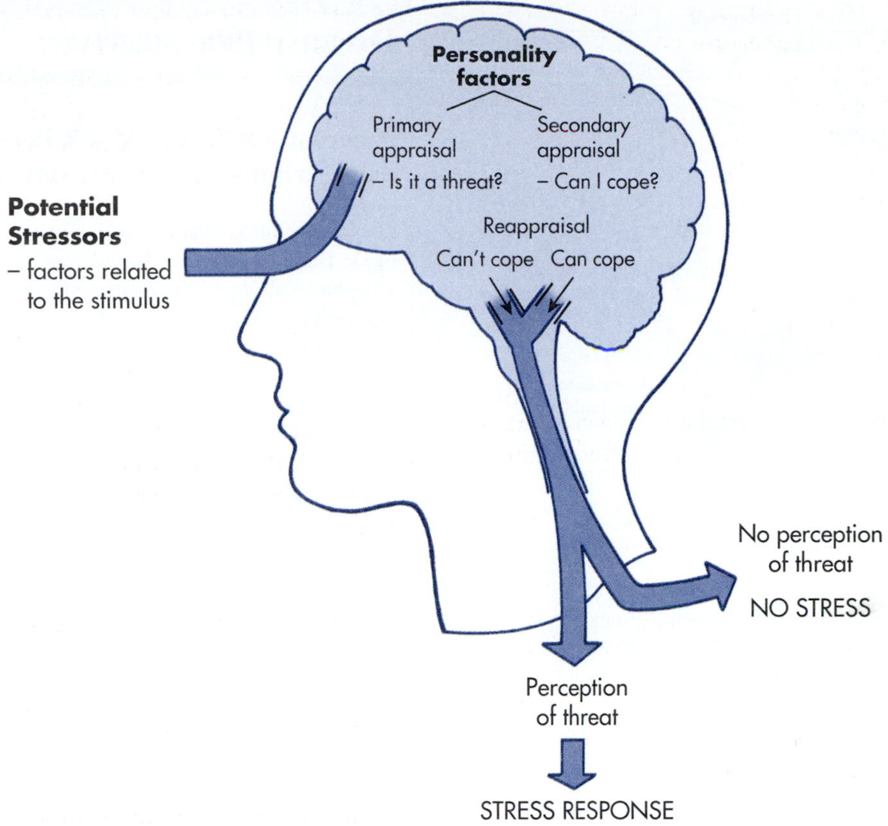

Figure 1-2

Incoming stimuli are neutral until they are perceived as threatening or nonthreatening. This is determined by a combination of stimulus and personality factors.

> **KEY TO UNDERSTANDING**
>
> Threats do not have to be real to be perceived as such. People can feel threatened even though they really are safe.

Stress as a Holistic Health Phenomenon

Stress as a holistic health phenomenon can be better understood when it is examined within the context of a person's level of functioning across the six dimensions of **wellness.**[7] The underlying premise of viewing stress this way (which we will investigate further in chapter 11) is the belief that the amount of stress in people's lives and their ability to manage it are strongly influenced by the degree to which they function optimally in the physical, social, spiritual, emotional, intellectual, occupational, and environmental dimensions of health (see fig. 1-3). Not only does each dimension and the overall level of functioning across the six dimensions play a role in the stress response, the balance of all six dimensions and the way they work together are important.

> **KEY TO UNDERSTANDING**
>
> The way you appraise a potential stressor is influenced by both how you feel (health) and what is going on in your life (environment) on any particular day.

Physical Wellness

Physical wellness relates to how well the body performs its intended functions. Absence of disease, though an important influence on physical wellness, is not the sole criterion for health. The physical domain is influenced by factors such as genetic inheritance, nutritional status, fitness level, body composition, and immune status.

> **wellness** a state of optimal health across six dimensions: physical, social, intellectual, emotional, spiritual, and environmental/occupational

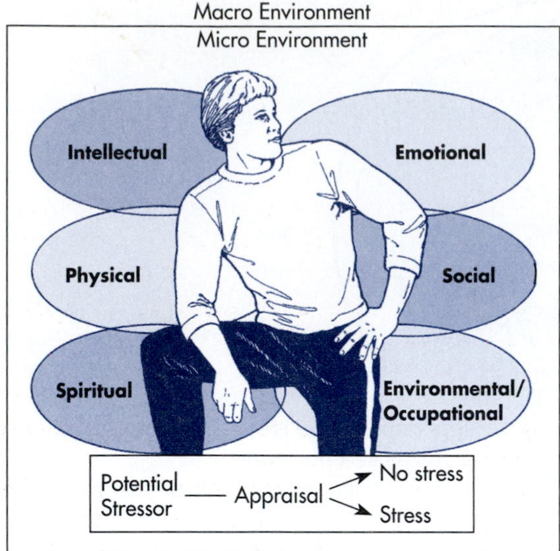

Figure 1-3
A holistic health model of stress places the stress appraisal process in the context of the individual's level of well-being across the six dimensions of health.

Social Wellness

Being connected to others through various types of relationships is the foundation of social wellness. Individuals who function optimally in this domain are able to form friendships, have intimate relationships, and give and receive love and affection. They are able to give of themselves and share in the joys and sorrows of being part of a community.

Intellectual Wellness

Our intellectual wellness depends on our ability to process information effectively. Intellectual wellness involves the ability to use information in a rational way to problem solve and grow. It also includes factors such as creativity, spontaneity, and openness to new ways of viewing situations.

Emotional Wellness

Being in touch with feelings, having the ability to express them, and being able to control them when necessary are the keys to emotional wellness. Optimal functioning involves understanding that emotions are the mirror to the soul and help us get in touch with what is important in our lives. Our emotions make us feel alive and provide us with a richness of experience that is uniquely human.

Spiritual Wellness

Feeling connected to something beyond oneself is the basis of spiritual wellness. One way to express spirituality is through participation in organized religious activities. This usually involves a belief in a supreme being or higher supernatural force as well as a formalized code of conduct to live by. In a secular sense, spirituality can manifest itself through a connection to something greater than oneself. Whether it is being part of a community, working to save the environment, helping to feed the needy, or committing oneself to world peace, the underlying feeling is one of a perception of life as having meaning beyond the self. In addition to traditional and familiar Western religions and secular spiritualism, useful coping techniques can be found in Asian philosophy, psychology, and spirituality. Throughout this book, we'll offer an

DIVERSE PERSPECTIVES

America, 1969: One Man's Perspective on a Turbulent Time in History

"I can remember what it was like in 1969," Aaron, a friend of Dr. Blonna's, recalls. "Here I was, an African American, a freshman at one of the Northeast's premier liberal arts universities, trying to cope with the normal pressures of college life: missing home, adjusting to the crushing academic workload, trying to figure out who I was and what I wanted to do when I graduated. It was very different from today, though, because 15,000 miles away there was a war in Vietnam going on. I'd start off every day by reading the newspaper to see what draft number the government was up to. Even though I was deferred from the draft because I was attending college, I worried that somehow, if my number was called, I'd have to give all of this up and go fight in Vietnam. Fortunately, I had number 312 and they were still way below that." Aaron continued: "Each day for me was filled with a roller-coaster ride of emotions: fear, anxiety, guilt, confusion. Even though I was in college, I had friends called to service. I'd look at the news and read the papers to see if any of my friends were listed among the casualties. I lost a few friends over there while I was in school. I feared for my friends and felt guilty at times because I was here, safe in college, while they risked their lives for all of us. It was a confusing time. Many people felt the war was unjust. Many of my black friends were militants and were against the war. They felt African Americans were being called to fight for a country that still didn't grant them the same rights as whites. Remember, the Civil Rights Act of 1964 had been passed only a scant five years earlier and many places still were not in compliance with it. I wasn't sure what I believed. I guess this added to my confusion and anxiety. It was hard for me to blot out all of this stuff going on outside the safe iron gates of my university and focus on being a college student when the world around me was at war. I hope my son, at college in Virginia, won't have to go through this as our government wages a war against terrorism in the Middle East."

Living Constructively

Basic Naikan Meditation

Throughout this book, we will be examining an approach to emotional and spiritual health that originated in Japan. This approach is rooted in Asian philosophy, psychology, and spirituality and their applications to life in contemporary Western society, and draws from two Japanese approaches to emotional well-being: Naikan and Morita therapies. Naikan therapy represents the self-reflective or introspective element of Japanese psychology. The cornerstone of Naikan practice is the daily self-reflection on three questions that help students gain insight into and a deeper appreciation of their connectedness and indebtedness to others. This forms the basis for the grace and expression of gratitude that Naikan helps foster. Developing grace and becoming more grateful for what you have and what others have done for you shifts the focus from you and your "problems" to others, what they have done for you, and what problems you have caused them. In time, such a shift in perspective helps you feel less distanced from others and more connected to them. Such feelings of interconnectedness are the hallmark of a heightened sense of spirituality.

Instructions:

1. For the next week, spend 30 minutes (10 minutes on each question) each night reflecting on the following three questions:
   - What did I receive from others today?*
   - What did I give to others today?
   - What troubles and difficulties did I cause others today?

   Keep a brief diary in which you record your answers.
2. At the end of the week review your daily lists and write a thank-you note to one person for something specific that the person gave you or did for you.**

**Try to broaden your scope on what you received from others. For example, think of that pizza you ordered last night.*

The pizza was delivered hot, to your door, in a sealed insulated bag by a delivery person who drove through the rain to get it to your home. The pizza was made by the pizza maker who spent twelve hours on his feet yesterday mixing dough, making sauce, grating cheese, and making pizzas in a hot oven.

Think of one of the ingredients of the pizza. The dough was made from flour, grown by farmers. It was harvested and sent to the mill where it was milled by millers who then bagged it and had it shipped to the wholesaler who sold it to a distributor who delivered it in 50-pound sacks to your local pizza maker. Many people contributed to the cultivation, processing, and delivery of that flour before it even got to your pizza parlor. The same can be said for all of the ingredients, many of which (like olive oil) traveled across oceans and continents in boats and trucks to get to your local pizza parlor. Although it may seem silly to you, consider what would your life be like without the interconnectedness of all these people, working together to bring you products such as pizza. When was the last time you expressed your gratitude for/to them?

***When writing your thank-you note, be specific. Make sure you thank the person specificially for what they did for you. For instance, imagine you are writing a note to your mom for cooking your dinner last night. Instead of just saying "thanks mom", try saying "thanks mom for cooking that delicious dinner. I really appreciate the time you spend in the kitchen preparing hot, nutritious meals for me."*

With permission from Krech, G (2002). *Naikan; Gratitude, Grace, and the Japanese Art of Self-Reflection.* Berkeley CA: Stone Bridge Press.

alternative spiritual view by exploring stress-management tools borrowed from Japanese psychotherapies, and examining their applications to life in contemporary Western society (see Living Constructively).

Environmental/Occupational Wellness

The physical and societal surroundings that affect individuals' functioning on both the micro and macro levels play a big role in the Environmental/Occupational dimension of wellness. The well-being of our *micro environment* includes the level of functioning of our school, home, work site, neighborhood, family, friends, and associates. Our social support system is also part of our micro environment. This micro environment greatly affects our health and affects our personal safety by influencing whether we are at risk for and fear such things as theft, crime, and violence. Air and water quality, noise pollution, overcrowding, and other factors that influence our stress levels are also affected by our micro environment.

The level of well-being of our *macro environment* (state, country, the world at large, and the universe) also affects our wellness. The effects of war, international disputes, famine, pollution, and ozone depletion all influence us to some extent. Decisions made by our political leaders also affect the way we think and live our lives. Our ability to stay focused and whole is constantly

> **KEY TO UNDERSTANDING**
>
> The stress response doesn't occur in a vacuum. It is influenced by what is going on in our immediate (micro) environment and in the world (macro) environment.

challenged by media that bring the entire world and its problems into our living rooms each night.

Defining stress as a holistic transaction between the individual, a potential stressor, and the environment incorporates the individual's overall level of wellness across the six dimensions of health.

A New Definition of Stress

Each of the common descriptions of stress described throughout this chapter has some merit, but remains flawed in one way or another. It is the premise of this book that to truly understand stress, we must consider not only our personal description of the stress response but also the importance of our perceptions about different stressors. The author borrows from each of these common ways of describing stress to create a more comprehensive definition of stress, which we will use in our discussions throughout this book. In this book we will define **stress** as a *holistic transaction* between an individual and a potential stressor resulting in a stress response.

To understand this explanation of stress, it is crucial that we acknowledge the difference between **potential stressors**—stimuli that *may* cause a stress response—and **actual stressors,** which *do* cause stress. The author believes that potential stressors only become actual stressors when they are perceived as being beyond one's ability to cope with. This is determined as a result of a transaction between the individual, the potential stressor, and the environment in which the transaction occurs. The transaction is holistic in nature because it is influenced by the person's overall level of physical, social, spiritual, emotional, intellectual, occupational, and environmental well-being at the time it occurs.

> **stress** a holistic transaction between an individual and a potential stressor resulting in a stress response
>
> **potential stressors** stimuli that may cause a stress response
>
> **actual stressor** a stimulus that does cause stress

Summary

In this chapter we examined the etiology of the author's definition of stress as a holistic transaction between the individual, a potential stressor, and the environment. We traced its roots in the four major ways of defining stress: stress as stimulus, stress as response, stress as a transaction, and stress as a holistic phenomenon. We clarified key definitions related to stress and briefly discussed the work of some of the pioneers in the field.

Claude Bernard, Walter Cannon, and Hans Selye were the pioneers in the research that qualified and quantified the effects of various stressful stimuli on the body. They showed us that the body attempts to maintain a balance, or homeostasis. When exposed to noxious stimuli that put demands on it, the body mobilizes energy and attempts to maintain homeostasis through a complex physiological response involving many different body parts and systems. This response changes over time, and if the source of stress is not removed, it wears the body down, and the body can become exhausted and break down.

Holmes and Rahe pioneered the investigation of the health effects of too many stressors. They coined the term *life events* to define everyday situations that place demands on people and force them to adapt. They quantified the effects of life events and their relationship to the stress response.

Psychological stress researchers such as Simeons examined the role of perception in the stress response. The stress response is viewed as a complex process involving factors concerning potential stressors, personality factors, and the resultant physiological changes that occur if stimuli are perceived as threats to our well-being. Richard Lazarus described various factors

Stress Buster Tips

Take a Vacation from the News

A simple way to reduce stress is to take a vacation from the news. Media coverage of world events can be overwhelming at times. With 24/7 coverage of global events available across a broad spectrum of media (print, radio, video, Internet, etc.), much of the coverage is overlapping, sensationalist, and unnecessary. Sometimes we need to take a temporary vacation from world events to clear our heads, reduce our worries, and put our lives in the proper perspective. Here's how to take a vacation from world events.

For one week do the following things:

1. Don't read the newspaper, news magazines, or Internet news pages.
2. Don't watch the news on television.
3. Don't listen to the news portions of radio programs.
4. Don't feel guilty. (Most of the important stories will still be around next week. If not, you can always go back and read them.)

Ease your way back to the news by limiting your exposure to bad news (front sections of newspapers, negative commentators and Web pages, etc.).

involving both the stimulus and the personality of the individual and examined the role of these factors in the assessment of potential stressors as threatening or not threatening.

A truly comprehensive view of health and stress, however, can never dismiss the effect of our environment on our attempts at achieving high levels of wellness and stress management. A wellness model of health adds an environmental dimension to the holistic definition. Our immediate micro environment can contribute to either our stress or our ability to cope. It will affect our quality of life, safety, support systems, resources, and countless other factors related to stress. Our stress level is also affected by the "big picture." Events going on in our state, our country, the world, and the universe (macro environment) filter through and affect our daily lives. Issues like war, international tension, the economy, and global warming affect the way we perceive our lives and our stress. Although we are ultimately responsible for how we interpret and cope with these events, they color our world and affect our lives.

Defining stress as a holistic transaction between the individual, a potential stressor, and the environment draws from all these classic definitions, weaving them together in an eclectic definition that incorporates all the critical variables involved.

STUDY QUESTIONS

1. Describe the major differences in the five ways (the author's and the four classic) of defining stress.
2. Compare the author's definition of stress with the four classic definitions.
3. Explain a holistic transaction by using a personal example.
4. What are life events, and how do they relate to stress?
5. What is homeostasis, and how does it relate to the stress response?
6. What does Selye mean when he characterizes stress as "the nonspecific response to any demand"?
7. Describe what happens during the fight-or-flight response.
8. What are a person's weak links?
9. What does Simeons mean by symbolic threats? Give an example of a symbolic threat to your well-being that is a source of stress.
10. What is the role of threat perception in the stress response?
11. Explain how levels of wellness are related to stress.
12. What are the micro environment and the macro environment? How are they related to stress?

DISCOVER OUR CHANGING WORLD

National Wellness Institute

http://www.nationalwellness.org

Founded in 1977, the National Wellness Institute (NWI) has steadfastly provided health promotion and wellness professionals with unparalleled resources and services that promote both professional and personal growth. Besides having a membership division, NWI hosts the National Wellness Conference. Held annually in Stevens Point, Wisconsin, at the University of Wisconsin–Stevens Point, for over 25 years, it is the most highly acclaimed conference for wellness and health promotion professionals.

Bill Hettler Home page

http://hettler.com/

Bill Hettler has been providing wellness/health promotion consultations and presentations since 1972. Bill is one of the cofounders of the *National Wellness Institute, Inc.,* and serves as president of the board of directors. Bill is probably best known as one of the creators of the National Wellness Conference. This weeklong conference has influenced the lives of thousands of people over the last twenty-plus years.

Critical Thinking Question

Complete the Wellness Test at the end of this chapter and describe your score. How does your overall level of health and wellness affect your stress in one positive way and one negative way? How has this changed in the past year? How do you think this will change in the coming year? Which of the dimensions of health impacts your stress the most?

ARE YOU THINKING CLEARLY?

In this chapter we discussed how your overall level of well-being across the dimensions of health influences how you perceive potential stressors. When you have high-level health, you perceive the world and potential stressors entirely differently than when your well-being is lower. Often, our perception of our well-being differs the reality of our health status as measured by tests and other assessments. This difference can sometimes stand in the way of us taking steps to improve our health and well-being. The following questions will help you assess whether or not your perception of your well-being measures up to the reality of your health status and if this is holding you back from improving.

1. Was your initial impression of your overall health status (before taking the assessment) much higher than your actual total score on the Wellness Test at the end of Chapter 1?

2. How have your thoughts about your health influenced your daily health behavior (eating, exercise, substance use, etc.) and lifestyle up to this point in your life?
3. How has your lifestyle impacted your stress up to this point in your life?
4. On a scale of 1–10 (10 being the most), how much control do you think you have over your lifestyle?

The answers to these questions should help you assess whether you are thinking clearly about your health and your lifestyle and how they relate to your stress. Of all the variables related to your health (genetics, the health care system, etc.), you have the *most* control of your daily behavior and lifestyle. Believing that you can control your behavior is a key step in managing your stress.

REFERENCES

1. Ardell, D.B. (1985). *The history and future of wellness.* Dubuque, IA: Kendall/Hunt.
2. Cannon, W. (1932). *The wisdom of the body.* New York: W. W. Norton.
3. Holmes, H.T. & Rahe, H.R. (1967). The social readjustment rating scale. *Journal of Psychosomatic Research,* 11, p. 213.
4. Lazarus, R.S. (1966). *Psychological stress and the coping process.* New York: McGraw-Hill.
5. Lazarus, R.S. (1977). *Stress and coping.* New York: Columbia University Press.
6. Lazarus, R.S. (1999). *Stress and emotion: A new synthesis.* New York: Springer.
7. National Wellness Institute. (2003). *Definition of wellness.* http://www.nationalwellness.org.
8. Rosch P.J. (2002). Hans Selye and the birth of the stress concept. In Everly, G.S., Jr. & Lating, J.M. (Eds.). *A clinical guide to the treatment of the human stress response,* pp. 353–364. New York: Kluwer Academic/ Plenum.
9. Selye, H. (1974). *Stress without distress.* New York: Signet Classics.
10. Selye, H. (1956). *The stress of life.* New York: McGraw-Hill.
11. Simeons, A.T.W. (1961). *Man's presumptuous brain: An evolutionary interpretation of psychosomatic disease.* New York: EP Dutton.

Name: ______________________ Date: 6/2

ASSESS YOURSELF 1-1

Wellness Test

Directions: Wellness involves a variety of components that work together to build the total concept. Below are some questions concerning the different aspects of wellness. Using the scale, respond to each question by circling the number that most closely corresponds with your feelings and lifestyle.

SOCIAL AND OCCUPATIONAL HEALTH	**Not True/ Rarely**	**Somewhat True/ Sometimes**	**Mostly True/ Usually**	**Very True/ Always**
1. I feel loved and supported by my family.	1	2	3	4
2. I establish friendships with ease and enjoyment.	1	2	3	4
3. I establish friendships with people of both genders and all ages.	1	2	3	4
4. I sustain relationships by communicating with and caring about my family and friends.	1	2	3	4
5. I feel comfortable and confident when meeting people for the first time.	1	2	3	4
6. I practice social skills to facilitate the process of forming new relationships.	1	2	3	4
7. I seek opportunities to meet and interact with new people.	1	2	3	4
8. I talk with, rather than at, people.	1	2	3	4
9. I am open to developing or sustaining intimate relationships.	1	2	3	4
10. I appreciate the importance of parenting the next generation and am committed to supporting it in ways that reflect my own resources.	1	2	3	4
11. I recognize the strengths and weaknesses of my parents' child-rearing skills and feel comfortable modifying them if I choose to become a parent.	1	2	3	4
12. I attempt to be tolerant of others whether or not I approve of their behavior or beliefs.	1	2	3	4
13. I understand and appreciate the contribution cultural diversity makes to the quality of living.	1	2	3	4
14. I understand and appreciate the difference between being educated and being trained.	1	2	3	4
15. My work gives me a sense of self-sufficiency and an opportunity to contribute.	1	2	3	4
16. I have equal respect for the roles of leader and subordinate within the workplace.	1	2	3	4
17. I have chosen an occupation that suits my interests and temperament.	1	2	3	4
18. I have chosen an occupation that does not compromise my physical or psychological health.	1	2	3	4
19. I get along well with my coworkers most of the time.	1	2	3	4
20. When I have a disagreement with a coworker, I try to resolve it directly and constructively.	1	2	3	4
	0	10	21	Points 29

ASSESS YOURSELF 1-1 (cont'd)

SPIRITUAL AND PSYCHOLOGICAL HEALTH	Not True/ Rarely	Somewhat True/ Sometimes	Mostly True/ Usually	Very True/ Always
1. I have a deeply held belief system or personal theology.	1	2	3	4
2. I recognize the contribution that membership in a community of faith can make to a person's overall quality of life.	1	2	3	4
3. I seek experiences with nature and reflect on nature's contribution to my quality of life.	1	2	3	4
4. My spirituality is a resource that helps me remain calm and strong during times of stress.	1	2	3	4
5. I have found appropriate ways to express my spirituality.	1	2	3	4
6. I respect the diversity of spiritual expression and am tolerant of those whose beliefs differ from mine.	1	2	3	4
7. I take adequate time to reflect on my life and my relationships with others and the institutions of society.	1	2	3	4
8. I routinely undertake new experiences.	1	2	3	4
9. I receive adequate support from others.	1	2	3	4
10. I look for opportunities to support others, even occasionally at the expense of my own goals and aspirations.	1	2	3	4
11. I recognize that emotional and psychological health are as important as physical health.	1	2	3	4
12. I express my feelings and opinions comfortably yet am capable of keeping them to myself when appropriate.	1	2	3	4
13. I see myself as a person of worth and feel comfortable with my strengths and limitations.	1	2	3	4
14. I establish realistic goals and work to achieve them.	1	2	3	4
15. I understand the differences between the normal range of emotions and the signs of clinical depression.	1	2	3	4
16. I know how to recognize signs of suicidal thoughts and am willing to intervene.	1	2	3	4
17. I regularly assess my behavior patterns and beliefs and would seek professional assistance for any emotional dysfunction.	1	2	3	4
18. I accept the reality of aging and view it as an opportunity for positive change.	1	2	3	4
19. I accept the reality of death and view it as a normal and inevitable part of life.	1	2	3	4
20. I have made decisions about my own death to ensure that I die with dignity when the time comes.	1	2	3	4

Points________

ASSESS YOURSELF 1-1 (cont'd)

STRESS MANAGEMENT	Not True/ Rarely	Somewhat True/ Sometimes	Mostly True/ Usually	Very True/ Always
1. I accept the reality of change while maintaining the necessary stability in my daily activities.	1	2	3	4
2. I seek change when it is necessary or desirable to do so.	1	2	3	4
3. I know what stress-management services are offered on campus, through my employer, and in my community.	1	2	3	4
4. When necessary, I use the stress-management services to which I have access.	1	2	3	4
5. I employ stress-reduction practices in anticipation of stressful events such as job interviews and final examinations.	1	2	3	4
6. I reevaluate the way in which I handled stressful events so that I can better cope with similar events in the future.	1	2	3	4
7. I turn to relatives and friends during periods of disruption in my life.	1	2	3	4
8. I avoid using alcohol or other drugs during periods of stress.	1	2	3	4
9. I refrain from behaving aggressively or abusively during periods of stress.	1	2	3	4
10. I sleep enough to maintain a high level of health and cope successfully with daily challenges.	1	2	3	4
11. I avoid sleeping excessively as a response to stressful change.	1	2	3	4
12. My diet is conducive to good health and stress management.	1	2	3	4
13. I participate in physical activity to relieve stress.	1	2	3	4
14. I practice stress-management skills such as diaphragmatic breathing and yoga.	1	2	3	4
15. I manage my time effectively.	1	2	3	4

Points__________

FITNESS	Not True/ Rarely	Somewhat True/ Sometimes	Mostly True/ Usually	Very True/ Always
1. I participate in recreational and fitness activities both to minimize stress and to improve or maintain my level of physical fitness.	1	2	3	4
2. I select some recreational activities that are strenuous rather than sedentary in nature.	1	2	3	4
3. I include various types of aerobic conditioning activities among the wider array of recreational and fitness activities in which I engage.	1	2	3	4
4. I engage in aerobic activities with appropriate frequency, intensity, and duration to provide a training effect for my heart and lungs.	1	2	3	4
5. I routinely include strength-training activities among the wider array of fitness activities in which I engage.	1	2	3	4
6. I routinely vary the types of strength-training activities in which I participate in order to minimize injury and strengthen all the important muscle groups.	1	2	3	4
7. I do exercises specifically designed to maintain joint range of motion.	1	2	3	4

ASSESS YOURSELF 1-1 (cont'd)

	Not True/ Rarely	Somewhat True/ Sometimes	Mostly True/ Usually	Very True/ Always
8. I believe that recreational and fitness activities can help me improve my physical health and emotional and social well-being.	1	2	3	4
9. I include a variety of fitness activities in my overall plan for physical fitness.	1	2	3	4
10. I take appropriate steps to avoid injuries when participating in recreational and fitness activities.	1	2	3	4
11. I seek appropriate treatment for all injuries that result from fitness activities.	1	2	3	4
12. I believe older adults should undertake appropriately chosen fitness activities.	1	2	3	4
13. My body composition is consistent with a high level of health.	1	2	3	4
14. I warm up before beginning vigorous activity and cool down afterward.	1	2	3	4
15. I select properly designed and well-maintained equipment and clothing for each activity.	1	2	3	4
16. I avoid using performance-enhancing substances that are known to be dangerous and those whose influence on the body is not fully understood.	1	2	3	4
17. I sleep seven to eight hours daily.	1	2	3	4
18. I refrain from using over-the-counter sleep-inducing aids.	1	2	3	4
19. I follow sound dietary practices as an important adjunct to a health-enhancing physical activity program.	1	2	3	4
20. My current level of fitness allows me to participate fully and effortlessly in my daily activities.	1	2	3	4

Points________

NUTRITION AND WEIGHT MANAGEMENT

	Not True/ Rarely	Somewhat True/ Sometimes	Mostly True/ Usually	Very True/ Always
1. I balance my caloric intake with my calorie expenditure.	1	2	3	4
2. I obtain the recommended number of servings from each of the food groups.	1	2	3	4
3. I select a wide variety of foods chosen from each of the food groups.	1	2	3	4
4. I understand the amount of a particular food that constitutes a single serving.	1	2	3	4
5. I often try new foods, particularly when I know them to be healthful.	1	2	3	4
6. I select breads, cereals, fresh fruits, and vegetables in preference to pastries, candies, sodas, and fruits in heavy syrup.	1	2	3	4
7. I limit the amount of sugar I add to foods during preparation and at the table.	1	2	3	4
8. I consume an appropriate percentage of my total daily calories from carbohydrates.	1	2	3	4
9. I select primarily nonmeat sources of protein, such as peas, beans, and peanut butter, while limiting my consumption of red meat and high-fat dairy products.	1	2	3	4
10. I consume an appropriate percentage of my total daily calories from protein.	1	2	3	4

ASSESS YOURSELF 1-1 (cont'd)

	Not True/ Rarely	Somewhat True/ Sometimes	Mostly True/ Usually	Very True/ Always
11. I select foods prepared with unsaturated vegetable oils while reducing consumption of red meat, high-fat dairy products, and foods prepared with lard (animal fat) or butter.	1	2	3	4
12. I carefully limit the amount of fast food I consume during a typical week.	1	2	3	4
13. I consume an appropriate percentage of my total daily calories from fat.	1	2	3	4
14. I select nutritious foods when I snack.	1	2	3	4
15. I limit my use of salt during food preparation and at the table.	1	2	3	4
16. I consume adequate amounts of fiber.	1	2	3	4
17. I routinely consider the nutrient density of individual food items when choosing foods.	1	2	3	4
18. I maintain my weight without reliance on over-the-counter or prescription diet pills.	1	2	3	4
19. I maintain my weight without reliance on fad diets or liquid weight-loss beverages.	1	2	3	4
20. I exercise regularly to help maintain my weight.	1	2	3	4

Points______

ALCOHOL, TOBACCO, AND OTHER DRUG USE

1. I abstain or drink in moderation when offered alcoholic beverages.	1	2	3	4
2. I abstain from using illegal psychoactive (mind-altering) drugs.	1	2	3	4
3. I do not consume alcoholic beverages or psychoactive drugs rapidly or in large quantities.	1	2	3	4
4. I do not use alcohol or psychoactive drugs in a way that causes me to behave inappropriately.	1	2	3	4
5. My use of alcohol or other drugs does not compromise my academic performance.	1	2	3	4
6. I refrain from drinking alcoholic beverages or using psychoactive drugs when engaging in recreational activities that require strength, speed, or coordination.	1	2	3	4
7. I refrain from drinking alcoholic beverages while participating in occupational activities, regardless of the nature of those activities.	1	2	3	4
8. My use of alcohol or other drugs does not generate financial concerns for myself or others.	1	2	3	4
9. I refrain from drinking alcohol or using psychoactive drugs when driving a motor vehicle or operating heavy equipment.	1	2	3	4
10. I do not drink alcohol or use psychoactive drugs when I am alone.	1	2	3	4
11. I avoid riding with people who have been drinking alcohol or using psychoactive drugs.	1	2	3	4
12. My use of alcohol or other drugs does not cause family dysfunction.	1	2	3	4
13. I do not use marijuana.	1	2	3	4

ASSESS YOURSELF 1-1 (cont'd)

	Not True/ Rarely	Somewhat True/ Sometimes	Mostly True/ Usually	Very True/ Always
14. I do not use hallucinogens.	1	2	3	4
15. I do not use heroin or other illegal intravenous drugs.	1	2	3	4
16. I do not experience blackouts when I drink alcohol.	1	2	3	4
17. I do not become abusive or violent when I drink alcohol or use psychoactive drugs.	1	2	3	4
18. I use potentially addictive prescription medication in complete compliance with my physician's directions.	1	2	3	4
19. I do not smoke cigarettes.	1	2	3	4
20. I do not use tobacco products in any other form.	1	2	3	4
21. I minimize my exposure to secondhand smoke.	1	2	3	4
22. I am concerned about the effect that alcohol, tobacco, and other drug use is known to have on developing fetuses.	1	2	3	4
23. I am concerned about the effect that alcohol, tobacco, and other drugs is known to have on the health of other people.	1	2	3	4
24. I seek natural, health-enhancing highs rather than relying on alcohol, tobacco, and illegal drugs.	1	2	3	4
25. I take prescription medication only as instructed and use over-the-counter medication in accordance with directions.	1	2	3	4

Points__________

DISEASE PREVENTION

1. My diet includes foods rich in phytochemicals.	1	2	3	4
2. My diet includes foods rich in folic acid.	1	2	3	4
3. My diet includes foods that are good sources of dietary fiber.	1	2	3	4
4. My diet is low in dietary cholesterol.	1	2	3	4
5. I follow food preparation practices that minimize the risk of food-borne illness.	1	2	3	4
6. I engage in regular physical activity and am able to control my weight effectively.	1	2	3	4
7. I do not use tobacco products.	1	2	3	4
8. I abstain from alcohol or drink only in moderation.	1	2	3	4
9. I do not use intravenously administered illegal drugs.	1	2	3	4
10. I use safer sex practices intended to minimize my risk of exposure to sexually transmitted diseases, including HIV and HPV.	1	2	3	4
11. I take steps to limit my risk of exposure to the bacterium that causes Lyme disease and the virus that causes hantavirus pulmonary syndrome.	1	2	3	4
12. I control my blood pressure with weight-management and physical fitness activities.	1	2	3	4
13. I minimize my exposure to allergens, including the ones that trigger asthma attacks.	1	2	3	4
14. I wash my hands frequently and thoroughly.	1	2	3	4
15. I use preventive medical care services appropriately.	1	2	3	4
16. I use appropriate cancer self-screening practices such as breast self-examination and testicular self-examination.	1	2	3	4

Assess Yourself 1-1 (cont'd)

	Not True/ Rarely	Somewhat True/ Sometimes	Mostly True/ Usually	Very True/ Always
17. I know which chronic illnesses and diseases are part of my family history.	1	2	3	4
18. I know which inherited conditions are part of my family history and will seek preconceptional counseling regarding these conditions.	1	2	3	4
19. I am fully immunized against infectious diseases.	1	2	3	4
20. I take prescribed medications, particularly antibiotics, exactly as instructed by my physician.	1	2	3	4

Points________

Sexual Health

	Not True/ Rarely	Somewhat True/ Sometimes	Mostly True/ Usually	Very True/ Always
1. I know how sexually transmitted diseases are spread.	1	2	3	4
2. I can recognize the symptoms of sexually transmitted diseases.	1	2	3	4
3. I know how sexually transmitted disease transmission can be prevented.	1	2	3	4
4. I know how safer sex practices reduce the risk of contracting sexually transmitted diseases.	1	2	3	4
5. I follow safer sex practices.	1	2	3	4
6. I recognize the symptoms of premenstrual syndrome and understand how it is prevented and treated.	1	2	3	4
7. I recognize the symptoms of endometriosis and understand the relationship of its symptoms to hormonal cycles.	1	2	3	4
8. I understand the physiological basis of menopause and recognize that it is a normal part of the aging process in women.	1	2	3	4
9. I understand and accept the range of human sexual orientations.	1	2	3	4
10. I encourage the development of flexible sex roles (androgyny) in children.	1	2	3	4
11. I take a mature approach to dating and mate selection.	1	2	3	4
12. I recognize that marriage and other types of long-term relationships can be satisfying.	1	2	3	4
13. I recognize that a celibate lifestyle is appropriate and satisfying for some people.	1	2	3	4
14. I affirm the sexuality of older adults and am comfortable with its expression.	1	2	3	4
15. I am familiar with the advantages and disadvantages of a wide range of birth control methods.	1	2	3	4
16. I understand how each birth control method works and how effective it is.	1	2	3	4
17. I use my birth control method consistently and appropriately.	1	2	3	4
18. I am familiar with the wide range of procedures now available to treat infertility.	1	2	3	4
19. I accept that others may disagree with my feelings about pregnancy termination.	1	2	3	4
20. I am familiar with alternatives available to infertile couples, including adoption.	1	2	3	4

Points________

ASSESS YOURSELF 1-1 (cont'd)

SAFETY PRACTICES AND VIOLENCE PREVENTION

	Not True/ Rarely	Somewhat True/ Sometimes	Mostly True/ Usually	Very True/ Always
1. I attempt to identify sources of risk or danger in each new setting or activity.	1	2	3	4
2. I learn proper procedures and precautions before undertaking new recreational or occupational activities.	1	2	3	4
3. I select appropriate clothing and equipment for all activities and maintain equipment in good working order.	1	2	3	4
4. I curtail my participation in activities when I am not feeling well or am distracted by other demands.	1	2	3	4
5. I repair dangerous conditions or report them to those responsible for maintenance.	1	2	3	4
6. I use common sense and observe the laws governing nonmotorized vehicles when I ride a bicycle.	1	2	3	4
7. I operate all motor vehicles as safely as possible, including using seat belts and other safety equipment.	1	2	3	4
8. I refrain from driving an automobile or boat when I have been drinking alcohol or taking drugs or medications.	1	2	3	4
9. I try to anticipate the risk of falling and maintain my environment to minimize this risk.	1	2	3	4
10. I maintain my environment to minimize the risk of fire, and I have a well-rehearsed plan to exit my residence in case of fire.	1	2	3	4
11. I am a competent swimmer and could save myself or rescue someone who was drowning.	1	2	3	4
12. I refrain from sexually aggressive behavior toward my partner or others.	1	2	3	4
13. I would report an incident of sexual harassment or date rape whether or not I was the victim.	1	2	3	4
14. I would seek help from others if I were the victim or perpetrator of domestic violence.	1	2	3	4
15. I practice gun safety and encourage other gun owners to do so.	1	2	3	4
16. I drive at all times in a way that will minimize my risk of being carjacked.	1	2	3	4
17. I have taken steps to protect my home from intruders.	1	2	3	4
18. I use campus security services as much as possible when they are available.	1	2	3	4
19. I know what to do if I am being stalked.	1	2	3	4
20. I have a well-rehearsed plan to protect myself from the aggressive behavior of other people in my place of residence.	1	2	3	4

Points__________

HEALTH CARE CONSUMERISM

	Not True/ Rarely	Somewhat True/ Sometimes	Mostly True/ Usually	Very True/ Always
1. I know how to obtain valid health information.	1	2	3	4
2. I accept health information that has been deemed valid by the established scientific community.	1	2	3	4
3. I am skeptical of claims that guarantee the effectiveness of a particular health care service or product.	1	2	3	4
4. I am skeptical of practitioners or clinics that advertise or offer services at rates substantially lower than those charged by reputable providers.	1	2	3	4
5. I am not swayed by advertisements that present unhealthy behavior in an attractive manner.	1	2	3	4
6. I can afford proper medical care, including hospitalization.	1	2	3	4
7. I can afford adequate health insurance.	1	2	3	4
8. I understand the role of government health care plans in providing health care to people who qualify for coverage.	1	2	3	4
9. I know how to select health care providers who are highly qualified and appropriate for my current health care needs.	1	2	3	4
10. I seek a second or third opinion when surgery or other costly therapies are recommended.	1	2	3	4
11. I have told my physician which hospital I would prefer to use should the need arise.	1	2	3	4
12. I understand my rights and responsibilities as a patient when admitted to a hospital.	1	2	3	4
13. I practice adequate self-care to reduce my health care expenditures and my reliance on health care providers.	1	2	3	4
14. I am open-minded about alternative health care practices and support current efforts to determine their appropriate role in effective health care.	1	2	3	4
15. I have a well-established relationship with a pharmacist and have transmitted all necessary information regarding medication and use.	1	2	3	4
16. I carefully follow labels and directions when using health care products such as over-the-counter medications.	1	2	3	4
17. I finish all prescription medications as directed rather than stopping use when symptoms subside.	1	2	3	4
18. I report to the appropriate agencies any providers of health care services, information, or products that use deceptive advertising or fraudulent methods of operation.	1	2	3	4
19. I pursue my rights as fully as possible in matters of misrepresentation or consumer dissatisfaction.	1	2	3	4
20. I follow current health care issues in the news and voice my opinion to my elected representatives.	1	2	3	4

Points ______

ASSESS YOURSELF 1-1 (cont'd)

ENVIRONMENTAL HEALTH	Not True/ Rarely	Somewhat True/ Sometimes	Mostly True/ Usually	Very True/ Always
1. I avoid use of and exposure to pesticides as much as possible.	1	2	3	4
2. I avoid use of and exposure to herbicides as much as possible.	1	2	3	4
3. I am willing to spend the extra money and time required to obtain organically grown produce.	1	2	3	4
4. I reduce environmental pollutants by minimizing my use of the automobile.	1	2	3	4
5. I avoid the use of products that contribute to indoor air pollution.	1	2	3	4
6. I limit my exposure to ultraviolet radiation by avoiding excessive sun exposure.	1	2	3	4
7. I limit my exposure to radon gas by using a radon gas detector.	1	2	3	4
8. I limit my exposure to radiation by promptly eliminating radon gas in my home.	1	2	3	4
9. I limit my exposure to radiation by agreeing to undergo medical radiation procedures only when absolutely necessary for the diagnosis and treatment of an illness or disease.	1	2	3	4
10. I avoid the use of potentially unsafe water, particularly when traveling in a foreign country or when a municipal water supply or bottled water is unavailable.	1	2	3	4
11. I avoid noise pollution by limiting my exposure to loud noise or by using ear protection.	1	2	3	4
12. I avoid air pollution by carefully selecting the environments in which I live, work, and recreate.	1	2	3	4
13. I do not knowingly use or improperly dispose of personal care products that can harm the environment.	1	2	3	4
14. I reuse as many products as possible so that they can avoid the recycling bins for as long as possible.	1	2	3	4
15. I participate fully in my community's recycling efforts.	1	2	3	4
16. I encourage the increased use of recycled materials in the design and manufacturing of new products.	1	2	3	4
17. I dispose of residential toxic substances safely and properly.	1	2	3	4
18. I follow environmental issues in the news and voice my opinion to my elected representatives.	1	2	3	4
19. I am aware of and involved in environmental issues in my local area.	1	2	3	4
20. I perceive myself as a steward of the environment for the generations to come rather than as a person with a right to use (and misuse) the environment to meet my immediate needs.	1	2	3	4

Points__________

YOUR TOTAL POINTS __________

Assess Yourself 1-1 (cont'd)

Interpretation

770–880 points
Congratulations! Your health behavior is very supportive of high-level health. Continue to practice your positive health habits, and look for areas in which you can become even stronger. Encourage others to follow your example, and support their efforts in any way you can.

550–769 points
Good job! Your health behavior is relatively supportive of high-level health. You scored well in several areas; however, you can improve in some ways. Identify your weak areas and chart a plan for behavior change.

330–549 points
Caution! Your relatively low score indicates that your behavior may be compromising your health. Review your responses to this assessment carefully, noting the areas in which you scored poorly. Then chart a detailed plan for behavior change.

Below 330
Red flag! Your low score suggests that your health behavior is destructive. Immediate changes in your behavior are needed to put you back on track. Review your responses to this assessment carefully. Then begin to make changes in the most critical areas, such as harmful alcohol or other drug use patterns. Seek help promptly for any difficulties that you are not prepared to deal with **alone,** such as domestic violence or suicidal thoughts. The information you read in this textbook and learn in this course could have a significant effect on your future health. Remember, it's not too late to improve your health!

From Payne, W.A. & Hahn, D.B. (2002). *Understanding Your Health,* 7e. St. Louis: McGraw-Hill.

CHAPTER

2

THE EMOTIONAL AND INTELLECTUAL BASIS OF STRESS

OUTLINE

The Emotional Basis of Stress
- Emotions and Stress
- Lazarus's Stress Emotions
- Emotions in Japanese Psychotherapy

Emotional Development and Personality
- Behaviorism
- Psychoanalytic Theory
- Piaget's Theory of Cognitive Development
- Kohlberg's Theory of Moral Development
- Maslow's Hierarchy of Needs Theory

Stress and Personality
- Stress-Prone Personality Types
- (Ellis's) Irrational, Illogical Personality
- Stress-Resistant Personality Types

The Intellectual Basis of Stress
- Intelligence
- Life Experience
- Verbal and Written Communication
- Creativity
- Problem-Solving Ability

Emotional Intelligence
- Emotions, Moods, Temperament, and Disorders of Emotion
- Five Criteria for Emotional Intelligence

The Convergence of Intellectual and Emotional Factors
- Primary Stress Appraisal
- Secondary Stress Appraisal
- Cognitive Reappraisal

OBJECTIVES

By the end of the chapter students will:

- Understand the influence of the mental and emotional dimensions of stress on health.
- Define personality and explain three different theories concerning its development.
- Explain how personality contributes to the stress response.
- Describe the role of anger and hostility in the development of the stress response.
- Explain the protective effects of the Type B and hardy personalities.
- Describe and compare Type A and C personalities in terms of how they contribute to stress.
- Describe the underlying assumptions of rational emotive therapy as it relates to the stress response.
- Describe emotional intelligence and explain how it relates to stress.
- Describe Millon's eight stress-prone personality styles.
- Describe the differences between primary and secondary stress appraisal.
- Describe the influence of perceived efficacy of coping in the stress appraisal process.
- List and describe how Lazarus's core relational themes relate to stress.

In this chapter we explore the emotional and intellectual basis of stress. In chapter 1 we defined stress as a holistic transaction between an individual and a potential stressor resulting in a stress response. The heart of defining stress this way is viewing it as a transaction. Lazarus and Folkman's[34] transactional stress appraisal model forms the foundation of this chapter and lays the groundwork for section II of the book devoted to coping with stress.

Although this model was not developed as a "health" or "wellness" model per se, it does take a holistic approach to explaining how emotional and intellectual factors are involved in the stress response. It shows how these factors are key personality attributes that are directly related to how we perceive potential stressors. Lazarus and Folkman's[34] model also shows how stress appraisals never take place in a vacuum. They always occur within a specific environmental context that can change over time. They are influenced by prior learning and coping success or failure. Stress appraisal is not static; it is a dynamic process that changes as we change and grow.

This is very similar to how we described health in chapter 1. Our health is ever changing. Our health status can improve as we eat healthier, exercise, and make other lifestyle changes. We'll start this chapter with a detailed description of the emotional basis of stress and a close look at the key "stress emotions" identified by Lazarus.[37]

THE EMOTIONAL BASIS OF STRESS

The emotional basis of stress revolves around the nature of feelings and their role in the stress response. Feelings and emotions are used synonymously and are related to stress in many ways. Daniel Goleman[18] (p. 289), in his groundbreaking book, *Emotional Intelligence,* defines an **emotion** as "a feeling, and its distinctive thoughts, psychological and biological states, and range of propensities to act."

Emotions and thoughts originate in different parts of the brain yet work together when processing sensations and other information. Emotions originate in a separate, more primitive, *feeling part* of the brain called the *limbic system* which we will discuss in detail in Chapter 5. Although we can identify electrical and biochemical signs of emotional activity in this feeling part of the brain, it does not act in isolation of the rest of the brain. The feeling part of the brain is nestled among the *thinking and sensing parts* of the brain (areas in the *cerebral cortex*) and because of this we must acknowledge the role that thoughts and sensations play in mediating emotions. Thoughts and sensations do not exist in a vacuum and often have a rich history of stored memories (yet another part of the brain exerting influence) and cultural influences. Additionally, Goleman[18] found that we have two sets of memories: one for ordinary facts and one for emotionally charged ones. *Stress-prone* or *stress-resistant* personalities might be more related to these emotional memories derived from people's *distinctive thoughts, psychological and biological states,* and *range of propensities to act* (in Goleman's [1997] words) than anything else.

Philosophers, psychologists, and others have argued for centuries about the organization and typing of emotions. Goleman[18] believes that there are *families of emotions* that derive their origins from a set of basic, or *primary emotions* (see Table 2-1, Families of Emotions).

Goleman[18] believes that all emotions are essentially impulses to act. They are the result of an evolutionary process that compels us to stop, pay attention, assess any potential danger, and act, all within a split second. As Goleman[18] points out, the root of the word *emotion* is

KEY TO UNDERSTANDING

A key to understanding emotions is realizing that although they originate in a separate, more primitive, *feeling part* of the brain called the *limbic system,* this feeling part of the brain is nestled among and influenced by the *thinking and sensing parts* of the brain (areas in the *cerebral cortex*) that play a role in mediating our emotions.

Table 2-1 Families of Emotions

Primary Emotion	Family Members
Anger	fury, outrage, resentment, wrath, exasperation, acrimony, animosity, annoyance, irritability
Sadness	grief, sorrow, cheerlessness, melancholy, despair, dejection, loneliness, self-pity
Fear	anxiety, apprehension, nervousness, concern, consternation, wariness, dread, fright, terror
Enjoyment	happiness, joy, relief, contentment, bliss, delight, thrill, amusement, rapture, pride
Love	acceptance, friendliness, trust, kindness, affinity, devotion, adoration, infatuation
Surprise	shock, astonishment, amazement, wonder
Disgust	contempt, disdain, scorn, aversion, distaste, revulsion, abhorrence
Shame	guilt, embarrassment, chagrin, remorse, humiliation, regret, mortification

Source: Derived from Goleman, 1997, p. 290.

emotions a feeling or state of mind, and the thoughts and physical reactions associated with it

> **KEY TO UNDERSTANDING**
>
> A key to understanding all emotions is realizing that they are essentially impulses to act; an evolutionary process that compels us to stop, pay attention, assess any potential danger, and act, all within a split second.

> **KEY TO UNDERSTANDING**
>
> People often confuse negative emotions with stress. A key to understanding negative emotions like anxiety is realizing that your anxiety only becomes a stressor when your brain perceives it as threatening and something you can't cope with.

from the Latin *motere* meaning "to move" while the prefix *e* added to the root means "to move away." As we'll see in this and later chapters, some of the stronger emotions like fear and anger are linked to the perception of threat and the mobilization of energy in the *fight or flight response.*

Emotions and Stress

Emotions can act as stressors, that is, stimuli that are capable of triggering a stress response. For example, a person could wake up one morning feeling anxious. This isn't unusual—in the course of any given day you could feel anxious, sad, troubled, happy, ecstatic, or a host of other emotions. However, if you perceive the anxiety you are feeling this morning as a *threat* and something you *can't cope with,* it can become a stressor and trigger a stress response.

Emotions can also be by-products of a stress response. Imagine that you are stuck in traffic and this will make you late for work. You can't control this, realize you will miss an important meeting, and feel threatened by being stuck in the traffic jam. Once the sense of threat and inability to cope kicks in, it triggers a stress response. Now you begin to feel your heart race, your breathing deepen, and sweat begins to accumulate on your forehead. Sensing this you get angry and begin to experience rage at the traffic, the accident that caused the traffic, and the drivers of the two cars that "did this to you." The emotions of anger and rage were triggered *because of* your stress response. Had you not become aware of the feelings of stress and loss of control, you may not have gotten angry.

Emotions can also sustain a stress response long after the initial threat is gone. For example, imagine you lied to your mother about something. Anticipating the confrontation with her, you felt threatened and unable to cope. This triggered a stress response that continued until you met her that evening and lied. Satisfied by your lie, your mother backs off and says everything is okay. Technically, the threat is now gone and things with your mother have been worked out. The only problem is that you are feeling guilty. The emotion of guilt, one of the strongest you can feel, keeps your stress response alive, even though your mom said everything is okay.

People often confuse negative emotions with stress. They are two different things. As we'll see later in the chapter, it is how you *perceive* the feelings and *deal (or not deal) with them* that triggers the stress response, not the emotions themselves. For instance, in the example above, when you woke up and felt anxious, you could have told yourself, "Huh, I'm feeling a little anxious this morning. I'll have to be extra careful to relax a little more today." Another way to deal with it would have been to do something productive, such as go for a run, or meditate for a few minutes. In either case you have not given into the anxiety and perceived it as meaning "I am stressed." The anxiety only becomes a stressor when your brain perceives it as threatening and something you can't cope with. Anxiety, like any other emotion, is a feeling, *not stress.*

Both the subjective experiencing and interpretation of emotions and the objective expression of them are intricately woven into the fabric of personalities. The myriad of factors that make up our personalities play a role in how feelings originate, how we perceive them, how we express them, and, ultimately, how we deal with them.

Lazarus's Stress Emotions

In his most recent book on stress appraisal and coping, Lazarus[37] describes a new synthesis of his previous ideas. Lazarus believes that stressful appraisals are linked to both ineffective coping and "stress emotions." Lazarus identifies the key emotions linked to stressful appraisals (see Table 2-2, Stress Emotions and Their Core Relational Themes).

Accompanying each of these emotions are what Lazarus terms "core relational themes." These core relational themes are linked to emotional narratives or scripts that accompany the emotions for the person. These emotional narratives develop as part of our personality structure. These emotional narratives are the inner dialogues we carry on with ourselves that tell us how we *should* or *must* react to the emotions (see Living Constructively Box on p. 30). Often these inner dialogues are negative and suggest unhealthy ways to deal with the emotions.

Let's use jealousy as an example. Years ago, one of Dr. Blonna's students gave an example of how not to deal with jealousy. The young man had just left Dr. Blonna's class on his way to the Student Center to pick up a snack. On his way there he saw his girlfriend under the eaves of the cafeteria building hugging another guy. She actually

Table 2-2 Stress Emotions and Their Core Relational Themes

The Nasty Emotions	
Anger	— demeaning personal offense to me or mine resulting in harm and the assignment of blame against another while in the presence of the person causing the harm.
Hostility	— latent, simmering angry disposition in the absence of the person causing the harm.
Envy	— wanting what someone else has, feeling deprived or being cheated out of the object of the envy.
Jealousy	— resenting a third party for perceived loss or threat of loss of another's bounty or affection.
The Existential Emotions	
Fright	— facing a sudden and overwhelming concrete physical danger.
Anxiety	— a slow, vague, anticipatory state of unease, concern, apprehension, and worry.
Guilt	— a real or imagined moral transgression that is compounded if we harm someone in the process.
Shame	— a sense of personal failure, of letting someone down. The presence of the other person can be literal (the person is there physically) or abstract (the person is *not* there physically).
Emotions Provoked by Unfavorable Life Conditions	
Relief	— removal from a frustrating or threatening life condition.
Hope	— fearing the worst yet yearning for the better regarding an unfavorable situation.
Depression	— a complex emotional mixture of anxiety, anger, guilt, and shame which accompanies a struggle to restore a worthwhile life after experiencing an irrevocable loss.
Sadness	— a wistful acceptance of a loss that cannot be restored accompanied by the loss of hope.
Empathic Emotions	
Gratitude	— the pressure to appreciate an altruistic gift that provides personal benefit.
Compassion	— being emotionally moved by another's suffering and wanting to help.

raised up on her toes and kissed the other guy on his cheek. Dr. Blonna's student was enraged. He assumed that his girlfriend was cheating on him with this other guy. Using Lazarus's core relational theme for the stress emotion *jealousy,* the student was *resenting a third party for a perceived loss of another's (his girlfriend's) affection.* This student went on to describe his reaction to this emotion and theme. He told Dr. Blonna he shut himself in his room and drank all day. He didn't return any phone calls, even his girlfriend's, and later that evening got into a fistfight with another student at the pub on campus and was almost arrested by the police from the adjoining community.

Needless to say, that was not a very healthy reaction to the stress emotion *jealousy*. Unfortunately, many people do not develop effective coping strategies as part of their personality development. Changing stress-producing inner dialogues is the focus of some of the stress management techniques we will discuss in chapter 7.

It is relatively easy to see in Table 2-2 how some stress emotions and their core relational themes are related to stressful appraisals. It is easy for most people to understand how anger and hostility, for example, can result in stress by linking these powerful negative emotions to people and situations that are appraised as threatening or harmful. Happiness-joy, pride, and love, the emotions linked to favorable life conditions, are not included in the table because they are generally positively toned and not related to stress. These emotions, however, can be linked to stress. The best way to understand how emotions linked to favorable life conditions can result in stress is to examine them within the framework of the entire stress appraisal model. One's perception of love, for instance, isn't always accompanied by altruistic feelings and logical thinking. Often love comes with emotional strings and historical baggage from previous relationships and interactions with significant others. Because of these emotional strings and historical baggage, we may have illogical expectations of love and potential loved ones. For instance, we may put loved ones on a pedestal and fail to see their flaws. We may expect too much from them. We all know people who fall madly in love with someone, rush headlong into the relationship, and refuse to accept obvious cues that the loved one is not the picture of perfection who will provide 24/7 bliss and happiness. When the reality of the loved one sets in (he or she is not that beautiful, sexy, intelligent, kind, patient, etc.), the appraisal changes. Love can also create stress when it steers us in directions that compromise our goals, values, morals, and ethics. Lovers often make demands on us that put us in positions where we are forced to choose between them and family, friends, careers, freedom, and so on.

The key to understanding the *stress emotions* is to realize that they are connected to commonly held *core relational themes* in which they are embedded. In the next section of this chapter we will explore how emotional and intellectual personality factors develop and are related to the stress response.

Emotions in Japanese Psychotherapy

As we have just seen in this chapter, Lazarus (1999) has clearly identified what he refers to as the fifteen "stress emotions," those feelings that are strongly associated with triggering a stress response. Further, these stress emotions are central to "core relational themes," our internalized personal scripts regarding what these emotions mean to us. The interpretation of the meaning of emotions and their place in these personal scripts is greatly influenced by culture and context. That is, we learn what these emotions are supposed to mean when they arise in specific situations and at certain times in our lives. This meaning does not exist independently from a cultural context. The same potential stressor might trigger different emotions and be linked to entirely different core relational themes in a different culture and in different times. In other words, the cognitive appraisal of stressors is influenced by cultural values and expectations.

Morita therapy represents the action element of Japanese psychology. A large part of Morita therapy teaches people how to accept and co-exist with unpleasant feelings. This is a major difference between the way Americans and other Western European cultures perceive emotions and the way the Japanese culture does. The Morita approach to dealing with feelings is very different from those emphasized in Western clinical psychology.

Shomo Morita (1998) described five guiding principles of feelings that formed the basis of his work in treating people with anxiety-based disorders. David K. Reynolds,[54,55] one of America's foremost experts in the application of Morita and Naikan therapies, adapted Morita's principles for use with his clients. Reynolds's adapted principles are described in the following Living Constructively Box.

KEY TO UNDERSTANDING

A key to understanding the interpretation of the emotions and their place in potentially-stressful personal scripts is realizing that they are strongly influenced by culture and context. In other words, the cognitive appraisal of stressors is influenced by cultural values and our expectations.

Living Constructively

The Five Principles of Feelings

The following five principles of feelings clearly illustrate the differences between Eastern and Western psychological traditions. They were synthesized by David K. Reynolds[54] in his classic work, *Constructive Living.*

Principle #1. Feelings are not controllable by the will.

While we might be able to clearly identify what we are feeling, and even understand its relationship to our stress, we can't switch feelings on and off. In other words, we can't make ourselves feel anything. Feelings come and go; we cannot directly control them by our sheer will alone. What we can control is our behavior, what we do in response to these feelings.

Principle #2. Feelings must be recognized and accepted as they are.

Rather than feel guilty or upset about feeling something, it is better to note what you are feeling, accept it, and move on. Since feelings arise on their own, and this is beyond our ability to control, it doesn't make sense to feel responsible for them and feel bad for being unable to control them.

Principle #3. Every feeling, however unpleasant, has its uses.

Acknowledging that you are feeling guilty, for instance, can cause you to examine your behavior. Admitting that you are feeling angry can help you identify the source of your anger and show you that something upsets you enough to trigger such strong emotions. Realizing that something causes you to feel afraid can motivate you to try to gain control over the situation.

Principle #4. Feelings fade in time unless they are restimulated.

Feelings, both positive and negative, diminish over time. Unless we do something to restimulate them (like constantly think about them and subvocally bring them up), feelings will start to fade.

Principle #5. Feelings can be indirectly influenced by behavior.

Feelings change in response to behavior. For instance, you can help negative feelings dissipate more rapidly by doing something productive. This will not only take your mind off your bad feelings, it will trigger new feelings of accomplishment. The worst thing to do whenever you are experiencing negative feelings is to sit around and think about them. This will constantly keep them in the forefront of your mind and keep them alive. It is better to do something productive so you stop thinking about the negative feelings.

The major difference regarding feelings in American versus Japanese approaches to dealing with emotions is what one *does* with them. Morita (1998) believed that since we cannot control or understand the etiology of our emotions, it is a waste of time to spend time trying to *work on* them. Rather, it is more important to acknowledge them, accept them for what they are, and stop blaming them for *causing* our behavior. Beyond this, attempts to change feelings by discussing them, trying to gain more insight into their etiology, or trying to understand them more deeply is wasted time. Morita also believed that since feelings are beyond our control we should not feel responsibility for them. Rather, we should shift that responsibility to what we can control, our behavior. A large part of Morita therapy is getting clients to believe this. Everyone has examples of things they do, despite not feeling great about them. From going to work to paying bills, we all engage in productive behavior, *despite* our unpleasant feelings about these behaviors.

Let's use going to class as an example. Imagine you have an 8:00 a.m. class and it is the winter session. It is dark, cold, and blustery as your alarm clock goes off at 6:45 a.m. to get ready for school. You lie around in bed telling yourself, "I don't feel like going to school today." You ask yourself, "Why did I ever sign up for 8:00 a.m. classes?" You continue to analyze this decision and your current feelings about going to class: "I wonder why I agreed to take this class. I really hate getting up early and going out in the cold. I don't like it when it is dark outside. I wonder whatever prompted me to take this class." As you sit in bed going through all of this self-analysis, you feel less and less like going to class. After twenty minutes of doing this you still feel miserable, and now, on top of everything, you are running late and worry about being late for class and finding a decent parking spot close to class.

Morita (1998) would propose that rather than lie in bed ruminating on how horrible it is having to face the cold, cruel morning and go to class, that it is better to just get up, jump in the shower, get dressed, and leave. In doing so you become involved in productive activity, get involved in morning preparation activities, and stop the chain of stressful thinking about how horrible it is to go to school on such a blustery day. Even if the feelings don't disappear completely, they cease to become the entire focus of your morning and are put in a different perspective. From this perspective they are not as dominant and will have a better chance of diminishing. You will also begin to see (if you allow yourself to) that your feelings don't drive your behavior. It is entirely possible to be productive *despite* feeling crummy. This is a major lesson that needs to be learned before you can manage your stress (and life in general). Just because you are anxious, worried, afraid, angry, etc., doesn't mean you can't go to school or work, take the dog for a walk, make breakfast for your kids, and do the countless things that need to get done.

KEY TO UNDERSTANDING

A key to understanding Morita therapy is realizing that your feelings don't drive your behavior. It is entirely possible to be productive *despite* feeling anxious, worried, afraid, angry, etc. If you shift your attention away from these, and other negative emotions, and onto productive behavior, in time, these feelings will pass.

EMOTIONAL DEVELOPMENT AND PERSONALITY

The **personality** is a collection of thoughts, attitudes, values, beliefs, perceptions, behaviors, and emotions that define who we are, how we view the world around us, and how others perceive us. Personality is constantly evolving and is the sum of everything we have experienced in our lives. Our emotional development occurs in parallel with all of the other facets of our personality.

There are many different theories regarding how personality develops. It isn't the purpose of this book to describe all of the traditional and nontraditional ways of explaining how personality develops. Instead, we will focus on a few of the most widely accepted theories to illustrate how personality and emotional well-being evolve. Table 2-3 summarizes the theories of six of the classic theorists and how they explain personality development.

Table 2-3 Traditional Models of Personality and Growth

View	Emphasis
Behavioralists	Responses to specific or generalized stimuli to explain human behavior
Freud	Growth as struggle between the unconscious-irrational forces and the conscious-rational resources of life
Erikson	Psychosocial aspects of growth
Piaget	Intellectual-maturational aspects of growth
Kohlberg	Moral-ethical dimensions of growth
Maslow	Growth in terms of inner needs and motivation

personality our unique collection of thoughts, attitudes, values, beliefs, perceptions, and behaviors that define who we are as people

Behaviorism

Behavioralism, developed by John Watson,[75] proposes that personality develops as a result of responses to generalized and specific stimuli. A stimulus-response model does not presuppose the existence of any innate, predetermined human personality attributes. Behavioralists believe our personalities are the result of a myriad of interactions between stimuli (people, places, events, situations, and images) and the responses they have evoked. Responses can be either positive or negative and can vary in their strength. The more powerful the response is, the more likely it is that we will either embrace (positive response) or reject (negative response) whatever stimuli prompted it.

Psychoanalytic Theory

Freudian psychoanalytical theory promotes the notion that human personality develops as a result of a struggle between conscious and unconscious forces in our lives.[22] These conscious forces struggle for control of our behavior. They struggle with the id, the unconscious and irrational mind, which is driven by eros, a powerful life force striving for the pursuit of pleasure. The fuel of this life force, libidinal energy, is channeled into various centers of our bodies during different stages of our development and creates a set of needs that must be satisfied. According to Freud, the personality develops in response to our ability to satisfy these needs. If these needs are not satisfied, we become fixated, or stuck, at various stages of life and develop neurotic personality traits. These traits carry over into the successive stages of development unless they are resolved at some point in time.

Eric Erickson,[10] who studied with Freud, also constructed a model that views personality development as a result of a struggle between opposing forces. These forces present themselves in a series of eight stages that occur throughout our lives. Erickson viewed development as a conflict between opposing psychosocial forces and qualities instead of a conflict between the id and the ego/superego. Healthy personality development results from accomplishing the developmental tasks required for each stage. Inadequate task resolution results in thwarted development in that particular area.

Piaget's Theory of Cognitive Development

Jean Piaget,[51] a Swiss psychologist, was another personality theorist who focused on stages of cognitive development. Cognitive development is one facet of personality that influences who we are and how we view ourselves. Like Erickson, Piaget felt that our cognitive abilities progress as we move through a series of stages. These stages require increasingly more sophisticated types of thought processes and abilities that depend on neurological development and mastery of previous tasks. These tasks range from the simple ability to manipulate objects to using logical thought and abstract reasoning.

Kohlberg's Theory of Moral Development

Lawrence Kohlberg[31] proposed another developmental approach to understanding personality—a theory that emphasizes moral development. Kohlberg suggests that there are stages of moral thinking and judging and that fully functioning adult moral reasoning occurs as a result of successful progression through those various stages and levels. Progression through Kohlberg's stages and levels is shaped by various influences, such as family, culture and subculture, and society.

Maslow's Hierarchy of Needs Theory

The last developmental theory we will examine is Abraham Maslow's[44] Hierarchy of Needs. Maslow, a humanist, believed that all humans are unique and are capable of growing and reaching their utmost potential. He believed that humans are essentially good and have the ability to make choices about the direction in which they want their lives to move. Maslow believed that all people are capable of reaching their highest potential if they progress through a series of development stages that meet various basic human needs. Figure 2-1 summarizes these needs.

Maslow was interested in human potential. He felt that all people are born with unique qualities and the ability to maximize their genetically determined potential. He was convinced that successful people, those who seem to live life to its fullest, share certain unique qualities that allow them to live to their fullest potential. He compiled a list of forty-eight of the most influential, historical, and contemporary figures of his time; people he considered to be fully self-actualized. Among those on his list were historical figures such as Abraham Lincoln, Henry David Thoreau, and Ludwig von Beethoven. Contemporary figures of his time included Albert Einstein, Eleanor and Franklin D. Roosevelt, Eugene V. Debs, and Amelia Earhart.

In studying these and other fully self-actualized people, Maslow identified the following sixteen common characteristics:

1. Do not distort reality
2. Have a high level of self-acceptance
3. Have loving and intimate relationships with others
4. Are autonomous and independent
5. Are spontaneous in thought and emotion
6. Are task-oriented rather than self-oriented
7. Are open to newness and change
8. View and appreciate familiar things in new and different ways
9. Possess a sense of spirituality that connects them to all living things and the universe

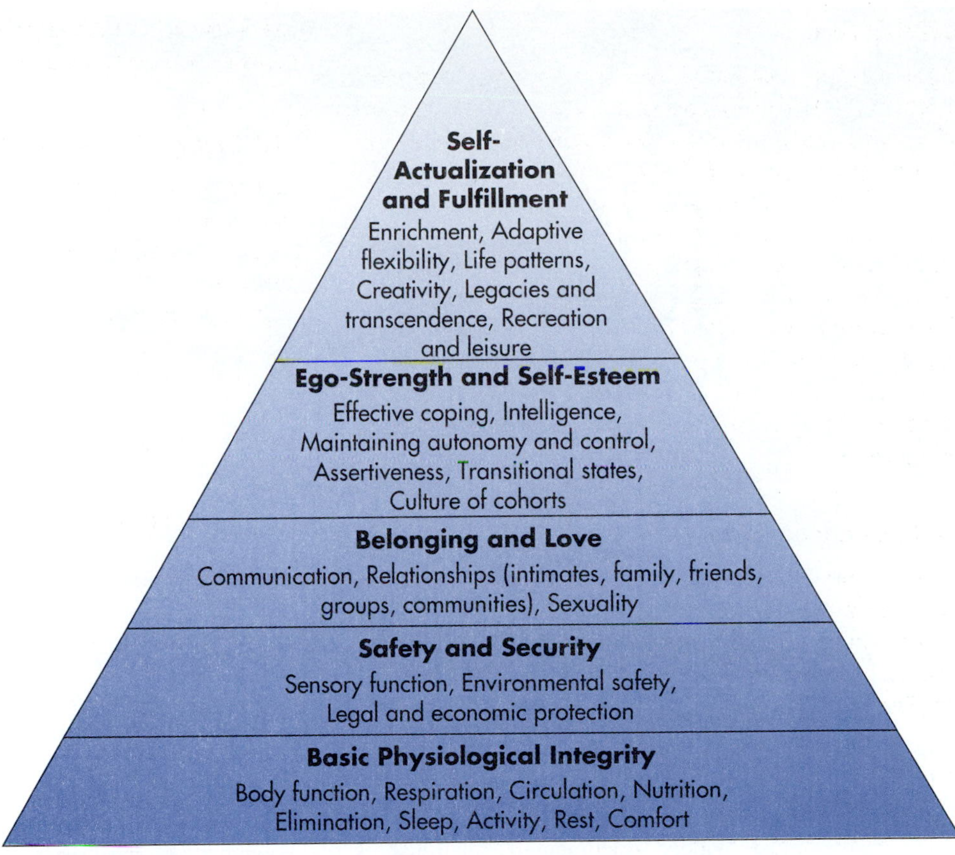

Figure 2-1
Maslow's hierarchy of needs.

10. Have empathy toward those from cultures other than their own
11. Relate to others as individuals
12. Have their own unique ethical sense of right and wrong
13. Resist acculturation
14. Are able to tolerate and enjoy silence and solitude
15. Are creative and inventive
16. Have a sense of humor and an appreciation of their own and other human failings

These characteristics set self-actualizers apart from others and enable them to continue to grow and fully develop their potential. These characteristics create and maintain a personality that enables self-actualizers to take advantage of situations that can contribute to their growth and to learn from negative experiences that could be detrimental to their well-being.

STRESS AND PERSONALITY

As we have seen, there are many different ways to describe the many facets of personality and how it evolves. Whether you believe personality develops in response to meeting inner needs, fulfilling developmental tasks, successfully completing stages of moral development, or any other criteria, there is an emotional component to this growth and development.

For instance, if you adhere to Maslow's Hierarchy of Needs theory, you would believe that successfully working your way up the hierarchy of needs contributes to healthy emotional development. Conversely, not fully meeting needs at any level of the hierarchy results in incomplete psychological growth and development with resultant retarded emotional development.

If you adhered to Freudian psychoanalytic theory you'd believe that healthy personality development occurs as a result of meeting instinctual needs that correspond to different stages of life. Failure to completely satisfy these instinctual needs will leave one stuck psychologically and emotionally at that level. Such people will carry around excess emotional "baggage" because of these unmet instinctual needs. In a sense, having this emotional baggage or retarded emotional development can result in a more "stress-prone" personality. Not having it can result in a more "stress-resistant" personality.

Stress-Prone Personality Types

Over the last forty years there have been many studies of the nature of personality and how it contributes to stress. While current studies tend to focus more on emotions and perception, earlier research focused on personality types, composites of personality characteristics, and behavior. We'll examine a few classic studies and models

Type A personalities are always trying to do more and more in less and less time.

of *stress-prone* personality and how they contribute to stress. We'll start this section of the chapter with a close look at the Type A Personality, a construct that has permanently etched itself into the consciousness of America.

The Type A Personality

One of the most widely documented relationships between personality, behavior, and stress is the link between the **Type A personality** and stress, pioneered by Friedman and Rosenman.[19] Friedman and Rosenman were *cardiologists* working in San Francisco. They first described the Type A behavior pattern in their patients.

Characteristics of Type As The Type A individual is someone who is always trying to achieve or acquire more and more things in less and less time. The Type A person is a chronic overachiever, usually in competition with others. Even though Type As put themselves under enormous pressure on a regular basis, they don't react to this by getting anxious. Rather, they confidently grapple with these self-imposed challenges.[53,73]

The typical Type A personality has the following characteristics:

- **Competitive**—Type As want to win at everything; even a child's board game can turn into a battleground. Type As often bring their competitive nature to their play, and recreational pursuits become competitive athletic events.
- **Verbally aggressive**—Often the speech of Type As, besides being rushed, is peppered with explosive accentuation of key words.
- **Hard-driving**—Type As push themselves to limits that most people resist. They routinely perform two or more tasks simultaneously and overbook their schedules. They jump from one task to another with little or no downtime. Because of this Type As are often rewarded for their efforts. They work long hours and still take work home.
- **Unable to relax**—Even while on vacation Type As tend to feel guilty about not doing something productive.
- **Very time conscious**—A Type A personality would have a very hard time getting through the day without a watch. Type As maintain strict schedules with little flexibility. They hate to "waste" time. Waiting in line at the supermarket or at a fast-food restaurant drives them up a wall because they are very impatient.
- **Easily angered**—Type As are easily angered. They have very short fuses. This anger or strong feeling of displeasure cuts across all barriers.
- **Hostile**—While anger is general and can be directed at events or objects, hostility is focused on people. Type As are hostile, and other people are the target of their anger (see Assess Yourself 2-1).

In addition to these traits, Type As exhibit body language and speech patterns that are noticeably different from those of non-Type As.[57,58]

The following body language and speech patterns typify Type As when responding to potentially stressful situations:

- **Tightening of facial muscles**—noticeably tense muscles of the face, neck, and forehead.
- **Gesturing with a clenched fist**—clench their fists and punch home their points.
- **Grimacing**—contort their facial muscles to express displeasure.

Type A personality a stress-prone personality characterized by aggressive, competitive, and hostile attitudes and behavior

- **Using explosive speech**—change their vocal intonation and use loud bursts of key words to make their points.
- **Interrupting the interviewer**—cut off the interviewer to make their points.
- **Hurrying the pace**—try to speed along the pace of the interview by finishing the interviewer's sentences and by other means.

This chronic combination of both substance (beliefs/behaviors) and style (the manner in which they are expressed) characterizes the Type A behavior pattern.

Type A personalities usually are highly successful people. Their hard work, fanatical drive, and competitiveness are rewarded with financial success and the admiration of their peers, who often wonder how they sustain their high level of activity. Unfortunately, there is a price to pay for this.

Type A and Health Friedman and Rosenman[19] wondered whether the presence of these personality attributes was merely a coincidence or whether there was some relationship between them and an increased risk for coronary heart disease. In looking back at the medical records of their patients, they examined whether those exhibiting Type A traits developed coronary heart disease (CHD) at a greater rate than did those with a calmer, more relaxed personality. CHD, also known as coronary artery disease, involves damage to the vessels that supply blood to the heart muscle.

Friedman and Rosenman found that Type As did in fact experience a greater rate of CHD than did patients not displaying Type A behavior patterns. Their research controlled the other factors associated with CHD, such as diet, lack of exercise, smoking, and high blood pressure. Their work has become so well known that the phrase *Type A* has become synonymous with people who are aggressive, competitive, and hard-driving. Their original studies and the countless studies that have followed have uncovered a strong relationship between the Type A behavior pattern and an increased risk for heart disease and premature death from all causes.[15,56]

Other subsequent long-term studies have noted similar associations between Type A behavior and increased risk for CHD in groups of healthy subjects.[23,53] The Type A personality is relatively stable; 61 percent of subjects rated as Type A between 1960 and 1961 retained that classification in a 27-year follow-up study.[4]

The increased risks associated with the Type A behavior pattern are not gender-specific. Although the majority of Type A studies are of men, research shows that both Type A men and Type A women are at increased risk for CHD.[1,32,47,48] One large research project, the Framingham Study, showed that Type A women are more than three times as likely to develop heart disease as Type B women.[23]

Recent studies of the Type A behavior pattern, stress, and cardiovascular reactivity clarify some of the earlier work concerning the specific relationships of these three variables. While the Type A personality was originally thought to be a causative factor in high blood pressure, recent evidence suggests that this may not be the case. Despite the tendency for Type As to show heightened responses under experimental conditions, these changes do not represent higher levels of blood pressure under normal circumstances.[54,55,56] However, there is a strong association between permanent elevations in blood pressure and people whose personalities might be characterized as hostile or angry.[58,60,61,62,63]

Because of inconsistencies in results[45,53] and problems in research associated with Type As,[71] some researchers have attempted to isolate which Type A factors are more significantly related to cardiovascular disease. Their studies point to two factors as the most predictive of all Type A variables: anger and hostility. **Anger** in general is directed at anything, and **hostility** is a type of anger that is directed specifically at people. Anger seems to be more of a reaction to a situation, while hostility is an enduring trait; it is difficult to isolate and measure either trait independently. Evidence supports that a significant relationship exists between hostility and anger and negative health outcomes.[2,42,43]

A significant relationship between the degree of hostility and the severity of the disease was found in the Williams et al.[76] study of subjects who already had coronary atherosclerosis. In healthy subjects, hostility level was significantly related to both heart attack and death from CHD.[46,71] Additionally, death rates from all causes were significantly related to high levels of hostility.[3,44,67] Two studies[9,45] discovered that men and boys have higher hostility scores than do their female counterparts, possibly explaining the heightened risk of CHD in males.

Type C Personality

In their book *Type C Behavior and Cancer,* Temoshok and Dreher,[72] describe yet another personality type, the Type C. The **Type C personality** is also referred to as the *cancer-prone personality* or the *helpless/hopeless personality* because of the prominence of these two emotions in this type of person. People with this type of personality respond to repeated failure and stress by giving up and developing a sense of hopelessness and helplessness about their problems. Rather than respond with greater anxiety and emotion, Type C persons show a suppression

anger a strong feeling of displeasure targeted at anything

hostility anger that is directed at someone

Type C personality a personality type also known as the helpless/hopeless personality because of the prominence of these emotions or absence of emotion.[14,27] While Type As are characterized by anger, hostility, and aggression, Type Cs show none of these traits and not only suppress their emotions but resign themselves to their fate.[12,28]

Type C personalities have also been referred to as "people pleasers" because of their desire to come off as more acceptable to others. They intentionally suppress anger and other negative feelings in an attempt to "be nice" rather than stand up for their own values. In a sense, this violates their integrity, contributes to their passivity, and reinforces their sense of helplessness and hopelessness.[25,72]

Studies point to a relationship between personality attributes and cancer.[13] Schmale and Iker[65] describe hopelessness as a key predictor of cervical cancer. In their study, Schmale and Iker[65] interviewed 68 women with evidence of suspicious cancer cells in the cervix. Interviews conducted with these women prior to their diagnoses measured their level of hopelessness. The researchers predicted which women were likely to develop the disease based on their higher levels of hopelessness. Of the 28 women who would ultimately be diagnosed with cervical cancer, 19 had high levels of hopelessness and were predicted to develop the disease. Other studies of different forms of cancer had similar results.[12]

Seligman[66] also studied hopelessness and helplessness and found them to be learned responses to failure. Seligman called this *learned helplessness.* In general, there are three components to the helpless/hopeless personality:

1. Cognitive—People with learned helplessness do not believe they can overcome their problems and succeed where they once failed.
2. Emotional—Repeated failure and lack of belief in their ability to overcome their problems result in chronic depression.
3. Behavioral—Depression and lack of faith in their ability to overcome their problems create inertia, a failure to attempt to change.

Rather than fight and attempt to overcome their problems, those with this personality construct tend to give up. Giving up rather than fighting back is implicated in a poor prognosis to overcome disease.

Greer et al.[21] characterized having a "fighting spirit" as a key variable in surviving cancer. Those with a fighting spirit were angry at being sick and wanted to fight back. Greer et al.[21] believe that this fighting spirit is the exact opposite of the helpless/hopeless personality which gives up. In a fifteen-year follow-up study of breast cancer survivers, those with a fighting spirit were more than twice as likely to be alive than were the helpless/hopeless personalities.[21]

Eysenck[12] cautions against using the word *causal* to describe the relationship between personality attributes and the development of cancer. Eysenck[12] believes that personality attributes such as the Type C personality interact synergistically with other risk factors, such as smoking and exposure to exogenous carcinogens. This relationship seems to hold true for both the development and the continued spread of cancer.[14]

In characterizing the helpless/hopeless personality as a form of learned helplessness, Seligman[66] opened the door to the possibility of being able to change. In his book *Learned Optimism,* Seligman[67] describes how people can change their helpless/hopeless personalities. Different counseling, psychiatric help, and stress-management interventions have been shown to work in helping individuals gain control of their lives, renew their hope, and feel more optimistic about their abilities to overcome their problems and diseases.[16,38,39,65] Such interventions have also been shown to improve the immune response, which can facilitate treatment and cure.[26]

(Ellis's) Irrational, Illogical Personality

Albert Ellis,[6,7,8] the founder of a type of therapy called rational emotive behavior therapy (REBT), has developed a group of personality attributes that he has labeled as *illogical beliefs* and that underlie his theory of stress and neurotic behavior. As touched on in chapter 1, Ellis believes people and things don't make us feel bad and behave neurotically. Instead, our negative thoughts and illogical beliefs about these people and things are the basis for our stress and neuroses. Ellis believes our perception of situations determines whether these situations become stressors.

The underlying theory of REBT is based on Ellis's ABC model. In this model the presence of an activating event, *A*, triggers a series of illogical beliefs. These illogical beliefs, *B*, cause a variety of negative mental, emotional, physical, behavioral, and social consequences, *C*. In essence, $A + B = C$.

The Role of Irrational Beliefs In his clinical work with patients, Ellis identified ten commonly held illogical beliefs about life (see Table 2-4). Such beliefs form the basis of an irrational **belief system** that gives a distorted perspective for assessing potentially stressful situations. Walen et al.[74] grouped the ten illogical/irrational beliefs into four categories:

1. "Awfulizing" statements—exaggerate the negative effects of a situation.

   People in this category could be referred to as "awfulizers" or "catastrophizers." The least little stressor is a catastrophe for them.
2. Shoulds/musts/oughts—set illogical demands on oneself and others.

belief system a collection of values, attitudes, and beliefs about the world and interactions between people

Table 2-4 Ellis and Harper's Ten Irrational Beliefs

Irrational Belief	Rational Belief
1. You must have love or approval from all the people you find significant.	1. Although it is *desirable* to have the approval of others, it isn't *necessary* for you to be happy with yourself.
2. You must prove thoroughly adequate, competent, or achieving.	2. Try to *do well* rather than do *perfectly.* Strive to do better and accept that there are things you won't do as well as others.
3. When people act obnoxiously or unfairly, you should blame and damn them and see them as bad, wicked, or rotten individuals.	3. Don't confuse people with their deeds. A person may *act badly* without being a *bad* person.
4. You have to view things as awful, terrible, horrible, and catastrophic when you get seriously frustrated, are treated unfairly, or are rejected.	4. Try to view negative outcomes as *undesirable,* not unbearable or intolerable. You *can* bear and tolerate them even if you are unhappy with them.
5. Emotional misery comes from external pressures, and you have little ability to control or change your feelings.	5. We create most of our misery *internally* through what we tell ourselves about undesirable life situations.
6. If something seems dangerous or fearsome, you must preoccupy yourself with it and make yourself anxious about it.	6. Living fully and creatively involves accepting the risks and dangers that accompany life. Seek ways to reduce the danger and risks to an acceptable level and move on.
7. You can more easily avoid facing many of life's difficulties and self-responsibilities than undertake more rewarding forms of self-discipline.	7. Immediate gratification only postpones facing responsibilities later. Determine what you need to do and do it.
8. Your past remains all-important, and because something once strongly influenced your life, it has to keep determining your feelings and behavior today.	8. While you can learn valuable lessons from your past, it doesn't *control and determine* the present and the future. It merely *influences* them.
9. People and things should turn out better than they do, and you must view it as awful and horrible if you do not find good solutions to life's grim realities.	9. People and things turn out the way they do. Accept this and realize that you have *limited ability* to influence their destiny.
10. You can achieve maximum human happiness through inertia and inaction or by passively and uncommittedly enjoying yourself.	10. In the long run, inertia and inactivity will cause stress because the only constant in life is *change.* If you do not adapt, you will be left behind.

People who view the world this way are referred to as "musterbators." Everything must be their way.

3. Evaluation of worth statements—imply that some people or things are worthless or a complete waste of time.

   People in this category could be called "evaluators." They commonly refer to people or situations as "worthless" or a "complete waste of time."

4. Need statements—set unrealistic, unattainable requirements for happiness.

   People who view the world this way are "needy" people. They are constantly finding fault with everything and are never happy. Nothing ever is good enough for them.

Ellis would argue that people who are awfulizers, musterbators, evaluators, and excessively needy are more predisposed to stress or neuroses than others because their distorted view of the world creates more potentially stressful situations. Relatively mild stimuli and situations are more likely to develop into stressors for people with an illogical belief system (see Stress Buster Tips: Minimizing *Shoulds, Oughts, Musts*). These people are unable to see the bright side or view the situation in a more rational way.[5]

Stress Buster Tips

Minimizing *Shoulds, Oughts, Musts*

1. For the next two weeks carry around a small spiral notebook and write down *every time* you use the word *should, ought,* or *must.*
2. Be sure to write down the *exact phrase* you used containing those words.
3. Put a check next to the entries that were used properly (for example, you told your 3-year-old he *must not* stick his finger into the electrical plug).
4. Count the number of times you used *shoulds, oughts,* and *musts* improperly.
5. Divide the total number of entries into the number used incorrectly to get the percent of incorrect use.
6. Start to use these words less.

Let's use Tom to illustrate this by showing how an awfulizer views the world (fig. 2-2). He woke up late for school because his alarm didn't go off. He had forgotten

Figure 2-2

Tom is late for school. His alarm did not go off. His pants are wrinkled. He has no time to iron them. The whole day is horrible for him.

to take his slacks out of the dryer the night before and had no time to iron them, and so he ran to class with wrinkled pants. Totally annoyed at the situation, Tom told himself, "How horrible! I can't go to class looking like this. This is awful." As he scurried across campus to get to class, Tom constantly reminded himself how terrible this all was and wondered, "Why does this always happen to me?" All day Tom stoked the fires of his stress by telling everybody about his misfortune. At three o'clock Tom was in the snack bar still recounting the morning's events. What could have been a minor annoyance or inconvenience (alarm not going off, being late for one class) turned into an all-day stressor that wasted a tremendous amount of energy.

KEY TO UNDERSTANDING

We all exhibit irrational tendencies at times. They are harmful only when they represent our predominate way of dealing with the world.

In trying to understand Ellis's illogical beliefs theory it is important to realize that all of us hold some of these views at one time or another. But people who hold several of these beliefs and regularly view the world in this irrational and illogical way are more stress-prone.

The Role of Negative Self-Talk A key aspect of Ellis's model is the role of negative **self-talk.** Self-talk is best characterized as an inner dialogue that you carry on with yourself as you think your way through a situation. Self-talk isn't always negative, or stress-producing. On the contrary, as illustrated in table 2-5, we often use little "pep talks" to boost our confidence, "get psyched" for some activity, or just reassure ourselves that we are doing the right thing or making the right decision. Ellis[7] discovered a relationship between negative emotions (sadness, anger, fear, anxiety, etc.) and negative self-talk. He found that illogical beliefs and the negative self-talk that accompanied them often triggered negative emotions. His clients would repeat negative messages about a stressful event to themselves. In addition, they would direct much of the negative subvocal speech inward, making themselves the target of the negative self-talk (see figures 2-2 and 2-3).

Negative self-talk influences stress transactions in several ways. When you engage in negative self-talk, it undermines your ability to appraise a potential stressor logically. You tend to blow it out of proportion and make it more threatening than it actually is. Further, when you listen to too much negative self-talk you begin to believe it and feel that you can't handle the situation. In other words, it affects your perceived ability to cope with the potential stressor. Once this happens, you feel threatened and unable to cope. As we've already discussed in chapter 1, this type of appraisal is what triggers a stress response. Even worse, negative emotions can perpetuate themselves and even grow when reinforced by negative self-talk. In other words, ongoing negative self-talk perpetuates negative emotions.

John is a perfect example (fig. 2-3). In this scenario, John was walking down the hall to class when a friend from an earlier class walked past him, oblivious to his presence. John immediately perceived this illogically by thinking to himself, "I can't believe she did that to me. How terrible!" He backed this up by asking himself subvocally, "What did I do wrong? I must be a total loser."

This interaction between the irrational/illogical thought pattern and the negative subvocal speech transformed a relatively benign event into a stressor that stayed with John all morning.

Negative self-talk, particularly if it persists beyond the stressful situation, transforms thoughts about the

self-talk a person's inner dialogue

Figure 2-3

John was just passed by one of his classmates who didn't even acknowledge his presence. John engages in subvocal speech.

primary stressor into a **secondary stressor** (see Assess Yourself 2-3). As you saw in the example of John, his self-talk about the friend passing by and not noticing him is a key factor in the initiation of his stress response. Not only is John's evaluation of the activating event (his friend passing by and not noticing him) illogical, so is his self-talk. Self-messages such as "I must be a total loser" contribute to his illogical perception of the activating event and himself. These types of negative self-statements undermine self-respect and self-esteem.

Negative self-talk is a source of secondary stress when a person keeps repeating these negative self-messages long after the activating event is over. In a sense, the self-talk replaces the activating event as the source of stress. John is stressed two hours later because all morning long he keeps telling himself what a loser he must be. Such protracted negative self-talk keeps the stress response alive long after it could have been stopped.

Over time, continued negative self-talk undermines self-esteem and can almost become a self-fufilling prophecy. If we really believe we are worthless or do not deserve to be treated better (because we tell ourselves this over and over), it is more likely that this is exactly what will happen. Do patterns of thinking make events worse than they truly are? Do negative beliefs about yourself become self-fulfilling prophecies? Substituting realistic self-talk for negative self-talk can help you build and maintain self-esteem and cope better with the challenges in your life. Table 2-5 describes typical examples of negative self-talk and more realistic self-talk.

Millon's Model

Millon[49] identified eight specific personality styles that he feels are particularly stress-prone: aggressive, narcissistic, histrionic, dependent, passive-aggressive, compulsive, avoidant, and schizoid. This should not be confused with acting aggressive, narcissistic, etc., on any given occasion. While all of us occasionally behave in an aggressive or narcissistic way, someone who would be characterized as having an aggressive or narcissistic *personality* is like this *most* of the time. It is their predominant way of relating to others. Everly and Lating[11] provide an excellent brief overview of these styles and how they contribute to increased vulnerability to stress.

Aggressive Personality—People who are exceptionally aggressive are more stressed because they mistrust others and are always on the defensive. They fear loss of control and use anger, intimidation, and dominance to retain control at all costs. This creates their heightened susceptibility to stress.[11]

Narcissistic Personality—People who are narcissistic are preoccupied with themselves and with being perceived by others as unique and special. They are self-absorbed to the point of being incapable of seeing any point of view but their own and lack empathy for others. Their stress comes from the fear of not being viewed as special, their inability to postpone gratification, and their inability to communicate with others.[11]

Histrionic Personality—People with a histrionic personality crave affection, support, constant stimulation, and interpersonal approval. This is accompanied by an exaggerated outpouring of affection and a flair for the dramatic. The histrionic personality is more stress-prone because of excessive fear of rejection, loss of approval and affection, and the constant need for stimulation and change.[11]

Dependent Personality—People who are overly dependent require unusually high levels of support from others. To gain this they will be passive and submissive. Their increased susceptibility to stress comes from their inability to view themselves as competent and their fear of loss of support or outright rejection.[11]

Passive-Aggressive Personality—People with passive-aggressive personalities are ambivalent, chronically negative, and pessimistic. They desire independence but lack the skills to achieve it. This causes dependency and a resultant passivity. Their increased susceptibility to stress comes from the struggle between the aggressive pursuit of independence and the passive need for peer-group approval.[11]

primary stressor the original stressor that triggers the stress response

secondary stressor our illogical thoughts about the primary stressor that keep the response alive long after the initial event has passed

Table 2-5 Negative Self-Talk/Realistic Self-Talk

Common types of distorted negative self-talk, along with suggestions for more accurate and rational responses.

Negative Self-Talk	Realistic Self-Talk
Focusing on Negative	
School is so discouraging—nothing but one hassle after another.	School is pretty challenging and has its difficulties, but there certainly are rewards. It's really a mixture of good and bad.
Expecting the Worst	
Why would my boss want to meet with me this afternoon if not to fire me?	I wonder why my boss wants to meet with me. I guess I'll just have to wait and see.
Overgeneralizing	
(After getting a poor grade on a paper) Just as I thought—I'm incompetent at everything.	I'll start working on the next paper earlier. That way, if I run into problems, I'll have time to consult with the instructor.
Minimizing	
I won the speech contest, but none of the other speakers was very good. I wouldn't have done so well against stiffer competition.	It may not have been the best speech I'll ever give, but it was good enough to win the contest. I'm really improving as a speaker.
Blaming Others	
I wouldn't feel so lousy today if I hadn't had so much to drink at the party last night. Someone should have stopped me.	I overdid it last night. Next time I'll make different choices.
Expecting Perfection	
I should have got 100 percent on this test. I can't believe I missed that one problem through a careless mistake.	Too bad I missed one problem through carelessness, but overall I did very well on this test. Next time I'll be more careful.
Believing You're the Cause of Everything	
Sarah seems so depressed today. I wish I hadn't had that argument with her yesterday; it must have really upset her.	I wish I had handled the argument better, and in the future I'll try to. But I don't know if Sarah's behavior is related to what I said or even if she's depressed. In any event, I'm not responsible for how Sarah feels or acts—only she can take responsibility for that.
Thinking in Black and White	
I've got to score 10 points in the game today. Otherwise, I don't belong on the team.	I'm a good player or I wouldn't be on the team. I'll play my best—that's all I can do.
Magnifying Events	
They went to a movie without me. I thought we were friends, but I guess I was wrong.	I'm disappointed they didn't ask me to the movie, but it doesn't mean our friendship is over. It's not that big a deal.

Source: Adapted from Schafer, W. (1995). *Stress management for wellness.* 3d ed. (Thomson Learning), pp. 227–231.[70]

Compulsive Personalities—People with compulsive personalities are rigid and inflexible and are driven by the need to behave in socially approved ways and maintain rigid self-control. Their increased susceptibility to stress comes from their inability to deal with ambiguity and abstraction. In a world of shades of gray, they see only black and white.[11]

Avoidant Personalities—These people desire social support and affiliation but fear rejection so much that social avoidance becomes a way of life. They are highly sensitive to interpersonal situations and relationships. Their stress-proneness comes from the combination of lack of social support and fear of interpersonal rejection.

Schizoid Personalities—These people are placid and bland, with virtually no desire for interpersonal contact. They might be viewed as the polar opposite of the histrionic personality. Schizoid personalities are more stress-prone because of hypersensitivity to social stimuli and fear of interpersonal intrusion. They also lack social supports.

Stress-Resistant Personality Types

Although no one is exactly sure how stress-prone personality types or individual traits develop, and the extent to which biological and psychosocial factors influence our personalities, it is safe to say that our perception of potential stressors is intricately linked to our personalities. Additionally, while the different stress-prone personality types just discussed are very diverse, they all increase susceptibility to stress and are accompanied by strong negative emotional states. In the next section we'll examine a couple of the classic *stress-resistant* personality types to see how they are protective against stress.

Type B Personality

In addition to identifying the Type A personality behavior pattern, Rosenman and Friedman[17] identified a second type of personality pattern, **Type B personality.** The Type B personality is the polar opposite of Type A. They defined the Type B personality behavior pattern in terms of the absence of Type A traits. In other words, Type B people could also be classified as non-As because of their absence of Type A traits.

Type B personalities are relaxed and easygoing. They are not time urgent or overly competitive. Type Bs do not exhibit the same patterns of hostility and anger. Type Bs do not exhibit the same physical manifestations of Type As. They do not show the same levels of facial and body tension or use explosive vocal tones or physical gestures (Rosenman & Friedman[19]).

Type Bs, in today's language, would be characterized as more "laid back" than Type As. This is not to say, however, that they are not high achievers, successful in business and government or other endeavors. Friedman and Ulmer[17] found that many leaders of industry, government, and science exhibited a Type B behavior pattern. In a study of 106 national leaders (college presidents, senators, congressmen, corporate chairpersons, Nobel Prize winners, etc.) forty-one (39%) were Type Bs. The majority sixty-five (61%) exhibited a Type A behavior pattern. While the Type A finding isn't surprising because they are the aggressive, time-urgent, competitive traits generally associated with success. What was surprising was the fact that the Type B behavior pattern did not preclude success and achievement.

Friedman and Rosenman[19] found that in subjects who are free from other risk factors for coronary heart disease (diabetes, hypertension, and elevated cholesterol), a Type B personality is protective against heart disease. Similar findings concerning the protective effects of Type B characteristics were also found in another study.[37] For example, Type B individuals have a lower incidence of daily hassles than Type A personalities because they are not as easily frustrated.[40]

Hardy Personality

Kobasa[29] identified another personality type, the **hardy personality.** Like Type Bs, the hardy personality may better fight stress and disease. Kobasa studied 430 male and female supervisors, managers, and executives of Illinois Bell Telephone (IBT) after the deregulation and divestiture of AT&T. All subjects took an initial battery of tests designed to measure their stress levels and illness levels. Each subject was given a total stress score and a total illness score based on the test results. Two groups were formed based on these scores—a high-stress/high-illness group and a high-stress/low-illness group. All low-stress subjects were removed from the study.[29]

To categorize the personality attributes of high-stress subjects, Kobasa administered a variety of psychological tests. When analyzing the results, she found that some subjects had certain personality traits that protected them against the ravages of stress. These subjects she entitled *hardy*. Hardy subjects do more than survive the daily pressures of corporate life; they thrive on pressure. Hardy subjects have the following characteristics: low blood pressure, few sick days, low triglycerides (compounds consisting of fatty acids and glycerol), happy personalities, and little psychological distress.[27] Additionally, three personality attributes are associated with hardiness: commitment, control, and challenge.

Commitment refers to having a sense of purpose and meaning in life and relationships. Kobasa describes this as being "committed to, rather than alienated from, oneself." Committed individuals are actively involved in life. Kobasa characterizes this as "vigorousness vs. a vegetativeness"[29] with their environment.

Closely related to commitment is control, a feeling of being in charge of one's life. People in control feel they are actors in life, not objects being acted on. This internal *locus of control* has been studied for several years. Rotter,[64] a pioneer in this area of research, found that people with a high internal locus of control feel in charge of their lives. These people also believe they are responsible for their actions and therefore are more likely to take steps to ensure their well-being.

KEY TO UNDERSTANDING

A helpful way to understand the Type B personality is to view it as the opposite of Type A.

Type B personality a personality type that is easygoing and noncompetitive and doesn't get angry or hostile easily

hardy personality a stress-resistant personality characterized by commitment, control, and ability to accept change

KEY TO UNDERSTANDING

People with an internal locus of control realize that regardless of the situation, we ultimately have the final word on our thoughts, feelings, and behavior.

KEY TO UNDERSTANDING

It is helpful when fearing change to realize that nothing in life is constant except change.

Even in situations where decisions are made above their level, subjects with high control scores believe they have the final word on events that affect their lives. Individuals who feel in control of their lives are better able to withstand the pressures of the business world, a place where few individuals have complete control of 100 percent of their work (see Assess Yourself 2-2).

The third personality attribute associated with hardiness is challenge, which relates to how people perceive change. Hardy individuals welcome change and view it as a normal part of life. They understand that no one is ever free from change. Instead, hardy people view change as the only constant in life. Hardy people are flexible and can adapt to life's changes.

As an example, hardiness is a buffer against stress and burnout among nurses.[78] Nurses who score higher than their peers on hardiness tests are more capable of combating the effects of job stress and burnout.

An outgrowth of the initial assessment of hardiness was the development and testing of a hardiness training program for the organization. Kobasa et al.[30] developed a multisession intervention that focused on helping subjects recognize stress, change their beliefs about the stressors, adopt positive (hardy) coping skills, and gain personal control over the stressors. Kobasa et al.[30] demonstrated a reduction in stress and an increase in measures of hardiness among the experimental group.

Maddi[41] developed a hardiness model based on his initial work with Kobasa and uses it in hardiness training programs throughout the country. In Maddi's Hardiness Model a breakdown in wellness (mental, behavioral, or physical) is due to the cumulative effects of excess strain and the ongoing stress response brought on by stressful circumstances (fig. 2-4). Inherited vulnerabilities can make us more susceptible to strain. Hardy coping and hardy health practices can interrupt the progression from stressful circumstances to wellness breakdown.

In this model, Maddi characterizes hardiness as "hardy coping." Hardy coping consists of hardy beliefs

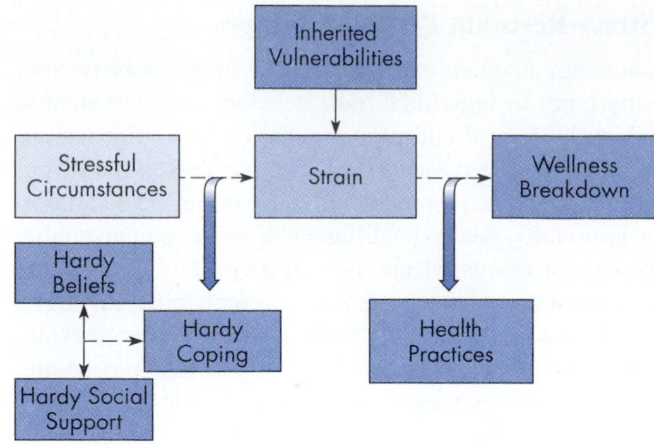

Figure 2-4

In Maddi's Hardiness Model, hardy coping (which results from hardy beliefs and hardy social support) can intervene and prevent strain. Hardy health practices can keep strain, which is influenced by inherited vulnerabilities, from resulting in a breakdown in wellness.

and hardy social support. In this model, hardy beliefs are the three Cs (commitment, control, and challenge). Hardy social support is the encouragement and helpful resources others can provide to help you cope. Hardy health practices are healthful behaviors such as physical exercise, relaxation, and good nutrition.

Although Maddi's work was built on his work with Kobasa, not everyone agrees with his principle. Kobasa's work has been criticized by Hull et al.,[24] who contend that all of Kobasa's three components of hardiness (commitment, control, and challenge) may not operate together in all stressful conditions. Hull et al. feel that hardiness may be more related either to a combination of control and commitment or to any of the three variables working independently. As discussed later in this chapter, Lazarus and Folkman's[34] model builds on Kobasa's concept of challenge and operationally defines it so that its role in personality and the stress response is clear.

THE INTELLECTUAL BASIS OF STRESS

Very little has been written about the intellectual basis of stress. Indeed, most of the literature on the personality attributes linked to stress-resistant or stress-prone personalities revolves around emotions. Only one theorist we have discussed so far, Ellis, recognizes the intellectual basis of stress. Ellis's REBT is in a sense an *intellectual* as much as a psychological theory of stress. As we have seen, *illogical thinking* is the foundation of his theory. Not surprising, then, is his recommendation of more *logical thinking* as the way to deal with stress. Further, Ellis believes that our illogical beliefs develop over the course of our lives. In a sense, he has suggested that we have learned to think illogically.

STRESS IN OUR WORLD 2-1

Shakir: The Hardy Personality at Work

Shakir is a perfect example of the hardy personality in action. Shakir is a midlevel bureaucrat in a large state agency that monitors federally funded family planning services for low-income populations. Shakir has seen it all in his fifteen years of state service. He has survived the policy changes of four U.S. presidents, two governors, three health commissioners, and three division directors. These policy makers have come and gone, each changing the face of Shakir's agency according to his or her political philosophy. Each has created new procedures, forms, and protocols that were scrapped as he or she moved on to other positions. Shakir has outlasted them all.

Shakir knows he could earn twice the salary he makes in his present job if he left for work in the private sector. His MBA from a premier graduate school, years of managerial experience, and polished communication skills would qualify him for a variety of high-paying, less politically volatile private-sector jobs. However, despite the constant change, lower salary, and lack of prestige, Shakir stays.

Shakir stays because he is committed and feels his work has some meaning. He realizes that by staying he provides the continuity needed to deliver important services to people in need. Besides doing a good job at work, Shakir volunteers his time to work with professional organizations and grassroots committees that are related to his profession.

Shakir also feels in control. He is the quintessential bureaucrat and is proud of that title. He operates smoothly within the slowly moving bureaucratic machinery and has learned how to get things done despite the bureaucracy. People respect him and help him overcome obstacles that others feel are beyond their control. Shakir is a valued and respected member of his division and is given a lot of authority to work within the parameters of the organization.

Even after fifteen years, Shakir feels challenged by his work. Rather than fearing change he looks forward to it. He views the policy changes that often accompany the political maneuvers in his state as healthy and challenging. Confident in his ability to adapt to change, Shakir views change as essential and actively solicits ideas from others concerning his work. He is more than a survivor; he has flourished.

Lazarus[36] uses the term *intellectual resources* to describe the personality attributes that are related to one's cognitive abilities. These intellectual resources include, but are not limited to, our intelligence, experience, ability to express ourselves orally and in writing, creativity, and problem-solving abilities. Our intellectual resources play a big role in how we perceive things; whether we think logically or illogically; our ability to express our wants, needs, and desires, our ability to articulate our point of view; our ability to assert ourselves; and a host of other factors that affect our level of stress.

Intelligence

Although studies have not demonstrated a statistically significant relationship between one's level of intelligence and one's stress level, intelligence plays a part in the appraisal of every potential stressor. **Intelligence** is defined as, " the faculty of understanding; the capacity to know or apprehend (grasp mentally)."[77] Clearly, many potential stressors could be defused as stressors if we understood them more completely. Ignorance is often the basis of fear and stress. We tend to fear what we don't understand, and this causes stress. Our intelligence also helps us decipher ambiguous threats to our well-being. The more completely we understand something, the less likely it is to feel threatening to us.

Life Experience

Life experience is a valuable intellectual resource. We draw from our past experiences when evaluating present potential stressors. If we have coped successfully with something in the past, we can draw on that experience to help manage it in the present. Remember, however, even though we have experienced it already, it will present itself differently in the present because of differences in the context, our level of health across the six dimensions (physical, social, etc.), and how successful we were in coping with it before.

As we age, we experience a host of different life events that help us put potential stressors in a different perspective. Americans tend to value youth to such an extent that they sometimes overlook the wisdom that age bestows on people merely by being a survivor. Many of our grandparents and other elders have survived at least two world wars, the Great Depression, the stock market crashes of the 1920s and 1980s, and other events that give them a unique perspective from which to evaluate present-day potential stressors.

intelligence the capacity to understand, know, or mentally grasp

Verbal and Written Communication

A large proportion of our stress arises from our inability to express ourselves and communicate clearly. A person's ability to communicate is directly related to that person's vocabulary. We have both thinking (cognitive) and feeling (affective) vocabularies. To express ourselves we have to be able to express what we are thinking or feeling in words. The more extensive our thinking and feeling vocabularies are, the easier it is for us to put our thoughts and feelings into words. Besides being able to capture these thoughts and feelings in words, we have to be able to transmit them to others. Some people are born great communicators; most of us have to learn how to express ourselves orally and in writing. It can be very frustrating and stressful to "be at a loss for words" when something that is potentially threatening occurs.

Creativity

Creativity is an intellectual resource that helps us discover new, innovative ways to perceive potential stressors and cope with them. Creativity allows us literally to "take the blinders off" and see things differently. Creativity is one of the intellectual resources Maslow identified that is related to self-actualization. Self-actualizers, according to Maslow, are people who reach their highest potential and make the most of their lives.[44] Often this is because they are able to come up with creative solutions to roadblocks and problems that would stop most people in their tracks. Payne and Hahn[52] describe five characteristics of creative people:

1. Creative people are intuitive and open to new experiences. They are not afraid of the unknown, the mysterious, the puzzling.
2. Creative people are idea people. They are less interested in the details and more interested in integrating and synthesizing information to make new constructs and theories.
3. Creative people do not follow the herd. They tend to be more independent in their thinking and actions and work best independently.
4. Creative people are flexible and can adjust rapidly to change. They also recognize that there are several ways to view any situation or problem.
5. Creative people move to a different drummer. They are driven by their own set of internal values, ethics, and goals.

As you can see, these traits can be very valuable in reducing stress. The flexibility and the unique perspective possessed by creative people allow them to appraise potential stressors very differently than do their less creative peers. Their ability to "think outside the box" helps diffuse potential stressors by providing more options.

Seward[69] identified four key mental barriers to creativity. The first barrier is the belief that for every problem there is only one right answer. In fact, there are several answers to most questions and several ways to solve any problem. The next barrier is the belief that one is not creative. The best way to inhibit creativity is to believe that one is not creative. We all have the ability to be creative if we allow ourselves that option. We will describe strategies for developing creativity in chapter 7. The third barrier is the fear of being foolish. Most people fail to dare to see things differently because they don't want to appear foolish in front of others. Students often don't ask questions in class because they don't want to ask "stupid questions." Remember, the only stupid question is the one you were too foolish to ask. The information you receive from the answer to a question might just be the insight you needed to find a creative solution to your problem. The last barrier, the fear of making a mistake, can also quash creativity. In reality, very few people get it right the first time. Our mistakes are the building blocks of our successes. With each mistake we learn something new and solve another piece of the puzzle.

Problem-Solving Ability

Problem solving and creativity go hand in hand. The more creative we are, the more options we can generate when tackling complex issues. As was just mentioned, there are several different ways to view and solve all problems. If you give ten computer programmers a problem, they will come up with at least ten different ways to program the solution. Our ability to problem solve and look at things from many different perspectives can help reduce stress by allowing us to see that there are many different ways to deal with potential stressors. Having a "plan B" or fallback position relies on our ability to be creative and solve problems.

Our ability (or lack of ability) to communicate also affects our assertiveness. Being able to stand up for what we need and want out of life while allowing others the same right hinges on our ability to communicate this to others. The ability to say no when we want to is a communication skill. We will discuss many strategies for enhancing these and other intellectual resources in chapters 6 through 11. They are presented here, in this brief overview, to help you understand how they fit into Lazarus and Folkman's[34] stress appraisal model.

KEY TO UNDERSTANDING

It doesn't matter whether something is truly threatening: if a person perceives something as threatening, it is.

EMOTIONAL INTELLIGENCE

Goleman[18] coined the term *emotional intelligence,* to refer to the intellectual attributes associated with understanding and managing emotions. Goleman explains how emotions are related to mood, temperament, and personality disorders (see figure 2-5, The Ripples of Emotions).

As we discussed at the beginning of this chapter, Goleman explains how emotions are primary feelings that are stored in the limbic system in the brain. Further, *stress-prone* or *stress-resistant* personalities might be more related to these emotional memories derived from people's *distinctive thoughts, psychological and biological states,* and *range of propensities to act* than anything else. These stored emotions are very volatile. They are strong, immediate, and short term.

Emotions, Moods, Temperament, and Disorders of Emotion

Emotions don't last long, but are capable of triggering action if allowed to. **Moods** are longer states, often lasting hours. According to Goleman,[18] people vary in the propensity for their emotions to spill over and create longer-lasting mood states. In other words, because of individuals' distinctive thoughts, psychological and biological states, and range of propensities to act, some people are more inclined than others to have their emotions shift into moods.

mood a state of mind dominated by a particular emotion or set of emotions

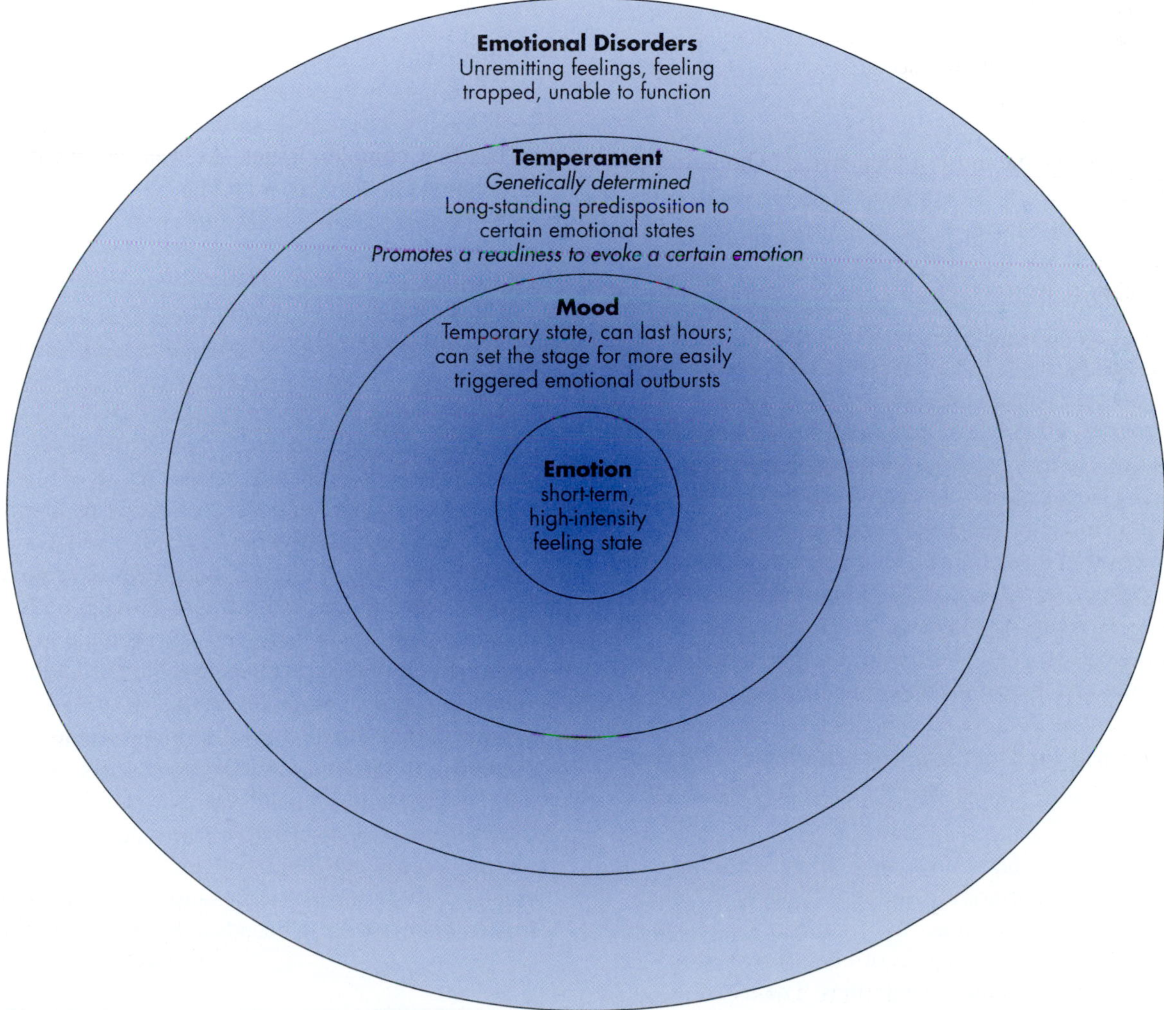

Figure 2-5 **The Ripples of Emotions**
Emotions are at the center of a ripple that spreads outward to moods, temperament, and emotional disorders.

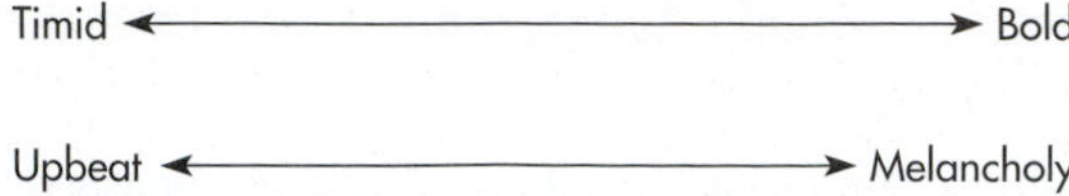

Figure 2-6 **Continuums of Temperament**

The four types of temperaments actually represent two continuums that constitute a range of emotions from those associated with being timid to bold or upbeat to melancholy.

Temperament is a long-standing predisposition to certain emotional states. Goleman[18] believes that there are four main temperaments: timid, bold, upbeat, or melancholy. The four actually represent two continuums (see figure 2-6, Continuums of Temperament). Timid and bold people are on opposite ends of one continuum while upbeat and melancholy people are on opposite ends of the other.

Timid people are prone to fearfulness and shy away from the unfamiliar and uncertain. They are more likely to suffer from anxiety than those who are not timid. Bold is the opposite temperament of timid. Bold people are outgoing, at ease, confident, and generally have short-lived fears. Upbeat people are cheerful and easygoing. They enjoy life, are frequently in good moods, and not too many things upset them. Melancholy people are the exact opposite. Goleman[18] feels that our temperament is a genetically influenced, biologically determined *emotional set* that is evident in newborns. Some babies are cheerful and easygoing while others seem more timid and fearful. Goleman believes that this genetic programming of temperament influences how easily emotions and moods are triggered, how long they last, and how intensely they are perceived to be.

Disorders of emotion such as panic, mania, and depression are clinically recognized psychological problems that often do not resolve without psychotherapy and medical treatment. They are long-standing emotional states that are covered in detail in chapter 6. Goleman feels that certain people are more susceptible to disorders of emotion such as depression because of their genetic preprogramming and susceptibility to strong emotional memories, moods, and temperaments (Goleman,[18] p. 215).

Five Criteria for Emotional Intelligence

Although there is ample evidence to suggest that our emotions, moods, and temperaments are influenced by genetic factors beyond our control, there are things we can do to live in harmony with them. Goleman[18] identified five specific domains of emotional intelligence that we can exert some degree of control over that will help us make peace with our emotions. The five domains are (1) knowing emotions, (2) managing emotions, (3) motivating oneself, (4) recognizing emotions in others, and (5) handling relationships.

- **Knowing Emotions** The first step in being able to understand the other four domains requires that people can identify what they are feeling. The ability to identify and monitor emotions is the cornerstone upon which all other emotional intelligence is built. Being unable to identify and recognize emotions leaves people at their mercy. Identifying what one is feeling is the first step in being able to manage emotions.
- **Managing Emotions** Once people recognize that they are feeling something and they can identify what they are feeling, they can decide upon a course of action. There are many different ways to manage stressful emotions. We will spend a lot of time in section II of this book describing how to cope with stressful emotions. A key to understanding how to manage emotions is realizing that culture plays a big part in what we do. In the Living Constructively box (see page 30) we compare how Eastern versus Western societies view emotions and what to do about them.
- **Motivating Oneself** Often even strong emotions can be used positively. Using fear or anger to motivate oneself to rise above these feelings is one example. A key to understanding how to use emotions to motivate oneself is realizing that the more time you intentionally allow an emotion to dominate your thinking, the longer it retains its ability to influence your behavior. We tend to think about this only in the negative sense such as when you continually go over and over how you failed at something and how miserable you feel because of it. Often, this kind of negative ruminating over emotions keeps you stuck and unable to do anything productive. You could just as easily use a strong emotion such as fear of failure to motivate you to identify and take the steps necessary to succeed.
- **Recognizing Emotions in Others** A key social skill is recognizing how other people feel and using this information in a positive way to help or comfort them. Often, this type of intelligence springs out of understanding how you did/would feel under similar circumstances. Being more adept at picking up non-verbal cues such as facial expressions and body language helps as does being sensitive to the nuances of tone and volume in others' speech patterns.
- **Handling Relationships** A key to success in relationships with intimate partners, co-workers, subordinates, etc., is managing the emotions in others that you recognized. Taking action in response to emotions is a quality of leadership. Good leaders realize when something needs to be done and they

temperament a long-standing predisposition to a certain emotional state take swift, decisive action. The ability to understand when the time is ripe to act on the behalf of others is learned in part from the emotional intelligence associated with knowing and managing your own emotions.

In the next section of this chapter we will refocus on Lazarus and Folkman's[34] stress appraisal model and examine where and how it integrates key emotional and intellectual factors into the assessment of potential stressors and the stress response. We will see how it is the best fit for understanding stress because of this.

The Convergence of Intellectual and Emotional Factors

In the preceding sections of this chapter we examined how intellectual and emotional factors relate to the stress response. Perhaps no theory better illustrates how the interaction of intellectual and emotional factors combine to create stress than Richard Lazarus and Susan Folkman's[34] stress appraisal model. Lazarus, working alone and with Folkman and other colleagues at the University of California at Berkeley, has spent the better part of four decades analyzing, assessing, dissecting, and synthesizing the relationship between potential stressors, personality attributes, intellectual resources, coping, and emotions. Lazarus,[33,34,35,36,37] provides a rich theoretical framework that ties together all the pieces of the emotional and intellectual bases of stress discussed earlier in this chapter.

Lazarus and Folkman's[34] model of stress revolves around the concept of threat. They believed that things stress us because they threaten our well-being in some way. Threat is a state of anticipated confrontation with a harmful condition and includes physical harm, emotional pain, and social discomfort. For instance, some people may perceive exercise as stressful because of the *physical* discomfort. Others may avoid becoming intimate with a partner because getting too *emotionally* close makes them vulnerable. Still others may avoid certain *social* gatherings because the environment makes them feel out of control. If the event provokes a perception of threat, it will lead to the stress response. Examine the case of Hiroko, a psychology major who has a midterm in her course on abnormal psychology. Hiroko has an A average in her major and has gotten excellent grades on all her midterms during the last two years.

As briefly discussed in chapter 1, the presence of a potential stressor initiates the stress appraisal process. There are three parts to the process: primary and secondary appraisal and cognitive reappraisal. The purpose of **primary appraisal** is to determine whether or not a potential stressor is threatening. The purpose of **secondary appraisal** is to determine if one can cope with it. Although Lazarus and Folkman[34] labeled them primary and secondary, they are equally important in the appraisal process and occur simultaneously. Both are followed by **cognitive reappraisal,** which involves looking at the potential stressor with the new information synthesized from the primary and secondary appraisals.

The appraisal process for a specific potential stressor is influenced by time and the environment in which the stressor presents itself. Each time the same potential stressor presents itself, it is appraised differently because the context in which it occurs is different from the original experience. People bring new insights and experience

primary appraisal the part of the initial appraisal of the potential stressor that answers the question: "Is it a threat to me?"

secondary appraisal the part of the initial appraisal of the potential stressor that answers the question: "Can I cope with this?"

cognitive reappraisal the process of reevaluating a potential stressor using information synthesized from the primary and secondary appraisals

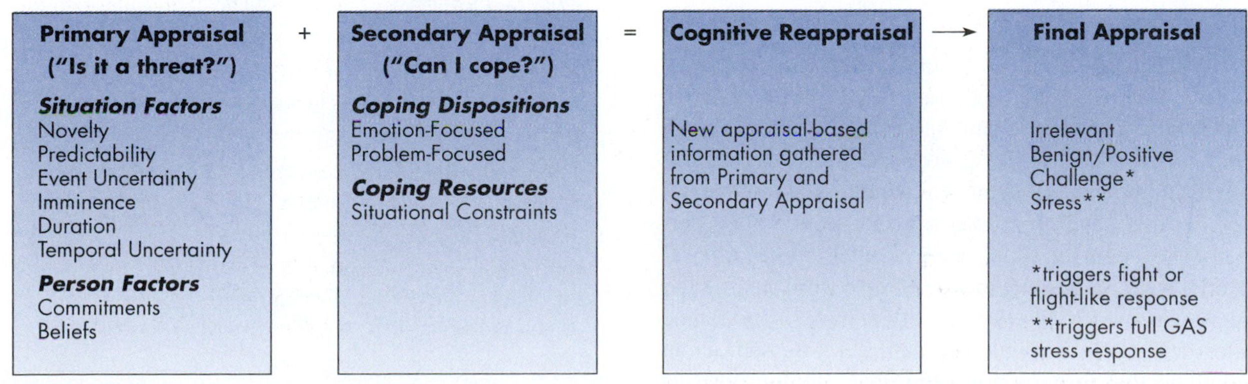

Figure 2-7
Lazarus and Folkman's[34] Stress Transaction Model

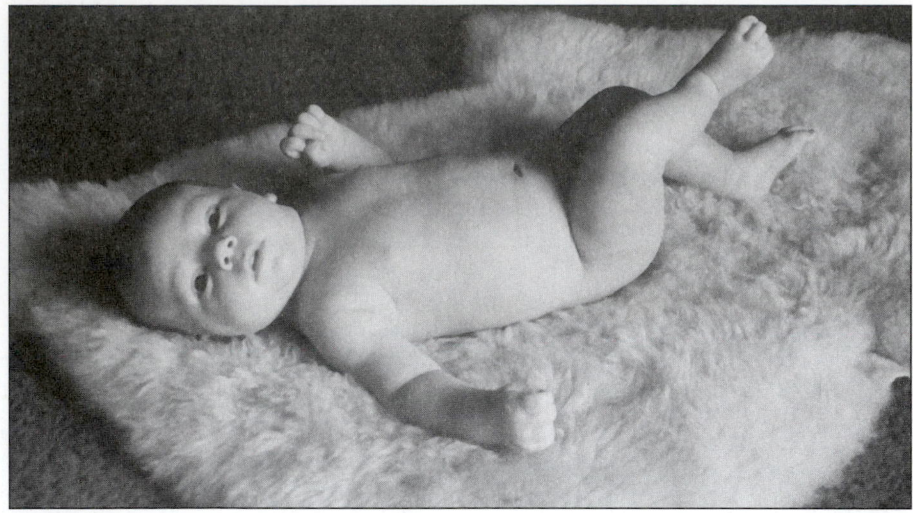

Positive events, such as the birth of a child, can energize and challenge us.

to each potentially stressful encounter. This influences their perception of threat and perceived ability to cope with it. Past experience and successful coping strengthen us and add new strategies to our coping skills. This feeds into the appraisal process and changes the way we view the same potential stressor. In essence Lazarus believes our past successes help reduce present and future stressors.

Another thing that happens during stress appraisal, especially with stressors that take a longer duration to unfold, is that the situation changes and things work out differently. In this sense space and time affect our ability to cope. Let's use Hiroko again as our example. When Hiroko first found out she had a midterm, essay examination six weeks into the semester, she could have perceived this as stressful. As the exam got closer, however, her study efforts began to pay off and she felt *less* threatened and *more* able to cope with the exam because she felt prepared and confident.

Primary Stress Appraisal

Lazarus and Folkman distinguish between three different types of primary appraisal: irrelevant appraisal, benign/positive appraisal, and stress appraisal.[34] The first two types of appraisals, irrelevant and benign/positive, do not result in the initiation of a stress response. **Irrelevant appraisal** is the assessment of encounters with potential stressors that have no relevance to us—there is no personal investment of time, energy, or emotions. Consequently, we have nothing to gain or lose from a particular experience, which is why we often have a hard time understanding how someone can get stressed about something that to us is not a big deal. **Benign/positive appraisal** is the assessment of encounters with people or situations that are perceived favorably with the potential to enhance our well-being.

Stress appraisal has three subtypes: threat appraisal, harm/loss appraisal, and challenge appraisal. The first two, threat appraisal and harm/loss appraisal, initiate a stress response, which, if allowed to continue, mimics Selye's General Adaptation Syndrome (GAS) described briefly in chapter 1 and in great detail in chapter 5. These two types of stress appraisals are accompanied by the negative stress emotions described by Lazarus earlier in this chapter.

Threat appraisal is an anticipatory appraisal because it is the assessment of harm or loss that has not yet occurred. As a result of threat appraisal, a person anticipates if exposure to a potential stressor will result in something bad happening to them. **Harm/loss appraisal** is similar to threat appraisal but involves the appraisal of potential stressors to which one has already been exposed. It focuses on the assessment of the consequences of exposure to the potential stressor.

irrelevant appraisal the assessment of potential stressors that have no relevance to us

benign/positive appraisal the assessment of encounters with people and situations that are perceived favorably by us

stress appraisal an assessment of a potential stressor that appraises it as a threat resulting in the initiation of a stress response

threat appraisal an anticipatory evaluation of harm or loss that has not yet occurred; during threat appraisal a person anticipates that something bad (threatening) will happen

harm/loss appraisal an actual assessment of situations that have already occurred; the evaluation of what harm or losses have occurred as a result of the potential stressor

A test could be appraised as an opportunity to showcase our talents or an opportunity to fail. Our perception of the test determines this.

Challenge appraisal is an assessment of a potential stressor that could possibly result in positive outcomes. Challenge appraisal involves looking at the exposure to a potential stressor in terms of what could be gained from it or the growth potential it entails. Challenge appraisal triggers a physiological response that mimics the *fight or flight* response mentioned briefly in chapter 1. Even though this energy mobilization is as intense as the energy resulting from threat appraisal, it is a short-term response. Unlike stress appraisal, challenge appraisal is not accompanied by stress emotions. Instead, when we are challenged we feel eagerness, excitement, and exhilaration, positive emotions that enhance our overall well-being and use of the energy mobilized.

Situation Factors in Primary Appraisal

Situation factors were originally called *factors in the stimulus configuration,* or *stimulus factors,* in Lazarus's original description of the model (Lazarus[33]). When the model was refined almost twenty years later, Lazarus and Folkman[34] used the term situation factors to replace the original. Situation factors include the potential stressor (originally called the stimulus) novelty, predictability, event uncertainty, imminence, duration, and temporal uncertainty.

KEY TO UNDERSTANDING

The difference between threat and challenge is realizing that though both trigger the same mobilization of energy, the latter is accompanied by positive rather than negative emotions.

Novelty, Predictability, and Event Uncertainty *Novelty* refers to newness. If a potential stressor is encountered for the first time, it is more likely to be perceived as threatening than one exposed to several times in the past. Part of the threat comes from not knowing what to expect. This is why most people perceive change as threatening; they do not know what to expect from something new. They are more comfortable with something known.

Predictability refers to the ability to forecast what is going to happen. It draws on experience associated with the potential stressor. If you've experienced this potential stressor several times in the past, you have some sense of what to expect from it. In this sense you can predict what will happen when exposed to it now. Predictability also revolves around having objective knowledge gained from learning about the potential stressor other than through firsthand exposure to it. You might have read about it or discussed it with others.

Event uncertainty refers to being uncertain about how the potential stressor can affect you. Sometimes potential stressors can be ambiguous or unclear, leading to uncertainty. Maximum uncertainty can cause mental confusion and increase threat.

challenge appraisal an anticipatory evaluation of a situation that focuses on positive things that can result from it; during challenge appraisal a person looks at a situation for its growth potential or for what might be gained from it

situation factors originally called *factors in the stimulus configuration,* or *stimulus factors,* situation factors include the potential stressor (originally called the stimulus) novelty, predictability, event uncertainty, imminence, duration, and temporal uncertainty

Let's look at how these play out with Hiroko's psychology midterm essay exam. Although the test is new (she never took it before), she is not new to taking essay exams in her major. In fact, she has done very well in the past on them. Hiroko feels that she can predict how the test will go because she has had this professor before, taken his tests, and knows how he grades. Further, the professor is not the kind who changes his procedures or employs assessments like pop quizzes. Lastly, Hiroko has little to be uncertain about. She knows when the test will be offered, how many questions will be on it, and has study questions provided by the professor.

Imminence, Duration, and Temporal Uncertainty *Imminence of confrontation* measures how close the threat is; the closer the threat, the greater the stress. Imminence could be either physical (distance) or temporal (temporal). Generally, the closer a potential stressor is, the more threat it poses. Potential stressors that are far removed (either physically or time-wise) are generally less threatening.

Duration refers to how long the exposure to the potential stressor is. While it is tempting to think that the shorter the duration, the less likely it is that a potential stressor would be perceived as threatening, this isn't necessarily true. As in Hiroko's midterm exam, the amount of time she and her classmates would have to both prepare for the test or actually take it, the less threatening it probably would be.

Temporal Uncertainty refers to being unsure when something will happen regarding the potential stressor. If you can see the potential stressor coming but don't know when it will arrive, it is more likely to be perceived as threatening. If you can see it and know when it will arrive, it is less likely to be perceived as threatening.

Let's look at how these play out with Hiroko's test. Since her test was about six weeks away, not very imminent, Hiroko didn't feel threatened by it. She felt that was ample time to prepare for it. Hiroko also felt that the duration of the test ($1\frac{1}{2}$ hours to take it) was adequate. In the past she did very well on essay tests of that duration. There was no temporal uncertainty with this test at all. She knew exactly when it would be offered and how long it would last. As a result of this appraisal, Hiroko did not find this exam very threatening. While Hiroko appraised little threat from this combination of situation factors, others might be very threatened by it because of differing emotional and intellectual factors in their personalities. Others might find that knowing about the exam too far in advance gave them extra time to worry about it. They also might think that $1\frac{1}{2}$ hours is not enough time to finish the test. Still others might not trust the professor and take him on his word for giving the test on the date indicated. They might catastrophize that he will try to trick them or give a pop quiz instead of the exam.

This is one of the fascinating things about appraisal. It really takes individual personality factors such as temperament and prior learning into account. People appraise potential stressors differently because of their temperament, past learning experiences, history of success or failure, or any of the emotional and intellectual factors we discussed in this chapter. Lazarus and Folkman's[34] model is flexible enough to accommodate and account for this diversity.

Person Factors in Primary Appraisal

Person Factors were originally called *personality factors* (originally including motivations, belief systems, and intellectual resources) in Lazarus's original description of the model (Lazarus[33]). Once again, when the model was refined by Lazarus and Folkman,[34] they used term person factors to replace the original. The two key person factors are commitments and beliefs.

As discussed earlier, commitments are an expression of what is important to people, what they are committed to. Commitments refer to one's values, goals, and ideals—in other words, what are important to people and give their lives meaning. A potential stressor could be anything that threatens a strongly held commitment. Commitments are the central components of our personalities. Our commitments are intimately related to our motivations or what drives our behavior. The stronger our commitments the more vulnerable we are to potential stressors that we appraise as threatening to these commitments.

Beliefs are personally formed or culturally shared notions about reality. Lazarus and Folkman[34] call them cognitive configurations about how the world is and how it should be. Our beliefs serve as our crystal ball through which we view the world. They are influenced by our genetic inheritance, learning, culture, and intelligence. Sometimes what we see is realistic, based on the best objective information available, and helps make us more stress-resistant. Other times what we see is distorted, unrealistic, based on subjective feelings, inaccurate data, missing information, and faulty logic and makes us more stress-prone.

Lazarus and Folkman[34] feel that beliefs about control are of particular importance in stress appraisals. Beliefs about self-control evolve as part of our personality development. Erickson[10] felt that a sense of trust in the world and belief in one's ability to control the events in one's life develop in infancy and early childhood respectively. Failure to meet the developmental tasks associated with developing trust and control results in unhealthy

person factors a person's commitments and beliefs, such as ideals, values, and faith; formerly referred to as *personality factors* emotional development and an inability to assess how much control individuals really have over situations in their lives. As Kobasa[29] showed, hardiness was linked to an *internal* locus of control. Hardy people felt in control of their lives and were more stress-resistant than their less hardy peers.

Lazarus and Folkman[34] theorized that stressful appraisals could occur when people either underestimate or overestimate how much control they have over certain potentially stressful situations. When people underestimate the control they have over potential stressors, they can easily be threatened by things that could have been appraised as irrelevant, benign, or challenging. When people overestimate the control they have over potential stressors and view them as benign/positive or challenging they can see these appraisals shift to stressful ones as the situations evolve over time. Going into a situation, these people were very confident and feeling in control but they soon realized that they were in over their heads and lacked the control necessary to manage the potential stressor. Once this happens they feel threatened and therefore stressed.

The last way beliefs influence appraisal is when they involve what Lazarus and Folkman[34] call *existential* beliefs. These are beliefs about faith, religion, God, fate, or spirituality. As we saw in chapter 1 and will cover in greater detail in chapter 4, existential beliefs can be a great source of comfort and strength when facing potential stressors. Sometimes the difference in appraising a potential stressor as stressful or challenging has to do with our faith in our ability to handle it. Faith, as we will discuss in chapter 4, is the belief in something/someone that cannot be proven empirically. Faith (or lack of it) is a key component of spirituality and something we will discuss in detail when we shift our attention to coping later in the textbook.

Let's look at how these person factors play out with Hiroko's psychology midterm essay exam. Hiroko is committed to doing the best that she can possibly do in college. She is acutely aware of her grade point average and strives to do her best on each assignment she is given. Academic success is something she values and her ideal is to earn a perfect 4.0 average. Because of this commitment to academic success, all tests are important. Initially, this test posed a slight threat because of this. She comes from a very high-achieving family that values academic success and from a culture (she is Japanese American) that values hard work and personal sacrifice. Hiroko feels pretty much in control of this potential stressor (the exam) because she has a strong history of success with essay examinations. She is trying not to overestimate the amount of control she has over this potential stressor. She has faith in her ability to do well on the test. She is intelligent, has excellent study habits, and other intellectual resources to draw on if needed.

Secondary Stress Appraisal

While primary stress appraisal determines whether a potential stressor is threatening, secondary appraisal is concerned with coping. It is crucial to remember that secondary stress appraisal occurs simultaneously with primary appraisal. All of the situation and person factors involved in primary appraisal are also used to decide whether or not one can cope with the potential stressor. These factors are used to help make a complex evaluation of what coping options are available, determine whether they can be achieved under the circumstances related to this potential stressor at this time, and discover whether there are any constraints to using these strategies.

The other key aspect of coping is how it relates to time. As the potential stressor becomes more imminent or of longer duration, the ability to cope with it changes also. The potential stressor might become easier to cope with or more difficult to manage. Part of it has to do with the changing nature of person and situational factors. Other things related to the ability to cope are coping dispositions and coping resources.

Coping and Coping Dispositions

Lazarus and Folkman[34] describe coping as the constantly shifting cognitive and behavioral efforts to manage potential stressors that are appraised as threatening. There are two types of coping: emotion-focused coping and problem-focused coping.

Emotion-focused coping revolves around techniques used to change the way one views potential stressors. In section II of this book this is referred to as rethink. In chapter 7 we will discuss several ways to change the way one can view potential stressors. Emotion-focused coping works by helping people defuse potential stressors from ever becoming threatening. **Problem-focused coping** works by changing either the environment related to the potential stressor or doing something to change the way the potential stressor affects the person. Rather than changing the way the potential stressor is viewed, one finds different ways of managing it.

Lets use Hiroko's test as an example. Hiroko never felt very threatened by this exam. If she did begin to feel threatened by her exam as it got closer to the date it was scheduled for, she could use emotion-focused coping to

emotion-focused coping coping that focuses on changing the way one views potential stressors in order to defuse their threat

problem-focused coping coping that focuses on changing either the environment related to the potential stressor, or doing something to change the way the potential stressor affects the person; rather than changing the way the potential stressor is viewed, one finds different ways of managing it reassure herself that she was still able to deal with it effectively. If self-doubts or negative self-talk began to creep into her consciousness, she could employ techniques to stop these negative thoughts and self-doubts and replace them with positive self-talk and remembrances of past successes. She could also use problem-focused coping to do things like getting a massage or doing some vigorous exercises to rid the tension building up in her neck in response to thinking about the test. She could also improve the lighting in her dorm room or buy a more ergonomically perfect chair to sit in when she studies. She could form a study group or use the computerized test bank to help her learn the material. All of these strategies attack the potential stressor without changing her thoughts about it.

Coping Resources

Lazarus and Folkman[34] describe six types of coping resources: health and energy, positive beliefs, problem-solving skills, social skills, social support, and material resources. As you can see just by quickly perusing the list, it is a well-rounded collection of resources that truly represents a wellness approach to stress advocated by this textbook.

Health and Energy To paraphrase Lazarus and Folkman,[34] a healthy and robust person has more energy to expend on coping than someone who is frail, sick, tired, or otherwise debilitated. High level health and energy is particularly important for dealing with long-standing chronic situations such as a family member's illness, a job that is not secure, serious debts, or a variety of other long-term conditions. In chapter 10 we will discuss how to use health and fitness to enhance coping.

Positive Beliefs As we've discussed, positive beliefs about oneself and one's ability to control one's life develop throughout the course of our lifetime. They can be rational and be rooted in objective data about past successes. They can also be reinforced by our faith in ourselves, others, or a higher being. As we discussed, even though this faith cannot be proven empirically, it can help us cope. Thinking positively helps people feel that they can cope and consequently are less threatened by potential stressors. We will discuss strategies for becoming more optimistic and using positive self-talk for coping in chapter 7.

Problem-Solving Skills As we discussed earlier in the intellectual basis of stress, problem solving is a resource that can help us defuse potential stressors by giving us more options for dealing with them. Problem solving helps reduce threat by helping people accurately appraise both potential threat and our ability to cope with it. Problem solving is based on flexibility and options. When people are able to solve problems successfully, they develop more confidence in their ability to cope with potential stressors.

Social Skills As we learned from Goleman,[18] effective social skills often revolve around the ability to have empathy and understand what other people are feeling when they experience stressful situations. Using this understanding to manage social relationships is a hallmark of emotional intelligence. One's perceived ability to cope with a social situation can greatly reduce any potential threat associated with it. Often, social skills learned and associated with one situation can be transferred to another. Many social skills revolve around effective communication and assertiveness which we will discuss in chapter 8.

Social Support In chapter 4 we will go into great detail regarding social support and how it is related to stress. Social support in general refers to having people available from whom one receives emotional, informational, or tangible support. Social support is related to coping in a couple of different ways. Often, just knowing that you have the support (material resources such as money or just someone to listen to you) of others can defuse a potential stressor from ever becoming threatening. Knowing you have the emotional, informational, or tangible support of others prevents potential stressors from ever becoming threats. The other way social support works is by having these resources kick in and short-circuit any threat that has begun to develop. This is especially beneficial with potential stressors that are of greater imminence or longer duration. These afford one the time to take advantage of their available social support resources.

Material Resources Material resources are the goods and services that money can buy that might help one cope with a potential stressor. Some stressors are particularly amenable to being defused as a result of purchasing something that can help cope with them. For instance, if one is threatened by having to commute to school in the winter because their car is not reliable, being able to buy a new car could dramatically reduce the potential threat involved in the commute.

Let's work through Hiroko's coping resources as an example. Hiroko is very healthy. She is a runner and eats a well-balanced diet low in saturated fat and calories. She

KEY TO UNDERSTANDING

The stress transaction doesn't take place in a vacuum; it takes place within a specific context of space and time. The same potential stressor, under different circumstances may not be perceived the same way. Your history, success at coping with this stressor in the past, and a host of other factors influence a stress transaction at any given time.

is a nonsmoker and does not use illegal drugs. She occasionally will drink alcohol socially. Hiroko's health contributes to her perceived ability to cope with this potential stressor (the exam). Hiroko is a Buddhist and has a lot of faith in her belief system, herself, and the support of loved ones. She uses meditation as a way to quiet her mind and think positively. Hiroko is excellent at problem solving. She is very creative and likes games such as crossword puzzles and mind twisters. She feels confident that if some unforeseen problem with the test presents itself, she will be able to handle it. If Hiroko has one weakness, it is her social skills. She has a hard time understanding assertiveness. In her culture certain assertive behavior would be considered rude, so she is still trying to understand this. She is not a very emotional person, so she has some problems seeing and interpreting emotions in others. For this potential stressor (the exam) she doesn't view this as a problem. While Hiroko does view her social skills as being a little deficient for interacting with the population at large, they work fine within her social support system. Her immediate and extended family (both here and in Japan) are always there to help her any way they can. Her dad is a well-educated man to whom she often turns for help studying. This support helps defuse the exam as a threat.

Hiroko has more than adequate material resources to deal with this potential stressor. She lives at home and her parents have the financial and other material resources she will need.

Situational Constraints

Situational constraints are circumstances and obstacles to taking advantage of ones coping resources. Situational constraints are temporal in nature. They may be present now but may not be there when confronted by the same potential stressor in the future. On the other hand, situational constraints that existed in the past with a potential stressor might not exist in the present with the current potential stressor. This could be the result of changes in coping resources or a new-found ability to use emotion-focused techniques.

Let's see how this plays out with Hiroko's exam. Hiroko remembers that the last time she had a similar exam and was feeling a little threatened, she went home and had a long talk with her brother who helped her put the situation in perspective. Eventually, after talking with him, she was able to refocus and did very well on her test.

> **KEY TO UNDERSTANDING**
>
> Expanding your repertoire of coping strategies will ensure that you don't get stuck if your only strategy won't work with, or is unavailable for your current stressor. The greater the number and more varied your coping strategies, the more likely it is that you will have something to draw on under any circumstance.

However, in this situation Hiroko realizes that she will not be able to employ this coping strategy. Situational constraints (her brother is overseas in the military) prevent her from using what worked in the past. She will have to use another coping strategy for this situation. Hiroko instantly reassesses the other coping strategies at her disposal and decides to form a study group with some students from the class. This helps defuse the threat associated with the exam.

Cognitive Reappraisal

After weighing all of the situational factors, her commitments and beliefs, and assessing her ability to cope, Hiroko reassesses the potential stressor to determine if it is a threat, something benign or positive, or a challenge to her intellectual abilities. Initially, Hiroko does perceive the test as a little threatening only because she is so close to graduating and doesn't want to have a blemish on her academic record. After a couple of days, however, as the situation unfolds, she talks to her mother and begins to review her class notes; she modifies her initial assessment, and the test loses its status as a stressor. Both the environment and the situation have changed, as well as Hiroko's perceptions of them. A stress transaction has occurred in Hiroko's life.

As you can see, Lazarus and Folkman's[34] Stress Appraisal Model is the perfect model for explaining how potential stressors become stressors. It takes into account emotions, intellectual resources, and personality attributes, and combines them into a comprehensive model for understanding stress. It is holistic because it takes one's environment into account when appraising potential stressors. We'll see how that plays out in the next chapter, "The Environmental and Occupational Basis of Stress."

SUMMARY

We began this chapter with an overview of the emotional basis of stress. We defined emotions and discussed how emotions can be grouped into families. We followed this with a look at Lazarus's analysis of stressful emotions. He believes that stressful emotions are linked to subvocal core relational themes, little internal scripts that tell us how these emotions should play out in our behavior. This was followed by a different look at emotions, one from another culture. We described Japanese cultural perspectives on emotions and their link to stress.

DIVERSE PERSPECTIVES

Zahava: Adjusting and Excelling

Zahava is a college senior majoring in business administration and is preparing to deliver an oral report on multinational marketing in the Middle East for her senior seminar class. As she goes over her notes in final preparation for tomorrow's report, she thinks back to her freshman year and how terrified she was over a similar assignment.

As a freshman Zahava was the first woman in her family to attend college. She came to college from a very traditional, religious Middle Eastern culture; her family emigrated from the Middle East when she was a freshman in high school. Zahava was taught to speak only when spoken to and to avoid bringing undue attention to herself. She had a very hard time adapting to college, where students were often asked to express and defend their opinions about various issues. Zahava thought she would never survive her first college oral presentation in macroeconomics. She was so afraid of standing in front of her class that she was sick for three days leading up to her presentation.

She smiles now as she looks back on those times. Tomorrow is a different story. She is much more comfortable with herself and her ability to deliver oral presentations. Her family members are thrilled by her academic success and now marvel at the well-rounded woman she has become. They have changed and accept her assertiveness as she articulates her needs and defends her own positions on issues. She no longer has the same internal conflicts about getting up in front of a room full of people and expressing and defending herself.

Besides resolving these issues about her cultural background, Zahava has become a better technical speaker. She has worked hard to improve her speaking ability. She has taken extra classes in communication and debate and, as a result, is a skilled public speaker. She feels no stress, only challenge, as she prepares for the last oral presentation she will give in college.

The next part of the chapter focused on personality theory. We examined several classic personality theorists, such as Freud, Piaget, and Maslow. We then examined several classic theories that link stress to specific personality attributes and personality types. We examined stress-prone personality and stress-resistant styles. Rosenman and Friedman and others present compelling evidence that the hard-driving, hurried, competitive, time-conscious man or woman is at an increased risk for cardiovascular disease. Their conceptualization of the Type A individual and the risks inherent in a Type A behavior pattern have become common knowledge and have helped us understand the role our personalities play in determining stress and health. Hostility and anger were identified as the two most destructive Type A attributes. Even a hard-driving, competitive person need not be at increased risk for stress or health problems if he or she is not hostile or angry. Hostility and anger seem to be the two attributes that account for most of the health risks associated with the Type A behavior pattern. The Type C personality, the next personality type examined in the chapter, is characterized by a sense of hopelessness/helplessness. People develop this personality construct over time as learned helplessness. Rather than actively confront his or her problems, the helpless/hopeless Type C person is emotionally subdued and resigned to his or her fate. This personality type has been shown to be related to cancer. Ellis shows how our belief system affects how we view things and whether these beliefs transform neutral situations into stressors. Ellis's work introduces the notion of thoughts as the mediators between potential stressors and the stress response. He clarified the idea that stress does not exist in situations and things but that it is our perception of situations and things that determines whether we make them into stressors. Million's model ties together many of the disparate personality factors and types uncovered by the researchers discussed earlier in the chapter into a comprehensive model for understanding the emotional makeup of stress-prone individuals. Million's model builds on the others that isolated individual personality factors or types.

We followed this discussion with a look at two stress-resistant personality types: the Type B and the Hardy Personality. Friedman and Rosenman described a Type B personality that is stress-resistant and the polar opposite of the Type A. Type Bs are more relaxed and easygoing and have a lessened risk of heart disease. Kobasa's work illustrates how people are more stress resistant if they are hardy. Hardiness refers to people who feel in control of their lives, are committed rather than aimless, and view situations as challenges rather than stressors. Kobasa's work ties research on Type As with accepted knowledge of the virtues of possessing an internal locus of control and the power of positive thinking. We then took a quick look at the intellectual resources that are associated with the stress response. Intelligence, life experience, oral and written communication skills, creativity, and problem solving were examined briefly to see how they are related to stress. The next part of the chapter focused on how emotional and intellectual factors converge in the stress response. In expanding his initial theory, Richard Lazarus joined with Susan Folkman to present a unified psychological theory of stress. Lazarus and Folkman's theory of stress appraisal and coping integrates emotional and intellectual factors and ties together the disparate research of the many theorists we have been discussing into a unified theoretical framework. It identifies the specific situational, personal, and coping factors that are involved in the appraisal of a potential stressor. The chapter ends with an application of their model to explain stress associated with a student, Hiroko's midterm. It shows how Hiroko appraises the exam as a potential stressor before determining that it was not a threat to her and she could cope with it. Once she decided this, the exam was defused as a potential stressor.

STUDY QUESTIONS

1. What is personality, and how is it related to stress?
2. Compare three different theories of personality development.
3. Describe the Type A personality behavior pattern.
4. List and describe the two key attributes of the Type A personality that are most related to stress.
5. Describe the Type B personality.
6. Describe the characteristics of the Type C personality.
7. Hardy personalities are characterized by what three attributes?
8. What is the underlying assumption of rational emotive psychotherapy concerning the role of perception in the stress response?
9. What is the significance of negative self-talk in the stress response?
10. Describe Lazarus and Folkman's stress transaction concept.
11. What is the difference between primary appraisal and secondary appraisal?
12. Describe the three types of primary appraisal.
13. What is the role of coping in stress appraisal?
14. What turns a potential stressor into a challenge?

DISCOVER OUR CHANGING WORLD

Visit the website for the Albert Ellis Institute for Rational Emotive Behavior Therapy, http://www.rebt.org/. Read about the mission of the institute and its activities/resources in the "What's New" link.

Critical Thinking Question

How can the Albert Ellis Institute help manage your stress as either a layperson or a future teacher, counselor, or other helping professional?

ARE YOU THINKING CLEARLY?

In this chapter we examined the nature and role of emotions in the stress response. Emotions, especially strong ones like anger and jealousy, have the *potential* to cause stress and inappropriate behavior if we feel threatened by them and that we can't cope with them. A key first step in stopping emotions from *automatically* triggering a stress response is examining what we think about them and how we act in response to them. The following questions will help you assess how you deal with potentially threatening emotions.

Imagine you start your day off on the wrong foot. Your alarm fails to go off and you are running late. As you are in the shower, your friend leaves a message for you saying that she is sick and can't pick you up on her way to school. You jump in your car and realize you never got gas last night (because your friend was driving) and must stop on the way to school, making you even later for your first class. As you drive to school you feel the anger begin to well up inside of you. Do you find yourself engaging in the following kind of self-talk?

1. I can't believe she (your friend) did this to me. What a #$%%@^&&!!!!! She better not call me later or I'm going to go ballistic on her over the phone!
2. Nobody better mess with me today or I am going to lose it!!!!
3. I better find a parking spot when I get to school or I am going to go crazy!!!!!!!
4. That stupid professor better not give me a hard time for being late or I'm going to give him a piece of my mind!
5. I am so pissed, I can't be responsible for what I might do today!
6. Those customers at work better watch out later or they'll get a hot cup of coffee in their laps!

If you think you would find yourself saying these kinds of messages to yourself if your day started off this way, you are allowing your emotions to control your thoughts and behavior. In chapter 7 we will learn how to shut down this kind of illogical, stressful thinking and behaving and replace them with more logical and productive ways to think and behave.

REFERENCES

1. Anderson, J.R. & Waldron, I. (1983). Behavioral and content components of the structured interview assessment of Type A behavior pattern in women. *Journal of Behavioral Medicine,* 6, pp. 123–134.
2. Barefoot, J.C. (1993). Keeping conflicting findings in perspective: The case of hostility and health. *Mayo Clinic Proceedings,* 68, pp. 192–193.
3. Barefoot, J.C., Dahlstrom, W.G., & Williams, R.B. (1983). Hostility, CHD incidence, and total mortality: A 25 year follow-up study of 255 physicians. *Psychosomatic Medicine,* 45(1), pp. 59–63.
4. Carmelli, D., Dame, A., Swan, G., & Rosenman, R. (1991). Long-term changes in Type A behavior: A 27 year follow-up of the Western Collaborative Group study. *Journal of Behavioral Medicine,* 14(6), pp. 593–606.

5. De Moor, W. (1988). A rational-emotive ABC model of emotional disturbances: A stress model. *Psychotherapy in Private Practice,* 6(2), pp. 21–33.
6. Ellis, A., Gordon, J., Neenan, M., & Palmer, S. (1997). *Stress counseling: A rational emotive approach.* New York: Springer.
7. Ellis, A. (1991a). The philosophical basis of rational emotive therapy. *Psychotherapy in Private Practice,* 8(4), pp. 97–106.
8. Ellis, A. (1991b). The revised ABC's of rational-emotive therapy (RET). *Journal of Rational-Emotive Therapy,* 9(3), pp. 139–167.
9. Engebretson, T. & Matthews, K. (1992). Dimensions of hostility in men, women, and boys: Relationships to personality and cardiovascular responses to stress. *Psychosomatic Medicine,* 54(3), pp. 311–323.
10. Erickson, E. (1986). *Childhood and society.* New York: WW Norton.
11. Everly, G.S. & Lating, J.M. (2002). *A clinical guide to the treatment of the human stress response.* 2d ed. New York: Kluwer Academic/Plenum.
12. Eysenck, H.J. (1996). Personality and cancer. In Cooper, C.L. (Ed.) *Handbook of stress, medicine and health,* pp. 193–215. Boca Raton, FL: CRC Press.
13. Eysenck, H.J. (1994). Synergistic interaction between psychosocial and physical factors in the causation of lung cancer. In Lewis C., O' Sullivan, C., & Baraclough, J. (Eds.) *The psychoimmunology of cancer,* pp. 163–178. Oxford, UK: Oxford University Press.
14. Eysenck, H.J. (1991). Personality, stress and disease: An interactionist approach. *Psychological Inquiry,* 2, pp. 221–232.
15. Eysenck, H.J. (1990). Type A behavior and coronary heart disease: The third stage. *Journal of Social Behavior and Personality,* 5, pp. 25–44.
16. Fawzy, F.I., Kemeny, M.E., & Fawzy, N. (1990). A structural psychiatric intervention for cancer patients. *Archives of General Psychiatry,* 47, pp. 729–735.
17. Friedman, M. & Ulmer D. (1984). *Treating Type A behavior and your heart.* New York: Knopf.
18. Goleman, D. (1997). *Emotional intelligence.* New York: Bantam Books.
19. Friedman, M. & Rosenman, R. (1974). *Type A behavior and your heart.* Greenwich, CT: Fawcett.
20. Girdano, D., Everly, G., & Dusek, D. (1993). *Controlling stress and tension: A holistic approach.* Englewood Cliffs, NJ: Prentice-Hall.
21. Greer, S., Morris, T., Pettingale, K., & Haybiottle, J. (1990). Psychological responses to breast cancer: A fifteen year outcome. *Lancet,* 1, pp. 49–50.
22. Hall, C. (1954). *A primer of freudian psychology.* London: World.
23. Haynes, S.G., Feinleib, M., & Kannel, W.B. (1980). The relationship of psychosocial factors to coronary heart disease in the Framingham Study: Eight year incidence of coronary heart disease. *American Journal of Epidemiology,* 111, pp. 37–58.
24. Hull, J.G., Van Treuren, R., & Virnelli, S. (1987). Hardiness and health: A critique and alternate approach. *Journal of Personality and Social Psychology,* 53(3), pp. 518–530.
25. Karren, K.J., Hafen, B.Q., Smith, N.L., & Frandsen, K.J. (2002). *Mind/body health: The effects of attitudes, emotions, and relationships.* 2nd ed. San Francisco: Benjamin Cummings.
26. Kiecolt-Glaser, J. & Glaser, R. (1992). Psychoimmunology: Can psychological interventions modulate immunity? *Journal of Consulting and Clinical Psychology,* 60, pp. 569–575.
27. Kissen, D.M. & Eysenck, H.J. (1962). Personality in male lung cancer patients. *Journal of Psychosomatic Research,* 6, pp. 123–137.
28. Kneier, A.W. & Temoshok, L. (1984). Repressive coping reaction in patients with malignant melanomas as compared to cardiovascular disease patients. *Journal of Psychosomatic Medicine,* 28, pp. 145–155.
29. Kobasa, S. (1979). Stressful life events, personality, and health: An inquiry into hardiness. *Journal of Personality and Social Psychology,* 37(1), pp. 1–11.
30. Kobasa, S., Maddi, S., & Kahn, S. (1982). Hardiness and health: A prospective study. *Journal of Personality and Social Psychology,* 42(1), pp. 168–177.
31. Kohlberg, L. (1981). *The philosophy of moral development* (Vol. 1). San Francisco: Harper & Row.
32. Lawler, K. & Schmied, L. (1992). A prospective study of women's health: The effects of stress, hardiness, locus of control, Type A behavior, and psychosocial reactivity. *Women and Health,* 19(1), pp. 27–41.
33. Lazarus, R.S. (1966). *Psychological stress and the coping process.* New York: McGraw-Hill.
34. Lazarus, R.S. & Folkman, S. (1984). *Stress appraisal and coping.* New York: Springer.
35. Lazarus, R. (1993a). From psychological stress to the emotions: A history of changing outlooks. *Annual Reviews in Psychology,* 44, pp. 1–21.
36. Lazarus, R. (1993b). Coping theory and research: Past, present, and future. *Psychosomatic Medicine,* 55, pp. 234–247.
37. Lazarus, R. (1999). *Stress and emotion: A new synthesis.* New York: Springer.
38. Le Shan, L. (1977). *You can fight for your life: Emotional factors in the causation of cancer.* New York: M. Evans.
39. Levy, S., Hoberman, R.B., Maluish, A.M., Schlien, B., & Lippman, M. (1985). Prognostic assessment in primary breast cancer by behavioral and immunological parameters. *Health Psychology,* 4, pp. 99–113.
40. Lyness, S. (1993). Predictors of difference between Type A and Type B individuals in heart rate and blood pressure reactivity. *Psychological Bulletin,* 114(2), pp. 266–295.
41. Maddi, S.R. (1998). The hardiness model. http://www.hardinessinstitute.com/model.htm.
42. Margiotta, E., Davilla, D., & Hicks, R. (1990). Type A-B behavior and the self-report of daily hassles and uplifts. *Perceptual and Motor Skills,* 70(3), pp. 777–778.
43. Maruta, T. (1993). Hostility's questionable role in heart disease. *Mayo Clinic Proceedings,* 68, pp. 109–114.
44. Maslow, A. (1968). *Toward a psychology of being.* Princeton, NJ: Van Nostrand.

45. Manuck, S. & Saab, P. (1992). The influence of age, sex, and family on Type A and hostile attitudes and behavior. *Health Psychology,* 11(5), pp. 317–323.
46. Matthews, K.A. & Haynes, S.G. (1986). Type A behavior pattern and coronary disease risk: Update and critical evaluation. *American Journal of Epidemiology,* 123(6), pp. 923–960.
47. Matthews, K.A., et al. (1977). Competitive drive, pattern A and coronary heart disease: A further analysis of the Western Collaborative Group study. *Journal of Chronic Disease,* 30, pp. 489–498.
48. Meninger, J. (1983). The validity of Type A behavior scales for employed women. *American Journal of Epidemiology,* 118, p. 424.
49. Millon, T. (1996). *Disorders of personality.* 2nd ed. New York: Wiley.
50. Morita, S. (1998). Morita therapy and the nature of anxiety-based disorders (shinkeishitsu). Translated by Akihisa Kondo. Edited by Peg Le Vine. Albany NY: State University of NY Press.
51. Piaget, J. *The psychology of intelligence.* London: Routledge and Kegan Paul.
52. Payne, W. & Hahn, D. (2002). *Understanding your health.* 7th ed. St. Louis: McGraw-Hill.
53. Ragland, D.R. & Brand, R.J. (1988). Type A behavior and mortality from coronary heart disease. *New England Journal of Medicine,* 318(2), pp. 65–69.
54. Reynolds, D. (1984). *Constructive Living.* Honolulu: University of Hawaii Press.
55. Reynolds, D. (2002). *A Handbook for Constructive Living.* Honolulu: University of Hawaii Press.
56. Rosenman, R. & Chesney, M.A. (1985). Type A behavior and coronary disease. In Spielberger, C.D. & Sarason, I.G. (Eds.) *Stress and anxiety* Vol. 9, pp. 207–229. Washington, DC: Hemisphere.
57. Rosenman, R. (1978). The interview method of assessment of coronary-prone behavior pattern. In Dembroski, T.M., Weis, S.M., Shields, J.L., Haynes, S.G., & Feinleb, M. (Eds.) *Coronary prone behavior.* New York: Springer.
58. Rosenman, R., Brand, R.J., Jenkins, C.D., Friedman, M., Straus, R., & Wurm, M. (1975). Coronary heart disease in the Western Collaborative Group study: A final follow-up of 8½ years. *Journal of the American Medical Association,* 233(8), pp. 872–877.
59. Rosenman, R.H. & Ward, M.W. (1988). The changing concept of cardiovascular reactivity. *Stress Medicine,* 4, p. 241.
60. Rosenman, R.H. (1996). Personality, behavior patterns, and heart disease. In Cooper, C.L. (Ed.) *Handbook of stress, medicine and health,* pp. 218–231. Boca Raton, FL: CRC Press.
61. Rosenman, R.H. & Hjemdahl, P. (1991). Is there a causal relationship of anxiety, stress or cardiovascular reactivity to hypertension? *Stress Medicine,* 7, p. 152.
62. Rosenman, R.H. (1991). Type A behavior pattern and coronary heart disease: The hostility factor. *Stress Medicine,* 7, p. 245.
63. Rosenman, R.H. (1990). Type A behavior pattern: A personal overview. In Strube, M. (Ed.) (1990). Type A behavior. *Journal of Social Behavior and Personality,* 5, p. 1.
64. Rotter, J.B. (1975). Some problems and misconceptions related to the construct of internal vs. external control of reinforcement. *Journal of Consulting and Clinical Psychology,* 43, pp. 56–67.
65. Schmale, A.H. & Iker, H. (1971). Hopelessness as a predictor of cervical cancer. *Social Science Medicine,* 5, pp. 99–100.
66. Seligman, M.E. (1975). *Helplessness: On depression, development and death.* San Francisco: Freeman.
67. Seligman, M.E. (1991). *Learned optimism: How to change your mind and life.* New York: Alfred A. Knopf.
68. Selye, H. (1956). *The stress of life.* New York: McGraw-Hill.
69. Seward, B.L. (2002). *Managing stress: Principles and strategies for wellbeing and health.* 3rd ed. Boston: Jones & Bartlett.
70. Shafer, W. (1995). *Stress management for wellness.* 3rd ed. New York: Thomson Learning.
71. Shekelle, R.B., Gayle, M., Ostfield, A.M., & Oglesby, P. (1983). Hostility, risk of coronary heart disease and mortality. *Psychosomatic Medicine,* 45(2), pp. 109–114.
72. Temoshok, L. & Dreher, H. (1992). *Type C behavior and cancer.* New York: Random House.
73. Thoresen, C. & Powell, L. (1992). Type A behavior: New perspectives on theory, assessment and intervention. *Consulting and Clinical Psychology,* 60(4), pp. 595–604.
74. Walen, S., DiGuiseppi, R., & Wessler, R. (1980). *A practitioner's guide to RET.* New York: Oxford University Press.
75. Watson, J. (1928). *Psychological care of infant and child.* Salem, NH: Ayer.
76. Williams, R.B., Jr., Haney, T.L., Lee, K.L., Kong, Y., Blumenthal, J.A., & Whalen, R.E. (1980). Type A behavior, hostility, and coronary atherosclerosis. *Psychosomatic Medicine,* 42, pp. 539–549.
77. Wordsmyth. (1999). *Wordsmyth online dictionary.* http://www.wordsmyth.net.
78. Wright, T., Blache, C., Ralph, J., & Luterman, A. (1993). Hardiness, stress and burnout among intensive care nurses. *Journal of Burn Care Rehabilitation,* 14(3), pp. 376–381.

Name: ______________________________ Date: __________

ASSESS YOURSELF 2-1

Type A Behavior

This scale, based on the one developed by Friedman and Rosenman,[17] will give you an estimate of your Type A tendencies.

Directions: Answer the following questions by indicating the response that most often applies to you.

Yes	No	Statement
____	____	1. I always feel rushed.
____	____	2. I find it hard to relax.
____	____	3. I attempt to do more and more in less and less time.
____	____	4. I often find myself doing more than one thing at a time.
____	____	5. When people take too long to make a point, I finish the sentence for them.
____	____	6. Waiting in line for anything drives me crazy.
____	____	7. I am always on time or early.
____	____	8. In a conversation, I often clench my fist and pound home important points.
____	____	9. I often use explosive outbursts to accentuate key points.
____	____	10. I am competitive at everything.
____	____	11. I tend to evaluate my success by translating things into numbers.
____	____	12. Friends tell me I have more energy than most people.
____	____	13. I always move, walk, and eat quickly.
____	____	14. I bring work home often.
____	____	15. I tend to get bored on vacation.
____	____	16. I feel guilty when I am not being "productive."
____	____	17. I tend to refocus other people's conversations on things that interest me.
____	____	18. I hurry others along in their conversations.
____	____	19. It is agonizing to be stuck behind someone driving too slowly.
____	____	20. I find it intolerable to let others do something I can do faster.

Scoring: Add up the number of items for which you checked yes. The greater the number of yes items, the more likely it is that you are a Type A personality.

Name: ______________________ Date: 6/3/08

ASSESS YOURSELF 2-2

Internal versus External Control

Directions: Circle the statement that best describes how you feel.

1. a. Children get into trouble because their parents punish them too much.
   b. Children get into trouble because their parents are too easy on them.
2. a. Many of the unhappy things in people's lives are partly due to bad luck.
   b. People's misfortunes result from the mistakes they make.
3. a. One of the major reasons we have wars is that people don't take enough interest in politics.
   b. There will always be wars no matter how hard people try to prevent them.
4. a. In the long run people get the respect they deserve in this world.
   b. Unfortunately, an individual's worth often passes unrecognized no matter how hard he or she tries.
5. a. The idea that teachers are unfair to students is nonsense.
   b. Most students don't realize the extent to which their grades are influenced by accidental happenings.
6. a. Without the right breaks one cannot be an effective leader.
   b. Capable people who fail to become leaders have not taken advantage of their opportunities.
7. a. No matter how hard you try, some people just don't like you.
   b. People who can't get others to like them don't understand how to get along with others.
8. a. Heredity plays the major role in determining one's personality.
   b. It is one's experiences in life that determine personality.
9. a. I have often found that what is going to happen will happen.
   b. Trusting to fate has never turned out as well for me as making a decision to take a definite course of action.
10. a. In the case of the well-prepared student, there is rarely if ever such a thing as an unfair test.
    b. Many times exam questions tend to be so unrelated to course work that studying is really useless.
11. a. Becoming a success is a matter of hard work—luck has little or nothing to do with it.
    b. Getting a good job depends mainly on being in the right place at the right time.
12. a. The average citizen can have an influence on government decisions.
    b. This world is run by the few people in power, and there is not much the little guy can do about it.
13. a. When I make plans, I am almost certain that I can make them work.
    b. I usually have little control over the outcome of my plans.
14. a. There are certain people who are just no good.
    b. There is some good in everybody.
15. a. In my case getting what I want has little or nothing to do with luck.
    b. Many times we might just as well decide what to do by flipping a coin.
16. a. Who gets to be the boss often depends on who was lucky enough to be in the right place first.
    b. Getting people to do the right thing depends on ability—luck has little or nothing to do with it.
17. a. As far as world affairs are concerned, most of us are the victims of forces we can neither understand nor control.
    b. By taking an active part in political and social affairs, people can control world events.
18. a. Most people don't realize the extent to which their lives are controlled by accidental happenings.
    b. There really is no such thing as luck.
19. a. One should always be willing to admit mistakes.
    b. It is usually best to cover up one's mistakes.
20. a. It is hard to know whether a person really likes you.
    b. How many friends you have depends on how nice a person you are.
21. a. In the long run the bad things that happen to us are balanced by the good ones.
    b. Most misfortunes are the result of lack of ability, ignorance, laziness, or all three.
22. a. With enough effort we can wipe out political corruption.
    b. It is difficult for people to have much control over the things politicians do in office.

ASSESS YOURSELF 2-2 (cont'd)

23. a. Sometimes I can't understand how teachers arrive at the grades they give.
    b. There is a direct connection between how hard I study and the grades I get.
24. a. A good leader expects people to decide for themselves what they should do.
    b. A good leader makes it clear to everybody what his or her job is.
25. a. Many times I feel that I have little influence over the things that happen to me.
    b. It is impossible for me to believe that chance or luck plays an important role in my life.
26. a. People are lonely because they don't try to be friendly.
    b. There's not much use in trying too hard to please people—if they like you, they like you.
27. a. There is too much emphasis on athletics in high school.
    b. Team sports are an excellent way to build character.
28. a. What happens to me is my own doing.
    b. Sometimes I feel that I don't have enough control over the direction my life is taking.
29. a. Most of the time I can't understand why politicians behave the way they do.
    b. In the long run the people are responsible for bad government on a national as well as on a local level.

Scoring: Give yourself 1 point for each of these circled choices: 1b, 2a, 3b, 4b, 5b, 6a, 7a, 8a, 10b, 11b, 12b, 13b, 15b, 16a, 17a, 18a, 20a, 21a, 22b, 23a, 25a, 26b, 29a.

Scores range from 0 (most internal) to 23 (most external).

Name: ______________________ Date: __________

ASSESS YOURSELF 2-3

Rational Beliefs Inventory

Directions: For each of the following twenty statements select 1 (most like me), 2 (somewhat like me), 0 (not sure), or 3 (not like me) to describe your feelings.

___ 1. I need approval from family, friends, and acquaintances.

___ 2. Things that happened to me in the past control who I am.

___ 3. I must be good at everything I try.

___ 4. I have little control over my emotions.

___ 5. Other people and things tend to make me feel bad.

___ 6. I deal with tough problems by avoiding them.

___ 7. Things should really turn out better than they do.

___ 8. My motto is "Never Volunteer."

___ 9. I can't seem to get fearful things off my mind.

___ 10. Unfair people are rotten and should be blamed for their misdeeds.

___ 11. It is terrible when things don't go my way.

___ 12. I really need love and approval from everyone.

___ 13. Worrying about fearful things helps me cope with them.

___ 14. Because the past strongly influences who we are, it determines our present emotions and behavior.

___ 15. It's really easier to avoid problems and responsibilities than to face them.

___ 16. I am happiest when I don't commit myself to things.

___ 17. There are some people who are just plain rotten and deserve all the misery they get.

___ 18. People really should do their best at everything.

___ 19. There really is a perfect solution to every problem—that's why it's so terrible when it isn't found.

___ 20. It's horrible when things in my life are not the way I want them to be.

Scoring: Add all the numbers you placed in the left-hand column.

The lower the score, the more illogical/irrational you tend to be.

0–20: If you scored in this range, you tend to believe in many of the ten illogical beliefs of rational emotive therapy.

20–40: You have a moderately illogical belief system.

40–60: You tend to be logical and rational.

Remember, this is an estimate of how your beliefs about life match up to the ten illogical beliefs of rational emotive therapy. All of us share some of these beliefs at times.

CHAPTER

3

THE ENVIRONMENTAL AND OCCUPATIONAL BASIS OF STRESS

OUTLINE

Our Personal Environment
- Environmental Stress and Strain
- Lighting Strain
- Climate
- Air Quality
- Noise Pollution

Ergonomics
- Ergonomics in the Home
- Ergonomics in the Workplace
- Ergonomics in Action: Computer Workstations

Work-Related Stress
- The Changing Workplace
- Measuring Occupational Stress

The NIOSH Model of Job Stress
- Stressful Job Conditions
- Individual and Situational Factors

A Transactional Model for Explaining Occupational and Environmental Stress

OBJECTIVES

By the end of the chapter students will:

- Discriminate between environmental and occupational strain and stress.
- Describe three sources of lighting strain.
- Describe three ways to reduce lighting strain.
- Explain how different temperature ranges contribute to strain.
- Explain how air exchange is related to indoor air quality.
- Explain why graffiti is considered a source of pollution.
- Describe three major sources of environmental noise.
- Compare and contrast firsthand and secondhand noise.
- Define ergonomics and explain how it relates to the design of computer workstations.
- Describe the components of the NIOSH model of job stress.
- Describe three potentially stressful job conditions.
- Compare the transactional model of occupational stress with other models used to explain the phenomenon.

In this chapter we will discuss the environmental and occupational bases of stress. While these two areas are introduced and treated separately for the purpose of discussing how they relate to stress, in reality they are inseparable. As we'll discuss in this chapter, one's environment includes the work place as well as one's college/university, neighborhood, state, country, and the world at large. We are faced with potential stressors in all of these environments. They all have their own unique set of factors that influence how we appraise them.

Our Personal Environment

For example, in your home environment, factors such as air quality, lighting, heating and cooling, security and safety, room size, total square feet of living space, how many people share that space, how those people get along, and other factors combine to create a context in which all stress transactions occur. In addition to influencing the context in which stress transactions occur, any of those factors individually could be a stressor if appraised as such. In other words, feeling crowded could be viewed as stressful by itself as well as factoring into how other potential home stressors are appraised.

Many college students live at home and commute to school. Many still share rooms with younger siblings and do not have an office or room in which they can read, study, write, and leave their books and other materials where they will be undisturbed. Still others live in homes with aunts, uncles, or grandparents, often with little privacy or respect for private space. This type of home environment can be very stressful for students who need private, quiet space to read, write, and study effectively. The inability to spread out books, papers, and other research materials and leave them without having to put everything back for fear that their things could be lost can be very stressful. Other students report having to share the family computer that is often located in a family or living room where it is difficult to concentrate and work effectively. Often these living conditions lead to interpersonal strife within the family. As you can see, any of the aforementioned factors can be stressors in themselves or they can combine to form a stressful home environment.

The same can happen at work where occupational factors combine to create stressful work environments. Students often report working in places that are dirty, unsafe, not heated or cooled efficiently, crowded, noisy, or lighted improperly. Others report a variety of stressful interpersonal issues related to their supervisors, owners, co-workers or customers. Still others report job insecurity or instability as common occupational stressors. As in the home environment, any of these occupational factors can be stressors in themselves or combine to form stressful work environments.

Most stress management textbooks discuss environmental and occupational factors as stressors, regardless of how they are appraised. Many don't even bring the appraisal process into the discussion of environmental and occupational stress. It is important to remember however that in keeping with our transactional model of stress, environmental and occupational factors must be viewed as *potential stressors* until appraised as threatening or harmful. Lazarus and Folkman (1984) pay particular attention to the environments in which stress transactions occur. They remind us that these environments change and over time present different contexts in which stress transactions occur.

Think about how roommates adjust to living together in a dorm, suite, or off-campus house. Initially, everyone is adjusting to the physical realities of sharing a kitchen, bathroom, living room, and often bedroom. Besides the initial adjustments to the physical realities of this new environment, there are interpersonal adjustments that have to be made regarding meeting and living with new people. Over the course of the semester and academic year, both the living environment and the relationships within it change. They may decide to divide the rooms differently, get different furniture, set up quiet study hours, or make other changes to the physical environment. They also make interpersonal adjustments. They get to know their room/house mates better. Maybe someone moves out and someone else moves in. Maybe someone doesn't return after the fall semester. In other words, their living environment changes in a hundred ways over the course of nine months. The exact same potential stressor faced today and back in October are appraised differently because of these changes to the living environment over time.

In the first part of this chapter we will focus on physical environmental factors such as lighting, temperature control, and noise, both individually and in combination. In the second half we will examine how these and other interpersonal factors combine in the work place to create occupational stress.

Environmental Stress and Strain

In chapter 1 we introduced the concept of strain to describe Selye's original conceptualization of the nonspecific response of the body to exposure to noxious environmental demands.[46] In Selye's view, the noxious environmental demands he subjected his laboratory animals to placed great *strain* on their ability to maintain homeostasis. The strain on their body parts and systems caused by the physiological adaptations necessary to maintain homeostasis in the face of those environmental demands eventually resulted in exhaustion and death. Selye, as we mentioned in chapter 1, inadvertently called this environmental demand *stress* instead of *strain.* In chapter 2 we described the importance of person and situation factors, coping, and time in the appraisal of *potential* stressors. It is in this vein that we will discuss environmental and occupational factors as *potential* stressors that exert *strain* on us. They become actual stressors when they are appraised as threatening, or harmful, or beyond our ability to cope with.

A lowering in air temperature, for instance, can strain the body's ability to maintain homeostasis. At a conscious level we are not aware of the physiological adaptations that are going on (increase in metabolic rate, mild shivering response) to keep things in balance. Since there is no appraisal, the temperature change is not yet a stressor; it is a potential stressor, or merely a demand to be dealt with, at this point. Once we begin to "feel cold" and realize that we can't cope with being cold, the potential stressor (change in temperature) becomes a stressor.

Lighting Strain

Lighting has become a major area of interest for experts on environmental and occupational health as they increase their understanding of the effects of natural and artificial light on the body and mind. Natural and artificial light often converge in work places where cubicles are encased in glass monolithic buildings that allow sunlight to stream in and bathe the workspace with **ambient lighting.** Both the amount and the type of lighting can create environmental strain and play a major role in visual discomforts such as eyestrain, burning or itchy eyes, headaches, and blurred or double vision.[40] All these conditions, if left unchecked over time, can become environmental stressors capable of triggering stress responses.

There are four sources of lighting conditions capable of causing strain: inappropriate luminance, reflected light, glare, and high contrast lighting conditions. These can exist separately or in combination in both indoor and outdoor environments.

Luminance is measured in candles per square meter, also called nits. The amount of indoor nits recommended for certain areas and tasks varies. Illuminating hallways in the home or office, for instance, requires about thirty nits. Retail stores generally require between sixty and one hundred nits. General office work requires about one hundred nits, while the luminance necessary for fine detailed workmanship is between 800 and 1000 nits.[20] Luminance that exceeds or falls below these recommendations can create strain and eventually induce a stress response.

Excess luminance *washes out* detail in the immediate field of vision, causing blurring and eyestrain as people make visual adjustments to focus and compensate for the inability to see things clearly. Outdoors, in bright sunlight, unshaded eyes can experience the effects of direct sunlight in a matter of minutes, forcing us to cover our eyes with our hands, a hat, or pair of sunglasses. Indoors, excessively

ambient lighting background lighting that encompasses the surrounding space in a room

luminance the level of brightness in an area as measured in candles per square meter, also called nits

Designers of large glass office buildings must think about the amount of light entering the work environment as well as the light reflected off the building's exterior.

bright ambient light is a problem when it washes out the detail on a computer or television screen, making it difficult for operators and viewers to see images clearly. Lighting should be bright enough to allow us to see items within the field of vision but not too bright that it washes out the detail. Another problem associated with a work site or television room is the relationship between excessive brightness and the creation of glare on computer monitors and television screens. Luminance that falls below the recommended levels can also cause blurring and eyestrain as people try to focus and make adjustments to the low lighting conditions and their inability to see things clearly.[40]

Reflected light is illumination that bounces or bends off another object and then enters a person's field of vision. Outdoors, reflected light is created by bright light bouncing off both natural and artificial surfaces. Snow, ice, sand, and water are notable sources of natural outdoor reflected light. Artificial sources of reflected light include cars (glass, metal, dashboards, etc.), building glass, signs, metal structures, equipment, and a host of other structures. Sun bounces off these sources and enters a person's field of vision directly. In addition to causing eye strain, many sources of outdoor reflected light contain ultraviolet rays, which can cause skin damage. Indoors, reflected light works exactly the same way. Indoor reflected light can reflect directly off a variety of surfaces, including window glass, countertops, floors, and mirrors, causing eyestrain.[40]

Glare is an uncomfortably bright reflection of light onto a viewing surface. Glare is similar to but somewhat different from excessively bright and reflected light. Whereas excessively bright light is not always reflective, glare is. Outdoors, glare can come from both natural and artificial surfaces. Snow, ice, sand, and water are notable sources of outdoor glare. Sun bounces off these sources and onto surfaces such as the pages of a book, a television screen, a laptop computer, or a wireless phone screen on which you are focusing. Indoor glare can be caused by natural or artificial lighting. Sunlight coming in through windows and doors, either directly or at an angle, reflects off television and computer screens, causing glare. It can also enter a room, bounce off another surface such as a mirror, and then hit a television or computer screen, causing glare. Artificial lighting such as desk lamps and overhead lighting can cause glare when it is excessively bright and bounces off a screen directly or at an angle. Glare on a screen can cause eyestrain, headaches, and fatigue. It forces continual contraction of a variety of facial muscles that can result in tension headaches.[40]

High-contrast lighting conditions create extreme differences in the foreground and background light. For instance, a typical computer workstation contains a computer, phone, lamp, and desk accessories. These items rest on a desk or built-in workstation area. The workstation or desk resides in a cubicle or office. Excessive contrast within this environment can cause an imbalance in the contrast in lighting conditions. For instance, if the computer equipment, lamp, phone, and desk accessories are white or tan but the desk/workstation or the cubicle/office walls and file cabinets are black or a very dark color, these competing shades may cause excessive contrast in lighting conditions, causing eyestrain.[40]

Climate

Both indoor and outdoor hot and cold temperatures that exceed recommended levels can cause strain. While people cannot control outdoor climate, they can regulate it to some extent by the amount and type of clothing that is worn. Other options include avoiding outdoor climate conditions (hot, cold, wet, snowy, etc., by staying indoors).

Indoor climate is determined by the levels of temperature and humidity in a building and are often outside the control of the people that live and work there. For example, the climate in dormitory and classroom space that most college students are exposed to is controlled by the administrators of the campus. Workplace climate is similarly controlled by others in administrative positions.

Most recommendations for work temperatures can also be applied to the home. One must also compensate for relative humidity, since high humidity can significantly alter the effects of temperature. In applying a standard of 50 percent relative humidity (a standard that most homes and worksites with proper humidifying and dehumidifying can achieve), the following temperatures are recommended to minimize strain. Sedentary work is best accomplished in temperatures between 70 and 75 degrees Fahrenheit for someone wearing a long-sleeved blouse or shirt and a suit. Work that involves standing and performing light physical labor is best performed at between 66 and 72 degrees. Manual labor is best done in temperatures a few degrees lower than that for light labor.[41]

Temperatures that are colder than those recommended above can also create strain and eventual stress. In colder temperatures blood begins to flow out of the hands and feet. When the temperature in the hands drops below 55 degrees Fahrenheit, fine motor coordination and control are affected.

Air Quality

Most people are familiar with the relationship between air pollution and health. Over the past twenty-five years in the United States and around the world, clean air standards have been established, legislation passed, and enforcement efforts have been implemented to control pollution. For

reflected light the illumination that bounces or bends off another object and then enters a person's field of vision

glare an uncomfortably bright reflection of light onto a viewing surface

high-contrast lighting conditions lighting that creates extreme differences in the foreground and background light

Stress Buster Tips

How to Reduce Lighting Strain

Take control of lighting strain. Most lighting strain can be controlled with a little planning and minimal cost. The following suggestions can help you reduce lighting strain before it becomes a stressor.

Outdoors

- Wear regular or wraparound sunglasses to keep excessive brightness from reaching your eyes.
- Use hats with wide sun brims to keep light from creeping over the tops of your sunglasses.
- Use umbrellas to block overhead sunlight. Umbrellas that tilt can adjust to provide maximum blockage of sun's rays.
- Use your car's sun visors to block direct sunlight.

Indoors

- Use blinds, drapes, and shades to control the amount of light allowed in and to keep it out of your direct line of vision.
- Always have shades or glare shields on lights and lamps and keep them angled at least 30 degrees from your direct line of vision.
- Reorient desk and television equipment to take it out of the direct line of light entering from windows.
- Use indirect or shielded light to control the overall brightness of a room.
- Install lighting diffusers that allow a range of lighting conditions.
- Use adjustable workstation lighting to control lighting conditions in a smaller area.
- Use glare-reducing filters on computer screens.
- Keep monitors clean to minimize dust-associated glare.
- Tilt a monitor down slightly to prevent it from reflecting overhead light.
- Use dark characters on a light background (they are less affected by glare than are light characters on a dark background) when determining the setting for a computer monitor.
- Adjust the contrast on all monitors to reduce extreme contrast.
- Try to keep colors light, muted, and matte in work areas to minimize high contrast.
- For workstations use diffuse lighting rather than spotlights, which tend to concentrate light and cause glare.

most people, air pollution is an outdoor issue. Air pollution conjures images of belching smokestacks, industrial complexes, and perhaps nuclear power plants. In fact, indoor air pollution can cause just as much a strain on people's lungs and health from the outdoors. In many cases indoor

When temperatures remain below 55 degrees Fahrenheit, workers must protect themselves against loss of coordination and fine muscle control.

air pollution is more concentrated and can therefore have more immediate and dramatic effects on people. In this next section of the chapter we will examine both indoor and outdoor air pollution as sources of environmental strain capable of becoming stressors.

Indoor Air Quality

Indoor pollution sources that release gases or particles into the air are the primary cause of indoor air quality problems in homes. There are many different types and sources of indoor air pollution:

- Combustion-based sources include particles from oil, coal, gas, kerosene, and wood that are released into the air as the fuel is burned for heating.
- Tobacco particulate matter is released into the indoor air in the form of secondhand tobacco smoke.
- Construction materials such as insulation, carpeting, and pressed wood products can also release particles into a home's indoor air.
- Pesticides applied around the foundation of a home or business can seep into indoor air.
- Naturally occurring radioactive particles in radon gas can escape from rock and soil and infiltrate indoor air.[8]

DIVERSE PERSPECTIVES

Graffiti: Art or Eye Pollution

Graffiti is a subject that people generally are rarely neutral about. To some, it is street art, free of convention and unrestrained in its expression of color, design, and bravado. To others, it is a form of eye pollution capable of acting as an environmental strain. Even government seems split on how to perceive it.

In some cities, local governments believe that the existence of graffiti causes damage to the public psyche by creating blight, marring the area's visual attractiveness, degrading its livability, and adversely affecting the quality of life of average citizens.[43] In Portland, Oregon, graffiti is illegal and considered a problem that causes millions of dollars in property value damage related to the defacing of public and private buildings and facilities. Graffiti is perceived as undermining civility. When graffiti is allowed to remain on public and private structures, it invites more markings and criminal activity, giving the impression that government has lost control of the area. This can strain the aesthetic sensibilities of the average citizen and lead to stress.[43]

In other places, such as San Francisco and Oakland, California, the cities support local graffiti contests that encourage young graffiti artists to pursue their craft. Marilyn Liu, a writer for the San Francisco area *Mercury News* calls graffiti *art* that was born on the streets and thrived on freeway underpasses, subways, and walls. The graffiti form *Tagging* (using spray paint to sign one's moniker) began in the early 1960s and was often used by gangs to mark their turf. In 1983 filmmaker Tony Silver documents the battle between the graffiti artists and mainstream society in his graffiti documentary *Style Wars.*

Since then graffiti has turned into more than just illegal writing on walls. It has become almost a mainstream form of art and has been featured on prime-time television shows. One of the tasks featured on the television show *The Apprentice* had contestants hiring a graffiti artist to create a billboard to advertise the racing video game *Gran Turismo 4.* Today you can even log onto the Internet and find *public walls* to tag and experiment on.

Graffiti artists have grown up and have begun to sponsor galleries and local, national, and international competitions that showcase the art and artists. In some European countries there are stores that sell paint specifically for graffiti and sponsor graffiti contests that award paint to winners. Taiwan recently opened five parks with public walls for anyone to paint on.

What do you think; is graffiti a viable art form or a public nuisance?

Source: Liu, M. (5/2/05, *Mercury News* http://www.mercurynews.com/mld/mercurynews/entertainment/columnists/marian_liu/11539895.htm?template=contentModules/printstory.jsp

Any of the materials described here, in high enough concentrations, can create strain and eventually stress. Sometimes the effects of exposure to these contaminants are irritation to the eyes, nose, and throat; headaches; dizziness; trouble breathing; and fatigue. Individual responses to these contaminants vary according to the level of exposure, the age of the person exposed, and the sensitivity of the exposed person to the materials.[8]

The primary reason for the buildup in the concentration of any indoor pollutant, causing it to exert strain and stress in humans, is poor ventilation in the building. **Ventilation** refers to the process of mixing outdoor air with indoor air, either through natural means (such as open windows) or artificial means (forced heating and cooling systems, fans). The level of ventilation is central to establishing indoor air quality. Inadequate ventilation can increase indoor pollutant levels by not bringing in enough outdoor air to dilute emissions from indoor sources and not carrying indoor air pollutants out of the structure. High temperature and humidity levels can also increase the concentrations of some pollutants.[8]

Ventilation is a combination of mixing outdoor air with indoor air and cleaning the air through filtering and, in some cases, washing. Some ventilation occurs naturally as a result of infiltration of air through cracks, vents, and joints, a process aided by wind and convection. The rest occurs through heating and cooling, the use of fans that vent individual rooms (bathroom fans are a good example), and ventilation of the whole house through the use of ceiling-mounted "whole-house fans." The rate at which new outdoor air replaces old indoor air is called the **exchange rate.** Local, state, and federal housing and building codes have established safe exchange rates for various residential and commercial buildings.[8]

Outdoor Air Quality

The effects of outdoor pollution are governed by the same principles as those associated with indoor pollution. The concentrations of pollutants in outdoor air, however, are much more variable and are subject to manufacturing and overall weather patterns and sunlight. These variables play a bigger role in keeping the pollutants out of the air in the first place and in influencing natural cleansing forces such as wind, which disperses pollutants from

ventilation the process of mixing outdoor air with indoor air through natural or artificial means

exchange rate the rate at which new outdoor air replaces old indoor air through natural or man-made ventilation an area. Some of the major sources of outdoor air pollution are:

- Ozone (caused by the reaction between nitrogen dioxide and volatile organic compounds in the presence of sunlight)
- Nitrous oxide (caused by the burning of gasoline, coal, and oil)
- Sulfur dioxide (caused by burning high-sulfur coal and oil)
- Lead (caused by various manufacturing emissions and fossil fuels)
- Volatile organic compounds (VOC) from fuel combustion, solvents, and paint
- Particulate matter (caused by a host of things ranging from burning wood to plowing fields)
- Mercury (caused by waste disposal, incineration, and smelting)[8]

It is much easier to control indoor air pollution than outdoor. Homes and worksites that employ hot air heating and cooling systems usually employ filters that can remove even microscopic particles from the air as it passes through the unit. Controlling outdoor air pollution is much more difficult. Outdoor air pollution is caused by a combination of natural and human conditions. Manmade pollutants are affected by weather conditions (temperature, moisture, air currents) to create conditions such as smog. In 1970 the United States Congress passed the Clean Air Act that set standards at the local, state, and national levels for pollution caused by humans. Since air pollution can cross national borders, international agencies such as the United Nations have tried to get countries to agree to worldwide air quality standards.

Noise Pollution

Sound is produced by any mechanical disturbance of the air at a speed exceeding 300 meters per second. Sound waves passing through the air at that speed enter the ear, reach the sensory areas of the brain, are interpreted as either sound or noise, and trigger a physiological response in the brain and nervous system. The main physical characteristics of sound are sound pressure level, sound frequency, type of sound, and variation in time. Sound pressure, the most commonly used standard, is measured in decibels. **Decibel** levels range from about 20 decibels in a very quiet rural area, to 50 to 70 decibels in towns during the daytime, to 90 decibels or more in noisy factories and discotheques, to well over 120 decibels near a jet aircraft at takeoff.[2]

Defining Noise

Noise is defined as any sound that is undesired or interferes with one's hearing of something (*Merriam-Webster,* 2005). A key to understanding noise is its subjective nature. A good example of this is how people perceive music. The loud, high-pitched guitar riffs of heavy metal or the deep, thumping bass of rap might be perceived as noise by someone who prefers classical music while those who prefer the former styles of music might view the strings and woodwinds of a classical ensemble as annoying fluff.

Noise is capable of creating strain when the type, frequency, and/or decibel level of sounds exceeds what is normally encountered by the individual. When sounds are consciously appraised as annoying or subjectively found to be displeasing because they intrude on people's ability to concentrate, function, or enjoy themselves, noise becomes a stressor. If we adhere to Lazarus and Folkman's stress appraisal model,[28] one must also take space and time into account when appraising the effects of sounds. Taking a ride through city traffic or listening to a rock song at high volume today may affect you entirely differently than it did last week when you experienced the same sources of sound. Today you are tired, are feeling rushed, or have a lot on your mind and feel that the traffic and/or song is too distracting. Last week, while on your way to an important meeting, feeling fully alive from the energy of the city and the pounding of the song's beat, you were uplifted by the same sounds.

Perceived noisiness is a term coined by researchers to acknowledge the subjective nature of noise. Perceived noisiness is similar to but distinct from decibel level, and that perceived noisiness may be a better predictor than loudness of adverse reactions to sound. Perceived noisiness takes into account qualities of sound/noise other than decibel level. For instance, mowing your lawn at 10 A.M. might produce the same decibel level of sound as mowing at 6:00 A.M., but because it is being performed at a time viewed as "appropriate" for such activity, it isn't necessarily perceived as noisy.[2]

We can be both the source and the victim of noise, as occurs when we are operating noisy household appliances or outdoor equipment. We can also be exposed to noise generated by other people. This **secondhand noise** affects us the same way people experience secondhand smoke. While we can control our own primary noise exposure, secondhand noise is often beyond our control and negatively affects both us and the community by broadcasting the sound throughout the immediate environment. One only has to imagine stretching out on a hammock to enjoy an outdoor snooze on a cool Sunday evening, only to be disturbed by a neighbor cutting the lawn and blowing the clippings away to appreciate the nature of secondhand noise.[38]

decibel a unit for measuring the relative loudness of sounds

noise a sound that is undesired or that interferes with one's ability to hear

perceived noisiness a subjective assessment of noise that combines the decibel level and the context in which a noise occurs

secondhand noise noise generated by others that invades your personal environment

> **KEY TO UNDERSTANDING**
>
> Defining noise is very subjective. People perceive sounds and volume levels very differently. Community standards and safe decibel levels are two standards commonly applied in defining what is "noisy."

Health/Stress Effects of Noise

Noise is associated with a variety of negative health outcomes. Hearing loss of varying degrees is a major problem that can range from having difficulty hearing sounds such as a telephone ringing or a clock ticking, to the inability to distinguish between consonants such as *s*, *sh*, *ch*, and *th*, to not being able to hear anything at all.[31] Hearing loss may also cause problems with concentration, fatigue, lowered self-confidence, irritation, misunderstanding, decreased working capacity, human relations, and stress reactions.[31,44,50]

Noise is also related to inadequate sleep. Regular and uninterrupted sleep is needed for good health. Noise is associated with the following sleep disturbance effects: difficulty falling asleep, awakening, and alterations in sleep stages or depth. Sleep loss as a result of noise can also induce increased blood pressure, increased heart rate, increased finger pulse amplitude, constriction of blood vessels, changes in respiration, irregular heartbeat, and an increase in body movements.[35] Secondary effects of sleep loss include increased fatigue, depressed mood or well-being, and decreased performance.[44,50]

Although environmental noise is not believed to be a direct cause of mental illness, it is assumed that it accelerates and intensifies the development of mental disorders. Studies on the adverse effects of environmental noise on mental health include the symptoms of anxiety, emotional stress, nervous complaints, nausea, headaches, instability, argumentativeness, sexual impotency, changes in mood, and increased social conflicts, as well as general psychiatric disorder such as neurosis, psychosis, and hysteria.[31,35,44,50]

Major Sources of Noise

Noise is among the most pervasive and destructive pollutants today. Noise from machinery and industrial plants; road, rail, and air traffic; business and community services; construction; domestic activities; and leisure are among the sources of hundreds of potentially stressful sounds that are routinely broadcast into the air.[38]

Machinery Noise: Noise from Industrial Plants Manufacturing and other forms of industry create serious noise problems which subject a significant proportion of the working population to potentially harmful noise on a daily basis. In industrialized countries, it has been estimated that 15 to 20 percent or more of the working population is affected by sound pressure levels of 75 to 85 decibels.[2] This noise is due to machinery of all kinds and often increases with the power of the machines. The Occupational Safety and Health Administration (OSHA) requires that employers have procedures in place to monitor noise exposure in a way that identifies employees exposed to noise at or above 85 decibels averaged over eight working hours. Procedures must measure all continuous, intermittent, or impulsive noise in the range of 80 to 130 decibels.[39] Employers are required to provide hearing protectors to all employees working under noise conditions that exceed that level. While the OSHA guidelines are designed to prevent hearing loss, they do not address noise stress, which may occur at much lower levels.

Construction and Public Works Noise OSHA hearing protection guidelines also cover those employed in the building construction (earth movers, carpenters, etc.) and public works (sanitation removal, road crews, etc.) industries. Both of these professions involve activities that can cause considerable noise. While OSHA guidelines protect workers, other citizens are exposed to noise that has the potential to be very stressful. Construction and public works equipment is often poorly silenced and maintained, and building and public works activities are often carried out without consideration of the environmental noise consequence. Garbage removal is a perfect example; it causes considerable noise and disturbance and is usually conducted in the early morning hours, when people are in their deepest sleep periods.

Road/Traffic Noise Road/traffic noise is a combination of noises produced by engines, exhausts, and tires on the road from the various vehicles using the roadways in a given area. The volume of noise generated by traffic depends on three factors: the volume of traffic, the speed

Many different types of barriers can be used to lessen the noise associated with road traffic.

Living Constructively

Environmental Naikan Reflection

In chapter 1 we identified the three essential skills of Living Constructively: coexisting with unpleasant feelings, paying attention to the world around us, and self-reflection. A particularly important thing to start paying attention to is the quality of your living environment and how you contribute to it. Performing Naikan self-reflection on your home is a good way to focus your attention on a very specific aspect of the environment and one you can exert substantial control over.

Instructions:

Spend 30 minutes tonight (10 minutes on each question) answering the following three Naikan questions:

1. How have elements of my home environment supported my health and well-being?

   Example:
   - I have clean water to drink.
   - I have a comfortable temperature in which to work and sleep.
   - I have walls that protect me from outside predators (etc.).

2. What have I contributed to my home environment to support my health and well-being?

   Example:
   - I recycle my glass and newspapers.
   - I mulch my grass clippings when I mow the lawn (etc.).

3. What troubles have I caused to others in my home environment?

   Example:
   - I do not shut off the water while I brush my teeth.
   - I flush pesticides and other toxic chemicals from the garden down the drain when I am finished using them (etc).

Answer the following critical thinking questions.

How has this activity changed your perception of your home environment?
What action can you take to change the way you act in relation to your home environment?
How do your personal environmental activities impact those beyond your home's boundaries?

Table 3-1 FHWA Noise Abatement Criteria (NAC)

Description of Activity Category	Interior (Decibels)	Exterior (Decibels)
Residences, motels, hotels, public meeting rooms, schools, churches, libraries, hospitals, and auditoriums	52	55
Lands on which serenity and quiet are of extraordinary significance and which serve an important public need and where the preservation of those qualities is essential if the area is to continue to serve its intended purpose	57	60
Picnic areas, recreation areas, playgrounds, active sports areas, parks, residences, motels, hotels, schools, churches, libraries, and hospitals	67	70
Developed lands, properties, or activities not included in categories above	72	75

Source: FHWA Noise Abatement Standards, 1995.[13]

of traffic, and the number of trucks in the flow of traffic. According to the Federal Highway Administration (FHWA),[13] traffic noise is increased by heavier traffic volumes, higher speeds, and a greater number of trucks. Additionally, road conditions such as steep inclines and uneven pavement increase road/traffic noise.[13;35]

Noise levels along federal highways are governed by the Federal-Aid Highway Act of 1970, which authorized the FHWA to develop noise level standards, regulations, and mitigation procedures for highway traffic noise on federally funded highways. The act set noise standards for existing and new road construction which included absolute decibel readings for the inside and outside of structures along roadways (Table 3-1).

These noise levels were set to determine noise impact and set a maximum allowable sound level. Any noises above these levels would require mitigation, which means lowering noise levels through various means, as shown in Table 3-2. In developing the standards the FHWA attempted to balance desirable noise levels with that which is feasible. The agency looked at three noise-related criteria before establishing the standards: (1) hearing impairment, (2) annoyance, sleep, and task interference or disturbance, and (3) interference with speech

Table 3-2 Controlling Road/Traffic Noise

Buffer Zones, Noise Barriers and Vegetation are the three main environmental controls used to regulate road/traffic noise.

Buffer Zones are open and undeveloped land that border a highway that are usually bought by highway agencies so that future dwellings and development cannot be built close to the highway. This regulates noise by increasing the distance from the roadway to the areas of human use.

Noise barriers are solid obstructions, either earth berms or freestanding walls, constructed between a highway and human use areas. Barriers must be long enough and tall enough to block the view of the highway, and must not have many breaks or openings.

Vegetation must be high, wide, and dense enough so that it completely blocks the roadway. The FHWA does not consider the planting of vegetation to be a noise abatement measure because it is almost impossible to plant enough vegetation along a roadway to achieve a meaningful level of noise reduction.

Source: FHWA[12] and Nadakavukaren.[35]

communication. Its research found that the level of noise generated by American roadways rarely lead to hearing impairment. Research on the annoying and interfering quality of road noise (criteria 2 and 3) was used to set the standards.[13]

ERGONOMICS

Ergonomics is an applied science concerned with designing and arranging things people use so that the people and things interact most efficiently and safely (*Merriam-Webster,* 2005). Also referred to as *human engineering,* ergonomics studies the physical and mental characteristics of people and the tasks they perform for the purpose of designing appropriate living and working environments. Ergonomics draws from a variety of disciplines, including psychology, sociology, kinesiology, physiology, biomechanics, applied physical anthropology, industrial and systems engineering, anatomy and physiology, and industrial hygiene. Ergonomics research focuses on the biomechanics involved in activities as well as products that can enhance efficiency while lowering risk of injury.

Ergonomics examines both human and manmade factors and conditions associated with efficient and safe performance of tasks. For example, driving a car involves both sets of factors. The human factors involve posture (how close/far one sits from the steering wheel; whether one slouches back and down in the seat), adjustments of controls (temperature controls, sound system, etc.), and one's sight lines (mirror adjustment and ability to see out of the windows without unnecessary straining). The manmade factors include the seating (number of possible adjustments to control height, proximity to the steering wheel, steering wheel height, etc.), access to controls (ease in which all controls can be reached), and sight lines (ease in which gauges and controls can be seen, ability to see other vehicles through the windshield, windows, and mirrors, etc.). Both sets of factors combine to create a driving experience that influences postural, visual, and climactic strain. Ergonomic specialists working in the automotive industry focus on these and other issues related to the human engineering of their cars.

Ergonomics in the Home

Many aspects of home life are influenced by ergonomics. Bathroom design, for example, has become a major focus of ergonomics in the home, especially as the population ages. Showers, sinks, toilets, even the bathroom mirror can cause strain if these items are located too high or low, or require excessive stooping, reaching, or stretching to access and use them. Ergonomic engineers have designed bathroom fixtures and accessories that enable universal access without stress or strain, for example with articulating mirrors that adjust for ease of use while shaving or applying makeup, and simple grab bars that allow for safe and sturdy access to showers and toilets. Similar improvements in the designs of common household objects have made such repetitive household tasks as chopping vegetables and talking on the phone less stressful on shoulder, hand muscles, and back muscles.

Automobile manufacturers lure customers with descriptions of cars that have ergonomically designed *cabins* to whisk you away in comfort and luxury. These cars feature dashboards with instrument clusters that are easily seen and reached with one hand. Instrument panels are tilted to face drivers more directly and gauges are illuminated in bright reflective colors. Outside and inside mirrors can be adjusted electronically from the inside while seated in the driver's seat. Seats in many cars can be adjusted in multiple directions as can steering wheels. Such adjustments can greatly reduce the strain on the shoulder, back, arms and legs, as well as enhancing auto safety by allowing the driver to focus on the road.

In addition to these aforementioned ergonomic aids, government at every level (local, state, and federal) and industry set safety and performance standards that are driven by ergonomic research. For instance, local building codes set standards for private home construction. Local and state governments set similar standards for school and public sector construction. Federal guidelines set standards for everything from appliances to automobile safety.

ergonomics an applied science concerned with designing and arranging things people use so that the people and things interact most efficiently and safely; also known as human engineering

Ergonomics in the Workplace

Individual workers' characteristics that are studied include age, size and shape, disabilities, previous injuries, educational level, job experience, comfort level with the technology under study, and expectations regarding the job and specific work tasks.[45]

Work tasks include the specific motion or motions involved in the tasks, the frequency and duration of the tasks, the importance of the tasks, the position of visual objects, the position and use of the hands when performing a task, the duration and use of all equipment associated with a task, and the interrelationships of these pieces of equipment. All these factors have implications for posture, reach, and risk of injury.[45]

Work environment issues include those related to the physical environment (lighting, temperature, noise, odors, furniture, equipment, machinery, workstations, layout, maintenance, etc.) and the psychosocial environment (job design, work organization, shifts, breaks, supervision, worker education and training, worker input, etc.).[45] Ergonomics explores how all these components mesh with the design of human-made living and work environments.

Most ergonomic research has been conducted on work-related environments in an effort to prevent work-related injuries and the costs associated with them. A major goal of ergonomics is to make work safer.[27] Another goal is to enhance worker and worksite well-being.[27] Although the worksite is the primary focus of most ergonomics research, many of these work-based findings can be applied to reducing strain associated with home living environments.

Ergonomics in Action: Computer Workstations

Americans are spending more and more time on their computers. Computers are used at home for everything from sending and receiving e-mail and pictures to telecommuting. Computers in the workplace have become so commonplace that they have replaced the typewriter as the staple of the American office. The role of computers in American life has sparked tremendous interest among ergonomic researchers.

Ergonomic research on computer workstations illustrates how personal and man-made factors in our environment can interact to create or minimize strain and stress. Research has analyzed every aspect of computer workstations: the computer (CPU, monitor, keyboard, mouse), the desk, the chair, lighting, noise, and temperature control. Computer workstation ergonomics findings can be generalized to both the home and office. Cornell University's Ergonomic Web[7] has developed designs for computer workstations based on sound ergonomic planning. The following ten guidelines for designing computer workplaces are recommended for both home and office environments.

1. **How will the workstation be used?** Ideally, computer workstations should be designed for one person to accommodate their size and shape and have features that are unique to that person, such as desk and chair adjustments. This is much more feasable at work than at home. Since most home computer use is shared, it is important to buy equipment that can be easily adjusted and is not fixed. If the computer is used only a few minutes a day, ergonomics will be of little concern. If it is used several hours a day, ergonomics will play a vital role in the strain associated with computer use.
2. **What kind of computer will be used?** Desktop computers have separate components (monitor, keyboard, etc.) that can be arranged with maximum flexibility. It is much easier to arrange separate components for maximum ergonomic efficiency. Laptops are much harder to adjust since the keyboard, monitor, and central processing unit cannot be adjusted much. If the computer is used literally on one's lap, watching television or lounging in bed will contribute to strain because of the poor ergonomics of these positions. If a laptop is used for extended periods of time, an external monitor, external keyboard, and external mouse are recommended to provide flexibility in adjusting the components for maximum ergonomic effects.
3. **What desk furniture will be used?** Whether at home or at work, components need to be on a stable work surface to minimize wobble and maximize proper arrangement. If the work surface will also be used to write on, it needs to be between 28 and 30 inches off the floor (average height for most people). A negative-tilt keyboard tray (see figure 3-1), which allows the keyboard to tilt down for better wrist posture and a more relaxed typing angle, is also recommended. The ideal mouse and keyboard alignment is to have the mouse on the desk surface above the keyboard, which is sloping downward (see figure 3-1).
4. **What chair will be used?** An ideal computer chair should have a lumbar support, a comfortable seat with adequate

Figure 3-1
The ideal typing position takes pressure off the wrists, forearms, elbows, legs, back, and neck.

cushioning, and a downward lip to take pressure off the back of the legs at the knees. It should be adjustable up and down. It should have optional armrests that can be removed or swung out of the way. The chair should have a locking tilt feature that allows it to be locked at a slightly backward tilt (100 to 110 degrees, not upright). The chair should have a five-wheel base that allows it to roll freely. Using kitchen chairs. sofas, or other seating arrangements at home will result in strain associated with poor posture, lack of support, or insufficient cushioning.

5. **What will be the primary use of the computer?** If the computer is used mostly for word processing, keyboard/mouse positioning and flexibility are of the utmost importance to ensure proper positioning to reduce strain. If it is used to surf the Net or primarily for graphic design, keyboard/mouse positioning is less important because the hands are not continually in the same position for extended periods of time.
6. **What are the sight lines?** The monitor should be directly in front of the keyboard (not to the side, which strains the neck). In the home, computers often share space with other objects such as television sets, stereo equipment, knick-knacks, etc., and monitors are often squeezed in wherever they can fit. A document holder should be used to keep documents at the same level and angle as the monitor. For the proper seat-to-monitor distance when seated, one should just be able to touch the center of the monitor with the middle finger of an outstretched hand. When you are seated comfortably, your eyes should be in line with a point on the screen about 2 to 3 inches below the top of the monitor casing (not the screen). Most of the time eye location is in the center of the monitor rather than at the top or bottom of the screen.
7. **How is your posture?** The chair, desk, and computer components should be adjusted to attain the following postural conditions (fig. 3-1):
   - You should be able to reach the keyboard keys with the wrists as flat as possible (not bent up or down or left or right).
   - Your elbow angle (from inner surface of upper arm to forearm) should be at or greater than 90 degrees to avoid elbow nerve compression. A negative-tilt keyboard can help keep the wrists flat while allowing for a slight bend in the elbows (see figure 3-1).
   - Your feet should be out in front of your knees, resting on either a built-in or a freestanding foot support.
   - Your head and neck should be as straight as possible.
8. **Is everything close, and are you relaxed?** Be sure that the things you use most frequently are placed closest to you so that they can be conveniently and comfortably reached. This is often difficult if the home computer is in the den or family room where space is at a premium. An ergonomically sound computer workstation should allow you to adjust everything so that you can work in a natural, relaxed, ideal typing posture.
9. **What are the other environmental conditions?**
   - Follow the lighting, noise, and temperature guidelines discussed at the beginning of this chapter.
10. **Are you taking enough breaks?**
    - Eye breaks. Every fifteen minutes look away from the screen at something more than twenty feet away and blink your eyes to refresh tear secretion.
    - Micro breaks. Follow bursts of typing with short (less than two-minute) breaks where you rest your hands and/or get up and move around or do something different (make a phone call, read something, etc.).
    - Rest breaks. Every thirty to sixty minutes take a brief rest break (get a drink, move around).
    - Exercise breaks. Get up and stretch at your workstation every hour or two.[7]

If you follow these ergonomic principles, you will greatly reduce your chances of suffering any computer related injuries or illnesses.

WORK-RELATED STRESS

So far in this chapter we have discussed potential environmental stressors such as lighting, temperature, and ergonomics that affect both the home and work environments. In the next section we will focus exclusively on work-related potential stressors. We will look at job conditions that make work stressful as well as the interpersonal dynamics that contribute to worker stress. Both have been studied around the world in a variety of countries and economies. There are several models used to explain job stress. We will focus on two models for understanding job stress, the model created by the National Institute for Occupational Safety and Health (NIOSH) and Lazarus and Folkman's Stress Appraisal Model.

The Changing Workplace

Print and other media have promoted the notion that job stress has been spiraling out of control over the last twenty years. This has been supported to a certain extent by a plethora of studies in academic journals and government reports.[23] While it is safe to say that workers today (especially in industrialized economies such as those of

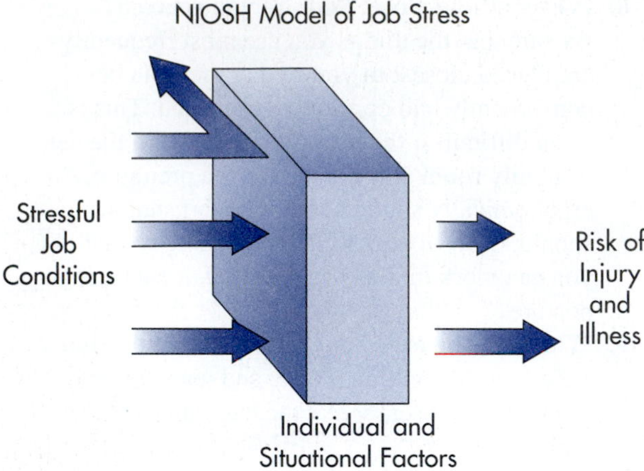

Figure 3-2

The NIOSH model of job stress shows how individual and situational factors can mediate stressful job conditions. One's personality and social support system (individual and situational factors, respectively) will affect how one appraises job conditions.

Source: NIOSH, 1999.[32]

the United States, Canada, and England) report high levels of occupational stress, we must be careful about statements claiming that these levels are much higher than those of twenty years ago and that the actual levels of work stress are increasing. Workers today are much more aware of occupational stress than they were twenty years ago. This increased level of awareness plays a significant role in the likelihood that they will report and rate it as high on a questionnaire or in an interview. It is likely that such increased reporting feeds into the overall level of awareness of work stress and contributes to the perception that occupational stress is increasing.[23]

While most research on occupational stress focuses on the factors that contribute to work strain and eventual stress, there is also a substantial body of literature documenting how changes in the workplace have created new opportunities and challenges for workers who perceive these changes in a positive light and take advantage of them.[23] These positive reports do not receive the same level of media coverage and are often overshadowed by more negative, sensationalistic reports. Take the case of muscoskeletal injuries associated with poor ergonomics. Today's understanding and use of technology to reduce worksite-related repetitive motion injuries were not available twenty years ago. This availability, coupled with a higher level of awareness on the part of workers and management, has set the stage for some very impressive worksite changes to reduce the incidence of such injuries.

In 2001 the state of New Jersey's Information Technology Division implemented a worksite-based program to reduce computer-related injuries. All employees in the division were initially surveyed to assess their incidence of computer-related injuries. About 84 percent of those surveyed reported no problems with backs, elbows, arms, hands, necks, or eyes. Employees in the program were then given ergonomic chairs that were adjustable and had good back support, negative-slope keyboard trays that were easily adjustable, and mouse platforms that sat over the keyboard. They were trained in the proper use and adjustment of the equipment and were offered accessories such as document holders, antiglare screens, and footrests to reduce computer-related strain. Eight months later the employees were surveyed a second time. In less than a year, there was a 40 percent reduction in computer-related health complaints. There are countless other examples where positive workplace changes have lessened the number of ergonomic-related injuries.

In addition, technological advances in the last twenty years have freed many workers from the shackles of space and time. Telecommuting has opened up windows of opportunity to workers who find the restraints of a daily commuting to a 9 to 5 job physically impossible, undesirable, or overly confining.

Measuring Occupational Stress

Part of the problem in understanding occupational stress lies in the limitations of the models used to measure and study it. Traditionally, research on occupational stress has focused on workplace "stressors." The stressors studied are typically characteristics of either the work (workplace, tasks, management, etc.) or the individual worker (personality attributes, demographic variables, level of training, etc.). The second type of study looks at the interaction between work and worker, examining how certain job characteristics combine with specific worker characteristics. The third type of study is a true transactional model, similar to that of Lazarus and Folkman[28] as discussed in chapter 2, which looks at the appraisal of potential worksite stressors by individual workers while taking into account their perceived ability to cope. Because of the complexity and expense of this type of research, most studies of occupational stress are on the former two types.[23] While these two types of occupational research should involve detailed interviews with workers and management, they theoretically could be conducted simply by analyzing statistical relationships between work and worker characteristics that were drawn from records without even talking to the principals involved. True transactional research cannot consist of mere chart review.

The NIOSH Model of Job Stress

The National Institute for Occupational Safety and Health (NIOSH) is the federal agency responsible for coordinating all work-related safety and health information.[36] NIOSH sponsors and conducts research and makes recommendations for preventing work-related injuries and illness. NIOSH is part of the U.S. Department of Health and

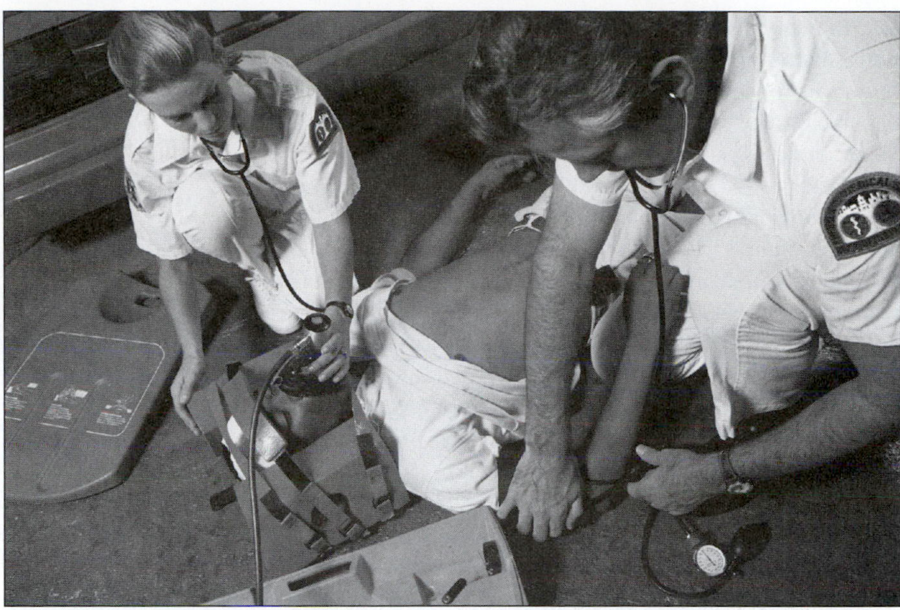

Being responsible in life-or-death situations can be very stressful to some people.

Human Services and is separate from the Occupational Safety and Health Administration, which is a regulatory agency in the U.S. Department of Labor.

NIOSH developed a model of job stress that combines stressful job conditions with individual and situational factors. This model proposes that while stressful working conditions play the primary role in creating job stress, they are mediated by individual and situational factors. In the NIOSH Model, stressful job conditions include: the design of tasks, management styles, interpersonal relationships, work roles, career concerns, and environmental conditions. Individual factors refer to the ability to maintain a relaxed and positive outlook. Situational factors include having a support network of friends and coworkers and being able to maintain a balance between work and family or personal life.

The NIOSH Model of Job Stress is consistent with the transactional view of stress proposed by this book. In a sense, what the NIOSH Model is proposing is very similar to Lazarus and Folkman's[28] Stress Appraisal Model. In a transactional view of stress, stressful job conditions are really potential stressors until appraised as threatening. The appraisal of potentially stressful job conditions is influenced by individual and situational factors (labeled person and situation factors in Lazarus and Folkman's model). Individual factors would include things such as a person's emotional and intellectual well-being, and situational factors would encompass their level of social well-being and social support.

Stressful Job Conditions

As we just discussed, the NIOSH model contends that the primary factor contributing to occupational stress is stressful job conditions. The six categories of stressful job conditions identified by NIOSH include factors related to all aspects of work: the tasks involved, work settings, human relations, the environment in which the work is performed, and a host of others. We will look at each job condition and the potentially stressful factors associated with it.

The Design of Tasks

The design of tasks refers to the actual activities associated with performing the job and the setting in which they are performed. NIOSH contends that some occupations are more stressful than others simply by virtue of these tasks and settings. The tasks are stressful because of the demands they impose on workers. The settings contribute to the demands of the tasks and are potentially stressful themselves. The major types of job demands and work tasks which can be stressful are critical decision-making responsibility, excessive complexity and/or difficulty, repetitiveness, simplicity, boredom, lack of personal safety, and excessive time urgency.

Some jobs require that workers be fully responsible for making critical or in some cases life-or-death decisions. Emergency medical workers arriving at the scene of an accident must quickly survey the scene and decide which victims require immediate care and which ones can wait. They must decide which procedures to institute immediately. Failure to act correctly could result in death. Police officers must make instantaneous decisions about drawing their weapons and firing or holding off and risking being shot.

Some jobs are exceedingly precise and complex. Girdano et al.[17] found that the higher the complexity of the job, the greater the stress. They found that the following factors are related to the complexity of a job: increase in the amount of information needed to be used, increase in the sophistication of skills, increase in the number of alternative ways of performing the job, and introduction of contingency plans (plan b).

In many cases, jobs follow procedures and protocols with several options along the way. For instance, nurses often make decisions about patient management that depend on the ways patients follow complicated diagnostic protocols.

Other jobs can be stressful because they are repetitive, boring, and monotonous or offer very little challenge and few chances to make decisions. The best example of this kind of work is the assembly line worker, who is responsible for performing countless repetitive tasks for an entire day. Whether it is bolting, welding, or soldering on one specific part of a machine as it moves along a conveyer belt or sewing a specific part of a garment on before it is passed along to the next seamstress, this type of work can be mastered in a short period.

Besides being tedious and repetitive, many assembly line jobs have been associated with **repetitive motion injuries.** These types of disorders result from the cumulative trauma of repetitive tasks such as operating a sewing machine as part of a clothing assembly line. Seamstresses are at increased risk for developing **carpal tunnel syndrome,** a painful disorder of the wrist and hand caused by the compression of the nerve running through the wrist. Seamstresses are required to perform the same short, stitching motions (such as sewing the sleeve into a garment) on their sewing machines for several hours in a row, each workday. The cumulative effects of performing such repetitive motions over time can result in traumatically compressing the nerve that runs along the underside of their wrists resulting in carpal tunnel syndrome.

This type of disorder results from the cumulative trauma of repetitive tasks. Girdano et al.[16] describe a condition called "assembly line hysteria" that is characterized by nausea, muscle weakness, severe headaches, and blurred vision. It was found to be caused by four conditions characteristic of assembly line work: boredom with the job, repetitive tasks on the job, lack of ability to communicate and converse with other workers, and low job satisfaction. In other cases, work can become a stressor when people feel underutilized and unchallenged. In these cases, skills and abilities go unused and frustration builds.

Other jobs are stressful simply because they are dangerous. For example, being on guard or under siege puts the body under continual stress. The work that police officers, firefighters, and soldiers do can be life threatening and unsafe.

Time Demands

Some jobs impose excessive time demands on workers. All jobs require that things be done on time. Excessive time demands are those based on unrealistic expectations of a worker's abilities. Time urgency comes in many forms: sales deadlines, production quotas, pay for piecework, seasonal work limitations, time estimates for specific jobs, and so forth. The negative effects of time urgency on cardiovascular function were documented thirty years ago by Friedman and Rosenman.[14] Other researchers have documented the relationship between time urgency and stress in work settings ranging from dressmaking to accounting.[4,6,19,37,49]

> **KEY TO UNDERSTANDING**
>
> Stress associated with role conflicts is associated with the way supervisors and managers require that jobs and policies be carried out, not with the jobs or policies themselves.

Another type of time stressor is **rotating shifts.** The body needs several weeks, for instance, to adjust fully to a switch from a day shift to a night shift. Typically, however, police officers, firefighters, and airline crews change shifts more often than that. Girdano et al.[17] found that such alterations in shifts can result in symptoms similar to jet lag, with headaches, gastrointestinal problems, loss of appetite, alteration of sleep patterns (insomnia, nightmares, etc.), and blurred vision. Jamal and Baba[21] also report shift change stress as a problem for nurses whose work schedules rotate constantly.

Permanent switches do not pose the same stress. After the body physiologically adjusts to the shift change, it is no longer a strain. An undesired shift change can be stressful because it interferes with a worker's lifestyle. This stress, however, is not due to the physiological adjustments that need to be made. It is due to the perceived harm or loss that will occur to the worker's lifestyle if the shift change interferes with the person's happiness and ability to continue in their present lifestyle.

Organizational policies regarding travel can be particularly stressful for both employees and their families. Overly frequent travel disrupts not only body cycles and biorhythms for the employee but also family schedules, patterns, and routines. Szwergold[48] noted that chronic travelers are constantly torn between their professional duties and their obligations to family members.

Management Style

Lack of participation by workers in decision making, poor communication within an organization, and lack of family-friendly policies can all lead to stress. Role conflicts caused

> **repetitive motion injuries** injuries to the soft tissues as a result of performing ergonomically incorrect tasks over and over, day in and day out
>
> **carpal tunnel syndrome** a painful disorder of the wrist and hand caused by the compression of the nerve running through the wrist
>
> **rotating shifts** work hour blocks that change or rotate on a regular basis; for example, switching from working days to working nights every two weeks

by the way jobs are assigned and carried out were cited in a number of studies as a source of stress.[5,16,17,42] In this case, workers felt that what they were being asked to do was in conflict with their stated job functions.

Ginsburg[16] identified specific supervisory behaviors that contribute to a management style that creates job stress for workers. This style includes the following behaviors, which are a reflection of the way a manager deals with workers: letting subordinates unfairly take the blame for problems, delegating too much or too little authority, displaying emotions that are inappropriate for the position, and being distrustful.

Communication styles were also cited as a source of stress. Er[11] stated that supervisors create unnecessary stress by confusing aggressiveness with assertiveness in their dealings with employees. Supervisors often must be assertive in enforcing organizational policies and goals. It is important for supervisors to use assertiveness correctly and not confuse it with aggressive behavior, which creates unnecessary stress in employees.

Interpersonal Relationships

A poor social environment and lack of support or help from coworkers and supervisors can also cause stress in the workplace. Power struggles are infighting scenarios where employees or groups of employees form political alliances and compete for positions, choice assignments, overtime, and the like. Power struggles can also refer to managerial styles that pit workers against management. Power struggles between peers are stressful enough. Power struggles that pit older, higher-salaried workers against newer, lower-paid employees in a cost-conscious job market are particularly frightening.

Discrimination Unequal status based on race, gender, age, or sexual orientation is also an abuse of power in which one group blocks another from equal participation. Title VII of the 1964 Civil Rights Act was passed to guarantee that such discrimination would be illegal in the United States. **Affirmative action** legislation was originally intended to ensure that all groups would have equal access to employment and promotional opportunities. Affirmative action guidelines were designed to assist employers in developing policies concerning the hiring and advancement of minority group members. The implementation of affirmative action policies can be a source of stress to nonminority candidates for employment and promotion if these policies are perceived by workers as a way of filling quotas rather than trying to enhance diversity by hiring minority applicants who are equally qualified.

Ageism is another form of discrimination that becomes very important and stressful in an era of downsizing as businesses look to purge older employees who are generally paid more and have more substantial benefits. Even Fortune 500 companies, which were perceived as unshakable in most economies and protective of workers, have fired what they label as "surplus employees—often the most senior staff members."[18]

Sexual Harassment Title VII of the Civil Rights Act of 1964 stipulates that it is an unlawful employment practice for a labor organization to exclude or to expel from its membership or otherwise discriminate against any individual because of his or her race, color, religion, sex, or national origin. Sexual harassment has been deemed a form of discrimination based on sex.

Sexual harassment is defined as any unwelcome sexual advances, requests for sexual favors, and other verbal or physical conduct of a sexual nature.

This type of behavior constitutes sexual harassment when:

1. Submission of such conduct is made explicitly or implicitly a term or condition of an individual's employment or academic advancement.
2. Submission or rejection of such conduct by an individual is used as the basis for academic or employment decisions affecting the individual.
3. Such conduct has the purpose or effect of unreasonably interfering with an individual's work or academic performance or creating an intimidating, hostile, or offensive working or educational environment. (EEOC, 2003)

A hallmark of sexual harassment is the use and abuse of power to secure sexual favors. Power differentials exist in the workplace and the classroom based on roles and responsibilities. The boss, the supervisor, and the professor have power over workers and students by the nature of their roles and authority. A boss or supervisor is responsible for evaluating work performance, giving assignments, and so forth. A professor evaluates papers, tests, and exams and ultimately assigns a grade to students in his or her class.

When someone holds power over another person by virtue of a "superior" role, the subordinate person has a harder time refusing the advances. The subordinates fear reprisal: in a poor performance review, no raise, undesirable work assignments, even termination. In a school environment, the students fear a less objective review of their work and lower grades. It should be noted that being approached in a respectful, inquiring way is vastly different from being approached in a harassing way.

affirmative action a part of the 1964 Civil Rights Act which was designed to ensure that all groups had equal access to work and advancement within a job

sexual harassment any unwelcome sexual advances or requests for sexual favors, and other verbal or physical conduct of a sexual nature

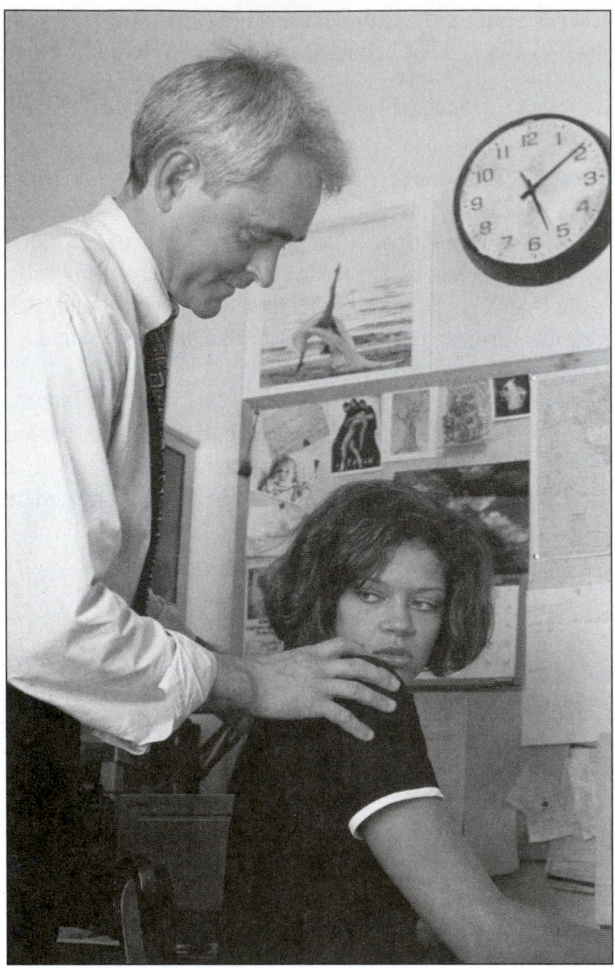

Inappropriate touching is a form of unwelcome sexual advance to many people.

Finally, if the pursuing person stops the pursuit once the subordinate has expressed a lack of interest or displeasure, it's not harassment. Persistence and an attempt to pressure the other person into responding, however, are more likely to be considered harassment, especially if the first two criteria are also present. Harassment relates in part to how males are socialized. Men tend to interpret women's friendliness as a sign of sexual interest, an invitation to pursue sexual involvement.[22,47] Men and women perceive sexual harassment differently. Men are much less likely to perceive certain behaviors as harassing than women are.[24] Thus, men have difficulty judging their behavior and its potential for harassment. The courts also have trouble determining whether certain actions cross the line between aggressive courting and sexual harassment.

Work Roles

Conflicting or uncertain job expectations, too much responsibility, and too many "hats to wear" can be sources of stress. Organizational policies also are a major source of stress. In general, ambiguous organizational policies are major contributors to employee stress. Areas of ambiguity include work objectives and goals, lines of responsibility, procedures and protocols, workers' and management's expectations about the job, and job performance. A relationship between ambiguous organizational policies and stress was found in both American and foreign studies of workers.[5,12,17,42]

Stress Buster Tips

Sexual Harassment: How to Fight Back

The following guidelines may be helpful in fighting back if you think you have been the victim of sexual harassment on campus or at work.

1. If the harassment includes rape or attempted rape, file criminal charges against the perpetrator.
2. Confront the person who is harassing you. Write a letter to the offender and follow up with a meeting. Be as clear and specific about the offender's actions as possible. Be specific about the incidents, times, and dates. Indicate that if the behavior doesn't stop immediately, you will press charges, using the letter as evidence.
3. Seek support. Don't hide what happened. Talk to significant other, coworkers, fellow students, and people identified with the issue. This may put pressure on the offender to stop.
4. If the behavior doesn't stop, meet with the offender's supervisor. In a work setting, this is the offender's immediate supervisor. In a college setting, this person may be the department chairperson, the head of the student center, a member of the sexual harassment panel, or the dean of students. Discuss the incidents and give a copy of your letter to the supervisor.
5. Know your rights. Sexual harassment is against the law. You do not have to put up with such behavior. Obtain the company's or school's sexual harassment policy. Read it thoroughly and make sure to follow its guidelines for handling your case. Identify the administrative office and the person responsible for handling sexual harassment violations in your workplace or school.

Source: Blonna and Levitan, 2005.[3]

Career Concerns

Job insecurity and lack of opportunity for growth, advancement, and promotion and rapid changes for which workers are unprepared can all contribute to stress. Another major organizational stressor is a lack of advancement or of the perception of a career ladder up which one cannot climb. Getting stuck in a dead-end job can be a major source of stress. Turnage and Spielberger[49] in a study of 68 managerial, 171 professional, and 68 clerical workers found lack of opportunity for advancement to be one of the most frequently cited job stressors. In many

STRESS IN OUR WORLD 3-1

The Smiths

The Smiths (not their real name) have moved six times in the last ten years as Craig Smith has pursued his dream of becoming a regional sales manager for his company, a large pharmaceutical firm in New Jersey. He; his wife, Mary; and their three children, Sharon (14 years old), Craig Jr. (12 years old), and Robbie (age 7) started in New Jersey ten years ago and moved to Buffalo, Indianapolis, San Diego, Houston, and then Chicago.

The moves were necessary, as the company put it, for Craig to learn new skills, understand the nuances of different territories and regions, and get experience at various levels of sales within the company. Craig has applied for what he hopes is his last transfer, back to New Jersey to become a regional sales vice president based in corporate headquarters.

Craig hopes this is his final move because the stress of moving and uprooting the family every time they have to make friends and put down roots is getting to everyone. Mary even put an ultimatum to Craig: one last move or she'll consider a divorce. Sharon and Robbie would like to go through their high school years at one school and see what it's like to hang on to friends for more than a year. Robbie's the only one who doesn't seem to mind too much.

Craig has had enough, too. With the sagging housing market over the last few years, they've really taken a beating when selling their houses. They'll also face a higher cost of living in New Jersey, but at this level, the company picks up all relocation costs and his raise will put them at a very comfortable earning level. Furthermore, he won't have to take another transfer, as this is the highest sales level within the company. At the age of 40, Craig is tired of fighting his way up the corporate ladder. He would really like to see what it's like to coach his son's little league team and watch his other kids grow up.

businesses and industries, advancement and promotion are contingent on relocation. Forced relocation is a potential stressor for many businessmen and businesswomen. Forced transfers can be very stressful to families as the children are forced to change schools, make new friends, and start all over in a new place. Spouses must also adjust and find new employment, make new friends, and establish new relationships with doctors, and dentists, and so forth.[34] The effect of having to do this every couple of years can lead to a sense of not wanting to unpack fully after each move. This sense is lessened if transitions are made easier by organizational policies which aid in the process of relocation.[14]

Environmental Conditions

As we mentioned at the beginning of this chapter, unpleasant or dangerous physical environmental conditions exert strain on workers and eventually turn into stressors if they are not remedied. Most physical environmental stressors seem to be related to blue-collar occupations that range from manufacturing to mining. Some of these stressors include excessive noise, poor temperature control, toxic chemicals, indoor pollution, overcrowding, poor arrangement and design of workspace, and lighting. For other workplaces, life-threatening environmental stressors include the presence of dangerous people such as enemies (soldiering) and criminals (policing).

Individual and Situational Factors

In the NIOSH model, individual factors refer to the personality attributes of the worker and the worker's level and quality of social support. Since we have discussed the emotional and intellectual factors in chapter 2 and will discuss social support in chapter 4, we will not spend time going over these factors here. Situational factors are more contextual and have to do with what else is going on in the balance between the individual's work and family or personal life. Situational factors will continue to play a major role in occupational stress as the lines between work and home become less clear. The interface of home and work has traditionally been explained using three models: the spillover hypothesis, the compensatory hypothesis, and the segmentation hypothesis.

The spillover hypothesis suggests that stressful home conditions "spill over" into the workplace and vice versa. Individuals with stimulating, varied, and satisfying work experiences have equally stimulating, varied, and satisfying home situations.[23] The compensatory hypothesis suggests a negative relationship between work and home. In other words, individuals may compensate for less than satisfying or boring, repetitive work experiences by engaging in exciting, interesting, invigorating home and leisure activities.[23] The segmentation hypothesis proposes that the work and home environments are essentially separate and that people "segment" their lives into things related to work and things related to home and leisure. They have different personas and activities for each part of their lives.[23] Research on all three hypothesis has been inconclusive in regard to which is the correct or best way to describe how people deal with the home-work interface.

A TRANSACTIONAL MODEL FOR EXPLAINING OCCUPATIONAL AND ENVIRONMENTAL STRESS

The best way to describe the effects of environmental and occupational strain and the subsequent stress is the transactional approach.[28,29,30] Essentially, the study of environmental and occupational stress is no different from the generic approach described in Lazarus and Folkman's

1984 stress appraisal model.[28] The transaction between the general or work environment and the individual is perceived as stressful to the extent that the individual perceives it as threatening, harmful, and beyond his or her ability to cope with.[23] Lazarus and Folkman's model is the central stress model used in this book.

A key to understanding environmental and occupational stress using the Lazarus and Folkman model is realizing that the individual and situational factors are related to one's overall level of wellness.

As has been espoused throughout this book, one's individual level of wellness greatly affects one's stress levels. This is especially true concerning environmental and work stress. One's overall level of well-being affects everything from the amount of energy and stamina a worker needs to keep up with the demands of the job to one's intellectual ability to keep pace with the demands of rapidly changing technological advances and one's willingness and ability to see things differently and creatively or learn new ways of getting the job done. One's level of well-being also affects one's perceived ability to cope with work stress.

Every source of environmental and occupational strain (potential stressors) is filtered through this level of wellness and perceived ability to cope and may or may not represent a stressor for a particular individual.

SUMMARY

In this chapter we examined the environmental and occupational basis of stress. We started by examining our personal environment and the factors in it that can exert strain and potential stress. We examined the most common potential environmental stressors: lighting, temperature, noise, and air and eye pollution. We discussed the sources and health effects of these potential environmental stressors and suggested ways to reduce their ability to become stressors. We explored how the science of ergonomics examines the interplay of these environmental factors and human characteristics in the creation of environmentally based stress. We showed how good ergonomic design features can reduce environmental strain associated with computer workstations.

The second half of the chapter was devoted to an exploration of occupational strain and stress. We examined models of occupational stress that focus on the individual worker, the workplace, or the interaction of the two. We discussed the NIOSH model, an interactive model that describes occupational stress and illness as resulting from an interaction between stressful job conditions and individual worker and situational characteristics. Stressful job conditions ranging from poorly designed tasks to unrealistic time requirements were examined. We discussed how an individual's personal factors were studied in chapter 2 and how situational factors are related to social support, which is the topic of chapter 4.

We ended the chapter with a description of a transactional approach to understanding environmental and occupational stress.

STUDY QUESTIONS

1. Describe how the concept of strain is related to occupational and environmental stress.
2. How is lighting related to environmental strain?
3. Compare and contrast three major sources of lighting strain.
4. What is a reasonable temperature for performing the following types of work: sedentary work, light physical labor, heavy manual labor?
5. How does inadequate air exchange in a room contribute to the room's air quality?
6. How does graffiti contribute to a community's aesthetic quality.
7. How can a person minimize his or her contributions to secondhand noise?
8. What can be done to reduce highway/traffic noise in a community?
9. Why is ergonomics important in setting up a computer workstation?
10. Why should the term *stressful job conditions* be changed to *potentially stressful job conditions?*
11. Why is the Lazarus and Folkman stress appraisal model included in this book, and why is it the best one to use in explaining environmental/occupational stress?

DISCOVER OUR CHANGING WORLD

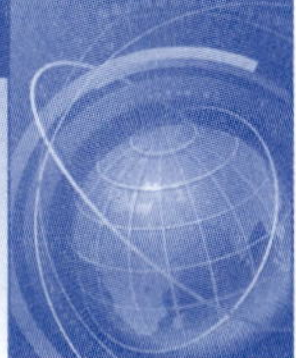

As we use our computers and the Internet more and more, it is essential that we begin to design and set up computer workspaces with ergonomics in mind. Healthy Computing.com is one of the most respected names in computer ergonomics and safety. Its corporate goal is to provide comprehensive, current, and unbiased information on ergonomics. Go to the company's website, http://www.healthycomputing.com/, click on the "office ergonomics" link, and review the information presented. Describe one new thing you learned about creating a more ergonomically sound workspace for yourself.

Critical Thinking Question

What specific steps can you take to improve the ergonomics of the workspace available to you at home or work?

ARE YOU THINKING CLEARLY?

In this chapter, we discussed noise pollution. Have you ever really thought about it? Did you ever wonder *why* you get dirty looks from people when you engage in activities that produce noise? Do you think it might be related to the amount of secondhand noise you contribute to *their* lives?

If you answer yes to any of these questions, it may be time to change the way you think about your contributions to secondhand noise.

1. Do you refuse to lower the volume and continue to blast your car radio at an ear-splitting decibel level when driving on local roads and/or when stopped at traffic lights?
2. Do you run loud home appliances such as a leaf blower or lawn mover before 9:00 A.M. or after 8:00 P.M.?
3. Have you intentionally modified your car/motorcycle exhaust system to make it louder?
4. When you are around others at the beach, lake, or park, do you blast your CD/cassette player at volume levels that interfere with others' peace and quiet?
5. Do you talk on your cell phone in public restaurants, at the movies, at plays, or on buses, subways, and trains?

REFERENCES

1. Aetna InteliHealth. (2003). *Complementary and alternative medicine,* August, 4, 2003. http://www.intelihealth.com/IH/ihtIH/WSIHW000/8513/8513.html?k=navx408x8513.
2. Berglund, B. & Thomas Lindvall, T. (1995). *Community noise.* Geneva: World Health Organization.
3. Blonna, R. & Levitan, J. (2005). *Healthy Sexuality.* Belmont, CA: Thomson/Wadsworth.
4. Brisson, C., Vezina, M., & Vinet, A. (1992). Health problems of women employed in jobs involving psychological and ergonomic stressors: The case of garment workers in Quebec. *Women and Health,* 18(3), pp. 49–65.
5. Buttner, E.H. (1992). Entrepreneurial stress: Is it hazardous to your health? *Journal of Managerial Issues,* 4(2), pp. 223–240.
6. Collins, K. & Killough, L.N. (1992). An empirical examination of the stress in public accounting. *Accounting, Organizations, and Society,* 17(6), pp. 535–548.
7. Cornell University. (2003). Computer workstation guidelines. Cornell University Ergonomics Web.
8. Environmental Protection Agency. (1995). *The inside story: A guide to indoor air quality.* EPA Document # 402-K-93-007. April, 1995. Pittsburgh PA: US Govt. Printing Office.
9. EPA 2003.
10. Equal Employment Opportunity Commission. (2003). *Sexual harassment charges: EEOC and Fair Employment practices agencies (FEPA) combined: FY 1002–FY 2001.* http://www.eeoc.gov/stats/harass.html.
11. Er, M.C. (1989). Assertive behavior and stress. *SAM Advanced Management Journal,* 54(4), pp. 4–5.
12. Erera, I.P. (1991). Supervisors can burn out too. *Clinical Supervisor,* 9(2), pp. 131–148.
13. Federal Highway Administration. (1995). *Highway traffic noise analysis and abatement policy.* Washington, DC: U.S. Department of Transportation.
14. Forster, N.S. (1990). Employee job mobility and relocation. *Personnel Review,* 19(6), pp. 18–25.
15. Friedman, M. & Rosenman, R. (1974). *Type A behavior and your heart.* New York: Knopf.
16. Ginsburg, S.G. (1990). Reducing the stress you cause others. *Supervisory Management,* 35(11), p. 5.
17. Girdano, D.A., Everly, G.S., & Dusek, D.E. (1990). *Controlling stress and tension.* Englewood Cliffs, NJ: Prentice-Hall.
18. Grant, L. (1993). White collar wasteland. *US News & World Report,* 114(25), pp. 42–52.
19. Homer, C.J., Sherman, J., & Siegal, E. (1990). Work-related psychosocial stress and risk of pre-term low-birthweight delivery. *American Journal of Public Health,* 80(2), pp. 173–175.
20. Hopkinson, R.G. & Collins, J.B. (1970). *The ergonomics of lighting.* London: MacDonald.
21. Jamal, M. & Baba, V.V. (1992). Shiftwork and department-type related to job stress, work attitudes, and behavioral intentions: A study of nurses. *Journal of Organizational Behavior,* 13(5), pp. 449–464.
22. Johnson, C.B., Stockdale, M.S., & Saal, F.E. (1991). Persistence of men's misperceptions of friendly cues across a variety of interpersonal encounters. *Psychology of Women Quarterly,* 15(3), pp. 463–475.
23. Jones, F. & Bright, J. (2001). *Stress: Myth, theory and research.* London: Prentice-Hall.
24. Jones, T.S. & Remland, M.S. (1992). Sources of variability in perceptions of and responses to sexual harassment. *Sex Roles,* 27(3–4), pp. 121–142.
25. Kaufman, L. (1997). A Report from the front: Why it's gotten easier to sue for sexual harassment. *Newsweek,* 129(2), p. 32.
26. Krech, G. (2000). *A Natural Approach to Mental Wellness.* Monkton, VT: The ToDo Institute.
27. Kroemer, H.E. (2002). *Ergonomics, National Safety Council,* October 9, 2002. http://www.nsc.org/issues/ ergo/define.htm.
28. Lazarus, R.S. & Folkman, S. (1984). *Stress appraisal and coping.* New York: Springer.
29. Lazarus, R.S. (1991). Psychological stress in the workplace. In P.L. Perrewe (Ed.). Handbook of job stress. Special issue of the *Journal of Social, Behavioral and Personality,* 6, pp. 1–13.
30. Lazarus, R.S. (1999). *Stress and Emotion: A New Syntheses.* New York: Springer.

31. Lercher, P. (1996). Environmental noise and health: An integrated research perspective. *Environment International,* 22(1), pp. 59–69.
32. Liu, M. (2005). Grafitti. *Mercury News,* May 2, 2005. www.mercurynews.com/mld/mercurynews/entertainment/columnists/marian_liu/11539895.htm?template=contentmodules/printstory.jvp
33. Merriam-Webster (2005). Online Dictionary. Merriam-Webster: www.m-w.com/cgl-bin/dictionary.
34. Munton, A.G. (1990). Job relocation, stress and the family. *Journal of Organizational Behavior,* 11(5), pp. 40–46.
35. Nadakavukaren, A. (2000). *Our global environment: A health perspective.* Prospect Heights, IL: Waveland Press.
36. National Institutes for Occupational Safety and Health. (1999). *Stress at work.* Washington DC: NIOSH.
37. Nelson, D.L. & Sutton, C.D. (1991). The relationship between newcomer expectations of job stressors and adjustment to the new job. *Work and Stress,* 5(3), pp. 241–251.
38. Noise Clearinghouse. (2003). http://www.nonoise.org/aboutno.htm.
39. Occupational Safety and Health Administration. (2002). *Hearing conservation.* Document 3074. Washington, DC: Occupational Safety and Health Administration.
40. Occupational Safety and Health Administration. (2003a). Indoor lighting. http://www.osha.gov/SLTC/computerworkstations_ecat/lighting.html. Washington, DC: Occupational Safety and Health Administration.
41. Occupational Safety and Health Administration. (2003b). *Heat stress. OSHA Technical Manual,* Section 3. Washington, DC: Occupational Safety and Health Administration.
42. Peiro, J.M., Gonzalez-Roma, V., & Ramos, J. (1992). The influence of work-team climate on role stress, tension, satisfaction and leadership perceptions. *European Review of Applied Psychology,* 42(1), pp. 49–58.
43. Portland City Council. (2003). *Graffiti policy.* Portland, Oregon.
44. Rosenlund, M., et al. (2001). Increased prevalence of hypertension in a population exposed to aircraft noise. *Occupational Environmental Medicine,* 58, pp. 769–773.
45. Safety Management. (2002). Designing the workplace with ergonomics in mind. *Safety Management,* 3, pp. 1–4.
46. Selye, H. (1956). *The stress of life.* New York: McGraw Hill.
47. Stockdale, M.S. (1993). The role of sexual misperceptions of women's friendliness in an emerging theory of sexual harassment. *Journal of Vocational Behavior,* 42(1), pp. 84–101.
48. Szwergold, J. (1991). Surviving the stress of business travel. *HR Focus,* 68(11), p. 5.
49. Turnage, J.J. & Spielberger, C.D. (1991). Job stress in managers, professionals, and clerical workers. *Work and Stress,* 5(3), pp. 165–176.
50. Van Kempen, E. M., et al. (2002). The association between noise exposure and blood pressure and ischemic heart disease: A meta-analysis. *Environmental Health Perspectives,* 110(3), pp. 307–317.

Name: ______________________________ Date: ____________

ASSESS YOURSELF 3-1

Do You Live/Work in a Sick Building?

Many well-known illnesses can be directly traced to specific building problems. These so-called, *building-related illnesses* can be toxic (carbon monoxide poisoning), infectious (Legionnaire's Disease), or Allergic (Asthma) in nature. Most of these diseases can be treated once they have been diagnosed properly. Sometimes, however, building occupants experience symptoms that do not fit the pattern of any particular illness and are difficult to trace to any specific source. This phenomenon has been labeled *sick building syndrome.* People may complain of one or more of the following symptoms: dry or burning mucous membranes in the nose, eyes, and throat; sneezing; stuffy or runny nose; fatigue or lethargy; headache; dizziness; nausea; irritability and forgetfulness.

Sick building syndrome is caused by indoor air pollution related to inadequate ventilation resulting in high levels of accumulated pollutants in the air. Other harmful indoor environmental conditions such as inadequate lighting, noise, vibration, and improper climate may also cause, or contribute to, the symptoms associated with sick buildings.

Physical Symptoms

Do you notice the following symptoms when you are in the suspected sick building? Do you notice a significant improvement or do these symptoms disappear when you leave the building?

	Symptoms Yes	Symptoms No	Improvement Yes	Improvement No
1. dry or burning mucous membranes in the nose, eyes, and throat.				
2. sneezing				
3. stuffy or runny nose				
4. fatigue or lethargy				
5. headache				
6. dizziness				
7. nausea				
8. irritability				
9. forgetfulness				

Building Symptoms

When you are in the home/building do you notice any of the following characteristics?

Presence of any of the following known indoor air pollutants;

	Yes	No
1. carbon monoxide (from unvented kerosene and gas space heaters, leaking chimneys and furnaces, woodstoves, fireplaces, etc.)		
2. organic gases (from paints, paint strippers, and other solvents; wood preservatives; aerosol sprays; cleansers and disinfectants; moth repellents and air fresheners; stored fuels and automotive products; hobby supplies; dry-cleaned clothing).		
3. respirable (breathable) particulate matter (from fireplaces, woodstoves, kerosene heaters, and environmental tobacco smoke).		
4. automobile exhaust from attached garages		
5. radon gas		
6. environmental tobacco smoke		
7. animal dander		
8. cat saliva		
9. house dust mites		
10. cockroaches		
11. pollen		

ASSESS YOURSELF 3-1 (cont'd)

SIGNS OF INADEQUATE VENTILATION

1. wet or moist walls, ceilings, carpets, windows or furniture
2. smelly or stuffy air
3. dirty central heating and air cooling equipment
4. mold in areas where books, shoes, or other items are stored

Any combination of personal symptoms and building symptoms might be indicative of a sick building.

WHAT TO DO IF YOU SUSPECT YOU LIVE/WORK IN A SICK BUILDING

If you think that you have symptoms that may be related to your home environment, discuss them with your doctor or your local health department to see if they could be caused by indoor air pollution. You may also want to consult a board-certified allergist or an occupational medicine specialist for answers to your questions.

Source: Adapted from United States Environmental Protection Agency (EPA) (1995). *The Inside Story: A Guide to Indoor Air Quality, EPA Document # 402-K-93-007.* Pittsburg PA: US Government Printing Office.

CHAPTER

4

The Social and Spiritual Basis of Stress

OUTLINE

OBJECTIVES

By the end of the chapter students will:

- Describe the components of the social dimension of health and explain how they relate to stress.
- Describe the relationship between social relationships and stress.
- Explain the types of resources one can get from social support systems.
- Understand the relationship between life events and stress.
- Understand the relationship between PTSD, life events, and stress.
- Describe the moderating effects of uplifts on daily hassles and stress.
- Describe the effect of chronic negative social conditions on stress.
- Explain the relationship between economic insecurity and stress.
- Explain how stereotypes, prejudice, and discrimination contribute to stress.
- Describe the differences between spirituality, religion, and faith.
- Explain how spirituality, faith, and religiosity are related to stress.

This chapter examines the social and spiritual basis of stress. Although it is impossible to discuss these dimensions of health without some reference to the issues discussed in chapter 2, the focus of this chapter is more on interpersonal factors. These **interpersonal** factors examine our connections with others and things beyond the self rather than focusing on **intrapersonal** issues, which are related to our personalities. We will examine the relationship between this sense of connectedness to something beyond the self and people's susceptibility to stress.

THE SOCIAL DIMENSION: SOCIAL SUPPORT AND STRESS

The social dimension of health is concerned with the nature, extent, and quality of a person's **social relationships.** These relationships can be studied at the individual, family, or network level. **Individual relationships** are our connections with significant individuals and groups. **Family relationships** are similar except that the connection is through blood or a civil bond. A **social network** is an interrelated chain, system, or group of relationships. A person's social network is composed of membership in both formal and informal groups and organizations. Formal social groups and organizations have specific membership requirements that must be met for one to be accepted. Often there are dues or tithes to pay. Churches and professional organizations are examples of formal groups or organizations. Informal groups and organizations have less structure, and gaining entry usually involves just signing up. Most community and school groups are considered informal.

A person's social network is really the composite of all of that person's individual relationships and group memberships. A synergistic effect can be created through the interaction of all one's individual relationships within a network. Simultaneously being part of multiple friendships, a family, a collegial group at work, a community group or two, and a national organization can create a support system that can help reduce stress. At other times one's network can actually create stress.

Social support can be defined as the resources people derive from their social relationships, membership in groups, and formation of networks. Generally, social support is broken down into three types of resources: (1) esteem or emotional support (comforting, congratulating, loving, etc.), (2) informational support (spiritual guidance, personal and professional advice, role modeling, skill building, job referrals, etc.), and (3) tangible support (help with various forms of labor, such as child care or housework, transportation, money, and emergency services such as shelter).

Our social support system changes as we age. When we are young, we turn mainly to the family; as we grow, our friends supplement whatever family support we have; and when we reach adulthood, our main source of support is our primary partner—our husband, wife, or lover. These primary support people are augmented by others who share our work, play, worship, and community involvement. The depth and richness of our involvement with these other people can make all the difference when we lose our primary support system.

KEY TO UNDERSTANDING

Social relationships make us feel connected to others—not separate and alone.

Measuring Social Support

Jones and Bright[53] discuss four functional measures of social support: (1) social embeddedness, (2) relationship quality, (3) perceived social support, and (4) enacted social support.

Social Embeddedness

Social embeddedness measures the connections individuals have to others in their social environments. There are two ways to measure social embeddedness. The first is to assess the number of connections, such as marital status, membership in groups, and number of friends, that a person has in his or her life. The second way is to go beyond membership and look at the stability and complexity of a person's connections.[53]

interpersonal events that go on between two or more individuals

intrapersonal events that go on within an individual

social relationships our interpersonal connections with other individuals and groups of people

individual relationships the social connections we have with significant individuals and groups

family relationships social relationships based on either a connection through blood or a civil bond

social network an interrelated chain, system, or group of relationships composed of membership in both formal and informal groups and organizations

social support the emotional (comforting, congratulating, loving, etc.), informational (spiritual guidance, personal and professional advice, role modeling, skill building, job referrals, etc.), and tangible (money, housing etc.) resources people derive from their social relationships

social embeddedness the number, stability, and complexity of connections individuals have to others in their social environments

Relationship Quality and Perceived Social Support

Relationship quality is measured by making a subjective assessment of the individuals being studied. Rather than look at the objective quantity of support (as in social embeddedness), this measure examines the subjective quality of the support one receives. Generally, studies examining relationship quality focus on the strength of one relationship rather than on the entire network.[53] **Perceived social support** is measured by asking participants to rate the satisfaction, adequacy, and availability of multiple supportive relationships.

Enacted Social Support

Enacted social support is measured by looking at the outcome of the support that is rendered. Studies of enacted support compare the quantity and quality of support (esteem/emotional, informational, tangible) with measures of stress. Studies of enacted support try to take an objective look at the effects of the support regardless of the level of embeddedness or perceived social support.

How Social Support Moderates Stress

Karren et al.[55] theorize that the health effects of social support revolve around the following five components:

1. Being cared for and loved and having the opportunity for shared intimacy.
2. Being esteemed and valued and from this gaining a sense of self-worth.
3. Having a sense of belonging through shared companionship, communication, and mutual obligations with others.
4. Having informational support from others that includes not only access to information but advice and guidance.
5. Having a safety net (access to physical or material assistance).

These five components work together to moderate stress in the following ways:

1. They provide a direct, protective effect that prevents potential stressors from becoming actual stressors.[55]
2. They buffer and reduce the severity of the effects of stress once the stress response occurs.[55,98]

The direct effects theory asserts that a high level of social embeddedness and enacted social support exerts a protective effect against stress regardless of the degree of stress one is experiencing.[74] In other words, if you have an extensive social network and it provides quality support, it will insulate or protect you from life's stresses. Its effects are *preventive* in nature, reducing the likelihood that potential stressors will become actual stressors.

The stress-buffering theory, in contrast, states that social embeddedness and enacted social support won't prevent stress from occurring but will help buffer (offset or disperse) the negative effects of stressors when you are exposed to them. In other words, the benefits of social support come into play when you need them.[74]

> **KEY TO UNDERSTANDING**
>
> We must continually evaluate our social relationships to see if their benefits outweigh the stress created by the time and energy we must use to maintain them.

The Value of Human Touch

An interesting benefit of some of the components of social support is human touch. The skin is one of the primary sensory organs and a giant communication system. A piece of skin roughly the size of a quarter contains over 3 million cells, 12 feet of nerves, 100 sweat glands, and over 50 nerve endings.[55] Touching, whether skin to skin or through clothing, is a primary (indeed, many believe *the* primary) mode of communication and an integral form of social support.

The early work of Harlow[43] demonstrated that monkeys deprived of social contact, physical touch, and nurturing do not develop normally and are significantly more likely to suffer premature disability and death than are monkeys that do receive social contact. Harlow demonstrated that even monkeys "cared for" by an artificial wire and cloth mother fared better than did the monkeys without any mother figure. Clearly, being touched, whether through a passionate embrace, a peck on the cheek, a cuff on the head or shoulder, holding hands, giving a massage, or a tousle of the hair, communicates love, intimacy, value, and worth as a human being. Touch in a sense reinforces our perceived social support.

The Value of Confiding in Others

Another benefit of social support is being able to confide in someone else. The act of confiding in others has been found to lower blood pressure, lower heart rate, and boost immune system competence.[35,39,79] You have probably heard the statements "I've been just bursting at the seams to tell someone this" and "It feels so good to get this off my chest." Although these are figurative statements, the results of confiding in someone or confessing

> **relationship quality** the subjective assessment of the quality of the support one receives from his/her social networks
>
> **perceived social support** the subjective rating of the satisfaction, adequacy, and availability of supportive relationships
>
> **enacted social support** the outcomes associated with the support that is rendered

Our social networks can be a rich source of support and enjoyment.

our transgressions can provide enormous physical and psychological relief.[35,79]

Pennebaker,[79] in his work with prisoners, found that relieving pent-up thoughts and feelings through verbal and written confessions was liberating even if it meant facing conviction and prison time. In their work with students, Francis and Pennebaker[39] found that stress-reducing benefits were associated with confiding in others through journal keeping. They found that writing about personal experiences initially increases blood pressure and heart rate. This is followed, however, by decreases in both. The effect of confiding seems to result in lower levels of arousal (lower heart rate and blood pressure) when one is subsequently stressed. Subjects also showed enhanced immune system functioning and improvement in a variety of physical symptoms.[39,79] Having strong social ties provides multiple opportunities to confide in others and confess our transgressions. We'll see later in this chapter how "confession" is also a benefit of organized religious practices.

Reduction of Loneliness

A final benefit from high levels of social support is reduced **loneliness.** Being lonely is different from being alone. You can feel content by yourself and lonely when surrounded by people who don't meet your expectations.[55] Loneliness is described as an unpleasant feeling that occurs when one's network of social relationships is significantly deficient in quality or quantity.[55]

Studies of loneliness show that living alone is not significantly related to feelings of loneliness.[12] Additionally, it isn't the quantity of persons with whom we surround ourselves but the satisfaction we get from those relationships that matters.[12] Hafen et al.[43] cite two major causes of loneliness: (1) predisposing and (2) precipitating. Predisposing factors have to do with distinctive social and personal characteristics such as extreme shyness and lack of social skills. This can occur for these individuals when introducing and talking about themselves, participating in groups, and making phone calls to initiate social activities. This lack of social skills often leads to living alone, not having many friends, and being unattached (no spouse, no sexual partner). Precipitating factors refer to the things that happen after a specific event, such as the breakup of a relationship, forced isolation (lack of transportation, being housebound, being hospitalized), and dislocation (being far from home in a new school or job, moving too often, being transferred too often).[76]

Bernikow[11] found that loneliness is related to a variety of medical ills ranging from heart disease and hypertension to addictions. She notes that many addicts refer to their addictive substances as their "best friends" in reference to how they help fill the loneliness. Others have linked loneliness to premature death, immune system suppression, and cancer. Social support can provide multiple opportunities for establishing friendships and minimizing loneliness.

As Lazarus and Folkman[64] put it, "without ongoing social relationships, much of the meaningfulness of human existence is lacking or impaired. Viable social relationships make possible identification and involvement which can be viewed as the polar opposite of alienation and anomie." Social interaction helps reduce our overall

loneliness an unpleasant feeling that occurs when one's network of social relationships is significantly deficient in quality or quantity; it can happen when one is alone or with other people stress level by making us feel connected and not separate and alone.

However, social networks also have the potential to create stress. To utilize the stress-reducing properties of social networks, you first have to invest a lot of time and energy to cultivate those relationships. Additionally, social relationships require nurturing, which also takes time. There is a certain amount of sacrifice involved in forming relationships and belonging to groups. A person must continually evaluate whether the stress-reducing benefits of extensive social networks compensate for the stress created by the demands of social networks.

Health Effects of Social Support

People with social ties (a spouse, a close-knit family, friends, church affiliation, and other group affiliations) live longer and have better health. People without such social ties have poorer health outcomes and die at a rate of two to five times higher than that of those with good social ties. These findings hold true regardless of socioeconomic status, race, gender, ethnicity, and overall health status.[55]

These results have been replicated in many studies across various cultures over the last thirty years. The Alameda County (California) Study is the classic research on social support and health outcomes. This study followed two groups of subjects (those with a high level of social embeddedness and those with a low level) for nine years. Social embeddedness was measured by self-reported affiliation in groups and marital status. Both groups were controlled for health risk factors such as smoking, obesity, exercise level, and alcohol use that could influence the study's results. The results were statistically significant and showed that those with low levels of social support died at a rate three times higher than that of those with higher levels of support. **Mortality** was inversely related to social embeddedness; those with the highest levels of embeddedness had the lowest mortality rates. Subjects with the lowest levels of social embeddedness had the highest mortality rates. A seventeen-year follow-up of the same subjects found the same results: High levels of social support were associated with the lowest death rates regardless of other risk factors, including smoking, obesity, and a sedentary lifestyle.[10]

Similar results were obtained in a study of 2,754 adults in Tecumseh, Michigan. The Tecumseh Study looked at both social embeddedness and enacted social support. It used an extensive array of psychological tests, personal interviews, and medical tests to measure these variables and rate the level of social support of study subjects. The study then followed this group and a matched control group for ten years. The results paralleled those of the Alameda County Study: Those with the highest levels of social support had the lowest mortality rates.[55,66]

In Sweden researchers studied a group of elderly men born in 1914 to assess the interdependence between relationship quality and perceived social support. The study found that men who were dissatisfied with the quality of their lives and the nature of their social relationships and support had higher mortality rates for all causes of death than did those who were satisfied with their social support.[44,55]

Syme[94] conducted a study of 12,000 Japanese men living in three locations (southwestern Japan, Hawaii, and San Francisco). Traditionally, men living in Japan have a much lower incidence of heart disease than Americans do regardless of diet, smoking, or exercise behavior. This has generally been attributed to their societal cohesiveness and high degree of social support. The Southwestern Japanese group was representative of this traditional Japanese population. The men in Hawaii had immigrated there, in general, to resist a Westernized lifestyle. The San Francisco men embraced American life while seeking to maintain their traditional cultural values. Of the three groups, they had the highest levels of social embeddedness, and perceived and enacted support. All three groups were controlled for other health risk factors. The results of the study showed that the San Francisco men, even though they were Westernized, had the lowest rates of death, heart disease, and morbidity of the three groups. These outcomes were attributed to their higher levels of social support.

In the literature associated with social resources and psychological stress, there is a growing body of work suggesting a link between social support and depression. Several studies point to the level of social support in an individual's life as the key moderator between life stressors and the development of depression. Higher levels of pessimism, depressive symptoms, and suicidal tendencies are found in subjects who report a lack of social supports.[98]

Physical illness is also related to social support. A study by Kiecolt-Glaser et al.[56] showed that social isolation is related to reduced immunity. In the study, subjects with the lowest levels of social support also had lower levels of killer cells, the immune system components responsible for destroying invading substances that cause the development of disease.

Although studies seem to indicate that extensive social networks are protective against disease, no one is exactly sure why this is so. It may be that people who are able to cultivate extensive social networks are also better able to take advantage of resources than are others. They may have better social skills that enable them to utilize the resources available to them more effectively. In other words, the protective effect may come not from the relationships per se but from individuals' ability to get what they need from these relationships.

mortality the number of deaths associated with a condition in a year

LIFE EXPERIENCES AND STRESS

Life is constantly changing. Even though we can be sure it will happen, the changing nature of life constantly tests the amount of control we think we have over our lives. Everyday life experiences exert strain on our lives, testing and often exceeding our ability to cope, pushing us into the stress response. In this next section we will take a closer look at major and minor life experiences and how they are related to stress. We'll also look at the effects of how traumatic personal (rape, incest, robbery, etc.) and community (earthquake, war, terrorism, etc.) events are related to acute and long-term stress.

In chapter 1 we introduced the concept of defining stress in terms of the number of major life events a person experiences over a short period of time. We examined the work of Holmes and Rahe[50] and presented evidence to support the notion that a person's physical and psychological well-being is related to the amount of major life-stress that person experiences in a given time. Since Holmes and Rahe pioneered the development of the first scale, several studies have been conducted using various types of life-events instruments. Measuring stress using life-events scales has become the dominant way of determining whether a person is stressed (see Assess Yourself 4-1, "Social Readjustment Rating Scale"). However, there are many troubling facts associated with this approach.

The most troubling aspect of a life-events approach to measuring stress and its effects on the body is the poor correlation found in the majority of research studies. Most statistical analyses of the relationship of life events to illness have been only weakly significant.[32,84] There have been many changes in an attempt to shore up the results. A tremendous amount of effort has gone into improving the Social Readjustment Rating Scale. Attempts have been made to weigh certain items more heavily than others, omit undesirable items, expand the breadth of the events, and make the evaluation less subjective.[54] However, those who have developed broader instruments, including various life-events categories, have found these changes to be problematic. Considerable variability was found within the categories—a fact attributed to the dependence of such instruments on subjects' personal biographical data.[33]

Another problem with using life events to measure stress is that this doesn't take into account a person's perception of the event or the specific context in which it occurs. Life-events scales assume that all persons will respond the same way to each occurrence of any event. However, each life event is part of a specific transaction involving the individual's perception of the stressor and perceived ability to cope with it.[34] It makes sense for people to avoid making too many major life changes in a short period and to be sure they give themselves a break to rest and rejuvenate after experiencing a particularly stressful period. However, not everyone perceives these changes in the same way, and care must be taken in generalizing about the effects of life events.

The benefit of using life events to help us understand stress is that this is a simple way to quantify potential stressors. Life-events scales are good tools for helping us assess the level of change in our lives (see Assess Yourself 4-2, "Student Stress Scale"). Coupled with an assessment of our physical, emotional, social, spiritual, and environmental well-being, they can help us know when we need to slow down.[28]

Daily Hassles and Uplifts

A better way to look at the influence of the psychosocial forces that affect our lives and cause us stress is to examine the role of daily **hassles** and **uplifts,** as discussed in chapter 1 and chapter 2. As defined by Kanner, Coyne, Schaefer, and Lazarus,[49] "hassles are the irritating, frustrating, distressing demands that to some degree characterize everyday transactions with the environment." They include everything from traffic jams to financial concerns, from arguments to bad weather. Uplifts are happy, satisfying experiences, ranging from hearing your favorite song on the radio to taking a day off work. Daily hassles and uplifts are much more individualistic than life events.

Hassles and Health

The centrality of hassles also plays a key role in their relationship to stress.[40,63] In studies, central hassles have been defined as those that reflect ongoing themes or problems in a person's life.[103] Even though the presence and quantity of central hassles were relatively constant for all studied subjects over time, types of hassles differed among the groups studied (elderly people, mothers with young children, older students, and a random sample from the community).[25] What was central differed from group to group, reflecting different interpersonal and social contexts.[42]

In addition to their link with stress, the frequency and intensity of daily hassles are significantly related to overall health. In fact, researchers have found that daily hassles are much more strongly related to health outcomes than are life events. The frequency and intensity of hassles has an especially strong association with psychological illness,[54] and similar results have been found

hassles irritating, frustrating, and/or distressing demands (such as traffic jams, arguments, bad weather, etc.) that characterize everyday transactions with the environment

uplifts happy, satisfying experiences (such as hearing your favorite song on the radio, eating your favorite food, taking a day off work, etc.) that characterize everyday transactions with the environment with regard to physical health problems.[32,64,105] Additionally, the association of hassles with the development of illness has been found to exist independent of major life events. That is, people who experience a lot of daily hassles are more likely to become ill than are people with fewer hassles, regardless of the overall number of life events they experience.[32] Stress-related illnesses, ranging from cardiovascular problems such as hypertension to disorders of the muscular system such as low back pain and tension headaches, will be covered in detail in chapter 6.

The Effects of Uplifts

The effects of uplifts on stress are less convincing than those of hassles. Uplifts by themselves seem to have little protective effect against stress. When examined in conjunction with hassles, however, they seem to play a mediating role. Uplifts seem to defuse the effects of daily hassles in people who have a lot of both.[32] In many instances people who are very productive and are involved in a variety of work, community, family, and social responsibilities experience more daily hassles than do those who are less involved. However, these people also seem to get many uplifts from their involvement in these activities. A key to understanding this is to view uplifts as having the ability to cancel out the negative effects of daily hassles.[66]

If one's activities are hassle-intensive but do not also produce many uplifts, they will be perceived as stressors. One's cognitive perception of the uplifts seems to imply that the work was worth it because the benefits outweighed the hassles.[32]

Although many major life events can and do appear suddenly and are beyond our immediate control, daily hassles usually are a result of forces which are within our ability to change. Because daily hassles are controllable and are more significantly related to the development of health problems than are life events, we can minimize our risks for stress-related illness by paying more attention to them (see Assess Yourself 4-3, "Hassles/Uplifts Inventory"). However, an integrated approach to studying both is needed. There is a need for longitudinal studies that will track individuals in their natural surroundings in order to examine the combined effects of life events and daily hassles over time.[100] Such studies would examine not only life events and daily hassles but the person-environment interactions in which they occur.

KEY TO UNDERSTANDING

Uplifts can cancel out the stress created by too many daily hassles.

Stress Buster Tips

Make Your Day More Uplifting

Think of uplifts as magical erasers capable of rubbing the daily hassles out of our day. Try these simple ways to make your day more uplifting:

1. Start each day by offering thanks for what you have and the opportunity to start anew. Such expressions of thanks build gratitude and spread grace.
2. Listen to natural sounds while eating breakfast. If you can, listen to the birds or the wind blowing through the trees as you eat (whether home or in a public park or sitting area at school or work). This will help you slow down and reconnect to the natural beauty that surrounds you.
3. Bring humor into your day (audio). Keep your favorite comedy CDs handy (or record them into your iPod) and play a cut or two at various times during the day when you have a few minutes.
4. Bring humor into your day (print). Cut out your favorite comic strip from the newspaper and tack it on your bulletin board to reread it during the day whenever you are hassled.
5. Bring beauty into your day. Bring a single cut flower to work or school and put it on your desk (or in your car) and admire its simple elegance.
6. Bring fragrance into your day. Wear your favorite cologne or perfume, burn incense, use cachet pillows and other means to bring beautiful fragrance to your life each day.
7. Bring inspiration into your day. Collect inspirational sayings and bring them with you so you can read them during the day, especially when you are hassled.

These simple strategies can start you on your way to start increasing uplifts and decreasing daily hassles. They are simple, inexpensive, and don't take much time.

Major Life Events and Stress

As we have discussed, one of the criticisms of using life-events tests as measures of stress is that they can be perceived differently by individuals. There are many different types of major traumatic events. What separates them from mere "life events" is near universality of the way they are perceived. Unlike life events such as marriage, divorce, loss of a job, etc., these events are catastrophic and devastating in their scope and effects.

These traumata are so far outside the realm of the usual human experience that they can cause enough intense fear, terror, and helplessness to leave their victims literally numb. Such traumata can be characterized as

The trauma associated with experiencing catastrophic events, like the bombing of the World Trade Center on 9/11/01, can result in posttraumatic stress disorder (PTSD).

either personal (rape, incest, robbery, torture) or community (earthquake, flood, war, terrorism). The most common traumata involve a threat to a person's life, serious personal physical harm, a threat to one's family or individual family members, catastrophic destruction of one's home or community, viewing another person being seriously harmed or killed, and learning about these events though not experiencing them firsthand. The event does not have to happen to the individual for it to be traumatic. It could affect a child, a spouse, a family member, a stranger, or the community as a whole.[1]

The terrorist attacks of the World Trade Center and the Pentagon on September 11, 2001, are examples of such traumata. The bombings not only were personally devastating to those who lost family members and friends, they shocked the entire nation. Although the first World Trade Center attack of 1993 and the subsequent bombing of the Alfred P. Murrah Federal Building in Oklahoma City in 1995 put us on notice about the possibility of major terrorist activity on American soil, the events of 9/11 were so horrific, they could not be ignored and will never be forgotten. Repeated television coverage of the terrorists flying American commercial airplanes into the World Trade Center, the Pentagon, and a lonely field in the middle of Pennsylvania brought the horror into everyone's life. For those with family members and friends working at the various sites, the intensity of their grief was magnified. We will discuss how such traumata are related to the psychological disorders Acute Stress Disorder and Post Traumatic Stress Disorder in detail in chapter 6.

Chronic Negative Social Problems

Chronic negative social situations such as poverty, unemployment, and discrimination fit somewhere on the spectrum of potential stressors between tragic life events and minor daily hassles. They are neither acute tragic life events nor minor hassles. Rather, they are ongoing sources of tension that often leave people caught up in a cycle of despair and hopelessness. These situations, lasting weeks, months, and even years, exert strain on both individuals and their social networks and their ability to cope, eventually resulting in stress.

Poverty

A key to understanding the effects of poverty on stress is to view it as a two-edged sword: It serves as both a source of stress and a barrier to effective coping. Poverty exposes people to a greater amount of traumatic situations, negative life events, and daily hassles. However, at the same time it attacks and limits many potential sources of social support.

Nowhere is this more evident than in the poorest urban areas. Ewart and Suchday[36] studied the effects of urban poverty on stress in a group of 212 high school students in inner-city Baltimore. The researchers constructed an instrument, the Neighborhood Stress Index, to assess the relationship between poverty, neighborhood violence and disorder, and chronic stress. The instrument combined elements of the census (income level, educational attainment, percentage of the population unemployed, percentage of the population living in the below poverty level, etc.) with neighborhood violence (self, family member, or friend attacked, beaten, mugged, shot, stabbed, etc.) and neighborhood disorder (saw people dealing drugs, know of shooting gallery in neighborhood, etc.). The results showed that poverty and the violence and disorder it brings contribute significantly to the amount of stress in the lives of inner-city youth in many ways. The level of "neighborhood stress" not only diminishes the daily quality of life, it affects the personalities of those living in the area. While the level of neighborhood stress on any specific day could be considered a "state" (point in time) measure of stress, a stressful personality is more of a "trait" (overall, ongoing nature) measure. This was verified in the study's findings. The high school students in the study who reported high levels of neighborhood stress had higher levels of anger, hostility, distrust, and irritability in meeting people and a sense of dejection when anticipating meeting others than did those with low levels of neighborhood stress.[36] As we described in chapter 2, personality characteristics such as hostility and anger are significantly related to stress.

KEY TO UNDERSTANDING

Poverty is a two-edged sword that is both a source of stress and a barrier to effective coping.

Poor women experience more frequent, more threatening, and more uncontrollable life events than does the general population. They are exposed to higher levels of violence, crime, and murder than the general population and suffer from a higher rate of illness and death among their children and a higher rate of imprisonment of their husbands. These traumatic situations and negative life events expose poor women to considerably more potential stressors than more affluent women experience.

Poverty also imposes chronic conditions that tax the coping abilities of the poor. Conditions that are endured daily include overcrowding, inadequate housing, dangerous neighborhoods, and financial uncertainty.[7,10,36] Also, role conflicts between poor women and their male partners often occur due to such issues as the high rate of unemployment and underemployment among poor men. Poor women are forced to work at unskilled jobs that provide limited salaries and inadequate benefits. Additionally, many poor women are forced to put their children in child-care arrangements that are less than adequate.[6]

While studies show that women with adequate social support systems are better able to cope with the stresses associated with being poor, poverty can erode these support systems. Many poor women are single parents and lack a working spouse, the financial cornerstone of most middle-class and affluent women. Poverty also takes its toll on friends and neighbors. With more affluent women, it is usually those friends and neighbors who come to the rescue in times of need; they provide the child care, emotional support, and financial resources to fall back on in times of need. With poor women, however, these friends, family members, and neighbors are often in the same dire straits. In fact, there is almost a contagion effect in such social networks where involvement in the social network exacts a higher cost than the benefits derived through participation.[7] Because everyone is in need, continually experiencing catastrophes and crises, involvement in these social networks is often more stressful than helpful.

Poverty takes many forms, and for most Americans it is a temporary condition lasting only one or two years. For certain groups, however, such as single mothers, poverty often is a chronic condition lasting several years.[7,18] As such, poverty can be viewed as a chronic, long-term stressor capable of creating the same negative physiological responses as any other stimuli.

Although being poor by itself is not a stressor and becomes one only when appraised as such, few people trapped in this condition are able to view it as a challenge rather than a threat. As a result, the association between poverty and mental health problems is one of the most well established in all of psychiatric **epidemiology.**[7] Low income and low socioeconomic status are associated with high rates of mental disease.

Economic Uncertainty

Economic uncertainty is reflected in how people feel about the economy in general and their personal job security. There are many things that factor into one's sense of economic uncertainty ranging from personality factors to global economic trends. Often, people will feel uncertain about the economy and their jobs despite encouraging economic trends and having a secure job. In the next section we'll refer to those two issues as economic insecurity and job insecurity.

Economic Insecurity

Economic insecurity refers to one's mistrust in the strength of the economy. The American economy has turned around significantly since the publication of the last edition of this text. As we go to print with this fourth edition, the American economy is in good shape. There have been 24 straight months of job growth resulting in the creation of 3.5 million new jobs. The jobless rate dropped to 5 percent, the lowest since September 2001. The month of June 2005 produced 146,000 new jobs. The economy has rebounded from much of the post 9/11 job losses.[58]

Job growth has occurred in many different sectors. The jobs created in June 2005, for instance, were spread across virtually all sectors except manufacturing, which continued the decline in job growth that began nearly three decades ago. Jobs grew in the following sectors of the economy just to name a few: construction, health care, business services, retailing, and architectural and engineering services.[73]

Besides job growth, other economic indicators point to a strong economy with steady growth. The cost of borrowing money, a key factor involved in purchasing power for large purchases such as homes (mortgages) and automobiles (auto loans) and smaller items (financed through credit cards), has gone down. Despite the Federal Reserve raising the short- and long-term interest rates to 3.25 percent and 4 percent respectively, the actual costs of borrowing money has not always been passed on to the

epidemiology the study of the distribution and determinants of diseases/conditions in populations

economic uncertainty how people feel about the economy in general and their personal job security

economic insecurity one's mistrust in the strength of the economy consumer.[26] For example, in an effort to keep applications for new first-time and refinanced loans high, banks and other mortgage lenders have kept mortgage rates at near to 50-year lows by *lowering* their profit margins (Muolo, 2005). Not only are rates low, consumers have a smorgasbord of mortgage options to choose from. Besides traditional 30-year fixed rate mortgages, there are shorter fixed rate options (15, 20 years, etc.), variable rate loans (rates vary according to the Federal Reserve rates), convertible loans (can convert from variable to fixed), and interest-only (pay only interest) loans. This has set up fierce competition between lenders for the consumer's attention.[49]

There are many other signs of economic growth and prosperity. This is the most entrepreneurial economy in a hundred years. Affordable technology has played a big part in the growth of small companies started by **entrepreneurs.** Advances in inexpensive computer hardware and software have enabled entrepreneurs to start up small businesses literally in their garages or basements. This technology has enabled them to cut costs on everything from printing and advertising to design of products. Small businesses account for about 75 percent of new job creation and the nation's total economic output.[4]

Two years of federal tax cuts has also fueled both the stock market and the availability of **venture capital** for new businesses. The stock market has rebounded and added about $2 trillion dollars in shareholder wealth to the economy.[101] Many entrepreneurs with visions of starting new companies who had been unable to obtain loans from banks and other lending sources are now finding that venture capital is more readily available. Leading economic analysts believe that the U.S. economy is in the beginning of a new growth cycle for venture capitalists with more money available to lend. They feel that this is a result of the new tax policies inaugurated by the tax cuts of 2003.[101]

With all of this terrific economic news, how can people feel any economic insecurity at all? Most of it has to do with how people *perceive* this news. Much of the good economic news has to do with changing economic times. The economy has changed. America has shifted away from being the world's foremost manufacturer of goods to the world's leader in providing information technology and services. The factory towns and industrial centers have been replaced by new corridors of information and other technologies, often emanating from universities and urban corridors. The new American companies are smaller, more fluid, with more flexible salary and benefit packages. Gone are the days of large manufacturing and corporate employers guaranteeing lifetime job and retirement security. These changes have forced us to re-examine our ideas about employers, jobs, borrowing money, saving for retirement, and a thousand other things. As the economy grows, it changes and these changes require that we change or get left behind. This growth and change can be perceived as threatening to many people and it taxes their ability to cope. Others thrive in it and see it as a time of unrivaled opportunity.

Job Insecurity

Job insecurity is reflected in how people feel about the stability of their job. Probst[81] proposes an interesting way to look at job insecurity. She proposes that job insecurity has two components: the likelihood of actually keeping one's job and the satisfaction with that job. She calls the former component *job security* and the later *job security satisfaction*. Probst's[81] work was motivated by the changing nature of employment over the past decade.

Business strategies such as **downsizing, reorganization,** and **outsourcing** have become increasingly more common over the past decade. Leaner, more efficient businesses of the 2000s may offer secure jobs to their employees, but the changed nature of these jobs forces workers (especially older workers who worked under the old systems) to view their organizations, and their positions within these organizations, differently. Despite being reassured that their jobs are safe, workers may feel insecure about them because they view the changes as threatening. In other words, one's perception of job security is influenced by both the continuance of one's job and stability with respect to desired features of one's job.[81]

Probst studied 500 state government employees from five different health and human services agencies that were in the process of being merged into one umbrella human services organization. Employees were not in danger of losing their jobs but did face possible job changes such as moving offices, changing supervisors, being demoted, learning new job-related technologies, a reduction in job status, and/or new work tasks. Within this umbrella agency, some employees were in danger of losing key

entrepreneurs one who organizes, owns, manages, and assumes the risks of a business

venture capital money available from private individuals and firms that specialize in lending capital to business ventures often deemed too risky by other financial institutions

job insecurity the way people feel about the stability of their job, including the perceived likelihood of actually keeping one's job and personal satisfaction with that job

downsizing cutting back on the number of employees and divisions, departments, and programs within an organization

reorganization changing the structure of the units within an organization; this affects whom they report to and how they work together or independently

outsourcing taking components of an organization (such as payroll, information technology, etc.) out and subcontracting them to independent contractors often working in other states or countries features of their job, or their current position, while others were essentially unaffected by the reorganization.

Probst[81] found that despite having a secure job (protected civil-service guarantee), workers still expressed job insecurity because of the changing nature of their workplace and job itself. In a sense the changes created a feeling of "what's next?" Rather than view the changes as a challenge, they were viewed as a threat. Part of this has to do with the importance of the job and what it means to the person.

The Value of Work

A job can provide many things other than income. Consequently, the loss of work can affect our lives in many ways. Lecrone[65] describes four major things that work provides:

1. A sense of purpose. A job can serve as a source of identity both individually and as a member of a family and a community. Not only do people see themselves as teachers, firefighters, stockbrokers, and so on, they view working as part of being a man, husband, woman, wife, and so on. They also see themselves as contributing members of their community through their employment.
2. Relationships outside the family. Friends at work augment family and neighborhood relationships. They serve as an outlet for certain types of communication and provide an opportunity to separate from our families in an acceptable way. Most psychologists agree that such separation is healthy.
3. A definition of time. When one is unemployed, the days just run together and weekends lose their meaning. Jobs help us structure the week and give us time periods to look forward to, such as weekends and vacations. They also help us define rest periods, which are the times used to wind down from work.
4. Exercise, a component of good health. Although many jobs are sedentary in nature they require us to get up and walk around, even if it is only to the water cooler and back.

Job Loss and Stress

A variety of potential stressors arise for someone who becomes unemployed. The challenge of meeting basic economic needs for survival, difficulty finding future work, loss of health and medical benefits, decline in lifestyle, and loss of self-esteem are just a few. Catalano[24] reviewed a variety of individual and ecological (community-based) studies concerning the health effects of economic insecurity. He defines economic insecurity as either the rate of unemployment in an area or losing a job and being unable to meet financial needs.

In Catalano's study economic insecurity tended to result in psychological distress and nonspecific physiological illness.[24] There was also a relationship, though weak, between economic insecurity and suicide,[34] child abuse, adverse birth outcomes, and heart disease.[24]

Among his findings, the least controversial was the strong association between psychological distress and economic insecurity. Several studies he reviewed point to the increased psychological distress associated with involuntary job loss.

Expectations about finding a new job and the length of job loss are significant mediators of unemployment.[5] The longer one is without a job, the greater that person's perception that he or she will be unable to find one. This combination has proved to be very stressful.

Not only did unemployed individuals have increased psychological distress, the effects of economic insecurity extended to their spouses.[7,56] In fact, in one study of stress and unemployment in rural nonfarm families, the wives of recently unemployed men suffered greater stress than did their laid-off husbands.[104] It was the wives in most cases who were responsible for the household budget. They were faced with the task of figuring out how to take care of the family's needs now that their husbands were unemployed.

The number of people seeking mental health services increases in times of high unemployment.[24] This phenomenon even extends to professionals in the upper socioeconomic brackets. Tetzeli[95] cites a 50 percent increase in visits to a major New York City hospital for stress testing among bankers, stockbrokers, and managers. Many of these people were still employed but anticipated being let go from their positions.

Catalano's[24] last finding was the strong association between economic insecurity and the level of physical illness among individuals and communities—what he refers to as nonspecific illness. The strong association between economic insecurity and nonspecific physical illness is consistent with the stress-illness model discussed in chapter 2. The chronic, low-level effects of unemployment and economic insecurity create an ongoing stress response that manifests itself in a variety of ways. In Catalano's research there were higher levels of illness even when other variables (age, sex, socioeconomic status, and other stressors) were controlled.

However, we must be careful in generalizing about the health effects of job loss. Many factors are involved in understanding how job loss results in a feeling of economic insecurity. Findings are mixed concerning the consistency of the effects of job loss across socioeconomic and demographic groups. For instance the effects of job loss among auto workers (a heavily unionized industry) were most pathogenic (disease producing) for minorities.[24] However, in some studies of representative samples across job categories, the effects of job loss were found to be as pathogenic for middle- and upper-income workers as they were for those with lower incomes.[24] Although it seems implausible, not everyone responds to losing a job in the same way.

Losing our jobs can be a source of economic insecurity and a major source of stress.

Gender and Ethnicity and Job Loss

In a study of Latinas (women of Latino origin), Romero et al.[87] found that few studies existed concerning the health effects of unemployment on women. They speculated that this was due to a large extent to the prevalence of sexist attitudes among researchers who assumed that the participation of most women in the workforce was an option, not a necessity. These subjects held very traditional viewpoints concerning the male partner's preeminence as the "breadwinner" in a family.[87] Consequently, these traditionalists viewed a woman's job loss as not being very stressful because it was just supplementary in nature. However, Romero et al.[87] proposed that most women are in the workforce not just to supplement their partner's income but because their salaries are needed to survive or sustain a standard of living higher than mere subsistence.

In their study Romero et al.[87] found that Latinas who lost their jobs due to the closing of a local manufacturing plant suffered from a variety of psychological stressors. The researchers grouped these stressors into three categories: family events, occupational events, and economic events.

More than half the women reported stress because of the effect their job loss had on family events. Losing their jobs meant that they couldn't provide the things to which their families were accustomed, and they had a hard time explaining this reduced quality of living to their children. Additionally, they reported that relationships with their children had deteriorated since their job loss.

Almost all the women reported feelings of sadness about the loss of their jobs and the loss of contact with former coworkers. A large majority also felt insecure about their ability to find another job, and almost all reported difficulties in making ends meet. They reported difficulties meeting both basic daily economic needs (food and other commodities) and special needs (presents for their children).

A job meant more than just a paycheck to these women, and their job loss presented stressors that went beyond the loss of income.[87] The extent of their stress depended on the length of unemployment and the age of the women. Those unemployed the longest reported the greatest stress levels. Higher stress levels were also reported among the older women. The older the woman was, the longer she needed to adjust to her job loss and cope with her stress.

Another study, this one of employed and unemployed male blue-collar workers, found mixed results concerning the effects of job loss.[40] The results challenged the notion that most people react to unemployment with loss of self-esteem, increase in stressful life events, and an external locus of control. The findings showed no significant relationship between being unemployed and the three expected outcomes.

The lack of self-esteem loss among the unemployed men is attributed to general levels of unemployment in the community.[40] There seems to be greater acceptance of one's lack of work if many others in the community are experiencing the same thing.

In cases where financial needs could be met with unemployment compensation benefits, job loss was actually perceived as a way to reduce stressful life events. Some of the men who were laid off viewed this as a time to rest, spend time with the family, pursue other interests, and investigate other jobs. Blue-collar workers seem to develop a tolerance of and expectation for periods of unemployment. This "it comes with the territory" attitude seems to have a buffering effect for a blue-collar worker when he actually loses a job.

Other studies have also identified variables that seem to mediate how one perceives the loss of a job. All these studies lend credibility to the perception of stress as a holistic transaction involving the perceived ability to cope with a potential stressor. In cases where job loss was perceived as an event that could be coped with, there was minimal stress. In other cases, such as with the Latina women, where job loss interfered with their ability to cope with economic needs, they felt stressed by the closing of the plant.

Job Loss and Violence

Campbell et al.[22] found that employment status was significantly related to femicide (the killing of women). Their study analyzed a variety of relationship and demographic variables associated with femicide. In their study, the strongest demographic factor associated with femicide was the abusers' lack of employment.

Another aspect of job loss and violence is its relationship to workplace violence. Contrary to popular belief and media hype, only a small percentage of workplace homicides are committed by disgruntled employees who leave work, return with a small arsenal, and open fire on coworkers. In the study *Workplace Violence: A Report to the Nation,* the University of Iowa's Injury Prevention and Research Center reported that in 1999 there were 645 workplace homicides. This was down from a record high of 1,080 in 1994. Among the 645 workplace homicides, the overwhelming majority (85 percent) were the result of criminal intent. Most of those homicides were committed by criminals who were not employees and whose primary purpose was robbery. Only about 7 percent of all workplace homicides are committed by current or former employees. In most cases these homicides are motivated by one or a series of interpersonal or work-related disputes.[52]

Discrimination, Prejudice, and Stress

Discrimination is the process of making a difference in the way one treats or favors one person or group over another on a basis other than individual merit. Discrimination is often based on **prejudice,** a preconceived judgment or opinion about someone or something. Typically those who face discrimination are usually the same people who face prejudice based on their race, age, ethnicity, gender, sexual orientation, or other factors that set them apart from those in positions to exert authority over them.

Although discrimination based on race, ethnicity, gender, age, or sexual orientation can be a tremendous source of stress, it is much more difficult to study empirically than are poverty and unemployment. There are few studies that examine the specific effects of discrimination on stress. Instead, most studies describe the effects of such issues as poverty, crime, violence, and unemployment and then analyze the demographics of those who are poor, involved in violent crimes, or unemployed. As we have discussed, nonwhites and women make up the largest segment of those affected by these conditions.

Many people make the argument that by virtue of the objective numbers alone, nonwhites and women are disproportionately represented in the statistics on poverty, crime, and unemployment—and the fact that such disparity is allowed to exist is cited as discrimination perpetuated by the dominant culture. Whether one agrees with this conceptualization or not, a case can be made for a relationship between stress and stereotypes, prejudice, and discrimination. One can carry the discussion further and argue that the net effect of this chronic stress is a collective outburst at the community level. It was just such a combination that precipitated the rioting in south-central Los Angeles in 1992.[100] After the acquittal of four white police officers caught on video tape and charged in the beating of Rodney King, Shoemaker et al.[100] assert that unequal distribution of civic and state resources in health care, education, and economic opportunities coupled with the paramilitary "law and order" posture of the police department created an incendiary community environment waiting to explode.

Stereotypes and Stress

A **stereotype** is a standardized mental picture that is held in common by members of a group and that represents an oversimplified opinion, prejudiced attitude, or uncritical judgment. Stereotypes abound for almost every class of people imaginable. People are stereotyped according to age, education, occupation, profession, national origin, religion, family role, interests, and disability status, just to name a few. Stereotypes related to gender, race, ethnicity, and sexual orientation seem to be the deepest seated and most disturbing in our culture.[29]

Although we hate to admit it, all of us use stereotypes at times. A key to understanding stereotypes is that they make it easy for us to categorize and make sense of people and experiences. Stereotypes are based in part on reality and personal experience. We tend to generalize to all members of a particular group attributes that we have observed as belonging to particular members of that group.

An example could be the stereotype that some people have about football players being insensitive brutes, pumped up on steroids and wanting to knock someone's head off. There have been enough reports about steroid abuse among football players to provide evidence that this exists and is a problem. In addition, most football fans have read books or interviews about hard-hitting linebackers and defensive backs who have had fantasies about tackling an opponent so hard that they literally take his head off. These kinds of reports create a stereotype

discrimination to make a difference in treatment or favor on a basis other than individual merit

prejudice a preconceived judgment or opinion about someone or something

stereotype a standardized mental picture of members of a particular group that represents an oversimplified opinion, prejudiced attitude, or uncritical judgment about football players that is somewhere between fact and fiction.

Stereotypes make us lazy; they can become substitutes for observation and for finding out what people and the world are really like.[44] Negative stereotypes can stand in the way of us really getting to know people who are different from ourselves. They can set up artificial barriers and fears that add to our mistrust of anyone or anything that is different from ourselves. Fearing and avoiding people and things that are different can create stress by making these people and things threatening to us.

Most of us resist being stereotyped. We want others to acknowledge our uniqueness and understand the characteristics that set us apart from others. We resent it when others categorize us in a stereotypical fashion, yet most of us use stereotypes at times to pigeonhole others. In particular, we apply stereotypes to those who are different from us. We do this because those who are different represent the unknown; they have unknown qualities, and they make us uneasy. We stereotype them because that makes it easier to categorize them. We can create a picture of who they are without having to take the time to get to know them.[48]

Being different affects people on the individual as well as on the group level.

Unfortunately, besides impoverishing us, stereotyping and seeing people as "other" sow the seeds of prejudice and discrimination. By stereotyping, we prejudge. Usually, when one stereotypes, the type of prejudging that accompanies this is adverse, not positive. Prejudice, or adverse prejudging, is easy to foster when one doesn't take the time to get to know or understand those who are different. When prejudice leads to unequal treatment, it results in discrimination.

A key to understanding stereotypes, prejudice, and discrimination is to plug them into Lazarus and Folkman's[64] transactional model to understand how they relate to stress. All three of these variables can fit into either stimulus configuration factors or personality factors.

In the book *Missing People and Others*[67] (see Stress in Our World box 4-1) Arturo Madrid refers to those who are different as "others." Being "other" means that you are dissimilar, on the outside, or excluded.

Being treated in a stereotypical fashion or not being allowed access to something, for instance, could be a stressor in itself (stimulus factors). Also, stereotypes, prejudice, and discrimination can negatively affect one's personality, reducing one's perceived ability to cope. We'll examine a few examples of this using different types of discrimination.

STRESS IN OUR WORLD 4-1

Missing People and Others

Being the other means feeling different. It is awareness of being distinct or consciousness of being dissimilar. It means being outside the game, outside the circle, outside the set. It means being on the edges, on the margins, on the periphery. Otherness means feeling excluded, closed out, precluded, even disdained or scorned. It produces a sense of isolation, of apartness, of disconnectedness, of alienation.

Being the other involves a contradictory phenomenon. On the one hand being the other frequently means being invisible. Ralph Ellison wrote eloquently about that experience in his magisterial novel *The Invisible Man*. On the other hand, being other sometimes involves sticking out like a sore thumb.

If one is the other, one will inevitably be perceived unidimensionally; will be seen stereotypically; will be defined and delimited by mental sets that may not bear much relation to existing realities. There is a darker side to otherness as well. The other disturbs, disquiets, discomforts. It provokes distrust and suspicion. The other makes people feel anxious, nervous, apprehensive, even fearful. The other frightens.[66]

Gender Role Stereotyping and Stress

Gender-role stereotyping begins in early childhood. By twenty-four months of age, a child is usually able to distinguish between males and females and has developed a **gender identity**—a clear understanding of being male or female—by the age of three.[13] Gender-role stereotyping, in which girls were raised to be pretty, nurturing, and domestic to the exclusion of being independent and earning a meaningful wage while boys were taught to be rugged, strong, and independent to the exclusion of being nurturing and able to openly express their emotions, is now thought to be damaging to children's overall health and survival.[16]

Children today do not experience the same rigidity in gender role learning as did those of previous generations.

KEY TO UNDERSTANDING

Stereotypes make it easy to categorize people. Instead of having to take the time to personally get to know people who are different from us, we can just lump them into an oversimplified perception of them as being a member of a group that we've already categorized.

KEY TO UNDERSTANDING

You can understand the effects of stereotypes, prejudice, and discrimination on stress by plugging each variable into Lazarus and Folkman's stress appraisal model.

It could be argued that the culture has changed somewhat in its tradition of "color coding" babies (boys wear blue and girls wear pink). Girls can now wear blue, but can boys wear pink? In most families, the answer is still no. This may reflect the unspoken parental fear that putting a boy baby in pink clothes will feminize him. The color pink is purported to "sissify" boys, yet girls seem to have the ability to develop normally in spite of wearing blue clothes.[13] Boys and girls today also can make freer choices for play and toys: boys and girls can play with kitchen sets; both are encouraged to play with blocks and other building toys.

No one is completely sure why children are drawn to certain types of toys and play activities, but stereotypical childhood play does reinforce stereotypical gender roles. Playing "house," for example, where the girls cook and set the table and the boys return from "work" to be served dinner, sets the stage for gender roles that play out in later life. The women's movement in the early 1970s called into question stereotyped gender roles and forced gender play. The prevailing wisdom was that both boys and girls would benefit from broader choices based on interest and skill. Slowly, barriers have broken down and public schools no longer have segregated areas such as the "boys' corner" or the "girls' corner" of old. Even with greater integration of boys' and girls' activities, there is still subtle gender stereotyping. Activities such as jumping rope, playing with dolls, and dressing up are more stereotypically female, whereas playing with toy guns, playing *Star Wars,* climbing trees, and so forth are more stereotypically male.[13]

In later life, stereotypical gender role expectations can be a source of stress when they force men and women into expected behaviors and lifestyles that are inconsistent with who they are as individuals. In his book, *The Male Role Stereotype,*[97] Doug Cooper Thompson describes how this plays out with the role men are expected to play in American society and how this can be a source of stress. Table 4-1 details his male stereotypical "code of conduct" and the psychic costs associated with it.

Table 4-1 Stereotypical Male Roles and Their Costs

Boys' Code of Conduct	Psychic Costs
Act tough—Most boys and men are brought up to believe that they have to show that they are strong and tough; they have to be able to "take it" and "dish it out."	Acting tough has its price. Men are far more likely than women to use violence to settle differences. Fighting is an accepted part of men's sports. Men commit a disproportionate share of violent crimes. Homicide is the leading cause of death for young black males.
Hide emotions—"Big boys don't cry" is an epithet that most men learn early and adhere to rigidly throughout their lives.	Hiding emotions can be a risk factor for mental and physical illness. Men who keep their emotions bottled up run the risk of contracting a variety of illnesses ranging from hypertension to depression. Hiding emotions or not clearly expressing them can also put a strain on most relationships in which clear, open communication is vital.
Earn "big bucks"—Most men are dissuaded from choosing careers that do not have great earning potential. Men are trained to believe that they have to be the family breadwinner.	The emphasis on having to be the breadwinner can put a tremendous amount of pressure on men. Some men choose careers that they really don't like but that pay well. Others put in an inordinate amount of time (overtime, nights, weekends) striving to get to the top. They have less time for themselves, their families, and their community.
Get the "right" kind of job—Boys learn early that men who pursue the wrong kinds of jobs (kindergarten teacher, nurse, secretary, librarian, etc.) are perceived as strange.	In striving for the big salary, many men forgo careers that would be more personally rewarding. Many men would be happier in less competitive jobs or jobs that are more nurturing and involve helping others.
Compete intensely—Boys learn early that to be a man is to be an intense competitor, whether on the playing field, in the classroom, or in the bedroom.	With its overemphasis on competition, the traditional male role carries over from work to play. There is no "downtime." Many men have not learned how to relax—to let down their guard and be playful. A casual jog with a friend often becomes a competitive race to the finish line.
Win—Men are taught to do almost anything to win. Getting ahead and winning, whether it is at Little League or in the boardroom, is crucial regardless of the personal or family sacrifice it may entail.	A "win-at-all-costs" attitude can be damaging both on the job and when it extends to home life and friendships. Much more in life is accomplished through compromise and accommodation than through winning and intimidation. Men who grow up learning to win at all costs have a harder time negotiating and compromising.

Source: Based on Doug Cooper Thompson, *The Male Role Stereotype.*

As you can see, the psychic costs associated with having to live up to stereotypical male roles that are inconsistent with who one really is can be very stressful. Women are exposed to similar unrealistic stereotypical roles. The successful woman of the 2000s is supposed to have a rewarding marriage, great sex life, wonderful children, high-level fitness, a meaningful career, and an active civic life. Her grandmother or mom would probably have been expected to have either a rewarding career or a marriage (rewarding or otherwise) with children (and no one expected children to be wonderful).

Racial and Ethnic Stereotypes

Sometimes stereotypes converge and create a special kind of stress. In Diverse Perspectives 4-1, Brent Staples[91] describes what it was like to grow up both black and male in urban America in the 1980s. Staples's depiction of what it is like being a black male in urban America is a vivid example of chronic exposure to a stressful situation and the adjustments he has had to make in his life as a result of this.

DIVERSE PERSPECTIVES 4-1

Just Walk On By: The Everyday Reality of Racial Stereotyping

My first victim was a woman—white, well-dressed, probably in her late twenties. I came upon her late one evening on a deserted street in Hyde Park, a relatively affluent neighborhood in an otherwise mean, impoverished section of Chicago. As I swung onto the avenue behind her, there seemed to be a discreet, uninflammatory distance between us. Not so. She cast back a worried glance. To her, the youngish black man—a broad six feet two inches with a beard and billowing hair, both hands shoved into the pockets of a military jacket—seemed menacingly close. After a few more quick glimpses, she picked up the pace and was soon running in earnest. Within seconds she disappeared into a cross street.

That was more than a decade ago. I was 22 years old, a graduate student newly arrived at the University of Chicago. It was in the echo of that terrified woman's footfalls that I first began to know the unwilling inheritance I'd come into—the ability to alter public space in ugly ways. It was clear she thought herself the quarry of a mugger, a rapist, or worse. Suffering a bout of insomnia, however, I was stalking sleep, not defenseless wayfarers . . . I was surprised, embarrassed, and dismayed all at once. Her flight made me feel like an accomplice in tyranny. It also made it clear that I was indistinguishable from the muggers who occasionally seeped into the area from the surrounding ghetto . . . I soon gathered that being perceived as dangerous is a hazard in itself.

Racial profiling is probably the best example of how stereotypes based on race and ethnicity converge to create stress. The origins of racial profiling is linked to the government's "war on drugs," a crusade embraced in concept by lawmakers, both parties at every level of government, and most Americans. Unfortunately, the war on drugs often turned into a war on people of color, with African Americans, Latinos, and other minorities bearing the brunt of the battle. The war on drugs spawned profiles of supposed drug couriers based on race and ethnicity. Police, ostensibly looking for drug criminals, used the established profiles to routinely stop drivers based on the color of their skin.

In the African-American community there is a term that captures the essence of racial profiling called *driving while black.* It refers to the discriminatory and prejudicial patterns of law enforcement directed at African Americans doing nothing more than driving their cars. Decades of research across the entire United States of America show that African Americans are pulled over and detained at a rate that far exceeds that of white motorists engaged in similar behavior. One example, taken from the American Civil Liberties Union's 1999 report, *Driving While Black: Racial Profiling on Our Nation's Highways,* clearly illustrates this disparity. In 1995 in Colorado, the settlement of a class-action lawsuit filed by the ACLU officials in Eagle County paid $800,000 in damages to more than 400 black and Latino motorists stopped on Interstate 70 because of racial profiling. Between August 1988 and August 1990 on I-70 between Eagle and Glenwood Springs, Colorado, 402 people of color were pulled over solely because they fit a drug courier profile. The payment made restitution to all 402 people stopped, none of whom were ticketed or arrested for drugs.[47]

Perhaps the outcry against racial profiling would not be so great if the nature of the stops were in line with routine police procedures for pulling motorists over and checking their motor vehicle documents. In most reported cases the stops were anything but routine, with countless reports of innocent people of color humiliated, threatened with dogs and beatings, handcuffed, thrown to the ground, maced, and in some cases beaten. Many cases were documented by police and bystander videotaping. A chilling example is an incident that occurred in Maryland in 1997. Charles and Etta Carter, an elderly African-American couple from Pennsylvania, were stopped by Maryland State Police on their fortieth wedding anniversary. The Carters were removed from their car and Mrs. Carter was not allowed to use the restroom during the search because police officers feared that she would flee. Troopers used drug-sniffing dogs to search

racial profiling the practice of singling out individuals as potential suspects based only on their race their car. In the course of the search their daughter's wedding dress was tossed onto one of the police cars and, as trucks passed on I-95, it was blown to the ground joining their other belongings that were strewn along the highway. These items were trampled over and urinated on by the dogs as the troopers went through them looking for drugs. No drugs were found and no ticket was issued. The Carters eventually reached a settlement with the Maryland State Police.[47]

Sexual Orientation Stereotypes

Homophobia is the irrational fear and hatred of homosexuality in ourselves and others. A key to understanding homophobia is to realize that it is based in part on prejudice founded on stereotypical assumptions about what it means to be gay or lesbian. Some stereotypes related to homosexuality are examined in the Diverse Perspectives box on page 102.

In 1990 the Federal Bureau of Investigation (FBI) began collecting data on hate crimes against gays and lesbians. As part of the national movement to identify and effectively deal with hate crimes, several states and municipalities have included sexual orientation in laws dealing with hate crimes. In the first year of data collection, hate crimes against gays and lesbians increased 15 percent. While this represents a dramatic increase, the real increase is probably much higher.[27] Many gays and lesbians fail to report hate crimes for fear of abuse at the hands of police, disclosure of their sexual identity to employers and the community, and fear that doctors will treat them badly. Even when gays and lesbians report hate crimes and win their cases in court, prosecutions often result in either acquittal or light sentences for those convicted.[70] This might reflect the homophobic attitudes of juries and judges and the pervasive belief that somehow gays provoke these bashings through sexual advances.

Being gay often means feeling pressured to hide these public displays of love and affection.

KEY TO UNDERSTANDING

Homophobia is based in part on a stereotypical assumption about what it means to be a gay man or lesbian.

SPIRITUALITY AND STRESS

The first half of this chapter examined the nature of social influences on stress. For many people, their spirituality is powerful enough to sustain their faith and help mediate even the most oppressive social conditions. The next half of the chapter will examine the nature of spirituality and how it relates to stress.

As you remember from chapter 1, the spiritual dimension is an integral part of health and affects stress in several ways. The key characteristic of the spiritual dimension is a sense of interconnectedness with a higher power or a greater meaning beyond the self. In this section, we will explore this interconnectedness and examine how spirituality is connected to faith and religion and how all three are related to health and stress.

Faith, Religion, and Spirituality: A Comparison

Faith, religion, and spirituality are separate entities, yet these terms are often used synonymously.[32] Part of the confusion lies in the fact that although all three are different, they are related. **Faith** is really the bedrock of both spirituality and religion, yet one can have faith (in the self, for instance) and be neither spiritual nor religious. The essence of **spirituality,** a sense of connectedness with a power greater than the self, is a cornerstone of religious participation and church membership, yet one can be spiritual and not be religious. One's sense of interconnectedness may be with the natural world or all human beings and not manifest itself in church membership. All religions of the world (Eastern, Western, and all others in between) are built on both faith and spirituality. The central focus of this faith and spirituality, however, is God or some supreme being.

homophobia the irrational fear and hatred of homosexuality in ourselves and others

faith the belief in something that cannot be proven empirically

spirituality a sense of interconnectedness with something or someone beyond the self

DIVERSE PERSPECTIVES 4-2

A Reality Check: Myth vs. Truth about Lesbian, Gay, and Bisexual People

In reality, gay and bisexual people tend to behave similarly to heterosexual people in terms of their lifestyles, behavior, and relationships. Yet there are countless myths and stereotypes surrounding homosexuality, most entirely unfounded and based on irrational fears, a lack of understanding, and a simple lack of familiarity with homosexual people.

Being gay is not contagious. Sexual orientation is not a disease that can be spread to other people. Most lesbian, gay, and bisexual individuals were raised by straight parents. No one knows for sure how sexual orientation develops.

Gay people don't recruit others to be gay. Sexual orientation can't be changed. You can't *recruit* someone into a sexual orientation. Gay people are attracted to other gays. Gay people do not sexually stalk straight individuals for casual sex, nor do they purposefully show an interest in seeking relationships with heterosexuals.

There are not necessarily specific gender roles in gay relationships. A variety of roles are adopted in gay relationships just as they are in heterosexual relationships. Most gay and bisexual men conform to cultural expectations for dress as do lesbian and bisexual women.

Being gay is not a conscious choice. While many heterosexual people believe that gay people could change if they wanted to, research has repeatedly shown this is not true. Psychologists don't consider sexual orientation for most people to be a conscious choice that can be voluntarily changed. The American Psychological Association has made several official statements that so-called conversion therapy is unethical. People who attempt to change their sexual orientation usually do so in response to internal or external pressure to be heterosexual.

Therapy cannot "cure" homosexuality. Treatments that claim to cure homosexuality are only successful in coercing heterosexual behavior—they do not change a person's inner feelings about their basic orientation.

Homosexuality is not "caused" by sexual abuse. Most people who were sexually abused as children grow into heterosexual adults. Gay and lesbian people, just as heterosexuals, may have been victims of sexual abuse, but this is not necessarily related to their sexual orientation.

Homosexuals are not child molesters. Approximately 95 percent of child molesters are heterosexual men. Many will abuse children of either gender.

Gay relationships are similar to heterosexual relationships in terms of stability and level of commitment. Just like heterosexual couples, many gay and lesbian couples form long-term, monogamous, stable relationships and consider themselves to have a lifetime commitment to each other; indeed, this is why gay activists lobby the government to permit gay marriage. As the nation's divorce rate indicates, many heterosexual people have trouble maintaining long-term relationships.

Gay people can and do have children. Many gays and lesbians are parents and have children from prior heterosexual relationships. Others choose to have children within their gay or lesbian relationship, by adoption or through other means, including artificial insemination or by enlisting a surrogate mother or father.

Homophobia is not limited to straight people. Gays, lesbians, and bisexuals often have homophobic feelings just as straight people do. They have internalized these feelings from the culture, and often have problems with self-hatred and lack of self-acceptance.

Gay people have the same range of sexual desire and self-control as heterosexuals do. Being gay is not indicative of having less or more control of one's sexual urges.

Being gay is not a mental illness. The American Psychological Association has determined that being gay is not a mental illness. Objective scientific research over the past thirty-five years has consistently shown that homosexual orientation, in and of itself, is not associated with emotional or social problems.

Source: Adapted from *Myths & Assumptions about LGB People.* The Texas Women's University Counseling Center. http://www.twu.edu/o-sl/counseling/SelfHelp042.html

Faith: Belief without Proof

Faith is a generic as well as dynamic human experience.[37] It is generic because faith cuts across all religions, races, ethnic groups, and cultures. It is dynamic because it is ever changing and adaptive. Faith evolves and develops as it passes through stages in our lives.

There are three dimensions to faith:

1. Faith involves a pattern of personal trust in and loyalty to a set of core values. These core values are referred to as our *centers of value*[37] and are made up of the people, institutions, ideals, and causes that give our lives meaning and direction.
2. Faith involves trust in and loyalty to images and realities of power. The biblical passage "the Lord is my shepherd, I shall not want" reflects an ultimate trust in the image of an all-powerful God who will watch over his flock. Others' faith may be in their government, spouse, father, or mother.
3. Faith involves trust in and loyalty to a master script or story for our lives. This master script is our

internalized picture of our lives. It evolves from our first day of life and provides a picture of who we are, where we are going, and what we shall do along the way. This vision, whether completely accurate or not, provides us with direction and meaning in our lives.

All three dimensions of faith rely on the underlying premise—trust and loyalty to that which cannot be proved empirically. Whether or not our beliefs have been explicitly nurtured through religious participation, we base our faith on forming relations of trust and loyalty to others with no guarantee of anything. Faith in this sense is a covenant.[38] We are not alone in our faith. Faith involves loyalty to others through a shared trust that involves our centers of value, images of power, and a master script. Beyond this, however, faith involves a trust in and loyalty to God, something, someone, or some reality that transcends us.

It is this transcendent nature of faith that distinguishes it from mere beliefs that are usually rooted in some empirical evidence. Faith is the belief in something that cannot be proved. One can have faith in a variety of things. One can be faithful without being spiritual or religious. However, faith is a key component of spirituality and religion (see Assess Yourself 4-4, "Spirituality and Faith Assessment").

Religion

Religion is an organized system of worship and belief. It includes faith and spirituality but goes beyond them by institutionalizing them. Each religion has its own interpretation of, guidelines for, and rules regarding specific issues of faith and spirituality. While all religions incorporate faith and spirituality, each has a different theological perspective on issues of faith and spirituality. This perspective has a cumulative historical tradition linking expressions of faith and spirituality by people of the past with those by people of the present and future.[38] At the core of all religions is a belief in God or a higher power. Religious faith is the personal appropriation of a relationship to this god or higher power. In most religions, there is a written master document or book (Bible, Koran, etc.) in which the word of God and God's disciples is recorded. The spokespersons chosen to deliver God's words vary according to the religion. It could be another congregation member (Quakers), a priest (Roman Catholics, Episcipalians), rabbi (Jews), imam (Muslims), medicine man (Native Americans), or monk (Buddhists), just to name a few.

Religions by their very nature are exclusionary. There are conditions for membership. One usually pledges his or her beliefs and a commitment to follow the tenets of the religion. There is often a ritualistic "cleansing ceremony" (baptism in Christian faith) where a person's previous sins are washed away and that person is allowed to start anew in the church. The faithful are expected to differ from the nonfaithful in their adherence to their religion's rules for membership and code of conduct. There are two basic orientations of religion: personal and institutional.[55]

The personal side of religion revolves around one's values, beliefs, attitudes, and behavior. Religion provides a forum for people to seek answers to questions such as, What is the meaning of life? Where did we come from? What happens to us after death? Additionally, religion provides a code of conduct and living that revolves around ethical principles and laws governing human behavior independent of the legal statutes of countries.[2] As we'll explore, many religions have specific health-related rules involving things such as alcohol, tobacco and other drug use, sexual behavior, and dietary practices. The personal side of religion also has to do with one's daily lifestyle and how church members integrate such health-related rules into their actions. It also involves prayer and altruistic behavior directed at helping others and building one's sense of interconnectedness.

The institutional side of religion includes but is not limited to church attendance, participating in church group activities, shared worship and study of scriptures, theology, ethical teachings, group praying, community outreach and activism, and contributing money to maintain the congregation.

Spirituality

Spirituality is a belief in or relationship with a higher power, creative force, divine being, or infinite source of energy.[37,38] This belief is manifested in a sense of interconnectedness, a feeling that somehow, some way, we are all in this together. The "we" spiritual people feel connected to can be members of one's religious group, other human beings, all living things, or all things living and dead from here ever after. For those whose spirituality is religion-based, it is ecumenical in scope.[85] It is part of but transcends individual religions. For those whose spirituality is **secular,** it is universal or even extraterrestrial. It is hard to lie on your back outside late at night looking at the stars in the sky and not feel a part of something that is bigger and never-ending, that is impossible to explain but somehow relates to us all. An exploration of this connectedness is provided in the Living Constructively box on page 104.

Our spirituality is a two-dimensional concept.[37,38] The vertical dimension is the relationship with the transcendent/God or set of supreme values that guide a person's life. The horizontal dimension is the person's

religion an organized system of worship and belief that includes faith and spirituality

secular something that is not overtly or specifically religious in nature

Living Constructively

Buddhism, Spirituality, and Constructive Living

Neither Naikan nor Morita therapies are religious practices. Both are Japanese psychological approaches to mental health founded by men who were devout Buddhists. While neither therapeutic approach directly addresses the subject of spirituality, both embrace its core sense of interconnectedness.

For example, the Morita principle of working with one's attention often uses activities that shift attention from the self to things in one's immediate environment. Clients might be given attention-building exercises that ask them to spend an hour examining a handful of beach sand or finding examples from nature of eight different shades of green. In performing these activities one often comes away with a renewed appreciation of the natural world and a different perspective of our connection to it. One of the clear purposes of doing Naikan self-reflection is to change how we view the support others have given us while reflecting on how our actions have troubled them. In doing this we gain a sense of how the actions of countless others have contributed to our lives. Let's use the personal computer I am using to write this book as a small example for the first Naikan self-reflection question, "What have others given me?"

What Have Others Given Me?

1. An affordable computer
   - a market-driven economy where prices reflect demand
   - a store in my neighborhood to buy the computer
   - excellent sales people to help me decide on a model
   - the Internet to check prices and compare features prior to shopping
   - a factory to build the computer
   - skilled workers who actually built it
   - workers who packed it and loaded it on a truck
   - the truck and everything and everyone who went into building it
   - truck drivers who drove it to a warehouse for my store
   - warehouse men and women who picked my order and loaded it on the truck going to my store
   - an excellent highway system that facilitated getting it to me in a reasonable amount of time
   - workers at the store who unloaded my computer and called me to let me know it was in
   - workers who delivered my computer, set it up, and trained me how to use it
   - the electricity that powers my computer and the oil, power station, wires, and people who maintain the entire electrical grid that services my home.

We could keep going when examining all of the people and factors that came together to bring this computer to me and grace me with its wonder. There are many places around the world where this isn't the case. There is no free press or Internet service where computers are marketed and advertised. The infrastructure to support getting access to computers is in disarray; electricity is often unavailable, roads are in disrepair, telephone service is unpredictable, and truck transportation is unreliable. These and many other basic essential people and services that I take for granted when I want a new computer do not exist in other places.

I am dependent on and blessed by all of the people and services that had to come together for me to obtain this computer and write this book. My accomplishment of writing the book might never have occurred if I didn't have access to this computer and the forces that connected to bring it to me. The interconnectedness of the world (a spiritual belief) is reinforced for me every time I think about this computer and place my fingers on its keys.

relationship with the self, others, and the environment. There is a perpetual interrelationship between the two dimensions (see fig. 4-1). The vertical axis gives us faith and hope and helps us believe we *can* cope. This, as you've seen, is central to managing stress. An essential stress-related part of the horizontal axis is what we do to show our spirituality. While the vertical axis relates to our beliefs and feelings, the horizontal axis embraces what we do. Those with a high level of spiritual health behave in an interconnected way. They take part in church and community activities. They help others. They get involved in causes and groups that are proactive, whether it involves cleaning up a vacant lot or beach with an environmental group or visiting the sick and infirm who are hospital-bound. It is in the "doing" that some of the greatest benefits of spirituality are derived. By sharing our love, our labor, our hope, and our faith with others we can reduce our stress.[55] It's hard to feel you can't cope when you are out helping others do just that.

M. Scott Peck, the author of *The Road Less Traveled,* was heavily influenced by James Fowler's[37,38] earlier writings concerning the seven stages of faith and the evolution of spiritual development. Although Peck is a Christian, he could just as easily be speaking for a

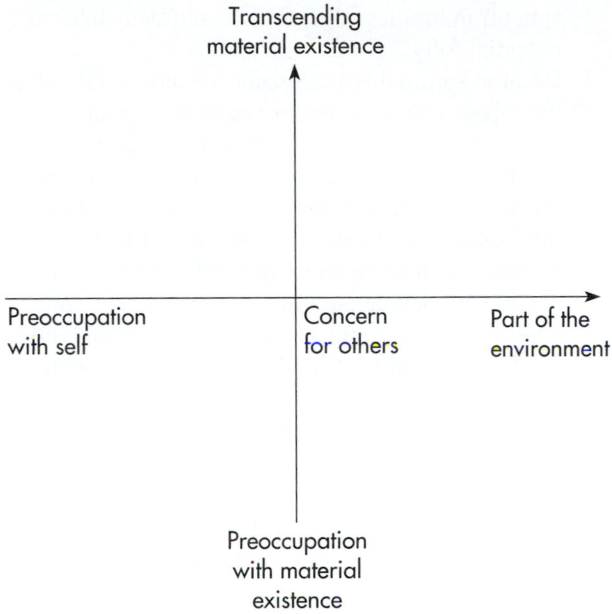

Figure 4-1

Spirituality involves movement along two dimensions. On the vertical dimension one transcends being overly concerned with the material world and earthly possessions. The horizontal dimension involves a lack of preoccupation with the self and a growing interest in others and the environment as a whole.

Buddhist or an atheist when describing spiritual development. In his book. *The Different Drum: Community Making and Peace,*[78] Peck describes spiritual development as a four stage process:

- Stage 1: chaotic and antisocial
  Stage 1 is made up of young children and perhaps one in five adults. It is a stage of undeveloped spirituality characterized as chaotic and antisocial. People in this stage are chaotic in the sense that their lives are basically unprincipled. There is nothing that governs them but their own will. They lack integrity, and their movement is guided by whim, not principle. Individuals in this stage are antisocial in that they are generally incapable of loving others. Their actions are self-serving and manipulative, even if they say otherwise. Many spend their entire lives at this level. Others move to the next stage.
- Stage 2: formal institutional
  Stage 2 is inhabited by the majority of churchgoers and believers as well as emotionally healthy children. In this stage of spiritual development, the person is strongly attached to the formal, institutional religious experience versus the essence of the religion. There is strict adherence to the traditions and dogma of the religion. Change and nontraditional interpretations of the religious experience are viewed with disfavor by persons in this stage.

Key to Understanding

A key to understanding spirituality is to view it as the exact opposite of social isolation and loneliness. Rather than feeling all alone and isolated, one feels connected to all people and forever in the presence of something beyond the self.

- Stage 3: skeptical and individual
  Stage 3 of spiritual development is characterized by an increasing skepticism about the formal interpretations and expressions of the religion. There is a focus on an individual interpretation of the teachings and practices that may include rejection of some things. However, this is not to be confused with the antisocial aspect of stage 1. Stage 3 individuals are often more socially committed and community-oriented than stage 2 people are. Their individuality often manifests itself in examining issues and seeking the truth—going beyond mere adherence to dogma.
- Stage 4: mystical and communal
  Stage 4, the mystic, communal part of spiritual development, includes people who have moved beyond narrowly defining their faith; the communal aspect of this stage is one of inclusiveness rather than exclusion. It is made up of people whose spirituality does not exclude others of a different faith or those who pray to a different god or don't believe in a god. It is made up of people who believe that all spiritual persons belong to the same group and that what connects them is a mystery. The interconnectedness of humans, and other life-forms and environments, cannot always be explained rationally or objectively. Stage 4 people believe that some things are beyond rational explanation and remain a mystery. They take comfort in the interconnectedness of life and revel in the mystery that surrounds their faith (see Stress Buster Tips, "Get Connected").

How Spirituality Moderates Stress and Health

Karren et al.[55] feel that spirituality is related to stress and health in four major ways:

1. Spirituality acts as a unifying force that integrates the other dimensions of health.

   As we learned in chapter 1, our stress is directly affected by our overall level of health and wellness across all six dimensions. Anything that can positively affect our stress can help us manage it.

   Emotionally, this gives us the courage to seek help when we are feeling desperate. Intellectually, it sparks our creativity and gives us the faith to go where no one else has gone. Socially, it provides a connection to another and faith in the love and trust

Stress Buster Tips

Get Connected

Spirituality is all about feeling connected to something higher than the self. Here are five simple ways to start getting connected.

1. Volunteer to work with people—There are hundreds of organizations looking for help. Find one that you think you'd enjoy being connected to and volunteer a few hours a week in helping it.
2. Volunteer to work with animals—There are many opportunities to help animals, ranging from walking an elderly neighbor's pet to spending time at the local animal shelter. Working with animals is a great way to get connected.
3. Join a church group—If you are a religious person, take a more active part in your congregation. Many religious people find the greatest sense of spiritual connectedness in engaging in fellowship activities and working with other church members.
4. Join an environmental group—Whether your spirituality is religious or secular, working with other people to help promote a cleaner, safer environment will get you connected to the natural world at a deeper level.
5. Join an online spiritual group—The Internet has opened up countless portals for connecting with spiritual seekers around the globe. It also provides a spiritual connection for the house-bound, shy, and disabled.

of another. Physically it motivates us to exercise and eat well and to engage in preventive activities now, despite their payout long in the future. Environmentally, it links us with all things on the planet. It makes us respect the flora and fauna that share a tiny planet in an infinite universe.

2. Spirituality helps create or bring into focus a meaning in life.

   We've all asked the questions What is the meaning of life? and Why should I carry on? Not having answers (or good answers) to these questions can be a major source of stress. Questioning the very purpose of one's existence can be the beginning of either a long philosophical quest or a short journey to suicide's doorstep.

   Being an interconnected part of something larger automatically gives our life meaning. Our role in life is to play out that part of the bigger whole by being ourselves. We *are* because we are a part of this great interconnected tradition of human history that came before us, is with us now, and will exist into infinity when we are gone. From this base we spin off in limitless directions to self-actualize our potential fully.

3. Because spirituality transcends the individual, it has the capacity to be a bond between individuals.

   Loneliness and social isolation are major sources of stress, as we saw in the beginning of this chapter. We also talked about some of the things that factor into isolation and loneliness. A sense of feeling different or disliked and a sense of feeling as though one did not belong are often cited as reasons for loneliness and social isolation. People with a high level of spirituality feel just the opposite. They feel connected to other individuals. They feel a kindship with them. They trust them and are willing to take a chance and try to get to know them. They realize how important connecting with others is and take steps to do that at every level of their lives.

4. Spirituality is based on individual perceptions of faith.

   The belief in something that can't be proved is the driving force behind much that is human in us. For instance, imagine not having faith in the future. People who do not have any faith in the future are afraid to enter relationships, afraid to change jobs, afraid to go back to school, afraid to enter a new career field, afraid to make a commitment, and afraid to move somewhere new, to mention just a few things. These fears always almost manifest themselves in stress. Imagine having no faith in yourself. Faith can be a major stress reducer.

Koenig[59,60] believes that asking for forgiveness (similar to confiding) exerts a stress-reducing and healing effect. Asking for forgiveness for your transgressions and believing you will receive it can have powerful affects. It can reduce anxiety and stress and provide a sense of control over one's life. Harris et al.[46] have encorporated the power of forgiveness into the therapeutic application of forgiveness-based interventions. Anadarajah and Hight[2] also suggest that health care providers utilize forgiveness and hope in their treatment regimens. They have developed a HOPE questionnaire to help clinicians assess a patient's spiritual beliefs in order to be able to use those beliefs to help them.

The Health Effects of Faith, Religion, and Spirituality

Most studies in this area are really studies of the relationship between religiosity and stress. Religiosity is generally measured by using one's reported membership in a church, attendance at services, participation in church-related activities, and level of prayer. These variables yield a composite "religiosity" score that can be compared to health and stress outcomes.[102] It is much more difficult to define either faith or spirituality operationally. It is

Prayer and other ritualistic and meditative behaviors can provide a soothing, stress-reducing effect.

generally assumed by researchers in this area that those who are religious also have faith and are spiritual. This assumption is partially grounded in the relationship between religion and spirituality for most Americans. Over 95 percent of all Americans believe in God. Among those people 74 percent report feeling close to God. Additionally, 77 percent feel that physicians should consider their spiritual needs and 73 percent believe that they should share these feelings with their physicians. About 66 percent want physicians to inquire about their religious and spiritual beliefs, while only 10 to 20 percent report that their physicians discuss religion or spirituality with them.[2]

The acceptance of the association between spirituality and improved health outcomes is so strong that fully 40 percent of all medical schools in the United States require that students take at least one course in the role of spiritual and religious factors in health and medicine.[82]

The Health-Promoting, Stress-Reducing Benefits of Spirituality

Several studies have shown associations between spirituality and religiosity and improved health and stress outcomes. Brown,[17] in a study of 1,473 Americans of similar age, income, and education, found that religious participation was almost as significant an influence on health as was age and social class. Those who were not regular participants in religious activities were more than twice as likely to report health problems as were participants. Age and social class are generally thought of by epidemiologists as *the* two most significant variables associated with morbidity and mortality. Brown's study[17] also found that among the religious, people who were members of more liberal denominations were in better health than were those in more conservative sects. Myers et al.[72] found a positive association between religiosity and physical and mental health outcomes. Religiosity was also found to be positively associated with preventing illness, including depression, substance abuse, and physical illness, as well as in coping with illness and recovering from illness.[9] Larson and Larson[62] found that recovery rates from illness and surgery were better for religious people than for the nonreligious. Oxman et al.[75] found that nonreligious patients were over three times more likely to die from cardiac surgery than were those who reported receiving strength and comfort from their religious convictions. Koenig et al.[60] found that almost half of the 298 patients involved in their study at the Duke Medical Center cited religion as the most significant factor in helping them cope with the stress associated with illness. Parmley[77] found that open-heart surgery survival rates were higher for the religious than for those who were not religious.

Strawbridge et al.[93] found that subjects who attend church on a regular basis live longer than those who don't attend. Idler and Kasl[51] found that the elderly who attend church regularly had significantly better mental health and lower death rates than did those who did not attend church. Argyle[3] found that those who attend church regularly had lower rates of heart disease, cirrhosis of the liver, and some forms of cancer than did nonchurchgoers and those who attended infrequently. Those who attended church infrequently or not at all were found to have four times the risk for developing cirrhosis of the liver and twice the likelihood of developing atherosclerosis compared with regular attenders. Wallace and Forman,[102] in a study of over 19,000 Michigan youth, found that adolescents with a strong religious affiliation were less likely to get into fights, carry weapons, smoke cigarettes, use marijuana, and drive while under the influence of alcohol. They were more also likely to eat well, have better overall nutrition, exercise more and get more, rest than their nonreligious peers.[102]

Brown[17] found that formal religious activity affects health in several ways. Some churches require healthful behavior, from avoiding cigarettes and alcohol to having only one sexual partner. Most churches advocate using the

Sabbath as a day of rest and reflection (a buffer against stress). Sharing a religion fosters networks of social support that one can turn to in times of need. Benson[9] believes that worship services provide certain therapeutic effects, such as sitting quietly in a soothing environment, listening to music, praying and taking part in other ritualistic and meditative behaviors, and removing oneself temporarily from the stressful activities of the day.

Prayer, Stress, and Health

All the great religions of the world use **prayer** as a technique for establishing the sense of connectedness with a higher being or consciousness that is the hallmark of spirituality. Studies of the benefits of prayer for health and avoiding stress are fraught with problems, primarily due to the difficulty in coming up with an operational definition of what constitutes a prayer.

There are generally four different types of prayers:

1. Meditative (feeling or quietly thinking about God)
2. Colloquial (asking for guidance and forgiveness)
3. Petitional (asking for help and specific favors)
4. Ritual (reading specific prayers)[50]

Studying the effects of any of these types of prayer on health and stress requires that one set parameters (duration, posture, breathing, etc.) for defining them. This has not been done except in studies in which prayer is used in a repetitive fashion to achieve a **meditative effect.** As we'll discuss in detail in chapter 9, Benson[7] called this meditative effect the "relaxation response." The relaxation response slows overall metabolic, breathing, and heart rates; lowers blood pressure; and slows brain wave activity.[8] Repetitive prayer can achieve the same effects. Benson[8] describes the four qualities necessary to achieve a meditative effect:

1. A quiet environment (no disruptions, minimal outside noise)
2. A comfortable position (sitting cross-legged on the floor)
3. A passive attitude (allowing intruding thoughts to pass without getting upset)
4. A focal point (something to focus one's attention on, in this instance a specific prayer)

Any of the four types of prayers can be used in a repetitive fashion to achieve a meditative effect by following these guidelines. Most prayers include the asking of forgiveness and confiding verses. While praying, the person usually asks for forgiveness, shares (confides) his or her sins or transgressions with God, and offers praise. It is the repetitive nature of praying, whether repeating the prayers subvocally or chanting and/or singing them, that is most capable of creating a meditative effect. One of the conditions for achieving a meditative effect is the continued repetition of the meditative saying or prayer over and over for fifteen to twenty minutes.[8]

Roman Catholics use rosary beads as a secondary focal point to help with meditative prayer. Each bead represents a prayer, and the person who is praying rolls the beads in his or her hand to help concentrate and recites the prayers over and over until all the beads have been used.

The United Church of Christ[99] has a simple formula for achieving a meditative state using prayer which is very similar to Bensons's[8] method for achieving the relaxation response. They recommend the following:

1. Find a comfortable place to sit.
2. Put both feet on the floor.
3. Sit upright and let your hands rest in your lap, palms upward.
4. Close your eyes and take a few moments to relax. Note all the noises and sounds around you and then let them go.
5. Start to repeat the meditative prayer (they use a special prayer).
6. If you hear anything while praying, recognize that it is there, say "God bless it," and return to your meditation.
7. Don't hurry the process or try to "get something out of it." Just allow yourself to "be" with God.
8. Repeat the prayer over and over.

Intercessory prayer is a more controversial type of prayer. This involves literally praying for someone else. Churches commonly organize "prayer chains" in which members of the congregation pray for others in the congregation or the community. These prayers are often aimed at helping a sick person recover completely or helping a person experiencing loss cope in a better fashion.

Byrd's classic study[20] involved 393 patients admitted to the coronary care unit of a major urban hospital. Byrd assigned subjects to either an intercessory prayer group or a control group. The subjects did not know to which group they were assigned. Byrd assigned a small group of intercessors (three to seven people who prayed for the others) to each of the experimental group subjects. The results indicated that the experimental group experienced a significantly lower need for antibiotics, diuretics, and intubation/ventilation and in general had better treatment outcomes. Other studies of intercessory prayer have yielded similar findings regarding improved treatment and recovery outcomes in the intercessory group. While all these studies had methodological flaws (mostly associated with the independent variable of prayer), if people

prayer an address (as a petition) to God or a god in word or thought

meditative effect a slowing or lowering of metabolic functions (breathing, heart rate, blood pressure, and brain wave activity)

intercessory prayer a type of prayer done for someone else; praying for another know that others are praying for them and that gives them comfort and a renewed optimism and sense of control, it is bound to help them get better.

Spiritual Distress and Illness

Spiritual distress is the inability to find sources of meaning, hope, love, peace, comfort, strength, and connection in life; it also occurs when there is conflict between one's beliefs and what is happening in one's life.[2] Spiritual distress is often associated with acute onset or terminal illness where the patient asks, Why is this happening to me? Spiritual distress revolves around a breach of faith and loss of spiritual connectedness as the patient confronts his or her illness. Individuals with spiritual distress are at risk of experiencing a disturbance in the belief or value system that provides strength, hope, and meaning in their lives.[23] Some of the defining characteristics of spiritual distress include questioning the credibility of one's belief system, feeling a sense of spiritual emptiness, expressing the feeling that there is no reason to go on living, feeling emotionally detached from oneself and others, and demonstrating discouragement and despair. Patients who are spiritually distressed are at greater risk for undesirable outcomes in their treatment and recovery. Spirituality affects patients' perceptions of their illnesses, faith in their ability to get well, will to live, sick role behavior, and preparation for death, to name a few things.

Types of Spiritual Distress

Spiritual distress can be grouped into three categories:

1. Inability to practice spiritual rituals
2. A conflict between religious or spiritual beliefs and the prescribed health regimen
3. The crisis of illness, suffering, or death

The inability to practice spiritual rituals can arise out of the constraints placed on patients by hospitalization or being in a nursing home. These constraints revolve around issues such as the inability to assume the normal physical position for prayer or meditation, the inability to maintain a religious diet or fast, and separation from spiritual articles, clothing, and texts.

Sometimes spiritual distress arises over a conflict between religious or spiritual beliefs and the prescribed health regimen. The person may object to prescribed or legally required medical procedures such as blood transfusions and immunization. Sometimes a prescribed diet or medication will conflict with spiritual dietary restrictions.

Finally, spiritual distress may be specifically related to the nature of the crisis, illness/suffering, or specter of death. In this case the distress is associated with a breach of faith rather than an inability to practice or conform to one's beliefs. The person asks questions such as, What did I do to deserve this? Is this God's will? Why is this happening to me? Is my faith too weak? Because spiritual and religious practices cut across all cultures and groups, it is important to utilize a multicultural approach in understanding these needs.

HOPE for Spiritual Distress

Anadarajah and Hight[2] use the acronym HOPE to describe an instrument with a series of questions that clinicians can use as a spiritual assessment.

The questions are used to assess the role of spirituality in a person's life for the purpose of minimizing spiritual distress. The responses help clinicians incorporate spiritual interventions into the patient's treatment regimen. The following are some examples of questions taken from the HOPE instrument.

> **H**ope
> What are your sources of hope, strength, comfort, and peace? What sustains you and keeps you going?
>
> **O**rganized
> Do you consider yourself part of an organized religion? How important is this to you?
>
> **P**ersonal
> Do you have personal spiritual beliefs and practices? What are they? What kind of a personal relationship do you have with God?
>
> **E**ffects
> What are the effects of your spiritual beliefs on your medical care and end-of-life issues?
>
> Answers to these questions allow the clinician to integrate spiritual concerns into the patient's treatment regimen.[2]

For many of us, spirituality includes peaceful, reflective moments outdoors.

SUMMARY

We began this chapter with an examination of the social dimension. We described social support and the nature of social networks and social resources. We then examined how social support is measured and its mechanisms for moderating stress. Finally, we examined the effects of social support on health and stress.

Keeping with our adherence to a transactional model of stress, we examined the role of perception while highlighting the need to weigh the costs associated with developing and nurturing extensive social networks against the benefits derived from them. The chapter examined the relationship between life events and stress, citing research criticizing a life-events approach. The use of daily hassles and uplifts was described as a more accurate method of analyzing social and spiritual stress. Research was presented that supports the notion that daily hassles are a more accurate indicator of a person's social stress than are life events. The role of uplifts was found to be relatively benign except in cases in which they coexisted with high levels of hassles, in which case, they had a moderating effect.

Chronic negative social problems such as poverty, unemployment, and discrimination were examined as middle-ground social stressors, falling somewhere between life events and daily hassles. Examples were presented concerning how these ongoing problems are related to chronic, low-level stress.

The second half of the chapter provided an analysis of how faith, religion, and spirituality are related to stress. Although they are used interchangeably, each represents a different phenomenon with its own relationship to stress. We examined the health effects of all three and explored the ways they moderate stress. We ended the chapter with a discussion of spiritual distress and the presentation of a model for exploring such distress with patients.

STUDY QUESTIONS

1. Describe the components of social support.
2. Describe the three measures of social support.
3. Explain how social relationships affect personal stress.
4. List and describe three different types of resources that people can get from social support systems.
5. Describe how touch and confiding are related to social support.
6. Describe how social relationships can be a source of stress in some instances.
7. Describe some of the health effects of social support.
8. Explain the theory behind life events and stress.
9. Explain two weaknesses in using life-events scales to assess personal stress.
10. How do uplifts work in moderating daily hassles?
11. Describe economic insecurity and explain how it is related to stress.
12. Explain how stereotypes, prejudice, and discrimination fit together.
13. Explain how stereotypes can create stress.
14. Describe the differences between spirituality and religion.
15. What is spiritual distress, and how is it related to stress?

DISCOVER OUR CHANGING WORLD

There are many examples of how spirituality manifests itself in people's lives. You have the option of visiting either of the two sites below, which represent distinctly different paths to discovering spiritual enlightenment.

Spirituality.com

The website, Spirituality.com, is maintained by the First Church of Christ Scientist, publisher of the *Christian Science Monitor.* It presents a very pro-Christian viewpoint of how spirituality manifests itself in people's daily lives.

1. Click on the following link and read one of the short articles under the heading "Exploring Your Inner Spiritual Resources."

   http://www.spirituality.com/tte/spirituality.jhtml;jsessionid=KHWBX4PTWRMUXKGL4L0SFEQ

2. Explain what the author said about achieving a spiritual connection through the activity described in the article.

Science of Spirituality

The second website is that of the Science of Spirituality, a non-profit organization whose goal is to help people achieve high levels of spiritual well-being through meditation.

1. Click on the link http://www.sos.org/whopage.asp?id=5 and read the full-text article on achieving spiritual well-being through meditation.
2. After reading the article, describe how Sant Rajinder Singh Ji Maharaj feels that meditation, spirituality, and the world's great religions are connected.

ARE YOU THINKING CLEARLY?

Your friends are supposed to be a major component of your social support network and a source of strength and comfort. Answer the following questions to help clarify this.

1. Do you associate with friends with whom you no longer feel a close connection to but feel obligated to be around?
2. Do you associate with friends you are uncomfortable being around?
3. Do you associate with friends who make excessive or unreasonable demands on you?
4. Do you associate with friends who behave in ways that make you unsafe?
5. Do you associate with friends who have betrayed your trust and in whom you can no longer confide?

If you answered yes to any of these questions, you may not be thinking clearly and logically about your friends.

REFERENCES

1. American Psychiatric Association. (2000). *Diagnostic and statistical manual of mental disorders.* (4th ed.). Washington, DC: American Psychiatric Press.
2. Anadarajah, G. & Hight, E. (2001). Spirituality and medical practice: Using HOPE questions as a practical tool for spiritual assessment. *American Family Physician,* January 1, 2001, pp. 1–16 (versionwww.aafp.org/afp/20010101/81.html).
3. Argyle, M. (1987). *The psychology of happiness.* London: Methuen.
4. Avalos, G. (2005). U.S. Jobless Rate dips to 9/11 levels. *Contra Costa Times.* Knight Ridder Business News (wire feed). July 9, 2005. p. 1, document # 865634821. Washington DC: Knight Ridder Business News.
5. Baik, K., Hosseini, M., & Priesmeeyer, H. R. (1989). Correlates of psychological distress in involuntary job loss. *Psychological Reports,* 65(3), pp. 1227–1233.
6. Beck, M. Rage, resentment, and a ruger: Motives of mass-murderer Colin Ferguson. *Newsweek,* 122(25), p. 3.
7. Belle, D. (1990). Poverty and women's mental health. *American Psychologist,* March, pp. 385–388.
8. Benson, H. (1975). *The relaxation response.* New York: Morrow.
9. Benson, H. (1996). *Timeless healing: The power and biology of belief.* New York: Scribner.
10. Berkman, L.R. & Syme, S.L. (1979). Social networks, host resistance, and mortality: A nine year follow-up of Alameda County residents. *American Journal of Epidemiology,* 109, pp. 186–204.
11. Bernikow, L. (1993). *Alone in America.* New York: Harper & Row.
12. Blaih, B. (1989). The health consequences of loneliness: A review of the literature. *Journal of American College Health,* 37, pp. 162–190.
13. Blonna, R. and Levitan, J. (2005). *Healthy Sexuality.* Pacific Grove, CA: Wadsworth Publishers.
14. Boulard, G. (2001). After September 11th students find themselves under a magnifying glass. *Community College Week,* 14(10), pp. 2–4.
15. Borysenko, J. (1993). *A fire in the soul: A new psychology of spiritual optimism.* New York: Warner Books.
16. Brody, L. (1997). Gender and emotion: beyond stereotypes. Journal of Social Issues (1997 Summer). 53(2) p. 369.
17. Brown, L. (1993). A prayer a day. *American Health,* March, p. 27.
18. Brunner, E. (1997). Stress and the biology of inequality. *British Medical Journal,* 314(7094), pp. 1472–1477.
19. Burg, B., et al. (1992). Loving women: Lesbian life and relationships. In Boston women's health collective, *The new our bodies ourselves.* New York: Touchstone.
20. Byrd, R.B. (1988). Positive therapeutic effects of intercessory prayer in a coronary care unit. *Southern Medical Journal,* 81, pp. 826–829.
21. Campbell, I. (2003). Global view: The tale told by jobs. United Press International, May 2.
22. Campbell, T.C., Sharps, P., Lanughton, K., et al. (2003). Risk factors for femicide in abusive relationships: Results from a multisite case control study. *American Journal of Public Health,* 93(7), pp. 1089–1098.
23. Carpentino, L.J. (1992). *Nursing diagnosis: Application to clinical practice.* (3rd ed.). Philadelphia: Lippincott.
24. Catalano, R. (1991). The health effects of economic insecurity. *American Journal of Public Health,* 81(9), pp. 1148–1152.
25. Chamberlain, K. & Zika, S. (1990). The minor events approach to stress: Support for the use of daily hassles. *British Journal of Psychology,* 81, pp. 469–481.
26. Cooper, J.C. and Madigan, K. (2005). The fed needs to do a little more fiddling. *Business Week,* July 18, 2005, issue 3943, p. 29. New York: Business Week.
27. Cotton, P. (1992). Attacks on homosexual persons may be increasing but many "bashings" are still not reported to police. *Journal of the American Medical Association,* 267(22), pp. 2999–3001.
28. Creed, F. (1993). Life events and stress. *Current Opinion in Psychiatry,* 6(2), pp. 269–273.
29. Cyrus, V. (1993). *Experiencing race, class, and gender in the United States.* Mountain View, CA: Mayfield.
30. Davey, J. (2002). One day in September. *Community College Week,* 15(4), p. 4.

31. Dettmer, J. (2001). New York shows strength in adversity. *Insight on the News,* 17(40), p. 13.
32. Delongis, A.D., Coyne, J.C., Dakof, G., Folkman, R.S., & Lazarus, R. (1982). Relationship of daily hassles, uplifts, and major life events to health status. *Health Psychology,* 1(2), pp. 119–136.
33. Dohrenwend, B.P., et al. (1990). Measuring life events: The problem of variability within event categories. *Stress Medicine,* 6(3), pp. 179–187.
34. Dooley, D., Catalano, R., Rook, K., & Serxner, S. (1989). Economic stress and suicide: Multilevel analyses. *Suicide and Life Threatening Behavior,* 4, pp. 337–351.
35. Dreher, H. (1992). The healing power of confession. *Natural Health,* July/August, p. 80.
36. Ewart, C.K. & Suchday, S. (2002). Discovering how urban poverty and violence affect health: Development and validation of a neighborhood stress index. *Health Psychology,* 21(3), pp. 1–16.
37. Fowler, J.F. (1986). *Stages of faith: The psychology of human development and the quest for meaning.* New York: Harper & Row.
38. Fowler, J.F. (1991). Stages in faith consciousness. In Oser, F.K. & Scarlett, W.G. (Eds.). *Religious development in childhood and adolescence.* San Franscisco: Jossey-Bass.
39. Francis, M.E. & Pennebaker, J.W. (1992). Putting stress into words: The impact of writing on physiological absentee, and self-reported emotional well-being measures. *American Journal of Health Promotion,* 6(4), pp. 280–287.
40. Frost, T.F. & Clayson, D.E. (1991). The measurement of self-esteem, stress-related life events, and locus of control among unemployed blue-collar workers. *Journal of Applied Social Psychology,* 21(14), pp. 1402–1417.
41. Garmon, J. (2001). Making sense, not war. *Community College Week,* 14(10), pp. 4–6.
42. Gruen, R., Folkman, S., & Lazarus, R. (1989). Centrality and individual differences in the meaning of daily hassles. *Journal of Personality,* 56, pp. 743–762.
43. Hafen, B.Q., Frandsen, K.J., Karren, K.J., & Hooker, K.R. (1992). *The health effects of attitudes, emotions, and relationships.* Provo, UT: EMS Associates.
44. Hanson, B.S., Isacsson, S.O., Janzon, L., & Lindell, S.E. (1990). Social network and social support influence on mortality in elderly men. *Advances* 7(1), pp. 16–18.
45. Harlow, H. F. (1953). Mice, monkeys, men and motives. *Psychological Review,* 60, pp. 23–32.
46. Harris, A.H.S., Thoreson, C.E., McCollough, M.E., & Larson, D.B. (1999). Spiritually and religiously oriented health interventions. *Journal of Health Psychology,* 4(3), pp. 413–433.
47. Harris, D.A. (1999). *Driving While Black: Racial Profiling on Our Nation's Highways.* American Civil Liberties Union Special Report (ACLU). NY: NY. ACLU Publishing.
48. Heilbroner, R. (1993). Stereotypes, prejudice and discrimination. In Cyrus, V. (Ed.). *Experiencing race, class, and gender in the United States,* pp. 144–145. Mountain View, CA: Mayfield.
49. Hevesi, D. (2005). Which mortgage? A complicated tale. *Wall Street Journal* (Eastern Edition). July 17, 2005, p. 11.1. New York: Wall Street Journal.
50. Holmes, T.H. & Rahe, R.H. (1967). Social readjustment rating scale. *Journal of Psychosomatic Medicine,* 11, pp. 213–218.
51. Idler, E.L. & Kasl, S.V. (1992). Religion, disability, depression and the timing of death. *American Journal of Sociology,* 97, pp. 1052–1079.
52. Iowa Public Research Center. (2001). *Workplace violence: A report to the nation.* Iowa City: University of Iowa.
53. Jones, F. & Bright, J. (2001). *Stress: Myth and theory.* Harrow, England; Pearson Education.
54. Kanner, A.D., Coyne, J.C., Schaefer, C., & Lazarus, R.S. (1981). Comparison of two modes of stress measurement: Daily hassles and uplifts versus major life events. *Journal of Behavioral Medicine,* 4(1), pp. 1–37.
55. Karren, K.J., Hafen, B.Q., Smith, N.L., & Frandsen, K.J. (2001). *Mind/body health: The effects of attitudes, emotions, and relationships.* (2nd ed.). San Francisco: Benjamin Cummings.
56. Kiecolt-Glaser, J.K., Kennedy, S., Malkoff, S., et al. (1988). Marital discord and immunity in males. *Psychosomatic Medicine,* 50, pp. 213–229.
57. Kirgiss, K. (2002). Taylor-made service: After the terrorist attacks, 99 students from Indiana's Taylor University drove to New York to help however they could. *Campus Life,* 60(7), pp. 62–64.
58. Knight Ridder. (2005). Good news. No, really. *Chicago Tribune.* Knight Ridder Business News (wire services). July 15, 2005, p. 1, document # 867841881. Washington DC: Knight Ridder Business News.
59. Koenig, H.G. (1997). *Is religion good for your health? The effects of religion on physical and mental health.* New York: Hayworth Press.
60. Koenig, H.G., Kvale, J.N., & Ferrel, C. (1988). Religion and well-being in later life. *The Gerontologist,* 28(1), pp. 18–27.
61. Lane, K. (2002). After the fall: Against the ruined backdrop of Ground Zero, the wounded Borough of Manhattan Community College is struggling to rebuild. *Community College Week,* 14(12), pp. 6–11.
62. Larson, D.B. & Larson, S.S. (1994). *The forgotten factor in physical and mental health: What does the research show?* Rockville, MD: National Institute for Healthcare Research.
63. Lazarus, R.S. (1990). Theory-based stress measurement. *Psychological Inquiry,* 1(1), pp. 3–13.
64. Lazarus, R. & Folkman, S. (1985). *Stress appraisal and coping.* New York: Springer.
65. LeCrone, H. (2001). Unemployment more than just loss of job. Cox News Service, September, 18.
66. Locke, S. & Coligan, D. (1986). *The healer within.* New York: Dutton.
67. Madrid, A. (1993). Missing people and others. In Anderson, M.L. (Ed.). *Race, class, and gender: An anthology,* pp. 6–11. Belmont, CA: Wadsworth.
68. Manisses Communication Group. (2002). Survey finds impact of September 11th stretches across the country. *Mental Health Weekly,* 12(35), pp. 1–3.

69. McFall, M., et al. (1989). Psychophysiologic and neuroendocrine findings in posttraumatic stress disorder: A review of theory and research. *Journal of Anxiety Disorders,* 3, pp. 243–257.
70. Minkowitz, D. (1992). It's still open season on gays. *The Nation,* 254(11), pp. 368–381.
71. Muolo, P. (2005). Strong volume, but price war. *National Mortgage News,* NY: July 8, 2005. Vol. 29, Issue 42, pp. 1–2.
72. Myers, J.E., Whitmer, M., & Sweeney, T.J. (1993). Spirituality: The core of wellness. *Wellness Connections,* 4(2), pp. 6–8.
73. O'Brien, C. (2005). Income gap widening in valley. *San Jose Mercury News.* Knight Ridder Business News (wire feed). Jan 24, 2005, p. 1, document # 783295331. Washington DC: Knight Ridder Business News.
74. Overholser, J.C., Norman, W.H., & Miller, I.W. (1990). Life stress and social support in depressed patients. *Behavioral Medicine,* Fall, pp. 125–131.
75. Oxman, T.E., Freeman, D.H., & Manheim, E.D. (1995). Lack of social participation or religious strength and comfort as risk factors for death after cardiac surgery in the elderly. *Psychosomatic Medicine,* 57, pp. 5–15.
76. Paloutzian, R.T. & Ellison, C.W. (1982). Loneliness, spiritual well-being, and the quality of life. In Peplau, L.A. & Perlman, D. (Eds.). *Loneliness: A sourcebook of current theory, research, and therapy.* New York: Wiley.
77. Parmley, W.W. (1996). Separation of church and state (of health). *Journal of the American College of Cardiology,* 28(4), pp. 1047–1048.
78. Peck, M.S. (1987). *The different drum: Community making and peace.* New York: Simon & Schuster.
79. Pennebaker, J.W. (1990). Opening up: The healing power of confiding in others. New York: Morrow and Company.
80. Pooley, E. (1994). Capitalizing on a killer: A spurious "black rage" defense. *New York,* 27(16), pp. 38–40.
81. Probst, T.M. (2003). Development and validation of the Job Security Index and the Job Security Satisfaction Scale: A classical test theory and IRT approach. *Journal of Occupational and Organizational Psychology.* Dec. 2003, vol. 76, p. 451.
82. Puchalski, C.M. & Larson, D.G. (1998). Developing curricula in spirituality and medicine. *Academic Medicine,* 73, pp. 970–974.
83. Pugh, T. (2003). Nation's jobless rate climbs to 6.4% in June. Knight Kidder/Tribune Business News (online), July 4.
84. Rabkin, J.G. & Streuning, E.L. (1976). Life events, stress, and illness. *Science,* 194, pp. 1013–1020.
85. Richards, P.S. & Bergin, A.E. (1997). *A spiritual strategy for counseling and psychotherapy.* Washington, DC: American Psychological Association.
86. Roberts, S.V. (1995). Staring back into the eyes of evil. *U.S. News & World Report,* April 3, p. 8.
87. Romero, G.J., Castro, F., & Cervantes, R.C. (1988). Latinas without work. *Psychology of Women Quarterly,* 12, pp. 281–297.
88. Roush, W. (1997). Herbert Benson: Mind body expert pushes the envelope. *Science,* 276, pp. 357–359.
89. Seong-Ngoo, K. (2002). Psychological burden after September 11th tragedy. *Student British Medical Journal,* May, p. 138.
90. Shoemaker, W.G., et al. (1993). Urban violence in Los Angeles in the aftermath of the riots: A perspective from health care professionals with implications for social reconstruction. *Journal of the American Medical Association,* 270(23), pp. 2833–2838.
91. Staples, B. (1993). Just walk on by. In Virgina Cyrus (Ed.). *Experiencing race, class, and gender in the United States,* pp. 180–182. Mountain View, CA: Mayfield.
92. Straw, D. (2001). A separate peace in a wartime classroom. *Community College Week,* 14(10), pp. 4–6.
93. Strawbridge, W.J., Cohen, R.D., Shema, S.J., & Kaplan, G.A. (1997). Frequent attendance at religious services and mortality over 28 years. *American Journal of Public Health,* 87, pp. 957–961.
94. Syme, S.L. (1987). Coronary artery disease: A sociocultural perspective. *Circulation,* 76, pp. 1–112.
95. Tetzeli, R. (1992). Economy creates more stress. *Fortune,* October, pp. 11–13.
96. Texan Women's University. http://www.twu.edu/o-sl/counseling/SelfHelp042.html
97. Thompson, D.C. (1993). The male role stereotype. In Virgina Cyrus (Ed.). *Experiencing race, class, and gender in the United States,* pp. 146–148. Mountain View, CA: Mayfield.
98. Turner, R.J. (1983). Direct, indirect, and moderating effects of social support on psychological distress and associated conditions. In Kaplan, H. (Ed.). *Psychosocial stress: Trends in theory and research,* pp. 357–367. New York: Academic Press.
99. United Church of Christ. (2003). Exploring your inner spiritual resources. Spirituality.com.
100. Wagner, B.M. (1990). Major and daily stress and psychopathology: On the adequacy of the definitions and methods. *Stress-Medicine,* 6(3), pp. 217–226.
101. Wall Street Journal (2005). The tax cut expansion. *Wall Street Journal* (Eastern Edition). July 12, 2005, p. A 16. New York: Wall Street Journal.
102. Wallace, J.M. & Forman, T.A. (1998). Religion's role in promoting health and reducing risk among American youth. *Health Education and Behavior,* 25(6), pp. 721–741.
103. Weinberger, M., Hiner, S.L., & Tierney, W.M. (1987). In support of hassles as a measure of stress in predicting health outcomes. *Journal of Behavioral Medicine,* 10, pp. 19–31.
104. Wilhelm, M.S. & Ridley, C.A. (1988). Stress and unemployment in rural non-farm couples: A study of hardships and coping resources. *Family Relations,* January, pp. 50–54.
105. Wolf, T.M., et al. (1989). Relationships of hassles, uplifts and life events to psychological well-being in 55 medical students. *Behavioral Medicine,* 15(1), pp. 37–45.

Name: ______________________ Date: ______________

ASSESS YOURSELF 4-1

Social Readjustment Rating Scale

The Social Readjustment Rating Scale was developed by Holmes and Rahe[44] to assist people in quantifying their level of stress. In this scale, events such as marriage, divorce, and retirement are given a score representing the amount of readjustment (and therefore stress) associated with the change. The score is measured in points called *life change units*. The events have been weighted so that more dramatic readjustments are worth more life change units.

To determine your score, check off the events that you have experienced in the last twelve months.

Rank	Life Event	Life Change Units
1	Death of spouse	100
2	Divorce	73
3	Marital separation	65
4	Jail term	63
5	Death of close family member	63
6	Personal injury or illness	53
7	Marriage	50
8	Fired at work	47
9	Marital reconciliation	45
10	Retirement	45
11	Change in health of family member	44
12	Pregnancy	40
13	Sex difficulties	39
14	Gain of new family member	39
15	Business readjustment	39
16	Change in financial state	38
17	Death of close friend	37
18	Change to different line of work	36
19	Change in number of arguments with spouse	35
20	Mortgage over $10,000	31
21	Foreclosure of mortgage or loan	30
22	Change in responsibilities at work	29
23	Son or daughter leaving home	29
24	Trouble with in-laws	29
25	Outstanding personal achievement	28
26	Spouse begins or stops work	26
27	Begin or end school	26
28	Change in living conditions	25
29	Revision of personal habits	24
30	Trouble with boss	23
31	Change in work hours or conditions	20
32	Change in residence	20

ASSESS YOURSELF 4-1 (cont'd)

Rank	Life Event	Life Change Units
33	Change in school	20
34	Change in recreation	19
35	Change in church activities	19
36	Change in social activities	18
37	Mortgage or loan less than $10,000	17
38	Change in sleeping habits	16
39	Change in number of family get-togethers	15
40	Change in eating habits	15
41	Vacation	14
42	Christmas	13
43	Minor violations of the law	11

Total ____

Here's how to interpret your score. Life change units are points assigned to various experiences. If your score is 300 or higher, you are at high risk for developing a health problem. If your score is between 150 and 300, you have a 50–50 chance of experiencing a serious health change within two years. If your score is below 150, you have a 1 in 3 chance of serious health change.

Reprint from *Journal of Psychosomatic Research*. 11:213. Holmes, T.H., and Rahe, R.H., The social readjustment rating scale, 1967. With permission from Elsevier.

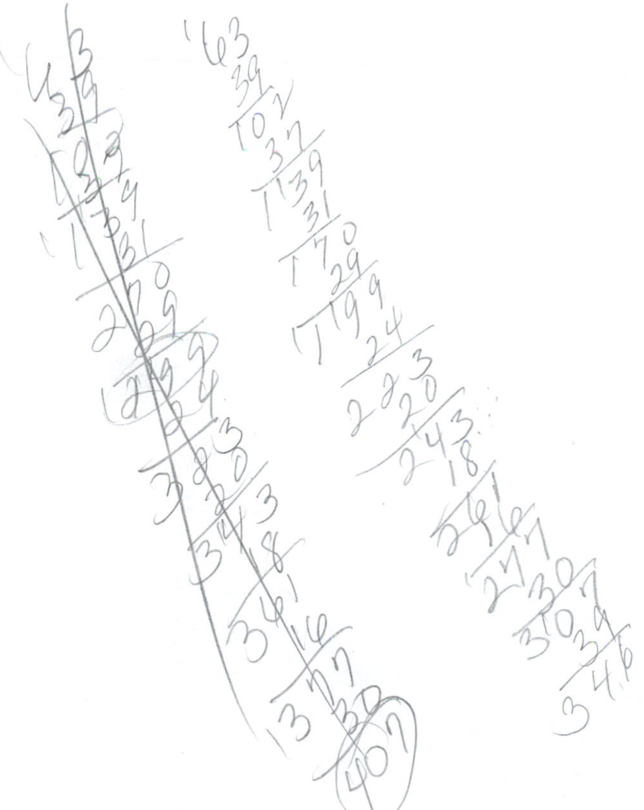

Name: ______________________________ Date: __________

ASSESS YOURSELF 4-2

Student Stress Scale

The Student Stress Scale represents an adaptation of Holmes and Rahe's Life Event Scale. It has been modified to apply to college-age adults and should be considered a rough indication of stress levels and health consequences for teaching purposes.

In the Student Stress Scale, each event, such as beginning or ending school, is given a score that represents the amount of readjustment a person has to make in life as a result of the change. In some studies, people with serious illnesses have been found to have high scores on similar scales.

To determine your stress score add the number of points corresponding to the events you have experienced in the last twelve months.

	Event		Points
1.	Death of a close family member	____	100
2.	Death of a close friend	____	73
3.	Divorce between parents	____	65
4.	Jail term	____	63
5.	Major personal injury or illness	____	63
6.	Marriage	____	58
7.	Firing from a job	____	50
8.	Failure of an important course	____	47
9.	Change in health of a family member	____	45
10.	Pregnancy	____	45
11.	Sex problems	____	44
12.	Serious argument with close friend	____	40
13.	Change in financial status	____	39
14.	Change of major	____	39
15.	Trouble with parents	____	39
16.	New girlfriend or boyfriend	____	37
17.	Increase in workload at school	____	37
18.	Outstanding personal achievement	____	36
19.	First quarter/semester in college	____	36
20.	Change in living conditions	____	31
21.	Serious argument with an instructor	____	30
22.	Lower grades than expected	____	29
23.	Change in sleeping habits	____	29
24.	Change in social activities	____	29
25.	Change in eating habits	____	28
26.	Chronic car trouble	____	26
27.	Change in the number of family get-togethers	____	26
28.	Too many missed classes	____	25
29.	Change of college	____	24
30.	Dropping of more than one class	____	23
31.	Minor traffic violations	____	20

Total ____

ASSESS YOURSELF 4-2 (cont'd)

Here's how to interpret your score. If your score is 300 or higher, you are at high risk for developing a health problem. If your score is between 150 and 300, you have a 50–50 chance of experiencing a serious health change within two years. If your score is below 150, you have a 1 in 3 chance of serious health change.

The following can help you reduce your risk:

- Watch for early signs of stress such as stomachaches and compulsive overeating.
- Avoid negative thinking.
- Arm your body against stress by eating nutritiously and exercising regularly.
- Practice a relaxation technique regularly.
- Turn to friends and relatives for support when you need it.

From Holmes, T.H., and R.H. Rahe, 1967. The social readjustment rating scale. *Journal of Psychosomatic Research,* 11, p. 213.

Name: ______________________________ Date: __________

Assess Yourself 4-3

Hassles/Uplifts Inventory

Directions: On the following pages, circle the events that have affected you in the last month. (This is not a complete listing.) Then look at the numbers to the right of the items you circled. Indicate by circling a 1, 2, or 3 how often each of the circled events occurred in the last month. If an event did not occur in the last month, do not circle it.

	How Often		
Uplifts	**Somewhat Often**	**Moderately Often**	**Extremely Often**
Getting enough sleep	1	2	3
Practicing your hobby	1	2	3
Being lucky	1	2	3
Saving money	1	2	3
Enjoying nature	1	2	3
Liking fellow workers	1	2	3
Not working (on vacation, laid off, etc.)	1	2	3
Gossiping; "shooting the bull"	1	2	3
Having successful financial dealings	1	2	3
Being rested	1	2	3
Feeling healthy	1	2	3
Finding something presumed lost	1	2	3
Recovering from illness	1	2	3
Staying or getting in good physical shape	1	2	3
Being with children	1	2	3
"Pulling something off"; getting away with something	1	2	3
Visiting, phoning, or writing someone	1	2	3
Relating well with your spouse or lover	1	2	3
Completing a task	1	2	3
Giving a compliment	1	2	3
Hassles			
Not enough money for food	1	2	3
Too many interruptions	1	2	3
Unexpected company	1	2	3
Too much time on hands	1	2	3
Having to wait	1	2	3
Concerns about accidents	1	2	3
Being lonely	1	2	3
Not enough money for health care	1	2	3
Fear of confrontation	1	2	3
Financial insecurity	1	2	3
Silly practical mistakes	1	2	3
Inability to express yourself	1	2	3

ASSESS YOURSELF 4-3 (cont'd)

HASSLES	Severity: Somewhat Severe	Moderately Severe	Extremely Severe
Physical illness	1	2	3
Side effects of medication	1	2	3
Concerns about medical treatment	1	2	3
Concerns about physical appearance	1	2	3
Fear of rejection	1	2	3
Difficulties with getting pregnant	1	2	3
Sexual problems that result from physical problems	1	2	3
Sexual problems other than those resulting from physical problems	1	2	3
Concerns about health in general	1	2	3

Scoring: Tally your scores for both the hassles and uplifts scales. There is no absolute cutoff score for either hassles or uplifts that you can use in evaluating your risk for stress-related illness. In general, the higher your hassles score, the greater your risk for stress-related disorders. The higher your uplift score, the greater your ability to cancel out the negative effects of hassles. Both scales should be taken and evaluated together.

Name: ______________________ Date: __________

Assess Yourself 4-4

Spirituality and Faith Assessment

1. Define spirituality and faith in your own words.

____

____

____

2. List three things in which you have faith.

____

____

____

3. Explain how this faith is related to your spirituality.

____

____

____

4. How does your spirituality and faith (or lack of them) affect your day-to-day stress?

____

____

____

Name: ____________________ Date: __________

ASSESS YOURSELF 4-5

Social Support Table

1. Draw a picture of a large table.

2. Place any number of chairs at the table. Each chair represents a person in your social support system.

3. Decide who sits where and why.

4. For each person in your support system, answer the following questions:
   - What type of support do I need from this person?
   - What type of support do I get from this person?
   - What type of support would I never ask for from this person?

5. On a scale of 1 to 10, rate the quality of support you get from your social support system.

6. What do I give up in return for this support?

7. Is it worth it? (If yes, why?)

8. If you could add one more chair, what type of support would you like to receive from the person who would occupy it?

CHAPTER

5

THE PHYSICAL BASIS OF STRESS

OUTLINE

OBJECTIVES

By the end of the chapter students will:

- Describe the basic functions of the major body systems involved in the stress response.
- List and describe functions of the four parts of the brain most directly related to the stress response.
- List and describe the three different stress pathways.
- Give an example of how sensory and motor brain areas work in initiating the fight-or-flight stress response.
- Trace the course of neural impulses through the central and peripheral nervous systems as they respond to a stressor.
- Compare and contrast the SAM and HPAC neural stress axes.
- Compare and contrast the role of neural impulses and circulating hormones during the alarm and resistance phases of the General Adaptation Syndrome.
- Define homeostasis and its relationship to the stress response.
- Describe how the sympathetic and parasympathetic nervous systems are involved in the stress response.
- Using a personal example, analyze the interplay between the cerebral cortex and the limbic system in the resistance phase of the stress response.
- Compare and contrast the role of the endocrine system in acute and chronic stress responses.
- Describe Selye's General Adaptation Syndrome.
- Critically analyze Selye's concepts of nonspecificity and eustress/distress.

Have you ever felt your mouth and throat dry up in the middle of addressing a large audience? How about having butterflies in your stomach as you waited to meet your girl/boyfriend's parents? Did you ever break out in a cold sweat as you heard the high-pitched whine of the dentist's drill as you sat in the chair waiting to get your cavity filled? Have you ever felt the heart-pounding exhilaration of psyching yourself up at the start of a race or some other athletic competition?

Most of us have felt these and other physical manifestations of the stress response as we placed ourselves in similar stressful and challenging situations. In this chapter we will examine the dramatic, observable physiological manifestations of the "fight-or-flight" acute stress response as well as the other subtle, nonobservable aspects of chronic stress.

Another term often used to describe an **acute stress response** is the *fight-or-flight response* that we mentioned in chapter 1. An acute stress response is a short-duration but high intensity response. The duration and intensity are determined by the seriousness of the threat that triggers it. For example, imagine you are driving down the highway in heavy traffic while moving at 65 miles per hour. Without any advanced notice someone cuts directly in front of you. This is an immediate, high-level threat to your well-being. If you do not react immediately, there is a good chance you will have a serious accident that could kill you. In response to this short-term, high-level threat, your brain triggers an acute stress response.

A **chronic stress response** is often referred to as an adaptive response because the initial threat either never was life-threatening or very intense to begin with or because it is of long duration and your body has adapted to it and is now in the resistance phase of the stress response. For example, imagine you are sharing an apartment with four other roommates. You get along great with three of them but the fourth just rubs you the wrong way. Initially, you got very angry whenever you were in the same room with this roommate. After a while, however, your body adapted to the presence of this threat (the roommate) and switched to a lower-level, less intense chronic response. Most of the things going on in your body during this lower intensity, chronic response (slightly increased blood pressure, production of stress hormones, etc.) occur without you being aware of them.

We begin our journey with an examination of the brain and what happens once it perceives a potential stressor as threatening. We will study the stress messages sent by the brain to the major body systems and examine in detail the direct effects on the body of the activation of these systems. We will see how the stress response changes in relation to whether the stressor is acute and life-threatening or chronic and less intense.

Although this chapter is devoted to physiology, in actuality we cannot separate the **psychological** from the **physiological;** all our thoughts, feelings, and beliefs have physiological components. A key to understanding this is to remember that the interpretation of our thoughts and feelings is influenced by our overall physical health and the condition of our body parts and systems. Conversely, all the bodily sensations we experience are interpreted by the brain and are subject to our mental health and the thoughts and feelings we have about those sensations.[4]

KEY TO UNDERSTANDING

Our thoughts and feelings are influenced by our physiological well-being. Conversely, our physical health is influenced by our thoughts and feelings about it.

OVERVIEW OF MAJOR BODY SYSTEMS INVOLVED IN THE STRESS RESPONSE

There are several ways to describe the systems of the human body. Most anatomy and physiology books describe the body by starting at the chemical level and working up through the increasingly complex levels of cells, organs, and then systems. Body systems are grouped and defined according to their functions. The five major body systems are (1) communication, control, and integration (nervous system, endocrine system, etc.), (2) transportation and defense (cardiovascular system, immune system, etc.), (3) support and movement (skin, skeletal system, muscular system, etc.), (4) respiration, nutrition, and excretion (respiratory system, digestive system, urinary system, etc.), and (5) reproduction and development (reproductive system). The last system doesn't exert a major impact on the stress response, and so it will not be discussed in this section of the text. To better understand the stress response, a brief overview of the nervous, endocrine, cardiovascular, immune, muscular, and digestive systems is necessary.[20,22,23]

acute stress response a short-duration but high intensity response triggered by a highly threatening (often life-threatening) stressor that is often referred to as the *fight or flight response*

chronic stress response an adaptive response to a non-life-threatening or low-threat stressor associated with the resistance phase of Selye's General Adaptation Syndrome

psychological pertaining to functions of the human mind; includes thoughts, feelings, memories, sensations, and associations

physiological pertaining to the functions of the human body and the body systems

Communication, Control, and Integration

The primary functions of the nervous and endocrine systems as they relate to stress revolve around receiving and sending information and initiating and ending physiological responses to perceived threats. For example, imagine you are in class and the professor announces a pop quiz (perceived threat). Your heart begins to race, your breathing quickens and deepens, and you begin to sweat (initial stress responses). As the professor starts to smile and says, "I was only kidding. I just wanted to see if you folks were awake this morning," the threat is removed (no pop quiz) and your heart rate, breathing, and sweating return to normal (ending of stress response).

The Nervous System

The nervous system is composed of two subsystems: the **central nervous system** and the **peripheral nervous system** (fig. 5-1). The central nervous system contains the brain and spinal cord. The peripheral nervous system consists of all other nerves emanating from the spinal cord and extending out to all tissues, muscles, and organs. The nervous system is responsible for communication, receiving and sending messages to and from the brain and to and from the rest of the body. Incoming messages can involve any of the five senses. Messages can also originate from within the brain in the form of memories and past associations. Once incoming messages are received, the brain interprets them and decides on a course of action in response to the messages. Outgoing messages travel from the brain through the central and peripheral nervous systems. The nervous system sends messages through the nerves via electrical impulses created by chemical reactions between nerve cells. The nervous system interacts with all other body systems during the stress response. Once the brain perceives stimuli as threatening, messages are sent through the nervous system and the stress response begins.[20,22,23]

Human growth and development are affected by both the endocrine and immune systems.

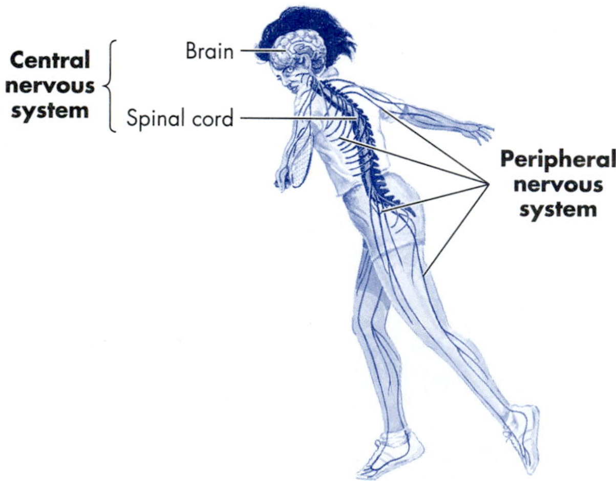

Figure 5-1

The nervous system is responsible for communication; receiving and sending messages to and from the brain to the rest of the body.

The Endocrine System

The nervous system cannot continue to send stress messages without help. Nerve pathways, like telephone lines, can overload and interrupt the flow of information to the body. To prevent this, the endocrine system gets involved. The endocrine system is made up of the pituitary gland, thyroid gland, parathyroids, adrenal glands, pancreas, thymus gland, pineal gland, and the testes in men and the ovaries in women. These glands produce and secrete various **hormones:** powerful chemicals that control a host of bodily functions ranging from growth to the metabolic rate. Endocrine glands secrete their hormones directly into the bloodstream, where they travel to meet specific targeted cells, tissues, and organs. This is why the effects of

central nervous system the part of the nervous system consisting of the brain and the spinal cord

peripheral nervous system all other nerves emanating from the spinal cord

hormones powerful chemicals that control a host of bodily functions ranging from growth to the metabolic rate hormones can be very dramatic, exerting an almost instantaneous effect on their targets as each heartbeat sends them coursing through the bloodstream. Endocrine glands can be activated electrically through direct nerve transmission from the brain and nervous system. Hormones secreted directly by the brain into the circulation can also activate endocrine glands chemically.[20,22,23] The endocrine system plays a major role in the stress response, releasing the key adrenal hormones adrenaline, noradrenaline, and cortisol. These and other hormones play major roles in mobilizing energy to combat stressors.

Transportation and Defense

The primary function of the cardiovascular system as it relates to stress is to move large quantities of blood to the parts of the body that need it the most by dilating blood vessels that service these areas. While this is occurring, the cardiovascular system restricts the flow of blood to less critical body parts by constricting blood vessels servicing these areas. The immune system responds to stress initially by mobilizing the spleen to produce extra blood in response to perceived threats that could result in injury and blood loss. The immune system responds to chronic stress in a negative way as the stress response creates changes in the delicate balance of immune components necessary for maximum immune system functioning.

The Cardiovascular (Circulatory) System

The cardiovascular, or circulatory, system can best be described as a closed system consisting of a pump, tubes, and fluid (fig. 5-2). The pump (heart) operates automatically at a predetermined rate, providing vital nutrients and removing waste products in the fluid (blood) as it moves under pressure through an interconnected network of flexible tubes (blood vessels) with different diameters. The role of the cardiovascular system is to supply the body with oxygen-rich blood and nutrients and remove waste products from the tissues and cells. It does this in conjunction with the lungs, which provide fresh oxygen to the blood and remove carbon dioxide waste. During the stress response, the heart and lungs work together to move huge quantities of oxygen and nutrients throughout the body to mobilize energy to combat stressors.[20,22,23]

The health of the cardiovascular system is vital during a stress response and is based on three factors. The first factor is the heart's ability to receive nourishment through its coronary arteries. For the heart to pump efficiently, it must receive nourishment from the blood through its own network of blood vessels. Although the heart's job is to pump blood to all body parts, it does not draw its own nutrients from this process. It is served by its own blood vessels, which must remain open and flexible, delivering an adequate supply of blood regardless of the demands made on the heart muscle. The second factor is the heart's ability to maintain a steady, rhythmic beat despite the varying demands made on it. Third, for a person to have a healthy heart, the blood vessels must be able to facilitate the passage of nutrient-rich blood by remaining open and flexible and maintaining normal pressure. The veins, venules, arteries, and arterioles facilitate the movement of blood by expanding and contracting in response to the heart's beating action. Blood vessels that are clear and pliable allow maximum blood flow under minimum pressure, a state that provides the optimal supply of nutrients and the efficient removal of waste without exerting undue wear and tear on the system. Stress affects all three components of the cardiovascular system: the heart, the blood vessels, and the blood itself.[20,22,23] The stress response increases heart rate and blood pressure. It also floods the blood with excess salts, sugars, and fats, dramatically altering blood biochemistry.

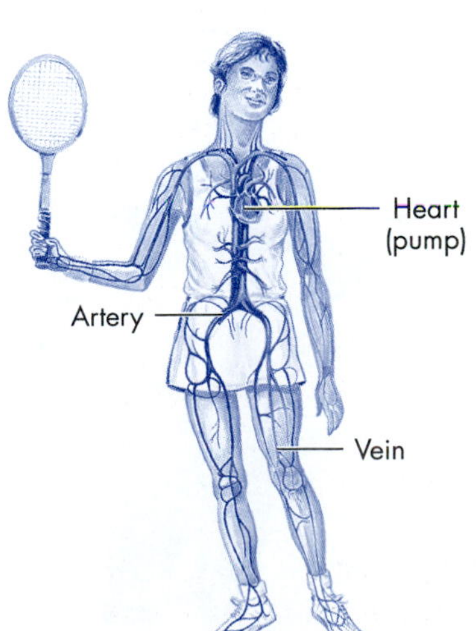

Figure 5-2

The circulatory system's veins, venules, arteries, and arterioles facilitate the movement of blood by expanding and contracting in response to the heart's beating action.

The Immune System

The immune system is a part of the body's defenses against illness and disease originating from factors and conditions both outside (exogenous) and inside (endogenous) the body. The immune system has five primary responsibilities:

1. Recognizing foreign substances that do not belong in the body, such as germs, allergens, and irritants.
2. Defending you by attacking foreign invaders.
3. Protecting you from reinfection from the same invaders in the future.
4. Performing surveillance for and destroying mutant cells before they can become cancerous.
5. Resisting recurrences of chronic infections caused by untreatable conditions such as viral infections.

The immune system is really a functional system rather than an organ system. This functional system is composed of various organs that have other functions but also produce a variety of immune system components.

Immune system organs are generally referred to as lymphoid organs because they are involved with the growth and utilization of lymphocytes, which are white blood cells that play a major role in immune system functioning. The lymph system is a major component of the immune system, with trillions of individual immune cells produced in bone marrow, the thymus, the lymph nodes, the spleen, the tonsils, the appendix, and other lymphatic tissue in the small intestine called Peyer's patches. As we will see in chapter 6, chronic stress can dramatically alter the delicate balance between the immune system components, resulting in increased susceptibility to illness.[20,22,23]

Support and Movement

The primary function of the muscular system as it relates to stress is to move us out of harm's way when we are confronted by threatening stressors. This positive response to life-threatening stressors has probably saved all of our lives at least once. If it were not for our muscular system's ability to support and move us out of danger in an instant, most of us would not be here today. Imagine all of the times when you were driving, skiing, walking, crossing a street, skateboarding, or participating in any event where you had to move out of harm's way in an instant or be killed. The muscular system responds to stress in a negative way by creating muscle tension that can lead to painful conditions like tension headaches if not intentionally released periodically during the day.

The Muscular System

The muscular system consists of three types of muscles: skeletal, smooth, and cardiac. Skeletal muscles attach to bones and provide movement through contraction and relaxation (fig. 5-3). The skeletal muscles are responsible for getting us moving during the fight-or-flight response in the presence of a stressor. The skin, another component of "support," helps us regulate temperature during vigorous skeletal muscle activity through the process of sweating. Smooth muscle tissue is distributed widely throughout the body. Visceral smooth muscle occurs in sheets and includes tissue of the digestive, reproductive, and urinary tracts. Cardiac muscle tissue is found only in the heart. Cardiac muscle tissue is responsible for the contractions and relaxation necessary for normal heartbeat. All three types of muscle tissue are influenced by nerve transmission and circulating hormones. Chronic stress can affect the functioning of all three types of muscle tissue, resulting in a variety of problems ranging from low back pain and tension headaches to anginalike pain in the heart.[20,22,23] (See Stress Buster Tips: "Physical Activity and Stress.")

Respiration, Nutrition, and Excretion

The primary functions of the respiratory and digestive systems as they relate to stress revolve around the rapid mobilization of energy by combining oxygen and other nutrients in the bloodstream. During the stress response the depth and rate of breathing increases bringing an increase in the amount of oxygen entering the bloodstream. This is combined with sugar (glucose) already circulating in the blood and extra amounts released from storage in the skeletal muscles. While this energy mobilization is occurring, digestion is shut down in an attempt to conserve energy and not waste it on a process that will not immediately get us out of harm's way.

Gas Exchange: The Respiratory System

The respiratory system interacts with the cardiovascular system to bring oxygen to the cells and remove waste gases. As deoxygenated blood is moved through the lungs, an exchange occurs (fig. 5-4). The lungs add oxygen to the blood and remove waste carbon dioxide gas. During the stress response, the depth and pace of breathing increase as the lungs work overtime to supply energy-producing oxygen to the cells.[20,22,23]

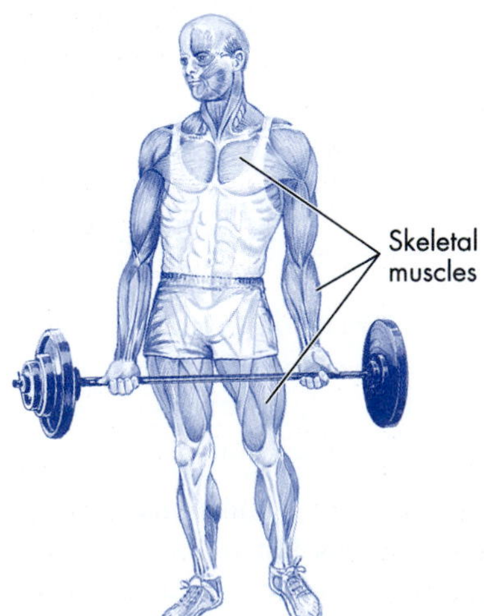

Figure 5-3
Skeletal muscles attach to bones and assist in movement of the body.

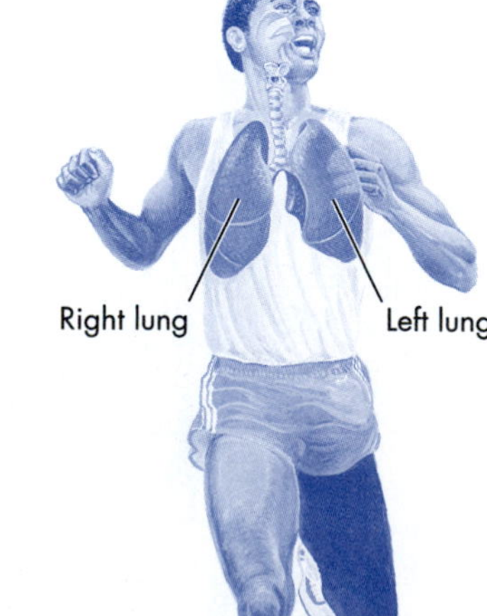

Figure 5-4
The respiratory system interacts with the cardiovascular system to bring oxygen-rich blood to the tissues and cells and to remove waste gases.

Stress Buster Tips

Physical Activity and Stress

As you can see, the stress response influences every major body system. One way to offset the negative effects of the stress response is to keep your body as physically fit as possible. This will help you minimize the wear and tear exerted by the stress response. It will also help provide an outlet for the tension and stress hormones produced during the stress response.

The Surgeon General recommends that every American get at least thirty minutes of moderate, continuous physical activity daily to promote health and prevent disease. Get your exercise by doing something *you* enjoy rather than following someone else's plan.

Nutrition and Excretion: The Digestive System

The digestive system consists of the digestive tube, which extends from the mouth to the anus, and the accessory organs and glands, which aid in the processing of food and waste. The organs of the digestive system are the mouth, pharynx, salivary glands, esophagus, liver, stomach, pancreas, gallbladder, appendix, small intestine, large intestine, rectum, and anus (fig. 5-5). The digestive system is responsible for the breakdown of food, separation of liquids and solids, assimilation of nutrients, and removal of the solid and liquid waste products left over from this process. The digestive process is facilitated by contractions of the smooth muscle tissue of the component parts of this system and the secretion of saliva, mucus, acids, and enzymes. The nervous and endocrine systems are capable of influencing the speed and nature of the digestive process through nerve transmissions and hormonal release into the circulation. The stress response wreaks havoc on digestion as changes in smooth muscle contractions, mucus secretion, and a host of other effects alter the normal pace and process of breaking down food and assimilating its nutrients.[20,22,23]

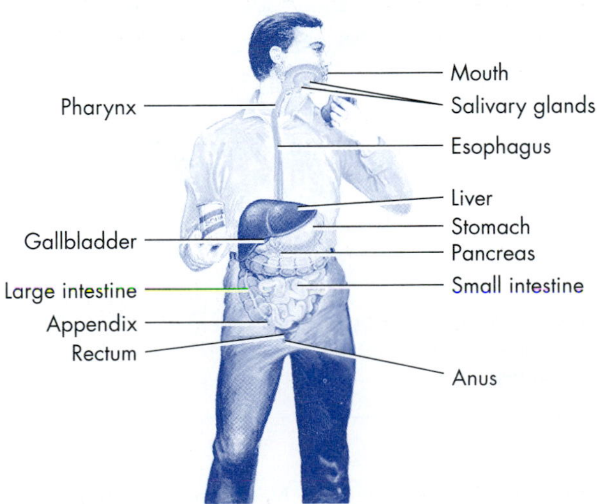

Figure 5-5
The digestive system is responsible for the breakdown of food, separation of liquids and solids, assimilation of nutrients, and removal of solid and liquid waste products.

Fight-or-Flight: An Alarm Reaction

A prehistoric man was crouching behind some brush at the edge of the savanna. Hunting a small deerlike creature, he was quietly stalking his prey. As he peered out from his hiding place, a large saber-toothed tiger was staring directly into his face.

Instantly the alarm was sounded. His eyes, picking up the image, sent to his brain a picture that was instantly deciphered as a clear and imminent threat. Instantaneously, messages were sent to various parts of his body to mobilize the energy needed to either stand and fight or run.

Nerves began to fire furiously; their targets were the muscles, organs, and glands involved in supplying the energy and force needed to combat this threat. Some of these nerve transmissions stimulated glands that dumped hormones into his blood, intensifying this state of readiness.

In a split second he was on his feet. Wild-eyed, nostrils flared, and muscles coiled like springs, he summoned all his courage and thrust into the belly of the beast the sharpened stick he used as a spear. With his heart pounding in his chest, his lungs gasping, and his muscles burning, he thrust his spear again and again until the tiger lay dying. Stopping only when he was sure he was out of harm's way, the man fell back onto the ground, exhausted but alive.

As a species for more than 2 million years, we have relied on the fight-or-flight stress response to help us get out of harm's way. Indeed, many of us would not be here were it not for our ability to mobilize such an intense, life-saving response to acute, short-term threats to our well-being. As we discussed in chapter 1, the fight-or-flight response is the net result of the alarm phase of Selye's General Adaptation Syndrome (GAS).[21] It is our first response to acute, life-threatening stressors such as Maya's (see the Stress in Our World Box 5-1). The alarm phase is triggered by direct nerve stimulation of targeted glands, organs, and muscles. The fight-or-flight response shuts down after the stressor is removed or is dealt with effectively.

When confronted with chronic, non-life-threatening stressors, fight-or-flight changes into a less intense response that makes up the resistance phase of GAS. If the stressor is not removed or coped with successfully, resistance eventually ends in the final phase of GAS, exhaustion. A key to understanding the stress response is to view it as a series of phases that continue to exact a toll

STRESS IN OUR WORLD 5-1

Maya: Fight-or-Flight in the Modern World

Two million years after our prehistoric man came face to face with his saber-toothed tiger, Maya puts on her left blinker and pulls onto the entrance ramp to the Los Angeles freeway. Not very far from the spot where her long-lost ancestor defeated the saber-toothed tiger, Maya, late for work, will have saber-toothed tigers of a different kind to deal with today on the job. As she slowly enters the traffic flow, mulling over how she will explain her lateness, out of the corner of her eye she catches an eighteen-wheel tractor-trailer bearing down on her. All at once the truck blasts its horn and jams on its brakes, causing the sickening combination of the smell of burning rubber and the screeching of brakes and skidding tires.

In a flash Maya's eyes, ears, and nose send images to her brain that are instantly deciphered as a clear and imminent threat. Her brain sounds the same alarm that saved her ancestor 2 million years ago. Nerves begin to fire furiously, sending muscles, glands, and organs into action. The mobilization is enhanced by hormones stimulated by nerve transmissions and by chemicals secreted from her brain.

Maya grips the steering wheel tightly, hits the gas, downshifts, and spins the wheel, throwing her small car off the road and careening down an embankment. Wild-eyed, nostrils flared, heart pumping, lungs and muscles aching, she holds the car on line until she comes crashing to a halt at the bottom. She slumps over the wheel of her car, exhausted but alive.

(1) Maya's brain senses danger and sounds the alarm. (2) Her body quickly responds by producing energy. (3) Fueled by the stress response, she flees the onrushing truck and seeks safety. (4) Safe at the bottom of the embankment, the threat removed, Maya's body begins to return to normal.

on our bodies until we remove or cope with the stressor that initiates it.

Everly and Lating[8] in a recent analysis of the stress response use the terms *axes* and *pathways* to describe the routes traveled through the body after a potential stressor is appraised as threatening. Neural and hormonal messages travel along each pathway to their targets. Those authors describe three different pathways: (1) the neural axis, (2) the neuroendocrine axis (also known as the sympathoadrenomedullary system, or SAM), and (3) the

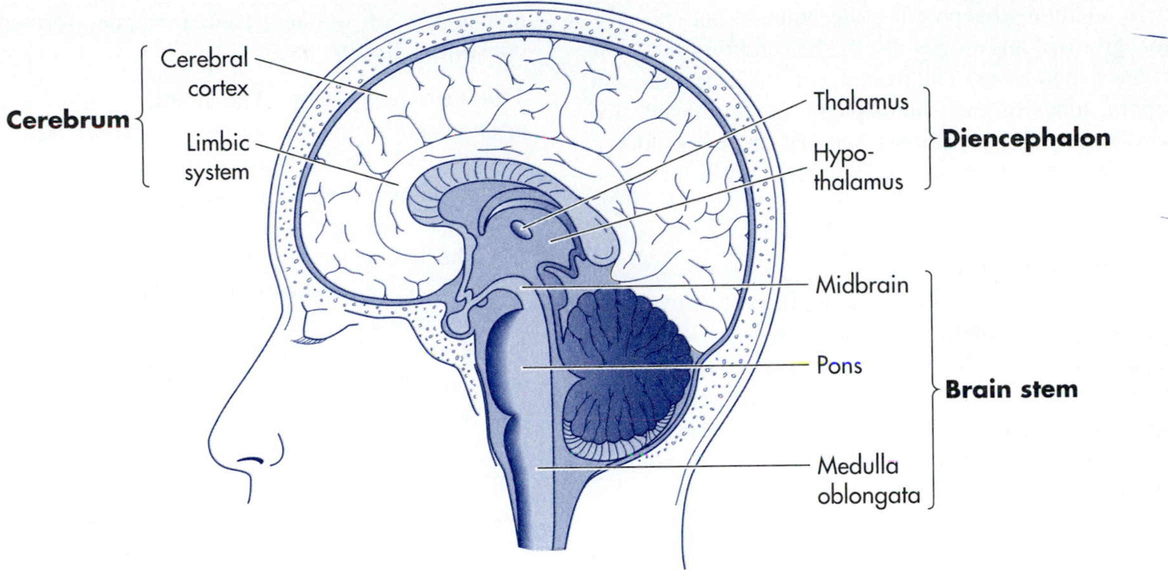

Figure 5-6
For the purpose of illustrating the stress response, we can divide the brain into three components: the cerebrum, the diencephalon, and the brain stem.

> **KEY TO UNDERSTANDING**
>
> The stress response can be viewed as a series of phases that continue to exact a toll on our bodies until we remove or cope with the source of stress.

endocrine axis (which contains the hypothalamic-pituitary-adrenal-cortical system, or HPAC). This newer "pathway" conceptualization of the stress response builds on the foundation laid out by Selye. You will see how the axes expand on Selye's earlier findings.[21]

The Neural Axis

The neural axis revolves around activity located in the human nervous system. As we mentioned earlier in this chapter, the human nervous system is composed of the central nervous system, which is made up of the brain and spinal cord, and the peripheral nervous system, which contains all the other nerve pathways. These two systems interact constantly during the stress response, receiving and interpreting information about potential threats and sending the alarm out throughout the body through electrical messages (nerve transmissions) sent out over an elaborate network of nerves. The same network is used to stop the stress response once the brain no longer perceives that the body is at risk.

The Brain

The fight-or-flight response originates with the brain's perception of threat. The average human brain weighs about 3.5 lb (1.58 kg) and is pinkish gray, wrinkled like a walnut, and about the size of two fists. Although there are several ways to divide the brain, for our purposes we will focus on the parts of the brain most directly related to the stress response: (1) the cerebrum, (2) the diencephalon, and (3) the brain stem (fig. 5-6). We will discuss how each part is involved in the fight-or-flight response.

The Cerebrum The entire surface of the brain is very irregular, with ridges (gyri), shallow grooves (sulci), and deep grooves (fissures) dividing it into sections. The deepest groove, the longitudinal fissure, divides the cerebrum into its two halves (hemispheres). The cerebral hemispheres form the outermost part of the brain. Each hemisphere is concerned with the **motor, sensory,** and **associational** functions of the opposite side of the body. The left hemisphere controls the right side of the body, and the right hemisphere is responsible for the left side of the body.

When Maya sensed imminent danger from the approaching tractor-trailer, motor activity on the right side of her body (removing her right hand from the steering wheel, downshifting, removing her right foot from the gas and applying it to the brake pedal, etc.) was directed by messages from the left hemisphere of her brain.

> **motor** relating to nerve impulses going out to muscles
>
> **sensory** relating to nerve messages coming into the brain
>
> **associational** connecting together individual sensory inputs

In addition to separating the brain in half, the fissures, grooves, and ridges divide the cerebrum into four sections called lobes. The frontal, parietal, occipital, and temporal lobes of each hemisphere are responsible for controlling a variety of motor, sensory, and associational brain functions which are directly involved in the stress response.

The Cerebral Cortex The entire cerebrum is covered by the cerebral cortex, a thin (1/8 in [.03 cm]) convoluted mass of neural cell bodies that makes up about 40 percent of total brain mass. This "executive suite" of the nervous system enables us to perceive, communicate, remember, understand, appreciate, and control voluntary movement. The cerebral cortex is the seat of consciousness and conscious behavior.[22,23]

The primary **motor area,** located in the posterior part of the frontal lobe of the cerebral cortex, controls the gross motor activity of the skeletal muscles. This is the part of the brain that allowed Maya to control her car and get out of harm's way. Messages from this part of her brain triggered the muscular activity she needed to focus her eyes, steer, brake, downshift, decelerate, and get to safety.

The conscious awareness of sensations, the **sensory areas** of the cortex (sight, sound, smell, taste, and touch), is controlled by the parietal, occipital, and temporal lobes of the cerebral cortex identified in fig. 5-6.

These are the parts of Maya's brain that transmitted the messages indicating the danger posed by the rapidly approaching tractor-trailer. Although it's hard to distinguish which messages arrived first, several sensations signaled imminent harm.

In one split-second glance into her left rearview mirror, Maya's visual cortex and association areas picked up the rapidly approaching image of the skidding, smoking truck; the visual cortex actually saw the image of the truck, and the association area determined what it was.

Simultaneously, as Maya saw the truck skidding, she heard the blast of its horn and the screech of its skidding tires. Those incoming sounds were received and interpreted as dangerous by the primary auditory cortex and auditory associational areas, respectively.

She's not sure when she first became aware of it, but Maya recalls almost becoming nauseated by the sickening smell of the burning rubber caused by the truck's tires trying to grip the pavement and stop. The olfactory cortex in the middle of the temporal lobes analyzed and interpreted the incoming smells as burning rubber.

Although the visual, auditory, and olfactory sensations involved in Maya's stressful interlude with the tractor-trailer entered as distinct, separate entities, they were quickly assimilated, sorted out, deciphered, and refitted together as a danger signal. This interplay relied on Maya's stored memories of past experiences that influenced her assessment of the present incoming stimuli. The combination of interpretation of new information and review of similar past experiences formed a new construct—I'm in danger.

The Limbic System The limbic system, a complex arrangement of nervous tissue, is also referred to as our "emotional brain." It links physical reactions to sensory and emotional stimuli. It encircles the upper part of the brain stem (see fig. 5-6).

The limbic system links the emotional brain with the thinking, rational brain (cerebral cortex). In this way the limbic system establishes a relationship between our thoughts and our feelings. Sometimes this relationship is clear-cut and appropriate as our emotions accurately reflect our knowledge about something. It was quite clear to Maya that the fear she was feeling as a result of the close call with the tractor-trailer was accurate and justified. At other times the intellect may inhibit us from expressing our emotions or our emotions may keep us from thinking clearly. Either of these situations can result in the triggering and perpetuating of a stress response.

The Diencephalon The diencephalon, which forms the central core of the brain, contains the **thalamus** and **hypothalamus** (see fig. 5-6). This area plays a critical role in the continuation of the stress response that begins with the interpretation of an incoming stimulus as potentially threatening.

The thalamus is a hidden region of the brain best described as the relay center for all inputs to the cerebral cortex. The sensations that informed Maya of impending danger all converged in her thalamus. The thalamus also plays a key role in mediating all sensations, motor activities, cortical arousal, and memory. The thalamus is truly the gateway to the cerebral cortex.[22,23]

If the thalamus is the gateway to the cerebral cortex, the hypothalamus, located directly underneath it and at the end of the brain stem, is the actual gate. Despite its small size, the hypothalamus exerts a tremendous amount of control over body functioning. It works in consort with the nervous and endocrine systems, sending its messages via

motor area the part of the cerebral cortex that controls nerve impulses going out to muscles

sensory area the part of the cerebral cortex that controls nerve messages coming into the brain from the senses

thalamus a hidden region of the brain often referred to as the gateway to the cerebral cortex, which serves as a relay center for all inputs to the cerebral cortex; plays a key role in mediating all sensations, motor activities, cortical arousal, and memory

hypothalamus an area of the brain located directly underneath the thalamus at the end of the brain stem that receives messages from the thalamus and works in consort with the nervous and endocrine systems, sending nerve and hormonal messages to the tissues, organs, and body systems involved in the stress response

KEY TO UNDERSTANDING

The stress response uses a tremendous amount of energy to adjust to demands made on our bodies by stressors.

direct nerve transmission and chemicals called **hormonal releasing factors.** These nervous and endocrine systems provide two of the main pathways of the fight-or-flight response.

You may remember from chapter 1 that Cannon hypothesized that our bodies continually adjust to demands from the environment to maintain a steady, homeostatic state in which metabolic processes function smoothly. Goldstein,[10] in a description of neurotransmitters and stress, explains that there actually are several homeostatic mechanisms that function similarly to thermostats. He refers to these mechanisms as **homeostats** and explains how they employ feedback from different body systems to regulate homeostasis throughout the body.

Normal, everyday occurrences such as standing up and digesting a meal throw the body out of equilibrium and force adjustments in a variety of systems that control homeostasis. Extreme threats to our well-being, such as Maya's impending crash, throw our bodies out of this steady state and force us to readjust rapidly. A key to understanding the stress response is to view it as a very energy-intensive adjustment to demands placed on the body. To meet the demands of stressors, the body must rapidly mobilize and use a tremendous amount of energy. These adjustments are mediated by the electrical and chemical messages sent by the hypothalamus.

When Maya perceived the tractor-trailer bearing down on her, her hypothalamus instantaneously sent direct nerve transmissions and hormonal releasing factors to the following targets involved in her fight-or-flight response: her heart, blood vessels, lungs, skeletal muscles, liver, spleen, salivary glands, sweat glands, and smooth muscles. Once stimulated, these target muscles, glands, and organs were responsible for saving Maya's life.

Her heart, responding to electrical and chemical stimulation, increased the volume of blood being pumped throughout her body by increasing its rate and pressure. This increased pumping of blood was necessary for supplying the extra oxygen and other fuels she needed in order to act.

Her blood vessels helped in this process. The blood vessels supplying her brain and skeletal muscles dilated, allowing increased blood flow to the areas that would be called on to save her life. Blood vessels to noncritical areas, such as her digestive system, constricted, facilitating the rerouting of the blood to where it was needed most.

Her lungs responded instantly by increasing her rate and depth of breathing. Her airways expanded, allowing maximum intake of air so that vital oxygen could mix with her blood.

Her skeletal muscles, fueled by her oxygen-rich blood and stored blood sugars, contracted to exert maximum force.

Her digestion shut down, and the blood used for that process was diverted. Smooth muscle contractions and salivation, necessary components of digestion, stopped, which is why Maya had a dry, cotton-mouth sensation after her ordeal was over.

Her liver started metabolizing additional sugar for energy. It also began liberating fats and converting them and proteins into usable energy sources to supply the tremendous amount of fuel needed to cope with the stressor.

Her sweat glands, preparing for the tremendous energy expenditure to come, initiated a cooling response by activating increased perspiration.

Maya's kidneys were stimulated to increase water volume and retention. This served to increase blood volume, raise blood pressure, and get more blood to where it was needed. Later this reaction triggered thirst receptors in her brain, causing her to drink to replace her lost fluids.

Finally, Maya's adrenal glands were activated and began to pump out adrenaline and noradrenaline, providing the chemical basis to enhance and sustain her stress response.

The Brain Stem The brain stem, consisting of three regions—the midbrain, pons, and medulla oblongata—produces the autonomic functions necessary for our survival and also serves as the pathway for connections between the higher and lower brain functions.

The reticular formation, also known as the **reticular activating system (RAS),** is a collection of neurons running through the three regions of the brain stem. It is responsible for sending messages between the higher parts of the brain that control thoughts and awareness to the lower parts that are responsible for the activities of organs, muscles, and glands. As is described later in this chapter, these organs, muscles, and glands are capable of activating the stress response as the body mobilizes

hormonal releasing factors chemicals secreted by the hypothalamus that trigger the pituitary to release specific hormones

homeostats thermostat-like mechanisms that regulate a variety of anatomic functions

reticular activating system (RAS) a collection of neurons running through the three regions of the brain stem that is responsible for sending messages between the higher parts of the brain (which control thoughts and awareness) to the lower parts (responsible for the activities of organs, muscles, and glands) tremendous amounts of energy to cope with threats to its well-being. The messages can travel in either direction; they can emanate from conscious thoughts and travel to organs, muscles, and glands, influencing their functions, or they can originate in the organs, muscles, and glands and send messages back to the brain, where this information is interpreted.

The RAS is responsible for both general and specific arousal of the brain. During general arousal the RAS is responsible for maintaining the alertness of the cerebral cortex. During specific arousal the RAS is responsible for magnifying and increasing our awareness of specific stimuli. It allows us to home in or focus on the details of a stimulus as messages are passed back and forth from various parts of the brain. With the help of associations, memories, feelings, and thoughts, we are able to decode and decipher the stimuli.

Because this complex set of neurons is capable of sending such an enormous amount of messages back and forth, the brain needs a filter to screen out unimportant messages. The RAS acts as that screen and disregards more than 90 percent of all familiar, repetitive, or weak sensory stimulation as unimportant while allowing new, unusual, or strong stimuli to penetrate. This helps us focus our attention on important stimuli. This also explains why Maya was oblivious to everything else going on around her as the truck was bearing down. She was no longer aware of the music on the radio, the other cars on the road, or the sun reflecting off her windshield. All her attention was riveted on the truck.

Think about a time when your attention was riveted on something as your brain tried to make it out. Have you ever been camping in the middle of the woods where, in the darkness of night, each new rustle of leaves or snapping twig is frightening until you figure out what they are? How about the creaks and pops that emanate from your basement, attic, or garage and always seem to occur late at night when everyone else is fast asleep? It seems as every fiber of your being is focused on the sounds that your brain furiously works to decipher what they represent.

If the RAS didn't screen out the majority of insignificant stimuli, we would be overwhelmed by overstimulation and in a state of chronic stress activation. The sensory stimulation of the average mall would be sheer madness. Driving in traffic would be impossible. Walking down a crowded city street would be mystifying as we examined each face, car, and passing building. Even sitting in a classroom would be difficult as we scanned the walls, ceilings, and desks.

Close your eyes for a minute and try to recount the composition of the classroom in which this course is being taught. What is on the walls? How many desks are there? How many windows? What color is the paint? What is the type, color, and pattern of the floor covering? Is the ceiling made of tiles, cement, or sheetrock? Most of us don't pay attention to these and many other similar details because they are unimportant or distracting.

As we will discuss in chapter 8, we are stressed because there are too many things going on in our lives. We run from one thing to the next. We are overbooked, overcommited, and pulled in several directions at the same time. When this happens, we are in a chronic state of RAS activation; our minds and bodies are continually aroused and need to slow down and rest.

The Spinal Cord

The 17-inch (43 cm) long, 3/4-inch (1.90 cm) thick, glistening white, ropelike spinal cord can be compared with a fiber optic telephone cable. Both are made of a multitude of threadlike fibers that are capable of sending and receiving a tremendous amount of electrical messages in a split second. The spinal cord is the lifeline between the brain and the rest of the body.

The initial information concerning the oncoming tractor-trailer was passed along as electrical impulses from Maya's brain, through her spinal cord, to her peripheral nervous system, and ultimately to the specific glands, organs, and tissues involved in the stress response.

The Peripheral Nervous System

The forty-three pairs of nerves which constitute the peripheral nervous system are made up of two divisions: the **somatic nervous system** and the **autonomic nervous system.** The somatic nervous system transmits messages that are under our conscious control. It comes into play during a stress response when we are aware that we are being stressed and consciously initiate some action as a result. We will discuss its role in the stress response later in this chapter when we meet Mario, a man with a different kind of stressor than the one Maya experienced. The autonomic nervous system controls functions that are unconscious and go on without our thinking about them. Body processes such as breathing, digestion, and heartbeat are operated by this system and go on without our conscious control.

The autonomic nervous system is the part of the peripheral nervous system that deserves the most attention as far as the stress response is concerned. The autonomic nervous system serves as the pathway for all the electrical messages sent by the hypothalamus to the myriad organs, glands, and tissues involved in maintaining homeostasis or adjusting to the demands of a stressor. The necessary body parts are activated in response to the perception of threat and are deactivated once the stressor is dealt with

somatic nervous system the part of the peripheral nervous system under our voluntary control

autonomic nervous system the part of the peripheral nervous system that is automatic and involuntary

Table 5-1 Effects of the Sympathetic and Parasympathetic Divisions of the Autonomic Nervous System

Target Organ/System	Sympathetic Effects	Parasympathetic Effects
Digestive system	Decreases activity of digestive system and constricts digestive system sphincters (e.g., anal sphincter)	Increases smooth muscle mobility (peristalsis) and amount of secretion by digestive system glands; relaxes sphincters
Liver	Causes glucose to be released to blood	No effect
Lungs	Dilates bronchioles	Constricts bronchioles
Urinary bladder/urethra	Constricts sphincters (prevents voiding)	Relaxes sphincters (allows voiding)
Kidneys	Decreases urine output	No effect
Heart	Increases rate and force of heartbeat	Decreases rate; slows and steadies
Blood vessels	Constrict blood vessels in viscera and skin (dilate those in skeletal muscle and heart); increase blood pressure	No effect on most blood vessels
Glands—salivary, lacrimal	Inhibit; result is dry mouth and dry eyes	Stimulate; increase production of saliva and tears
Eye (iris)	Stimulates dilator muscles; dilates pupils	Stimulates constrictor muscles; constricts pupils
Eye (ciliary muscle)	Inhibits; decreases bulging of lens; prepares for distant vision	Stimulates to increase bulging of lens for close vision
Adrenal medulla	Stimulates medulla cells to secrete epinephrine and norepinephrine	No effect
Sweat glands of skin	Stimulates to produce perspiration	No effect
Arrector pili muscles attached to hair follicles	Stimulate; produce "goosebumps"	No effect
Penis	Causes ejaculation (emission of semen)	Causes erection because of vasodilation
Cellular metabolism	Increases metabolic rate; increases blood sugar levels; stimulates fat breakdown	No effect

KEY TO UNDERSTANDING

Sympathetic nervous system responses can be called stress responses, while parasympathetic responses can be labeled relaxation responses.

or removed. This activation and deactivation is controlled by the two branches of the autonomic nervous system: the **sympathetic** and **parasympathetic** branches of the autonomic nervous system (Table 5-1). A key to understanding these branches is to refer to sympathetic responses as *stress responses,* while parasympathetic responses are referred to as *relaxation responses*.

Goldstein[10] refers to these two branches as the most sensitive, rapidly acting, and powerful of the body's stress systems.

In Maya's case her sympathetic nervous system was responsible for passing along nerve transmissions sent from her hypothalamus in response to the presence of the tractor-trailer bearing down on her. These messages triggered the initiation of her stress response, leading her to swerve her car off the road and down the embankment.

Once her car came to a halt and the threat of the accident was gone, her parasympathetic nervous system took over, initiating responses that began to reverse those set in motion sympathetically. Her heart rate, respiration, and muscle tension began to return to normal; hormone and blood sugar levels began to drop off and get back to their normal ranges.

The Neuroendocrine Axis

The neuroendocrine axis is also known as the sympathoadrenomedullary system because it mobilizes energy through a combination of direct nerve stimulation and hormonal stimulation of target body parts (fig. 5-7). This system activates the adrenal medulla to secrete epinephrine and norepinephrine. The addition of these powerful hormones, triggered chemically, enhances and prolongs the initial response mediated by direct nerve transmission.

The neural and neuroendocrine axes comprise the alarm phase of Selye's General Adaptation Syndrome (see Figure 5-7).

sympathetic nervous system the part of the autonomic nervous system that is responsible for activating the organs that maintain homeostasis

parasympathetic nervous system the part of the autonomic nervous system responsible for turning off the autonomic system

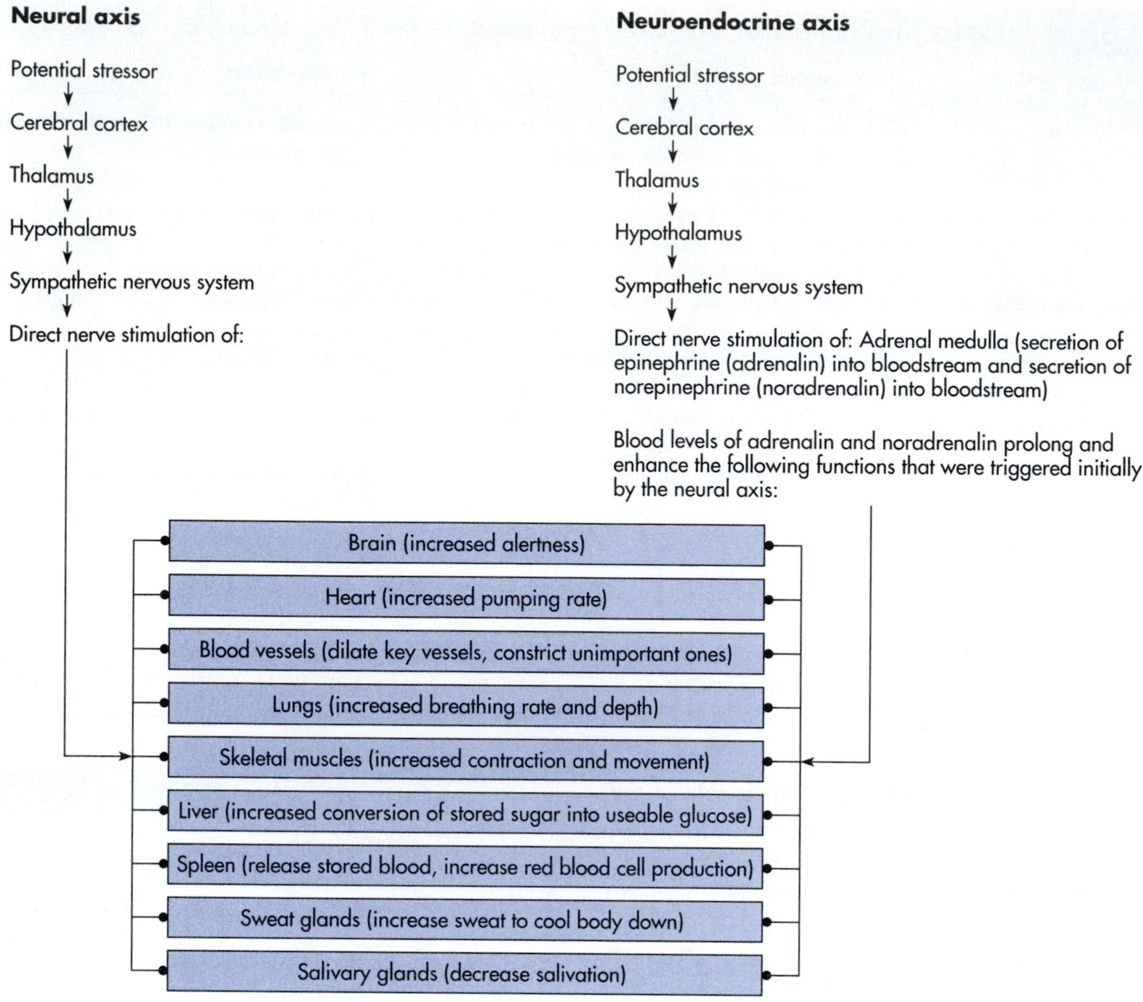

Figure 5-7

The neural and neuroendocrine axes comprise the alarm phase of Selye's General Adaptation Syndrome.

The Endocrine System

The endocrine system works on the principle of feedback, with the hypothalamus acting as a thermostat that senses the level of a particular hormone circulating in the bloodstream. Just as the thermostat in your home senses the level of heat in the house and turns on the heating or cooling system, your hypothalamus regulates the functioning of various organs, glands, and systems by sensing their levels of activity and turning them on and off as needed.

If the level of a particular hormone is too low, the hypothalamus secretes specific releasing factors into the bloodstream. The pituitary gland, sensing the presence of those releasing factors, secretes one of its own hormones, **ACTH,** which travels through the bloodstream to the target endocrine gland, prompting it to begin producing hormones. The **pituitary gland** has earned the nickname "the master gland" because of its role in orchestrating this complex regulatory process.

The Role of the Adrenal Glands

The adrenal glands play the most significant role in the stress response. They are the primary endocrine glands involved in fight-or-flight acute stress responses like Maya's. They also are the key endocrine glands involved in the resistance phase of the General Adaptation Syndrome when stressors are low-level and chronic.

ACTH the abbreviation for adrenocorticotropic hormone, a powerful hormone produced in the adrenal cortex (the outer part) that is indicative of the resistance phase of Selye's General Adaptation Syndrome

pituitary gland a pea-sized endocrine gland nestled in a bony shell at the base of the brain; often referred to as "the master gland" because of its role in secreting a variety of hormones that orchestrate several complex physiological functions from growth to ovulation

Living Constructively

Mistaken Attention

As we've mentioned throughout the text so far, paying attention to the world around us is one of the three essential skills of the Japanese therapies and living constructively. When we are suffering from chronic stress, we often begin to make simple mistakes in our life. Little mistakes such as missing a turn while driving, misplacing a cup as we put it on the counter, or typing in the wrong e-mail address because we misread the correct spelling often represent an inattentiveness that is the result of chronic stress. The following activity, Mistaken Attention, will help you begin to pay attention to the little mistakes you are making and help you begin to slow down and start to correct them and deal with the stress that is causing them.

Instructions:

1. Keep track of all the mistakes you make today and every day for the next week. Keep track of all mistakes in all aspects of your life (work, home, driving, paying bills, etc.)
2. At the end of the day identify those mistakes that you made because you were not paying full attention to the task you were involved in.
3. What were you doing with the rest of your attention?
4. How much time did you waste because of these mistakes?
5. What can you do to avoid such mistakes in the future.

Source: Adapted from Krech G. (2005) *Working with your attention. Exercises and Daily Journal.* Monkton Vt: ToDo Institute.

For the purpose of understanding their role in the stress response, the adrenal glands can be divided into two primary parts—the medulla and the cortex. The medulla, or inner part, comes into play during the initial mobilization of energy needed to fuel the fight-or-flight response, and the cortex, or outer shell, plays the key role in sustaining stress responses of longer duration. Hormones secreted during such long-term stress responses are associated with the resistance and exhaustion phases of the GAS.[21]

A key to understanding the endocrine system's role in the stress response is to realize that it gets involved because nerves can't continue to fire indefinitely without malfunction. In a sense, nerves will short-circuit without adequate downtime.

The hypothalamus gets the adrenal glands involved in the stress response in two ways. The first way is by sending direct nerve transmissions to the **adrenal medulla** during fight-or-flight (1). This can be referred to as the adrenomedullary stress system because it revolves around the actions of epinephrine and norepinephrine (also known as adrenaline and noradrenalin), the hormones secreted by the medulla.[2,9]

Adrenaline and noradrenaline are powerful hormones that stimulate almost all body systems. Their role in the fight-or-flight response is to enhance and prolong the activation of the various muscles, glands, and organs that are triggered by direct nerve stimulation from the hypothalamus.

The second way the hypothalamus gets the adrenal glands involved in a stress response is through the secretion of releasing factors (2) that trigger the pituitary gland to activate the production of adrenal cortical hormones necessary for longer-lasting stress responses. One of these adrenal cortical hormones, cortisol, does this by inhibiting the breakdown of epinephrine and norepinephrine. Cortisol also provides additional fuel for the stress response by helping the body convert stored fats and proteins to usable glucose energy.[4,5]

KEY TO UNDERSTANDING

The endocrine system keeps the stress response going by chemically regulating physiological processes initiated by direct nerve stimulation.

RESISTANCE: A CHRONIC, LONG-TERM STRESS RESPONSE

The alarm response is acute, intense, and necessary for survival. It does not cause harm to the body; rather, it is designed to save our lives. Without it we would not have an immediate response to life-threatening situations. If, however, the stressor is not dealt with through fighting or fleeing, or if it is chronic and persists for long periods (see Stress in Our World 5-2), our bodies must shift into a lower-level type of stress response. We simply cannot

adrenal medulla the inner core of the adrenal gland

STRESS IN OUR WORLD 5-2

Mario: Living with Chronic Stress

Mario hasn't been feeling very well lately. He's had nagging muscle tension in his neck, he thinks he's developing an ulcer, and he hasn't been feeling rested even after ten hours of sleep. He's been thinking about going to the doctor to see what's wrong.

Mario has been in a very unhappy relationship for more than a year now. There have been times when he's felt like he was going to blow his top. He gets so angry at his wife that he screams and calls her names that surprise even himself. He feels his heart pounding in his chest, his muscles tightening, and his breath coming out in gasps. Unable to vent this rage, he turns it inward, bites his lip, and goes into another room to simmer down. In time his symptoms disappear, and he falls asleep, exhausted by his ordeal.

After a few of these confrontations without any resolution, Mario has realized that he isn't ready or able to rectify the problems in his marriage. He also feels that he has no options and has to stay in it. He has resolved that he isn't going anywhere and, sadly, will have to endure things.

Over the last few months since he made this decision to maintain his status quo, Mario has begun to feel ill because his body has been experiencing a different kind of stress response—one that is less intense but every bit as complex and energy-intensive as the life-saving alarm response. His body simply cannot maintain the high levels of activation mobilized during his initial confrontations with his wife. Since he has neither fought not fled and because the source of his stress (his wife) still exists, his body has shifted into a lower-intensity response.

Daily, Mario's senses and brain sound the alarm-signaling threat, but his body's response is less intense. His heart and lungs are still working overtime, but he doesn't realize it until the end of the day, when he is exhausted and wonders why. If he checked it, he would see that his heart rate, blood pressure, and respiration are all elevated. It is his body's way of mobilizing the energy needed to meet the threat that his brain and senses are perceiving. Every time he sees his wife, smells her scent on his clothing, or thinks about her, his brain receives these messages, mixes them with memories and past associations, and interprets this as a threat, keeping the stress response alive.

This routine requires a tremendous amount of energy. To keep this stress response alive, his body uses energy from all available sources. It takes the calories from the food Mario eats and also draws extra energy from reserves in his skeletal muscles. This, however, isn't enough, and so his liver is triggered to synthesize energy from other sources, such as protein and fats. Hormones also help out; various glands secrete a variety of hormones into his bloodstream to provide energy, raise blood pressure, and increase his metabolic rate.

Mario doesn't even realize all this is going on. It is only after he begins to feel tired all the time, starts developing an ulcer, and can't get his muscle cramps to stop that he realizes that something is going wrong. Mario is in the resistance stage of a long-term stress response and is on the verge of exhaustion.

keep the intense, energy-demanding alarm response alive indefinitely. To cope with chronic stressors that are not life-threatening, we move into the resistance phase of Selye's stress response.

The Physiology of Resistance

The resistance phase of the General Adaptation Syndrome is similar to the fight-or-flight response or alarm phase in that it requires the body to mobilize energy to meet the demands imposed by stressors. However, it differs in several key ways. The same body parts and systems mobilized during alarm are still working, but at a less intense level. The body is not at rest and also is not in the throes of the alarm response; it is somewhere in between. The result is similar to an automobile that idles faster than it should. The engine works harder simply to keep its operating parts in balance. It uses more gas, performs less efficiently, and will break down sooner than will a car idling at the proper rate.

Mario's body in resistance works the same way. He feels chronically fatigued, is more susceptible to illness, and is less efficient and happy. He suffers from a decreased quality of life; all the energy he uses in maintaining the stress response is lost. Rather than use all this energy to try to maintain homeostasis in the face of his constant stressor, he could be putting it to much better use. He could be using that energy to enjoy and get the most out of his life rather than having to use it to cope with the stress of his relationship.

The Brain and Resistance

One big difference between Maya's and Mario's stress responses is the role of conscious thought and emotions. In Maya's case her alarm response was triggered by a direct, immediate, life-threatening stressor (the tractor-trailer). It was mediated primarily by sensations (visual images, sounds, smells) that were clear-cut warning signs of imminent harm. In Mario's stress response his stressor (his relationship) is less direct, more diffuse, and not immediately life-threatening.

At times Mario isn't completely sure that his relationship is as bad as it often appears. He has doubts about his wife's words and actions and isn't always clear about their intentions and meaning. His feelings often cloud his ability to think rationally, making it hard to sort things out. The past and the present seem to merge, confusing things even more.

Unfortunately, it isn't always easy to differentiate between direct, life-threatening events and symbolic, less-threatening stressors. Mario responds to his less-threatening, symbolic stressor the same way Maya does to her immediate, life-threatening one. The difference is the role played by the thinking, analyzing, and emotional parts of Mario's brain.

The Cerebral Cortex Mario spends a good part of his waking day sorting through the myriad of thoughts and emotions associated with his deteriorating relationship. He sifts through the hundreds of bits of information about his life, his wife, and their relationship, trying to figure out where, why, and how things began to turn the way they did.

This rational, analytical assessment is carried out by the cerebral cortex, the part of the brain responsible for rational thought processes such as judgment, reasoning, planning, and producing abstract ideas. It also plays a role in mood and is linked to the limbic system, the emotional brain. This is why his feelings keep creeping into what he wishes could be an entirely rational assessment of his situation.

The cerebral cortex is the part of the brain that decides whether Mario has the resources to cope with his relationship. If you remember from chapter 1, Lazarus and Folkman[13] referred to this decision-making process as the stress transaction. Mario uses his brain to assess factors concerning his potential stressor and his personality. If he had decided that the potential stressor could be improved and had the personality resources to do that, the situation would pass and he would not be stressed. However, he is stressed because he feels that the problems in his relationship are too large and deep-seated, and he simply can't cope with them.

The importance of cortical functions in initiating and sustaining the stress response cannot be understated. The greatest distinction between the work of the stress pioneers such as Selye and Cannon and those who have followed, such as Mason[15] and Lazarus and Folkman, is the understanding and documentation of the role of perception in the stress response. A stress response can be triggered merely by our thoughts and feelings. We do not need to be confronted with immediate threats to our well-being, such as Maya's tractor-trailer. If we feel something is a threat, regardless of the accuracy of this assessment, we will trigger a stress response. A key to understanding this is to realize that our perception of people and situations determines whether they are stressors. They are only potential stressors until we perceive them as otherwise.

KEY TO UNDERSTANDING

Our perception of situations determines whether they will become stressors.

The Diencephalon, Limbic System, and Brain Stem Mario's stressor is much more complex than Maya's. In fact, at times, things seem to be going fine between Mario and his wife. Sometimes he's not really sure what their problems are or whether his wife's comments and behavior are intentionally hurtful.

For example, last night as they were getting ready to go out to dinner with friends, Mario's wife made a comment about his suit. "Nice suit. It makes you look twenty years younger," she said. It was not so much what she said, but the way she said it. Mario's limbic system was working overtime as thoughts and emotions intermingled and were relayed through his thalamus, back and forth between his cortex and limbic system. Mario's mind was racing as his wife made her comment. Twenty years worth of feelings for this woman, their relationship, himself, and his life blended with each other and with Mario's attempts to think through the moment rationally.

The tension built up inside him as his hypothalamus set a variety of physiological responses into motion. Mario did everything he could to resist the temptation to strike back or break down and scream, thus totally sabotaging a potentially enjoyable evening out with friends.

Mario tried to relax but seemed supersensitive to everything going on around him; he was acutely aware of every detail of the rest of the evening. Getting dressed seemed to take forever because he felt his wife was evaluating everything about him. Their silence in the drive to their friends' house seemed deafening because his RAS had his brain aroused and focused on every sensation. He tried to shut down his brain a little by having a few drinks, but he drank too much and wound up getting his wife even more irritated with him. Unfortunately for Mario, his body would soon suffer the toll for turning his rage inward. His developing ulcer and muscle spasms were the price he was paying.

The Endocrine Axes

As we discussed earlier in this chapter, Everly and Lating[8] describe four endocrine axes that exert the greatest

KEY TO UNDERSTANDING

Chronic stress responses reduce our day-to-day quality of life by wasting energy we could be using more productively.

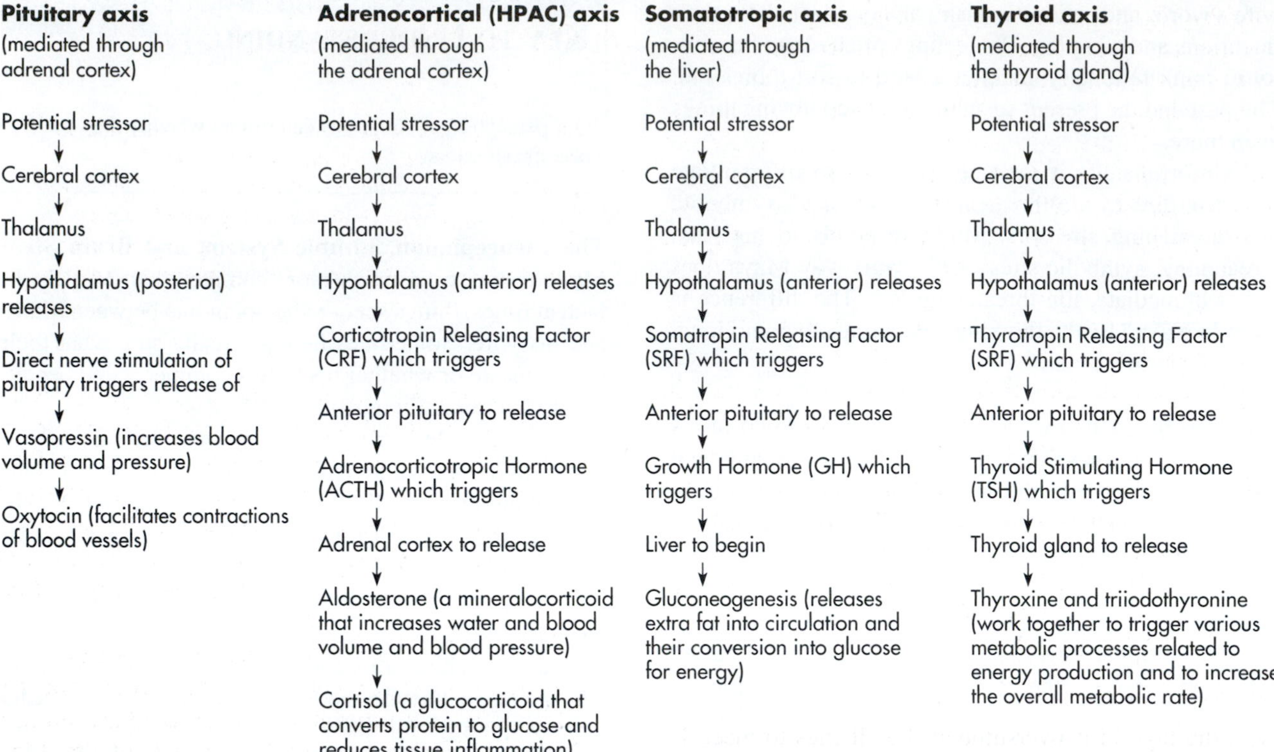

Figure 5-8 **The four endocrine axes at work during the resistance phase of Selye's General Adaptation Syndrome (GAS)**

During the resistance phase of GAS, all four of the endocrine axes work together to mobilize energy to help the body maintain homeostasis in the face of a chronic stressor.

influence on the resistance stress response. The four endocrine axes are: (1) the adrenocortical axis (also known as the hypothalamic-pituitary-adrenal-cortical system, (2) the somatotropic axis, (3) the thyroid axis, and (4) the posterior pituitary axis (see figure 5-8). All four neuroendocrine axes will be discussed next.

The Adrenocortical Axis During resistance the hypothalamus produces releasing factors that stimulate the pituitary to activate the outer shell of the adrenal glands. The outer part, the **adrenal cortex,** plays a major role in perpetuating his stress response. This is also known as the hypothalamic-pituitary-adrenal-cortical system because of the interaction of the hypothalamus and pituitary glands and the primary role played by adrenal cortical hormones.[1,3,4,15,25] Mario's adrenal cortex produces hormones called **corticoids.** Two major types of corticoids, *glucocorticoids* and *mineralocorticoids,* are involved in perpetuating his stress response.[2,3,5,19,26]

Glucocorticoids work with other hormones by maintaining Mario's increased metabolism; they make sure enough energy is available. *Cortisol* is the glucocorticoid responsible for providing the gas needed to fuel the stress response. Cortisol provides fuel by working with Mario's liver to create new sources of *glucose,* the body's main source of fuel.

The liver plays a major role during the resistance phase of Mario's stress response. The liver is responsible for producing energy by absorbing nutrients from recently eaten food and converting them into glucose. In addition, the liver can change excess simple sugars called monosaccharides into glycogen and fat and store them for later use. When Mario's glucose is exhausted, he taps into the glucose stored in his skeletal muscles and liver. This stored glucose provides additional fuel to keep his stress response alive and maintain homeostasis.

Eventually, Mario uses all his glycogen reserves. Once they are depleted, cortisol helps his liver synthesize **amino acids** into glucose. Additionally, cortisol increases the level of fats in his bloodstream by releasing free fatty acids from stored fat tissue to be used as a source of fuel. This process of converting amino acids and fats into energy for the body is called gluconeogenesis.

Mineralocorticoids, the second group of adrenocortical hormones, help control the volume of water and

adrenal cortex the outer shell of the adrenal gland

corticoids adrenal cortical hormones

amino acids organic chemical compounds that are the building blocks of protein electrolytes in Mario's body by maintaining his levels of sodium and potassium. Working in a feedback system with the hypothalamus, kidneys, and adrenal glands, mineralocorticoids keep his body's essential fluids in balance. Aldosterone, a key mineralocorticoid, helps prevent the rapid loss of sodium from Mario's body by conserving sodium ions and eliminating potassium. This increases Mario's blood volume, thereby raising his blood pressure.

The Somatotropic Axis Activation of the somatotropic axis results in the secretion of growth hormone. The hypothalamus secretes somatotropin-releasing factor (SRF), which stimulates the anterior pituitary. Once it is stimulated, the anterior pituitary releases growth hormone into circulation. Although its role in the stress response is not completely understood, it is believed that growth hormone helps mobilize fats stored in the body and resist the effects of insulin. These actions mobilize energy by increasing free fatty acid conversion into glucose and increasing the level of glucose in the blood.[8]

The Thyroid Axis During prolonged exposure to stressors the thyroid is overstimulated as it tries to meet the body's demands for fuel for the stress response. The thyroid gland helps keep Mario's stress response alive during the resistance phase by increasing his metabolic rate and assisting in gluconeogenesis. Two thyroid hormones, thyroxine and triiodothyronine, work together to affect virtually every cell in Mario's body. These hormones are linked to increasing the metabolic rate, heart rate, heart contractility, peripheral blood flow, and blood pressure.[8] Historically, the role of the thyroid is well documented in Selye's work.[21] Hyperthyroidism, caused by excessive thyroid stimulation, was part of the key triad Selye documented as indicative of exhaustion.

The Pituitary Axis Besides secreting releasing factors that trigger the adrenal and thyroid glands, the pituitary gland is stimulated by the hypothalamus during the stress response and secretes vasopressin and oxytocin. Vasopressin, also known as antidiuretic hormone (ADH), works with the kidneys to retain water to elevate the total body water content.[1] This increases blood volume and pressure. Oxytocin causes constriction of the smooth muscles in the walls of the blood vessels, resulting in increased blood pressure.[7,12] Oxytocin also causes psychogenic labor contractions in pregnant women. This can cause premature labor and delivery.[1,8]

The Physiology of Exhaustion

After a period of time, Mario's body simply won't continue to run at this increased level of energy demand. The stress response, fueled by the hormonal influences of his adrenal, thyroid, and pituitary glands, will begin to exact a toll. Something has to give, and what goes first is what we referred to in chapter 1 as Selye's[21] "weak link." Selye believed that we have a finite amount of energy available to adapt to the demands of stress. After we use it all, we suffer from exhaustion. This adaptation energy, or stored reserve, is systematically depleted during the resistance phase if we don't remove the source of stress or do things to relax and offset the demands of the stressor.

> **KEY TO UNDERSTANDING**
>
> Like your car battery, you have a finite amount of energy available to meet the demands of life. If you don't eliminate or cope with stressors and instead repeatedly go through long periods of resistance followed by bouts of exhaustion, you will use up too much of your adaptation energy supply, resulting in premature disability and death.

A key to understanding adaptation energy is to compare it to another energy source that is finite; your car battery. Like your car battery, you have a finite amount of energy available to meet the demands of life. Most car batteries, if treated with care last from thirty-six to forty-eight months. If you leave your lights on overnight or your door ajar and you run your battery down, you can recharge it. After too much abuse and too many recharges your battery will die prematurely. As an American, you can expect to have over eighty years of adaptation energy. If you take care of your body and remove or cope with stressors before they result in long periods of resistance and exhaustion, you can look forward to a full life span. If however you don't eliminate or cope with stressors and they repeatedly result in long periods of resistance followed by bouts of exhaustion (physical or mental), they will force you to use too much adaptation energy resulting in premature disability and death.

Selye[21] believed the weak link to be a body part or system that is predisposed to break down due to some inherent weakness. According to Selye, this inherent weak point, whether due to heredity or to environment, is the most likely part to falter when faced with the ravages of stress. It seems clear now, decades after Selye introduced this concept, that exhaustion occurs as a result of three physiological causes: (1) loss of potassium ions, (2) loss of adrenal glucocorticoids, and (3) weakening of vital organs.

The long-term effect of mineralocorticoids keeping sodium levels high through the suppression of potassium and hydrogen ions is that cells begin to die. Potassium, the chief positive ion in cells, plays a vital role in the effective functioning of cells. When potassium levels fall, cells function less effectively and eventually die. Exposure to chronic, low-level stress can contribute to this process.[20,23]

The long-term result of excessive adrenal gland stimulation is the depletion of adrenal glucocorticoids. When this happens, blood glucose levels fall dramatically, resulting in the loss of nutrients to the cells.

As these physical responses indicate, chronic stress resulting from long-term resistance puts a heavy demand on strategic body parts (see Assess Yourself 5-1, "Physiological Symptom Checklist"). The heart, blood vessels, and adrenal and thyroid glands are particularly susceptible to sudden breakdown from the strain of this continual stress response.[20,23] We will examine in detail in chapter 6 the effects of stress on the development of disease.

A Critical Look at the General Adaptation Syndrome (GAS)

Selye's[21] three-phase General Adaptation Syndrome has remained among the most accepted and well-known explanations of stress in the field. In recent years, however, the two key elements of Selye's theory—nonspecificity and the comparability of eustress and distress—have been challenged.

If you remember from chapter 1, nonspecificity refers to Selye's belief that all stressors trigger the same kind of response in the body. Selye believed that there are no specific stress responses matched to specific stressors. In other words, you don't have one stress response for relationship problems, one for traffic, and one for flunking a test. According to Selye, your body responds the same to each of these. Additionally, he believed that the body responds the same to positive (eustress) and negative (distress) stressors; all stressors throw the body out of equilibrium, forcing adaptation. This adaptation puts increased demands on the body, and in Selye's eyes, positive events exact the same toll as negative events. These two issues represent the core of Selye's definition of stress. Doubts about their validity challenge the very notion of stress held by many people in the field.

Much of Selye's initial work on the General Adaptation Syndrome occurred prior to 1950 and was hampered by a lack of sophisticated instruments and measurement techniques now available for the study of biochemical activity within the human body. As a result, many of his findings and interpretations of the effects of stress were attributed to **morphological** changes in the adrenal and thyroid glands rather than actual measurement of the hormonal activity of those glands while his subjects were under stress. In the 1960s and 1970s, however, advances in instrumentation and scientific technology and the emergence of the field of neuroendocrinology, which studies the relationship between the brain and the endocrine system, began to cast serious doubts about Selye's findings concerning nonspecificity.

David Goldstein,[10] a researcher at the National Institutes of Health in Maryland, poses a fundamental challenge to Selye's nonspecificity concept, a challenge based on the acceptance of evolutionary theory. Citing evidence stemming from Darwin's work, Goldstein claims that a nonspecific response to any demand is contrary to accepted beliefs about the evolutionary process. In fact, Goldstein asserted, stress responses have a "primitive specificity" that makes sense in terms of processes that go on during evolutionary adaptations to these situations.[10]

Additionally, Goldstein[10] has identified different responses to seven specific stressors: water deprivation, salt deprivation, changes in posture, eating a large meal, exercise, hemorrhage, and alterations in temperature. During exposure to each of these stressors, different homeostats regulate different systematic responses. This seems to indicate that there are at least seven specific stress responses to environmental stimuli alone.

If in fact there are seven specific responses to simple environmental stressors, it is logical to assume that there also might be different responses to specific psychosocial stressors. Most of us are much more likely to be stressed by emotional arousal stemming from psychosocial stressors than by the extremes in noxious environmental conditions created by Selye in the lab. In fact, as Mason[15] reported, emotional stimuli are among the most potent in stimulating pituitary-adrenal-cortical activity.

It is hard to sort out the emotional arousal caused by stimuli from the actual stimuli. There is a high degree of intercommunication between psychosocial or emotional inputs and physiological outputs.[6] Citing research that minimizes psychological reactions to physical stimuli, Mason[15] provides evidence that contradicts Selye's nonspecific-response concept. In certain studies where psychological reactions to increased physical stimuli were minimized, human and monkey subjects did not react with a nonspecific triggering of adrenal hormones.[16] This information lends credibility to the idea that the psychological perception of threat posed by Selye's noxious environmental stimuli was the key variable—not the actual noxious stimuli themselves. This distinction fundamentally changes the view of the stress response from that of a nonspecific response elicited by a diversity of stimuli to that of a hormonal response elicited largely by a single stimulus or stimulus class.[15]

In other words, stress isn't the nonspecific response to *any* demand—just those demands capable of triggering emotional arousal. **Emotional arousal** is another term for

morphological concerned with the structure and function on an organism

emotional arousal another way of saying feeling threatened or harmed using Lazarus and Folkman's threat appraisal model

KEY TO UNDERSTANDING

The difference between the stress response and the challenge response lies with our perceived ability to cope with the potential threat to our well-being. While both mobilize energy through the neural axis, only stress proceeds through the neuroendocrine with the resultant production of cortisol.

feeling threatened or harmed, which supports Lazarus and Folkman's[13] view of the stress response as being mediated by the perception of threat/harm or challenge.

Cortisol seems to be the main hormone whose presence indicates stress rather than challenge.[11,16] Frankenhaeuser[9] has shown that cortisol secretion is linked to the perception of threat. She studied subjects exposed to threatening and nonthreatening tasks. Both types of tasks were considered potential stressors. Each threw the body out of equilibrium, required energy to accomplish the task, and elevated the level of norepinephrine, the hormone related to sympathetic nervous system arousal. When the tasks were accomplished, the level of norepinephrine returned to normal.

A key to understanding the difference between the stress response and the challenge response is our perceived ability to cope with the potential threat to our well-being. While both mobilize energy through the neural axis, challenge doesn't proceed through the neuroendocrine with the resultant production of cortisol. When we are threatened, we feel that we can't cope and are overwhelmed by negative emotions such as fear, anxiety, and loss of hope. When we are challenged, we feel that we can cope and this feeling is buoyed by the presence of positive emotions such as happiness, pride, and hope.

Being challenged can bring you to the edge of peak performance.

DIVERSE PERSPECTIVES 5-1

Dave, Wheelchair Wizard

Dave is a student at the university where Dr. Blonna teaches. He is a 24-year-old sophomore who recently returned to college after losing both legs in an automobile accident when he was 18. Dr. Blonna met Dave after helping him find his classroom on his first day of school and was amazed at Dave's positive attitude. Dr. Blonna asked Dave how he was enjoying school so far. Dave responded, "So far, so good. Everyone here has been pretty cool. I get the typical stares, and sometimes people turn their heads away when we make eye contact. I guess they're afraid I'll think they are staring or something. Mostly people are real helpful with directions or help me maneuver around little obstacles like these high door sills on the floor." Dr. Blonna asked Dave if he found it very stressful returning to college and dealing with the added burden of having to get around the hilly campus in a wheelchair. Dave looked at him quizzically and said, "Stressful, nah. Seeing my friends get killed in the same car and me surviving, that's stressful. Not knowing if I'd survive or ever be able to get around again, that was stressful. I'm just glad to be here. I'm trying to look at the hills, these crazy door sills, and the slow elevators more as challenges. You know, before I got into the accident, I was a pretty decent basketball player. People always told me I'd never make varsity because at 5 feet, nine inches I was too small. I never did believe them or let them get me down. I just turned it into a challenge and used it to keep me motivated. I did make the varsity in my senior year and played pretty well. I look at college the same way. Its been a long time since I've been on a college campus, and I am glad to be back and look forward to whatever challenges it throws my way."

In addition to heightened norepinephrine levels, the threatened group had elevated blood levels of cortisol. This seems to lend credibility to the specificity of a stress response in relation to one's perception of the stressor. Also, it seems that the perception of threat is necessary for continued activation of the stress response. Other studies have also reported presence of cortisol in subjects exposed to threatening and challenging tasks.[14]

These findings seem to indicate that there is not just one, nonspecific stress response to all demands; there are in fact different responses that occur depending on whether one perceives stimuli as a threat, harm/loss, or challenge. Therefore, eustress may be an outdated concept and, at the very least, a misnomer.

Although positive, challenging stimuli throw us out of equilibrium and force our bodies to adapt through increased energy utilization, our perception of these stimuli surely determines the extent and duration of our bodily involvement. Getting psyched up for an athletic competition, for instance, gets our "juices flowing" in a positive way.

We perceive such a stimulus as a challenge, and our bodies respond by producing extra energy through glycogenesis and gluconeogenesis. However, this mobilization ceases once the stimulus is removed and the challenge is over. This is different from the kind of energy mobilization that occurs during the resistance phase in response to a chronic stressor such as a relationship gone bad. Lazarus and Folkman would say that our perception (and therefore the body's involvement) of the latter is different from that of the former. Although the types of physiological processes triggered for energy mobilization are similar, the perception of the stimuli and the duration and intensity of exposure are entirely different. Activation of adaptive mechanisms that enable the body to adjust to the demands of challenge are not the same as those involved in adjusting to harm, loss, or threat.

Further, our sense of being clear about and in control of the athletic competition is likely to be very different than it is for the relationship stressor. We can consciously focus on the challenge and, through the cerebral cortex, trigger the mobilizing of the energy needed to get us through the ordeal.

In the short term the hormones that mobilize blood sugars and fats enable extra effort and higher performance levels. In the long term sustained release of these chemicals in response to situations involving perceived harm, loss, or threat leads to fatigue and the depletion of reserves.

There is evidence to support the theory that chronic stressors can leave the body in a state of excessive sympathetic arousal. It has been found that individuals suffering from post-traumatic stress disorders (PTSD) have abnormally high levels of adrenal hormones and elevated blood pressure and heart rate.[6,7,9,10] Reactivation of memories, thoughts, and feelings about traumatic events is presumed to be the cause of the continual stimulation of the adrenal glands in PTSD sufferers.[16,18,19]

Though short-term eustress demands energy, there is little evidence that long-term eustress leads to the negative health effects associated with distress. It may well be that the cognitive stress appraisal of situations that could be labeled eustress eventually reduces them to what Lazarus and Folkman[13] would refer to as benign/positive events that are no longer capable of triggering a stress response.

SUMMARY

We started this chapter with an overview of the major body systems involved in the stress response. This is a critical first step in understanding what the stress response is and how it manifests itself throughout our bodies. We then discussed the fight-or-flight response and traced it from its origins in the various sensory and motor centers of the brain to its end points throughout the body. The anatomy and physiology of the brain were discussed in detail, with particular attention paid to the way the various components of brain functioning come into play during the stress response. It should now be understood how potentially stressful stimuli are received and interpreted and how they are reacted to by the body.

The brain's relationship to the central and peripheral nervous systems was compared to that of a switchboard and a telephone system, with the brain receiving and routing incoming messages. These messages travel along different circuits, ultimately reaching their destinations and transmitting their messages. The transmissions fired off by the nervous system can be considered electrical message units carried along the various branches of the nervous system. They stimulate the organs and tissues involved in initiating the stress response and mobilizing the energy needed to maintain homeostasis in the face of a stressor.

We discussed the endocrine system and focused on its role in keeping the stress response alive once nerve transmissions have been stretched to their limit. A detailed discussion of the various endocrine glands and hormones was presented, and the complexity of this system and its role in the stress response should now be understood.

We discussed the three major axes or pathways by which neural and hormonal messages are sent throughout the body during the stress response. We examined the neural, SAM, and HPAC pathways and described their relationship to Selye's findings. Selye's General Adaptation Syndrome, the classic model used to describe the physiological changes associated with the stress response, was presented in detail and was tied in to all the information in the first part of the chapter. We also discussed the three phases of GAS (alarm, resistance, and exhaustion), citing the involvement of the various body parts and systems. The chapter ended with a critical analysis of Selye's work, citing areas where it diverges from more recent insights gleaned from the fields of psychoneuroendocrinology and stress appraisal.

Study Questions

1. List and describe the major body systems involved in the stress response.
2. What are the four parts of the brain most directly related to the stress response? Describe their components and functions.
3. Describe the fight-or-flight response and its primary purpose.
4. What are the major differences between the neural, SAM, and HPAC stress pathways?
5. How do nerve impulses and hormones send stress messages during the alarm and resistance phases of the General Adaptation Syndrome? What are their similarities and differences?
6. What is the relationship between homeostasis and stress?
7. What are the effects of sympathetic nervous system activation and parasympathetic deactivation?
8. How do higher (cortical) and lower (limbic) brain functions interact during a chronic stress response?
9. What are the three phases of the General Adaptation Syndrome? Discuss the relationship of timing in these phases.
10. What are the major challenges to Selye's concepts of nonspecificity and eustress/distress?

Discover Our Changing World

The Medical Basis of Stress

http://www.teachhealth.com.

This free online guide to stress provides an overview of the medical aspects of stress as well as information on coping with stress. Scroll to the section titled "Brain Chemical Messengers" and read about "sad messengers" and "happy messengers."

Critical Thinking Question

How does the concept of sad and happy messengers fit with belief that stress messages reside in the brain (a "bag of hormones," as she calls it) and are transmitted hormonally as neurotransmitters?

Are You Thinking Clearly?

Many of us keep on pushing to finish tasks and take on more responsibilities even after we begin receiving messages from our bodies that are warning signs of stress. Rather than viewing these as signs that we need to back off and do less, we drink another cup of coffee or set our alarms an hour earlier thinking these short-term strategies will solve our problems. Take a minute and answer the following questions regarding how you perceive the early warning signs of stress.

1. When you notice a chronic problem like low back pain that isn't due to overuse or an injury, do you find yourself saying something like, "It's probably nothing. I'll just ignore it and it will go away" (and it doesn't)?
2. Do you find yourself saying the following in response to feeling overwhelmed by stress? "I'll cut back after next semester," or " I'll cut back when I graduate and then only have to worry about work."
3. Do you find yourself saying, "It can't be stress, it must be something else," when you experience common physical and emotional stress symptoms?
4. Do you tell yourself, "I'm too busy to do anything about my stress. I'll take care of it when I have some time," when you feel worn out by your stress?

If you answered yes to one or more of these questions, there is a pretty good chance that you are not thinking clearly about stress and need to rethink your position. The longer you put off dealing with stressors, the greater the likelihood that you will suffer from the wear and tear of resistance.

References

1. Antoni, F.A. (1993). Vasopressinergic control of pituitary ACTH secretion comes of age, *Frontiers of Neuroendocrinology,* 12, p. 76.
2. Baum, A. & Grunberg, N.E. (1995). Neuroendocrine measures of stress response. In Cohen, S., Kessler, R.C., & Gordon, L.G. (Eds.). *Measuring stress: A guide for health and social scientists,* pp. 175–192. New York: Oxford University Press.
3. Chrousos, G.P. (1992). Regulation and dysregulation of the hypothalamic-pituitary-adrenal axis: The corticotropin releasing hormone perspective. *Endocrinology Metabolic Clinics of North America,* 21, p. 833.
4. Cohen, S. & Kessler, R.C. (1995). Strategies for measuring stress in studies of psychiatric and physical conditions. In Cohen, S., Kessler, R.C., & Gordon, L.G. (Eds.). *Measuring stress: A guide for health*

and social scientists, pp. 3–26. New York: Oxford University Press.

5. Cohen, S., Kessler, R.C., & Gordon, L.G. (Eds.). (1995). *Measuring stress: A guide for health and social scientists.* New York: Oxford University Press.
6. Daruna, J.H. & Morgan, J.E. (1990). Psychosocial effects on immune function. *Psychosomatics,* 31(1), pp. 4–11.
7. Dembroski, T.M. & Blumchen, D. (Eds.). (1983). *Behavioral bases of coronary heart disease.* Basel, Switzerland: Karger.
8. Everly, G.S. & Lating, J.M. (2002). *A clinical guide to the treatment of the human stress response.* New York: Kluwer Academic/Plenum.
9. Frankenhaeuser, M. (1983). The sympathetic-adrenal and pituitary-adrenal responses to challenge: Comparison between the sexes. In Dembroski, T.M. & Blumchen, D. (Eds.). *Biobehavioral bases of coronary heart disease.* Basel, Switzerland: Karger.
10. Goldstein, D.S. (1990). Neurotransmitters and stress. *Biofeedback and Self-Regulation,* 15(3), pp. 243–271.
11. Kasl, S. (1996). Theory of stress and health. In Cooper, C.L. (Ed.). (1996). *Handbook of stress, medicine and health.* New York: CRC Press.
12. Krantz, D.S. & Falconer, J.J. (1995). Using cardiovascular measures in stress research: An introduction. In Cohen, S., Kessler, R.C., & Gordon, L.G. (Eds.). (1995). *Measuring stress: A guide for health and social scientists,* pp. 193–212. New York: Oxford University Press.
13. Lazarus, R.S. & Folkman, S. (1985). *Stress appraisal and coping.* New York: Springer.
14. Lovallo, W.R., Pincomb, G.A., Brackett, D.J., & Wilson, M.F. (1990). Heart rate reactivity as a predictor of neuroendocrine responses to aversive stimuli and appetite changes. *Psychosomatic Medicine,* 52, pp. 17–26.
15. Mason, J.W. (1975). A historical view of the stress field. *Journal of Human Stress,* June, pp. 22–36.
16. McFall, M.E., Murburg, M.M., Roszell, D.K., & Veith, R.C. (1989). Psychophysiologic and neuroendocrine findings in post traumatic stress disorder: A review of theory and research. *Journal of Anxiety Disorders,* 3, pp. 243–257.
17. Pert, C. (1999). *Molecules of emotion.* New York: Simon & Schuster.
18. Sapolsky, R.M. (1997). Stress and glucocorticoid response. *Science,* 275(14), p. 1663.
19. Sapolsky, R.M. (1996). Why stress is bad for your brain. *Science,* 273(13), p. 749.
20. Seely, R.R., Stephens, T.D., & Tate, P. (1995). *Anatomy and physiology.* St. Louis: Mosby.
21. Selye, H. (1956). *The stress of life.* New York: McGraw-Hill.
22. Thibodeau, G.A. & Patton, K.T. (1993). *Anatomy and physiology.* St. Louis: Mosby.
23. Tortora, G.J. & Anagnostakos, N.P. (1987). *Principles of anatomy and physiology* (5th. ed.). New York: Harper & Row.
24. Trachtman, P. (1998). Molecules of emotion. *Smithsonian,* 6(98), pp. 136–139.
25. Tsigos, C. & Chrousos, G.P. (1996). Stress, endocrine manifestations and disease. In Cooper, C.L. (Ed.). *Handbook of stress, medicine and health.* New York: CRC Press.
26. Yehuda, R. (1997). Stress and glucocorticoid. *Science,* 275(14), p. 1662.

Name: ______________________________ Date: ____________

ASSESS YOURSELF 5-1

Physiological Symptom Checklist

Circle the number which indicates the frequency of occurrence of each symptom.

		Never	> 1 × in past 3–6 months	> 1 ×/month	> 1 ×/week
1.	Tension headache	0	1	2	3
2.	Migraine (vascular) headache	0	1	2	3
3.	Stomachache	0	1	2	3
4.	Cold hands	0	1	2	3
5.	Acid stomach	0	1	2	3
6.	Shallow, rapid breathing	0	1	2	3
7.	Diarrhea	0	1	2	3
8.	Muscle cramps	0	1	2	3
9.	Burping	0	1	2	3
10.	Gasiness	0	1	2	3
11.	Increased urge to urinate	0	1	2	3
12.	Sweaty hands/feet	0	1	2	3
13.	Oily skin	0	1	2	3
14.	Fatigue/exhausted feelings	0	1	2	3
15.	Dry mouth	0	1	2	3
16.	Hand tremor	0	1	2	3
17.	Backache	0	1	2	3
18.	Neck stiffness	0	1	2	3
19.	Gum chewing	0	1	2	3
20.	Grinding teeth	0	1	2	3
21.	Constipation	0	1	2	3
22.	Tightness in chest or heart	0	1	2	3
23.	Dizziness	0	1	2	3
24.	Nausea/vomiting	0	1	2	3
25.	Butterflies in stomach	0	1	2	3
26.	Skin blemishes	0	1	2	3
27.	Heart pounding	0	1	2	3
28.	Blushing	0	1	2	3
29.	Palpitations	0	1	2	3
30.	Indigestion	0	1	2	3
31.	Hyperventilation	0	1	2	3
32.	Skin rashes	0	1	2	3
33.	Jaw pain	0	1	2	3

Interpretation:

Add up your total score.

< 38 = low physiological symptoms score
38–50 = moderate physiological symptoms score
51–75 = high physiological symptoms score
76–99 = excessive physiological symptoms score

CHAPTER

6

THE EFFECTS OF STRESS ON THE BODY AND MIND

OUTLINE

OBJECTIVES

By the end of the chapter students will:

- Define psychosomatic illness.
- Differentiate between psychogenic and somatogenic diseases.
- Describe the effects of chronic stress on the following body systems:
  - Endocrine system
  - Muscular system
  - Cardiovascular system
  - Immune system
  - Nervous system
  - Digestive system
- Define and describe acute traumatic stress disorder and post traumatic stress disorder (PTSD) in terms of their causes, symptoms, and criteria for diagnoses.
- Describe the role of chronic stress in the development of a variety of diseases and illnesses.
- Describe the role of stress in the development of a variety of psychological problems.

As we discussed in chapter 5 the stress response causes many acute and chronic physiological changes in the body. Some of the changes are health-enhancing and mobilize energy to help us perform tasks or flee danger. Other changes, however, are destructive and sap us of vital energy and wear our bodies down resulting in a host of physical and psychological illnesses. In this chapter we will examine in depth how acute and chronic stress affects the physiological functioning of key body systems and how breakdowns in those systems lead to specific types of illnesses and diseases. Finally, we will review critically some of the problems associated with stress research in the hope that such a review will empower readers to become better judges of the quality of the stress studies they read.

FROM STRESS TO DISEASE

In chapter 5 we discussed how stress affects various body parts and systems. We briefly touched on how the final stage of Selye's General Adaptation Syndrome (GAS) is exhaustion, a state of breakdown. In this section we will examine a host of theories, including Selye's, that attempt to explain exactly how this occurs. We will examine both medical and psychosomatic explanations for the jump from stress to disease.

The Medical Model

Traditional medical practice is steeped in the medical model of disease development. The medical model has a long history that is based on the separation of the mind and the body. This mind-body separation laid the foundation for the model which Edward Koch refined through his work with infectious diseases in the late nineteenth century. "Koch's Postulates" was a theory based on the belief that every disease has a single etiologic agent, a microorganism. The model makes no reference to the role of the mind in the disease process. Further, Koch believed that the following conditions have to exist for a disease to occur: (1) the microorganism must be observed in all cases of the disease, (2) the microorganism must be isolated and grown in pure culture, (3) the microorganism, when extracted from the pure culture and inoculated into a new host, will cause disease in the new host, and (4) the microorganism can be observed and recovered from the newly infected host.

The medical model was used not only to explain disease development but also as a blueprint for the treatment of disease. The model focused on the defect or dysfunction in the person, using a problem-solving approach. Analysis of the medical problem focused on evaluating the patient's medical history, symptoms, diagnostic test results, and physical examination to diagnose a specific illness. The medical model focused on the physical and biological aspects of the specific illness and did not evaluate that information in the specific psychosocial context of the individual. It did not recognize the mind-body interaction in the diagnosis and treatment of disease.

Although Koch's Postulates are very valuable in the study of infectious communicable diseases, they are of less use in understanding the etiology of and treating the majority of illnesses that threaten industrialized societies today. The greatest threats to our well-being are the diseases and conditions of lifestyle, including cardiovascular disease, cancer, depression, and suicide. Epidemiology has shown that these problems are not caused by a single microorganism but by a host of psychological and physical risk factors, including stress.

Psychosomatic Models

The term **psychosomatic** was coined by Philip Deutsch[28] to illustrate the interaction between the mind and the body in the disease process. Diseases associated with stress have often been trivialized as being "all in one's head," or psychosomatic. In our culture there seems to be a bias against diseases that are not linked to a clear, causative organism or a germ that is responsible for the problem.

In actuality, susceptibility to infectious diseases and the development of any type of illness, whether caused by an infectious or a communicable organism, never occurs without mental processes. As we have seen in chapters 2 and 5, our brains are intimately linked with physiological functioning at the cellular level. Our perception of the events going on around us affects nerve impulses, chemical reactions, and other physiological processes. Why one person develops a disease and another similarly receptive person does not often has to do with a variety of factors beyond the disease-producing germ. **Psychogenic** and **somatogenic** are two categories of psychosomatic disease.[13,36] Psychogenic disease refers to psychosomatic illnesses that are without a causative organism, or germ. These diseases, such as bronchial asthma, chronic backache, migraine headaches, peptic ulcers, and colitis, are conditions that arise when the structure and function of body parts and tissues are altered by a chronic stress response.

Chronic stress is a risk factor that contributes to the development of some diseases, such as cardiovascular disease. The degenerative process of atherosclerosis is

psychosomatic the interaction of the mind and body in the disease process

psychogenic psychosomatic illnesses without a causative germ

somatogenic psychosomatic illness that involves a causative germ

Key to Understanding

A common misunderstanding is the belief that psychosomatic diseases are *all in one's head.* Actually, the disease process involves both psychological and somatic factors. The progression of all diseases (even infectious diseases caused by an identifiable organism) is influenced by the combination of the mind and the body working together.

worsened by the physiological changes in the body caused by the ongoing stress response. There is, however, no causative germ involved.

With somatogenic disease, a causative organism exists. The long-term effects of the stress response weaken the body's defenses, making a person more susceptible to infection and the development of disease. A person in college may be susceptible to mononucleosis, for instance, due in part to the effects of chronic stressors on his or her immune system. The link between somatogenic disease and stress is less direct and more difficult to prove because many other factors, ranging from a person's behavior to the virulence of the invading germ, must be taken into consideration.

Selye and the General Adaptation Syndrome

Selye's work[67] was a clear break from a medical model approach to understanding disease development. As we discussed in chapters 1 and 5, Selye[67] proposed that the link between stress and disease came during the exhaustion phase of his General Adaptation Syndrome (GAS). During GAS, the body tried to maintain homeostasis in the face of threat by mobilizing the stress response. A sequential response, GAS moved from the initial acute shock or "alarm," to the system (alarm phase), to a less intense level of arousal (resistance phase) which resulted in chronic activation of major body systems (cardiovascular, nervous, endocrine, etc.). Selye believed that that chronic activation drained vital reserves of energy (adaptation energy) stored in cells, tissues, organs, and body systems. Evidence of this draining of vital reserves of adaptation energy included (1) loss of potassium ions, (2) loss of adrenal corticoids, and (3) weakening of vital organs through atrophy or hypertrophy. If the stress response persisted for too long, those reserves would be depleted and lead to a breakdown (exhaustion phase) of a body part or system (weak link).

Everly and Lating[33] provide an exhaustive expansion of Selye's research on the stress response. They identify six major psychophysiological theories to explain the link between stress and disease: (1) Lachman's model, (2) Sternbach's model, (3) Kraus and Raab's hypokinetic disease model, (4) Schwartz's dysregulation model, (5) Conflict theory, and (6) Everly and Benson's disorders of arousal model.

Lachman's Autonomic Learning Theory Model

Lachman[49] believed that learning and autonomic nervous system arousal work together to create a learned pattern of responses to intense or chronic stressors. Autonomic nervous system activation is paired with stimuli that individuals have identified as stressors, resulting in a "learned pattern of emotional arousal." This learned pattern combines with certain genetic and biological predispositions that determine which end organs are affected and how. Lachman felt that genetic and environmental factors (such as nutrition, physical trauma, and previous infections) combine to create a threshold of resistance to autonomic activation. Body parts and systems break down once the demands of autonomic system activation exceed that threshold. A person's learned pattern of emotional arousal influences the frequency, intensity, and duration of stimulation of the body parts affected by autonomic arousal and their subsequent susceptibility to becoming diseased and breaking down. Some people become emotionally aroused (stressed) more easily and more intensely than others. The way this affects their bodies and their susceptibility to stress-related disease is determined by their threshold, which is a combination of genetic and environmental influences.

Sternbach's Psychophysiologic Model

Sternbach[72] felt that individuals have a specific stereotypical response to stressors. This results in a characteristic individual psychophysiological response to stressors, creating a unique weak link for the person. The stereotypical response and the subsequent weak link may be genetically determined or may result from trauma or an unknown reason. Frequent activation of the autonomic nervous system taxes the resources of the body and the weak link. Deactivation of autonomic responses does not work properly. The return to homeostasis is slow and results in continued activation of target organs. This eventually causes too great a strain on the organs or systems, resulting in their breakdown.

Kraus and Raab's Hypokinetic Disease Model

Kraus and Raab[47] felt that the body has a natural antidote to stress: physical activity. They believed that continuous striated muscle (skeletal) activity results in increased circulation, healthy metabolic activity, and endocrine balance. Such activity doesn't necessarily prevent stress but essentially counteracts the effects of the stress response on the body. In a sense, they believed that stress-related diseases are as much related to the absence of strenuous physical activity as they are to the presence of stressors.

Schwartz's Dysregulation Model

Schwartz[66] believed that body systems work on the principle of feedback. Neural and biochemical messages are sent to and from various organs and systems to switch on and shut down functioning. The endocrine system is a perfect example. The level of specific hormones in the blood is regulated by a thermostat (the hypothalamus). The thermostat monitors and controls blood hormone levels by either switching on or shutting down the organs that secrete the hormones. When the system works properly, it is self-regulating and keeps blood hormone levels where they should be.

Schwartz believed that chronic overstimulation of organs by stress activation disrupts the normal feedback process. Chronic overstimulation of body parts and systems results in miscommunication (think of telephone lines and communication systems overwhelmed with messages during an emergency). When the normal feedback process is disrupted through miscommunication, organs and systems do not work the way they should, are overtaxed, and break down.

Alexander's Conflict Theory Model

Alexander[2] theorized that different types of conflict trigger specific physiological mechanisms that result in direct organ-specific illnesses. Alexander suggested the following possibilities for conflict-organ relationships: guilt leading to vomiting, alienation leading to constipation, and dependence leading to asthma. Subsequent studies, however, have not demonstrated significant relationships between specific types of conflict and disease outcomes.

Everly and Benson's Disorders of Arousal Model

Everly and Benson's[31] disorders of arousal model provides the most comprehensive analysis of the mechanisms by which the stress response manifests itself in disease. Their model (fig. 6-1) synthesizes all the salient parts of the other models used to explain the link between stress and disease. The model starts with a potential stressor. That stressor can be cognitive, affective, or environmental or can be a personologic predisposition. The leap from potential stressor to stress arousal, however, is mediated by the limbic system. Everly and Benson theorized that people with stress-related diseases are highly susceptible to limbic system arousal. They called this the limbic hypersensitivity phenomenon (LHP). LHP, Everly and Benson believed, develops as a result of either acutely traumatic or repeated extraordinary limbic excitation. Once limbic arousal occurs, the stress response is triggered along the various neurological, neuroendocrine, and endocrine stress axes described in chapter 5. If the stress response is evoked too often or sustained too long, it results in overstimulation. Overstimulation leads to wear and tear and the eventual breakdown of target organs and systems. This breakdown can be the result of biochemically induced trauma or toxicity or actual overwork. The resultant "disorders of arousal" include all the classic stress-related physical disorders but also most anxiety and adjustment disorders and some forms of depression.[33]

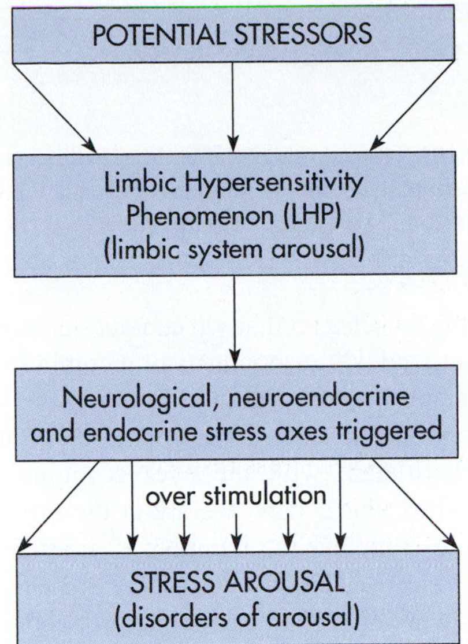

Figure 6-1
In Everly and Benson's model, a potential stressor arouses the limbic system and triggers a stress response along the neurological, neuroendocrine, and endocrine stress axes. If the stress response is evoked too often or sustained for too long it will result in over stimulation leading to breakdown of target organs and systems and disorders of arousal.

The Effects of Acute, High-Level Stress on Disease

In this next section we will examine the effects of acute, high-level stress on physical and psychological illness. Acute stressors are generally life-threatening and short term. As we have seen in chapters 1, 3, and 5, our bodies are equipped with the ability to mobilize tremendous amounts of energy to fight-or-flee, thus ensuring our survival. In this section we'll examine how such a potent response influences our physical and psychological well being.

Acute Stress Effects on Physical Illness

As we described in chapter 5, in acute, alarm-phase stress, we are in a state of complete mental and physical readiness. We have an abundance of energy at our disposal because the digestive system shuts down and the liver works overtime to convert all available energy sources, such as sugars, fats, and proteins, into a usable state.

The endocrine system contributes to this energy mobilization by secreting the powerful adrenal hormones adrenaline and noradrenaline. The cardiovascular system pumps oxygen and energy-rich blood through the arteries at a greater rate and force, supplying every critical area in the body from the brain so that we can think clearly to

> **KEY TO UNDERSTANDING**
>
> Although the effects of acute, high-level stress are intense, they are short-lived and begin to reverse once the source of stress is removed or coped with effectively.

the skeletal muscles so that we can act quickly. The nervous system quickly responds to all incoming stimuli and fires off nerve impulses at an astounding rate. The muscles are contracted, energized, and ready to move. The pupils are dilated, with the eyes scanning the scene clearly. In this alarm state, we are at the brink, ready to fight or flee. Whether the stimulus is a perceived harm, loss, or challenge, and whatever the stressful situation may be, we are energized and primed for action.

The effects of acute, or alarm-phase, stress responses are usually not harmful as long as we take action and utilize this energy. The rapid mobilization of energy created to assist us in confronting a threat, a harm, or a challenge is, in most cases, a positive, life-saving adaptive mechanism. Although the effects are intense, they are short-lived and begin to reverse once the source of stress is removed or coped with effectively. The result of this type of stress response on the body is fatigue. Maya's near-fatal car accident in chapter 1 is the perfect illustration of this adaptive response. If Maya has a lifestyle that is balanced and includes proper nutrition, exercise, and adequate rest, her body will rejuvenate itself and she will not suffer any harm from this acute stress response.

The more often people experience events that provoke alarm reactions, however, the greater their need for rest to help the body restore the energy that was used up in coping with the stressor. The effects of a moderate amount of short-term stress on psychogenic and somatogenic disease is negligible.

Acute, short-term stressors however can become problematic if they are intense enough or occur too frequently. As we just discussed in Everly and Benson's *Disorders of Arousal Model,* the effects on the limbic system due to repeated activation or exposure to extremely traumatic stressors can result in the limbic hypersensitivity phenomenon (LHP), which is a risk factor for a host of physical and psychological illnesses.

Acute Stress Effects on Psychological Illness

An acute stress response can be triggered by a number of potential stressors ranging from traumatic events such as a terrorist bombing to being in an elevator full of people. In this section we'll examine how such stressors manifest themselves in a variety of anxiety disorders.

Anxiety Disorders

Anxiety is a vague uneasy feeling whose source is often nonspecific or unknown to the individual.[6] Anxiety can be caused by threats to both biological integrity (unmet needs for food, water, or sex) and security of the self (unmet needs for self-respect, approval, or status). Mild anxiety is frequently coupled with fears, doubts, guilt, and obsessions. Higher levels of anxiety are characterized as the most uncomfortable feelings an individual can have, a terror so strong that individuals try to get rid of it as soon as possible.[29,79]

Stress and Panic Attack **Panic attacks** are discrete periods of intense fear and discomfort that come on unexpectedly and reach their peak within ten minutes. A person is diagnosed as having a **panic disorder** when he or she has experienced four or more attacks in a four-week period or one or more attacks followed by a period of at least a month of persistent fear or worry about having another attack. Additionally, sufferers experience at least four of the following symptoms:

- shortness of breath
- racing heartbeat
- chest pain
- smothering, choking sensation
- dizziness, vertigo, or unsteady feelings
- tingling in the hands or wobbly legs
- hot and cold flashes
- sweating
- feelings of unreality
- faintness, trembling, or shaking
- nausea, vomiting, or diarrhea
- fear of going crazy or dying.[4]

There are three characteristic types of panic attacks: unexpected (not linked to a situational cue), situational (linked to a situational cue), and situationally predisposed. *Unexpected* panic attacks occur spontaneously and are not linked to any internal or external trigger. *Situational* panic attacks are ones that occur immediately on exposure to or in anticipation of a trigger (for example, during or before giving a speech in front of a class). *Situationally predisposed* panic attacks are similar to situational panic attacks because they are linked to a specific trigger. They differ in that they do not always result in panic.[4] In community-based epidemiological studies it is estimated that 3 percent of the adult population experiences recurrent panic attacks, approximately 10 percent of the adult population has isolated or infrequent attacks, and about a third of all young adults have had at least one panic attack.[46] Although the causes of generalized

> **anxiety** a vague, uneasy feeling of nonspecific or unknown origin
>
> **panic attack** discrete periods of intense fear and discomfort that come on suddenly, without warning, and reach their peak within ten minutes
>
> **panic disorder** a condition in which a person suffers from frequent panic attacks

STRESS IN OUR WORLD 6-1

Bill

Bill is 58 years old. A high school graduate with a year of college education, Bill has been in the building supply business for over twenty years. He's been the manager of a large building supply store in the central New Jersey area, where at one point in time there were about twelve of those stores in the tristate area. They serviced local contractors and other smaller building supply outlets. Bill's company was owned by a much larger corporation that was involved in many other facets of the building trade, ranging from construction to logging. Much of the parent company's business was international in scope.

Bill's company, the smallest and least profitable of all the ventures, was sold to another company last year because it had consistently lost customers to large national home supply businesses. As it turns out, those businesses are able to offer consumers rock-bottom prices because they buy and sell much larger quantities than Bill's business ever could.

Bill was given his pink slip this morning. Although he's seen the writing on the wall for over a year (his store dropped from ten full-time employees to three in the last year, with much of the work picked up by part-timers and the remaining full-time staff), he still can't believe it. Bill's boss said he was sorry to have to do this, but the parent company wants to "clean house" and bring in "their own people." Bill will be offered six months of severance pay and a lump sum for his retirement, but all his medical and other benefits will cease in one month.

Bill is in a state of shock. He's got a son finishing his third year at an expensive private college. His daughter will be graduating high school next year, and her plans are uncertain. Bill's wife, a high school graduate, has a part-time job as a secretary, but it doesn't pay well and the benefits won't carry the family. They've managed to put a small amount aside in savings to help defray the costs of their son's final year of college. Bill is concerned that he may have a hard time finding a job with adequate benefits at his age. At 58 he feels too old to shift gears into a new occupation and too young to retire. Even if his severance package is enough to retire on, he still needs medical care coverage.

Bill has suffered from high blood pressure and ulcers for the last few years. In addition to this, Bill has struggled all year with chronic worry and panic attacks as he's watched his job disappear. He hasn't had a good night's sleep in months and has lived on antacids, antidepressants, and a little too much alcohol. He is not sure how he is going to cope with losing his job.

anxiety, phobias, and panic attacks are many and varied, stress is implicated in all three.[29] Perceived threats are a major cause of anxiety and panic. These threats, whether real or imagined, focus on two areas: biological integrity and security of the self. People who feel in danger of impending physical or psychosocial harm become anxious, and if the threats are not removed or coped with effectively, a generalized state or anxiety can result in or lead to a breakdown or panic attack (see Stress in Our World 6-1: "Bill").

Acute Stress Disorder The essential feature of **acute stress disorder** is the rapid development of characteristic anxiety, dissociation, and other symptoms that occur within one month of experiencing an extremely traumatic stressor.[4] As was described in chapter 4, these traumata are so extreme and outside the realm of the usual human experience that they are capable of causing enough intense fear, terror, and helplessness to leave their victims literally numb.

Such traumata can be characterized as either personal (rape, incest, robbery, torture) or community (earthquake, flood, war, terrorism). The event does not have to happen to the individual for it to be traumatic. It could affect a child, a spouse, a family member, a stranger, or the community as a whole. The most common traumata involve a threat to one's life, serious personal physical harm, a threat to one's family or to individual family members, catastrophic destruction of one's home or community, viewing another person being seriously harmed or killed, and learning about these events though not experiencing them firsthand.[4] As we mentioned in chapter 4, traumatic events such as the suicide terrorist attacks on the World Trade Center and Pentagon of 9/11 are so horrific, they have the potential to affect millions of people watching from a safe distance. The sheer horror of the event and the perceived vulnerability it creates combine to trigger the disorder.

To make a diagnosis of acute stress disorder, the following criteria must be met:

1. The person has been exposed to a traumatic event in which both of the following occurred:
   a. the person experienced, witnessed, or was confronted with a traumatic stressor that involved actual or threatened death or serious injury to himself or herself or to others.
   b. the person's response was one of fear, helplessness, or horror.

acute stress disorder a disorder characterized by the rapid development of anxiety, dissociation, and other symptoms following within a month after experiencing an extremely traumatic stressor

2. The person has three or more of the following associative symptoms while experiencing or after experiencing the traumatic event: a sense of numbing or emotional detachment, being in a daze, loss of reality, no longer has a sense of self, amnesia regarding the traumatic event.
3. The traumatic event is persistently reexperienced through recurrent dreams, flashbacks, thoughts, illusions, or reliving of the event.
4. The person demonstrates a marked avoidance of all stimuli (people, memories, thoughts, places, activities) that arouse recollection of the event.
5. The person experiences heightened levels of arousal (insomnia, can't concentrate, startled easily).
6. The disturbance causes clinically significant distress or impairment in social, occupational, or other functioning and impairs the individual's ability to seek help.
7. The disturbance lasts from two days to four weeks and occurs within four weeks of experiencing the traumatic event.
8. The disturbance is not due to exposure to a substance or a general medical condition.[4]

Post-Traumatic Stress Disorder (PTSD) The essential features and diagnostic criteria for **Post-Traumatic Stress Disorder (PTSD)** are essentially the same as those for acute stress disorder. The major difference is that the symptoms associated with PTSD persist for more than one month; therefore, diagnosis of PTSD cannot be made until that time.[4] Although the trauma associated with PTSD is experienced as an acute stressor, it is reexperienced in many ways by the sufferer, leading to a state of chronic stress arousal. The trauma can be relived through dreams that recreate the event or parts of it. Occasionally sufferers dissociate from reality and slip into trancelike states for seconds, minutes, hours, and even days as they relive the traumatic event. In other cases, daily activities that contain aspects of the traumatic experience can symbolize the event and trigger intense psychological stress.

Sleep disorders are common among PTSD sufferers who have difficulty falling asleep as well as staying asleep. Recurrent nightmares involving the reliving of the event can disturb the duration and depth of sleep. Increased emotional arousal can make concentrating on tasks difficult (see Diverse Perspectives 6-1: "Nikki"[10]). Many sufferers with milder cases report an increase in aggression manifested as increased irritability and tension. In more severe forms, particularly among war veterans who have committed acts of violence, the sufferer may experience unpredictable outbursts of aggressive behavior and expressions of anger. This heightened level of arousal is related to chronic neuroendocrine and autonomic nervous system activation.[33] Persons suffering from acute stress disorder and PTSD have been found to have higher resting heart rates, blood pressure, and levels of circulating adrenal hormones than nonsufferers.[43]

DIVERSE PERSPECTIVES 6-1

Nikki

Nikki, a 20-year-old Muslim student from Pakistan, attended one of Dr. Blonna's stress management classes in 2002. She had been under a tremendous amount of stress since 9/11 and came to see him one day after class to discuss what was going on in her life. "Dr. Blonna," she said, "I think I am going to drop the class and take a leave of absence from school. Even though I have just one year left and I really like school, I just need to take a break. I can't continue." When asked to explain her problem, she admitted to being under terrible stress. "I'm just very afraid to live here lately," she explained. "Our mosque in Paterson has been vandalized several times, and my mother has been the victim of many abuses this past year. People have thrown garbage at our mosque, painted hateful things on its walls, and thrown bricks through the windows at least five times. My mother still wears our traditional clothing [Nikki stopped wearing it right after 9/11] and has been cursed and spit at several times while walking down the street. For the past year I have constantly been afraid for my family and for myself. I worry that one day someone will do something more serious than just yell filthy things or throw garbage at us. My stomach is in knots every day, and I have been having a hard time sleeping and concentrating. I am even afraid to work in my uncle's store anymore. He has had his windows broken so many times this past year that he has put up very heavy mesh steel over them and locks the door after each customer comes in." After explaining the daily stresses of her life, she concluded by saying, "I think I am going back to Pakistan for a while, at least until my family thinks it is safe to return. I can live with my aunts and uncles and find work there. At least I will be among my people and feel safe. I just want to be able to smile and laugh again."

People suffering from PTSD make deliberate attempts to avoid all stimuli in hopes of suppressing the psychological distress associated with them. This often leads to distancing oneself from others and social isolation. A "psychic numbing" or "emotional anesthesia" begins soon after the experience and leaves the person with an overall inability to feel emotions of any type. It is as if the pain associated with the trauma is so deep that it deadens any feelings at all. PTSD sufferers often feel detached from others and generally uninterested in life and the things that used to bring them happiness and joy.

The author saw examples of this psychic numbing on campus in the weeks following the events of September 11, 2001. The author works at a university where the World Trade Center and the skyline of Manhattan are

post-traumatic stress disorder (PTSD) a form of acute stress disorder that persists for more than one month visible from the highest point on campus. Some of his students were directly involved with 9/11 by working and volunteering at the site, and others were connected to those who died. He will never forget how students, faculty, and staff wandered around campus screaming and sobbing, frantically trying to place cell phone calls to loved ones. The author's son, a freshman at the college at that time, recalls sitting on top of his dormitory roof watching in disbelief as the World Trade Center lay in ruins over twenty-five miles away, smoldering long into the night. Students were crying and trying to console each other as they attempted to make sense of what had happened earlier in the day. The impact of that day lingered at the campus for the entire semester like a thick fog. Many students, faculty, and staff barely survived the semester, sometimes just going through the motions. Many class sessions started out with a moment of silence to honor the dead, the missing, and the heroic rescuers. Many professors, like the author, started each class by forming a circle, holding hands, and sharing each other's strength. Some of his students remain in therapy years after the events of 9/11. Researchers estimate that tens of thousands of New Yorkers suffered from post-traumatic stress disorder in the months after the attack on the World Trade Center.[68] Additionally, about 17 percent of the U.S. population *outside* New York City reported symptoms of PTSD two months after the terrorist attacks.[53] Events such as the terrorist attacks of 9/11, war, and chronic and traumatic stress changed the campus and the outside culture.[50] On campuses around the country, grief counselors were brought in to help students cope with their losses. Campus counseling centers were inundated with students, faculty, and staff seeking help. Students from around the country made a pilgrimage to New York City to help out in any way they could.[45] Loss, grief, and fear brought on by these events have changed our collective culture and have many implications for personal wellness and sexuality. They affect our trust, our ability to relax, and our faith in the culture.[26,27] Debra Straw, a professor from Burlington, Vermont, writing in *Community College Week,* describes this eloquently in the following passage: "One young woman, normally an A student, told me last week that she has been getting Bs and that she has been taking depression medication and getting therapy as a direct result of what has been happening in the larger world. These young people now live in fear and uncertainty. Their American Dream seems to have been blown away."[74] The terrorist attacks of 9/11 threatened the diversity that is vital to a well-rounded college experience.[34] Terror, fear, anger, and suffering affected the previous level of acceptance and understanding of students from different cultures, particularly those from the Middle East. On some campuses across the nation, there were reported backlash incidents against Middle Eastern students, professors, and staff and Islamic studies and culture.[12] This creates a campus climate that is not healthy or safe.

KEY TO UNDERSTANDING

The essential features and diagnostic criteria for PTSD are essentially the same as those for acute stress disorder. The major difference is that the symptoms associated with PTSD persist for more than one month; therefore, diagnosis of PTSD cannot be made until that time.

THE EFFECTS OF CHRONIC, LOW-LEVEL STRESS ON DISEASE

We've just described how acute stressors exert a very dramatic and noticeable effect on physical and psychological illness. The effects of chronic stress are much more insidious because the symptoms it causes are usually unnoticeable. Physical and psychological symptoms of chronic stress, such as elevations in blood pressure, changes in blood chemistry, imbalances in immune system components, loss of concern for others, and mild depression, often go unnoticed until it is too late and illness has already taken hold. In the next section we will examine the effects of chronic stress on physical and psychological illnesses.

Effects of Chronic Stress on Physical Illness

The effects of chronic low-level stress on disease are most clear with psychogenic diseases. Over time the stress response exerts a generalized wear and tear on the body. When body parts and systems are forced to work overtime for long periods without rest and rejuvenation, they begin to malfunction and eventually break down. The relationship between stress and psychogenic disease is most direct with five body systems: the endocrine, muscular, cardiovascular, immune, and digestive systems. Excess strain on these systems results in inefficiency and a gradual breakdown in their performance, followed by increased susceptibility to a host of illnesses.[32] In the next section we will examine this phenomenon, first by explaining the relationship between stress and the body system under study and then by looking at individual diseases and conditions that are associated with malfunction of each system.

Stress and Endocrine System Disorders

The stress response is intimately linked to endocrine system functioning. Besides being the key component in perpetuating the chronic, low-level stress response, the endocrine system is responsible for a variety of other functions, ranging from reproduction to growth. Chronic stress has the potential to interfere with and shut down these endocrine functions.[18]

KEY TO UNDERSTANDING

When body parts or systems are forced to work overtime for long periods without rest and rejuvenation, they begin to malfunction and eventually break down.

The endocrine system, as discussed in chapter 5, relies on a feedback mechanism involving the hypothalamus, the pituitary, other endocrine glands, the bloodstream, and hormones. The whole system must work together; if one component breaks down, the whole system can go down.[19]

Research in this area was hampered for years by a lack of sophisticated instruments and methodology. Selye[67] and others, working with laboratory animals, observed structural changes in their subjects caused by exposure to acute and chronic stressors. Because they lacked the sophisticated instruments and methods needed to pinpoint and quantify specific hormones, they used morphological changes such as enlarged adrenal glands and heavier pituitary glands to indicate the response to stressors. Adrenal gland weight before and after exposure to stressors was used as an indicator of adrenal functioning while a person was under stress.[55] Selye[67] characterized the following syndrome associated with chronic stress: increased activity followed by enlargement of the adrenal cortex, swollen lymph glands, atrophy of the thymus, and stomach ulcers.

Early findings in animal research have been replicated with human subjects. The same physiological changes have been noted in humans, and the link between these responses and the brain has been clarified, establishing the relationship between our thoughts and the stress response.[54]

There are many varied effects of the disruption in normal endocrine functioning. Chronic hormonal imbalance is related to a host of illnesses, ranging from sexual dysfunction to lowered immune system functioning.

In chapter 5 we discussed how hormones are associated with the stress response. In this section we will examine how the three hormones epinephrine (adrenaline), norepinephrine (noradrenaline), and cortisol are implicated in a variety of medical problems.

Stress and Heart Disease Epinephrine and norepinephrine work together to speed up circulation, helping to mobilize the energy needed to fight or flee. Epinephrine causes blood vessels, especially the smaller ones in the extremities, to constrict, thereby forcing the heart to pump under greater pressure. Chronically increased blood pressure results in a condition called **hypertension,** which is a primary risk factor for stroke and heart attack.

Norepinephrine also causes blood vessels to constrict and interferes with blood platelets and red blood cells. Platelets are cell fragments found in blood and are involved in clotting. Red blood cells are primarily involved in transporting oxygen throughout the body. Excess norepinephrine has been shown to disturb platelets and red blood cells, causing damage to the endothelium, which is the lining of the heart and blood vessels.[40] Damage to the endothelium is considered a precursor to the development of atherosclerosis, or hardening of the arteries. Norepinephrine also converts another stress hormone, testosterone, into estradiol, a little-understood chemical that is significantly elevated in men who have heart attacks.[44] Although not completely understood, estradiol and other estrogens play a role in controlling fluid and electrolyte balance, which contribute to the regulation of blood pressure.

Cortisol, a very potent hormone, inhibits the breakdown of epinephrine and norepinephrine and increases the body's sensitivity to those substances. In doing this, it interferes with the body's ability to relax and reverses the process of stress activation. Cortisol increases blood cholesterol and fat levels by releasing these substances from fatty tissue so that they can be converted to energy through gluconeogenesis. A chronic stress response can result in continual activation of this process, unnecessarily elevating serum cholesterol and fat, which are recognized risk factors for heart disease. Excess cortisol levels have also been connected to damage to the endothelium.[44]

Stress and Sexual Dysfunction Perhaps nothing illustrates the interaction between the mind and the body better than human sexual response and dysfunction. The interaction of all five senses plays a key role in the sexual response: becoming sexually aroused, maintaining interest, having an orgasm, and feeling satisfied. Sensory arousal combines with emotional arousal (limbic system) and conscious thought (cerebral cortex) as the sensing, feeling, thinking brain triggers and directs the organs, glands, and tissues that regulate the sexual response. Although responses as common as developing and maintaining an erection and maintaining sufficient vaginal lubrication (classic signs of sexual arousal) seem to be simple, primitive responses, in reality they are the complex result of many reactions within a complicated and interdependent system. Thus, sexual response isn't always an all-or-nothing phenomenon. Levels of performance and satisfaction vary. Everyone experiences some level of dysfunction throughout the course of life. Sometimes it is produced by illness, stress, fatigue, or a variety

hypertension another name for high blood pressure, meaning elevated blood pressure that consistently exceeds 140/90 mmHg

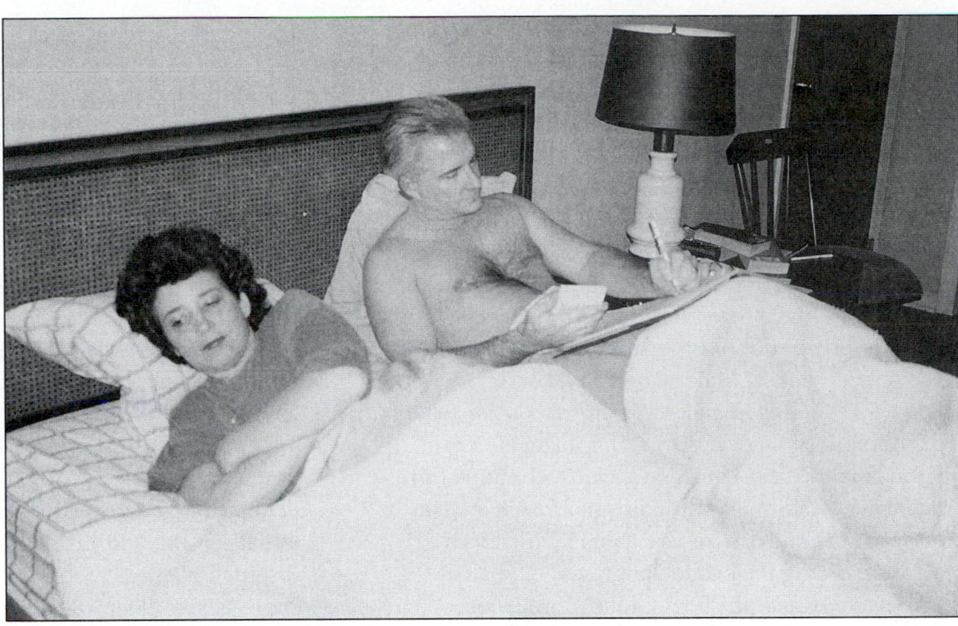

Stress can diminish your interest in sex.

of other causes. Dysfunction is not just a heterosexual issue either. Gay, lesbian, and bisexual people also experience sexual dysfunction.[10]

According to the *Diagnostic and Statistical Manual,* sexual dysfunction is a disturbance or disorder in desire, excitement, orgasm, or resolution of the sexual response cycle.[4] The American Psychiatric Association (APA) classification of sexual dysfunctions is based on traditional models of sexual response and a four-phase conceptualization of human sexual response (desire, excitement, orgasm, and resolution).

- **Desire Phase** The desire phase originates with fantasizing and thinking about engaging in sexual activities. Sexual dysfunctions that relate to this phase are called **sexual desire disorders.** These disorders include hypoactive sexual desire disorder and sexual aversion disorder.

  Hypoactive sexual desire disorder is a dysfunction characterized by very low levels (or complete absence) of sexual desire. Individuals with this condition do not initiate sexual activity and may engage in sexual relations only begrudgingly at the insistence of their partners. They have little or no motivation to seek sexual stimulation and are increasingly undisturbed by this lack of desire. Sexual aversion disorder is characterized by disgust and active avoidance of any genital sexual contact with a sexual partner.[4]
- **Excitement Phase** The excitement phase is characterized by the buildup of sexual excitement and tension, manifested through vasocongestion. Penile swelling and erection are physical evidence of desire in men. In women, vaginal lubrication and expansion and swelling of the vulva indicate arousal. Sexual dysfunctions related to this stage are called **sexual arousal disorders.** These disorders differ from sexual desire disorders in that the latter are related to lack of desire and the former are related to inability to achieve sufficient levels of arousal. The major characteristic of a female sexual arousal disorder is persistent or recurrent inability to attain or maintain sufficient vaginal lubrication and swelling to complete sexual activity. Vasocongestion is impaired, and the vagina and external genitalia do not become fully engorged with blood. As a result, penetration is restricted, which may result in painful intercourse, avoidance of sexual relations, and a disturbance of the relationship. Female sexual arousal disorder is often accompanied by a sexual desire disorder and female orgasmic disorder.[4] Male erectile disorder, previously called "impotence," is the persistent or recurring inability to attain or maintain an adequate erection for the completion of sexual activity. This disorder has different patterns. Some men with the disorder are unable to attain an erection at all. Others are able to get an erection but lose it upon penetration. A third group of males are able to attain an erection and complete penetration but lose the erection while thrusting.[4]
- **Orgasm Phase** In the orgasm phase, built-up sexual tension is released, followed immediately by

sexual desire disorders sexual disfunctions that relate to the desire phase of the sexual response cycle

sexual arousal disorders sexual dysfunctions related to the arousal phase of the sexual response cycle psychological feelings of satisfaction and satiation. Sexual dysfunctions related to this phase are referred to as **orgasmic disorders.** These disorders center on the inability of men and women to release pent-up sexual tension through orgasm. These people are interested in sexual relations and are able to become sexually aroused. Their problems relate to their inability to move to the next stage of sexual response: orgasm. Female orgasmic disorder, formerly known as "inhibited female orgasm," is a persistent or recurring delay in or absence of orgasm after a typical excitement phase.[4] Male orgasmic disorder, formerly known as "inhibited male orgasm," is a persistent or recurrent delay in or absence of orgasm after a normal excitement phase. In its most common form, men who have this condition cannot reach orgasm during intercourse. They are able to experience pleasure during the excitement phase of sexual activity and enjoy the beginnings of a sexual encounter but rapidly lose interest. For these men, thrusting and prolonging sexual activity are a chore rather than a pleasure.[4]

- **Resolution Phase** The resolution phase is characterized by a physiological return to the predesire stage. Sexual pain disorders may be present during intercourse or in the resolution phase. The most common sexual pain disorders are dyspareunia and vaginismus. **Dyspareunia** is genital pain associated with sexual intercourse. It may be present before, during, or after intercourse and can affect both men and women. Symptoms range from mild discomfort to sharp pain. **Vaginismus** is the recurrent or persistent involuntary contraction of the perineal muscles surrounding the outer third of the vagina during attempted penetration with a penis, finger, tampon, or speculum. In some cases, even the anticipation of vaginal penetration can cause muscle spasms. Symptoms range from mild discomfort and tightness to severe contractions and cramping.

Chronic and acute stress can affect all four phases of the sexual response cycle and can be a contributing factor to sexual dysfunction. The relationship between chronic stress and endocrine system functioning plays a key role in sexual dysfunction. Chronic stress has been implicated in the development of problems associated with sexual desire and sexual arousal disorders for years.[43,52] The profound physiological and endocrine changes that accompany depression, fatigue, and stress contribute to a loss of sexual desire in both men and women.[7,8,9,43,51] These factors seem to disrupt the production of neurotransmitters that influence the production of androgens, including testosterone. Testosterone, although once considered a "male" hormone, is produced in both men and women and is the key hormone linked to sexual desire. Although it is produced by men and women, the actual amounts vary for each gender and a much smaller quantity seems necessary to achieve the same arousal effects in women.[10] Dropoffs in testosterone levels lead to reduced sexual desire and sexual arousal disorders. The mechanism of this action, although not completely understood, centers on messages passed from the hypothalamus to the pituitary in response to perceived stress. The hypothalamus triggers a decrease in the secretion of pituitary hormones, follicle-stimulating hormone (FSH), and luteinizing hormone (LH). This decreased level of FSH and LH results in decreased levels of testosterone, which affect the sex centers in the brain and result in a loss of sexual desire and sexual arousal disorders. Excess corticosteroid production is also related to the suppression of testosterone production. In a classic piece of sex research, Kaplan[43] demonstrated the relationship between stress, low testosterone levels, and diminished sexual desire and arousal disorder. Kaplan[43] showed that men under chronic stress show a significant and consistent depression in levels of testosterone. When the source of stress is removed or coped with (through therapy and stress-management training), testosterone levels return to normal, sexual desire increases, and arousal occurs.

Basson et al.[8] believe that emotional and intimacy issues are the central factors in understanding the sexual response and dysfunction in women. Women, according to Basson et al.,[8] are much more likely than men to have intimacy issues as the basis of low sexual desire and sexual arousal disorders. In fact, in their studies of women with sexual desire and arousal disorders, many of the women with low sexual desire had no problem becoming aroused physiologically (evidence of lubrication, etc.) and achieving orgasm.[7,8] This provides more evidence of the delicate interplay between the mind and the body (in this case the endocrine system). Chronic stress can easily disrupt this interplay, for instance, by flooding the blood with excess hormones that can disrupt the normal transmission of hormonal messages from the brain to the organs and glands involved in the sexual response.

Stress and Premenstrual Syndrome Another endocrine disorder affected by stress is premenstrual syndrome (PMS). PMS is characterized by myriad physical and psychological symptoms that appear from two to six days before the onset of menstruation. Psychosocial symptoms include negative emotions such as anxiety,

orgasmic disorders sexual dysfunctions related to the orgasm phase of the sexual response cycle

dyspareunia genital pain associated with sexual intercourse

vaginismus recurrent or persistent involuntary contraction of the perineal muscles surrounding the outer third of the vagina irritability, depression, anger, insomnia, confusion, and social withdrawal. Physical symptoms include fluid retention, breast tenderness, weight gain, headaches, dizziness, nausea, increased appetite, and a craving for sweets.[40]

Most discussions of PMS emphasize its negative physiological and psychological aspects. PMS has been used as a legal defense for women who have committed violent acts, implying that the overwhelming power of their emotional distress rendered them incapable of controlling their behavior. The politicizing of PMS and its use as a legal defense may work against women since this feeds into continuing negative sex-role stereotypes of female emotions, menstruation, and the inability of women to hold positions of responsibility.[24] This emphasis on the negative aspects of the syndrome ignores the fact that for many women menstruation is a time of peak creativity and productivity.[61]

Research about the causes, nature, and treatment of PMS lack consistency. Although most PMS researchers believe that shifting hormonal balances play a key role in the etiology of the condition, the specific hormones and exact mechanisms of action are unclear. A change in the ratio of estrogen to progesterone has been implicated, as has a change in the level of mineralocorticoids that control fluid retention. Still other theorists propose that the key hormones involved in menstruation are those of the brain that influence mood.[40]

While estimates of the number of PMS sufferers vary from 20 to 75 percent of women, most researchers agree that 3 to 5 percent of women have symptoms serious enough to interfere with normal daily functioning. One of the many problems in studying the extent and nature of PMS is the fact that symptoms are often transient, do not always occur, and are often unobservable.[61]

An interesting aspect of PMS is the relationship between women's moods, attitudes, and emotions and the physiological symptoms that characterize the syndrome. Researchers are still trying to ascertain whether it is the negative emotions about menstruation and PMS that trigger the hormonal and other physiological changes or whether it is the physical discomfort that precipitates the psychological and social distress. As we have seen in this chapter, the two are intimately related through cortical, hypothalamic, and pituitary and adrenal functioning. There is evidence that dissatisfaction with one's gender role and marriage can increase the severity of PMS symptoms.[24] Marital distress, as discussed in chapter 2, can be the cause of chronic, resistance-level stress capable of causing imbalances in circulating hormones.

For years stress management has been advocated as part of a comprehensive PMS treatment program.[29] Stress-management techniques such as meditation and diaphragmatic breathing can help control the negative emotional and negative physical symptoms of PMS. Carefully controlled studies examining the role of stress management in the treatment of PMS are needed.

Stress and Muscular System Disorders

Each muscle is actually a mass of millions of muscle cells capable of being stimulated by nerve innervation during a stress response. When muscle contraction occurs, muscles are stimulated fully. They shorten, and movement, or work, is accomplished. When they are stimulated partially, **tension** occurs, but no work is accomplished.[36] Muscles that are chronically tense, or partially contracted, result in a state of **bracing.**

Overview of the Muscular System

The three types of muscles are skeletal, smooth, and cardiac.[76] Skeletal muscles are also known as striated muscles because they have long bands of fibers called striations. These muscles can be controlled voluntarily. Skeletal muscles attach to and cover the skeleton. They are remarkably adaptable and allow us to perform a variety of tasks, ranging from playing a piano to lifting massive weights.

Unlike skeletal muscles, smooth muscles are neither striated nor capable of voluntary action. Smooth-muscle tissue is found in the walls of vital internal organs such as the stomach, bladder, and lungs. These muscles contract involuntarily in response to chemical and nerve messages. We do not have to contract our intestines voluntarily, for instance, to move food along as it is digested.

Cardiac-muscle tissue, like skeletal-muscle tissue, is striated. However, unlike skeletal-muscle tissue, the movement of cardiac muscle is involuntary. The steady rates of a heartbeat are set by a natural pacemaker that electrically stimulates the heart, causing it to beat.

Chronic Muscle Tension and Disease

Chronic, low-level stress results in constant muscle tension in all three types of muscle tissue. Acute, strenuous muscle contractions are not as harmful as chronic, mildly tensing contractions. Chronic muscle tension is a by-product of resistance-phase stress, which is the mild, low-level state of activation that our bodies are put in when we are continually stressed. Often the effects of chronic muscle tension go unnoticed until symptoms present themselves.

The usual symptom of chronic muscle tension in striated, skeletal muscles is pain in a muscle or muscle group. This pain is not attributed to acute overexertion, such as the muscle pain you feel after vigorous physical work. Pain symptoms can range from mild tension headaches to very painful spasms requiring rest and treatment. Symptoms of chronic smooth-muscle tension are disrupted functioning, such as a case of chronic constipation when tensing of the smooth muscles of the digestive system results in changes in digestion and elimination.

tension partial shortening of a muscle

bracing a state of chronic muscle tension

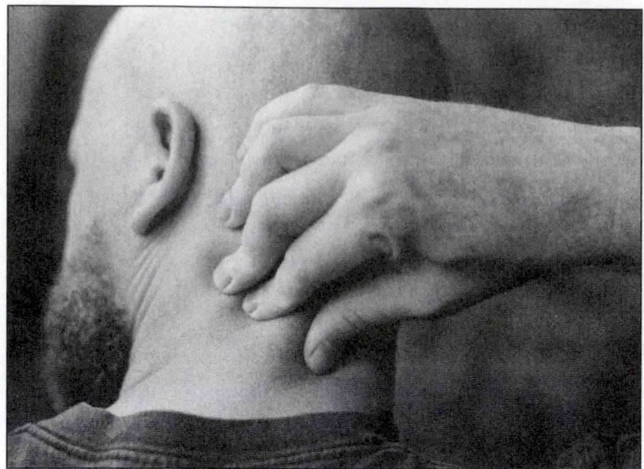
When our muscles are tense, our brains tell us we are stressed.

Furthermore, chronic muscle tension contributes to the perception of stress in the mind by conveying messages that are perceived by the brain as stressful.[30] In other words, when our muscles are tense, we feel "stressed" and this perception reinforces the tension. It is a vicious cycle that is broken only when we can get our muscles to relax.

Chronically tense muscles have been associated with negative health conditions related to skeletal muscles. These health conditions include headache, backache, temporomandibular joint (TMJ) disorder, and muscle spasms, pulls, and tears.[36]

Stress-Related Headache Headache associated with chronic muscle tension is caused by involuntary contractions of the muscles of the eyes, forehead, neck, and jaw which are usually unnoticable. Chronic tension in this region results in tension headaches. Tension headaches have a close relationship to emotional conflict, and, like migraines, can be painful and debilitating.[65]

Stress-Related Backache Backache, especially in the lower back region, is often the result of chronic muscle tension. As with tension headaches, backaches result from chronic, involuntary contractions of skeletal muscles. People who have lower back problems due to other conditions, such as obesity, poor posture, or disc injury, can compound their illness if they are also chronically stressed.

Stress-Related TMJ Syndrome Temporomandibular joint syndrome is a disorder of the jaw. Bruxism, a chronic grinding and clenching of the teeth, can exacerbate the syndrome. This behavior occurs most often at night. In TMJ syndrome, a combination of facial pain, sensitive teeth, headaches, ringing in the ears, and clicking or popping sounds when a person opens and closes the mouth often occurs.[36,75]

Stress-Related Muscle Pain Chronically tense muscles are muscles that are constantly overworked; therefore, these muscles are more susceptible to pulls, spasms, and tears. Muscle spasms, which are unrelenting, extreme contractions of a muscle or muscle group, are often the end product of ignoring the early warning signs of muscle tension, such as mild pain and tension.[36]

Stress and Cardiovascular System Disorders

The relationship between stress and cardiovascular disease is perhaps the most studied and documented stress-related disorder. The cardiovascular system does not work entirely independently of other body systems, especially the endocrine system. Because of this, there is a considerable connection between the two systems in relation to the effects of the stress response.

As described in chapter 5, the cardiovascular system can best be described as a closed system consisting of a pump, tubes, and fluid (fig. 6-2). As we will see, stress affects all three components of this system.

The role of the cardiovascular system is to supply the body with oxygen-rich blood and nutrients and remove waste products from the tissues and cells. It does this in conjunction with the lungs, which provide fresh oxygen to the blood and remove carbon dioxide waste. These functions are critical not only for the long-term health of the entire body but also for a zestful day-to-day quality of life.

People with impaired cardiovascular functioning simply do not have the amount of energy and ability necessary to perform at high levels for long periods of time; their bodies are being robbed of the vital nutrients and oxygen supplied by efficient heart and lung operation. Because all living tissue requires an ongoing, fresh supply of blood to perform effectively, cardiovascular problems affect all body systems. Long-term problems of the cardiovascular system can lead to malfunctioning, premature aging, and death of body parts, body systems, or the individual.

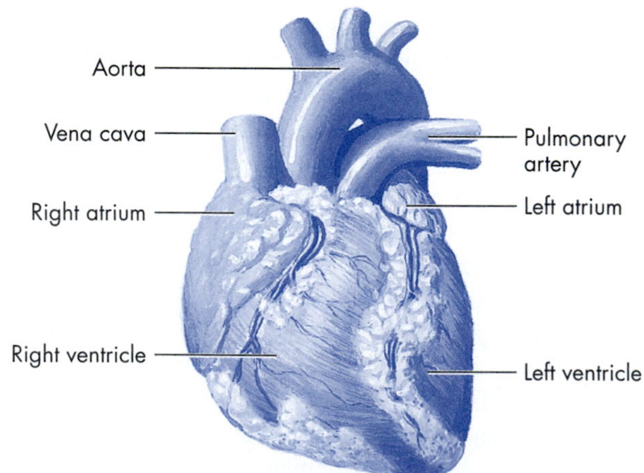

Figure 6-2
The cardiovascular system can best be described as a closed system consisting of a pump (the heart), tubes (blood vessels), and fluid (blood) that constantly supplies the body with oxygen-rich blood and nutrients while removing waste products from the tissues and the cells.

The health of the cardiovascular system is based on three factors. The first factor is the heart's ability to receive nourishment through its coronary arteries. For the heart to pump efficiently, it must receive nourishment from the blood through its own network of coronary blood vessels. Although the heart's job is to pump blood to all body parts, it does not draw nutrients from this process. It is served by its own blood vessels, which must remain open and flexible, delivering an adequate supply of blood regardless of the demands on the heart muscle.

The second factor critical for heart health is the heart's ability to maintain a steady, rhythmic beat despite the varying demands made on it. For the heart to supply blood to critical parts of the body (the brain and heart muscle in particular) on a continuous basis, it must pump rhythmically in all situations. **Arrhythmias, spasms,** and irregular beating patterns are potentially life-threatening because they could possibly lead to a failure to maintain an adequate supply of blood to critical tissue, especially in the brain.[63,64]

Finally, for a person to have a healthy heart, the blood vessels must be able to facilitate the passage of nutrient-rich **blood** by remaining open and flexible and maintaining normal blood **pressure.** As noted in chapter 5, the veins, venules, arteries, and arterioles facilitate the movement of blood by expanding and contracting in response to the heart's beating action. The beating of the heart and the pumping of blood exert pressure against the walls of blood vessels. This pressure is mediated by the blood vessels' ability to stretch during the work, or systolic, phase and bounce back during the rest, or diastolic, phase of a heartbeat. Blood vessels that are clear and pliable allow maximum blood flow under minimum pressure, a state that provides the optimal supply of nutrients and removal of waste without exerting undue wear and tear on the system.

Effects of Stress on the Cardiovascular System Chronic, low-level stress can affect all three components of the cardiovascular system and jeopardize the health of the entire body. It is impossible to isolate these effects from endocrine system functioning in many cases because hormones are directly involved in stimulating cardiovascular functioning on several levels.

Chronic, low-level stress can accelerate the heart rate, making the heart pump faster and under greater pressure than necessary. It can also change the chemistry of the blood, flooding it with excess, life-threatening cholesterol, fats, and other substances. Finally, low-level stress can change the makeup of the blood vessels, speeding the process of **atherosclerosis,** or hardening of the arteries.

Chronic stress can also speed the development of cardiovascular disease in persons with other risk factors, such as sedentary lifestyles, smoking, and diets high in fats and cholesterol. The combination of chronic stress and other risk factors can often be synergistic, resulting in negative consequences beyond the individual risks attributed to each factor separately.

Stress-Related Heart Disease As we have already examined in detail, chronic, low-level stress results in accelerated heart rate and elevated blood pressure. What makes this combination a potentially deadly result of the chronic stress response is its insidious nature. Often, because these effects in resistance are less dramatic than is the case during an alarm reaction, we do not notice them. Unless we check our resting pulse routinely and monitor our blood pressure with a sphygmomanometer, we are usually unaware of elevations in either.

Additionally, it is long-term elevation of these functions that can cause severe health problems. Heart rate and blood pressure normally respond to increased demands by elevating, thereby supplying extra blood to meet energy needs. When these needs are met, heart rate and blood pressure should return to their normal ranges.

Problems arise when they remain elevated for long periods. Chronic **hypertension** damages the **endothelium** of the blood vessels, making them more susceptible to the development of atherosclerosis. Chronic hypertension is also a major risk factor for stroke and heart attack. The increased blood pressure can dislodge **plaques** and send them coursing through the blood vessels. If they lodge in a blood vessel servicing the brain, a stroke occurs. If one lodges in a blood vessel servicing the heart, a heart attack results. Acute stress can also trigger a heart attack due to the dramatic increase in stimulation. Both a stroke and a heart attack can be fatal.

KEY TO UNDERSTANDING

The cardiovascular system is a closed system consisting of a pump (the heart), tubes (blood vessels), and fluid (the blood).

arrhythmias irregular heart rhythms

spasms sudden, involuntary muscle twitches that range in severity from mild to very painful

blood pressure the pressure created against the walls of blood vessels in response to the beating of the heart and the pumping of blood

atherosclerosis the buildup of plaques on the inner walls of arteries

hypertension another name for high blood pressure, meaning elevated blood pressure that consistently exceeds 140/90 mmHg

endothelium squamous tissue that lines the walls of the heart, blood vessels, and lymphatic vessels

plaques accumulations of fat and cholesterol on the endothelium

Stress-Related Changes in Blood Chemistry Chronic stress also affects blood chemistry, which contributes to changes in the structure of the blood vessels themselves. As we discussed in chapter 5, under normal conditions the liver is responsible for producing more than 75 percent of all the cholesterol needed by the body. Any excess cholesterol that is not needed by the body is removed by the liver. The liver works overtime when under chronic stress, producing extra cholesterol to fuel the stress response, while at the same time trying to get rid of any cholesterol that is not needed by the body.

When the liver simply can't keep up with these demands, a certain amount of the cholesterol in circulation is deposited in the interior walls of the blood vessels. Eventually, these deposits accumulate, resulting in atherosclerosis. Besides increased levels of cholesterol, hormonal changes disrupt the normal chemistry of the blood, making this a contributing factor to the hardening process in atherosclerosis.[44,57,79]

Stress-Related Changes in the Blood Vessels **Arteriosclerosis** is the general term used to describe any of a number of degenerative changes in the arteries leading to their decreased elasticity and reduced blood flow. But *atherosclerosis,* as mentioned earlier, is a specific term used to describe changes in the walls of large arteries caused by deposits of fatty plaque, called fibrin (a clotting factor); cholesterol; and calcium (fig 6-3). These changes decrease the diameter of the artery's interior and make the arterial walls brittle. Once the blood vessels lose their elasticity, they become less efficient in transporting and processing nutrients and waste products.

Atherosclerosis is directly linked to increases in blood pressure. When the diameter of the blood vessels gets smaller and the body still requires the same volume of blood, the heart must pump more frequently and under greater pressure to meet this need. The loss of elasticity also contributes to the demands for increased pressure.

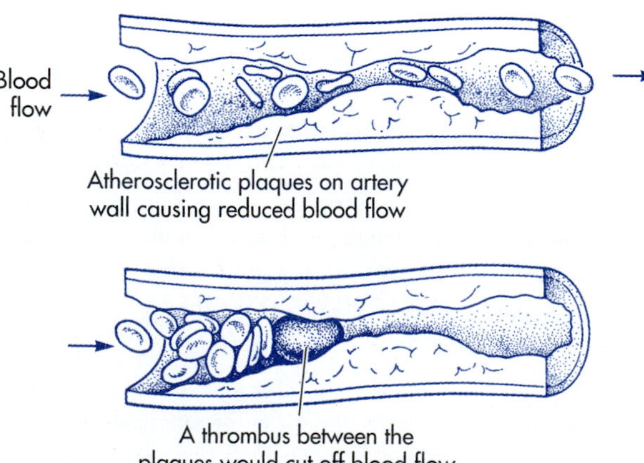

Figure 6-3
Atherosclerotic plaque in an artery.

This deadly combination contributes to both stroke and heart attack.

Stress-Related Migraine Headaches **Migraine headaches** are another major problem associated with stress and the cardiovascular system. Migraine headaches are also referred to as vascular headaches because they involve the carotid artery. The common carotid artery that carries blood from the heart up each side of the head splits into two branches: the external carotid, which terminates in front of the ear, and the internal carotid, which disappears under the bones of the skull.

Migraine headaches typically affect only one side of the head. At some point prior to the migraine attack, the carotid arteries on the affected side of the head narrow, which may result in a flushing, or pallor, of the skin. This narrowing of the arteries before the actual onset of a migraine produces a collection of symptoms called the **prodrome.** These prodromal symptoms include increased irritability, nausea, sensitivity to noise and light, and a sensation of seeing flashing lights. The prodrome starts one to two hours before the actual headache.[38]

Following the prodrome and a period of constriction, the carotid arteries begin to swell. This dramatic constriction, followed by expansion, is responsible for the onset of the headache. Migraine headaches produce painful throbbing and intense pain that can last for several hours or days. Other accompanying symptoms can include nausea, vomiting, chills, sweating, edema, irritability, and extreme fatigue. An attack is often followed by dull neck and head pains and a great need for sleep. The constriction and dilation are believed to be associated with the release of the potent chemicals serotonin, a vasoconstrictor, and bradykinin, a vasodilator, which mediate, respectively, the narrowing and widening of the carotid arteries.

Both physiological and psychological factors seem to be involved in migraine headaches. Migraines often run in families; an inherited migraine trait, due to a recessive gene, is thought to be the cause.[65] Low serotonin levels, or deficiencies in the enzyme that metabolizes it, are believed to be related to the onset of migraines.[38]

Migraine-headache sufferers also share a personality type characterized as ambitious, perfectionistic, rigid, tense, or resentful, yet efficient and poised. In many cases these individuals have experienced emotional crises

arteriosclerosis a general term used to refer to a number of degenerative changes in the arteries that lead to decreased elasticity and blood flow

migraine headache a type of headache caused by the constriction followed by rapid expansion of the carotid arteries in the neck

prodrome a group of symptoms occurring before the onset of illness before the onset of the headaches.[59] They often harbor resentment and hostility and are unable to vent those emotions. Feelings of anger and repressed rage are often present. These emotions are often well concealed and sometimes not even realized by migraine sufferers. Psychotherapists treating patients with migraines find that symptoms are sometimes short-circuited when patients are able to vent their underlying hostility.[58]

As we discussed in chapter 2, there is considerable evidence to support the relationship between illness and stress, anger, and hostility. Emotions, especially powerful emotions such as hostility, rage, and anger, are capable of triggering an alarm response, which can evolve into chronic, resistance-level stress if the source is not alleviated or coped with effectively.

Stress and Immune System Disorders

As we discussed in chapter 5, the immune system is a part of the body's defense network against illness and disease originating from factors and conditions both outside (exogenous) and inside (endogenous) ourselves. Our bodies are equipped, through mechanical and chemical defenses, with the ability to protect us from exogenous invaders such as microorganisms, allergens, and other substances as well as endogenous factors such as mutating cells and improperly functioning tissue.[60,70,71]

A breakdown in any part of the immune system can compromise its ability to perform and lead to a variety of health problems, including immunosuppression and hyperimmunity.[23,37,73] Immunosuppression results in a diminished ability of one or more of the components of the system. Hyperimmunity has the opposite effect, resulting in uncontrolled activation of one or more parts of the system. In either case there is an imbalance in the finely tuned precision required for the system to work at peak efficiency.

Much of what we know about the relationship between the brain, the nervous system, and the immune response has come out of the field of **psychoneuroimmunology** (PNI). PNI was developed in 1964 by Dr. Robert Ader, the director of the Division of Behavioral and Psychosocial Medicine at the University of Rochester.[1]

Psychoneuroimmunology is the study of the intricate interaction of consciousness (psycho), the brain and central nervous system (neuro), and the body's defense against external infection and aberrant cell division (immunology).[59] Although PNI is a relatively new medical discipline, the philosophical roots of the connection between physical health, the brain, and the emotions can be traced to Aristotle.[39] Much of what we know about the effects of stress on the body has come from this science. Cohen, Miller, and Rabin,[23] Cohen and Herbert,[22] Herbert and Cohen,[41] Volhardt,[80] O'Leary,[56] and Pelletier and Herzing[59] all provide detailed reviews of the literature and meta-analyses of the links between immunity and stress.

Stress-Related Immunosuppression Cohen and Herbert[22] and Herbert and Cohen[41] found substantial evidence linking stress to decreased immune system functioning. They found that stress is significantly related to the absolute numbers and percent of circulating white blood cells and immunoglobulin levels. Additionally, they found that these immune system changes are directly related to the duration of stress activation. Vollhardt[80] found that according to most major PNI theorists, stress and psychiatric disorders such as depression and anxiety are the most common neurological links to immune system dysfunction. Vollhardt chronicled some of the major studies implicating such negative emotional states and immune suppression. Pelletier and Herzing[59] and others[71,78] also described the role of stress, loneliness, hopelessness, and depression in immunosuppression. O'Leary[56] described the effects of chronic stress on immunosuppression, paying particular attention to the variables of social disruption, psychological depression, and negative personality attributes.

Several studies have shown that chronic stress exerts a general **immunosuppressive effect** that suppresses or withholds the body's ability to initiate a prompt, efficient immune reaction.[37,41,44] This has been attributed to the abundance of corticosteroids produced during chronic stress, which produces an imbalance in corticosteroid levels and weakens immunocompetence.[60] This weakening of immune system function is thought to be associated with general strain on the various body parts associated with the production and maintenance of the immune system.

As discussed in chapter 5, atrophy of the thymus, a key component of the immune system, has been documented by Selye.[67] Shrinking of the thymus results in its inability to produce T cells or the hormones needed to stimulate them. This can lead to an imbalance and inefficiency of the entire immune response.

Furthermore, chronic stress can deplete nutritional factors associated with immune system functioning. Key nutrients, particularly the water-soluble vitamin C and B complex vitamins, are depleted as a result of chronic stress.[60]

Stress has also been implicated in weakening the part of the immune system responsible for surveillance of the body's mutating cells. During stress these mutant cells are not destroyed because they are not identified by the weakened immune system. Left unchecked, they proliferate and spread, causing cancer.[48,60]

Stress-Related Hyperactive Immunity The effects of stress and other psychological attributes on hyperactive

psychoneuroimmunology the emerging field that studies the effects of stressful emotions on immune functioning

immunosuppressive effect anything that slows down or interferes with the correct immune response

Living Constructively

Accepting and Learning from Disease

One of the most dramatic and useful applications of Naikan self-reflection is in accepting and managing illness. As Krech* points out, it is easy and very common for people who have developed a serious illness to cry out, "why me?" and remain locked in a self-focus that can hinder both their immediate prognosis and future growth. As we've just learned from psychoneuroimmunology, negative emotional states can add to immune suppression, thereby hindering the healing process. Krech* proposes that rather than focus on the self, continually asking, "why me?" why not welcome the illness with "open arms" and shift the focus to what others have done for you. This shift of attention can help you hang onto or enhance the faith you have in your ability to get better and in turn, your immune system's ability to work for you.

Example:

Seven years ago, on December 5, the author's wife Heidi was suddenly stricken with adult-onset Acute Lymphoblastic Leukemia (ALL). With no warning Heidi found herself in a hospital critical care unit at death's doorstep for nineteen days. Although she got perilously close to death on several occasions, she never lost her faith in her doctors, her family, and God. She vowed, "If I can get home by Christmas Eve I'll make it all the way back." Although Heidi did not know about Naikan self-reflection then, here is how she feels she would have answered the three questions:

1. **What Have others Done for Me?**
   - "I have the benefit of one of the leading Cancer specialists putting me on a cutting-edge new treatment regimen."
   - "I am blessed that one of the most impressive cancer specialty units is in a hospital only fourteen miles from my home so it is easy for my family to visit."
   - "The nurses and the doctors in my unit are so caring and supportive. I have the ultimate faith in them."
   - "Rich has been here every day for me, bringing me comedies and musicals that we watch in bed every day and laugh at."
   - "Michael and Will visit almost every day. It is so wonderful for Mike to snuggle up and give me a kiss, despite having these seven tubes connected to my body."
   - "My sister Jane has been so wonderful, bringing me anything I want, especially those peanut butter and jelly sandwiches."
   - "I know God is looking out for me. He won't let me die with so much to live and be grateful for."
2. **What Have I Done for Others?**
   - "I wish I could do more but I have tried to make the nurses' job easier by only ringing them when I really need them."
   - "I have tried to talk with or smile at the other patients and their families in the unit whenever I get the chance. I want them to have the same faith I do."
   - "I have tried to stay positive for the boys, hiding whatever fear I might be experiencing from them. They are so young and I want to stay strong for them."
   - "I have complied with all of the doctor's orders. I will do my best to get the medicine to work."
   - "I have accepted Rich's crazy ideas about visualizing my immune system kicking in. I have even held both of his hands in mine and closed my eyes in an attempt to share his strength and energy."
3. **What Troubles Have I Caused Others?**
   - "I really put a crimp in everyone's Christmas plans. I hope I can get home so they can have a normal holiday."
   - "I am such a burden to Rich. I hate to see him sleep on that pull-out chair in my room every night. He needs a good night's rest."
   - "So many people have taken time off work to come visit me and bring me things. I am really making their lives more complicated than they need to be."
   - "I made my mom so sad. She feels so bad that she is healthy and her daughter is so near death."
   - "I have really given the boys a rude awakening that life is so tenuous. One day I am their invincible mom and the next I am at death's doorstep."

Heidi rarely complained for the nineteen days she was in the hospital (she made it home on Christmas Eve to spend it by the fireplace with her family). She admits to being afraid and having to redirect her feelings away from her fear and onto those around her who were caring for her. She is convinced that doing this helped her marshal all of her energies to getting better not feeling sorry for herself. Heidi is still in remission seven years later.

*Krech, G. (2002). Naikan: gratitude, grace, and the Japanese art of self-reflection. Berkeley CA: Store Bridge Press.

immunity have also been examined.[80] Although most PNI research focuses on immune suppression and its effects on disease, there is research linking stress and psychological disorders with hyperimmunity. **Hyperimmunity** is characterized as an exaggerated autoimmune response, meaning that the body literally turns on itself, perceiving self as an antigen. Autoimmune disorders linked to stress include, but are not limited to, rheumatoid arthritis, ulcerative colitis, psoriasis, and systemic lupus erythematosus.[17,18,19,20,78]

There are both behavioral and immunological adaptations that occur during stressful situations. Because of a central nervous system link mediated by the production of corticotropin-releasing hormone, the stress response can affect certain inflammatory diseases, such as rheumatoid arthritis.[73] The perception of stress activates not only the stress response but also an autoimmune inflammatory response. Because of the link, ongoing stress and affective psychological disorders such as depression may be related to the chronicity of the inflammatory response.[17,77]

Hyperactive immunity also plays a big part in allergies. Common allergens, ranging from pollen and household dust to foods such as chocolate, are responsible for triggering an immune response in susceptible individuals. The presence of these allergens, which are perceived by the body as invaders (antigens), triggers the production of a potent immune system chemical called histamine. In a normal immune response histamine deactivates the invading antigens, rendering them harmless to the body. However, in hyperactive immunity excess histamine is responsible for triggering an inflammatory response that can include swollen tissues, mucus secretion, and constricted air passageways. These reactions result in a runny or stuffy nose, watery eyes, itching, and difficulty breathing—all characteristic of an allergic reaction.[18,60]

In someone with irritable lung syndrome who is susceptible to asthma, exogenous allergens can trigger an asthma attack. During an asthma attack, the large air passageways (bronchi) of the lungs swell, become clogged with mucus, and constrict, making breathing extremely difficult and often frightening.

Stress and negative emotions can serve as endogenous factors capable of triggering an asthma attack in an asthmatic, further demonstrating the mind-body connection in the absence of exogenous antigens. Stress can also exacerbate existing attacks when an attack is perceived negatively, thus creating a feedback loop of attack, causing physical symptoms that the body perceives as stressful, thus perpetuating the attack (see Stress Buster Tips: "Coping with Asthma Attacks").

Stress Buster Tips

Coping with Asthma Attacks

The last thing you want to do if you are having an asthma attack is punish yourself with negative self-talk and self-blame. This will not help and could worsen and prolong the attack. Instead, try this:

1. Accept the fact that you are having an attack and continue to tell yourself, "I will not let this attack get the best of me."
2. Slow down and use your inhalation medication properly (rushing the use of your inhaler will decrease its effectiveness by keeping much of the medicine from reaching the deeper recesses of your lungs).
3. Systematically contract and release the muscles of your neck, shoulders, chest, and abdomen. This will relax your upper body and help your lungs.

Take a break and slowly drink a cup of coffee or tea. Caffeine is a bronco dilator and will help open your airways.

Stress and Digestive System Disorders

As discussed in chapter 5, the digestive system is responsible for processing food from ingestion to elimination. It is directly related to the muscular system because much of the work associated with digestion is controlled by autonomic, smooth-muscle contractions and the release of digestive juices. Refer back to figure 5-7 illustrates the organs involved in digestion.

Chronic stress upsets the digestive process; chronic smooth-muscle tension, combined with excessive levels of stomach acids and decreased levels of saliva, leads to a variety of digestive difficulties. These problems are even worse in people who are chronically stressed and have a genetic predisposition to digestive disorders.

Chronically tense smooth muscles can result in diarrhea, constipation, spasms of the esophagus and colon, and ulcers.[36] Chronic smooth-muscle tension also affects the **peristaltic action** of the digestive system, slowing it down and sometimes causing spasms associated with colitis or irritable bowel syndrome. Partially digested food is not moved smoothly through the digestive system, resulting in constipation or diarrhea.[44] Mucus production in the stomach lining is also diminished during chronic stress, resulting in a greater susceptibility to the effects of digestive juices, particularly hydrochloric acid, which has been implicated in the development of ulcers, erosions in the lining of the stomach.[44]

hyperimmunity an exaggerated autoimmune response, meaning that the body literally turns on itself, perceiving itself as an antigen

peristaltic action contracting and relaxing of the smooth muscles of the digestive system that pushes partially digested food along along the gastrointestinal tract

KEY TO UNDERSTANDING

Stress is both a risk factor for psychological illness and a symptom of a broader problem.

Effects of Chronic Stress on Psychological Illness

Exposure to both acute, traumatic stressors and chronic, low-level hassles may be viewed as a contributing factor in a variety of psychological problems and in some cases may be considered the first stage in the development of certain forms of these illnesses (see Assess Yourself 6-1, "Determining Your Stress Level"). Chronic stress is a risk factor for psychological problems such as burnout, anxiety disorders (general anxiety, panic, phobias, acute stress disorder, post-traumatic stress disorder), mood disorders (major depressive disorder, dysthymic disorders, bipolar disorders), and suicide.[4,13]

Stress-Related Burnout

Burnout, although not an officially classified psychological illness, is a condition in which people lose their concern and feelings for others. Burnout can be defined as a way "to deplete oneself, to exhaust one's physical and mental resources. In effect, to wear out oneself by excessively striving to meet unrealistic expectations imposed by oneself or by the values of society."[13] In most cases, burnout is a response to self-induced psychological stress caused by illogical and irrational beliefs about work and job performance.[6]

Risk factors for burnout include having extreme dedication to work, putting in long hours, taking work home on a regular basis, taking personal responsibility for all uncompleted work (even if the amounts are unrealistic), and feeling anxiety and guilt about undone work.[5,15,16,42] Although burnout has been studied mostly among social workers, psychologists, child-care workers, prison personnel, and other service-oriented professionals whose jobs revolve around helping others, burnout can affect anyone.[15,16,21,30] People who are burned out lose their concern and empathy for those around them and begin to treat them in a detached, mechanical way. Cherniss[15] noted the following symptoms of burnout in the human service workers he studied:

- Loss of concern for clients
- Tendency to treat clients in a detached, mechanical fashion
- Increasing discouragement, pessimism, and fatalism about work
- Decline in motivation, effort, and involvement in work
- Apathy, negativism, irritation, and anger with coworkers and clients
- Preoccupation with one's own comfort and welfare on the job
- Tendency to rationalize failure by blaming clients and "the system"
- Resistance to change, growing rigidity, and loss of creativity

Burnout is a response to the intense, unrelenting stress of caring for others' interpersonal needs. There are four stages of burnout:

1. Enthusiasm—positive feelings about self, work, and ability to help.
2. Stagnation—feelings of a lack of personal or organizational growth and/or progress; sense of sameness; sense of not moving forward.
3. Frustration—feeling that nothing can be done or no one is willing to try.
4. Apathy—no longer caring; more concern for personal comfort.[5,15,16]

Workers experiencing personal stress from non-job-related sources tend to carry this over to their work. This contributes to their overall stress levels and enhances the opportunity for burnout.[5,13]

Stress and Anxiety Disorders

As we mentioned anxiety is a vague uneasy feeling whose source is often nonspecific or unknown to the individual.[6] Chronic anxiety can be specific or generalized.[4,25] In **specific anxiety disorders** there is an identifiable object, event, or situation that is linked to the anxiety.

Stress-Related Specific Phobia The essential feature of Specific Phobia is a marked and persistent fear of clearly discernible objects or situations. There are five subtypes of Specific Phobia:

1. Animal type—Phobic object is an animal or insect such as a dog or spider.
2. Natural environment type—Phobic object is something in the natural environment such as water, storms, or heights.
3. Blood-injection-injury type—Phobic object is blood, a personal or observed injury, or injection.
4. Situational type—Phobia is triggered by being in a situation such as being in an elevator, on a bridge, flying, or driving.
5. Other type—Phobia is triggered by fear of something, such as choking, falling, or catching an illness.[4]

Exposure to these objects and situations causes phobic reactions that can leave a sufferer with feelings of faintness, fatigue, nausea, tremors, palpitations, and panic.[4]

specific anxiety disorder a type of anxiety disorder linked to an identifiable object, event, or situation

The causes of phobias are not entirely clear, although a very stressful, traumatic life event or generalized fear about life is commonly reported.[4]

Stress-Related Generalized Anxiety Disorder Generalized anxiety disorder is characterized as unrealistic, excessive anxiety about two or more life circumstances for a period of six months or longer. The focus of the anxiety is not on another classifiable disorder such as a phobia, panic attack, or obsessive-compulsive disorder. The disturbance is also not due to the effects of substances such as drugs or a general medical problem, and it does not occur exclusively during other types of disorders, such as mood disorders or psychoses. Instead, an individual suffering from general anxiety is bothered by his or her circumstances almost continuously.

General anxiety sufferers feel irritable and tense and have difficulty concentrating. These mental signs are coupled with physical symptoms such as shortness of breath, increased heart rate, cold and clammy hands, a dry mouth, nausea, diarrhea, chills or hot flashes, muscle tension, aches, and soreness.[4]

Stress and Mood Disorders

Mood disorders are psychological illnesses that have disturbances in mood as their characteristic feature. Mood disorders are broken down into major depressive disorder, dysthymic disorders, and bipolar disorder.[4,28]

Stress-Related Major Depressive Disorder The essential feature of major depressive disorder is the presence of one or more major depressive episodes. A **major depressive episode** is characterized by a depressed mood or loss of interest or pleasure in almost all activities. This must persist for most of the day, nearly every day, for at least two consecutive weeks and be accompanied by at least four of the following additional symptoms: changes in appetite or weight, sleep, and psychomotor activity; decreased energy; feelings of worthlessness or guilt; difficulty thinking, concentrating, or making decisions; recurrent thoughts of death or suicidal ideas, intentions, or plans. The intensity of the episode is great enough that it results in sufficient distress to disrupt normal daily functioning.[4]

People suffering from major depressive disorder not only feel "down in the dumps," they also suffer from an ever-present loss of pleasure or interest in most things in life. Things that were previously enjoyable are no longer fun, and their general demeanor is one of not caring about anything anymore. The average untreated episode typically lasts for four months or longer.[4] Over 50 percent of all people having one major depressive episode will have another before returning to normal functioning. Estimates of major cases of depression range from 4.5 percent to 9.3 percent of the adult female population and 2.3 percent to 3.2 percent of adult males.[4]

Stress-Related Dysthymic Disorder The essential feature of dysthymic disorder, also referred to as chronic depression, is a mild, low-level depressed mood that lasts for more than two years (one year for children and adolescents). The diagnosis is based on a person never being without symptoms for more than two months during a two-year period. It differs from major depressive disorder in intensity and duration. Although individuals with chronic depression are able to function, they do so at a less than optimal level. They may experience constant fatigue, feel hopeless, have difficulty making decisions, have low self-esteem, and have difficulty concentrating. They may have a poor appetite or overeat and may have difficulty sleeping or oversleep regularly.[4,28]

Stress-Related Bipolar Disorders The essential feature of bipolar disorders is an alternation between major depressive episodes and **manic states.** Manic states are characterized by high levels of energy, psychomotor activity, and productivity and a decreased need for sleep. Extreme increases in self-esteem, rapid flights of ideas, easy distractibility, and irritability are also characteristic of the manic state. The depressive state, in contrast, is characterized by a depressed mood or loss of interest or pleasure in almost all activities for a period of at least two weeks.[4]

Depression is a normal reaction when we suffer a loss or tragedy or when things don't work out the way we would like. However, when depression lasts more than two to three weeks, it's time to seek help. Although there are many causes of depression, acute and chronic stress are considered major risk factors. Many people become depressed after suffering a traumatic life event. In some cases, events that occur early in a person's life, such as the loss of a parent through death or divorce at a critical stage of development, undermine the development of self-esteem. For others, a chronically stressful environment, whether at work or at home, is a trigger for depression. These stressful life events make some people vulnerable to depression.[4,19,25,33,71]

The shift from manic to depressive states can be influenced by conditions called specifiers.[4] One common specifier is the **seasonal pattern specifier.** Formerly called Seasonal Affective Disorder (SAD), it occurs during the short gray days of winter (see figure 6-4). The lack

major depressive episode a period of depressed mood or loss of pleasure that lasts at least two weeks

manic states distinct periods when a person's predominant mood is elevated, expansive, or irritable and is accompanied by other manic symptoms

seasonal pattern specifier a shift from manic to depressive states that is influenced by the change in seasons, and concurrent weather and daylight changes; formerly called *seasonal affective disorder (SAD)*

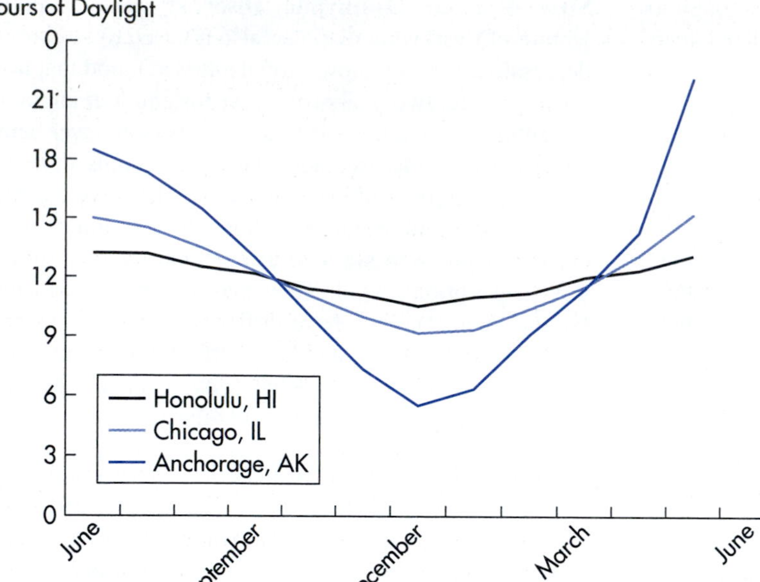

Figure 6-4
People who live further from the equator, and thus experience shorter days during the winter months, are more likely to suffer from mood disorders with a seasonal pattern specifier (commonly called Seasonal Affective Disorder, or SAD).

of exposure to sunlight is perceived as a stressor. From October to March, people with this disorder are depressed and lose interest in work, sex, and other pursuits while craving sweets and rich foods. A seasonal pattern specifier form of depression is related to latitude and is more common among people living in the northern United States where there are longer, more harsh winters.[4]

Stress and Suicide

Suicide can be characterized as a permanent solution to a temporary problem. However, people who take their own lives are desperate; they do not see the options that may be open for solving or reducing some of their problems. They cannot cope with their lives and feel lonely, ashamed, and hopeless.

Suicide rates for adolescents and college-age people are rising.[11] Suicide is now the second leading cause of death for young adults between the ages of 15 and 24.[69] Because of the pressures of modern life and the inability of youth to cope, depressed young people see suicide as a way of dealing with their insurmountable problems.

Although there are many risk factors for suicide among the adolescent and college-age population, three of them are stress-related: depression, major loss, and stressful life events. Other risk factors include demographic factors (nonmedical background data such as the person's age, sex, race, and socioeconomic status), psychiatric disorders, and biological problems, such as decreased levels of serotonin, growth hormones, and corticotropin-releasing factor. However, depression is linked to more than two-thirds of all suicides.[62]

SUMMARY

In this chapter we examined the relationship between acute and chronic stress responses and the development of health problems. We began with a discussion of the concept of psychosomatic illnesses. We then differentiated between the two types of psychosomatic illnesses, psychogenic and somatogenic, and discussed the interplay between the mind and the body in the development, onset, and progression of disease.

We explored several theoretical frameworks that attempt to explain the link between stress and disease development. Among the theories discussed were the medical model, Selye's GAS, and Kraus and Raab's hypokinetic model. We ended this section with a thorough analysis of Everly and Benson's disorders of arousal model, the most comprehensive explanation of the link between stress and disease.

We discussed how acute stress responses, or alarm reactions, help us mobilize the intense amount of energy needed for the fight-or-flight response to save our lives. We discussed how this energy mobilization is crucial to our well-being and can be used positively when we are meeting challenges as well as threats. We also discussed how acute stress can trigger extremely negative health outcomes such as sudden heart attack and acute stress disorder.

We discovered that chronic stress responses, low-level physiological reactions to persistent unrelieved stressors, although milder in nature, ultimately cause us more harm. We explored this in detail, examining the effect of chronic stress on the body parts and systems most directly affected by it. We detailed how stress on these body parts and systems leads to their decreased efficiency, their breakdown, and sometimes the person's death.

We ended the chapter by exploring the relationship between stress and the development of psychological illnesses. Several categories of psychological problems, ranging from burnout to suicide, were examined, with a focus on the role of stress in their development.

STUDY QUESTIONS

1. What is psychosomatic illness?
2. List and describe the two different types of psychosomatic disease.
3. Compare and contrast Everly and Benson's disorders of arousal model to Selye's General Adaptation Syndrome.
4. Compare and contrast the medical model to a psychosomatic view of disease.
5. Discuss the similarities and differences between acute and chronic stress responses.
6. Describe the role of chronic stress in the weakening and eventual breakdown of various body parts and systems.
7. How does chronic stress affect the muscular system?
8. Describe the effects of chronic stress on the endocrine system.
9. How does chronic stress affect the digestive system?
10. Discuss how chronic stress affects the three components of the cardiovascular system.
11. Describe how chronic stress upsets the functioning of the immune system.
12. Describe how stress is related to anxiety disorders.
13. Describe how stress is related to mood disorders.
14. Describe the role of stress in suicide.

DISCOVER OUR CHANGING WORLD

Go to the home page of the National Institute for Stress Physiology http://www.nisp.org/index.html

1. Click on the link "Breaking News."
2. Click on any link to any breaking news story related to stress. These links are updated daily.
3. Write a short summary of the late-breaking news story, connecting it to something in chapter 6.

ARE YOU THINKING CLEARLY?

Many people deny that they are suffering from the effects of stress. They make illogical statements such as "I work best when I am under pressure" and "I'm not stressed, I'm just a little run-down" when in fact they are suffering from stress. One clear way to determine whether you are thinking clearly about this and gauge how stress is affecting you is to compare your current beliefs with an objective assessment.

1. List three beliefs you have about the effects of stress.
2. Take the assessment at the end of this chapter ("Determining Your Stress Level") and evaluate your results.
3. Compare the results of this assessment with your initial beliefs about how stress is affecting you.
4. Are you thinking clearly about stress?

REFERENCES

1. Ader, R. (1981). *Psychoneuroimmunology*. New York: Academic Press.
2. Alexander, F. (1950). *Psychosomatic medicine*. New York: Norton.
3. Amkraut, A. & Solomon, G. (1974). From symbolic stimulus to the pathophysiologic response: Immune mechanisms. *International Journal of Psychiatry in Medicine,* 5, pp. 541–563.
4. American Psychiatric Association. (2000). *Diagnostic and statistical manual of mental disorders.* (4th ed.). Washington, DC: American Psychiatric Association.
5. American Psychiatric Association. (2003). *The road to burnout.* Adapted from Miller, L.H. & Smith, A.D. *The stress solution.* http://helping.apa.org/work/stress6.html.
6. Anderson, K.N., Anderson, L.E., & Glanze, W.D. (1994). *Mosby's medical, nursing, and allied health dictionary.* (4th ed.). (Rev. ed.). St Louis: Mosby.
7. Basson, R., (2000). The female sexual response: A different model. *Journal of Marital Therapy,* 26, pp. 51–65.
8. Basson, R., Berman, J., Burnett, A., et al. (2000). Report of the international consensus development conference on female sexual dysfunction: Definitions and classifications. *Journal of Urology,* 163, pp. 888–893.
9. Berman, J., Berman, L., & Goldstein, I. (1999). Female sexual dysfunction: Incidence, pathophysiology, evaluation, and treatment options. *Urology,* 54, pp. 385–391.
10. Blonna, R. & Levitan, J. (2004). *Healthy sexuality.* Atlanta: Wadsworth.
11. Blumenthal, S.J. (1990). Youth suicide: The physician's role in suicide prevention. *JAMA,* 264(24), pp. 3194–3196.
12. Boulard, G. (2001). After September 11th students find themselves under a magnifying glass. *Community College Week,* 14(10), pp. 2–4.
13. Brown, G.W. (1993). Life events and affective disorders: Replications and limitations. *Psychosomatic Medicine,* 55 pp. 248–259.
14. Chance, P. (1981). That burned out, used-up feeling. *Psychology Today,* January, pp. 88–92.

15. Cherniss, G. (1992). Long-term consequences of burnout: An exploratory study. *Journal of Organic Behavior,* 13(1), pp. 1–11.
16. Cherniss, G. (1980). *Burnout in human service professionals.* New York: Praeger.
17. Chicanza, I.C., Chrousos, G.P., & Panayi, G.S. (1992). Abnormal neuroendocrine-immune communications in patients with rheumatoid arthritis. *European Journal of Clinical Investigation,* 22, p. 635.
18. Chrousos, G.P. (1995). The hypothalamic-pituitary-adrenal axis in immune-mediated inflammation. *New England Journal of Medicine,* May 18.
19. Chrousos, G.P. & Gold, P.W. (1992). The concepts of stress systems disorders: Overview of behavioral and physical homeostasis, *JAMA,* 267, p. 1244.
20. Chrousos, G.P. (1992). Regulation and dysregulation of the hypothalamic-pituitary-adrenal axis: The corticotropin releasing hormone perspective. *Endocrinology Metabolic Clinics of North America,* 21, p. 685.
21. Clark, C.C. (1980). Burnout, assessment, and intervention. *Journal of Nursing Administration,* 10(9), pp. 39–43.
22. Cohen, S. & Herbert, T.B. (1996). Psychological factors and physical disease from the perspective of human psychoneuroimmunology. *Annual Review of Psychology,* 47, pp. 113–142.
23. Cohen, S., Miller, G.E., & Rabin, B.S. (2001). Psychological stress and antibody response to immunization: A critical review of the human literature. *Psychosomatic Medicine,* 63, pp. 7–18.
24. Coughlin, P. (1990). Premenstrual syndrome: How marital satisfaction and role choice affect symptom severity. *Social Work,* 35, pp. 351–355.
25. Cummins, R. (1990). Social insecurity, anxiety, and stressful events as antecedents of depressive symptoms. *Behavioral Medicine,* Winter, pp. 161–164.
26. Davey, J. (2002). One day in September. *Community College Week,* 15(4), p. 4.
27. Dettmer, J. (2001). New York shows strength in adversity. *Insight on the News,* 17(40), p. 13.
28. Deutsch, P. (1959). *On the mysterious leap from mind to body.* New York: International Universities Press.
29. Endler, N.S. & Parker, J.D.A. (1990). Stress and anxiety: Conceptual and assessment issues. *Stress Medicine,* 6, pp. 243–248.
30. Evans, B.K. & Fischer, D.G. (1993). The nature of burnout: A study of the three factor model of burnout in human service and non-human service samples. *Journal of Occupational and Organizational Psychology,* 66, pp. 29–38.
31. Everly, G.S. & Benson, H. (1989). Disorders of arousal and the relaxation response. *International Journal of Psychosomatics,* 36, pp. 15–21.
32 Everly, G.S. & Rosenfeld, R. (1981). *The nature and treatment of the stress response.* New York: Plenum.
33. Everly, G.S. & Lating, J.M. (2002). *A clinical guide to the treatment of the human stress response.* New York: Kluwer Academic/Plenum.
34. Garmon, J. (2001). Making sense, not war. *Community College Week,* 14(10), pp. 4–6.
35. Gerber, R. (2000). *Vibrational medicine for the 21st century.* New York: HarperCollins.
36. Girdano, D.A., Everly, G.S., & Dusek, D. (1990). *Controlling stress and tension; A holistic approach.* Englewood Cliffs, NJ: Prentice-Hall.
37. Glaser, R., Rice, J., Sheridan, J., et al. (1987). Stress-related immune suppression: Health implications. *Brain Behavior-Immunity,* 1(1), pp. 7–20.
38. Goodell, H. (1967). Thirty years of headache research in the lab of the late Dr. Moward G. Wolf. *Headache,* 6, pp. 158–171.
39. Hall, S.S. (1989). A molecular code links emotions, mind, and health. *Smithsonian,* June, pp. 67–71.
40. Harrison, M. (1982). *Self-help for premenstrual syndrome.* Cambridge, MA: Matrix Press.
41. Herbert, T.B. & Cohen, S. (1993). Stress and immunity in humans: A meta-analytic review. *Annals of Behavioral Medicine,* 55, pp. 364–379.
42. Huebner, H.S. (1992). Burnout among school psychologists: An exploratory investigation into its nature, extent, and correlates. *School Psychology Quarterly,* 7(2), pp. 129–136.
43. Kaplan, H.S. (1974). *The new sex therapy.* New York: Brunner Mazel.
44. Karren, K., Hafen, B.Q., Smith, N.L., & Frandsen, K.J. (2001). *The health effects of attitudes, emotions, and relationships.* (2nd. ed). San Francisco: Benjamin Cummings.
45. Kirgiss, K. (2002). Taylor-made service: After the terrorist attacks, 99 students from Indiana's Taylor University drove to New York to help however they could. *Campus Life,* 60(7), pp. 62–64.
46. Klerman, G.L., Weissman, M.M., Ovellette, R., Johnson, J. & Greenwald, S. (1991). Panic attacks in the community: Social morbidity and health care utilization. *JAMA,* 265(6), pp. 742–746.
47. Kraus, H. & Raab, W. (1961). *Hypokinetic disease.* Springfield, IL: Charles C. Thomas.
48. Kune, S. (1993). Stressful life events and cancer. *Epidemiology,* 4, pp. 395–397.
49. Lachman, S. (1972). *Psychosomatic disorders: A behavioristic interpretation.* New York: Wiley.
50. Lane, K. (2002). After the fall: Against the ruined backdrop of Ground Zero, the wounded Borough of Manhattan Community College is struggling to rebuild. *Community College Week,* 14(12), pp. 6–11.
51. Lieblum, S.R. (2000). Redefining female sexual response. *Contemporary ObGyn,* 45(11), pp. 120–131.
52. Lief, H. (1985). Evaluation of inhibited sexual desire: Relationship aspects. In Kaplan, H.S. (Ed.). *Comprehensive evaluation of disorders of sexual desire,* pp. 59–76. Washington, DC: American Psychiatric Press.
53. Manisses Communication Group. (2002). Survey finds impact of September 11th stretches across the country. *Mental Health Weekly,* 12(35), pp. 1–3.
54. Mason, J. (1968). A review of psychoendocrine research on the pituitary-adrenal cortical system. *Psychosomatic Medicine,* 30(5), pp. 576–580.
55. Mason, J. (1968). The scope of psychoendocrine research. *Psychosomatic Medicine,* 30(5), pp. 565–576.

56. O'Leary, A. (1990). Stress, emotion, and human immune function. *Psychological Bulletin,* 108(3), pp. 363–382.
57. Oliver, M.F. (1981). Diet and coronary heart disease. *Behavioral Medical Journal,* 37, pp. 49–58.
58. Pelletier, K.R. (1977). *Mind as healer, mind as slayer.* New York: Dell.
59. Pelletier, K.R. & Herzing, D.L. (1988). Psychoneuroimmunology: Toward a mind-body model: A critical review. *Advances,* 5(1), pp. 27–56.
60. Reichlin, S. (1993). Neuroendocrine-immune reactions. *New England Journal of Medicine,* 13, p. 61.
61. Reid, R.L. (1991). Premenstrual syndrome. *New England Journal of Medicine,* 25, pp. 1208–1211.
62. Rosenfield, A.H. (1985). Depression: Dispelling the despair. *Psychology Today,* June, pp. 29–34.
63. Rosenman, R.H. (1996). Personality, behavior patterns, and heart disease. In Cooper, C.L. (Ed.). *Handbook of stress, medicine, and health,* pp. 218–231. Boca Raton, FL: CRC Press.
64. Rosenman, R.H. (1991). Type A behavior pattern and coronary heart disease: The hostility factor. *Stress medicine,* 7, p. 245.
65. Sargent, J.D., Green, E.E., & Walters, E.D. (1973). Use of autogenic feedback techniques in the treatment of migraine and tension headaches. *Psychosomatic Medicine,* 35, pp. 129–133.
66. Schwartz, G. (1977). Psychosomatic disorders and biofeedback: A psychobiological model of disregulation. In Maser, J. & Seligman, M. (Eds). *Psychopathology: Experimental models.* San Francisco: Freeman.
67. Selye, H. (1976). *The stress of life.* New York: McGraw-Hill.
68. Seong-Ngoo, K. (2002). Psychological burden after September 11th tragedy. *Student British Medical Journal,* May, p. 138.
69. Shafer, D., Vreeland, V., Garland, A., Rajos, M., Underwood, M., & Busner, C. (1990). Adolescent suicide attempters: Response to a suicide prevention program. *JAMA,* 264(24), pp. 3151–3155.
70. Staines, N., Brostoff, J., & James, K. (1993). *Introducing immunology.* (2nd ed.). St Louis: Mosby.
71. Stein, M., Miller, A.H., & Trestman, R.L. (1991). Depression, the immune system, and health and illness. *Archives of General Psychiatry,* 48, pp. 171–177.
72. Sternbach, R. (1966). *Principles of psychophysiology.* New York: Academic Press.
73. Sternberg, E.M., Chrousos, G.P., & Gold, P.W. (1992). The stress response and the regulation of inflammatory diseases. *Annals of Internal Medicine,* 117(10), pp. 854–866.
74. Straw, D. (2001). A separate peace in a wartime classroom. *Community College Week,* 14(10), pp. 4–6.
75. Tasner, M. (1986). Temporomandibular-joint (TMJ) Syndrome. *Medical Self Care,* pp. 47–50.
76. Thibodeau, G.A. & Patton, K.T. (1993). *Anatomy and physiology.* (2nd ed.). St. Louis: Mosby.
77. Tsigos, C. & Chrousos, G.P. (1994). Physiology of the hypothalamic-pituitary-adrenal axis in health and dysregulation in psychiatric and autoimmune disorders. *Endocrinology Clinics of North America,* 23, p. 451.
78. Vamvakopoulos, N.C. & Chrousos, G.P. (1994). Hormonal regulation of human cotricotropin releasing hormone expression: Implications for the stress response and immune/inflammatory reaction. *Endocrinology Review,* 15, p. 409.
79. Van Dorner, C.J.P. & Orlebeke, K.F. (1982). Stress, personality and serum cholesterol level. *Journal of Human Stress,* December, pp. 24–28.
80. Vollhardt, L.T. (1991). Psychoneuroimmunology: A literature review. *American Journal of Orthopsychiatry,* 61(1), pp. 35–47.

Name: ______________________________ Date: ____________

ASSESS YOURSELF 6-1

Determining Your Stress Level

1. Take the following stress assessment from the McGraw-Hill health assessment web page, http://www.mhhe.com/hper/health/personalhealth/labs/Stress/lab10-1.html.
2. Evaluate your score.
3. Write a short overview of your stress level based on the results of this assessment.

Determining Your Stress Level

To evaluate your level of stress and help you identify changes that you need to make, circle the number under the appropriate response to each question.

Use the following guidelines in making your decisions:
Rarely: almost never
Sometimes: once or twice each week
Often: four or more times each week

How Frequently Do You:	**Rarely**	**Sometimes**	**Often**
1. Experience one or more of the symptoms of excess stress, such as tension, pain in the neck or shoulders, and headaches?	1	3	5
2. Find it difficult to concentrate on what you are doing because of deadlines or other tasks that must be completed?	1	3	5
3. Become irritable when you have to wait in line or get caught in a traffic jam?	1	3	5
4. Eat, drink, or smoke in an attempt to relax and/or relieve tension?	1	3	5
5. Worry about your work or other deadlines at night and/or on weekends?	1	3	5
6. Wake up in the night thinking about all the things you must do the next day?	1	3	5
7. Feel impatient at the slowness with which many events take place?	1	3	5
8. Find yourself short of time to complete everything that needs to take place?	1	3	5
9. Become upset because things have not gone *your* way?	1	3	5
10. Tend to lose your temper and get irritable?	1	3	5
11. Wake up in the night and have a hard time getting back to sleep?	1	3	5
12. Drive over the speed limit?	1	3	5
13. Interrupt people while they are talking or complete their sentences for them?	1	3	5
14. Forget about appointments and/or lose objects or forget where you put them?	1	3	5
15. Take on too many responsibilties?	1	3	5

Add together the numbers that you circled.

Enter your score here _____

Evaluate your score according to the following criteria:

Potential level of stress
Low: < 35
Moderate: 35–42
High: 43–50
Very high: > 50

PART

II

The Five Rs of Coping with Stress

In chapter 6 we discussed Everly and Benson's (1989) disorders of arousal model. As we discovered, this model provides the most comprehensive analysis of the mechanisms by which the stress response manifests itself in disease. In essence, the link between stress and disease is arousal.

Everly and Lating (2002) used this model to identify the three key elements of arousal that characterize the stress response and are the precursors to the development of stress-related diseases. The three elements are (1) increased neurotransmitter arousal and activity, (2) increased neuromuscular arousal, and (3) increased negative cognitive arousal. All three levels of arousal are linked and work together in initiating and sustaining the stress response. A comprehensive model for coping with stress should incorporate strategies designed to break this chain, stop the stress response, and initiate a relaxation response.

The Five Rs of Coping with Stress

Part II of this book revolves around self-help strategies for coping with stress that you can learn without the aid of professional counselors or therapists or expensive high-tech gadgets. While there is no doubt that professional counseling and psychotherapy can be very helpful (and indicated) for certain people and expensive equipment can sometimes make coping easier, you will not find much about these types of interventions in this book. There are many other stress management books on the market that cover these. Instead, what you'll find in Part II of this book is a myriad of simple, easy-to-learn, coping strategies that are organized into five levels of defense against stress. This approach to stress management is called the Five Rs of Coping.

The Five Rs of Coping Model provides a variety of strategies and levels of coping that can be used

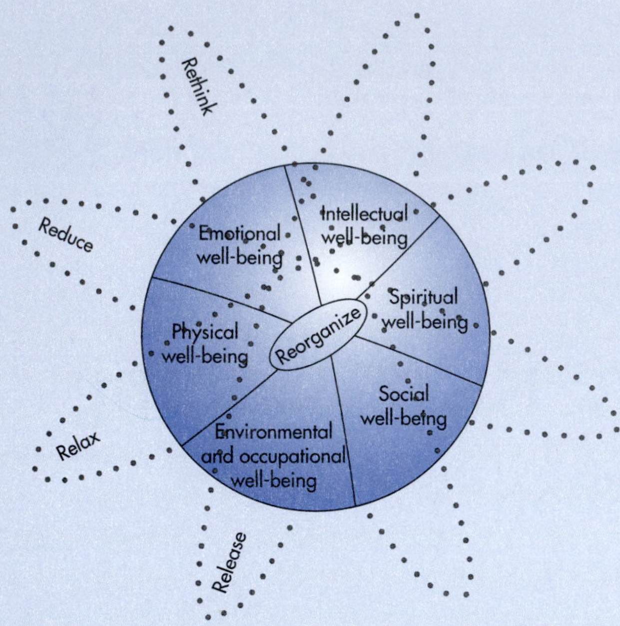

This wellness model of stress management integrates high-level health and five levels of coping.

independently or together. A key to effective stress management is realizing that different techniques and potential stressors are influenced by space and time. What worked for you in coping with a potential stressor on a specific occasion may not be effective the next time you confront the same potential stressor. Having a stress management plan that incorporates different kinds of strategies and levels of coping is flexible and enables you to meet the challenges of coping with stress in a changing world.

The five Rs of coping are rethink, reduce, relax, release, and reorganize, and they represent a multilevel wellness-based approach to stress management. The stress management strategies incorporated into the five Rs of coping are designed to combat one or more of the three levels of arousal identified by Everly and Lating. Throughout chapters 7 through 11 we will discuss how the strategies and levels of coping (Rs) work independently and together to reduce arousal and the stress associated with it. A *synergistic* effect occurs when all the levels of coping are working together simultaneously. The combined result is much greater than the sum of the individual parts.

Rethink strategies, which are presented in chapter 7, help us minimize cognitive (and subsequent neurotransmitter and neuromuscular) arousal and decrease repetitive negative self-talk. Rethink strategies work by helping us examine our thoughts and illogical beliefs about life and potential stressors and replace illogical, irrational beliefs with more logical, rational ones. This helps us defuse potential stressors by changing the way we view them.

Reduce strategies, which are presented in chapter 8, help us minimize all three levels of arousal by focusing on reducing the amount of stressors in our lives. Even when we are involved in too many enjoyable activities and demands, we reach a point of physical, intellectual, and emotional overload and feel we no longer can cope; then these things become stressors. These strategies reduce arousal by reducing stressors.

Relax strategies, which are presented in chapter 9, work by inducing a relaxation response. Relaxation is incompatible with stress and works by decreasing neurotransmitter, neuromuscular, and cognitive arousal. The relaxation techniques described in chapter 9 work in a variety of ways to reduce arousal. The chapter presents a variety of techniques you can learn to perform by yourself in the privacy of your own home.

Release strategies, which are presented in chapter 10, work by providing a positive, vigorous physical outlet for the energy produced by the stress response to maintain homeostasis in the face of threat. Release strategies help reduce all three levels of arousal by inducing a state of fatigue associated with physical activity. The fatigued, relaxed state that follows the activity is incompatible with the stress response.

Reorganize strategies, which are presented in chapter 11, work by integrating techniques from chapters 7 through 10 into a wellness framework for a more stress-resistant lifestyle. Daily practice of these techniques creates a hardier, more stress-resistant lifestyle by increasing your level of wellness across all seven dimensions (physical, social, spiritual, emotional, intellectual, occupational, and environmental). Such a lifestyle is designed to reduce the frequency and intensity of your stress arousal.

CHAPTER

7

RETHINK: CHANGING THE WAY YOU VIEW THINGS

OUTLINE

Rethinking Your Perspective on the World

- Knowing What You Value
- Purposeful Living and Goal Setting
- Putting Things in Their Proper Perspective
- Reducing Stress by Enjoying Life More
- Changing Your Perspective by Slowing the Pace of Your Life

Rethinking the Way You View Stressors

- Becoming More Logical and Optimistic in Our Thinking
- Where East Meets West: Using Morita and Naikan Therapies to Rethink How We View Potential Stressors
- Changing Our Perspective by Rethinking Road Rage—Anger on the Highway
- Using Rational Thinking and Japanese Psychology to Rethink Road Rage

OBJECTIVES

By the end of the chapter students will:

- Analyze and clarify their personal values on a number of issues.
- Evaluate how a perspective on life relates to stress.
- Explain and give examples of the three humor skills.
- Apply Ellis's ABCDE model of rational emotive therapy to coping with a personal stressor.
- Analyze how Morita psychotherapy relates to coping with stress.
- Apply Seligman's ABCDE technique to coping with a personal stressor.
- Describe Seligman's concept of learned optimism.
- Explain the role of humor in stress management.
- Demonstrate competency with a variety of humor skills.
- Demonstrate competency with a variety of anger-management skills.

The concept of *Rethink* as a defense against stress revolves around the belief, reinforced in many places in this book, that most of our stress is determined by the way we view the world in general and potential stressors in particular. As we've mentioned several times in this book, our perception of potential stressors determines whether or not they become stressors and trigger the stress response. Often, our appraisal of potential stressors and the emotions aroused by them is inaccurate and based on a distorted world view or faulty and illogical thinking. This chapter will review several different strategies for examining how we view the world and potential stressors and changing this view if it contributes to our stress.

RETHINKING YOUR PERSPECTIVE ON THE WORLD

Becoming more logical and rational regarding how we view the world often requires that we change our **perspective.** In a sense, this is our *big picture* of how the world and the people in it *should be*. This broad perspective view is generally colored by our values, ethics, and goals, essentially what is most dear to us and central to who we are as people. When this world view is *threatened,* we feel unable to cope and are therefore stressed. If we can change our perspective, we often can reduce our stress. Sometimes it is as simple as realizing that a situation or person is potentially stressful to us because they represent something different, new ideas or behaviors that are foreign to us. Often if we can just shift our focus off ourselves and try to view the situation from their perspective we can reduce the stress. There are many different ways to change one's perspective for the purpose of reducing stress.

Changing the way we view individual potential stressors requires that we step back and distance ourselves from them and then reexamine what emotions they trigger and what we are telling ourselves about them. In doing this we can use techniques that will help us examine whether we are thinking clearly, logically, and optimistically (less likely to be stressed) about those stressors or lapsing into muddled, illogical, catastrophic thinking (which makes us more likely to be stressed). If we prefer, we could also shift our attention off ourselves (our thoughts and feelings) and onto the world around us or the task at hand. As we'll see, this is the preferred approach of Morita and Naikan therapies, and a fundamental tenet of Living Constructively.

This chapter is divided into two halves. The first half will examine how to *Rethink* your worldview. It is devoted to helping you know who you are, what you value, how your goals and purpose reflect this, and how all of this relates to your stress. The second half focuses on helping you examine your thoughts and actions when confronted with potential stressors and how to think more logically and/or act more purposefully when dealing with them. By the end of the chapter you should be on your way to *Rethinking* how you view the world and potential stressors.

Knowing What You Value

Our **values** are the mirror of our personalities and are central to defining who we are as people. While our knowledge, attitudes, and beliefs strongly influence who we are and paint a picture of us for others, it is our values that are the foundation on which those other facets are built. When we are children and young people, our values usually mirror those of our parents. As we move through adolescence and young adulthood, our values often change and become more personal, a mixture of what we have learned from our parents and what we have chosen to embrace from our culture. Sometimes our values are threatened and cause us stress when they clash with those of our parents or our culture. When this happens, clarifying our values and understanding what is central to who we are as people can be very helpful in reducing the stress associated with this threat (see Stress in Our World 7-1: "Maria: An Inner Values Conflict").

Values Clarification

Values clarification is a process of helping individuals clarify and stand up for what they truly value. It is a three-part process involves prizing, choosing, and acting on one's values.[29,34]

- Prizing beliefs and behaviors—During the first step of values clarification, individuals explore their values and are given opportunities to affirm and prize them publicly. This process allows individuals to stand up for the things they hold sacred.
- Choosing beliefs and behaviors—The second value-clarification step involves examining values against other options. After consideration of the consequences, people are allowed to choose either their values or other values from the alternatives examined in clarification activities.
- Acting on beliefs—The third and final step involves taking action that is consistent with one's beliefs. Students are supported in their attempts to use their values to shape a lifestyle that helps them act with consistency.[29,34]

Figure 7-1 portrays a hierarchy of values. The **core values** are the things that are central to who you are and for

rethink changing the way we think about the world and potential stressors

perspective a person's relative mental picture, or point of view, in regard to a particular situation or event

values personal beliefs, morals, ethics, and/or ideals

core values our most deeply held beliefs about the things that are central to who we are as people

STRESS IN OUR WORLD 7-1

Maria: An Inner Values Conflict

Maria is feeling stressed. She is in the middle of her first examination for her philosophy class and notices that the woman next to her, Dawn, is cheating. Dawn has a small piece of paper with tiny notes written on it taped to her arm and covered by her sweatshirt. Every time the professor turns his head or walks away, Dawn rolls up her sleeve and glances at her notes. Other students seem aware of this but go about their business and ignore Dawn.

Maria is not used to this. As a Roman Catholic of Italian-American descent, Maria grew up in a strict Catholic family and attended religious schools through the primary and secondary grades. She was taught that cheating is a sin against God. To view another person cheating and not do something was considered almost as bad.

As a result, Maria is feeling confused. Although she has heard other students talk about cheating, she has never observed such a blatant attempt. Should she say something to Dawn, the professor, her classmates? Why doesn't somebody else say something to Dawn? Why doesn't the professor see what is going on? Why is Dawn cheating? Isn't it immoral to cheat? Why should I care so much? These and a hundred other questions go through Maria's mind as she becomes increasingly more distracted by Dawn's cheating.

She finds herself thinking more about Dawn than about her own performance on the test. Maria then gets angry. She realizes that she is becoming stressed by this inner-values conflict brought on by Dawn's cheating. Maria is in the throes of an intrapersonal conflict.

which you would fight or die. Students typically identify such things as country, spouse, children, religion, and freedom as core values. These are the values that are most likely to cause stress when they are threatened. Surrounding this core are lesser-held **satellite values** that you hold dear but to which you are not as strongly committed. Students identify things such as political beliefs, cultural traditions, personal attributes such as intelligence and beauty, pursuits such as recreation and sports, and so forth. These types of values are more amenable to "rethinking" for the purpose of stress management.

Not surprisingly, when we are put into situations in which we perceive that our values are being threatened, we often become stressed. We might refer to this type of potential stressor as an **intrapersonal conflict.** Understanding our values helps us view potential stressors in the proper perspective. A key to understanding what stresses us and then coping with it effectively is being clear about the things we value. Take a moment to complete Assess Yourself 7-1, "Strength of Values." This activity will help you clarify your values and understand how they relate to your stress.

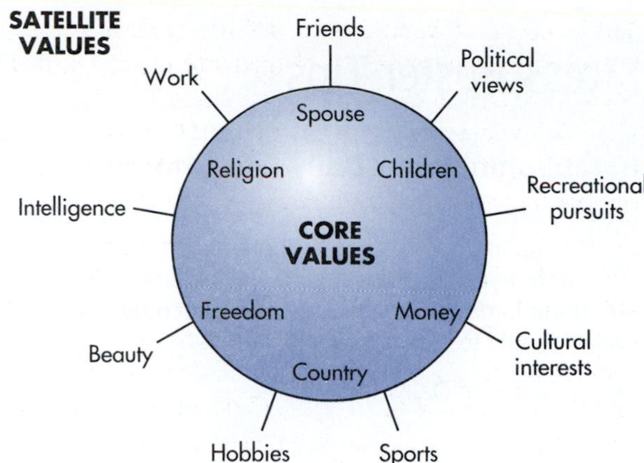

Figure 7-1

Our core values represent our most deeply held beliefs about the things that are central to who we are as people. Our satellite values are less important to us and more open to compromise and change.

Using Daily Life Criteria to Rethink Your Perspective

Another way to understand what you value and how it affects your life and stress is to approach this topic from the opposite direction by assessing what it means to you to have a *good* day or *stress-free* day. Generally, these good days are those that are free from major conflicts between who you truly are and how you live your life. These days don't include having to play roles that make you uneasy or compromise the things that have value and meaning for you. They usually include engaging in fun activities, and time just seems suspended as the day passes. Most students, when asked to keep a stressor log or diary have entries labeled stress-free day or good day, usually followed by a smiley face ☺. These are days that generally were calm and happy or afforded them the opportunity to do what they truly wanted to do or to just be themselves without pretenses. While they may have experienced slight fluctuations in mood or external events during this time, they were generally offset by the overall *goodness* of the day. It is this author's belief that these days were good because they represent a state where there is no (or minimal) conflict between one's values and one's behavior. It is an idyllic state where who we truly are and what we do mesh seamlessly for a short period.

Anderson & Krech[1] call this a day in which we meet our Daily Life Criteria (DLC), our standards for living life well. For the most part, one's DLC are concrete activities that are done on a daily or regular basis. Some examples Anderson and Krech[1] cite from their work with

satellite values values that are less important to us and more open to compromise and change

intrapersonal conflict problems arising because of conflicts within a person, such as an assault on a person's values

Stress Buster Tips

Establishing Your Daily Life Criteria

Imagine a perfect day *for you* and what it would include. Where would you be living? What would you be doing? Who would you be doing it with? Would you write, sing, run, create, make love, cook extravagant meals or serve simple meals to others in a soup kitchen?

List up to seven Daily Life Criteria:

1. ____________________________
2. ____________________________
3. ____________________________
4. ____________________________
5. ____________________________
6. ____________________________
7. ____________________________

How do these DLCs represent your core and satellite values?
How do these DLCs relate to the purpose and direction of your life?
What is standing in the way of you meeting these criteria for living a good life?

clients are: exercising three times a week for one hour, meditating twenty minutes each day, writing for one hour each day, having breakfast with one's partner each morning, etc. One's Daily Life Criteria set standards for how you want to live your life. They touch on every facet of life from diet to how you want to live your life with your partner, to where you want to live. The more one lives in consort with one's DLC, the less stress one will experience because one is being true to one's values.

DIVERSE PERSPECTIVES 7-1

Whose Life Is It Anyway: Americans Out of Control?

In *How I Found Freedom in an Unfree World,* Harry Browne[3] suggests that most Americans are caught up in living someone else's life. Often we live by an agenda that is set by someone else. Though American culture encourages independence, at the same time it romanticizes the idea of being out of control. Soap operas, song lyrics, and romantic novels are full of characters who are passionately overwhelmed and out of control of their emotions and behavior. Carol Cassell[4] in her book *Swept Away* describes how American women grow up believing that losing control of their emotions and sexual behavior while in the throes of passion is acceptable and even desirable. A by-product of this attitude, however, is the abdication of responsibility for one's behavior. Being *out of control* becomes an excuse for not assuming responsibility for behavior. Our popular culture makes it seem as though we have no control over our emotions or behavior once life throws us a curve. People love to share in our grief and wallow in our self-pity. They feel cheated if we handle things and don't get swept away. Network news thrives on stories that focus on this lack of control. People who can adjust, who can pick themselves up and get on with their lives if things don't go their way, are viewed as emotionless automatons or *boring*.

The downside of being out of control as far as stress management is concerned is being less hardy and *stress resistant*. Susan Kobasa[18] found that people who are more hardy feel *more* in control of their lives. They have an internal locus of control and are able to *pull their own strings.*[7] People who pull their own strings resist being swayed by others. They make their own plans and decisions, based on a rational assessment of the issues and how these issues relate to their lives.[8] They sometimes go against conventional wisdom because it isn't right for them, and they don't buy into illogical assumptions about potential stressors.[3]

Purposeful Living and Goal Setting

If you take the time to ask ten people what their purpose in life is or what they are purposefully pursuing, you'll be amazed at their answers. Some of them will just look at you strangely and start to back away slowly. Others will stop and scratch their head and say, "Purpose, you mean like what's my plan?" Many will describe their purpose in terms of their short-term or long-term goals. They'll answer with statements such as: "I am planning on going to law school and becoming a lawyer" or "I am in a technology school learning computer programming" or "I am working with my band on a demo CD and we plan on going on tour next year." Such purposes are specifically linked to career or job plans. Still others will admit to a higher calling. They'll respond with answers such as: "I want to give something back to my community" or "I want to work to save the environment" or "I want to stop the war in Iraq and all future wars." One's purpose in life is very personal and can be defined in many different ways.

A key to understanding purposeful living in terms of stress management isn't having the *right* purpose as defined by others; the key is *having* a purpose, one that meshes with who you are, your values, and your daily life criteria. People who have no purpose are like the wind, they are unpredictable, they change direction for no apparent reason, and they often are dormant for days on end. Finding purpose in life is central to managing stress. Examining your values and your daily life criteria are tools that can also help you think about your purpose in

KEY TO UNDERSTANDING

Effective goal setting requires setting small, manageable goals that you have a realistic chance of achieving.

life. Once you start finding your purpose you can start setting goals for achieving purposeful living.

Setting Realistic Goals

When we are thinking clearly and being true to ourselves, our **goals** are directly related to our values. For instance, we set a goal to finish college because it is a prerequisite for acquiring the type of career and lifestyle we value. We have a goal of choosing a partner because he or she shares our values and sense of what is important and meaningful in life.

When we are not thinking clearly or being true to ourselves, we let others set goals for us that are not consistent with our values. When we let pressure from parents, friends, or others determine what college major we take, which career path we choose, or who we pick as a partner, our values are threatened, we feel we can't cope, and we become stressed.

Often, when we are without focus or direction in our lives, we are like ships adrift at sea without anchors. We move in and out of relationships, schools, and jobs, seemingly at the whim of fate.

Our goals can be as lofty as we want; however, the best goals are ones that are realistically within reach. By setting realistic goals, we can guarantee ourselves a better chance of success. A key to understanding realistic goals and objectives is realizing that they are rooted in action. Goals such as finishing college, starting one's own career, buying a house, and serving in the Peace Corps revolve around behavior. To realize our goals we need to take action. It is not enough merely to dream about what we want. We have to be willing to do the work. When we reach our goals, it enhances our self-esteem and motivates us to set bigger and more difficult goals. Setting unrealistic goals sets us up for failure. Continual failure to reach our goals can lead to disappointment and reinforce doubts and negative beliefs we may harbor about our abilities. In actuality, all of us have had our share of success. We just tend to forget this. Take time to assess your life goals by doing Assess Yourself 7-2, "Goals and Objectives Worksheet."

Setting Measurable Objectives

One way to ensure that your goals are met is to set concrete, measurable objectives for each goal. Because our goals are often lofty and immeasurable, establishing measurable objectives helps us keep our focus. Measurable objectives answer the following question: Who will do how much of what by when? John's case is a perfect example. His overall goal is to get better grades in college. He could refine that goal by restating that he would like to raise his grade point average by 0.5 of a point. To accomplish this, he could set the following objective: "By the end of next year (by when), I (who) will earn at least a B (how much) in all five of my classes (what) each semester."

It is also important to remain flexible when we set our goals and evaluate our results. Sometimes things happen that change the course of events midway through the process of working toward our goal. We need to be fluid and adapt to these new demands. Sometimes we will need to reformulate our goals, but other times just stretching the time frame for completion will suffice (see Stress Buster Tips: "Effective Goal Setting").

Stress Buster Tips

Effective Goal Setting

1. Complete Assess Yourself 7-1, "Strength of Values."
2. Decide which aspects of your life you want to work on, improve, or explore (for example, improve your level of fitness, save some money, learn a new hobby). Remember, you cannot meet all your goals at the same time.
3. Prioritize your goals. Rank them on a scale of 1 to 10 (1 being the most important) and start working on the most important ones.
4. Break large goals down into smaller segments. If you eventually want to be able to run marathons, start by getting into shape for a 10,000-meter run.
5. Set goals you can reach. You can ensure success by setting goals that are within your reach. Success in reaching these smaller goals will eventually get you to your overall goal.
6. Make your goals measurable. Be as specific as possible. "I would like to lose ten pounds in the next three months" is an example of a specific, measurable goal.
7. Set a reasonable time frame for each goal. Without linking your goal to a time frame, you may lose your commitment. Make sure you give yourself enough time to reach your goal.
8. Reward yourself for success. Put some money aside or get someone you love to commit to doing something nice for you. Your reward could be as simple as putting aside the time to take a bubble bath and relax.

Expecting and Embracing Change

"The only constant in life is change!" Perhaps if we all grew up believing this, we would be less stressed when

goals an end toward which we direct out effort

KEY TO UNDERSTANDING

Understanding that life is constantly changing will help us accept change and rethink it as a potential stressor.

life throws us a curve. All one needs to do is look around at nature to see examples of change. The seasons change, ushering in times to plant and harvest. The weather changes, bringing with it much-needed rain, breaks from scorching heat, refreshing wind. Animals adapt to threats from predators or changes in their environment. People change as they adapt to new technology, new information, new insights. If we stop to really look at and think about change, we can begin to expect it and not fear it. Expecting that change is an inevitable part of life puts it in a new perspective. No longer is it some unknown entity; it is a normal part of life. Accepting change and viewing it as healthy and growth-enhancing can go a long way to reducing the stress most people associate with it.

Instead of embracing change, most people in our culture grow up believing in the fallacy that someday we will be "home free." We believe that if we control as many variables as possible, everything will work out as planned. If things don't work out, we get stressed, angry, or depressed. "How can life be so unfair?" we lament when things don't go our way. It would be nice if life did always work out according to plan. Unfortunately, however, the best intentions sometimes go awry. Just when everything is going the way we want it to, something happens to set us back or force us to shift to "plan B."

To thrive, not merely survive, we must adapt to change or be left behind. We must always be ready with a plan B, even if that plan is simply to be open enough to allow ourselves to view something differently than we have in the past. Rethinking starts with the acceptance of change and ends with the creative application of new ways to manage it. Believing that change is the only constant in life doesn't mean letting go of all control over our lives. Rather, it means developing a mind-set that allows us to be fluid and adapt to the inevitable change that being truly human entails. Hardy people embrace change and are able to adapt to it and thrive under changing circumstances. Such an attitude enables us to see stressful situations in the proper light. We are at least in control of the way we view our lives. This is exactly the attitude that Kobasa[18] found equates to hardiness.

KEY TO UNDERSTANDING

A key to understanding change is realizing that to thrive—not merely survive—we must embrace change or be left behind as the world passes us by.

Putting Things in Their Proper Perspective

Sometimes we become stressed as a result of losing our perspective on an issue or a problem. For example, we might blow something that someone said to us out of proportion. We may make a big deal out of a little problem or setback that, when viewed in a broader perspective, is really not that important. Somehow we lose our ability to view the issue from a broader perspective and overemphasize our needs or problems while everything else takes a back seat to us. We become, in Metcalf and Felible's[25] words, "the center of the universe." In other words, our concern or our problem becomes so important in our own minds, we think everyone and everything revolves around us. Therefore the things that involve us take on added significance. If anything goes wrong with them, it is very stressful. When we have a more realistic perspective, we step back from the problem or issue and take a more objective look at it. Our perspective is not clouded by our overblown sense of importance or urgency.

How do you know when you are acting like you are at the center of the universe? Metcalf and Felible[25] describe two different *center-of-the-universe* types. The first type of center-of-the-universe person feels that nothing is ever their fault. They blame others when things go wrong. Someone else always screws up, never them. By blaming others they have an illusion of control. The second type feels so important that whenever something goes wrong it is *always* their fault. They feel that their importance extends to the accomplishments and failings of others. They do not think the units they are connected to (family, work, social) could possibly survive without them, and therefore they want to be connected to everything involved about them. They do not delegate responsibilities. Whenever something goes wrong, they always blame themselves. They feel as if they should be able to plan for and control even the most minute details of their lives and relationships. Lastly, center-of-the-universe types often exhibit both characteristics: sometimes feeling that nothing is their fault and other times believing that everything is their fault.

Why do people develop this *center-of-the-universe* position and take on such an attitude of importance? Probably because they have a hard time accepting the absurdity of life.[25] They may have grown up with the belief that they could control all the variables in life. However, just when they think everything is under control, life throws them a curve. Metcalf and Felible[25] developed three strategies, entitled the three humor skills, for changing one's perspective and escaping from the center of the universe. The three skills which we will discuss in the next section of this chapter are: (1) the ability to see the

KEY TO UNDERSTANDING

Sometimes the best way to deal with absurd people and situations is to laugh at them rather than thinking about how unfair or crazy or stressful they can be.

absurdity in difficult situations, (2) the ability to take yourself lightly while taking your work seriously, and (3) having a disciplined sense of joy in being alive.

Embracing the Absurdity of Difficult Situations

According to Metcalf and Felible,[25] one must develop the first skill, accepting **absurdity,** to escape from the center of the universe. They firmly believe that since you can't control everything in life, you might as well laugh over the absurdity of it all. Some things you will encounter are so ridiculous that the only way to deal with them is to laugh at them. To do this, however, takes training. In many cases we have to relearn just how absurdly funny life can be.

Life and people can be very absurd when you think about it. In a recent nationally televised, professional football playoff game, the favored team was getting blown out. Everything it tried backfired. On-target passes were dropped, tackles were missed, balls were fumbled and then recovered by the opposing team. By the end of the first half, the favored team was down 35 to 3—a truly absurd situation for the quarterback of this team. It would have been easy for him to give in to the temptation to quit.

Instead, however, he gathered his team and said, "Listen, we've got nothing more to lose. Let's go out there, open it up, and have some fun. Let's take it one down at a time." In doing this he took the pressure off. Sometimes it takes getting to a point where we feel we have nothing more to lose before we can lighten up and see the absurdity of it all.

That quarterback was able to march his team back, play by play, to tie the game at 38 and throw it into overtime, when his team won it on a field goal (see Stress Buster Tips: "Creating an Absurdity Library").

Focusing on the Bright Side

Another way to put things into a different perspective is to focus on their bright side. We can learn something from even the most absurd or painful situations if we allow ourselves to. Norman Vincent Peale[27] wrote a book more than fifty years ago that is as timely today as the day it was written. His message is: There is incredible power in thinking positively about things. We have already seen in chapter 2 how our brains translate neutral stimuli into either stress or no stress according to our perception of harm, challenge, or ambivalence. Peale explains not only how we can use positive thinking to reduce stress but also how we can use it to maximize psychological well-being.

Although Peale's message is delivered in religious terms and his ultimate source of strength is belief in God, secular people can learn a great lesson from it as well. In a sense what Peale is saying is that it is up to the individual. You can focus on the dark side, the negative, debilitating aspects of your life, and be stressed, or you can cut those loose and focus on the bright side, the positive aspects of any situation (see Stress in Our World 7-2, "The Fisherman").

F. Scott Peck[28] in *The Road Less Traveled* in a way shares this sentiment with Peale. Peck believes that we need to acknowledge the fact that life is difficult and that sometimes we will find it very hard to keep going. However, we need not fixate on this. By focusing on the dark side and wallowing in self-pity, we can miss out on all of the beauty and fun in life. Peck[28] believes that we need to acknowledge that life is tough before we can move on and get beyond the negative aspects of situations.

Focusing on the bright side does not mean denying the existence of pain. It simply means making the most of a bad situation without denying its existence. It also

Stress Buster Tips

Creating an Absurdity Library

This tool is designed to help us remember how absurd and humorous the world can be. When we get caught up in taking things too seriously, we sometimes need to be reminded of the absurdity of it all.

Instructions:

1. Starting today, begin to put together your own personal absurdity library. Compile cartoons, song lyrics, stories, letters from friends, advertisements, and photographs. You can even add records, tapes, and videos to your collection. In no time, your collection will be overflowing with goodies to dig into when the need arises.
2. Look for things that have personal meaning for you, even if others do not view them as special.
3. Add to your collection daily.
4. Whenever you feel the need, stop what you're doing and go to your absurdity library.

Adapted from Metcalf, C.W. and Felible, R. (1992). *Lighten up: Survival skills for people under pressure.* New York: Perseus Books Group.[25]

absurdity a sense of amusement at the silliness and irony of a situation

STRESS IN OUR WORLD 7-2

The Fisherman

There is an old fable about a fisherman who went out to sea one day with his two sons. The day started off like any normal day in their Mediterranean fishing village. The men in the village would spend time getting their hand-held nets ready as their sons prepared the twenty-foot wooden rowboats for the day's fishing. In the fable, the fisherman and his two sons did the same and then took turns rowing out to the fishing grounds a couple miles offshore. It was a beautiful day, and the fishing was good.

Around noon, however, their luck changed. The skies began to darken quickly as the wind picked up. Before they knew it, a storm roared in and they were being tossed around in twenty-foot waves, their sense of direction gone. Not knowing which way to row, they let the tide take them and prayed for the best. Conditions worsened, and the father feared for the lives of his sons. All seemed lost when suddenly a beacon appeared in the darkness, pointing the way to shore. Summoning all their strength, they rowed toward the beacon, crashing through the waves and moving steadily toward the shore.

As the boat neared safety, the old fisherman realized what the beacon was. Apparently, his house had been struck by lightning during the storm and the resulting fire was lighting the way home. As they approached the smoking, charred remains, the fisherman's wife came running up and threw her arms around her men, thanking God for their safe return.

Have you ever experienced anything like this in your life? Could you turn a tragedy around and see the bright side? Has it proved true in your life that there is a silver lining to every dark cloud?

means cutting loose from the experience once you have grieved long enough. Assess Yourself 7-4 helps you focus on the bright side.

Taking Yourself Lightly While Taking Your Work Seriously

This second humor skill is one that exemplifies grace and modesty, two qualities sorely lacking in most of us. It is characterized by a humble attitude and a proper perspective. As we have already discussed in this chapter, it is hard to take yourself lightly when you view yourself as the center of the universe.

Metcalf and Felible[25] use the example of a young boy with cancer to explain what they mean by this second humor skill. When undergoing chemotherapy, this young cancer patient would imitate the sounds of various animals. He would squeal like a pig, bark like a dog, and cluck like a chicken. The medical staff would go along with him, and his treatment sessions would be lighthearted exchanges of animal sounds. For most people chemotherapy is a painful, serious situation. Metcalf and Felible couldn't understand how this boy could be so playful under such circumstances. The boy explained it by saying that he was not the cancer. Cancer was only part of his life. He took the disease seriously and attended treatment faithfully, believing that the discipline involved in seeing it through just might save his life. However, he didn't dwell on it. He was doing all he could do. He didn't take himself so seriously that he had to stop being a kid and having fun. In fact, the silliness helped; it made him and everyone else feel better.

Stress Buster Tips

Photo Funnies

Photo funnies are just the thing for a quick, simple reality check whenever you begin to take yourself too seriously.

Instructions:

1. Go to an arcade where they have an inexpensive photo booth.
2. Make the most ridiculous, silly faces you can muster.
3. Take a few pictures.
4. Pick the silliest and keep them with you in your wallet or purse.
5. Whenever you begin to take yourself too seriously, put yourself at the center of the universe, or deal with someone or something that is truly absurd, pull out your pictures and take a good look at yourself.
6. Remember, you are not just the problem you are having—you are this too.

From Metcalf, C.W. and Felible, R. (1992). *Lighten up: Survival skills for people under pressure.* New York: Perseus Books Group.[25]

Having a Sense of Joy in Being Alive

The third humor skill is having a sense of joy in being alive. How many of us stop long enough to reflect on how great it feels to be alive? Sometimes we take it for granted. Do you know someone who has been very close to death—someone who has suffered a life-threatening illness or accident? These individuals often seem like changed people. Suddenly they are able to see the absurdity of life and all the time they wasted on meaningless things. They sense the preciousness of each day and live it as if it were their last. These people have a renewed zest for living and joy in the simple things in life. Assess Yourself 7-6 encourages you to create your own joy list.

Putting More Humor and Laughter into Life One of the best ways to change the way we view the world is to

STRESS IN OUR WORLD 7-3

Rich: Naikan and the Fallacy of the Self-Made Man

Rich is a very successful professor, writer, consultant. He recently attended a ten-day retreat in Japanese psychology to see how the material and concepts would *fit into* his existing work. He went into the experience a self-confessed *self-made man* and left a changed person humbled by his lack of gratitude. Rich had always believed that he had achieved his success the American way, through hard work, self-sacrifice, and having the courage to take advantage of opportunities when they presented themselves.

After describing such sentiments to his teacher, he was instructed to pick one aspect of his success and to do Naikan self-reflection on it, examining what others did for him as well as the troubles he caused others while achieving his success. Rich chose his textbook writing as the area to do Naikan on. Here is what he discovered:

A. What have I done for others (regarding my writing)?

1. I have offered to include others in my writing projects.
2. I brought two colleagues on as co-authors on two different books.
3. I have shared data and information gained from researching my books in conference presentations and other forums.
4. I have brought material from my books to my classes to enrich them.
5. I have included some of my students' writing and research in my books.
6. I have given my books away for free to friends, the library, and certain students.

B. What have others done for me?

1. Someone invented personal computers, without which it would have been much more difficult to write my first book.
2. Market forces combined to reduce the price of personal computers so I could afford one.
3. I received free computer training at my university.
4. My wife allowed me to divert a sizeable chunk of our money to buy the computer, a fax machine, cable Internet access, and other items needed to write.
5. My job (college professor) afforded me the time to write. The four-day schedule, breaks during the day, and summer months all contributed to finding the time to write.
6. The university library, complete with Internet access, made doing the research manageable.
7. The reference librarians at the library are at my disposal to search databases and assist me in researching material for the book.
8. Having fast (cable modem), affordable Internet access at home made doing the research easy.
9. My editors were instrumental in helping me get through the initial first and second drafts of my manuscripts. Their expertise in composition, grammar, and aesthetics really made the final drafts a reality.
10. My publishing house had everything needed to create, publish, distribute, and market the book. I did not have to even think about that stuff.
11. The publishing industry is supported by the trucking, train, warehousing, retailing, and college bookstore industries that were instrumental in selling the book and returning the profits to me.
12. I was fortunate that other publishers saw my success with my initial book and offered me contracts to write subsequent books in other areas.
13. My wife put up with my needs for privacy, time, and delayed gratification.
14. My wife supported me emotionally over the years when I wanted to quit writing and doubted my abilities to write books.
15. My kids respected my need for privacy and allowed me to write for several hours each day during the summers when they wanted me to take them somewhere or play with them.
16. My friends and colleagues at work supported me emotionally as I struggled to complete my first book.
17. My chairperson at work has helped me craft work schedules that maximized my writing time.
18. My university supported my writing and rewarded me with a promotion, merit raise, and recognition, in large part because of my writing.
19. My parents expressed pride in my writing.
20. My mother-in-law spoke often, and kindly, of my writing and brought copies of my books to her senior citizen's meetings.
21. Earnings from my first book made it easier and more motivating to write.

C. What problems have I caused others?

1. I am sometimes short-tempered with people who waste my time because it is so important to my writing.
2. My work scheduling needs make it harder for my chairperson to fill other class time slots.
3. I am often unavailable for friends and family because I am writing.
4. I don't always answer the phone and talk to people when I am writing.
5. I don't always respond to e-mails promptly because I am writing.
6. I sometimes neglect my wife because I am writing or doing research on my books.
7. I am not the best neighbor because I don't take the time to socialize with my neighbors. I use that time to write or escape from the pressures of writing by being alone or with my wife.

(Continued)

Stress in Our World 7-3 *(Continued)*

8. I don't spend a lot of free time on campus because I'd rather use it to write.
9. I have little patience for friends and colleagues who are not *productive* with their free time and sometimes view them as lazy.
10. I am often self-centered and guard against sharing my time with others.

Rich's Conclusions:
I never really realized how much support others had given me for my writing until coming to this retreat and doing Naikan on just one aspect of my life and my success. After examining other aspects of my life throughout the week using Naikan self-reflection, I realized that even highly motivated, hard-working people like myself would be nowhere without the support of others. I had never really thought about how living in such an affluent, free state and country really sets the stage for my success.

I used to take things such as affordable technology, reliable energy, clean water to drink, free libraries to access, etc., for granted. I don't take these things for granted anymore. I am grateful for them and have started expressing my gratitude for them whenever the opportunity presents itself.

take it less seriously and laugh at it more often. We need to put some humor back into our lives. Humor has as its root the Latin word *umor,* which means fluid, like water. Humor helps us be more fluid and go with the flow of our lives. Fluid is also the opposite of rigid and tense. It is not coincidental that when we laugh, we can't be stressed. It is physiologically impossible to be laughing (a relaxation response) and stressed at the same time. **Humor** can be "a set of survival skills that relieve tension, keeping us fluid and flexible instead of allowing us to become rigid and breakable in the face of relentless change."[25] Viewing humor this way is empowering because it implies that we can learn these humor skills. Like any new skills, we must practice the skills for them eventually to become conditioned responses to the absurdity of life and the reality of change.

Reducing Stress by Enjoying Life More

How much do you enjoy your life? Are you having as much fun now as you would like to be having? Are you doing the things you enjoy, or have you lost sight of the notion that life is supposed to be enjoyed and that you deserve to have fun? Assess Yourself 7-5, "Am I Having Fun Yet?" is a quick activity designed to help you assess your fun level.

If there isn't much fun in your life at this time, lighten up—you're not alone. Many of us have lost sight of the fact that we need and deserve to have fun. As a culture we have become so self-conscious about having to be good at everything we do that we have lost our ability to try something that looks like fun, even if we can't be good at it. The childlike innocence we are born with—the ability to let loose spontaneously, free from concern about what other people might think—has been replaced with a concern for how well we can do things. Our fun has become so organized that we feel we can't even play unless we have taken lessons first.

In some cases we simply have forgotten how to laugh. We have been surrounded by so much sadness that we forget what it means to be happy. Our home life, instead of contributing to our happiness, has robbed us of the joy we should be experiencing. Sometimes we surround ourselves with people who are joyless. Like the mythical Scrooge, they scowl their way through life, "bah humbugging" everything that is happy. They overanalyze and approach life through a pseudosophisticated cynical haze that finds most simple and fun things boring. In other cases we may just work too hard. We have bought into the Puritan work ethic to such an extent that we have forgotten that the purpose of work is to enable us to live the kind of life we truly enjoy. Instead of trying to work smart, we are obsessed with working hard. Instead of working to live, we live to work. Our work becomes our life (see Stress Buster Tips: "Learn How to Play Again").

Most Americans define themselves by their jobs rather than by how they live their lives off the job. As a culture we are obsessed with work. We have bought into the belief that we should feel guilty if we don't strive our hardest to work our way to the top. And today simply working is no longer good enough; we now must have careers. Instead of viewing work as a way to provide for our needs, most people view work itself as a need. It is no wonder that people have a hard time leaving their work at

Key to Understanding

A key to enjoying life more is surrounding yourself with people who have a zest for living.

humor a quality or sense of silliness, absurdity, or amusement

Stress Buster Tips

Learn How to Play Again

What did you do with your extra day off last Memorial Day weekend? Did you spend it picnicking with friends? Taking the first swim of the season? Enjoying the latest box-office hit?

Or did you feel compelled to spend the long holiday weekend involved in much less pleasurable pursuits, such as painting the house, cleaning the yard, or, worst of all, catching up on work that you brought home from school or the office? If you did any of these things or were plagued with guilt because you did not do anything "productive" with your weekend, you are not alone.

The following are some tips to make your leisure time more fun:

- Keep work and play separate.—Although the weekend golf outing with the boss is inevitable, keep this and other forms of mixing work with leisure to a minimum.
- Do not turn play into work.—Do not turn each game of tennis into the finals at Wimbledon. Leisure-time sports and hobbies are played for fun, not to win at all costs.
- Find new playmates.—If you spend most of your free time with the same circle of friends, you are probably doing the same things. Meet new people and create new play opportunities by changing your socializing patterns.
- Expand your leisure horizons.—Devote one day a month or every other month to trying a different play activity.
- Do what you really enjoy, not what you think you should do.—Rollerblading may be all the rage, but if it is not for you, participating will be a source of stress.
- Don't rule something out because you think you will not excel.—Skiing the novice trails can be just as exhilarating as doing the expert slopes. You do not have to be an expert at an activity to enjoy it.
- Do not put off until tomorrow the fun you can have today.—Too many of us promise that someday when we have the time we will try this or that. Make the time today! Pencil into your schedule a certain amount of "fun" time each day.

A good way to have fun is to combine socializing with good friends with healthy activities.

the office. Taking work home or on vacation, or feeling that one is too valuable even to take a vacation are other examples showing that our work has become central in our lives. This partially explains why many of us have a hard time relaxing on our days off.

Other cultures perceive work in an entirely different light. Southern European and Latin American cultures build breaks or siestas into the middle of the day. These extended "lunch hours"are not spent hunched over a desk, furtively munching a sandwich while trying to get in extra work. Rather, they are spent in the company of family or friends, sharing a meal, and often include a restful nap or break. Work is resumed after this break. Additionally, in most European countries people go "on holiday" for at least four weeks in the summer. The pace of work slows down, and operations revolve around human needs. However, productivity in these countries remains high, in some cases higher than in the United States. West Germany, for instance, before its merger with East Germany, enjoyed a standard of living second to none though its workers toiled for fewer hours on the job than Americans did.[21] Even Japanese workers, famous for their intensity, long hours, and level of commitment, try to infuse into the work environment activities that reduce stress and increase productivity. Exercise sessions, singing, and team-building efforts all work to build the body and the spirit and help diffuse the pressures of the job.

Changing Your Perspective by Slowing the Pace of Your Life

Think about the pace of your life. How would you characterize it? Is it about average, faster than average, slower than average? What are some examples of things that contribute to the "pace" of living?

Students typically list things such as the speed at which people talk, drive, and complete work as examples of the pace of living. Others mention drive-through windows at banks, drugstores, fast-food outlets, dry cleaners, and other places as examples of a fast-paced life. Some students point out "express" checkout lines in supermarkets and other stores as an example of a faster pace. Others describe the way in which people on the street greet or don't greet each other and how service workers in stores and restaurants either take the time to talk to you or not.

The author lives and works in a very fast-paced part of the country (central and northeastern New Jersey, respectively). People routinely drive twenty miles over the speed limit and tailgate those who are not driving at least ten miles over the limit. People work and talk at breakneck speed, leaving little time to express pleasantries with neighbors or strangers. Everything is available through a drive-through lane, and heaven forbid that someone should have one item over the limit in an express checkout line.

Living Constructively

Changing Your Perspective by Paying Attention

As we've mentioned a few times in this text, one of the three primary skills involved in Living Constructively is working with your attention. To help fully understand what that means, Krech (2005) developed the following Seven Basic Assumptions about Attention:

1. **Your experience of life is not based on your life, but on what you pay attention to.**
   Although you might have been exposed to something, if you did not pay attention to it, you missed it.
2. **Psychological suffering is generally associated with a heightened degree of self-focused attention.**
   Research has shown that focusing on such emotions as depression and anxiety doesn't always help resolve them. In many cases such self-focused attention to one's experience of these problems will magnify them.
3. **What you pay attention to grows.**
   This has both positive and negative connotations. For example; paying attention to the sounds of birds in your garden will heighten your awareness of them and help you discriminate between the various sounds. Paying attention to your anger will fuel it and keep it alive.
4. **Different tasks/situations require different attention skills.**
   Being able to discriminate subtleties in color, for instance, requires enhanced visual attentiveness while being able to put together your child's bicycle that came in 100 parts requires the ability to pay attention to details and following instructions in a particular order.
5. **Most of us exercise little voluntary control over our attention.**
   Television, multitasking, and other forms of stimulation have trained us to attend to fast-moving, varied stimuli. This has made it difficult for us to focus our attention on a single item for a sustained period of time.
6. **When you shift your attention, "lead" with the body, not the mind.**
   Krech (2005) recommends engaging in physical activity that involves using the large muscles (arms, legs, shoulders, etc.) of the body in moderate to fast repetitive activity if you want to shift your attention away from your thoughts. It is harder to worry about what happened yesterday when you are stacking firewood or shoveling the snow off your driveway.
7. **Working with your attention is a skill and competence that requires practice.**
   Increasing your attention isn't mystical or impossible. Anyone can do it if they work at it and practice regularly.

These assumptions underlie many of the activities and assessments contained in this chapter and the rest of the sections of the book dealing with attention.

When we live in a very fast-paced environment, everything speeds up and we literally get swept away in the rush. We get tense, continually feel rushed, become excessively time-urgent, and feel there aren't enough hours in the day. When this happens, it is easy to lose one's perspective on time and life. We begin to develop illogical beliefs about how quickly things need to get done and how fast we should live our lives. We rush our way through the day, often at such an intense pace that we miss many of the details that give our lives texture, depth, color, and richness. We keep putting things off because we can't afford to "waste" the time. And then, one day, we simply run out of time.

We do not have to become slaves to someone else's beliefs about time and the necessity to live our lives at a breakneck pace that detracts from the quality of our lives and creates stress. All we need do is intentionally *slow down*. We can also begin intentionally to build things into our lives that force us to slow down and live at a slower pace. Assess Yourself 7-8 provides a quick assessment of the pace of your life. You can use the various activities mentioned in this assessment as "slow the pace" techniques to work into your daily schedule. Incorporating these types of activities into your daily routine will increase your awareness of a reasonable pace of living and help you slow down.

Working with Your Attention

One of the best ways to slow our pace and change our perspective on life is to slow our thinking down. Our brain is a remarkable organ that can do more than one thing at the same time. Take engaging in a conversation with a friend as an example. The average person speaks at a rate of about 125 words per minute. Our brains can think at a rate between 500–1000 words/minute.[5] In other words, if we allow it to, our brain will be able to listen to our friend while we think about something else at a rate of between 375–875 words per minute (the difference between listening to our friend and thinking about something else). Because our brain is capable of doing more than one thing at the same time, it is easy for us to focus part of our attention on something other than the task at hand. How often have you found yourself doing that while talking to a friend, listening to your professor, talking with your parents? How often have you allowed your brain to be somewhere other than being fully focused on what you were engaged in *right now,* whether it was a conversation with someone, making love with your partner, or listening to music?

This is just one example of what John Kabat Zinn,[14] inventor of the Mindfulness-based approach to stress management, describes as evidence of our evolution from human *beings* to human *doings*. Many of us, Kabat-Zinn notes, have lost our ability to merely *be in the present.*[15] Whether we are sitting in a hammock or a chair by the pool or at the shore or in our favorite chair listening to the radio, we often find our minds mulling over things from the past or planning what we will be doing in the future instead of just simply enjoying *being* in the hammock or chair and enjoying the moment.

Kabat-Zinn describes a funny story about how on one occasion he was taking his morning shower and found himself holding a meeting with colleagues that would occur later on during that morning. He was literally going through the entire script for the meeting in his head, literally describing his positions on the key issues to be discussed, forming his colleagues' comments and mouthing his rebuttals. He describes how he completely missed out on the experience of *being* in the shower, the warm water cascading down on his body, the fragrant soap washing away the prior day's remnants, and the warmth loosening his muscles and getting him ready to face the day. While such an example might seem innocuous and for some people even a good idea, focusing on the future or the past at the expense of the present can result in our inability to **be** in the present when it *really* counts; like when we are in a real meeting, or making love with our partner, or in a concert hall listening to a concert.

Our attention is usually misdirected by focusing on three areas: the past, the future, and on the self rather than the present. Focusing on any or all of these can sidetrack you from paying attention to the present and also on what needs to be done. Obviously, there are times when it is perfectly acceptable to focus on any of those three areas. We often focus on the past when trying to remember some person, place, or event. We focus on the future when making plans and setting goals, and we focus on the self when we reflect on our thoughts and feelings about something. These are all appropriate examples of focusing on the past, future, and self. Inappropriate focusing on the past, future, or self occurs when we do this when engaged in something in the *present* that demands our full attention. This type of focusing is really misdirected attention and can have stressful consequences.

KEY TO UNDERSTANDING

When you are really paying attention you are focusing all of your thinking and senses on what you are engaged in at the present moment.

The Costs of Misdirected Attention

Misdirected attention is intimately related to stress because of the repercussions we often face when we don't pay full attention to life. It affects our personal lives, our work, our safety. Krech[20] describes ten costs associated with misdirected attention:

1. *Psychological Suffering*
   The more self-focused one's attention is, the more it contributes to problems such as anxiety, depression, shyness, etc. By constantly going over problems, it keeps them in the forefront of one's awareness.
2. *Making Mistakes*
   When people don't pay attention to what they are doing, they make more mistakes.
3. *Increased Safety Risks*
   A major risk associated with all types of accidents (from motor vehicle to home), injuries (at work and at play), and crime (both violent and other) is failure to pay attention to safety procedures and protocols.
4. *Oversensitivity to Changes in the Body*
   Hypochondriacs have misdirected attention. Every subtle normal body change is perceived as a potential problem (often exacerbating existing problems).
5. *Not Appreciating the Support of Others*
   When our attention is constantly turned inward, on the self, we fail to notice what others are doing to support us.
6. *Boredom/Lack of Interest*
   When we pay attention to life's details, the world becomes very interesting (much more interesting than us). When we are bored, we are not paying attention to the richness around us.
7. *Not Noticing What Needs Doing*
   When our attention is misdirected we often confuse *what we feel like doing* with *what needs to be done.*
8. *Forgetfulness*
   When our attention is misdirected we forget where we put things, forget appointments, and forget items on our *to do* list.
9. *Wasting Time*
   Misdirected attention takes our attention away from what we need to be doing, wasting time, and setting us back.
10. *Causing Unnecessary Trouble to Others*
    You are not an island. The costs of your misdirected attention is passed on to others .

KEY TO UNDERSTANDING

Multitasking can become problematic when it becomes your normal way of attending to tasks without realizing it.

One of the main culprits of misdirected attention is **multitasking.** Multitasking basically means doing more than one thing at the same time. How many people do you know who watch television, listen to music, send instant messages on the computer or text messages on their cellular phones all while doing homework? In our fast-paced world it has become common place to *have* to do more than one thing at a time. Is there a price to pay for all of this divided attention? Once again it comes down to deciding when multitasking becomes harmful. No one can argue that intentionally multitasking when doing homework, for instance, won't result in you being more productive in terms of the *volume* of other things (in addition to the homework) that you can accomplish. You can simply do more by doing many things at once. The question is whether the *quality* of your homework and other things that you have just accomplished is acceptable. If you are doing homework while sending and receiving text or instant messages, watching television, and listening to music, how high is the quality of that work? How much better would it be if it received your *full* attention? Only you can decide this for yourself based on your morals, ethics, and personal standards.

The second potential problem with multitasking is when it becomes your *unintentional* standard operating procedure and you don't realize it. Many people become so caught up in multitasking that they either do not realize they are doing it or they cannot turn it off. They find themselves automatically doing more than one thing at the same time to the detriment of everything they do. Not only does this involve physical tasks, it can also involve thinking and this can lead to problems. This typically happens during school when your mind wanders in class and you start thinking about other commitments or events later in the day instead of paying full attention to the professor. It is also common during lovemaking when people are thinking about other things (bills, the kid's dentist appointment, etc.) instead of focusing fully on their partners and what is going on physically between the two of them. Unintentional multitasking is insidious and can take over without you realizing it.

RETHINKING THE WAY YOU VIEW STRESSORS

If you agree with the central premise of this book that stress is the result of an appraisal process that leaves us believing that we can't cope with a potential stressor, you certainly realize how important our thoughts and beliefs are in this process. Illogical thinking about potential stressors and our ability to cope with them is the single greatest cause of stress today. By thinking illogically, blowing things out of proportion, and misunderstanding the potential consequences of potential stressors, we create the bulk of the stress associated with modern living. There are thousands of minor potential stressors for every life-threatening stressor or major life event we encounter in any year. If we can learn how to appraise potential stressors more positively by thinking more logically about them, we can drastically reduce our stress levels without even having to remove the potential stressors. We can defuse them as stressors simply by changing the way we think about them.

Becoming More Logical and Optimistic in Our Thinking

As we discussed in chapter 2, rational emotive behavior therapy (REBT) uses logical thinking and positive self-talk as aids in reducing stress and neuroses. In fact, the underlying premise of REBT is that people or things do not cause stress—our illogical beliefs and irrational self-talk are the culprits. Logically, REBT techniques revolve around understanding our illogical beliefs and replacing them with more rational thoughts.[9]

Using Ellis's ABCDE Model to Think More Logically

Ellis and Harper's[8] ABCDE technique for reducing distress embraces this concept. Figure 7-2 outlines what the letters ABCDE stands for and defines each step.

We can illustrate the ABCDE technique further by discussing Rich, a first-semester college senior who wants to change his major from international marketing to education. After an intern experience during the summer, Rich decided that the high-powered world of international marketing was not for him. He thinks that he really wants to work with young people, teaching business to high school students. After making the decision to switch his major, he informs his girlfriend. She is very upset by the news. Disappointed that he wants to teach, she claims that he will never be able to support a family on a teacher's salary. She is annoyed that he didn't know what he wanted sooner. His parents are also worried about him changing focus so late in his college career.

In Rich's situation, the ABCDE technique would work like this:

A.—Rich's girlfriend and parents react negatively to Rich deciding to change his major.

multitasking the practice of attending to more than one thing or activity at the same time

 (Activating event)—the primary stimulus that activated the stress response

 (Belief system)—our illogical beliefs about **A** (accompanied by the specific negative self-talk)

 (Consequence)—the negative physical, mental, and behavioral effects of **B**

 (Dispute)—a process of substituting more rational, logical beliefs and self-talk for each **B**

 (Effects)—an assessment of the effects of the dispute process on **C**; Did **D** result in diminished consequences?

Figure 7-2
The ABCDE technique for reducing stress.

B.—As a result of all the flak he is getting, Rich subvocalizes the following illogical beliefs:

1. "I shouldn't make this change so late in my college career."
2. "I should really enter a career in which I can earn more money than I can earn teaching."
3. "I should have known sooner what I wanted."
4. "I shouldn't disappoint my girlfriend and my parents."
5. "I'll never amount to anything."
6. "As a teacher, I'll never be able to support a family."
7. "I never do anything right. What's wrong with me?"

C.—As a result of all of this negative self-talk and illogical thinking, Rich is experiencing the following symptoms:

1. Physical
   Muscle tension in his neck and upper back
   Tension headaches
   Difficulty sleeping
   Fatigue
2. Mental
   Loss of self-confidence
   Anxiety
   Difficulty concentrating
3. Behavioral
   Not wanting to go out much on the weekend
   Not seeing his girlfriend in a week
   Arguing with his parents over little things almost every day
   Going out late a few nights a week, drinking by himself at the local bar

D.—Rich decides to tackle his problem by analyzing each of these illogical beliefs and substituting more rational thoughts in their place.

1. "I know it's not going to be easy, but I need to make this change now. I know I will not be happy and productive if I stay in international marketing."
2. "Money is important, but I'll never be good at something I don't want to be doing."
3. "It certainly would have been easier if I had known at 19 that I wanted to teach. The truth is, I didn't find out until this summer when I did some work with a neighborhood youth group. Besides, most of my marketing courses will fit with my new major: business education."
4. "Although I don't like to cause my family and girlfriend pain, I've got to be true to myself if we are to have honest relationships."
5. "I've already accomplished a lot. There is no reason to believe I can't be an excellent teacher."
6. "It may be difficult on a teacher's salary, but there are a lot of men who teach and support their families. If I ever marry, I need to have a wife who also wants to earn part of the family income."
7. "I've made tons of correct decisions in the past. This is the right decision for me."

E.—As a result of working through the dispute and coming up with a more rational belief system concerning his decision, Rich experiences the following changes:

1. Physical
   Muscle tension relaxes
   Tension headaches lessen
   Is able to sleep soundly
2. Mental
   Regains confidence in decisions
   Is still anxious but is able to discuss that
   Regains concentration
3. Behavioral
   Is spending more time with his girlfriend
   Has stopped arguing with his parents
   Is more social
   Is seeking support of his friends

Work through your own ABCDE scenario in Assess Yourself 7-3.

Using Seligman's Learned Optimism to Think More Logically

In chapter 2 we introduced Seligman's concept of learned helplessness and the helpless/hopeless personality. A key component of the helpless/hopeless personality is the sense of **pessimism** that accompanies it. Seligman would call this a person's **"explanatory style."**[33] In a sense, a

pessimism a generally negative interpretation of life and events

explanatory style the way in which a person views the world and explains his or her misfortune person's explanatory style is the way that person views the world and explains his or her misfortune. While pessimism leads to negative interpretations of life and events, **optimism** leads to positive interpretations. It is very similar to what Ellis and Harper[8] would call our illogical belief system. While Ellis and Harper feel that most people's illogical beliefs can be captured under their "ten illogical beliefs" umbrella, Seligman feels that a person's explanatory style is composed of three components: permanence, pervasiveness, and personalization.

Permanence refers to how long we believe stressful events will persist. People who view stressful events as permanent tend to be pessimists and are more stressed than optimists who view them as temporary. Pessimists use words such as *always* and *never* to describe stressors.[33] Their illogical beliefs would sound like this:

> "Why do these things *always* happen to me?"
>
> "I *never* can get it right."

Optimists tend to view stressful events and situations as temporary, and their beliefs would sound like this:

> "Although this is a very painful thing to go through, it too will pass."
>
> "I am really upset over this, but I'll get over it in a couple of days."

Optimists can even admit to feeling *temporarily* overwhelmed and unable to cope. The difference is their belief (and consequent optimistic subvocal speech) that this feeling is transitory and does not represent a permanent condition that will never pass.

While permanence relates to time, pervasiveness relates to one's sense of space. Pessimists tend to view the effects of stressors as pervasive, affecting every aspect of their lives. Pessimists are "catastrophizers," to use Ellis and Harper's conceptualization.[8] Optimists tend to view stressors as context-specific and not affecting all other facets of their lives or well-being. For instance, pessimists might view flunking a test in one class as a measure of their lack of intelligence and likelihood of flunking other tests in other classes (despite never having done so). They might tell themselves things such as:

> "I am really stupid"
>
> "I'm probably going to flunk the midterm in my other classes also."

Optimists would view flunking the test as something specifically related to that particular test and the specific course the test was associated with and not universally associated with *all* tests, courses, or their overall intelligence. They would use the following self-talk to explain the failing grade:

> "Boy, that test was hard. I'll have to study harder to pass the next one."
>
> "I guess I really screwed up on that particular test. I'll have to see how it will affect my overall grade for the course."

Personalization refers to taking responsibility for stressors. Pessimists tend to have an external view of personal responsibility for stress. They tend to blame others or society for their problems and stress. Optimists tend to take personal responsibility for feeling bad and being stressed. We discussed this internal versus external locus of control in chapter 2.

Pessimists would engage in the following kinds of personalization self-talk:

> "She or he really made me feel bad."
>
> "Everybody is always making me do things that take up my time and make it impossible to get my homework in on time."

An optimist probably would react in the following way to these situations:

> "I really feel bad when she or he acts that way."
>
> "I need to start saying no to things I really have no time to do."

Seligman[33] believes that optimists and pessimists experience the same setbacks and tragedies in life. The difference is that the optimist bounces back from defeats and weathers them better than does the pessimist. The other thing to remember, Seligman[33] notes, is that almost all optimists admit to feeling pessimistic at times. The techniques pessimists must learn to help them become more optimistic are the same techniques optimists can practice to help them remain optimistic in the face of pessimism.

Seligman's Model Seligman[33] admits to being a devotee of Ellis and Harper's generic ABCDE model[7] for coping with stress and emotional problems. The difference is that Seligman applies this model to specific potential stressors that focus on optimism and/or pessimism. Seligman's ABCDE acronym also stands for slightly different terms than does Ellis and Harper's. Figure 7-3 illustrates Seligman's model of learned optimism.

There are a few differences between Seligman's and Ellis and Harper's models. Seligman's A is entitled "adversity" instead of "activating event." It is essentially the same thing: the situation or event that triggered the stressful response.

Seligman's Bs are similar to Ellis and Harper's. They are illogical beliefs but are slightly different in that they are also pessimistic statements. The tip-off to their pessimism

optimism a generally positive interpretation of life and events

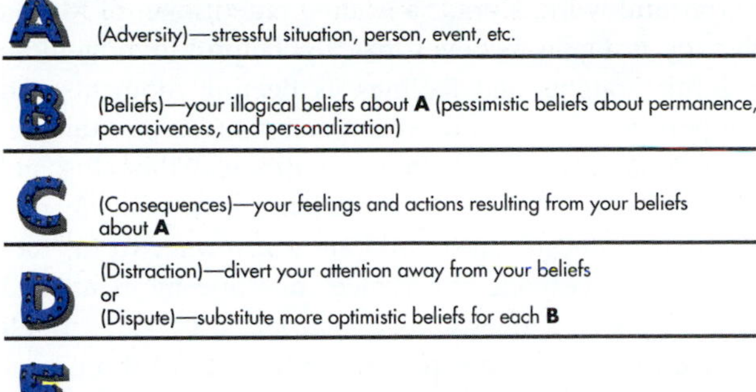

Figure 7-3

Seligman's ABCDE model for coping with stress and emotional problems is similar to Ellis and Harper's but focuses on potential stressors that are related to optimism and pessimism.

lies in their permanence, pervasiveness, and personalization. In evaluating these Bs, one must refer back to a pessimistic explanatory style to assess them properly.

A major difference in the use of Seligman's model relates to the dispute stage. For this stage, Seligman has two Ds: distraction and dispute.[33] Distraction is simple. It is the first line of defense (D) to use when you don't have the time to dispute each B fully. Seligman recommends a quick thought-stopping strategy by suggesting you write illogical thoughts down and then redirect your thoughts away from the illogical Bs that have taken hold. Seligman recommends wearing a rubber band around your wrist and snapping it as a way to stop your thoughts. Another strategy is to slap your wrist hard against a desk or wall. Finally, he recommends keeping a 3- by 5-inch file card with the word *stop* preprinted on it. Pull this card out of your wallet to stop your illogical thoughts.

Once you have stopped your illogical thoughts, Seligman recommends that you write them down so that you can examine them later, when you have more time to dispute them fully. Another distraction tip Seligman recommends is to refocus your attention on something else for several minutes and give that thing your full attention. You could focus on an inanimate object on your desk or take an action such as eating an orange. In any case, the idea is to take your time and fully experience whatever you focus on with all your senses, making sure to keep your mind off the potentially distracting As and Bs.

Seligman's dispute is much the same as Ellis and Harper's. Instead of merely substituting a more logical belief (D) for each illogical B, however, Seligman's model also encourages you to choose a more optimistic one. These new Ds should be based on more optimistic statements regarding permanence, pervasiveness, and personalization.[33]

Seligman's E (energization) is synonymous with Ellis and Harper's effects. In this step you evaluate how your new, optimistic thoughts and subsequent stress reduction "energize" you.[33]

Learning to Argue with Yourself Most students find the dispute phase very hard. They need guidelines for evaluating whether their beliefs are logical or illogical, optimistic or pessimistic. Seligman[33] offers four things to look for when disputing your Bs: evidence, alternatives, implications, and usefulness.

- **Evidence**—The best way to show that a belief is illogical or pessimistic is to prove that it is factually incorrect. For instance, if you flunk a test and make negative self-statements about your lack of intelligence and generalize the pervasiveness of this to how you will now start flunking more tests in other classes, *stop* and examine the evidence. If there is little other evidence of your low intelligence (your overall grades are good, etc.) or flunking other classes and/or tests (you haven't flunked any other tests in other classes, etc.), you can safely assume that your beliefs about this test are illogical and pessimistic.
- **Alternatives**—The alternative way to view your illogical feelings about this test and your intelligence is to look at other explanations for flunking the test. Almost nothing in life is the result of a single cause. Maybe your flunking the test has as much (or more) to do with the professor's poor teaching abilities, misleading questions, lack of adequate class coverage, or a host of other factors outside yourself. Pessimists tend to see things as having a single cause. Optimists look for multiple causes. If there are multiple causes, maybe your thinking (as stated in your Bs) is illogical.
- **Implications**—Pessimists tend to be catastrophizers. They project the worst-case scenario as a consequence of their As. As a result of flunking this test, how likely is it that you will flunk the class or flunk other tests? If the answer is "not very," it is likely that your Bs are illogical.
- **Usefulness**—Sometimes our Bs become self-fulfilling prophecies. They become very useful in giving us a way out of meeting potential stressors head on. For instance, by believing that flunking this test sets the stage for flunking other tests or the class, you allow yourself to throw up your hands and say, "What's the use in studying anymore? I'm going to flunk any way." If you are using your Bs to avoid confronting your stressors, they are probably illogical and/or pessimistic.

Where East Meets West: Using Morita and Naikan Therapies to Rethink How We View Potential Stressors

As we have just described, the work of Lazarus and Folkman, Ellis and Harper, and Seligman illustrate how illogical, irrational, and pessimistic thinking are associated with negative emotions and a threatening appraisal of potential stressors. This kind of appraisal leaves us feeling that we can't cope with the threat and this triggers a stress response. The best way to deal with this, according to Western, cognitive psychologists, is to *work on* changing these illogical, irrational, pessimistic thoughts. This will reduce the negative emotions associated with such thinking and short-circuit the stress response.

As we have seen, this works quite well with potential stressors that lend themselves to such a detached, analytical approach. It also is especially beneficial for people who enjoy such intellectual activity and are able to spend the time analyzing their illogical thinking and substituting more logical thinking in its place. It may not be as applicable, however, with potential stressors that trigger very strong emotions such as anger or hate or for people who are unable or unwilling to take the time to analyze and categorize their thoughts and feelings.

The Japanese therapies might be better suited for such potential stressors and people. The three fundamental skills that Morita and Naikan use to help people deal with negative thoughts and painful emotions are generalizable to all potential stressors and types of people. In the next section we'll examine how to use these skills (co-existing with painful thoughts and feelings, shifting your attention, and self-reflection) to reduce stress.

How to Co-Exist with Painful Thoughts and Feelings

Instead of analyzing and trying to change the negative thoughts and painful emotions that accompany potential stressors, a Moritist approach to them is to *acknowledge* that they exist, *accept* them, and *co-exist* with them while redirecting your focus away from yourself and onto engaging in purposeful work. As we mentioned in chapter 2, the Japanese call this *arugamama,* accepting reality for what it is. Accepting reality for what it is implies two things: (1) you accept whatever thoughts and unpleasant feelings you are experiencing at the moment and (2) you accept that experiencing painful and troubling thoughts and feelings is part of being human. If you can accept these two fundamental truths, you can begin to shift your attention away from these troubling and painful thoughts and emotions and begin focusing on some purposeful work. In time the negative thoughts and emotions fade and are no longer stressful. Moritists feel that stressful thoughts and emotions do not hide in the unconscious when this happens. These thoughts and emotions are simply replaced by new ones that are associated with the work and the positive outcomes related to performing purposeful work. Kora,[19] a leading practitioner of Morita therapy in Japan, believes that it is helpful to view these painful thoughts and feelings as fleeting moments and temporary reflections of your personality. For example, when you feel overwhelmed by illogical thoughts and painful emotions you are experiencing *a neurotic moment*. This doesn't mean you are *a neurotic*. Kora[19] believes that everyone experiences neurotic moments and rather than view oneself as *a neurotic,* it is better to tell yourself that you are experiencing another of those *neurotic moments* that are difficult if not impossible to control and in time will pass. It is best to acknowledge the feelings, accept them, and let them run their course. Most people, however, in an attempt to minimize the pain and suffering associated with the thoughts and emotions, are too eager to eliminate them right away.[19]

KEY TO UNDERSTANDING

A key to understanding neurosis is realizing that everyone has neurotic moments. Having neurotic moments does not make one a neurotic person.

Shifting Your Attention to Manage Stress

Krech[20] believes that the best way to shift your attention away from yourself (and your thoughts and feelings) is to engage in productive labor that involves the large muscle groups working at a moderate to fast pace in nonrepetitive activity. Any kind of work or play that involves this kind of activity will eventually take your mind off yourself and your problems. Krech's personal favorite is playing basketball. Basketball is a fast-paced game involving explosive use of the legs and arms. It involves random, fast-paced motion and is physically demanding. Chopping firewood, turning over soil in the garden, raking leaves, and washing the floor by hand are all examples of household activities that involve larger muscle activity and are physically demanding.

Besides engaging in the work, it is also important to focus your attention on the work. This is called being fully involved in the moment. If you find your mind drifting back to your problem and the negative thoughts and painful feelings that accompany it, you must shift your thoughts to the basketball game or the household chores. For example, pay attention to the feel of the basketball itself. A basketball has a pebbled finish (little rubber dimples that improve your grip) and is criss-crossed by recessed seams. When you are dribbling and shooting, pay attention to the feel of the finish and the seams. Use the seams to get a better grip and put rotation on your shot as it releases from your fingertips. Pay attention to the release. Can you feel the ball spin off your fingertips as it leaves them? This is one of the greatest joys for basketball shooters; watching their shot spin off their fingertips, reach the zenith of its arc on the way to the basket, and hearing the swish of the cord as the ball falls directly through the center of the hoop. The same can be done with the leaf raking, soil digging, or floor washing. You can fully immerse your attention into all the motions involved in these activities if you allow yourself to fully pay attention to what is going on. In time, you can actually learn to enjoy even the most mundane household

Stress Buster Tips

Close Up

Instructions:

Take a walk with a magnifying glass today and inspect 10 things close up. Examine things using the magnifying glass for detail related to color, texture, patterns, shapes and outlines. Describe what you saw for each of the 10 items.

____

____

____

____

____

____

____

____

____

____

Source: Anderson & Krech,[1] 1996.

chores by viewing them as helpful ways to shift your focus and improve your attention.

There are many other ways to improve your overall ability to pay attention to things other than yourself and your thoughts and feelings. Meditating on a regular basis helps you focus your attention on one thing at a time. Stress Buster Tips: "Close Up" is one example of an attention-building activity taken from the ToDo Institute's distance learning program entitled "Working with Your Attention" (ToDo, 2005).

Using Self-Reflection to Manage Stress

Many of the Living Constructively boxes and Stress Buster Tips used throughout the text so far are examples of Naikan self-reflection. Naikan self-reflection is an excellent way to change your perspective on your stressors. As we mentioned previously in this chapter, sometimes by changing your perspective on a stressor can change your stressful appraisal of it. For example, imagine that you are working as a waiter/waitress in a restaurant and your manager wants you to go out of your way to treat each customer to the best service possible, regardless of how obnoxious or unappreciative he or she may be. One day you wait on a party of eight who came in to celebrate a silver anniversary. The party includes a forty-something-year-old couple, their four kids, and their grandparents. The kids range in age from 2 to 16 years old, and grandma and grandpa are in their seventies and can't hear all that well. From the beginning you tell yourself, "Oh great, why do I get all the families? They'll probably be a lot of trouble and not tip so well." As you are trying to describe the day's specials, grandma keeps interrupting you because she can't hear you, the oldest daughter's cell phone rings, and the youngest child starts to cry. You lose your patience with the group and for the rest of the meal are very curt, unfriendly, and avoid them as much as possible. They respond to this by leaving you a minimal (10 percent) tip and complaining to the manager about your lack of friendliness and attentiveness to their needs. Your boss chews you out in front of the rest of the waitstaff and sends you home early. This would be a great example to use Naikan self-reflection on.

1. What did I do for this family?
2. What did this family do for me?
3. What trouble did I cause for this family?

As a result of shifting the focus off yourself and your needs, can you put yourself in their shoes and try to imagine what the experience was like for the family? You can use Naikan self-reflection to change your perspective on any stressor or potential stressor.

Combining Positive Self-Talk with Morita and Naikan Techniques

As we just described, both Morita and Naikan therapy are based on the Japanese principle of arugamama, or accepting life as it is. If you agree with this premise, your self-talk about reality should reflect this perspective. In other words, when you are experiencing unpleasant thoughts and feelings, you should tell yourself, "Oh, I am experiencing unpleasant thoughts and feelings. I'll just have to let them pass while I do what I have to do." Accepting reality as it really is (in this case it includes unpleasant thoughts and feelings) would be a *logical* and *rational* way for you to view the world. It would be *illogical* and *irrational* for you to say something to yourself such as; "I am experiencing negative thoughts and feelings. Maybe if I try hard enough to understand why I am feeling this way I can get them to disappear." This type of self-talk is illogical and irrational because it is inconsistent with the concept of arugamama. It would not be inconsistent with Morita or Naikan principles to substitute more logical and rational thinking using a combination of techniques from Ellis and Harper's[8] and Seligman.[33] Here is an example using library research as the activating event.

Example:

Activating Event: Conducting online research for a paper at the campus library.

Illogical Beliefs

"I hate doing research using the Internet."

"I'm no good at doing research using the Internet."

"I wish this was quicker. I can't stand spending so much time on this."

"I can't look at this stuff for another minute. I am so bored."

Consequences

Feeling anxious, annoyed, and bored

Mind wanders, have to reread material several times

Dispute (using Morita and Naikan skills and arugamama)

"I am feeling anxious, annoyed, and bored; in time these feelings will pass."

"It is OK for me to hate doing Internet research but I still must do it."

"I often spend lots of time doing things I do not enjoy doing because they need to get done."

"Even though I am bored, I'll just try rereading the material I just printed off."

Distract (can use by itself if the dispute doesn't work)

"I'll take a brisk walk around the library a few times and come back to what I am doing until I finish."

Such an approach is not inconsistent with the Japanese therapies because you are not trying to *find out why* you are thinking or feeling the way you do, nor are you denying reality as it really is. You are merely replacing your illogical thoughts about conducting the research with more realistic thinking based on arugamama. Further, you are redirecting your focus towards doing what needs to get done (conducting the research). An action option, taking a brisk walk and then returning to the research would combine the *Distract* element from Seligman's ABCDE Model[33] with the *Dispute* element of Ellis and Harper's ABCDE Technique.[8]

Changing Our Perspective by Rethinking Road Rage—Anger on the Highway

As was mentioned in chapters 2 and 6, anger is a negative emotion associated with a variety of physical, emotional, and behavioral consequences. Anger is a very strong emotion, a powerful internal feeling. In many cases, anger is an illogical, irrational response to a potential stressor. Angry feelings often persist long after their source has disappeared. As you've seen, this feeling of anger is capable of switching on the stress response and perpetuating it, keeping it alive long after the source of stress has disappeared. Mismanaging anger can result in a host of physical, emotional, behavioral, and interpersonal consequences. There is probably no better example to use than road rage to illustrate the effects of mismanaging anger.

Road rage is a stress reaction characterized by feelings of extreme impatience, anxiety, and intense anger (rage). In a sense, road rage could be considered having an extreme temper tantrum while driving a vehicle. People who suffer from road rage do not make good driving judgments. A few even become temporarily psychotic.[24] Road rage is an extreme form of aggressive driving. Aggressive driving embraces a variety of behaviors, including running red lights and stop signs, speeding, changing lanes without signaling, tailgating, making obscene gestures, and getting road rage.[2] Road rage rarely seems to be the result of a single incident. Rather, it seems to be an outward manifestation of personal attitudes and stress in the motorist's life. The traffic incident is the catalyst that triggers the rage.[24]

The May 1997 report of the American Automobile Association (AAA) Foundation for Traffic Safety found that 12,828 people, including 94 children under the age of 15, were injured or killed in traffic accidents involving road rage. The study found that violent traffic incidents increased 7 percent a year since 1990.[24] The National Highway Traffic Safety Administration estimates that one-third of 6.84 million crashes and two-thirds of 41,907 traffic fatalities in 1996 were linked to aggressive driving and road rage.[2] According to the AAA study, road rage often leads to a violent confrontation between the enraged driver and his or her victim. The most popular weapon used in these violent altercations was the vehicle being driven. In 12 percent of the AAA-reported incidents, the driver used the vehicle to cut off, ram, or run over the victim. Other weapons reported were firearms, knives, clubs, tire irons, golf clubs, pepper spray, eggs, and, in one instance, a crossbow.[24]

Using Rational Thinking and Japanese Psychology to Rethink Road Rage

The following six-step procedure is an example of how to combine Western and Eastern strategies to manage our inner anger and rethink Road Rage.

Step 1. Acknowledge that you are angry and identify the response.

Anger-management experts generally agree that the first step in anger management is acknowledging the existence of anger. This is also central to arugamama, accepting reality as it really is. Identifying exactly how your body is responding can help you realize that you are angry. Everyone responds to anger differently.[35,36,37] Some people respond internally and literally feel as if they are going to explode. They feel their blood pressure and temperature start to rise. Others respond externally. They explode at the least little provocation and let loose a torrent of verbal abuse directed toward others. Still others sulk, turn inward, and punish themselves. They get angry at themselves for getting angry!

Step 2. Accept your anger.

Accepting your anger is slightly different than merely acknowledging it because acceptance implies personal responsibility and ownership of the

road rage a stress reaction characterized by feelings of extreme impatience, anxiety, and intense anger while driving a vehicle anger. Often we do not admit we are angry because we do not like ourselves when we are angry and we don't like how anger feels. It is not a pleasant emotion. The second part of arugamama is acknowledging that you accept this unpleasant feeling and can co-exist with it.

Step 3. Target the source of your anger.
Understanding what you are angry about is different from understanding *why* you are angry. "Why" questions about anger are generally more difficult to answer than are "what" questions. When you target the source of your anger, you are identifying what the activating or adverse event followed by your illogical beliefs to use Ellis and Harper's[8] and Seligman's[33] terminology respectively. For example:
Source (activating/adverse event)
— slow drivers in the fast lane
Illogical Beliefs
— " these idiots *shouldn't* be in this lane"
— "why is the fast lane *always* full of slow drivers"
— "these @#%!~~**## drivers only think of themselves"
— "if I had a tank I'd run them all over"
— "I'll *never* get to work with these idiots on the road"
The source of this person's rage is the presence of people in the left lane driving *slowly*. In reality, these drivers are usually driving within the legal limits of that lane, but it is still too slow for someone experiencing road rage. The words used to characterize the other drivers are illogical because they leave no room for interpretation. The fast lane isn't *always* filled with slow drivers who *only* think of themselves. In fact, sometimes the slow drivers *should* be in the fast lane (like when they are passing someone else or can't get back into the middle lanes).

Step 4. Do not give in to uncontrolled venting of anger.
Tavris[35] was one of the first to demystify the popular notion of releasing anger in a cathartic way. She found that the uncontrolled purging of anger not only did not get rid of the anger completely, it often made matters worse. Uncontrolled venting of anger increases one's focus on the anger. This self-focus, as we've learned from the Japanese therapies, reinforces it and keeps the anger alive longer. If we can accept the anger and shift our attention away from it, the anger will begin to dissipate. As the AAA study (1997) showed, the uncontrolled venting of anger through aggressive driving often results in accidents, injuries, and death to both the perpetrator and victim. Additionally, the uncontrolled venting of anger during episodes of road rage can increase our risk of becoming a victim of a violent crime perpetrated by the targets of our venting (AAA, 1997).

Step 5. Dissipate anger in a healthy way.
The following five tips will help you get rid of your anger in a healthy way:

- *Shift Your Attention.*
  Stop focusing on your anger and the drivers in the left lane. Shift your attention to something else. If the road is very scenic, you can focus on the beautiful trees and rolling hills that this road cuts through. You can shift the focus to music and put in your favorite CD. You can shift your attention to comedy and put on your favorite comedy CD. You can shift your attention to your breathing and practice slow, deep breathing, focusing on the air entering and leaving your body.
- *Get Physical.*
  While this is difficult to do while driving, it is not impossible. If you can, pull over onto the shoulder of the road or into the next rest area. Take a few deep breaths and spend a few minutes contracting and relaxing the large muscles of your body (see examples in chapter 9). If you can pull into a rest area, get out of your car and take a brisk walk or do some push-ups.
- *Replace illogical beliefs and negative self-talk with ones that accept reality as it is.*
  You can do this one-for-one as Ellis and Harper[9] and Seligman[33] advocate, or replace them all with a Morita approach and just accept reality as it is. Here is an example using the illogical beliefs from above:
  — "these idiots *shouldn't* be in this lane"
  I don't know if these people are really idiots and maybe they just can't get back into the middle or right lanes because of the traffic.
  — "why is the fast lane *always* full of slow drivers"
  The fast lane isn't always filled with slow drivers. Most of the time the fast lane moves pretty smoothly.
  — "these @#%!~~**## drivers only think of themselves"
  I have no idea what these folks are thinking.
  — "if I had a tank I'd run them all over"
  I'd wind up in jail for the rest of my life if I did this.
  — "I'll *never* get to work with these idiots on the road"
  I'll get to work. I might be a few minutes late, but that is better than getting a ticket for reckless driving or getting into an accident.
  Or
- *Deal with anger promptly.*
  Don't let unchecked anger fester. As soon as you recognize your road rage beginning to appear, do something.

Step 6. Become pro-active in your anger management. Keep an anger diary. Whenever you identify what makes you angry, write it down. Look for patterns in the things that make you angry. Identify people, places, and situations that arouse anger in you. Use this information to prevent becoming angry in the first place. Try to plan in advance how you can avoid these anger-producing stimuli in the first place or cope with them if you have to experience them. Think your way through these situations *before* they occur.

SUMMARY

This chapter introduced the first level of coping with stress—*Rethink.* It started with a discussion of values clarification. By clarifying our values we examine the things in life that are most central to who we are. We discussed how values fit into our Daily Life Criteria, the habits and behaviors that contribute to us enjoying life fully. Clarifying values and criteria for happiness are a critical step in stress management because this gives us a frame of reference and helps us understand why we get stressed when we are in situations in which things that we value and add meaning to our lives are threatened. The chapter examined the relationship between purposeful living and goals. Having a purpose in life guides us in setting goals for our future. Goals help shape our lives and give them meaning. Goals put us on a course and give our lives direction and purpose.

The next part of the chapter examined how our perspective on life influences our stress. Our overall views about how the world and the people in it *should be* play a major role in our stress levels. This section describes how, when our perspective changes, we sometimes lose sight of what is important to us and begin to view ourselves as the center of the universe instead of a small part of it. The chapter continued with a discussion of ways to see ourselves and our problems from a different perspective. It explored Metcalf and Felible's three skills, and the role of fun, humor, and laughter in changing our perspective on life and coping with stress. This part of the chapter also examined how the pace of our lives affects our perspective and is related to our stress. It described how multitasking and constantly rushing about from one commitment to another speeds us up and contributes to our stress. It gave suggestions for slowing the pace of our lives.

The next part of the chapter examined ways to change our perspective on individual stressors. The two primary strategies covered focused on how to become more logical and rational in our thinking about potential stressors. The chapter described Ellis and Harper's[8] ABCDE technique for appraising potential stressors more rationally by examining and disputing our illogical beliefs about them. Seligman's[33] model for learning to be more optimistic was also described in detail. Seligman's model, derived from Ellis and Harper's ABCDE model, uses dispute to change our pessimistic, illogical beliefs into more rational, optimistic beliefs, thereby reducing stress.

The chapter then shifted to an examination of how the three primary skills of Morita and Naikan therapies could be used to rethink potential stressors. It described how coexisting with negative emotions, shifting one's attention away from stressful thoughts and feelings, and using self-reflection could all be used to rethink potential stressors. This was followed by a discussion of how Japanese and Western therapies could be integrated into one comprehensive way of changing the way we view potential stressors. The chapter ended with an example of how to integrate the two schools of thought using coping with road rage as the example.

STUDY QUESTIONS

1. What is values clarification?
2. How is values clarification related to coping with stress?
3. Compare and contrast selective awareness and perspective awareness.
4. What are Metcalf and Felible's three humor skills? Give an example of how any one of these skills helped you cope with a stressful incident in the past.
5. Describe each component of Ellis ABCDE model of rational emotive behavior therapy.
6. Use Ellis's ABCDE model to work through a personal stressor that originated in your illogical thinking.
7. How can co-existing with feelings be used to reduce stress?
8. Apply Seligman's ABCDE technique to a specific stressful situation that was based on illogical thinking.
9. Describe what Seligman means by "learned optimism."
10. How is change related to stress?
11. How do humor and laughter physiologically alter the stress response?
12. Describe the 6 steps involved in anger management.
13. How does shifting one's attention help one cope with stress?
14. How can self-reflection be used to cope with stress?
15. What are Daily Life Criteria?

DISCOVER OUR CHANGING WORLD

The ToDo Institute
http://www.todoinstitute.com

The ToDo Institute is one of only two centers for Japanese therapy in North America. Go to its home page and read about the institute. When you are done, click on any link and read more about the Japanese therapies.

Describe one new thing you learned about any of the Japanese therapies. How does this compare to what you have been exposed to (through the media, personal experience, etc.) regarding the way Western counselors or therapists might approach mental health issues?

Are You Thinking Clearly?

As we have discussed, many people are stressed because they allow others to determine the course of their lives, relationships, career paths, and the like. Take a minute and honestly answer the following questions regarding the path of your life up to this point:

1. Are you in college because you really want to be there or because someone else (parents, etc.) thinks this is where you should be?
2. Are you in your degree program because you find it interesting and it has some meaning for you, or are you there because of pressure from someone else?
3. Are you staying in your current relationship because you really want to be with this person, or are you in it because of a less healthy reason (pressure from someone else, fear of being alone, too lazy to break up, etc.)?
4. Are you staying in your current job merely to earn income even though it no longer interests you or provides a meaningful outlet for your creativity?
5. Are you involved with friends you no longer feel close to, you have outgrown, who are excessively negative or destructive?

If you answered yes to any of these questions, you may not be thinking clearly about your life and someone else may be pulling your strings rather than your being in control.

References

1. Anderson, L. & Krech, G. (1996). *A finger pointing at the moon.* Monkton, VT: ToDo Institute.
2. Bowers, B. (1997). Getting aggressive about road rage. *Bests' Review-Life-Health-Insurance Edition,* 98(7), pp. 61–64.
3. Browne, H. (1973). *How I found freedom in an unfree world.* New York: Macmillan.
4. Cassell, C. (1984). *Swept away: Why women fear their own sexuality.* New York: Simon & Schuster.
5. Cicatelli, B. (1985). *Ten Bad Listening Habits: and What to Do about Them.* New York: Cicatelli Associates.
6. Dryfoos, J. (1985). What the United States can learn about prevention of teenage pregnancy from other countries. *SIECUS Report,* 14(2), pp. 1–7.
7. Dyer, W. (1978). *Pulling your own strings.* New York: Crowne.
8. Ellis, A. & Harper, R. (1975). *A new guide to rational living.* North Hollywood, CA: Wilshire Books.
9. Ellis, A. (1993). Reflections on rational emotive therapy. *Journal of Consulting and Clinical Psychology,* 61(2), pp. 199–200.
10. Fergusen, A. (1998). Road rage. *Time,* 151(1), pp. 64–69.
11. Gard, C.J. (1996). Humor helps: Managing stress and anger. *Current Health,* 24(8), pp. 22–24.
12. Goddard, K. (1991). Morita therapy: A literature review. *Transcultural Psychiatric Research Review,* 28(2), pp. 93–115.
13. Jemmott, J.B., Jemmott, L., & Fong, G.T. (1992). Reductions in HIV risk-associated behaviors among black male adolescents: Effects of an AIDS prevention intervention. *American Journal of Public Health,* 82(3), pp. 372–377.
14. Kabat-Zinn, J. (1995). *Mindfulness Meditation* (audiotape). New York: Simon Schuster.
15. Kabat Zinn, J. (1994). *Wherever you go you are there.* New York: Hyperion.
16. Kobasa, S. (1979). Stressful life events, personality and health: An inquiry into hardiness. *Journal of Personality & Social Psychology,* 37(1), pp. 1–11.
17. Kemp, S. & Strongman, K.T. (1995). Anger theory and management: A historical analysis. *American Journal of Psychology,* 108(3), pp. 379–418.
18. Kobasa, S. (1979). Stressful life events, personality and health: An inquiry into hardiness. *Journal of Personality & Social Psychology,* 37(1), pp. 1–11.
19. Kora, T. (1995). *How to live well.* New York: State University of NY Press.
20. Krech, G. (2005). *Working with Your Attention: Exercises and Daily Journal.* Monkton VT: ToDo Institute.
21. Lawday, D. (1991). Letter from a productive lover of leisure. *U.S. News & World Report,* 111(6), pp. 6–8.
22. Martinson, F.M. (1982). Against sexual retardation. *SIECUS Report,* 10(3), p. 3.
23. McMillan, L. (1997). Dealing with life's anger. *Vibrant Life,* 13(6), pp. 28–31.
24. McMurry, K. (1997). Stick it in your rearview mirror: Aggressive driving is all the rage. *Trial,* 33(7), pp. 94–97.
25. Metcalf, C.W. & Felible, R. (1992). *Lighten up: Survival skills for people under pressure.* New York: Perseus Books Group.
26. Nathan, J. (1990). Sitting, laboring, and changing: A critical examination of the indigenous Japanese psychotherapies. *Psychologia: An International Journal of Psychology in the Orient,* 33(3), pp. 163–170.
27. Peale, N.V. (1952). *The power of positive thinking.* Greenwich, CN: Fawcett Crest.
28. Peck, F.S. (1978). *The road less traveled.* New York: Simon & Schuster.
29. Raths, L., Harmin, M., & Simon, S. (1966). *Values and teaching.* Columbus, OH: Charles E. Merrill.
30. Reynolds, D. (1984). *Playing ball on running water.* New York: William Morrow.
31. Reynolds, D. (1986). *Even in summer the ice doesn't melt.* New York: William Morrow.
32. Reynolds, D. (1992). The teacher-student relationship in Japanese culture and Morita Therapy. *International Bulletin of Morita Therapy,* 5(1), pp. 18–21.
33. Seligman, M.F.B. (1998). *Learned optimism.* New York: Simon & Schuster.
34. Simon, S.B., Howe, L.W., & Kirschenbaum, H. (1978). *Values clarification: A handbook of strategies for teachers and students.* Hadley, Mass: Values Press.
35. Tavris, C. (1982). *Anger: The misunderstood emotion.* New York: Touchstone.
36. Warner, N. (1983). *Make anger your ally: Harnessing our most baffling emotion.* New York: Simon & Schuster.
37. Weisinger, H. (1996). *Anger at work: Learning the art of anger management on the job.* New York: William Morrow.

Name: ______________________ Date: __________

ASSESS YOURSELF 7-1

Strength of Values

PURPOSE

This strategy provides students with an opportunity to assess the strength of their feelings about the issues they themselves identify.

PROCEDURE

This worksheet contains several unfinished sentences (see below). Students use the stems to write complete sentences or paragraphs if they wish.

The worksheet may then be filed for later reference, or an optional class discussion or small group discussion might follow.

WORKSHEET

Complete the statements below. You may write one sentence or a whole paragraph. Write "nothing" for any sentence for which you have no answer or "pass" if you would prefer not to answer.

1. I would be willing to die for . . .

2. I would be willing to physically fight for . . .

3. I would argue strongly in favor of . . .

4. I would quietly take a position in favor of . . .

5. I will share only with my friends my belief that . . .

6. I prefer to keep to myself my belief that . . . (for your's private record.)

From Simon, S.B., Howe, L.W., & Kirschenbaum, H. (1978). *Values clarification: A handbook of strategies for teachers and students.* Hadley, Mass: Values Press.[37]

Name: ______________________________ Date: ____________

ASSESS YOURSELF 7-2

Goals and Objectives Worksheet

Accomplishing your goals takes planning, hard work, discipline, determination, organization, and faith. This worksheet will help you organize your goals and set objectives to keep you on course.

LIFE GOALS

A. Personal Goals

First Goal

____

____

Objectives

a. ______________________________

b. ______________________________

c. ______________________________

Second Goal

____

____

Objectives

a. ______________________________

b. ______________________________

c. ______________________________

Third Goal

____

____

Objectives

a. ______________________________

b. ______________________________

c. ______________________________

B. Professional Goals

First Goal

____

____

Objectives

a. ______________________________

b. ______________________________

c. ______________________________

Assess Yourself 7-2 (cont'd)

Second Goal

____

____

Objectives

a. ______________________________________

b. ______________________________________

c. ______________________________________

Third Goal

____

____

Objectives

a. ______________________________________

b. ______________________________________

c. ______________________________________

Name: ______________________________ Date: ____________

ASSESS YOURSELF 7-3

ABCDE Scenarios

Think of a situation in which you became stressed because of your illogical beliefs about that situation. Make sure the beliefs you had really were illogical and inappropriate for the situation. For instance, it is reasonable to be upset if a good friend lets you down, but it is illogical or inappropriate to blame yourself and use negative self-talk.

Work through your scenario using Ellis and Harper's[7] ABCDE technique. Refer to the list of illogical beliefs from chapter 2 for help in identifying your illogical beliefs about the situation. Make sure to list each belief separately. Share these scenarios with your classmates in small groups.

A.—Activating event (the stressor that activated your response)

B.—Illogical beliefs (the specific illogical beliefs and negative subvocal self-talk related to the activating event)

C.—Consequences (the negative effects of your beliefs—could be mental, physical, social, behavioral, etc.)

D.—Dispute (rephrasing each belief into a more logical/rational statement)

E.—Evaluate effects (the effects of the dispute on the consequences)

Name: ____________________ Date: __________

ASSESS YOURSELF 7-4

Bright-Side Scenarios

There are at least two ways to view every situation. Often we choose to focus on the negative side of a situation. Try to focus on the bright side of the following scenarios. Describe as many bright-side interpretations as possible for each scenario.

1. You lose your job

2. You do your best but are beaten by an opponent in the championship (individual or team sport).

3. Your company relocates to another part of the country and offers to take you along.

4. Your boyfriend or girlfriend wants to date other people.

5. Your parents get divorced.

6. Your parents get remarried to someone else.

7. Your old clunker car dies in the driveway.

8. You flunk the CPA exam the first time around.

9. You must do your term paper over because it is unacceptable.

10. It rains for the first two days of your vacation.

Name: ____________________ Date: ____________

ASSESS YOURSELF 7-5

Am I Having Fun Yet?

INSTRUCTIONS

1. List ten things that are fun and that you love to do.
2. Indicate how many times you engaged in one of these activities in the past week and past month.
3. Check off whether this activity is something you have done alone or with a partner.
4. Check off whether this activity can be done for under $5.
5. Check off whether this activity involves some degree of controlled psychological (taking an honors course, reading a difficult book), social (meeting new people, joining a new group), or physical (rock climbing, mountain biking) risk.

	Activity	Number of Times in the Past Week	Number of Times in the Past Month	Do it Alone or with Partner	Under $5	Psychological, Social, Physical Risk?
1.						
2.						
3.						
4.						
5.						
6.						
7.						
8.						
9.						
10.						

ACTIVITY

If you can't come up with ten things that are fun and that you enjoy doing, you need to ask yourself, "What am I doing with my life and time?" and start trying to add more fun to your life.

NUMBER OF TIMES IN THE PAST WEEK AND NUMBER OF TIMES IN THE PAST MONTH

Research shows that doing fun things fewer than seven times a week and thirty times a month is associated with higher levels of mental illness.

ALONE OR WITH PARTNER

Look for balance. We all need fun things to engage in alone and with others.

UNDER $5

The more inexpensive or free things we have on our fun list, the easier it is to have fun at any time.

PSYCHOLOGICAL, SOCIAL, OR PHYSICAL RISK

Taking risks can be fun and add spice to our lives. Look for one or two things to do that add controlled risk to your fun list.

Name: ______________________________ Date: ____________

Assess Yourself 7-6

Joy List

Here is the perfect companion when you begin to question what life is all about. It is called the joy list, and it takes off where Assess Yourself 7-5 leaves off. It is amazing how many people cannot come up with ten things they really enjoy. This activity will help you keep track of the things that bring joy to your life.

INSTRUCTIONS

1. Dedicate a small spiral pad for this activity.
2. Carry the pad with you daily.
3. Every time you do something you enjoy, write it down.
4. Look back over your list frequently.
5. Try to build these things into your schedule.
6. Share your list with someone you love.

Start now by writing down ten things that bring you joy.

1. ______________________________
2. ______________________________
3. ______________________________
4. ______________________________
5. ______________________________
6. ______________________________
7. ______________________________
8. ______________________________
9. ______________________________
10. ______________________________

From Metcalf, C.W. & Felible, R. (1992). *Lighten up: Survival skills for people under pressure.* New York: Perseus Books Group.[25]

Name: ______________________________ Date: ______________

ASSESS YOURSELF 7-7

Humor Inventory

The Humor Inventory is really a simple tool. It consists of four parts:

1. What happened?
2. How did it make you feel?
3. What were you left with?
4. What can you do about it?

Instructions:

- What happened?
  Describe the event that contributed to distorting or blocking your sense of humor.
- How did it make you feel?
  List the specific feelings you can remember about this incident.
- What were you left with?
  Discuss the belief(s) about humor you took away from this.
- What can you do about it?
  Consider how you can take this information and change your views about humor and the way you use it.

Example:

1. What happened?
   When I was about 5 years old, I remember waiting with my father and brother outside a hospital as my mother visited a sick friend. The hospital had a fringed awning covering the walkway into the front door. To amuse ourselves, we had a contest to see who could jump up and touch the fringe. My father easily reached it. My older brother got very close. I, chubby and sickly, could barely get off the ground. This was hilarious to my father and brother, who laughed heartily, rolled on the ground, and made remarks such as "What a load" and "Fat boy."
2. How did it make me feel?
   I was embarrassed. I wanted to run away and hide from them and all the people on the street who I imagined were staring at me.
3. What was I left with?
   I realized that humor could be a powerful weapon. Teasing and bringing attention to someone's shortcomings could bring someone to his knees.
4. What can I do about it?
   I am trying to stop using this kind of humor against my own sons. I slip up occasionally but always apologize and try not to repeat my mistakes.

Divide your life up into the following segments:

- Grade school (ages 5 to 11)
- Junior high (ages 12 to 15)
- High school (ages 15 to 18)
- College and career (ages 18 to 29)
- Parenthood
- Middle years (ages 36 to 65)
- Elder years (70+)

Take a humor inventory for all the stages that are appropriate for you. Share them with your classmates in small groups.

From Metcalf, C. W. & Felible, R. (1992). *Lighten up: Survival skills for people under pressure.* New York: Perseus Books Group.[25]

Name: ______________________________ Date: ______________

Assess Yourself 7-8

Slow the Pace: When Was the Last Time You . . .

Check off whether you performed this activity in the past month.

	Yes	No	Activity
1.			Walked instead of driving or taking the bus
2.			Intentionally took the back roads or streets so you could take your time
3.			Took the train or bus so you could sit back and gaze out of the window
4.			Took a walk in the woods or a park
5.			Took a bicycle ride off the beaten path
6.			Went on a nature walk
7.			Stopped to smell or observe the flowers or scenery along the side of a road
8.			Watched a sunset
9.			Sat quietly and listened to the birds in the trees
10.			Listened to the wind blowing through the trees
11.			Sat on the beach and just watched and listened to the waves
12.			Rocked a baby to sleep
13.			Explored a tide pool, pond, or frozen shoreline
14.			Examined a handful of beach sand or snow
15.			Planted a garden
16.			Watched the clouds roll by
17.			Looked at the stars and the moon on a clear night
18.			Brushed your pet's fur or someone's hair
19.			Gave someone a shampoo

Scoring: Yes ______ No ______

Add up the total number of responses for the past month. The greater the number of yes responses, the better. If you did not have at least four yes responses, you need to slow down and rethink the pace of your life before it slips away or you forget how to slow down.

These are just a few activities that require you to slow down and pay attention to the small things that give our lives the richness that makes us fully human. These things will also help you reduce your stress by helping you rethink your priorities and the relative unimportance of all the rushing around you do.

CHAPTER

8

REDUCE: FINDING YOUR OPTIMAL LEVEL OF STIMULATION

OUTLINE

OBJECTIVES

By the end of the chapter students will:

- Define Reduce, the second level of coping with stress.
- Compare and contrast Rethink and Reduce, the first and second levels of coping with stress.
- Analyze the relationship between level of stimulation and efficiency.
- Describe the triple As of coping, using a personal stressor as an example.
- Assess and evaluate their time management.
- Using personal examples, describe the ACT method of time management.
- Explain the relationship between stress management, assertiveness, nonassertiveness, and aggressiveness.
- Describe the three-part communication model used in the text.
- Describe the relationship between communication and stress.
- Identify aspects of their lives that may be areas for downscaling.

Reduce, the second level of defense against stress, revolves around strategies designed to help you find your optimal level of stimulation by cutting back on the overall volume of potential stressors and actual stressors in your life. We will discuss how even activities that are stimulating and fun can become potential stressors when we take on more of them than we can handle. In this chapter we will examine many different ways to *Reduce* the volume of stressors we face in our lives and find our optimal level of demand or stimulation. In chapter 7 we explored the relationship between illogical thoughts, negative emotions, and stress. We learned that much of our stress is influenced by our perspective on life and the events that happen to us. In this chapter we will focus mainly on our *actions,* how we actually *live* our lives. This chapter will concentrate very closely on the *choices* we make regarding how we spend our time on a day-to-day basis. Obviously, the way we live our lives is influenced by our thoughts and emotions—you can't separate the two—but in this chapter we will focus mainly on ways to change our *behavior,* on how we *act* on these thoughts and feelings. An example of this would be how we often take on too many responsibilities because we believe that we can't say no or be assertive in certain situations. Although the behavior of taking on too many responsibilities is the actual stressor, our irrational beliefs and feelings, such as guilt about not being able to say no or assert ourselves, factor into the problem. Because of this we will examine strategies for both cutting back on stressors and preventing them from occurring in the first place by being more assertive and communicating more clearly.

Stimulation, Demand, and Stress

Have you ever had so many things to do or so many decisions to make that you were mesmerized into inactivity, paralyzed to the point where you were unable to start? The sheer volume of things to do and consider seemed so impossible to overcome that you simply couldn't get started. On the other hand, have you ever been so bored or not challenged by a simple task that you were totally uninterested in taking the first step to complete it? Your boredom, in time, became a stressor because while you knew you could accomplish the task quickly, your procrastination began to cause problems. As you sat at your desk, not performing the task, the time seemed to pass incredibly slowly as your guilt over your procrastination mounted with each passing hour.

If you remember from chapter 1, Selye[31] defined stress as the nonspecific response of the body to any **demand.** When Selye referred to demands, he was referring to conditions such as food deprivation, extremes in climate and lighting, and other stimuli that he could control in a laboratory setting. They were considered demands because in order to maintain homeostasis in the face of this stimulation the laboratory animals had to adapt. In other words, these stimuli demanded adaptation in order to maintain homeostasis. In a similar fashion, when we are stimulated too much and too many demands are placed on us (by ourselves or by others), we must adapt. All forms of stimulation, both positive and negative, use energy and force our bodies to adapt. This is why even activities that are fun can become stressors if they require too much of our time and energy or if we engage in them without cutting back on other activities. When we try to do too much at the same time, even if it involves doing things we really like, we can burn out. The pressures of trying to juggle too many demands can lead to too much stimulation.

One of the most fascinating things about stress management is the incredible diversity in the type and level of stimulation that causes people to either be stressed or to thrive and reach their maximum potential. As we have discussed throughout this text, stress is a very individualistic phenomenon. What stresses one person out doesn't even affect another and can be exactly what a third needs to reach his or her maximum potential. Some stimuli that may drive you crazy roll right off your one friend's back and are exactly what a third friend is looking for. Just as the nature of these stimuli is individually perceived by each of you as either stressful or not, so is the amount of stimulation you all need to maximize your potential.

Finding Your Optimal Level of Stimulation

As we just discussed, each of us needs a certain number of demands to be stimulated enough to reach our potential but not too much to become stressed. The amount of **stimulation** that challenges you to dig down and work harder may mesmerize your friend into inactivity. Trying to keep up with the pace that challenges you may render your friend useless; some people simply cannot keep up because they are stressed to the limit. What amount of stimulation will get us to perform at our peak efficiency without burning out? The inverted U-shaped curve (fig. 8-1) will help us answer these questions.

This curve clearly illustrates the effects of excess demands or stimulation on our level of functioning. The horizontal axis plots the level of stimulation or demand and runs from low to high. The vertical axis plots the

reduce the second level of defense against stress; revolves around finding one's optimal level of stimulation by cutting back on the overall volume of stressors in one's life

demand a positive or negative condition or activity or stimulus that forces the body to use energy

stimulation the state of being aroused, excited, energized, or forced to react in some way

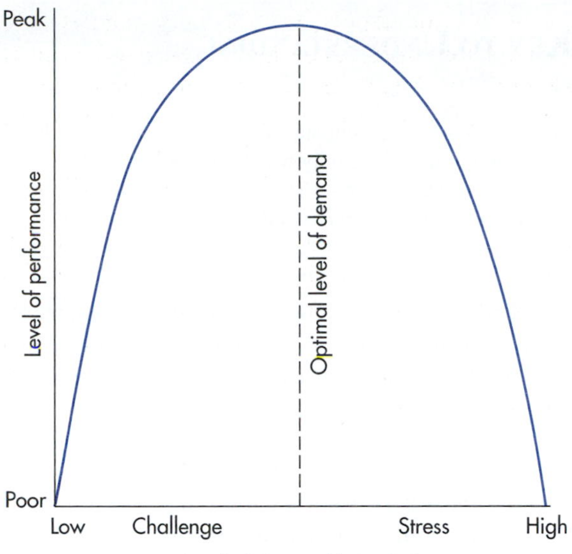

Figure 8-1

This drawing illustrates how our level of performance is related to our level of demand. As our level of demand/stimulation increases, we are challenged and our performance increases. When we reach our optimal level of demand, we reach peak performance. If we exceed our optimal level of stimulation, the same demands that challenged us become stressors.

level of performance, ranging from inefficient to optimal efficiency. The curve shows that too low a level of stimulation results in inefficient functioning. In other words, when we are not stimulated and challenged, we become less productive, less engaged, and unmotivated.

As we take on more responsibilities and demand more of ourselves, we begin to perform at a higher level of efficiency. This is what was referred to in chapter 2 as being challenged. Because we perceive it positively, it is not stress. Rather, we sense the exhilaration and energy it mobilizes. As we near our optimal level of stimulation or challenge, we approach peak efficiency. A key to managing stress is finding your optimal level of demand.

Without this illustration one would logically think that if a person is performing at peak performance at this peak level of demand, there is no reason to think that that person cannot do even better with a little more stimulation. In fact, however, the opposite is true. A little more demand results in a decrease in performance. We begin to miss deadlines, hand in sloppy work, forget meetings, and so forth. With a lot more demand, challenge is replaced by stress and we sink to the same level of inefficiency as when we were not challenged enough. Good coaches realize this and strive to challenge each player and the team just enough to reach that point of peak efficiency. In addition, they try to have this peak coincide with the end of the season's drive for the playoffs (see Stress in Our World 8-1: "Coach Brown").

But what do you do if you do not have a personal coach? How do we determine how much stimulation is enough? How do we know what the effects of a certain level of demand will be? Trial and error is the key to finding out how much stimulation is appropriate. We take on a certain amount of work and commitment and assess how well we are performing. We examine not only the end result of our labor but also how we feel during the labor. Do we feel challenged or stressed? Are our emotions positive or negative?

An example might be the amount of credit hours you choose to register for in a semester. How do you know where to start? Your school adviser may advise you to take sixteen credits because that establishes a rough parameter for how many credits you need to graduate in four years.

KEY TO UNDERSTANDING

A key to understanding your level of demand is realizing that a certain amount of stimulation is necessary to improve your performance and enjoyment of life. Too many demands (even fun ones), however, can result in overstimulation and having those demands become stressors.

STRESS IN OUR WORLD 8-1

Coach Brown: Finding the Optimal Level of Demand

Coach Brown is a good example of someone who knows just how far to push his players to get them to perform at optimal efficiency. When he accepted the coaching position, he inherited a team that many people felt had failed to live up to its potential by not making the NCAA playoffs the year before. However, in his first year Brown took the same team to the playoffs and within a game of beating the NCAA champions.

He was able to achieve this in part because he is a master of determining how hard to push his players. Brown pushed when he needed to and laid back when his team needed to regroup. Rather than treat each player the same, Brown worked with the individual men, using the appropriate type and amount of stimulation to push each to his highest level of efficiency.

Have you ever had a similar experience with a coach, parent, or other leader? Have you ever had an experience with a person who was not very skillful in motivating you and pushed you too hard or not hard enough? What kinds of pressure and how much pressure motivates you toward peak efficiency?

One of your friends is doing quite well with sixteen credit hours per semester. He has a very respectable grade point average, has time to study and complete his assignments, and is involved in a couple of extracurricular activities. Another friend has found that fourteen credits is too many. He can't manage to keep up with the reading and work associated with fourteen credits because the class those credits represent is too much for him to handle. It's funny because when you listen to the two of them talk about this, the one with sixteen credits explains that he'd be bored and unmotivated with a lower credit load while the friend with fourteen credits can't imagine carrying more than that. While it is helpful to hear both friends describe how their credit load affects them, you will ultimately have to find out, through trial and error, what your own optimal level of academic demand is.

Part of your decision will be based on how well you are functioning across the six dimensions of health. If you have high levels of physical, mental, emotional, spiritual, social, and environmental well-being, you will have more energy and a zest for life. You will feel more able to cope with the demands of extra work.

Regardless of what you ultimately decide, it is your decision. No one else can tell you how much is right for you. Trust your intuition and stand by your decision. Keep in mind, however, that the only constant in life is change and that you might be better positioned next year to push yourself harder. At any given point in your life, your six dimensions of wellness will influence your perceived ability to cope.

Categories of Stressors

The first step in reducing your overall stress level is taking an inventory of the amount and types of stressors in your life. Keep a personal stressor diary for several weeks to help you understand what stresses you, the intensity of those stressors, and how you respond to them (see Assess Yourself 8-2 Stressor Diary).

If you have determined that there are too many stressors in your life, you need to take action. You need a plan to control as many of those stressors as possible. Unfortunately, you never will be able to control all your stressors. Some of the things that cause us stress come without warning. It is important to realize this so that you do not set up unrealistic expectations about being able to control all your stress. Psychologist David Elkind[7] describes three categories of stressors: stressors that are foreseeable and can be controlled, stressors that are foreseeable and cannot be controlled, and stressors that are neither foreseeable nor controllable.

Category One Stressors

Category One Stressors are those that are foreseeable and can be controlled. They are stressors that you know about in advance and have time to work on. For instance, if you know that driving in a crowded city such as New York is very stressful, you can choose not to drive there. If you wish to visit, you can use public transportation. You can foresee this stressor and control it.

KEY TO UNDERSTANDING

There is no way to anticipate what your exact optimal level of demand will be. The only way to find it is through trial and error. You will know when you have passed it because your level of performance will drop.

Category Two Stressors

Category Two Stressors are those that are foreseeable but cannot be controlled. These stressors require different coping strategies because you cannot control or avoid them. An example of this kind of stressor would be having to wait in line for hours to buy tickets to a concert. You are generally stressed by waiting in line for hours at a time, but this is the only way you can purchase the tickets and you really want to go to the concert. The only way tickets are being sold is on a first-come, first-serve basis in person. This stressor is foreseeable, but you cannot control it.

Category Three Stressors

Category Three Stressors are those that are neither foreseeable nor controllable. These are the ones that catch you completely off guard. An example of this type of stressor is a traffic jam caused by a major accident. You leave your house a half-hour early to go somewhere and are making good time driving on a three-lane highway. As you crest the ridge of a hill, traffic is at a complete standstill. The cars fill in behind you, and there is nowhere to go. You turn on the radio and learn that there has been a ten-car pile-up and traffic is backed up for five miles and three hours. You could neither foresee this happening nor control it when it did. Because we can't do much in advance to prepare for the third category of stressor, do not worry about it. When things happen unexpectedly, you need to adapt to the change and go with the flow. A key to stress management is not getting overly upset about things that are beyond your control.

Category One Stressors stressors that are forseeable and can be controlled; you know about them in advance and can do something about them

Category Two Stressors stressors that are foreseeable but cannot be controlled; you see them coming but cannot do anything about them

Category Three Stressors stressors that are neither foreseeable nor controllable; these are the ones that catch you completely off guard

Living Constructively

Thirty Thousand Days

In a fascinating book about how to use your eyes to pay full attention to the world around you, James Elkins (2000),* a professor of art, talks about fully attending to the ordinary things in life, like grass. In writing how to view grass the way an artist would, Elkins recounts that up until writing that chapter of his book, he had not paid much attention to grass, figuring he had his whole lifetime to do it if he ever desired to do so. When he actually sat down to write the chapter, Elkins was shocked about how little time he actually had to observe grass fully, over the changing course of the seasons.

Elkins calculates that the average person has about 30,000 days (slightly over eighty-two years) to appreciate grass. Grass is actually in bloom about 10,000 of those days. At 40+ years old Elkins estimates that he used up more than half of those opportunities and had about thirty summers left to watch the grass. He further estimated that each summer has about sixty days of good weathers and maybe twenty days that he actually was able to get outside and have some time to spare. He figured that gives him about 600 chances to see the grass. Those few days can easily slip away.

When we realize that our lives are finite and how quickly time passes, it makes us stop and question how we want to spend our remaining time. Do we want to waste it doing things we really don't want to do? Do we want to spend it in relationships that are not fulfilling, with people who drag us down? The following activity is designed to help put your 30,000 days into clearer focus and help you decide on the things you might want to abolish.

Instructions:

1. Calculate the exact number of days you have lived. Count the number of full years you have lived up until this year and multiply those by 365. Next add up all the months and days (including today) that you have lived *this* year.
2. Subtract this number from 30,000. This is the number of days you have left.
3. Make three lists: (1) things I want to start doing, (2) things I want to continue doing, and (3) things I want to stop doing.
4. Describe how you want to spend the rest of your life using information gathered from these three lists.
5. What is keeping you from doing this?

(With permission from ToDo Institute.)

* Elkins J. (2000). How to use your eyes. NY, NY: Routledge Pub.

We can, however, work with categories 1 and 2. Once you have kept your personal stressor diary for a few weeks, you will begin to get a handle on the kinds of things that cause you stress. Look for patterns: types of people, kinds of situations, and combinations of events. After you know the kinds of things that are stressors for you, examine whether you can anticipate these things in advance and whether you can exert any control over their occurrence. If you do have some control over their occurrence (category 1), you can formulate a plan for reducing their likelihood. If you cannot control the occurrence of this stressor (category 2), you have to use a different type of strategy to cope with it.

Key to Understanding

Do not get overly concerned about stressors that are beyond your control. Since there is nothing you can do to see them coming or manage them when they occur, you need not feel responsible for them.

The Three As of Coping

There are three ways (three As) of coping with some category 1 stressors: (1) *Abolish* means completely eliminating stressors, (2) *avoid* refers to minimizing your exposure to stressors, and (3) *alter* means somehow changing the way you are exposed to the stressor.

Take traffic as an example. Suppose, after keeping your stressor diary for a few weeks, you find that your commute to school is a major source of stress for you. You have 9:00 A.M. classes four days a week, and getting to school at this time puts you right in the middle of rush-hour traffic.

Abolish the Stressor

Using the triple As of coping, you begin with *abolish*—you consider dropping out of school. This way you have no school and therefore no commute. Realistically, however, you still want to attend school, and so you shift to plan B—abolish your 9:00 A.M. classes. By taking either 8:00 A.M. or 11:00 A.M. classes, you change your commute, leaving either before or after the rush hour. Using your problem-solving skills and knowledge of the area and assessing your time needs for the rest of

If there really is such a thing as a universal stressor, it is traffic. Traffic is the bane of commuters everywhere.

the day and week, you decide which classes will better fit your schedule.

Avoid the Stressor

If the first A is impractical, you can shift into the second A, *avoid*. Using this strategy, you do not completely eliminate the stressor—you simply minimize your exposure to it. Using the rush-hour traffic as an example, you can simply choose to expose yourself to it less frequently. Instead of taking 9:00 A.M. classes four days a week, you may choose to take them only twice a week. In a sense, you cut your stress in half by cutting your exposure in half.

Alter the Stressor

If neither of these solutions is acceptable, you can use the third A, *alter,* to change the stressor or your exposure to it somehow. Again taking the commute as an example, you can alter this stressor to defuse it. You may decide to carpool. By being a passenger, you can sit back, read the paper, or take a nap during the ride to school. Some people, however, might find being a passenger more stressful than driving. You also could try a different route; a back road may take a little longer but could provide a break from the traffic. The change of scenery might be enough to defuse the commute as a stressor. You could also install a cassette deck or compact disk player in your vehicle and listen to comedy or peaceful music while stuck in traffic. You might even choose to listen to notes from class, using the commute as a time to study (see Assess Yourself 8-3, "Triple As Scenarios").

Managing Your Limited Resources

As we discussed earlier in the chapter, we all have approximately 30,000 days to live. How many of those days are spent engaged in activities that really mesh with our purpose in life or doing things that give our life meaning? A key to understanding how this relates to reducing your overall volume of potential stressors is to think of your time and energy as limited resources. As Selye[31] taught us, since we all have limited energy available to adapt to life's changes, we need to conserve it as much as possible. The same can be said for other resources such as time and money. For most people the two are related: people use increasing amounts of time to earn the money they need to meet their expenses. Unless one has additional sources of money available from investments or inheritance, the usual source of their income is their work and wages. Understanding the relationship between expenses, work, and time is an essential part of stress management. Generally, as expenses increase, the number of available nonwork hours in a day, week, or month decreases. Having fewer nonwork hours in the day, week, or month is stressful for most people because it limits the amount of time they have for fun, leisure, and maintenance (shopping, cleaning etc.) activities.

Managing Our Scale of Living

Our society has a tendency to equate money and material possessions and prestigious accomplishments with our **scale of living.** The *good life* is often referred to as more upscale living. We want upscale houses in upscale neighborhoods and to drive upscale cars.

We want our children to attend more prestigious upscale preschools, private academies, and colleges or universities. We are pushed from preschool through graduate school to want fast-track careers and the money, power, and prestige that accompany them. We learn to compete at everything, to expect and push for more, bigger, and better everything. Having the best of everything becomes our main goal in life and we convince ourselves that it is worth it to work long hours in jobs we hate to obtain these symbols of upscale living, of *the good life.* Sometimes, however, all this pushing and striving for the best of everything results in creating lives that have gotten away from us. We lose our purpose, our daily life criteria for happiness get lost in the mad rush to acquire wealth and more possessions.

The Simple Living Network[29] was started by people who reject the notion that the good life is based on amassing as much material wealth and as many prestigious accomplishments as possible. What voluntary simplicity is really about is helping people live more simple lives that revolve around their values and purpose. As we've mentioned, sometimes this is hard to do if our lives become too busy working long hours to acquire things. It really becomes a matter of not having enough time to both work to maintain an upscale life style and engage in activities that give life meaning.

scale of living an arbitrary measure of personal affluence and comfort in terms of income, possessions, and achievements

Downscaling is a term used to describe voluntarily cutting back on one's lifestyle so one can afford to do what one really wants to do. Often this involves working fewer hours, but it can also mean working the same amount of time but in a job or career that is less lucrative but more consistent with one's values and purpose. It could be viewed as an unburdening one's life and living more lightly and with fewer distractions that interfere with the quality of one's life. Of the people who are drawn to this movement, many are former executives, entrepreneurs, government officials, public servants, and others who have forsaken their successful, high-profile lives for much simpler, less lucrative, but more personally rewarding ways of living.[11]

The Living Simply Network (Simple Living.com[33]) is a national organization devoted to living more simply. It advocates living a more environmentally friendly, spiritual lifestyle that embraces self-actualization without exploitation of others or natural resources. Some of the guiding principles of those involved in living simply are:

- *Eliminating excess possessions and activities that produce physical or mental clutter*
  As we'll discuss later in the chapter, sometimes the volume of possessions we own and are responsible for can be overwhelming and require so much of our time just to maintain that they take away from our ability to live our life according to our criteria for happiness. For example, a bigger house and property means more time is required to clean the extra rooms, mow the lawn, trim the shrubs, and shovel the snow in the winter. It also means having to earn more money to pay the heating and cooling bills, property taxes, and other expenses.

  Additionally, the more activities we are involved in, the harder it is to do any of them well or sometimes even enjoy. This is especially true if we engage in activities that we really do not want to be involved in but are not assertive enough to refuse volunteering for. When we are involved in fewer activities we can devote more time to the ones we participate in. Think about activities such as playing a musical instrument or painting. These and other artistic endeavors require long periods of practice. Finding the time to engage in these types of activities often means cutting back on other less meaningful pursuits.
- *Limiting consumption of material goods to items that are truly needed or valued*
  This is an example of the environmental consciousness of people who live simply. They realize that production of consumer goods requires use of natural resources such as paper, electricity, and gasoline, resources that are not renewable and that come at a cost to society and the planet. Adherents of living simply believe that we can live meaningful lives and still consume fewer unnecessary products. For example, if we don't need a second car and can avoid buying one by using public transportation or carpooling occasionally, we shouldn't purchase the second vehicle.
- *Preserving the earth's resources*
  This is another example of the environmental consciousness of people who live simply. Recycling, using less water, oil, and electricity helps preserve the earth's resources while cutting one's cost of living and making it easier to keep work hours to a minimum.
- *Engaging in meaningful, satisfying work that uses one's uniqueness*
  As we've already mentioned, work should be an expression of our purpose in life. Living simply makes it easier to choose a job based on this and not merely financial concerns.
- *Investing time to develop close, rewarding relationships*
  Living simply means having more time to spend developing meaningful relationships with friends, neighbors, and family members. Developing relationships takes time and living a more simple life frees up more time to devote to this.
- *Exploring one's spirituality*
  Part of becoming more spiritual involves spending time engaging in introspective activities such as meditation and self-reflection. It also involves engaging in activities that involve others, whether it is members of your community, congregation, or organization. People who spend long hours commuting and at work often find it difficult to find the time to participate in such spirituality-building activities.
- *Becoming more peaceful by learning to live more in the present*
  This is a direct outcome of a more self-reflective, spiritual life. Research on meditation shows that regular meditators feel a greater sense of inner peace and are more mindful of the activities they are engaged in and the world around them.
- *Becoming more self-reliant*
  Living simply means doing more things for yourself rather than paying others to do them. This covers things from household chores to repairing items rather than throwing them away and buying new ones. It means having the time and desire to fix a small appliance if it only needs a minor repair rather than throwing it away.
- *Taking good care of one's body and overall health*
  Living simply means taking more personal responsibility for one's health and relying on the health care system less[29]

downscaling voluntarily cutting back on one's lifestyle so one can afford to do what he or she really wants to do

Regardless of our current lifestyle, each of us can find ways to live a more simple life according to some of the tenets described above. We can all find some way to downscale, free up more time to truly live, and reduce some of our stress.

Only you know whether this needs to be done. It is so easy to get caught up in other people's expectations of how much you should be doing that it can be a challenge to take charge and say, "Enough is enough." Sometimes this means letting other people down or failing to live up to others' expectations. However, for you to be productive and whole, you need to live and work within your limits. Pushing too hard can be counterproductive. Downscaling can be achieved in several ways. It may simply involve cutting back your number of commitments. You may be happy with the lifestyle you have and the direction of your life but simply are too busy. In this case downscaling does not mean changing the direction and focus of your life. All that is required is to cut back on your activities and responsibilities. In other cases downscaling may involve changing the present focus and future direction of your life. You may decide that you are in a rut and your life is moving in a direction that is more stressful than enjoyable. If this is the case, you will not only have to cut back on activities but also change the course of your life. You will need a new direction and a new plan to get where you want to be. The blueprint for downscaling is very similar to everything else we have been discussing in this chapter in that it begins with a look at your values and goals. Try to identify areas in your life where you might be able to live more simply. The next part of the chapter will examine how to manage limited financial and time resources.

Managing Limited Financial Resources

As we mentioned in chapter 7, our purpose in life is shaped by our values and daily life criteria. When we stray from this purpose or when it is threatened, we are often stressed. In our consumption-based American economy it is easy to get pushed off course and wind up owing more than we can afford. When this happens we usually wind up feeling stressed about how we are going to pay for our immediate expenses and debts and where are we going to find the time to take care of life's necessities, let alone have any time left over for fun. This is especially true for college students who have to find the time to juggle both academic and financial stressors.

Dealing with College Debt

Most college students view college-related expenses as a financial burden they must assume in order to meet their educational and career goals. The share of family income required to pay college expenses in the 2000s has surpassed the percentage required in the 1980s and 1990s. This percentage has gone up most for students at the lowest end of the economic scale.[4]

College tuition, room and board, and fees have soared. Thirty years ago, the average annual tuition and fees at private and public four-year colleges were about $7,500 and $1,750 respectively. In the 2004–2005 academic year, the average tuition and fees for a four-year private college were $20,082 (up 6 percent from 2003–2004) and $5,132 (up 10.5 percent from 2003–2004) at a four-year public institution.[5] The average total charges (tuition, fees, room and board) for four-year private institutions was $27,516 ($1,459 more than 2003–2004's $26,057—a 5.6 percent increase) and for four-year public institutions was $11,354 ($824 more than 2003–2004's $10,530—a 7.8 percent increase).[5] As tuitions have continued to rise, more than half of recent college graduates report owing between $10,000 and $40,000 in student loans, with the average debt increasing to $20,000 from $17,000 in 2002. Almost 60 percent of undergraduate students receive some form of financial aid. This translates into a higher level of debt for students in the 2000s compared with many of their parents who went to college in the 1960s, and 1970s and relied on government grants and subsidized loans. Most students have a manageable debt level, especially those who complete their degrees. Many, however, especially those who do not complete their degrees, are left with a heavy debt they can't repay.

Even students who can borrow and afford to repay loans are concerned about their ability to repay their college debts once they graduate. More and more students are facing increasingly heavy debts not only from the escalating costs of tuition, room and board, and fees but from credit card debt. Gallo[9] describes student credit card use as "out of control," citing studies that show that 71 percent of undergraduates have three credit cards and that 62 percent of those with credit cards carry an average credit card debt of $1,366.25. The relative ease of obtaining credit cards, low interest rates, and aggressive on-campus and direct mail marketing, along with escalating college costs, have led to an increase in credit card use among college students.[14] Over 80 percent of colleges permit on-campus solicitation by credit card vendors which offer students *t*-shirts, low introductory rates, and other perks for signing on. College bookstores and even alumni associations receive rebates from credit card companies for sponsored credit card programs.[8]

Unfortunately this heavy debt load often influences the choices students make regarding academic majors and careers. Kim[14] reports that heavy debt forces more than 30 percent of college graduates to take jobs other than the ones they trained for and really wanted to pay off their loans and credit card debt. This is a sure-fire prescription for stress as it sets the stage for a conflict between one's values and daily life criteria and one's work. Working in a job or career because it pays more than the one you trained for and really want is not the best way to spend eight to ten hours a day, Monday through Friday.

Budgeting Your Limited Financial Resources: How Much Money Do You Really Need?

We don't often think logically when it comes to money. People often underestimate the amount of money they spend and the amount they really need to meet their financial obligations. The same kind of illogical thinking that contributes to interpersonal stressors factors into financial stress. Most financial experts agree that the first step in managing your limited financial resources is taking an inventory of how much money you actually spend during the month.[6,39] Each dollar spent is put into a specific category and at the end of the month you can examine how much you spent on each category. Here are some common categories used to calculate actual expenses:

Rent or Mortgage

Utilities (gas, electric, water-garbage removal, sewer, etc.)

Food (include eating out, even small items like coffee, etc.)

Transportation (car payments, fuel, maintenance, parking, etc.)

Insurance (homeowners/renters, auto, medical, dental, life)

Personal Expenses (entertainment, clothing, gifts, education, travel, pocket money, etc.)[6,39,40]

The key to developing an effective budget is being completely accurate in compiling your expenses. Even failing to list that morning coffee and newspaper that you buy on your way to school/work can throw off your budget. In an era of designer coffee shops, these two expenses can contribute several dollars to daily expenses.

Once you have assessed your actual level of spending and categories, you are ready to construct a **budget.** A budget is nothing more than a system for allocating your net income to meet your actual expenses. A balanced budget means that you spend what you take in. When you spend more than you take in (usually through loans or credit card spending), you have a deficit budget. When you have money left over after accounting for all of your expenses, you have a surplus budget (see Assess Yourself 8-1, Developing a Budget).

Any of the three types of budgets can be a potential stressor depending upon what your beliefs are about the relationship between net income and expenses. For example, some people feel that money is a stressor even though they can meet all of their expenses and have a balanced budget. Others who run deficits month after month don't get stressed at all. Still others, who manage to have a surplus which they save, feel they are still not saving enough (see the Are You Thinking Clearly? box at the end of this chapter on p. 228).

Managing Your Limited Time

Do you feel that there is not enough time in the day to do what needs to be done? Do you feel that you could use a couple of hours at night to finish up things? Are you the kind of person who would be lost if one day you forgot to wear your watch? Most people feel that they could use a little more time. Unfortunately, we cannot add more hours to our days or more days to our lives. What we can do is examine how we spend our time and find ways to use it more efficiently. We may not be able to add any extra hours to the day but almost everyone can save one hour by becoming more efficient.[17]

Goal Setting and Time Management

The first step in time management is setting goals for our lives. As we discussed in chapter 7, having a set of clear goals for your life helps reduce stress because it provides structure and purpose. It also serves as a basis for the planning and use of time.

This emphasis on efficiency and use of time does not mean we should not have time to relax. Indeed, people who manage their time effectively realize that building free time into their schedules is just as important as building in time to study and work. One of the things **time management** teaches us is that there is enough time for both work and play if we plan wisely.

Assessing Your Use of Time

Once you have clarified your goals and decided they are worthy of serious time considerations, you are ready to examine exactly how you use your time. You need to take a look at a few weeks worth of time logs to get a sense of how you use your time (see Assess Yourself 8-4, "Time-Management Log"). Once you have completed your assessment, you can begin to look for patterns and trends in your use of time. Can you identify blocks of time that are not being used efficiently? Is your log so cluttered with commitments that there is very little time left for personal use? Remember, the most important thing to assess is how your use of time either complements or works against your values and goals.

If your use of time inhibits your values and goals, you need to specify exactly how and where this is occurring. It

budget a system for allocating net income to meet actual expenses

time management the process of systematically allocating one's time to maximize one's use and enjoyment of it may be that your schedule is not whole or balanced. You may spend too much time engaged in things such as watching TV and talking with friends. Or you may find that too much of your time is spent in work-related activities and that you do not allow yourself to indulge in a little "vegging out" now and then. There are seven different types of time we will discuss in the next section of this chapter: self-care, school, work, commuting, play, sleep, and before and after time.

Each type of your time can be analyzed for quantity and quality. You need to ask yourself not only how much time you are spending but whether it is quality time. Once again, remember that you are the ultimate judge of what works for you.

Self-Care Self-care time is the amount of time you spend in activities related to your appearance and health. It includes your morning routine activities such as showering, styling hair, applying makeup, etc. It also includes health-related activities (time spent exercising, meditating, going to the doctor, etc.).

School Time School time involves the hours spent in all the activities related to completing assignments. This includes time spent in class, studying, going to the library, writing papers, and attending performances. Students often underestimate the amount of out-of-class time that is required to be successful in college.

Work Time Work time is that period of the day when you are engaged in tasks that are required of you according to your role. Obviously, the job you work at for pay is the type of work most people include in this category. Other types of labor, ranging from child care to community service, can also fall into this category and must be assessed.

For instance, a person engaged in full-time child care who is also active in community service may actually put in more work hours than does a person with a traditional 9-to-5 office job. The former does not share the same schedule of mandatory coffee breaks, free lunch hours, and personal time afforded by the for-pay work world of many people. Students engaged in classwork, homework, part-time jobs, child care of siblings, housework, and community service can be stretched to the limit. These types of activities need to be evaluated as work when one is assessing time use. People engaged in this type of labor can easily find themselves as overextended and stressed out as the typical harried executive.

Commuting Time In today's society we are dependent on automobiles and spend much of our time in transit. Commuting time needs to be taken into account in examining our schedules. How many hours do we spend getting to and from school and work? How is this commuting time spent? Are there ways to alter it to make it less stressful?

Before and After Time Often we get into trouble with our use of time by not scheduling enough before and after time. We cut things so close that the slightest deviation from normal can throw off our schedule for the rest of the day. Students are notorious for scheduling three or more classes back to back in an effort to use time more efficiently. In actuality what this does is set them up for stress because invariably things happen between classes that throw off these precise schedules. A class running overtime or a long line in the school cafeteria can wreak havoc on tight schedules.

Playtime is critical for combating stress. Make sure you build some into every day.

Playtime Playtime is important for total wellness and needs to be built into each day as a stress-preventive strategy. Playtime needs to be scheduled in just as work time does. Playtime also needs to be given the same priority as work time. Remember the efficiency curve—more is not necessarily better in dealing with stress and time demands.[23]

Playtime is usually the first to be sacrificed when we overbook our commitments. Rather than accept this practice as standard operating procedure, we need to view this loss of playtime as a warning of a lack of balance. We also need to assess our playtime constantly to ensure that it stays play and not work. All too often our competitive instincts take over, and a relaxing game can become a struggle for dominance. Instead of using the game to relieve stress and tension, the game becomes a stressor itself. There is nothing wrong with competitive play as long as it is not the sole source of play.

Sleep Time Sleep time is another highly variable phenomenon. While some of us get by on five hours of sleep and feel refreshed, others need eight to nine hours to recharge their energy. Sleep needs vary from day to day and are influenced by a host of variables, ranging from overall level of health to energy expended during the day. Sleep needs also vary throughout the life cycle. Your body will let you know if you are not getting enough sleep.

Stress Buster Tips

What to Do about Sleep Deprivation

1. Don't get stressed about it. It's bad enough that you are not sleeping enough; don't compound the problem.
2. Don't combine sleep deprivation with driving and/or alcohol. The combination of too little sleep and driving is dangerous. Add alcohol to this mix and it becomes fatal.
3. Catch up. Studies show that after two full, unrestricted nights of sleep, your body will recover, even from chronic sleep deprivation of a week or two.
4. Break the habit of watching late-night TV in bed. Use your VCR to tape late-night shows and watch them during the day, after a good night's sleep.
5. Take a fifteen-minute warm bath before bed. After you soak, cool off a little. The natural drop in body temperature is a natural sleep inducer.[35]
6. Get some exercise. Vigorous exercise performed at least four hours before bedtime will help you fall asleep more easily.[35]
7. Give yourself thirty minutes to get to sleep. If you don't fall asleep after this time, get out of bed, do something physicial like wash the dishes or clean your room, and try again when you're feeling drowsy.
8. Reduce. Cut back on the demands on your time that force you to stay up late and get up early. When you get opportunities to drop responsibilities, do so.
9. Downscale. If you can reduce your overhead and cost of living, you might be able to employ number 8 more easily.
10. Change your illogical thoughts about sleep. It's not good to deprive yourself of sleep; it's stupid. Start telling yourself you need and deserve more sleep.

Any time you are relying on an alarm clock to wake you up, you are not getting enough sleep. If your brain needs an alarm clock to wake it up, it needs more sleep.[22] Most people need eight hours of sleep to function optimally. A small fraction of people can function normally on six hours of sleep, while another small percentage needs nine hours.[22]

A sleep foundation survey found that nearly two of three people do not get the required eight hours of sleep. Of these people nearly one-third get less than six hours of sleep.[15]

Sleep is not a luxury. Your body and brain need restful sleep to recharge so that they can perform at peak efficiency. A sleep cycle can be broken into two parts: rapid eye movement (REM) (dreaming occurs during this time) and nonrapid eye movement or deep sleep. Each part of the sleep cycle is responsible for important brain and body functions.

Most researchers generally agree that dreaming is the time when the brain tries to sort out the events of the day. Think of your brain at the end of the day as a cluttered desktop. Dreaming helps you sort out and organize the clutter, preparing you for the next day's work.[38]

During deep sleep your brain biochemically recharges itself. Your body replenishes the brain's stores of adenosine triphosphate (ATP)—energy molecules that were used up during the day.[15] During deep sleep our bodies also circulate approximately 70 percent of our daily dose of growth hormone and prolactin needed for tissue repair and growth and immune-system competence.[35] Depriving yourself of sleep short-circuits your brain and body's ability to recharge.

The loss of an hour or two of sleep over two successive nights can lead to a substantial sleep debt, with a decrease in performance. After seventeen hours of being awake, your body functions as if impaired with a blood alcohol level of 0.05 percent (a level approaching legal intoxication in most states).[23]

Four hours of sleep loss (two days in a row sleeping six hours instead of eight) can slow reaction time by 10 to 15 percent.[35] Continued sleep debt not only further reduces energy levels and performance but makes you more susceptible to infection and illness.[35]

Unfortunately, in our culture much sleep deprivation is intentional. It is considered a characteristic of hard work and upward mobility (work hard, stay late, get up early). We often falsely equate hard work and late hours with productivity. Even more ironic is the idea of staying up late, setting the alarm for 5:00 A.M., and going out for a run or to the gym. We might be better off sleeping in rather than further depleting our energy reserves (see Stress Buster Tips: "What to Do about Sleep Deprivation").

Prioritizing Your Time by ACTing

Time management revolves around prioritizing how you use your time. In the previous sections of this chapter we spent a lot of time deciding *what* you want to spend your time on. In this section we will discuss *how* to use your time more effectively to achieve this. Combining the two is the key to a productive life. It is not enough to just *talk* about what you want to do in life. You must also *act* on it.

There are several ways to approach prioritizing what you spend your time on. The **ACT Model** is an approach to time management that revolves around making priority lists of things that you need and would like to accomplish during any given day. Each activity is assigned a different

ACT Model an approach to time management based on prioritizing tasks to be accomplished in a given time period priority status and is acted upon based of its priority. In other words, activities with the highest priority (called *A List* activities) are acted upon first. Activities of lesser priority (*C* and *T List* activities) are acted upon only after A List demands are met.

> *A List Activities*—activities that *absolutely* must be done today or you will suffer immediate, severe consequences. These are things you cannot put off until tomorrow. Only you can determine what these activities are, but for the most part these are things such as paying bills, handing in school and work assignments, and meeting personal obligations. Remember, playtime is essential. Do not neglect to schedule some in as an A-list activity.
>
> *C List Activities*—activities that *could* get done when the A-list tasks are finished. Working on an assignment that is due next month is an example of this kind of task. Although you would like to begin the project, failure to do so will not result in any negative consequences today. C-list activities will become A-list activities in time as their deadlines approach.
>
> *T List Activities*—activities you could *try* to do if all of your As and Cs get finished. Things such as shopping for a new car and writing a letter you have been meaning to get to would be T-list activities.

The best time to make up these priority lists is at the end of the day. You begin by assessing which C- and T-list activities remain from during the day. Taking these and tomorrow's A-list activities, you plan your schedule for the next day. If you have fewer As, today's unfinished Cs may move up and become A-list activities as their deadlines approach. You may even be able to get to some T-list entries.

Some people simply tape these lists to their desks and check things off as they are finished. Others spend lots of money on color-coded schedule books or notebook computers. Others keep a daily calendar datebook that comes in handy when scheduling future commitments.

A word about working through your A list: some people like attacking the more difficult items first. In this way they attack the most difficult problems when they are the freshest and have the most energy. Others like to knock off several smaller tasks first to get a sense of accomplishment right off the bat. There is no correct formula; whatever works for you is the best approach.

The key aspect of a priority system such as this is to finish your A list before moving on to your C or T list. It is tempting to stop doing what has to be done to pursue something else that is more fun or less important. This invariably leads to stress, however, as A-list deadlines get closer and you have not made the necessary progress in meeting them. This is when you find yourself taking unfinished work home or staying up late to accomplish things that could have been finished on time.

Stress Buster Tips

Protecting Your Time

How many times have you begun a project or started to write a paper or finish a report when someone walks into your room or office and interrupts you? How about those never-ending phone calls that constantly interrupt your flow of thoughts as you try to compose that paper or memo? Here are some simple strategies to combat these distractions and protect your time.

Let People Know about Your Intensions
Let your boss, coworkers, family, and friends know about your desire to create uninterrupted time. Tell them that at certain hours (be specific) you will be unavailable except for emergencies. Explain to them that you will be more productive and less stressed if they will accept this.

Abolish Your Open-Door Policy; Close Your Door
Whether you are in your office at home or work or in your room, close the door. Everyone needs peace, quiet, and privacy to think and complete work. This time is just as, if not more, crucial to your effectiveness as time spent in meetings, informal discussions, and socializing. An "open door" policy invites interruptions.

Post Your "Office Hours"
Schedule time at work and home for meetings and consultations. Choose times that correspond with your "off-peak" productivity time. Don't have office hours when you are most productive. Use a clock-face (can set the hands of the clock) message board to let people know when you will be available.

Change Your Illogical Thinking about Interruptions
You have the right to not be interrupted constantly. You have the right to tell someone who interrupts you, "I'm busy at the moment. Come back at (suggest a time) or I'll call you when I'm finished."

Use Your Answering Machine
If you don't have one, buy one. Let the machine answer all your phone calls. If you can monitor the call, listen to the message but don't feel you have to pick up at that very moment. Better yet, turn the monitor off and listen to your messages when you are done with work.

Use Public Space
If you can't avoid interruptions at home, in the dorm, or at work, leave the area and do your work in one of your town's public facilities. Many local libraries have "quiet rooms" where you will not be interrupted.

One way of really enjoying your playtime is to become more organized and use time effectively. This way, when you are off, you do not worry about unfinished business because there is none. You can be concerned

KEY TO UNDERSTANDING

Finish your A-list activities first.

about one thing—the pleasure that you can get out of this free time.

There is one final thing to remember about managing your time; be prepared to fight for your time. Just when you become organized and find the extra time you've been searching for, someone will come knocking (literally) and try to take it away. See Stress Buster Tip protecting your time on previous page.

Managing Time Resources by Limiting Procrastination

Procrastination is one of the biggest wasters of time regardless of what kind of work you are involved in (school, house, full-time job, etc.). Chances are, you're a procrastinator if you answer yes to one or more of the following questions:

- Do you tend to leave unpleasant projects to the last minute?
- Do you hope that if you put off certain tasks, they will go away or someone else will do them?
- Have you ever thought that you could do a better job if you just had more time?
- When you fail to get a job done on time, do you blame someone else?
- Do you set unrealistic deadlines for yourself which practically guarantee that you won't finish on time?
- Do you overload yourself with work and then complain that there is too much to do?
- Are you running out of excuses and alibis for not getting your work done on time?[20]

Reasons for Procrastination There are three major reasons for procrastination: fear of failure, laziness or apathy, and the need for instant gratification.[20,32] The number one reason why most people procrastinate is fear of failure. We postpone doing something because we're afraid we won't do it right. We become mesmerized into inactivity. Rather than take a stab at trying, we are frozen into inactivity. Many of us, as a defense mechanism, set unreasonably high standards for performance. When we set standards so high that we can never meet them, we don't even have to try.

Fear of failure can be a self-fulfilling prophecy and can lead to a cycle of failure if we are not careful. By putting off starting a big project and waiting until the deadline looms near before even beginning it, we set ourselves up for failure. By procrastinating too long, we can assure failure. Our failure then reinforces our initial fears about being able to perform the task. We complete the cycle by using negative self-talk and telling ourselves things such as "See, I knew I couldn't do that" and "I never should have started that project." This sets the stage for avoiding difficult tasks in the future. We begin to anticipate failure.

Laziness and apathy also contribute to procrastination. Laziness has two components: physical (amount of energy) and emotional (motivation or apathy). Laziness is often related to overall energy level. People vary in their daily amount of available energy and what they bring to any task. Low energy levels can sap any motivation for taking on difficult tasks. Low motivation and apathy can be part of one's overall personality or can be task-specific. In general some people aren't as motivated as others to work and perform at their highest levels. We all know people who are seemingly "up," highly charged and motivated all the time. Others are usually motivated for most work but might be apathetic about specific tasks.

People who procrastinate because they need instant gratification put off detailed and tedious tasks because they realize those tasks will take time. People who are able to delay gratification until a tedious task is complete will have less of an inclination to put a task off.

Break the Procrastination Habit To break the procrastination habit, we need to generate success in managing our time more efficiently. The following strategies are especially helpful for procrastinators:

1. *Don't Overbook.* Since procrastinators use overloaded schedules as an excuse for avoiding certain tasks, they need to pay particular attention (at least until they begin to stop procrastinating) to reducing unimportant responsibilities at school and work. Do not volunteer for unimportant tasks. Save your limited energy for the things you *must* do. You need to start doing these things better.
2. *Give Yourself More Time.* Stop using lack of time as an excuse. Intentionally build in extra time to accomplish your A-list activities. Give yourself 50 percent more time for larger tasks than you currently allot. Spend less time doing less productive things.
3. *Ensure Privacy and Limit Interruptions.* Procrastinators more than anyone else must guard their privacy and limit interruptions. Procrastinators will use the least little distraction to get sidetracked. Not finishing the task, they will blame these distractions for their failure. Use the privacy-ensuring tips already mentioned in this chapter.
4. *Complete More Important Tasks First.* We've talked about the concept of developing master lists of tasks

procrastination a tendency to put tasks off until later

and prioritizing activities according to the ACT formula. Most people are able to attack their A lists in any order. It doesn't matter if they complete several smaller A activities before they move on to the more difficult tasks. Procrastinators do not have this self-discipline. They will use this to avoid difficult tasks. Therefore, procrastinators need to finish the most difficult tasks *first*. Only after finishing these tasks should procrastinators move on.
5. *Break Large Tasks into Smaller, More Manageable Units.* Sometimes attacking a large task can seem daunting for anyone, let alone a procrastinator. By breaking large tasks into smaller units, they are less intimidating. Try interspersing small, household A List tasks like doing the wash into work or school projects that you are working on at home. This will give you a chance to get up and move your body. Use a timer to limit the amount of time you devote to these breaks to ten or fifteen minutes maximum.
6. *Reward Yourself.* Set up a reward system for yourself. It is going to be difficult to start being able to delay gratification. Reward yourself for your efforts. Rewards can match the task—small rewards for small tasks, larger rewards for more difficult work. Make the reward match your interests (try to avoid using candy or nonhealthy rewards that can rob your energy).

Managing Limited School, Work, and Home Space Resources

A final category of limited resources related to stress is space. Whether we realize it or not, we all have our personal requirements for space. We usually think about them or even realize they exist when we start running out of space. Running out of space is primarily related to two things: having more material objects than your current space can hold and/or being disorganized. As with all potential stressors, space requirements vary from one person to the next and one's appraisal of space is individually determined. Some people perceive clutter (knickknacks, magazines and newspapers on tables and furniture, etc.) as a sign of hominess while others view it as a mess that needs to be cleaned up.

As we mentioned earlier in this chapter, one of the guiding principles of living simply is getting rid of unnecessary material possessions. A side benefit of ridding your life of excess material possessions and buying fewer things in the future is that it frees up additional space. Paring away nonessential items also helps you manage the second cause of running out of space, lack of organization. It is simply harder to organize your limited space when it is overflowing with things that need to be put somewhere.

Jeffrey Mayer,[21] the time-management guru of the 1990s, believes we all can reduce stress by wasting less time. When your home or office space is disorganized, it simply takes you longer to find things. In addition to wasting time, the process of having to look for something that is either misplaced or doesn't have its own place to begin with can be stressful. It often seems that when we need something the most we are least likely to locate it quickly and efficiently. Mayer believes that the extra seconds devoted to finding misplaced items add up to several minutes of *lost time* each day. Becoming more organized can help us recover this lost time *and* reduce our stress. Rather than looking for large blocks of wasted time, it may be more efficient to save time in smaller pieces. Having thirty seconds every five minutes might be easier than trying to free up a block of thirty minutes.[19] Using time efficiently begins with becoming organized.

Three Steps to Organizing Limited School and Work Space

1. **Start with Your Desk** Start getting organized by cleaning your desk. You'll need about two hours of uninterrupted time to do this. Mayer[19] recommends that you schedule an appointment with yourself to do this. Write it in your appointment book, pull the plug on the phone, lock the door, and get to work. Bring a large garbage can!

   Begin with the top of your desk. Take a look at every piece of paper in every pile. Be prepared for a shock. If you're like the average person, you'll uncover letters, memos, assignments, returned assignments, and other items that have long since been completed or have been abandoned. In many cases it is too late to respond to the item. Toss it out! Move on to the next item. Ask yourself, "Why am I keeping this?" If you don't have a *good* answer, throw it out. Return the items you do not throw out to a pile that contains similar items.

   Move to your desk drawers. Go through the same process with the papers and miscellaneous items ("Do I really need that plastic spoon that has green mold around the edges?"). Try to separate desk hardware (pens, pencils, paper clips, and other items) from assignments, notes, and other work.
2. **Start a File System** Your ultimate goal in this step is to take everything off your desk and put it into a system of file folders in your desk or file cabinet. Make up a set of folders with appropriate headings: Assignments Due, Memos to Respond To, Phone Calls to Return, and so on. The headings should be clearly legible on the folder tabs and should be staggered so that they don't block each other when you put them away. You should be able to see each tab clearly when you open your desk file drawer or file cabinet. Make as many headings and files as you feel are necessary.

   Organize the folders in a portable accordion file or hanging folders. (Mayer advises against using hanging folders because he feels they take up too much space in a file drawer or cabinet and tend to pinch the tabs as you close the drawer.[19])

3. **Develop a Master List** The key to Mayer's[19] time-management system is developing a master list of all work, phone calls, memos, and other items. The master list serves as the index to your file system. You must put everything on your master list before you insert any of the items from your desk into the appropriate folders. This allows you to keep just three items on your desktop: your list, a phone, and your computer. You can keep your master list on a yellow legal pad.

   As you complete tasks, cross them off the master list. It is all right if your list takes up more than one page. You'll be surprised at how quickly it gets reduced now that you've become more organized. You may want to condense sheets as you complete most of the items on any given page.

   You can combine Mayer's master list concept with the ACT prioritization system by marking *A*, *C*, or *T* next to any item on the list as you enter it.

Becoming Organized at Home

You can also find more time by wasting less time finding things in your home. The rest of your cluttered home (or dormitory room), like your desk, can rob you of precious time by making it more "time-consuming" to find things. Everyone can recall at least one occasion when a simple task (such as replacing the batteries in a flashlight) took ten times longer than necessary because you couldn't find what you needed to accomplish the task. Sometimes the problem is simply not being organized enough. Our living space, like our desks, can get overrun with piles. The problem centers on getting organized. At other times the problem has to do with excess junk and clutter. We become junk men and women. We hold on to useless junk that has long since lost any meaning or value in our lives. When meaningful possessions become junk, we need to throw them out so that we can get organized. Clutter guru Don Aslet[1] offers a twelve-step program for decluttering and organizing your limited home space in the Stress Buster Tips on this page.

Reducing Stress By Communicating More Effectively

Miscommunication is a major source of interpersonal stress. As we'll discuss in this section of the chapter, a dialogue involves clear, direct communication and feedback between two people. When two people communicate clearly, they each know where the other stands and there is little chance of misunderstandings occurring. Conversely, ineffective communication or miscommunication *often* results in misunderstandings and this can become a source

Stress Buster Tips

A Twelve-Step Guide for Junkaholics

Here are some ideas from cleaning expert Don Aslet on how to get clutter out of your home—and banish it forever.

Start small. Go through one drawer or one shelf per session—not the whole closet. Otherwise you'll just feel overwhelmed.

Get tough. Dump the contents of the whole drawer, box, or shelf onto the floor. That'll force you to consider each object as a potential discard. Ask yourself, Is this object earning its keep? If not, out it goes. If you're undecided, put the possession on probation: Give it three months to reveal its usefulness.

Don't get sidetracked. If you stop to read every old letter and look at every batch of photos, you'll never get anywhere.

Lend what you can't bring yourself to toss. Nine times out of ten you'll never want it back.

Take stuff to the dump or Goodwill the same day. If not, don't be surprised if the next day you reconsider.

Go through your mail daily while standing by the recycling bin. To have your name removed from mailing lists for credit card solicitations, catalogs, and other advertisements, contact Direct Marketing Association, www.dmaconsumers.org/consumerassistance.html to have your name removed from the mail-preference service.

Set a limit on saving bags, containers, and boxes. Ten shopping bags or yogurt containers is reasonable. Fifty is not.

Save magazine articles, not whole magazines. Tear out the pages you're interested in. And if you haven't read or filed the articles in three months, toss them.

Treat unwanted gifts like flowers. Yes, they express a sentiment that you appreciate. No, that doesn't mean you have to keep them forever.

Get rid of two old garments every time you buy a new one. This rule works for shoes, appliances, books, records, and toys.

Miniaturize mementos. Got a sentimental side? Keep the Girl Scout badges instead of the whole uniform. Take a great portrait of yourself with your trophies or standing next to that nostalgic car in your garage—then trash the trophies and put the car up for sale.

Have your kids give something back to Santa. Hold a pre-Christmas de-junking day to clear out toys from Christmases past and donate them to charity. The kids probably won't mind making room for more.

From Aslet, D. Clutter's last stand. *Health,* October 1994.[1]

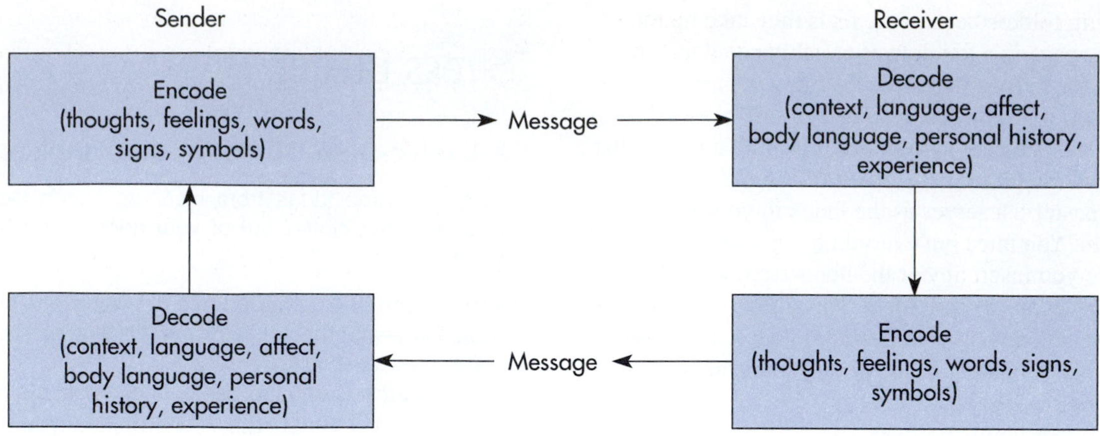

Figure 8-2

This illustration represents a model of communication.

of stress. As we discussed in chapter 2, regarding Lazarus and Folkman's[17] stress appraisal model, most people feel threatened when things are ambiguous. Think about what it feels like to have a conversation with someone close to you (your boss, spouse, boyfriend/girlfriend) that you walk away from saying to yourself, " I wonder what s/he meant by that." The ambiguity seems to hang over your head like a dark cloud until you get it cleared up. When people are unsure of the intent or meaning of a message, they feel threatened by it and therefore become stressed. Allowing ambiguous communications to linger for days, weeks, months, and even years is a sure-fire way to strain relationships. Almost everyone knows someone who is estranged from a friend or family member because of something that was said a long time ago that never was resolved. Communicating clearly initially and taking responsibility for clearing up misunderstandings as soon as possible are the two best ways to reduce stressors associated with miscommunication.

A Model for Effective Communication

Communication is defined as the process by which information is exchanged between individuals through a common system of symbols, signs, or behaviors. It involves all the modes of behavior an individual uses to affect another person, including spoken and written words as well as nonverbal messages such as gestures, facial expressions, bodily posture, and artistic symbols.[7]

Effective communication is a process that involves sending and receiving coded messages. Figure 8-2 illustrates what happens when a message is sent, received, and responded to.

A sender wishing to communicate puts the idea and feeling of the message into a form that can be transmitted. This process of formulating a message and choosing appropriate words, symbols, tone, and expressions to represent it is called **encoding.**

The encoded message is transmitted and received by the receiver and then translated by the receiver's personal storehouse of knowledge and experience. This perceiving and translating process is called **decoding.**

As you can see in Figure 8-2, both encoding and decoding take place in the context of the interpersonal and physical relationship of the communicants. What is being said involves not only the actual message but also the physical environment and the relationship between sender and receiver. A sender might alter the message depending on whether the environment is friendly or unfriendly, familiar or unfamiliar, safe or unsafe, formal or informal. Additionally, a sender might send a different message in the same environment depending on the nature of the relationship with the receiver. The message might be affected by whether the sender and receiver are friends or enemies, strangers or acquaintances, peers or of unequal status.

As can be seen in Figure 8-2, communication involves sending and receiving both verbal and nonverbal messages. Each type of message is capable of transmitting information and is part of the encoding and decoding process.

Verbal Communication

Verbal communication is two-dimensional in that it involves transmitting both thoughts and feelings by putting them into words. The cognitive dimension is concerned with communicating thoughts about things, while the affective dimension involves putting feelings into words. Most people find communicating cognitive information easier than expressing feelings.

encoding the selection of signs, symbols, emotions, and words to transmit a message

decoding the use of knowledge, memory, language, context, and personal history and experience to interpret a message

Both dimensions of verbal communication can translate into potentially stressful communications. For instance, someone can say something to you and that person's actual *words* are interpreted by you as stressors. A professor might make a comment such as "John, I can see you are not prepared for today's discussion." This is interpreted by you as a stressor because you feel embarrassed in front of the class.

Other times, it isn't *what* someone says that is stressful, it is *how* he or she says it. The tone or inflection makes you wonder what the person really means. The same professor could say something like "Well, John, I can see that you are *certainly* well prepared for today's lesson." Even though these words seem complimentary, the way the professor said them (emphasizing the *you* and the *certainly* after John stumbled on his answer to a question) is perceived as a stressor.

Specificity is crucial in effective verbal communication; the more specific the message is, the more likely it is to be transmitted clearly. Vocabulary plays a big part in the specificity of verbal communication. Having a large working vocabulary allows us to specify exactly what we want to say.

Nonverbal Communication

How we say things is as important as what we say. **Body language** is a term used to describe the nonverbal messages we send through our posture, gestures, movements, physical appearance, and even silence. Our body language intentionally or unintentionally sends messages to receivers.

Positive Body Language Positive, or open, body language involves a relaxed posture, steady eye contact, nods of the head, and an occasional smile or happy expression. All are cues that you are an approachable sender or a receptive receiver (fig. 8-2).

Negative Body Language Negative, or closed, body language includes visible signs of tension, such as clenched fists, tight jaw muscles, a "closed" posture (arms folded, body shifted sideways, etc.), and facial expressions ranging from anger to disbelief. Negative body language can indicate that you are either apathetic or disturbed about something.

We've all had someone (a teacher, mother, father, or other adult) stand over us with his or her arms folded across his or her chest, head lowered, giving us "the stare." Without a word being said we begin to sweat and wonder, "What did I do wrong this time?" Other nonverbal messages are not as powerful but often result in our feeling threatened and therefore stressed.

Physical Appearance Physical appearance can convey a variety of messages. A messy or ungroomed appearance may represent a variety of encoded messages ranging from positive (comfortable and relaxed) to negative (apathic and not respectful). Clothing and adornment might be intentionally or unintentionally erotic and seductive. This can affect both the encoding and the decoding process; the sender might be trying to convey one message (I'm trying to look my best), while the receiver may perceive another (This person is trying to manipulate or come on to me).

Silence Silence is a form of nonverbal communication that can be both a source of stress and a sign of comfort (see Diverse Perspectives 8-1: "Cultural Considerations in Communication"). Silence is a stressor when wordless pauses are perceived as signs of a breakdown in the communication process. At other times silence communicates comfort and acceptance between friends and lovers who understand that a loving bond exists despite a lack of conversation. Silence is a necessary part of effective communication and is often overlooked. People need time to listen to, digest, and understand messages. Silent time allows us the opportunity to reflect as we formulate our thoughts and words.[13]

Touch and Space Touch is another way to communicate a wide range of messages nonverbally. A firm handshake, a pat on the head, a gentle squeeze of the shoulder, and a reassuring touch on the arm all convey messages without speaking a word. Appropriately used, they add another dimension of communication that sometimes reaches deeper than mere words. When touch is used inappropriately, however, its effects can be devastating. A simple pat on the head can be a sign of endearment to your child but can embarrass or infuriate another adult. A squeeze on your friend's shoulder can show him you understand his problems, but the same squeeze on your secretary's shoulder can be a form of sexual harassment.

The space between sender and receiver also affects communication. Hall[13] has identified four space zones common to communication in North America:

1. Intimate space (less than 18 in.)—space reserved for communication between intimate partners
2. Personal space (18 in.–4 ft.)—space appropriate for close relationships that may involve touching
3. Social/consultive space (4–12 ft.)—space for nontouching, less intimate relationships that may involve louder verbal communication
4. Public space (more than 12 ft.)—space used for formal gatherings, such as addressing a large group

Stress can arise when senders and receivers violate these commonly accepted space parameters. For instance, we are stressed by situations in which nonintimate persons

body language a term used to describe the intentional and unintentional messages we send through our posture, gestures, physical appearance, and even silence

DIVERSE PERSPECTIVES 8-1

Cultural Considerations in Communication

Communicating effectively requires awareness of and sensitivity to various cultural influences related to verbal and nonverbal communication. The following are a few examples of common cultural considerations to keep in mind.

Verbal Communication

Not all cultural groups and subcultures share a common language. Although English is the first language spoken by most Americans and common discourse is the level most frequently used to communicate, this is not the case for many individuals and groups. For many Americans, English is a second language and common discourse is not always completely understood.

Some subjects and forms of communication may be unacceptable to certain cultures. Such forbidden topics of discussion may include emotions, feelings, and intimate sexual and other personal matters. The use of humor as a form of communication may also be disagreeable in some cultures.

Nonverbal Communication

Just as there are cultural differences related to the spoken word, there are a variety of nonverbal factors that vary according to culture. For example, there are differences in territoriality and personal space. In general, people of Arabic, southern European, and African origin frequently sit or stand relatively close to each other when talking. People in Asian, northern European, and North American countries are more comfortable talking farther apart.

Perception of time and the relationship of the past, present, and future also vary by culture. Americans and Canadians are very time- and future-oriented; in daily life, these people are triggered to action at specific times of the day and schedules are strictly adhered to. However, in other cultures people are much less concerned with the future and do not follow such rigid schedules. Many Native American homes do not even have clocks because people are more concerned about the present and live one day at a time.

Body language also varies significantly according to culture. European Americans like to maintain and place a high value on direct eye contact when speaking to one another. Native Americans, however, view continuous direct eye contact as insulting and disrespectful. Rules about eye contact also vary by gender in certain cultures. In Islamic cultures, for example, women are taught to avoid eye contact, though it is acceptable for men. The meaning and acceptability of nonverbal behaviors such as pointing fingers, shaking hands, and other forms of touch also vary by culture.

The following can be helpful in managing cultural considerations with verbal and nonverbal communication:

1. Slow down—People for whom English is a second language can have a hard time keeping up with and understanding the speech of someone whose first language is English.
2. Minimize nonverbal distractions—Be conservative rather than flamboyant in your use of gestures, personal space, and so on.
3. Look for feedback—People who do not understand, cannot keep up, or are uncomfortable with something you do or say will often send nonverbal or verbal cues. The cues can be as blatant as asking for clarification or as subtle as a turned head or lack of eye contact. It is your responsibility to seek clarification of these cues.
4. Use an interpreter—Get someone to translate your message into the other person's language of choice.
5. Avoid talking loudly—When we are not sure we are being understood, we sometimes raise our voices, assuming the person cannot hear us. Talking loudly can be perceived as threatening or condescending and is rarely helpful.
6. Show respect—Even if you make a mistake, being humble and respectful of cultural differences will convey the message that you care and want to understand and improve communication.[15]

get within the boundaries of intimate space. We find ourselves backing up to reclaim our violated space. Sometimes we place objects as barriers between us and others to define our space and set allowable communication zones.

Building Communication Skills

We can reduce stress by becoming more confident and skilled communicators. Communication involves three sets of skills: initiating, listening, and responding (fig. 8-3).[18] Improving our initiating skills can reduce stress by helping us take responsibility for communicating our needs and wants, clear up miscommunications, and be more assertive. Strengthening our listening skills can help reduce stress by improving our ability to understand what

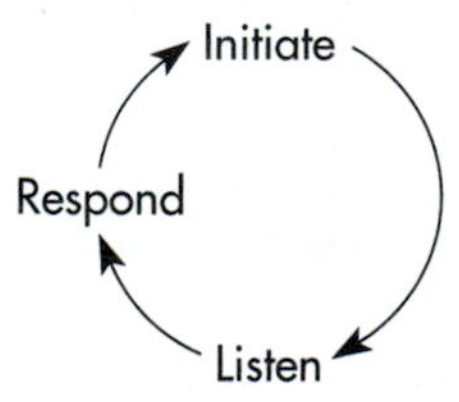

Figure 8-3
This model illustrates the circular nature of a dialogue. Each person is actively involved in giving messages, listening, or responding.

> **KEY TO UNDERSTANDING**
>
> Effective communication requires assuming responsibility for clearing up misunderstandings.

others say and mean. Listening skills help us become more disciplined communicators who pay attention to what others say. Improving our responding skills helps us reduce stress because it enables us to clarify potentially stressful miscommunications, provide feedback, and show others that we understand (or don't understand) what they are saying and what they mean.

Initiating Skills

Initiating skills are encoding techniques you can employ to begin to express yourself. The key in communicating to reduce stress is understanding that it is your responsibility. If you have a problem with something someone says or does, it is your responsibility to bring it to that person's attention. The speaker may or may not be aware of the way his or her words or actions affect you. Furthermore, the fact that the person said it is evidence that he or she does not realize the power of the words or that he or she does and did it intentionally. In either case it is illogical to wait for the person to apologize or bring it up. It is not the speaker's problem but yours.

The best time to clear up problems associated with communication is when they first occur. Taking time to clear things up before they are allowed to progress can prevent the problem from escalating. Often, however, it is impossible to do this because of situational constraints. In these cases tell the other person that you need some time alone with him or her to discuss something important. Try to get the person in a neutral place where you feel safe and emotionally strong. Make time to talk.

Important in initiating communication is the use of *I* language. When you use *I* language, you take responsibility for your feelings. *I* language does not blame your feelings on other people. For example, let us say your friend made fun of you in front of three other common friends. Rather than blame your friend by saying, "You really made me feel terrible," you could say, "I really feel terrible when you . . ." Rather than blame your friend for what you are feeling, you own up to your feelings and state them in *I* language.

It is important to describe both the situation and your feelings about what happened in clear, simple terms. Try to avoid general statements such as "I hate it when you treat me bad" or "I hate it when you do things like that." It is better to specify exactly what the other person did that you dislike. It is better to say things like "I hate it when you make fun of me in front of our friends" or "I really feel like a fool when you make fun of me in front of our friends." The phrase *in front of our friends* clarifies the situation by making it more specific.

It is also important to criticize the behavior, not the person. You must be sure that the person understands that you still like him or her but that you do not like it when he or she behaves a certain way. Remember, the person probably is totally unaware of the nature of his or her language and behavior and its effects on you. The more precise you are in describing exactly what is bothering you, the better the chance you have for clearing up the problem without hurting the person's feelings.

Initiating also includes nonverbal messages. As we have discussed, posture, position, and expression all factor into the verbal message that is being sent. Sometimes we initiate by using only nonverbal communication. A simple stare can send a message that is infinitely more powerful than a hundred words.

Listening Skills

Once you have expressed yourself clearly, the second phase of the communication cycle, listening, comes into play. Effective listening is a critical decoding skill.

There are two types of listening: passive and active. **Passive listening** is one-way listening; the listener merely absorbs what is being sent by the initiator. Passive listening is what we do when watching television or a movie or listening to the radio. Passive listening, however, is not the most effective form of listening to another person when you are trying to reduce stress.

Active listening is much better for dealing with interpersonal communication because it requires feedback. Active listeners show that they are listening by providing both nonverbal and verbal feedback. For this reason active listening is very demanding. It takes a lot of energy and concentration, and it is very easy to get distracted and lose interest.

Simple verbal and nonverbal cues such as a nod followed by "uh huh" are enough to let the speaker know

> **KEY TO UNDERSTANDING**
>
> Effective communication uses *I* language, which assures the listener that the speaker takes responsibility for his or her feelings.

initiating skills encoding techniques you can employ to begin to express yourself and to start a dialogue

passive listening one-way listening that provides no feedback

active listening listening with understanding and feedback

Stress Buster Tips

Open-Ended Statements for Keeping People Talking

Open-ended statements tend to begin with different words than do closed-ended questions, which for the most part can be answered with one- or two-word replies. Open-ended statements require the person to elaborate and typically begin with the following words:

Are? How?
Do? Why?
Who? What?
When, where, which?

The following are examples of open-ended statements.

1. "No kidding, tell me more."
2. "Tell me how you feel about . . ."
3. "What are your thoughts about . . . ?"
4. "I'm not sure I understand; please explain that . . ."
5. "In what way did . . . ?"
6. "Why do you think that?"
7. "How did you come to that . . . ?"

From Garner, A. (1980). *Conversationally speaking.* New York: McGraw-Hill.[6]

you are listening. Once the initiator is finished, you then move into the third phase of the cycle: responding.

Responding Skills

Responding skills involve reacting to the initiator's message and encoding some type of feedback by using verbal and nonverbal communication. If the message is clear and no further clarification is necessary, a simple declarative statement can be used to acknowledge that you hear and agree or disagree or have new information to provide. If you disagree or have problems, remember to use *I* language to express your opinions.

Often responding skills are used to get additional information needed to understand an issue or solve a problem. Keeping the conversation going or requesting more information relies on being able to draw more information from the initiator. Four techniques for doing this follow.

Open-Ended Statements Using **open-ended statements,** such as "Tell me more" and "What else do you know about that?" are easy ways to get information and keep a conversation going. They require the initiator to provide additional information beyond a simple yes/no answer. Stress Buster Tips: "Open-Ended Statements for Keeping People Talking" provides more examples.

Paraphrasing **Paraphrasing,** putting the person's message into your own words and interpreting what he or she means, is another way to provide feedback and get more information. You can start off a paraphrase by stating, "So, what you're saying is . . ." or "I sense that you . . ." When you paraphrase, you interpret the person's message, and he or she will usually let you know if you are on target or off base concerning your interpretation of what was said.

Mirroring A more powerful technique for keeping a person talking is **mirroring.** Mirroring is restating the person's exact words while mimicking his or her body posturing. This is done intentionally for impact. Mirroring is not mimicking. It is not intended to make fun of what is being said. It is only used to encourage the person to continue describing their story. Mirroring is very useful when someone says something that has strong emotional connotations. The message was so powerful that you want to hear more before risking weakening or misinterpreting it. For example, if a friend told you she was so angry at her boyfriend that she could kill him, you would mirror it by saying in a surprised and questioning tone of voice, "You're so angry at him that you could kill him!" This usually will provoke the person to continue and go into the greater detail you desire.

Yes/No Questions The weakest type of response in a dialogue, and the way most of us seek additional information, is to ask direct yes/no questions. Yes/no questions do not require explanation as paraphrasing and mirroring do because they can be answered by a simple yes or no. Although they are very useful for verifying facts, they are easy to overuse and can shut down a dialogue.

Once the receiver encodes a response by using one or more of the four techniques, the communication process shifts back to the sender. We have now come full circle with sender encoding, receiver decoding, and receiver encoding and providing feedback that now becomes information to be decoded by the sender as the cycle begins all over again.

Gender Differences in Communication

Do men and women communicate differently? Does the difference increase when they're communicating about

responding skills verbal or nonverbal feedback skills used to respond to an initiator of a dialogue that involve reacting to the initiator's message

open-ended statements statements that can't be answered with a simple yes/no answer

paraphrasing repeating back your version of the initiator's message

mirroring repeating the initiator's exact words while mimicking his or her exact body language problems? Can gender differences in communication be a source of stress? The answers to these questions are yes, yes, and yes! Numerous studies conducted over the last twenty years have found that not only do men and women communicate differently, this is especially true in discussing problems and is a major source of stress.

Men and women are socialized differently, and many researchers believe this shows in the way we communicate. In general, women in America are socialized to show their feelings while men are taught to keep their feelings hidden. Men have been taught to keep their fears and doubts hidden because in American culture showing them is considered a sign of weakness. Men are socialized to believe that admitting weakness is unmanly. Studies have found that for most women, conversation is a way of establishing connections and negotiating relationships. The emphasis is on displaying similarities and matching experiences.[24,37] Tannen[37] found that for men, the basis of conversation is entirely different. For most men, conversation is a means to preserve independence and negotiate and maintain status in a hierarchical order. In a sense women seek inclusion and equality, while men seek independence and differences in status.

Because of men and women's different orientations toward communication, they handle problems (or "troubles talk" as Tannen labels it) differently.

Women are much more likely than men to talk about their troubles by describing them in great emotional detail. In turn women listening to other women are much more likely than men to respond to such talk by sharing a similar problem or expressing sympathy or empathy. When confronted with troubles talk, men are much more likely than women to give advice, tell a joke, change the subject, or remain silent (ways of exhibiting expertise or avoiding emotional expression).

Michaud and Warner[24] believe that these gender differences in the way men and women respond to "troubles talk" can lead to communication problems when people receive (or do not receive) the responses they feel are most appropriate. According to Michaud and Warner,[24] since most women give sympathy and share problems, they expect to receive sympathy and sharing in response to their troubles talk. Since men deal with troubles by joking or giving advice, that is what they expect in return. Noller and Fitzpatrick[25] found similar results when they studied the communication of husbands and wives. Wives tend to send clearer messages and frame them in an emotional context, while husbands send more neutral, less expressive messages that are harder to interpret.

When women receive advice or joking in response to sharing their troubles, they tend to feel that their feelings are being invalidated, their problems are insignificant, and the partner is being condescending by telling them how to "fix" their problems. Conversely, when men are offered sympathy and sharing, they feel they are being placed in a lower-status position and being condescended to.[24,25]

KEY TO UNDERSTANDING

Lack of assertiveness is a key factor in becoming overburdened.

What are your thoughts about this? Do you think men and women communicate the same or differently? How does your partner communicate about something that is troubling?

REDUCING STRESS BY LEARNING TO SAY NO

So far in this chapter we have discussed the first step in reducing stress: finding your optimal level of demand and deciding how you want to live your life and spend your time. The second step is learning how to assert yourself and say no to others who try to infringe on your plans.

Reducing activities, whether they involve the three ways of coping, time management, or downscaling, often require that we assert ourselves in regard to our desire to cut back on life demands. In many cases these demands on our time and energy revolve around the needs of other people, and the decision to downscale will affect others who will try to pressure us to get their needs met. Therefore, if our attempts at reducing stress are to succeed, assertiveness is key.

Asserting Yourself

Assertiveness is often confused with **aggressiveness,** and many people fail to develop assertiveness skills because of this confusion. In their attempts to control what they perceive as aggressiveness, they act nonassertively and fail to get their needs met, allowing hostility and frustration to build up inside.

In actuality assertiveness is not a negative attribute. It is based on mutual respect and democracy in relationships. Assertiveness is understanding your wants and needs and pursuing them without infringing on the wants and needs of others.[2] Aggressiveness, in contrast, is pursuing your needs and wants without any regard to how this affects the rights of others; often, aggressive people get their needs met at the expense of others.

assertiveness understanding your wants and needs and pursuing them without infringing on the wants and needs of others

aggressiveness understanding your wants and needs and pursuing them at the expense of others, with little or no regard to how this affects the rights of others

Nonassertiveness is failing to pursue your needs and wants while allowing others to meet theirs. Nonassertive people frequently fail to stick up for their rights and allow others to take advantage of them, often denying that this is going on.[33] Lack of assertiveness is a key factor in becoming overburdened with commitments that demand time and interfere with doing what you want or need to do.

Nonassertive people are also often filled with resentment and hostility toward others. Originally, in an attempt to avoid conflict, the nonassertive will say yes when they really mean no. This temporarily relieves them from feeling guilty. Unfortunately, however, when they do this, they get trapped into doing things they do not want to do or do not have the time to do. When this happens, they begin to feel miserable because they have lost control of their lives and time. They are constantly fighting back anger and hostility directed at other people. They also realize that the only way this will stop is if they begin to say no, which brings them full circle to the same situation as the initial one—having to say no. If they were assertive to begin with, they could have avoided all that aggravation and stress (see Stress Buster Tips: "How to Say No").

Assertiveness begins, as do all the reduce strategies, with an assessment of our use of time, level of commitment, goals, and values. Once we have evaluated these areas, we can decide whether to allow new demands on our time. Saying no and meaning it are the hard parts.

Often lack of assertiveness is a cultural issue that transcends stress management. Some cultures require the subjugation of personal desires for the good of a larger whole. Children are expected to put their needs behind those of others and respect the wishes of parents, grandparents, and elders.

The conflict between these traditional ways of behaving and American cultural values that focus on the individual and self-actualization can be a source of stress for traditional students (see Diverse Perspectives 8-2: "Susie Chen").

Stress Buster Tips

How to Say No

Saying no is not always easy, but it is essential if you are to be assertive and reduce your stress. Remember, you have the right to say no. The following are clear guidelines for saying no.

1. Face the other person from a normal distance.
   - If you are too far away, you may appear timid.
   - If you crowd the person, you border on being aggressive.
2. Look the other person directly in the eye.
   - Averting eye contact is a sure giveaway that you will cave in.
3. Keep your head up and your body relaxed.
   - Don't be a shrinking violet.
4. Speak clearly, firmly, and at a volume that can be heard.
5. Just say no.
   - You do not need to clarify why.
6. Be prepared to repeat it.
   - Sometimes people are persistent.
7. Stick to your guns.
   - Do not give in—it gets easier with practice.

If you feel a need to explain why you are declining, here are a few tips for setting the stage:

1. Thank the person for the offer.
2. Express appreciation.
3. Affirm your friendship.
4. Reject the offer, not the person.

Verbal Assertiveness: The DESC Model

One useful technique that combines both assertiveness and effective verbal communication is the DESC model.[2,10] It is a powerful tool that will help you become more precise in asserting yourself and an excellent technique to use when the source of your stress is interpersonal, such as another's behavior or remark or a social situation.

The DESC model has four parts:

1. **D**escribe—paint a verbal picture of the situation or other person's behavior that is a source of stress. Be as precise as possible.
2. **E**xpress—express your feelings about the incident using *I* language.
3. **S**pecify—be specific in identifying alternative ways you would prefer the person to speak or behave.
4. **C**onsequences—identify the consequences that will follow if the person does or does not comply with your wishes.

Example: Mary has just walked out of a meeting with her sorority sisters when the president of the sorority walks up and announces in a loud voice, "Mary, you did such a good job chairing last year's homecoming float committee, I'd like you to do it again this year." Mary really does not want the job again. It took a lot of time and required a tremendous amount of work. Feeling trapped, however, Mary says, "Sure, Erica, I'd be glad to do it." As she walks away, Mary's stomach is churning and she is angry with both Erica for putting her on the spot and herself for agreeing to something she does not want to do.

nonassertiveness failing to pursue your needs and wants while allowing others to meet theirs, often at your expense

DIVERSE PERSPECTIVES 8-2

Susie Chen

Susie Chen was a senior marketing major and was the youngest daughter in a first-generation Chinese-American family. Susie's two sisters were married and worked with their husbands in the family business, which consisted of three laundries. Susie, the first in the family to attend college, managed one of the three laundries.

Susie enrolled in a stress-management class because she needed help managing her time more efficiently. She attended college during the day and worked at the family business more than forty hours a week and on weekends. She also lived at home with her mother, father, and grandparents.

After a few weeks of class, it became apparent that time management was not Susie's problem; she had excellent time-management skills. Susie's real problem was that she was feeling extremely anxious and stressed anticipating her impending graduation. Upon her graduation her family expected her to become more involved in the family business, perhaps opening a fourth outlet, and continue to live at home. The issue was never discussed—they just assumed that Susie would obey their wishes.

However, Susie had no desire to remain in the family business or continue to live at home. She longed to join a multinational company and see the world as an international marketing representative. She also wanted her own apartment.

When she was asked by her professor whether she had explained these desires to her family, she exclaimed, "Oh, no! I couldn't do that. They would never understand or accept it. Plus, it would be considered impolite." When her professor probed further concerning how she was going to pursue her plans, Susie explained that they would have to wait until her parents died or she ran away, leaving them a letter praying for their future forgiveness.

The professor was dumbfounded. He really did not know what to do. It was obvious that cultural reasons were keeping Susie, an excellent student with great communication skills, from using the assertiveness techniques her professor recommended. They decided that she was better off learning how to live with this stressor and cope with it by using other techniques such as meditation and exercise than trying to eliminate it through the use of assertiveness.

Instead, Mary could have used the DESC model to respond to Erica's request.

1. **D**—Erica, when you come up to me in front of several sisters and ask me to do something . . .
2. **E**—I feel trapped, angry, and taken advantage of.
3. **S**—I'd prefer that you either bring this up at our meeting or speak to me about it personally.
4. **C**—In the future if you do this again, I won't volunteer and it will hurt our friendship. Furthermore, I'll be less likely to do anything for the sorority if you continue to behave this way. If you do change, I still may not volunteer for everything, but at least I'll think about it and we'll remain friends.

When using this model, be as precise as possible in describing the other person's offending behavior or actions. Remember, do not criticize the person, just the offensive behavior. It is also very important to take responsibility for your feelings and use *I* language when describing them. Rather than blaming Erica, Mary was very clear in saying, "I feel trapped, angry, and taken advantage of."

SUMMARY

This chapter introduced Reduce, the next level of defense against stress. Reduce works by helping us find our optimal level of demand and stimulation. It is based on the principle that we do not function efficiently when we are overbooked, overcommitted, and unable to say no to people who pressure us into taking on too much in our lives. Even activities that we enjoy can become too demanding and result in overstimulation and stress. The unifying thread in all Reduce activities is cutting back on the volume of potential stressors in our lives.

We began the chapter with a discussion of the concept of demand and the relationship between one's level of demand or stimulation and stress. Demands or stimulation can be related to work, family, school, community, and so on. We discussed the variable nature of demands and how the amount of tolerable stimulation varies from person to person and day to day. We discussed the fine line between attaining an optimal level of stimulation and overstimulation. Without any demands or stimulation, we don't get very much out of life. As our level of demand rises, we are challenged and our level of performance increases until we reach our optimal level. Once we exceed the optimal level of demand, the same stimuli that challenged us become stressors as we feel we can no longer cope.

This chapter presented many strategies for reducing the level of demand in our lives. It started with a discussion of the three ways of coping—abolish, avoid, and alter—that allow us to eliminate, minimize, or change our exposure to potential stressors.

The next section focused on skills that help us manage limited resources. We only have so much time and money and when we place too many demands on these resources we become stressed. Living beyond our means, or on a grander scale than we can support, taxes our limited resources and can cause stress. Strategies were presented for living a simpler life on a scale more consistent with our resources and budget. In the next part of this section on limited resources we looked at ways of evaluating whether our use of time is consistent with our values and goals. We discussed ways of assessing our use of time and a model for prioritizing the activities that make up our days and use this valuable resource. We discussed how lack of organization wastes time and proposed ways to organize school, work, and home space to maximize efficiency and conserve the time it takes to find things and perform activities. In the final part of this section we examined the role of miscommunication as a source of stress. We discussed the components of communication and how to communicate effectively to reduce the ambiguity that often causes stress. We discussed a four-part communication model that emphasizes personal responsibility for clearing up communication breakdowns before they become sources of stress.

We ended the chapter with a discussion of learning how to say no to people and demands that create overstimulation and stress in our lives. We defined assertiveness and described how nonassertive behavior often results in taking on too many demands and taxing our limited resources. We discussed strategies for saying no and assuming control of the level of commitment in our lives. We ended the chapter with a discussion of the DESC Model, a specific technique for communicating more assertively.

Study Questions

1. How does Reduce work in coping with stress?
2. How does Reduce differ from Rethink as a defense against stress?
3. Describe the inverted U-shaped stress curve.
4. How does a person find his or her optimal level of stimulation or demand?
5. What does Mayer say about freeing up an additional thirty minutes of time?
6. What are the effects of clutter on time management and coping with stress?
7. Describe the ACT method of time management.
8. What is the Living Simply Movement's philosophy about lifestyle and stress?
9. How do men and women differ in the way they communicate?
10. Describe the DESC model of verbal assertiveness and explain the relationship between lack of assertiveness and stress.

Discover Our Changing World

The Simple Living Network

http://www.simpleliving.net/default.asp

The Simple Living Network is an organization devoted to helping people simplify their lives. It contains hundreds of pages with strategies for simplifying your life. Visit the Simple Living Network's home page and click on the "About Us" link. Read about who they are, their history, and the scope of their services.

Next, go to Duane Elgin's page and read his essay entitled "The Garden of Simplicity." Read all ten of his approaches to simplicity: http://www.simpleliving.net/webofsimplicity/the_garden_of_simplicity.asp.

Critical Thinking Question

Think about your own life and the path you have chosen. How does the life you are leading relate to the philosophy expressed in Elgin's ten approaches to living simply?

Are You Thinking Clearly?

In this chapter we discussed a variety of strategies to help you learn how to reduce the overall volume of stressors in your life. Students often report that they are too busy to deal with their stress. If they only had the time, they say, they'd do something about it. They promise they'll start reducing "next semester" or "after I graduate." They feel that reducing one's stressor level is important, but they are just too busy to do it. If you find yourself saying these things regarding the reduction of your level of stressors, *stop* and ask yourself the following questions:

1. Can I still honestly say, "Things will get better next semester or after I graduate"?
2. Isn't it more logical to believe that I will find other demands to take the place of this semester's or school's demands when I graduate?
3. Wouldn't getting rid of some demands that I don't need or enjoy anymore make my life more enjoyable and less stressed?

4. Who is in charge of my life, my time, and my demands?
5. Do I equate being this busy with being a more important person?
6. Do I feel guilty about doing less than other people think I should be doing?

The answers to these questions should help you assess whether you are thinking clearly about reducing your stress. If you are not, try using the Ellis and Harper's (1975) ABCDE technique to work through your illogical thoughts about relaxing as a line of defense against stress.

REFERENCES

1. Aslet, D. (1994). Clutter's last stand. *Health,* October, pp. 64–67.
2. Bower, S.A. & Bower, G. (1976). *Asserting yourself: A practical guide for positive change*. Reading, MA: Addison-Wesley.
3. Cicatelli Associates. (1985). *Ten bad listening habits and what to do about them*. New York: Cicatelli Associates.
4. College Board (2003). College costs: Keep rising prices in perspective. http://www.collegeboard.com/article/0,1120,6-29-0-4494,00.html?orig-sec.
5. College Board (2004). *Trends in College Pricing 2004–2005*. Report # 040341319. Washington DC: The College Board.
6. Dunleavey, M.P. (2004). Battle your budget back in shape. *The Jacksonville Free Press*. November 4, 2004. Vol. 18 (42), pg. 2.
7. Edelman, C.L. & Mandel, C.L. (1994). *Health promotion throughout the lifespan*. St. Louis: Mosby.
8. Elkind, D. (1984). *All grown up and no place to go: Teenagers in crisis*. Reading, MA: Addison-Wesley.
9. Gallo, E. (2003). Strategies and trends. *Journal of Financial Planning,* 16(6), p. 26.
10. Garner, A. (1980). *Conversationally speaking*. New York: McGraw-Hill.
11. Gorney, C. (1994). Step off of the fast track. *Health,* October, pp. 64–67.
12. Greenberg, G. (1993). *Comprehensive stress management*. St. Louis: McGraw-Hill.
13. Hall, E. (1973). *The silent language*. Menlo Park, CA: Benjamin Cummings.
14. Kim, J.J. (2003). College grads, student loans, and job hunting. *Wall Street Journal,* September 2, 2003, p. D2.
15. Kotulak, R. (1998). You'd better not cheat on sleep. *Wisconsin State Journal,* June, 7, p. 3A.
16. Kozier, B., Erb, G., & Olieveri, R. (1991). *Fundamentals of nursing*. Redwood City, CA: Addison-Wesley/ Benjamin Cummings.
17. Lazarus, R. & Folkman, S. (1985). *Stress appraisal and coping*. New York: Springer.
18. Mandel, B. (1980). Communication: A four-part process. *Hotliner,* 1(4), p. 6.
19. Mayer, J. (1990). *If you haven't got the time to do it right, when will you find the time to do it over?* New York: Simon & Schuster.
20. Mayer, J. (1995). *Time management for dummies*. New York: IDG Books.
21. Mayer, J. (1996). *No trespassing: Avoiding interruptions*. ACT http://www.actnews.com/articles/11-1996/N . . . tm#No Trespassing: Avoiding Interruptions.
22. Mayo Clinic (1996). How much sleep do you need? *Mayo Oasis Newsletter,* October 28. http://mayohealth.org/mayo/9610/htm/sleep/htm.
23. Mayo Clinic (1997). Asleep at the wheel. *Mayo Oasis Newsletter,* October 8. http://mayohealth.org/mayo/ednote/htm/ed971008.htm.
24. Michaud, S.L. & Warner, R.M. (1997). Gender differences in self-reported response in troubles talk. *Sex Roles: A Journal of Research,* 37, pp. 7–8, 527–571.
25. Noller, P. & Fitzpatrick, M.A. (1991). Marital communication. In Booth, A. (Ed.). *Contemporary families: Looking back, Looking forward.* Minneapolis: Council on Family Relations.
26. *Parade.* Do you really know how to play? (1992).
27. Payne, W. & Hahn, D. (1998). *Understanding your health*. St. Louis: McGraw-Hill.
28. Pierce, L.B. (1998). The Pierce Simplicity Study. http://www.mbay.net/~pierce/more.htm.
29. Pierce, L.B. (2003). *Simplicity Lessons.* Carmel, CA: Gallagher Press.
30. Roach, M. (1994). De-junk your life. *Health,* 87, pp. 86–89.
31. Selye, H. (1956). *The stress of life*. New York: McGraw-Hill.
32. Seward, B.L. (1997). *Managing stress: Principles and strategies for health and wellbeing*. Boston: Jones & Bartlett.
33. SimpleLiving.Com (2005). About the Simple Living Network. http://www.simpleliving.net/about/default.asp
34. Smith, J.C. (1993). *Creative stress management*. Englewood Cliffs, NJ: Prentice-Hall.
35. Sipe, J.R. (1997). New day is dawning on sleep research. *Insight on the News,* 13(3), p. 38.
36. Sturz, J. (1997). The rest of your life. *Men's Health,* 12(6), pp. 74–76.
37. Tannen, D. (1990). *You just don't understand: Women and men in conversation*. New York: William Morrow.
38. TeRRAP. (1991). *Assertiveness bill of rights.* Menlo Park, CA: TERRAP Phobia Treatment Center.
39. Trippon, J. (2004). *How millionaires stay rich forever.* Bretton Woods, NH: Bretton Woods Press.
40. Villa, S. (2003). Spending and saving strategies for singles. *New Pittsburgh Courier,* July 30, 2003, Vol. 94 (61), page B1.
41. Watzalawick, P., Beavin, J.H., & Jackson, D.D. (1967). *Pragmatics of human communication*. New York: Norton.

Name: ______________________________ Date: __________

ASSESS YOURSELF 8-1

Developing a Budget

In developing a budget the most important thing to keep in mind is honesty. Be truthful with what you know about your earnings, expenses, ability to save, and so on. The best-looking budget will work only if it is adhered to. The following is a sample budget.

Expenses		**Income**	
School	$3,500	College savings	$7,500
*tuition/fees		Summer job (net)	2,000
*books			
Room and board or	5,000	Part-time job (net) (during year 15 hrs/week/ $5/hr net for 36 weeks)	2,700
*rent (monthly)	300		
*utilities (monthly)	50		
*telephone (monthly)	15		
*food (monthly)	190		
Clothing	125		
Travel/car			
*car payments (monthly)	150		
*insurance (monthly)	67		
*gas/oil (monthly)	75		
*repairs (monthly)	15		
Savings	320		
Miscellaneous	400		
Totals	$11,900		$11,900

The proposed budget is for a typical college student sharing an off-campus apartment with two other roommates. Room and board–associated costs would be similar to those for dorm students.

In this budget the student is drawing $7,500 a year from a college savings plan that is already established for him or her. This budget also assumes that the student worked over the summer and cleared (after taxes) $2,000. The student also works fifteen hours a week during the school year, netting $5 an hour.

This is a fairly tight budget, even though the source of income is high. It does not include any available income for credit card debt or extensive travel, such as a trip at spring break.

What this budget does do is break down expenses (including anticipated car-maintenance expenses) into monthly amounts and compares these with available income. This budget could be tightened considerably if the student would forgo a car entirely (savings of $3,680) or for go a new car ($1,800 yearly car payment).

Obviously, this budget is not typical for all students. What it does illustrate is that students need to set their budgets according to their available income and ensure that they plan for foreseeable expenses in advance and have some money left in reserve for emergencies. Credit cards should be utilized only in emergencies. Debit cards (payment due in full at end of the month) are preferable because balances do not build.

Name: ______________________________ Date: ____________

ASSESS YOURSELF 8-2

Stressor Diary

For the remainder of the semester, keep a personal stressor diary. Keep track of your stressors, how you appraise them (illogical self-talk), how your body/mind responds to them, their level of intensity, and how you cope. This will help you identify trends or patterns in your stressors and assist you in your stress-management plan.

Day/date	Potential Stressor	Appraisal (illogical self-talk)	Mind/Body Response	Intensity	Coping
Example: Monday 9/1	Stuck in traffic	"I'll never make it to class." "The professor will hold this against me all semester."	Muscle tension in neck, anger	8–9	Nothing except scream at the driver in front of me.
Tuesday 9/2	Fight with girlfriend over comment made by TV anchorman	"What a total idiot I am for going out with her." "Why do we always argue over everything? I'll bet other couples don't argue over stuff like this."	Stomach churning, anger	8–9	Yelled at her and stormed out of the room.

ASSESS YOURSELF 8-2 (cont'd)

Day/date	Potential Stressor	Appraisal (illogical self-talk)	Mind/Body Response	Intensity	Coping

Name: ______________________________ Date: ______________

Assess Yourself 8-3

Triple As Scenarios

The following scenarios represent common stressors that respond very well to a triple As approach. Work through each of the As—*abolish, avoid,* and *alter*—for each scenario. Do all three apply to each scenario? If not, why?

1. You love your mother, but she can drive you nuts. She insists on having you come over two nights a week for dinner. You do not mind seeing her, but her apartment is cramped and parking is very difficult. Besides that, you really do not want to commit to such a rigid schedule.

   ____
   ____
   ____
   ____
   ____

2. Your roommates seem to think that college is a nonstop party. They are up late five nights a week and out the other two. They never study and are on academic probation.

   ____
   ____
   ____
   ____
   ____

3. Although your apartment is small, the housework seems never-ending. You do not get much help from your roommate, who abuses your generosity in preparing food, shopping, and cleaning up.

   ____
   ____
   ____
   ____
   ____

Name: ______________________ Date: __________

ASSESS YOURSELF 8-4

Time-Management Log

Day/Time	Activity
5:00 A.M.	
5:30 A.M.	
6:00 A.M.	
6:30 A.M.	
7:00 A.M.	
7:30 A.M.	
8:00 A.M.	
8:30 A.M.	
9:00 A.M.	
9:30 A.M.	
10:00 A.M.	
10:30 A.M.	
11:00 A.M.	
11:30 A.M.	
12:00 P.M.	
12:30 P.M.	
1:00 P.M.	
1:30 P.M.	
2:00 P.M.	
2:30 P.M.	
3:00 P.M.	
3:30 P.M.	
4:00 P.M.	
4:30 P.M.	
5:00 P.M.	
5:30 P.M.	
6:00 P.M.	
6:30 P.M.	
7:00 P.M.	
7:30 P.M.	
8:00 P.M.	
8:30 P.M.	
9:00 P.M.	

ASSESS YOURSELF 8-4 (cont'd)

Day/Time	Activity
9.30 P.M.	
10.00 P.M.	
10.30 P.M.	
11.00 P.M.	
11.30 P.M.	
12.00 A.M.	
12.30 A.M.	
1.00 A.M.	
1.30 A.M.	
2.00 A.M.	
2.30 A.M.	
3.00 A.M.	
3.30 A.M.	
4.00 A.M.	
4.30 A.M.	
5.00 A.M.	

Name: ______________________ Date: __________

ASSESS YOURSELF 8-5

How Well Do I Communicate?

Answer by circling 0 (rarely), 1 (sometimes), or 2 (often).

	Rarely	Sometimes	Often
In conversation, how frequently do you interrupt?	0	1	2
How often do you joke, saying in a funny way something that is really important to you?	0	1	2
Do you think that if your partner or friend really cared about you, she or he would understand your needs without your having to explain everything?	0	1	2
When you do not understand something, do you dislike having to ask questions?	0	1	2
How often do you hint about things you want rather than asking directly?	0	1	2
How frequently do you say yes when you really want to say no?	0	1	2

Total 7

INTERPRETATION

If your score is around three, you are an above-average listener and communicator. You understand and get your message across. If you score around six, you are like most people. Sometimes you do not understand what another person wants or are not able to get your own meaning across. Scores of eight to ten suggest that you frequently do not communicate well. A careful reading of this chapter should help you listen and speak much more effectively, greatly increasing your ability to communicate and enjoy good relationships.

TO CARRY THIS FURTHER . . .

Having completed this personal assessment, did you find that you are a more or less effective communicator than you would have anticipated? Do you better understand why a high score in a particular area might be perceived as unsupportive of effective verbal communication?

From Payne, W. & Hahn, D. (2002). *Understanding your health*. St. Louis: McGraw-Hill.[22]

CHAPTER

9

RELAX: USING RELAXATION TECHNIQUES TO OFFSET THE EFFECTS OF STRESS

OUTLINE

OBJECTIVES

By the end of the chapter students will:

- Define relaxation.
- Compare and contrast the relaxed and stressed states.
- Analyze how and why relaxation is incompatible with stress.
- Describe passive relaxation.
- Explain how breathing is related to all forms of relaxation training.
- Demonstrate proper deep-breathing techniques.
- Describe three different types of meditation.
- Demonstrate Benson's relaxation response.
- Describe the role of imagery in relaxation.
- Describe the role and limitations of biofeedback in stress management.

In chapters 7 and 8 we explored coping with stress by changing the way we think about potential stressors and reducing the volume of stressors in our lives. What do you do, however, when this is not possible? Even though you try, you just can't seem to change your thoughts. What do you do when you are unable to think logically and feel overwhelmed by the sheer volume of stressors in your life? When this happens, you need to use strategies that work differently. This chapter introduces techniques that can be used to offset the effects of stress arousal by putting your body into a relaxed state. These techniques act like stress-free mini-vacations for your body and mind. All of the strategies presented in this chapter can be practiced in the privacy of your own home without more formal instruction or purchasing expensive equipment. Some of these techniques, such as meditation, have been used for thousands of years to help people gain control of their bodies and minds. All of these techniques require a mindful, but **passive mental state.** The passivity associated with these techniques has as much to do with the mental state you achieve while performing them as it does with their level of physical exertion. A key to being truly relaxed is achieving a passive mental state. Essentially, this means allowing your mind to slow down and, as thoughts and emotions arise and enter consciousness, accepting them for what they are and then allowing them to pass.

THE STRESSED STATE COMPARED TO THE RELAXED STATE

Engaging in activities to relax, and achieving a state of relaxation mean different things to different people. While there is a certain amount of subjectivity involved in defining relaxing activities, one can apply clear, objective standards to measure the state of relaxation. Table 9-1 indicates the physiological processes associated with the stress response. Each of these has a baseline reading for when we are in a state of balance or homeostasis. We can then measure what their levels are when we are stressed. Essentially, the rates increase when we are stressed and decrease when we are relaxed.

The Stressed State: A Quick Review

In chapter 6 and the introduction to Part II of this book we explored Everly and Benson's disorders of arousal model which provides the most comprehensive modern analysis of stress arousal.[16] Essentially the model describes how the stress response starts in the brain's limbic system, proceeds along the neurological, neuroendocrine, and endocrine stress axes, and if allowed to continue for too long, results in overstimulation, wear and tear, and eventual breakdown of target organs and systems. The resultant "disorders of arousal" include all the classic stress-related physical and psychological disorders discussed in chapter 6. Everly and Lating[17] use this model to identify the three key elements of arousal that characterize the stress response and are precursors to the development of disorders of arousal. The three elements are (1) increased neurotransmitter arousal and activity, (2) increased neuromuscular arousal, and (3) increased negative cognitive arousal. All three levels of arousal are linked and work together in initiating and sustaining the stress response.[17]

Cannon[10] and Selye[44] long ago realized the negative effects of sustaining the stress response. Cannon and later Selye believed that our bodies have a finite amount of energy available for adapting to the demands of stress in our lives.[12,44] They believed that if we manage our stress

passive mental state a state achieved by allowing your mind to slow down and, as thoughts and emotions arise and enter consciousness, accepting them for what they are and then allowing them to pass.

Table 9-1. Relaxation Versus Stress

Stress	Relaxation
Increased body metabolism	Decreased body metabolism
Increased heart rate	Decreased heart rate
Increased blood pressure	Decreased blood pressure
Increased breathing rate	Decreased breathing rate
Increased oxygen consumption	Decreased oxygen consumption
Increased cardiac output	Decreased cardiac output
Increased muscular tension	Decreased muscular tension
Decreased blood-clotting time	Increased blood-clotting time
Increased blood flow to the major muscle groups involved in fight-or-flight (including the arms and legs)	Normalized blood flow to the major muscle groups

Source: From Curtis, J. and Detert, R. (1985). *Learn to relax: A 14-day program.* LaCrosse, WI: Coulee Press.[12]

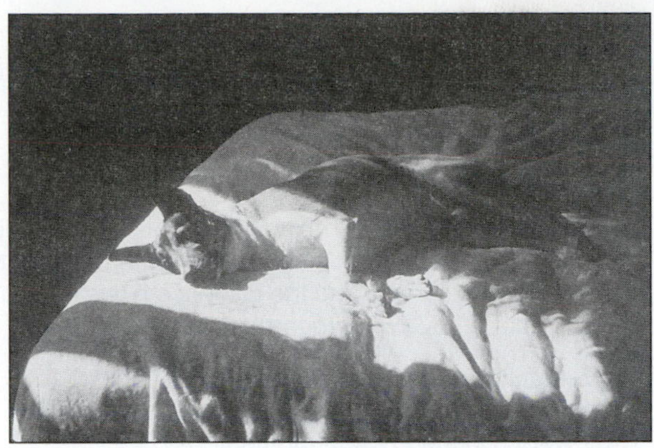

To understand what relaxation is about, watch a dog have a good stretch and lie down in front of a warm window.

properly, this adaptation energy should last a lifetime. However, if we expose ourselves to enough chronic stress, we will exhaust this energy prematurely, wear our bodies down, become exhausted, and die. A key to understanding this is to think of our bodies as car batteries. Like car batteries, our bodies come with a finite amount of energy that should last a lifetime with proper care. As with the batteries, if we run our bodies down, we can recharge them (through relaxing) several times and bring them back to full power. Eventually, however, if we run them down too often, we will use up their adaptation energy too soon and they will not recharge at all.

The Relaxed State

To get a sense of what it means to be truly relaxed, watch a dog or cat seek out a warm spot in the sun. It finds a quiet spot away from the main traffic of the house, circles it a few times, stretches its legs, rolls its head and neck, lies down and fully arches its back, takes a deep breath and exhales deeply, and then curls up or sprawls in the warm rays. As you can see in Table 9-1, the **relaxed state** is the exact opposite of the stressed state. It is characterized by the decrease of key physiological processes such as muscle tension, heart rate, breathing rate, and blood pressure. It is also accompanied by a passive mental state.

When we are relaxed, there is a decrease in both skeletal and smooth muscle tension. Our muscles are not in the chronic state of mild contraction that characterizes the stress response. This protects them from the cumulative negative effects of being constantly tensed. The breathing rate decreases, and the depth of breathing increases. We breathe more evenly and fully, allowing efficient oxygen utilization and carbon dioxide removal. The number of times the heart beats per minute decreases, and blood pressure also decreases; both reduce wear and tear on the cardiovascular system. In addition, we have more efficient circulation. Blood is allowed to move freely throughout the body, no longer pooling in the internal organs. The extremities warm up as circulation is restored. When we are relaxed, our blood volume decreases and normal water balance is restored because we no longer are producing extra mineralocorticoids that retain sodium and increase blood volume and pressure. Our metabolic rate returns to normal, and the parasympathetic nervous system exerts control over the many processes that are set in motion by sympathetic activation.

In this relaxed state, we simply cannot be stressed. The two states are diametrically opposed and cannot coexist. A person cannot be stressed and relaxed at the same time. The whole purpose of practicing the activities in this chapter is to put your body into a relaxed state on a regular basis. These relaxed periods will stop the stress response and offset its effects. Think back to the car battery analogy when you spend time performing these relaxation activities and view it as time spent recharging your battery. When you engage in these activities, you are shutting off the demand for energy (canceling the effects of stress) and bringing your battery back to full power.

KEY TO UNDERSTANDING

A key to understanding the importance of relaxation is realizing that when you are relaxed it is impossible to be stressed at the same time. They are incompatible states of being.

KEY TO UNDERSTANDING

A key to understanding adapting to stress is realizing that we have a limited amount of energy available to use for this purpose. When we exceed it, we begin to wear down.

BREATHING AND RELAXATION

Breathing is the basis of both life and relaxation. At any given point in our day we are only a few breaths away from being out of this planet, out of this life. One of the ironies of breathing is how important it is, yet how little attention we pay to it. Kabat-Zinn[26] believes that our breath is symbolic of our life; right beneath our noses (literally) is a gold mine that we take completely for granted.

relaxed state a state of being characterized by the decrease of key physiological processes such as muscle tension, heart rate, breathing rate, and blood pressure; it is also accompanied by a passive mental state

Breathing, he states, is our biological and spiritual connection with the cycles of the universe. We breathe in life-giving oxygen and recycle this back into the universe by exhaling carbon dioxide. This cycling of breath in and breath out is, at the atomic and molecular levels, our connection to the universe and the cycle of life we share with other living things such as the trees and animals around us. In this sense, our breathing is a spiritual process also as this cycle illustrates our interconnectedness to our planet and the universe beyond.

In *Peace Is Every Step*[19] Thich Nhat Hahn, the world-renowned Zen Master, scholar, and author, explains that the simple practice of being more conscious of our breathing can help relax us. When we practice conscious breathing, our thinking slows down. Conscious breathing helps us stop thinking so much, especially about past and future worries. The parts of the brain that control breathing are intimately related to the parts that control stress arousal. Controlled, deep, even breathing facilitates relaxation. Rapid, shallow, irregular breathing disrupts relaxation. One of the main bases for understanding whether you are stressed is the pace and depth of your breathing. If it is rapid and shallow, chances are that you are stressed. Becoming aware of your breathing pattern is the first step in learning how to slow down your breathing and reduce stress.

Learning to control your breathing will provide immediate benefits in learning to control your stress responses. By breathing correctly we can strengthen and train lung functioning, increase cardiovascular response, increase oxygenation of the blood, calm the nerves, and increase restfulness. There are many different ways to work with breathing to help offset the effects of stress. All of the relaxation techniques discussed in the rest of this chapter begin with getting in touch with the pace and depth of one's breathing.

We will discuss how to perform mindful breathing, a form of meditation a little later in the chapter. Stress Buster Tips offers a simple breathing activity taught by Thich Nhat Hahn.[19] In the next section we will discuss how to use diaphragmatic breathing, a specific deep breathing technique to slow the pace of breathing and increase the depth and duration of respiration to reduce stress.

Diaphragmatic Breathing to Reduce Stress

Most of us use only a portion of our lungs when we breathe. We tend to breathe with only the top third of the lungs. To receive the stress-reducing benefits of breathing, we must learn how to get our entire lungs involved. We need to learn how to fill our lungs from the bottom up, a process called **diaphragmatic breathing.** You do this by pushing your stomach out as you inhale, making room for the air to fill the lower portion of your lungs. Refer back to chapter 5, fig. 5-6, to see the shape of your lungs.

Stress Buster Tips

Conscious Body

In *Peace Is Every Step,* Thich Nhat Hahn[19] offers this simple breathing activity to help you become more conscious of your breathing and the influence it has on your life. The activity revolves around four simple lines:

1. Breathing in I calm my Body.
2. Breathing out I smile.
3. Dwelling in the Present Moment.
4. I know this is a wonderful moment.

Repeat lines 1 and 3 when you inhale and lines 2 and 4 when you exhale. Make sure you breathe slowly, and focus your attention on the line and your breathing. If other thoughts or feelings enter your consciousness, accept this and get back to reciting the lines to yourself while you breathe.

Practice this simple activity several times a day. It is particularly important to do this when you anticipate being in a stressful situation or are already feeling stressed.

Key to Understanding

Proper breathing is the key to all relaxation.

As you slowly take air in, your lungs begin to fill from the bottom up. Sometimes it helps to let the shoulders rise and fall with inhalation and exhalation, respectively.

Most of us breathe too quickly. Breathing slowly means that it should take several seconds to fill your lungs with air. It is not unusual to take ten seconds or longer to inhale or exhale in breathing exercises. The following instructions will help you begin to breathe deeply.

1. Find a quiet place away from others to practice.
2. Minimize distractions by closing doors and turning off the radio, television, and phone.
3. Sit on a chair with your back straight, head up.
4. Visualize a picture of your lungs.
5. Slowly breathe in through your nose.
6. As you breathe in, push your stomach forward.
7. Let your ribs expand and your shoulders rise as the air fills your lungs completely from the bottom up.

diaphragmatic breathing a deep breathing technique that uses the diaphragm to assist in completely filling the lungs from the bottom up

8. When your lungs feel full, slowly begin to exhale through your mouth.
9. Let your shoulders fall and your ribs shrink back as the air slowly passes through your mouth.
10. Gently pull your stomach back in with your stomach muscles, fully draining all the air from the lower portion of your lungs.
11. Repeat this activity for five minutes.
12. Practice this activity a few times a day.

In time, with regular practice, you will automatically shift into a deeper, more even breathing pattern whenever you feel stressed. Deep breathing is an excellent first choice for reducing stress. It is also the starting point for the other techniques described in this chapter.

MEDITATION

When most people think of meditation, they visualize an old man in diaphanous robes with a long white beard and dark, leathery skin. This imaginary man sits alone, in a full lotus position, on top of a mountain in Tibet or some other exotic location. He is in a deep trance, engaged in a mystical communication with a higher being. Seated at his feet is a disciple who, after making the long, arduous climb to the mountaintop, seeks the true meaning of life.

In fact, there is nothing mystical or mysterious about meditation at all. Meditation, according to Kabat-Zinn,[26] is about paying attention, on purpose, in the present moment. There are many different definitions of meditation. One of the best is that of Kabat-Zinn[26] who defines it this way: "**Meditation** is the process by which we go about deepening our attention and awareness by refining them and putting them to greater practical use in our lives."

In truth, most meditators are average people like you and me. Some are young; others are old. Most do not have long, flowing beards, and very few are interested in sitting on top of high mountains for extended periods.

Historical and Cultural Origins of Meditation

The practice of meditation dates back to prehistoric times. The earliest evidence of meditation comes from anthropological findings that prehistoric cultures used meditative chants as part of sacrificial rituals designed to please various gods.[24]

The written history of meditation dates back to the origins of the great Eastern religions of Hinduism (2500 B.C.), Buddhism (560 B.C.), Taoism (600 B.C.), and Confucianism (550 B.C.). All these religions employed meditative techniques as a way to clear the mind and transcend the body to achieve a greater spiritual connection.[8]

Meditative practices also became a part of Western religious practice. The great Western religions of Judaism (1250 B.C.), Christianity (28 A.D.), Protestantism (1500 A.D.), and Islam (570 A.D.) all incorporated meditative practices such as repetitive prayer to achieve spiritual transcendence.[8] These religions also used meditation and repetitive prayer as a means of seeking forgiveness and purging sin.

Meditation in its religious or spiritual context is intended to train disciples to achieve the fullest possible control over their minds. Yogis claim that in achieving this control and heightened awareness, disciples can transcend normal stages of consciousness and reach the highest levels of connectedness and spirituality. One form of meditation, **transcendental meditation (TM),** derives its name from this belief in transcendence to another plane.[3]

Meditation in general and transcendental meditation in particular received a lot of attention in the 1960s and 1970s when the Beatles, an English rock group, studied TM with the Maharishi Mahesh Yogi. Millions of Americans became acquainted with this previously unknown practice. The Maharishi's face was on the cover of almost every major magazine, and TM training courses and schools popped up all over the country.

Benefits of Meditation

There are many physiological benefits of meditation, ranging from reduced muscle tension to increases in brain-wave patterns that were more conducive to relaxation. These claims were studied and well documented in the 1970s when the Harvard Medical School undertook a group of research studies to examine the physiological benefits of TM. Through a series of carefully controlled studies, Harvard researchers were able to reach the following conclusions concerning the benefits of meditation:

1. Decreased metabolic rate and oxygen consumption, called hypometabolism or the **hypometabolic state,** occurs only during two other states: sleep and hibernation. Meditators were able to achieve hypometabolism without being asleep or hibernating. The meditative state is a restful but awake state. During meditation the body needs and burns less energy. It slows down and, as with sleep, provides a period of rest. The meditative state, however, uses even less oxygen than the sleeping state.[23]
2. Brain-wave activity also changes during meditation (fig. 9-1). **Alpha waves** increase in intensity and

meditation the process by which we go about deepening our attention and awareness by refining them and putting them to greater practical use in our lives

transcendental meditation (TM) a type of focused meditation popularized by Maharishi Mahesh Yogi from India

hypometabolic state a restful waking state characterized by decreased metabolic rate and respiration

alpha waves slow, low-amplitude brain waves associated with a wakeful, resting state

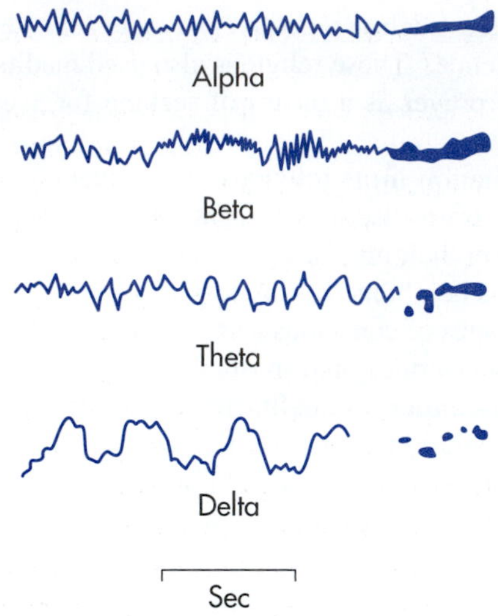

Figure 9-1
Alpha waves are the slow, low-amplitude waves associated with a restful waking state.

frequency. These low-amplitude, slow, synchronous brain waves are the type associated with the restful awake state.

3. Heart rate decreases during meditation. In the Harvard study the researchers found that heart rate decreased by an average of three beats per minute during meditation.
4. Blood pressure remains unchanged during meditation, but the researchers found that regular meditators had lower blood pressure than nonmeditators before, during, and after meditation suggesting the long-term effects of the practice.
5. Respiration decreases during meditation. The rate and depth of breathing slow down. There is a decreased need for oxygen because of the lessening of the metabolic rate.[3,50,51,52,53]

Other studies have documented findings that go beyond those in the Harvard research. Two studies[21,46] found that meditators experience a carryover of the effects of meditation. Although many studies document that meditators experience various short-term stress-reducing effects, these characteristics become a more stable trait for regular meditators. The benefits, particularly a calmer, more peaceful view of the world, become a part of a meditator's day-to-day existence.

In general, the meditative state is relaxed and restful, ideal for canceling the effects of stress. Being in a meditative state is incompatible with stress. You cannot be stressed and relaxed at the same time. For this reason, and for practice, teachers of meditation urge their students to meditate for twenty minutes twice a day. This successfully cancels the effects of the stress response and trains the mind to sink more easily into the meditative state.

In a sense, what meditation does is help us unclutter our minds. It slows our minds and limits our thoughts, giving us a temporary break from the countless thoughts and feelings our brains encounter each day.

Focused and Open Meditation

The many different forms of meditation can be grouped into two broad categories; focused or open. **Focused meditation** uses a focal point to direct one's attention to. In focused meditation the focal point can be anything from an object to a phrase. We will discuss meditating using three major types of focal points: objects, words/phrases, and the breath. During focused meditation people direct all of their attention to the established focal point, and when distractions occur, they note the distraction mentally and then redirect their attention to the focal point. **Open meditation** is also referred to as non-focused or mindful meditation. Open meditation is a process of directing one's full attention to the experience of existing in the present moment. It does not shift attention to a single focal point. Instead, during open meditation people direct their attention and awareness to whatever is going on within and around them at the present moment. It is not *thinking about* what is going on but rather *noticing and paying full attention* to what is going on. There is no attempt to censor incoming thoughts, sounds, and other stimuli and redirect one's attention to some focal point designed to *limit* awareness as is the case in focused meditation. Instead, thoughts, feelings, and other stimuli are *fully attended to* as long as they are related to the present moment. As with focused meditation, any thoughts or feelings that are related to the past or the future are noted but then attention is redirected to the *present moment.* In the next section of this chapter we will discuss focused and open meditative practices in greater detail.

Object Meditation

In **object meditation** the focal point is an object such as a candle, a hanging crystal, or a **mandala.** Others simply focus on a point in the room, such as where the ceiling meets the wall. Often the objects have an added spiritual

focused meditation a type of meditation that uses a focal point (an object, word/phrase, sound, breathing etc.) to direct one's attention to

open meditation a type of meditation, also referred to as nonfocused or mindful meditation, that does not employ a focal point but instead directs one's full attention to the experience of existing in the present moment

object meditation a form of focused meditation that uses an object such as a candle, a hanging crystal, or a mandala as the focal point

mandala a Hindu or Buddhist graphic symbol of the universe in its ideal form depicting the transformation of a universe of suffering into one of joy or metaphysical significance. A mandala, for instance, is a Hindu or Buddhist graphic symbol incorporating a circle enclosing a square with a deity on each side. It represents the universe in its ideal form, where suffering has been transformed into joy. It is used to help the meditator envision how to achieve the perfect self. Secular mandalas vary tremendously but usually employ a graphic design pattern in the form of a circle divided into four separate sections or bearing a multiple projection of an image. Many people who meditate using crystals believe that they represent a perfect natural (a mineral from the earth) geometric form that works directly with the light, color, and beauty to help one add balance to one's life. Among those who believe in **feng shui,** crystals are said to possess the *light cure,* which brings healing energy to the surrounding area. Whether one believes this or not, hanging crystals are beautiful and provide a mesmerizing focal point because of the way they reflect light. Many people like to use a lighted candle as their focal point because they find the dancing flame an easy object to focus on. Students report "losing themselves" in the flickering flame of the candle as it hypnotically waves back and forth. Try several different focal points and compare how you enjoy meditating to them. Focused meditation is often used when teaching people how to meditate for the first time because it provides an easy to understand way to redirect past and future thinking back to the present (back to a single object like a candle).

Word/Phrase Meditation

In **word/phrase meditation** the focal point used is a word or a phrase. The words or phrases are chosen because of their simplicity or relaxing or spiritual significance. For example, some people focus on simple words such as *one* when inhaling and *two* while exhaling. These words themselves are meaningless except they represent a simple, easy-to-remember focal point. Often, one's **cadence** of footsteps, breathing pattern, or strokes can be used to meditate while performing physical activity. One actually counts "one, two, three, four," etc., in synchrony with the beat, time, and rhythm of their steps, breath, and strokes. The focus is on the *words* that accompany the cadence, not the actual activity. This is different from moving meditation where the focus is on the *activity,* not the words. Others choose a word that helps create a relaxing visual image. Words such as *beach* and *sun* are often used because of their association with warm, relaxing images. Obviously, not everyone finds the beach relaxing and some people visualize exposure to the sun's rays as harmful. Some people use words and phrases that represent relaxing colors, shapes, or places. One can use any word or phrase as long as it is relaxing. A **mantra** is a special word or phrase used by those practicing transcendental meditation that has added personal spiritual significance for the individual. In transcendental meditation the bestowing of a mantra by the teacher is a sacred ritual. One's personal mantra is a secret that is not to be shared with others.

Some people find a secluded beach on a warm day an ideal place to meditate. The combination of warm sun, gentle wind, and the hypnotic pounding of the waves is hard to match.

Sound Meditation

The focal point of **sound meditation** is manmade or natural sounds. Some people like to meditate to music. Music has been shown to affect the following physiological processes: metabolic rate, muscular activity, respiration, heart rate, and blood pressure. Music also has the ability to affect our emotions profoundly. Music can act in positive, stress-reducing ways by slowing physiological processes and producing positive emotions. Unfortunately, like noise, it can also act as a stimulus that increases these responses and creates negative emotions.[20] One person's music, however, is often another person's noise; therefore, the subject of which music will relax versus which will stress continues to be controversial. Common sense will tell you which types of music and artists help relax you. If you feel agitated or rushed, try music with a more melodic composition and a slower rhythm. There are many companies that specialize in Indian and other eastern musical forms that are specifically designed for meditation.

Other people find it relaxing and helpful to meditate to natural sounds ranging from thunderstorms to the sound of waves to the wind whistling through the trees.

feng shui a Chinese practice in which a structure or geographical site is chosen or configured so as to harmonize with the spiritual forces that inhabit it

word/phrase meditation a form of focused meditation where the focal point used is a word or a phrase

cadence the beat, time, or measure of rhythmical motion or activity

mantra a special word or phrase used by those practicing transcendental meditation that has added personal spiritual significance for the individual

sound meditation a form of focused meditation where the focal point used is man-made or natural sounds

To do this, meditate outdoors or listen to commercially prepared audiotapes and CDs.[19]

A third type of sound that people use to meditate is the sound associated with a repetitive physical activity. Some people even combine physical activity with meditation. To achieve a meditative state, one focuses on the rhythmic sounds of things such as breathing (as they walk, run, swim, bike, etc.), footsteps (as they walk, run, hike, etc.) splashing (as they swim, canoe, kayak, etc.), swooshing (as they cross-country ski), and other sounds. The repetitive nature of the activities is perfect for meditation, because people can tune in to these sounds while tuning out external stimuli. Often people combine focusing on these sounds and their cadence. Using these two focal points (word and sound) can often make it easier to practice object meditation because they naturally accompany each other.

Breath Meditation

The focal point of **breath meditation** is one's breathing. Watching the air travel in, around, and out of the nose, throat, and lungs helps meditators maintain concentration on their focal point while forgetting about everything else going on in their lives. You can learn to watch the air go in and out by first looking at a picture of the respiratory system to visualize the structure of the body parts involved in breathing. After you can visualize the body parts used in breathing, close your eyes when you breathe and, using your imagination, follow the flow of the air. This will help minimize distractions.

Applying Focused Meditation: Benson's Relaxation Response

The **Relaxation Response** is a very popular form of focused meditation developed by Benson[3] from Harvard University. It uses the key elements of practice associated with transcendental meditation but demystifies the practice by removing the personal mantra component and deemphasizing TM's spiritual and metaphysical aspects. Benson[3] identified what he considered to be the four components of meditation necessary to achieve relaxation or what he coined as the relaxation response.

Learning the Relaxation Response Benson's[3] four components are: a quiet environment, a mental device, a passive attitude, and a comfortable position. As we will discuss, there is much flexibility involved regarding how people structure these components.

For most people, meditating requires a quiet environment with minimal distractions. The choices are endless. Some people prefer to meditate outdoors, where they can experience the warmth of the sun, the sounds of birds, or a running brook. Others prefer the peace and solitude of a carpeted room with the shades drawn and the windows closed. It is not a good idea to meditate in an area with people entering and leaving, or other distractions. Turn off the television, radio, or stereo. Temporarily disconnect the phone or turn the volume down.

Benson[3] and his colleagues referred to a focal point as a mental device. Since the relaxation response is a type of focused meditation, one's focal point can be any of the types previously discussed (object, word, etc.). If the focal point is a sound or word/phrase, Benson recommends closing your eyes while meditating. This will help you stay focused. Match the repeated sound, word, or phrase to the inhalation and exhalation of your breath. Some people use two different words: one to repeat while inhaling and one to repeat while exhaling. For example they might say "in" on inspiration and "out" on exhalation.

A passive attitude refers to an accepting mental state. The passivity has to do with not fighting distractions because they are inevitable and will occur. The phone will ring, other noises will occur, and your focus will be disrupted by competing thoughts. When this happens, simply acknowledge the distractions and refocus. Do not worry about your performance.

A comfortable position is one you can maintain, without tension, for twenty to thirty minutes. You do not have to be a yoga master and sit in a full lotus position to meditate. You need only be comfortable and relaxed. Stretch beforehand, loosen or remove any tight clothing, and make sure you are not chilled. Sitting in a chair with a straight back and sitting on the floor with your legs crossed are good positions for meditation. Do not meditate while lying down. You will have a tendency to fall asleep.

Instructions for the Relaxation Response

1. Sit quietly in a comfortable position.
2. Close your eyes or focus on your visual focal point.
3. Completely relax all your muscles from your feet to your head. Contract and release your major muscles in your hands, arms, feet, legs, neck, shoulders, and the rest of your body.
4. Breathe easily and naturally through your nose. As you breathe repeat your word, phrase, or sound with every inhalation and exhalation.
5. Continue for ten to twenty minutes. You can check your watch, but do not use an alarm to signal the end. When you finish, sit quietly with your eyes closed initially. Avoid abruptly sitting up or standing.
6. Maintain a passive attitude. Get back to your focal point when you are distracted. Initially, ten minutes will seem like an eternity. Be patient. With practice you will come to enjoy the time and be surprised that it passes so quickly.

breath meditation a form of focused meditation where the focal point is one's breathing

Relaxation Response a popular form of focused meditation developed by Herbert Benson of Harvard University that incorporates the key elements of transcendental meditation (TM)

Open/Mindful Meditation

Open meditation is also known as mindful meditation. As we mentioned earlier in this section, during open meditation there is no attempt to censor incoming thoughts, sounds, and other stimuli. Rather, these stimuli are allowed to enter and be given one's full attention. Kabat-Zinn[25] describes this as a detached observation of things as they actually exist.

Many people are frustrated when they initially learn how to perform object meditation because their focus is interrupted by competing thoughts, feelings, and external stimuli. When they become aware of these aspects of things, they perceive them as distractions, and often react emotionally, becoming upset with themselves for *allowing* the distraction. Rather than ignoring, suppressing, or evaluating these disruptions and thus getting emotionally involved with them, Kabat-Zinn[25] recommends that you merely note the presence of these stimuli and observe them in a nonjudgmental way. This is your reality as it truly exists for you.

A key to understanding open meditation is realizing that it is based on developing an accepting attitude toward reality. When you practice open meditation, you become more mindful of the moment fully attending to your thoughts, your feelings, and any internal and external stimuli. The idea is to detach yourself from these thoughts and feelings and observe them in a noncritical way. In essence, you are stepping back from them to gain a different perspective. By stepping back and noting these thoughts and feelings, you gain a deeper understanding of them that is not biased by an emotion-laden evaluation.[25]

In essence, mindfulness teaches us to see things as they really are, not the way we think they should be. This is often very hard to do. We are used to filtering our thoughts and feelings through a layer of experience and a list of *shoulds, oughts,* and *musts* (how things should, ought to, and must be) rather than seeing them the way they actually are. Because of this, open meditation is much more difficult than object mediation for many beginners. Beginners often have a tendency for their minds to wander and to be unsure what they should do when this happens.

To better understand this technique, let's imagine you are practicing open meditation. You are comfortably dressed, sitting quietly on an exercise mat, legs gently crossed, hands folded and gently resting in your lap. You've taken a few deep diaphragmatic breaths and are starting to pay attention to your thoughts and feelings and the sensations in your body and all around you. As you do this, you start thinking about a homework assignment that is due tomorrow *(thinking* ahead instead of *paying attention* to the present). You start an inner dialogue with yourself and tell yourself, "I better remember to get my studying done tonight." The next thing you are aware of is an emotional response. You start to criticize yourself for not studying more: "I'm such a jerk for not studying more." You continue by saying, "I'm probably going to do really poorly on this test." At this point you realize that your thoughts and emotions drifted from the present, back to the past, and into the future.

According to Kabat-Zinn,[25] to correct this you would simply note that this happened, accept it without being judgmental, and get back to paying attention to the present moment. Rather than continuing with this self-critical debate about your study habits, you would simply tell yourself, "How interesting, here I am having this debate about the test. When I am done meditating, I'll start thinking about it more." After this happens you would get back to paying attention to the present moment and resume meditating until your session was over. Eventually, with practice and time, you become more proficient at staying focused and it becomes easier to note the distractions in a nonjudgmental way and get back to paying full attention to the present moment.

Formal and Informal Mindfulness

Mindfulness is generally taught and applied two different ways, formally and informally. **Formal mindfulness** meditation practice as developed and taught by Kabat-Zinn[26] and his associates is implemented over an eight-week period and is designed to have people practice for forty-five minutes a day. This training model was designed to work with people who had been referred for training by their health care providers because of stress-related illness. The training emphasizes that stress is something that is part of life and that stressors are often uncontrollable but can be managed using mindfulness.

Informal mindfulness is the application of mindful behavior into daily experience. In addition to the forty-five-minute formal training sessions, persons enrolled in the program are taught how to incorporate informal mindfulness into their daily activities—in a sense, to become more mindful of every activity they are engaged in. Two common examples of informal mindfulness training as taught by Kabat-Zinn[26] are mindful eating and mindful walking. Mindful eating is often taught to people with eating disorders to help them become more mindful of their eating behavior.[31] People are taught during mindful eating to slow their eating behavior. For people viewing mindful eating it looks like a movie being shown in slow motion; people sitting quietly, observing their food,

open meditation a type of meditation, also referred to as nonfocused or mindful meditation, that does not employ a focal point but instead directs one's full attention to the experience of existing in the present moment

formal mindfulness a type of mindfulness meditation training implemented over an eight-week period and designed to have people practice for 45 minutes a day

informal mindfulness the application of mindful behavior into daily experience

STRESS IN OUR WORLD 9-1

Frank and The Garden

When I was a young man in my 20s I was always on the go and could never sit still very long. I had big plans and lots of energy to accomplish them. I remember always feeling that there was so much to do and so little time to do it in. I think I spent about half of my time *thinking about* what I needed to do and most of the other half actually *doing* it. I don't think I spent more than 10 percent of my time actually *being* in the present moment. My thoughts were always drifting off into the past ("Why did this or that have to happen?" or "I wish I had done this or that differently") or the future ("I think I'll try this tomorrow" or "I better get ready for that next month"). I got a lot accomplished, advanced in my education and career, and made some money, but never seemed to be very happy or aware of the present moment, content to just *be* myself. I was always in the process of *becoming* someone, never *being* myself.

At the time, my wife and I had a third-floor attic apartment that a *paisano* from my family was renting to us for a minimal amount. Frank and his wife Fanny were an old Italian couple from the same village in Italy as my father. Their grown children were married and had moved out and into houses of their own. Frank and Fanny were both well into their 80s at the time but had a vibrant quality that made them seem years younger. I think they enjoyed having Heidi and I on the third floor. It was like having their kids home.

Frank had an amazing capacity for just *being* in the present moment. Although his three-story apartment building was in a very developed urban area, he had this amazing garden that took up most of his 800-square-foot yard. In his garden he planted tomatoes, peaches, figs, and other fruits but his pride and joy were his grapes from which he made wine in his basement. On more than a couple of occasions I enjoyed the pleasure of a lunch comprised of Fanny's homemade pasta with marinara sauce made from their tomatoes and Frank's wine that seemed to have the maximum alcohol achievable under normal fermentation.

I used to watch Frank walk in his garden: back and forth, back and forth, hands clasped behind his back, half-lit stogie in his mouth, pacing the same twenty-five-foot horizontal east-to-west path, pausing only to change directions and pace north to south. I remember saying to myself, "What a crazy old dude, all he ever does is pace *mindlessly* back and forth through his garden." How silly I was. What I didn't realize then was that Frank's pacing was *anything but* mindless. I remember now how he would stop and lean his head back, eyes closed, nostrils flared, experiencing his garden through its aromas, moisture, and sounds. I recall how a thin smile would cross his face as he stopped to examine a grape, taste a fig, caress a tomato. His actions were hardly mindless. What I now realize is that Frank epitomized mindfulness. *Everything* he did was mindful. It would frustrate me to watch him pick a tomato. He would carefully examine each fruit before he picked it, choosing only the ripest for Fanny's sauce. He would gently pluck the fruit from the vine, being oh so careful not to disturb the other pieces that were still ripening. Then he would hold the piece to the sunlight, wipe it off on his shirt, and examine it one last time before gently placing it in his basket. He would then move on to the next tomato, repeating the procedure. It could take him a good twenty minutes to pick the day's tomatoes. I would say to myself, "What a waste of time. I could have done that in five minutes." I think Frank realized how I felt because he would give me a knowing look, as if to say, "Slow down, Rich, and enjoy the full experience of these wonderful tomatoes, a gift to us from nature."

I miss those early evenings spent with Frank in his garden. How I wish he and Fanny were still around, so I could tell them how much I can now appreciate their simple, honest lives, and the mindfulness they brought to each moment. How much I would now give for a wordless walk in the garden with Frank, stopping now and then to smell the air, sift through the soil, and sit on the garden swing, merely *being* in the presence of such beauty.

slowly picking up small pieces with their utensils, gradually lifting the food off their plates and bringing it to their mouths, taking slow bites and chewing thoroughly. For those engaged in the practice, they experience eating like never before. They are taught to pay attention to the presentation of the food before eating it—the color, shape, placement, aromas, etc. They begin to marvel at things like how the fingers, hands, and arms work in consort with their brain to pick the food up and bring it into the mouth, the process of chewing, the experience of tasting something anew.

Mindful walking (also known as walking meditation or moving meditation) is a similarly slow process. Unlike a normal walk which is usually designed to get you somewhere, mindful walking is not designed to get anyplace (see Stress in Our World 9-1). Mindful walking in a sense is more like pacing because one walks back and forth or around in a loop.[26] During mindful walking people are taught how to focus on the individual components of a step (lifting the leg, bending the knee, stepping forward, heel touching, toe touching, etc.) and the process of walking (feelings in the feet, legs, back, etc., one's balance and sensation of movement). The distance one travels is not important, it is the process of walking that counts.

One can incorporate the principles of moving meditation into other physical activities, such as hiking, cross-country skiing, swimming, and so on. This can be done when engaged in the activity alone or in the company of others. In these adaptations of moving meditation, you typically would perform them at a normal pace but just become more mindful of the moment, paying attention to each footfall, stroke, glide, etc. This should not be confused with sound meditation, where one concentrates and focuses on sounds of rhythmic inhalation/exhalation or foot pounding to the exclusion of everything else. Instead, during moving meditation, one is open to the sights and sounds of the immediate environment. The idea is to be immersed in the immediate environment, to be fully open to it while shutting off distracting thoughts and ideas (usually about the past or future) and any judgmental thinking ("Am I doing this right?") that drift in.

One of the goals of mindfulness training is to slow down and become more mindful of all activities. This, according to Kabat-Zinn[26] will help them chart a course toward "greater sanity and wisdom in their lives."

VISUALIZATION

Visualization goes hand in hand with several relaxation techniques. Visualization, or the mental creation of relaxing visual images and scenes, can be used with other techniques, such as deep breathing, yoga, stretching, and meditation.

Visualization, by itself or in conjunction with the aforementioned techniques, works by using relaxing images to facilitate a relaxation response. It does this in two ways: by offsetting the effects of stress-arousing scenarios and by creating relaxing scenes.

Think for a moment about a scary scene from a horror movie. Think about all the ways you might describe your reaction: "It made my flesh crawl," "It was hair-raising," "It made me shiver," "I got a lump in my throat." All these statements reflect the physiological processes set into motion by the stress response. In fact the visual images we have can be as arousing as the actual events. Although viewing a horror film can set these physiological processes in motion, just recalling the scene in our minds can have the same effect.

Conversely, if we visualize a relaxing scene, our bodies can achieve a relaxed state. Such stress-reducing visual imagery can be focused on our own bodies or on outside scenarios. For instance, if we envision warm sensations in our arms and legs, we actually feel the legs getting heavy and warm. If we focus on the sun's warming rays, we feel them radiating over us, making us warm and relaxed.

In deep breathing we visualize air entering the deepest passageways and spaces of our lungs, filling them with oxygen. In meditation we might focus on a warming word, such as *sun,* or a warming scene, such as the image of floating on a raft in a pool with the warm sun beating down. All these positive images can help us relax, warm up, and cancel the negative effects of stress. Because these warming words and scenes are so personal and subjective, what works for one person may be ineffective for another.

> **KEY TO UNDERSTANDING**
>
> Minimal distractions are important for successful meditation.

> **KEY TO UNDERSTANDING**
>
> Do not worry about your performance during meditation.

Creating Personal Visualization Scripts

Many commercially available visualization tapes utilize imagery activities that may be incompatible with what you find relaxing and warming. For instance, if the tape uses an image of you floating on your back on a raft in the middle of a lake and you hate lakes and feel nauseous floating on anything, these images will create (rather than reduce) stress.

Smith,[48] has developed a very creative format for developing personal relaxation "scripts" that allow you to tailor your relaxation activities to your personal likes and dislikes. Table 9-2 is an adaptation of Smith's format for use in developing visualization scripts.

Let's use Heidi to illustrate how to develop a personal visualization script.

Develop Script

Heidi's unifying idea for the images in her visualization script is the relaxing nature of a Caribbean beach. She remembers spending one of the most relaxing days of her life on a deserted beach in the Bahamas with her husband about ten years ago.

Unifying Idea

- The relaxing nature of a Caribbean beach

Table 9-2 Developing a Personal Visualization Script

Develop Script

1. Unifying idea of script
2. Specific images to be used
3. Sequence of images

Elaborate on Script

1. Write actual script dialogue
2. Incorporate personally relaxing meaningful words
3. Finalize sequencing

Refine Script

1. Reinforce personal ability to relax
2. Incorporate pauses and silences
3. Write ending segment

Some specific images that stick in Heidi's mind about the day have to do with the sky, the color of the water, and the warmth of the breeze.

Specific Images

- The sky was a deep blue the color of a robin's egg.
- Huge white clouds drifted across the sky the entire day.
- The ocean was a deep aquamarine greenish blue with pure white waves cresting over deep green coral reefs.
- There was a steady, warm, gentle breeze all day.
- The sound of the waves created a hypnotic beat.
- The sand was warm, soft, and powdery to touch.
- Palm trees and flowering bougainvillea plants created a roof of natural shade.

Sequence of Images

- Walking down the steep path, over and through coral cliffs to the edge of the beach
- Walking down the beach through the warm sand to find the perfect spot
- Spreading the blanket under a canopy of vegetation
- Stretching out on the blanket
- Listening to the waves
- Gazing out at the water
- Watching the clouds
- Drifting off to sleep
- Waking and stretching
- Walking back to the cottage

Elaborate on the Script

During the elaboration stage, Heidi would craft the actual relaxing dialogue, incorporating specific details and reinforcing words. Heidi's relaxing words are *deep green, warm, aquamarine water, soft,* and *gentle.*

Write the Actual Dialogue and Incorporate Final Sequencing

- "It is a beautiful day, sunny, 88 degrees, clear blue skies, a gentle breeze, and wispy clouds that drift by effortlessly."
- "Hand in hand, my husband and I walk down the rugged path to the beach, admiring the moonlike appearance of the coral cliffs that rim the beach."

Incorporate Personally Relaxing, Meaningful Words

- "As we walk on the beach, the *warm,* fine white sand is *soft* and *gentle* on my feet."
- "We spread our blanket under the shade of palm trees and flowering bougainvillea."
- "I lie back on the blanket and watch the white crests of the waves break over the *deep green* coral reefs and slide over the *aquamarine water* of the shoreline."
- "I lie back, close my eyes, and breathe in the fragrant scents as a *warm, gentle* trade wind caresses my body."
- "I am feeling very relaxed as my body sinks deeper and deeper into the *soft* sand."
- "I am feeling more and more relaxed as the *gentle* trade winds carry fragrant air over my body."
- "I am feeling very relaxed as the gently crashing waves slowly lull me to sleep."

Refine Script

To reinforce her ability to relax, Heidi adds empowering dialogue and pauses to her script.

Incorporate Pauses and Silence

- "It is a beautiful day, sunny, 88 degrees, clear blue skies, a gentle breeze, and wispy clouds that drift by effortlessly."

  Pause for a few seconds . . .
- "Hand in hand, my husband and I walk down the rugged path to the beach, admiring the moonlike appearance of the coral cliffs that rim the beach."
- "As we walk on the beach, the warm, fine white sand is soft and gentle on my feet."

Reinforce Personal Ability to Relax

- *"I am warm, relaxed, and in control."*

  Pause for a few seconds . . .
- "We spread our blanket under the shade of palm trees and flowering bougainvillea."
- "I lie back on the blanket and watch the white crests of the waves break over the deep green coral reefs and slide over the aquamarine water of the shoreline."
- "I lie back, close my eyes, and breathe in the fragrant scents as a warm, gentle trade wind caresses my body."
- *"I am feeling very relaxed, as my body sinks deeper and deeper into the soft sand."*

  Pause for a few seconds . . .
- *"I am feeling more and more relaxed as the gentle trade winds carry fragrant scented air over my body."*
- *"I am feeling very relaxed as the gently crashing waves slowly lull me to sleep."*

  Pause for thirty seconds . . .

Write Ending Segment

- "I slowly start to wake up."
- "I stretch my arms and legs and take a couple of deep breaths."
- "I take five seconds to slowly open my eyes."
- "I slowly rise and fold up our blanket."
- "Hand in hand, we slowly walk back to our cottage."
- "Refreshed, we sit on the cottage steps, ready to take on the evening."

Although this script was for visualization, you could develop one for any of the other relaxation activities discussed in the chapter. Use it to create activities that are tailored to your relaxing words, images, and sounds.

DIVERSE PERSPECTIVES 9-1

A World of Relaxing Images

One of the most fascinating things about having students write their own visualization scripts is the diversity and richness of their relaxing images and scripts. Having people read their Personal Imagery Scripts is an excellent way to illustrate exactly how variable relaxing environments are. Here are some of the memorable images from former students:

Francesca (23, born in Puerto Rico): "The lush rain forest of my native Puerto Rico. I am sitting on a my blanket in a small clearing off a winding path that leads up from the valley floor to the top of the mountain. Everything is green and moist. There is a waterfall on my right and I listen to the water crashing against the walls of the gorge as it falls from the top."

Lauren (46, born in Italy): "I can see a beach close to Naples, where my mother was born. The sky is deep blue and matches the water. There are wispy white clouds that drift over the top of the mountains in the distance. There is a gentle warm breeze."

Scott (19, born in New Jersey): "I love the Jersey shore. I am sitting on a ¼-mile-wide beach with sand dunes stretching ten miles in either direction. It is 6:00 P.M. on a warm Saturday at the end of September, so there are very few people on the beach. I watch the sandpipers running back and forth with the waves, their skinny legs always one step ahead of the water. They move in unison, bathed in the orange glow of the sun sinking over the dunes."

Jesse (20, born in Colorado): "My dad used to take me on a hike to a lake high in the Rockies. The thing I remember the most was walking through the evergreen forest. I can picture that image now; the air is fragrant with the smell of pine in the air. The temperature is cool, even on this hot summer day. The pine needles cover the path through the forest, giving into our weight as we walk. I remember spreading out a blanket and laying on my back, gazing up through the tall pine trees. The bottom twenty or thirty feet were pretty sparse, but the tops were covered with dense green branches that swayed in the breeze, occasionally giving us a peek of the clear, blue skies."

Monica (22, born in New York City): "I live in West New York, N.J., right on the Hudson River. It is 2:00 A.M., on a cool dark summer's night and everyone is asleep in my apartment. I spread a cushion on my balcony and look at the lights of Manhattan Island. The sky is pitch black, but the full moon, the stars, and the lights of the city cast this surreal glow on places that almost make it seem like daytime. It is quiet and I am hypnotized by watching the movement of red tail lights on the West Side Highway that seem to float by on their way to who knows where."

Living Constructively

Letting Go Mindfully

Being mindful goes beyond just paying attention to the world around us. It also involves paying attention to our actions, becoming more deliberate in what we do. It reminds me of walking gently in the woods, being careful not to disturb the natural order of the place and to leave no tracks as you pass through. Often, when we engage in common, everyday activities like getting things from a cabinet or moving from room to room, we operate as if on automatic pilot, opening and closing doors, drawers, and cabinets a little too quickly, often slamming them in our haste and creating unnecessary noise or damage.

Krech (2003)[29] has a wonderful activity to help remind us of this and to increase our attentiveness to such daily activities. It is called *Letting Go* and revolves around becoming more mindful of how to touch and then let go of things.

Instructions for Letting Go:

1. Pay attention to every time your hand lets go of something today. This could involve letting go of a cup or glass, door handle, cabinet or drawer pull, your pen, or a person's hand.
2. Be mindful of exactly what is going on. Note how you put that glass down. Notice the movement of the door knob when you turned it slowly and gently closed the door or forgot and just let it release from your fingers.
3. Pay attention to the texture, weight, shape, and feel of everything you handle and then let go of. How does this influence how you release these things?
4. What are the consequences of the way you let go of things today. Did you get a certain look from a person when you released his/her hand? Did a door or drawer slam (or not slam) when you were mindful of how you released them?

When the day is over write down what you learned from this activity. How do you think being more mindful of letting go can impact your life if you practiced this on a regular basis?

AUTOGENICS

Autogenic training is a form of hypnosis that incorporates visual images of our bodies becoming warm and relaxed. Two normal by-products of hypnosis—warmth and a feeling of heaviness in the limbs—are associated with increased peripheral blood flow and reduced muscle tension. They are also associated with other techniques designed to facilitate a relaxation response similar to what you would experience through meditation. Autogenics just gets you there in a different way. Meditation relaxes your mind first, which leads to your body relaxing and getting warm. Autogenics begins with your body, and your mind in turn slows down and relaxes.[33,34]

Autogenic means self-generating. Essentially, autogenic training is a type of self-hypnosis that uses imagery to relax and warm our bodies systematically. Instead of focusing on external scenarios, the images conjured up through autogenics are of the arms, legs, stomach, and forehead. These body parts are imagined to be warm, heavy, and relaxed.

Autogenics was developed by a Johannes Schultz, a German psychiatrist, and his student, Wolfgang Luthe, for use in the practice of psychotherapy.[41] They used hypnosis as a tool to help relax their patients by reducing muscle tension, increasing blood flow to the periphery, and slowing heart rate and respiration. They were able to teach their patients to induce this state themselves, thereby facilitating their psychotherapy and helping them gain some control over their lives.

It became apparent that the use of autogenics could be expanded to include nonpsychotherapeutic settings where clinically well people could use the technique for stress reduction.[2,32]

Instructions for Performing Autogenics

There are five steps involved in performing autogenics. As you move from step 1 (breathing and visualization) through step 5 (wrap up), you will redirect blood flow from your heart and other internal organs out to your arms and legs, hands and feet, bringing relaxing heaviness and warmth.

Step 1: Focus on Breathing and Visualization

Take a few deep abdominal breaths and contract and relax any muscles that are tense. Repeat the following sentences to yourself: "My breathing is slow and even," "My breathing is smooth and rhythmic," "My breathing is effortless and calm."

> **KEY TO UNDERSTANDING**
>
> During autogenic training, visualize that your body is heavy and warm.

As you continue to breathe, visualize yourself on a warm, sunny beach. As the waves move in, they cover your body with warmth and relaxation. Feel the waves of warmth and relaxation wash over your shoulders and chest and through your arms and hands. Feel the waves of warmth rush over your stomach and hips, down your back, and through your legs and feet. Feel the warmth and continue to breathe.

Step 2: Focus on the Heart

As you continue to breathe slowly and deeply, visualize your heart and say to yourself, "My heartbeat is calm and regular."

As you continue to repeat this message to yourself, visualize your heart beating calmly and regularly, sending warm blood throughout your body. See the blood flow out of your heart, through your internal organs and your brain, and out through your arms and legs, all the way out to your fingers and toes. Continue for a few seconds to breathe slowly and deeply, watching your blood course slowly throughout your body.

Visualize the center of your body, your solar plexus, that part of your body right behind your navel. Imagine it is warm and relaxed and repeat, "My solar plexus is warm and relaxed."

Repeat to yourself, "I am relaxed. I am calm. I am quiet. My breathing is smooth and rhythmic. My heartbeat is calm and regular. My solar plexus is relaxed."

Step 3: Focus on the Arms and Hands

Starting with your right arm, repeat the following statement as you continue to breathe slowly and deeply and visualize the warm blood flowing throughout your arm all the way to your fingers: "My right arm and hand are heavy and warm." Switch your focus to the left arm and hand and, following the same instructions, repeat: "My left arm and hand are heavy and warm." Now focus on both arms and hands and repeat, "Both of my arms and hands are heavy and warm. It would take a great effort to raise my arms." Continue to breathe slowly and deeply, watching the blood flow into your arms and hands, making them feel heavy and warm.

Step 4: Focus on the Legs and Feet

As you continue to breathe slowly and deeply, visualize the blood traveling throughout your legs, bringing with it feelings of heaviness and warmth. Continue to breathe slowly and deeply and repeat, "My right leg and foot are heavy and warm." Shift your focus to your left leg and repeat, "My left leg and foot are heavy and warm." Shift your focus to both legs and repeat, "Both of my legs and feet are heavy and warm. It would take a great deal of effort to lift my legs and feet."

Step 5: Wrap Up

Continue to breathe deeply and slowly, visualizing the waves of warmth and relaxation washing over your body, and realize that you are totally and deeply relaxed. It is only in this state that you should repeat the statement

"I am calm and relaxed." Continue to breathe deeply and slowly, repeating the message to yourself. After a few breaths begin to get back in touch with where you are: the room and the time. You are safe, secure, and relaxed. Begin to count down from five:

5—Take a deep breath and visualize the room.
4—Take a deep breath and begin to stretch.
3—Take a deep breath and slowly open your eyes.
2—Take a deep breath. You are now mentally alert and ready to get back to whatever you were doing before this activity.
1—You are fully awake and ready to go.

To get the full benefits of autogenics, you will need to practice it on a regular basis. Slowly, you will find it easier to relax and fall into the autogenic state.

The Quieting Reflex and the Calming Response

The quieting reflex and the calming response are eclectic interventions that combine aspects of breathing, visualization, and autogenic training into simple, quick interventions that can be used anywhere. We will discuss the quieting reflex first since the calming response was derived from it.

The Quieting Reflex

Dr. Charles Stroebel[46] developed a quick six-second relaxation technique called the *quieting reflex*. He named it this because with practice it can be triggered almost reflexively. The quieting reflex incorporates deep breathing, muscle relaxation, and visual imagery and can be used with any type of stressor.

Instructions for the Quieting Reflex

1. Think about whatever it is that is making you stressed.
2. Smile to relax facial muscle tension.
3. Repeat to yourself, "I can keep a calm body and an alert mind."
4. Take a quiet, easy breath.
5. Exhale through parted teeth, allowing your jaw to go slack.
6. Visualize heaviness and warmth flowing throughout your body.

The Calming Response

Dr. Jay Segal[62] from Temple University developed a slightly modified version of the quieting reflex called the *calming response*. This technique also is quick and utilizes deep breathing, muscle relaxation, and visual imagery.

Segal's technique, like Stroebel's,[46] can be used anywhere and any time you are stressed or are anticipating stress. It is designed to help you relax quickly and stop the stress response from progressing.

Six Steps of the Calming Response

1. Take a personal inventory of stressors.
2. Whenever you are stressed or are about to be confronted with any of your stressors, stop what you are focusing on and get in touch with the depth and pace of your breathing. Is your breathing shallow, irregular, and uneven?
3. Think of a relaxing, warming word and visual image.
4. Take three deep abdominal breaths. On the first breath, repeat to yourself, "I will not let my body get involved" or "My body will stay uninvolved."
5. On the second breath, identify any muscle or muscle group that is tense and:
   - On inhalation, contract and hold it for three seconds.
   - On exhalation release the contraction.
6. On the third deep, slow breath, close your eyes and think of your calming word and relaxing image.

You can repeat this sequence again if you are still tense and use it as often as you want during the day (see Stress Buster Tips: "Using the Calming Response Preventively").

Stress Buster Tips

Using the Calming Response Preventively

The calming response is a simple, easy-to-use tip for reducing stress once it occurs. It can be done anywhere and takes only a few seconds. The beauty of this technique is that it can also be used to prevent stress from occurring. Try using it in the following way:

1. Keep a stressor diary for at least one month.
2. Identify stressors that are foreseeable and avoidable (see chapter 8).
3. Use the calming response just before exposure to these stressors.

By using the calming response this way, you can prevent potential stressors from turning into actual stressors.

Biofeedback

The final activity we will explore in this chapter is biofeedback. **Biofeedback** is a technique that employs instruments that measure body functioning associated with stress (usually temperature, muscle tension, brainwave activity, and perspiration). If a stress response is present, that information is fed back to you through a signal such as a buzzer, light, or beeper.

biofeedback a technique for evaluating the effects of stress on the body by using instruments that monitor body functions, such as temperature, muscle tension, brain wave activity, and perspiration

How Biofeedback Works

The physiological processes that are measured by the biofeedback equipment occur automatically as a result of involuntary, autonomic nervous system functioning. As you might recall from chapter 5, it was previously thought that people have no conscious control over these involuntary processes. As we have discussed, however, with practice we can slow down our breathing rates, increase our blood flow, and influence our brain waves.

Biofeedback provides us with information about these various involuntary body processes, information that is used in two ways:

1. It makes you aware that these body functions have been activated (meaning you are stressed).
2. It helps you regulate these functions once you are aware they are operating.

As you are learning how to regulate the body processes associated with the stress response, biofeedback provides instant information about the success of your efforts. With the aid of biofeedback machines, you can train yourself to recognize stress and put your body in a relaxed state.

In time you can wean yourself off the machines, because you no longer need them to tell you either that you are under stress or that you are relaxing properly. The techniques you would use to relax are those we have already discussed: deep breathing, muscle relaxation, visualization, and autogenics. The main difference with biofeedback is that you would employ those techniques while being hooked up to a biofeedback machine.

Biofeedback has been shown to be very effective in treating some stress-related disorders.[5,42] It seems to be most effective in dealing with cardiovascular disorders because of subjects' ability to increase circulation to the periphery and relax constricted blood vessels. Migraine headache, hypertension,[5,6,36] and Raynaud's syndrome, a disease characterized by reduced blood flow to the extremities,[5] have all been treated successfully with biofeedback. Biofeedback is also used in the treatment of muscle-tension-related disorders, though there have been mixed results concerning the application of biofeedback in the treatment of tension headache.[6]

Types of Biofeedback

There are four main types of biofeedback machines: electroencephalographic (EEG), thermal, electromyographic (EMG), and electrodermal (EDR).[17] Each works differently according to the type of information it measures.[40]

- EEG biofeedback machines measure brain waves. As was discussed earlier in this chapter, brain-wave patterns change during the stress response. EEG biofeedback machines use various auditory (tones) and visual (computer images) forms of feedback to let you know which wave pattern is present. Eventually, you begin to associate changes in tone or in visual images with a relaxed state and learn how to induce these changes by using relaxation activities.
- Thermal biofeedback machines measure temperature at the extremities. During the stress response, temperature at the extremities drops as the blood vessels servicing those areas constrict and reduce blood flow, concentrating blood in the vital organs. Sensors are usually clipped to the fingers and are used to provide feedback as relaxation efforts warm the extremities by increasing their blood supply. A light, buzzer, or bell signals that you are relaxed and that blood flow to the fingers has increased.
- EMG biofeedback machines measure tension in striated muscles. Both acute and chronic muscle tension associated with stress can be measured this way. Once muscle relaxation activities are begun, the machine provides feedback, again in the form of lights, bells, or buzzers, to let you know whether you have successfully relaxed your muscles.
- EDR biofeedback machines measure the body's electrical activity. One of the oldest applications of EDR involves galvanic skin response (GSR). GSR biofeedback works by sensing excess perspiration that enhances the electrical conductivity of the skin. This phenomenon is referred to as skin conductance. Increased sweating is a normal by-product of the stress response as your body prepares for fight-or-flight. The machine provides feedback concerning your success in reducing the stress-associated perspiration.[17,42]

Biofeedback equipment ranges in price from under $100 for simple, palm-size, battery-operated GSR machines to several thousand dollars for more complex machinery that measures different functions. Each has its own limitations because conditions other than stress can influence temperature, skin conductivity, and muscle tension.[42]

Remember, biofeedback is just a means of providing information concerning your body and your relaxation activities. Signals such as lights and buzzers tell us when our bodies have relaxed and help condition us concerning what relaxation feels like. You still must learn how to relax through breathing, muscle relaxation, and imagery. Biofeedback does not take the place of these techniques. However, it can provide positive reinforcement to people who have tried these techniques and others but are not sure they are doing them properly or have doubts about their effectiveness.

KEY TO UNDERSTANDING

Remember that a biofeedback machine does not take the place of learning how to breathe and relax your muscles.

HOBBIES, ENTERTAINMENT, RECREATIONAL ACTIVITIES AND STRESS

Many people confuse being entertained and engaging in nonphysical hobbies and recreational activities with true relaxation. If you remember from the beginning of this chapter, a truly relaxed state is the opposite of a stressed state. When you are truly relaxed, your breathing and heart rates slow down, muscle tension is reduced, and you are fully mindful of what you are involved in at the present moment. Although you have a passive and accepting mental state (you do not fight the drifting in and out of thoughts and sensations), your mind is completely engaged in what you are doing, paying full attention.

Relaxation vs. Entertainment

The activities we have discussed in this chapter so far have all been studied empirically and have been shown to be capable of inducing a truly relaxed state if done properly and practiced regularly. This isn't the case with most of the activities people say they engage in to *relax*. People cite everything from watching television to going camping as activities they engage in to relax. While these and other activities people use to relax are enjoyable (usually) and provide a certain level of relief from the demands of the day, they have not been found to induce the same deeply relaxing state as the ones we have discussed in this chapter.

Being entertained and engaging in hobbies or recreational activities has the potential to be relaxing if engaged in *mindfully.* Unfortunately many hobbies, recreational activities, and forms of entertainment are pursued *mindlessly* and used to *deaden* one's awareness of reality, not *heighten* it. Indeed, many people refer to these pursuits as "vegetating" or "vegging out." If you ask people how they relax after a busy day, it is not uncommon for them to say, "I just veg out in front of the TV" or "I have a drink or two and just veg out." Some even turn to illegal psychoactive drugs to try to become "dazed and confused" or achieve some other form of altered consciousness that *disengages* them from reality and what they are engaged in.

Besides being pursued mindlessly, some activities used to relax often *create* stress by speeding up body functions or arousing strong emotions. Playing video games is a prime example of this kind of *relaxing entertainment.* While these games often demand the full attention of those who play them, it is not a relaxed attentiveness. The attention one gives to video games often becomes a source of stress because it is often accompanied by muscle tension and a sense of competitiveness as one tries to *beat* the game, or one's opponent, or *increase* one's score. To get a sense of this just watch a couple of kids or adults *play* these games. They often look anything but playful. It often looks more like work than play as they frantically manipulate the joysticks and controllers and exert body English to get the figures in the game to do what they want them to do. People become addicted to these games, playing for hours on end and staying up all night to *master* them and *get to the next level.* Often, instead of the game being a relaxing diversion and escape, it becomes a stressful obsession.

Other forms of *relaxing entertainment* actually stimulate brain activity and trigger behavior that is neither healthy nor conducive to mindfulness. Take watching the typical 30- or 60-minute prime-time network television show as an example. The typical show is broken up into short clips that move the viewer through the story or action at an accelerated pace. In real life, conversations, events, and stories proceed at a real pace that is much slower and take time to unfold. It is not unusual for the average situation comedy to take you through an entire day (or multiple days) in a person's life in a 30-minute segment broken up every few minutes by commercial advertisements that zip along at an even faster pace. Often, subliminal eating messages are directed at the audience that can trigger unnatural eating patterns (eating something when you are not really hungry for instance) in viewers. The unnatural pace of most network television is designed to keep the viewer stimulated (and watching), provide instant gratification (by delivering story lines quickly and easily), and reward short attention spans. Viewers do not have to be fully engaged in the show to get the meaning or the final point. It is delivered mindlessly for them at the end of thirty or sixty minutes. Many people use *mindless viewing* of television as a drug, something to partake of to *escape* their troubles. They will turn the television on and watch whatever happens to be on that particular time. Often, they will *channel surf* to find something *better* to view *while they are still watching the other program.* This kind of distracted viewing is the *exact opposite* of mindfulness.

Does this mean that playing video games and watching television are harmful or bad for you? Neither playing video games nor watching television are inherently harmful or bad for you. There are many creative, enjoyable video games that are fun to play and are enjoyable ways to spend time. They are exciting and entertaining. There are also many entertaining television shows, sporting events, and educational programs that are well worth seeing. However, they should not be confused with legitimate relaxation activities capable of inducing relaxation and managing stress.

Using Hobbies, Entertainment, and Recreational Pursuits to Relax

First of all it is important to realize that even though an activity might not be as completely relaxing as meditation or biofeedback, it can still be enjoyable and fun to engage in. As we discussed in chapter 7 it is important to have fun and engage in fun activities daily. Just accept that if you are using these to truly relax, they are not going to have the same effect as the more traditional stress management activities. The best way to make any hobby, recreational pursuit, or form of entertainment more relaxing is to engage in it more mindfully. Almost any activity can be pursued more mindfully if it is:

1. Nonconceptual—mindful activity involves awareness of *being* rather than thinking about what one is doing.
2. Present-centered—mindful activity focuses on the present moment, what you are doing now. It doesn't look ahead or backward.
3. Nonjudgmental—being judgmental involves focusing on what you'd like the activity to be rather than what it actually is. Awareness cannot flow freely if we'd like our experience to be something other than what it is.
4. Intentional—mindful activity intentionally directs (or redirects) the attention to what one is experiencing in the present moment.
5. Participatory—mindful activity is not detached witnessing. It involves active participation by the body and the mind.
6. Nonverbal—mindful activity cannot be captured in words because awareness occurs before words to describe it are formulated.
7. Exploratory—mindful activity is always looking for more subtle levels of perception, finding new things out about yourself and the activity.
8. Liberating—mindful activity removes you from your suffering and is enlightening.[18]

As you can see from these characteristics of mindfulness, almost any hobby, recreational activity, or form of entertainment can be engaged in more mindfully if you follow these guidelines and give it your full attention. Listening to music is a good example. Some people put music on as a background diversion while they do other things such as clean, cook, etc. While this is fun and can brighten your mood, it really isn't the same as listening to music mindfully. When you listen to music mindfully, you give it your full attention and do nothing else. You tell yourself that you will be spending the next (so many) minutes intending to do nothing but listen to this music. You listen for variations in the melody, rhythms, etc., and pay attention to all of the nuances. At the same time you let your mind just focus on the music and not the events of the day, the meal that needs to be cooked, or anything else. If you listen to the music this way, you will be much more likely to achieve more of the benefits of the more traditional relaxation strategies discussed in the first half of this chapter.

SUMMARY

This chapter introduced *Relax,* the fourth line of defense against stress. The chapter began with a description of relaxation as a physiological state that is incompatible with stress and explained why the body cannot be stressed and relaxed at the same time. All the techniques discussed in the chapter are designed to put the body in a relaxed state.

The chapter started with a discussion of breathing and how conscious breathing is a form of relaxation training. The chapter described how to perform diaphragmatic breathing, a technique commonly used to reduce stress. Diaphragmatic breathing is a form of deep, slow, controlled breathing that works by filling the lungs completely from the bottom up.

The next strategy described was meditation. Meditation was examined from a variety of perspectives. The health benefits of meditation, from lowered respiration to changed brain waves, were discussed. Several different types of meditation were described. Focused meditation techniques including object, word/phrase, sound, and breath meditation were discussed. All of these forms of meditation use a focal point to fix one's attention on while practicing. Benson's relaxation response, a simplified way to meditate, was described in some detail. Open or mindful meditation was also extensively described. Unlike focused meditation, open meditation does not use a focal point to narrow attention.

Visualization was discussed next. Visualization revolves around the idea that visual images can induce either a stress or a relaxation response. By visualizing warm, relaxing images, we can facilitate a relaxed state of being. Conversely, by conjuring up uncomfortable images, we can induce a stress response. A model for developing personal visualization scripts was introduced.

Autogenics, a form of self-hypnosis that incorporates breathing and visualization to help us relax, was the next technique discussed in the chapter. Autogenic training uses images of warm, relaxed body parts to induce a tranquil state that is incompatible with stress. From autogenics, the chapter moved to a description of biofeedback. Biofeedback uses various instruments to monitor the autonomic processes set into motion as part of the stress response. These responses are fed back through lights and buzzers to help us monitor our efforts to relax. In time, we can learn to do this without the aid of the equipment.

STUDY QUESTIONS

1. What are some of the physiological changes that occur during relaxation?
2. How does relaxation work in reducing stress?
3. Describe what the author refers to as a "passive mental state."
4. Why is deep breathing the foundation of all relaxation activities?
5. What are the four conditions required for performing Benson's relaxation response?

6. What is the quieting reflex?
7. What is visual imagery, and how is it used to reduce stress?
8. Define autogenics, and describe how it works to reduce stress.
9. What is biofeedback?
10. What is the ultimate goal of using biofeedback equipment?

DISCOVER OUR CHANGING WORLD

Center for Mindfulness in Medicine, Health Care, and Society (CFM)

http://www.umassmed.edu/cfm/

This is the home page for the Center for Mindfulness in Medicine, Health Care, and Society (CFM) founded in 1995 by John Kabat-Zinn. The Center is dedicated to furthering the practice and integration of mindfulness in the lives of individuals, institutions, and society through a wide range of clinical, research, education, and outreach initiatives in the public and private sectors. These initiatives include the renowned Stress Reduction Program—the oldest and largest academic medical center-based stress reduction program in the country—as well as a range of professional training programs and corporate workshops, courses, and retreats.

Click on the various links and read about the history of the center, its mission, and the programs it provides.

Critical Thinking Question

After reading about mindfulness in this chapter and the services provided by this center, how do you think your life would change if you enrolled in their eight-week mindfulness-based stress management program?

ARE YOU THINKING CLEARLY? RELAX

In this chapter we discussed a variety of strategies to help you learn how to use a variety of techniques for relaxation. Often students report that they do not have time to relax or do not know how to relax. They feel that relaxation is important but just can't seem to work it into their day. If you find yourself saying these things regarding relaxation, *stop* and ask yourself the following questions:

1. Can I still honestly say "I don't know how to relax" after completing this chapter?
2. Is my problem really that I don't know how to relax or is it that I just won't allow myself the luxury of relaxing?
3. Have I really tried practicing all the strategies in the chapter in order to find one that is right for me?
4. Do I like being a martyr, having people feel sorry for my stressed-out persona?
5. Do I feel guilty about relaxing and think I should be "doing something else"?
6. If I can learn new things, such as how to play tennis and use a new software program, why can't I learn how to relax?

The answers to these questions should help you assess whether you are thinking clearly about relaxing as a way to cope with stress. If you are not, try using the Ellis and Harper's (1975) ABCDE technique to work through your illogical thoughts about relaxation as a line of defense against stress.

REFERENCES

1. Anasari, M. & Lark, L. (1998). *Yoga for beginners.* New York: HarperCollins.
2. Anderson, N.B., Lawrence, P.S., & Olson, T.W. (1981). Within-subject analysis of autogenic training in the treatment of tension headache pain. *Journal of Behavior Therapy and Experimental Psychology,* 12, pp. 219–223.
3. Benson, H. (1975). *The relaxation response.* New York: Avon.
4. Benson, H. & Stuart, E.M. (1993). *The wellness book.* New York: Fireside.
5. Blanchard, E.B. & Haynes, M.R. (1975). Biofeedback treatment of a case of Raynaud's disease. *Journal of Behavioral Therapy and Experimental Psychiatry,* 6, pp. 230–234.
6. Blanchard, E.B., et al. (1982). Biofeedback and relaxation training with three kinds of headaches: Treatment effects and their predictions, *Journal of Consulting and Clinical Psychology,* 50, pp. 562–575.
7. Blonna, R. & Levitan, J. (2005). *Healthy sexuality.* Belmont, CA: Wadsworth.
8. Bradley, D.G. (1968). *A guide to the world's religions.* Englewood Cliffs, NJ: Prentice-Hall.
9. Bynner, W. (1980). *The way of life: According to Lao Tzu.* New York: Perigee Books.
10. Cannon, W.B. (1932). *The wisdom of the body.* New York: Norton.
11. Crompton, P. (1987). *The t'ai chi workbook.* Boston: Shambhala.
12. Curtis, J. & Detert, R. (1985). *Learn to relax: A 14-day program.* LaCrosse, WI: Coulee Press.
13. DiFilippo, J.M. & Overholser, J.C. (1999). Cognitive behavioral treatment of panic disorder: Confronting

situational precipitants. *Journal of Contemporary Psychotherapy,* 29(2), pp. 99–113.
14. Dunn, T. (1987). The practice and spirit of t'ai chi ch'uan. *Yoga Journal,* November/December.
15. Environments (disc 9). (1979). New York: Syntonics Research.
16. Everly, G.S. & Benson, H. (1989). Disorders of arousal and the relaxation response. *International Journal of Psychosomatics,* 36, pp. 15–21.
17. Everly, G.S. & Lating, J.M. (2002). *A clinical guide to the treatment of the human stress response.* New York: Kluwer Academic/Plenum.
18. Germer, C.K. (2005). Mindfulness: What Is It? What Does It Matter? In Germer C.K., Siegel, R.D. & Fulton, P.R. (Eds.) *Mindfulness and Psychotherapy.* New York: Guilford Press.
19. Hahn, N.T. (1991). *Peace Is Every Step.* New York: Bantam.
20. Hasner, S. (1985). Music therapy and stress reduction research. *Journal of Music Therapy,* 22, pp. 193–206.
21. Holmes, D.S. (1984). Meditation and somatic arousal reduction: A review of the experimental evidence. *American Psychologist,* 39, pp. 1–10.
22. Inkeles, G. & Austin, K.K. (1992). *The new sensual massage.* Bayside, CA: Arcata Arts.
23. Jevning, R., Wallace, R.K., & Beidebach, M. (1992). The physiology of meditation: A review. *Neuroscience and Biobehavioral Reviews,* 16, pp. 415–424.
24. Joseph, M. (1998). The effects of strong religious beliefs on coping with stress. *Stress Medicine,* 14, pp. 219–224.
25. Kabat-Zinn, J., et al. (1992). Effectiveness of a meditation based stress reduction program in the treatment of anxiety disorders. *American Journal of Psychiatry,* 149, pp. 936–943.
26. Kabat-Zinn, J. (1994). *Wherever you go you are there.* New York: Hyperion Press.
27. Karren, K.J., Hafen, B.Q., Smith, N.L., & Frandsen, K.J. (2002). *Mind/body health: The effects of attitudes, emotions, and relationships.* (2nd ed.). San Francisco: Benjamin Cummings.
28. Kirlian, S. & Kirlian, V. (1961). Photography and visual observation by means of high-frequency currents. *Journal of Scientific and Applied Photography,* 6, pp. 145–148.
29. Krech, G. (2003). Working with Your Attention: Exercises and Daily Journal. Monkton UT. ToDo Institute.
30. Krieger, D. (1979). *The therapeutic touch: How to use your hands to help or heal.* Englewood Cliffs, NJ: Prentice-Hall.
31. Kristeller J. & Hallet C. (1999). An exploratory study of meditation-based intervention for binge eating disorder. *Journal of Health Psychology,* 4(3), pp. 357–363.
32. Lehrer, P.M., et al. (1983). Progressive relaxation and meditation: A study of the psychophysiology and therapeutic differences between the two techniques. *Behavior Research and Theory,* 21, pp. 651–652.
33. Linden, W. (1994). Autogenic training: A narrative and quantitative review of clinical outcome. *Biofeedback and Self-Regulation,* 19(3), p. 227.
34. Linden, W. (1999). The autogenic training method of JH Schultz. In Lehrer, P.M. & Woolfolk, R.L. (Eds.). *Principles and practices of stress management.* (2nd ed.). New York: Guilford.
35. Lusk, J.T. (1992). *Relaxation imagery and inner healing.* New York: Whole Person.
36. Miller, N.E. (1989). What biofeedback does (and does not) do. *Psychology Today,* November, pp. 22–24.
37. Montague, A. (1986). *Touching.* (3rd ed.). New York: Columbia University Press.
38. Naliboff, D.B. & Tachiki, K.H. (1991). Autonomic and skeletal response to nonelectrical cutaneous stimulation. *Perceptual and Motor Skills,* 72(2), pp. 575–584.
39. Roberts, D. & Mosley, B. (1978). A Father's Time, *Psychology Today,* June/July, pp. 48–70.
40. Rokicki, L.A., et al. (1997). Change mechanisms associated with combined relaxation/EMG biofeedback training for chronic tension headache. *Applied Psychophysiology and Biofeedback,* 22(1), pp. 21–41.
41. Schultz, J. & Luthe, W. (1959). *Autogenic training: A psychophysiological approach to psychotherapy.* New York: Grune & Stratton.
42. Schwartz, M.S. (1995). *Biofeedback: A practitioner's guide.* (2nd ed.). New York: Guilford.
43. Segal, J. (1975). *The calming response.* Philadelphia: Temple University Press.
44. Selye, H. (1956). *The stress of life.* New York: McGraw-Hill.
45. Shapiro, D.H. (1978). *Precision nirvana.* Englewood Cliffs, NJ: Prentice-Hall.
46. Stroebel, C. (1978). *The quieting response training: Introduction.* New York: BMA.
47. Shapiro, D. & Surwit, R.S. (1979). Meditation. In Pomerlau, O. & Brady, J.P. (Eds.). *Behavioral medicine: Theory and practice.* Baltimore: Williams & Wilkins.
48. Smith, J.C. (1993). *Creative stress management: The 1,2,3, cope system.* Englewood Cliffs, NJ: Prentice-Hall.
49. Van Peski-Oosterbaan, A.S., et al. (1997). Cognitive behavioural therapy for unexplained noncardiac chest pain: A pilot study. *Behavioural and Cognitive Psychotherapy,* 25(4), pp. 339–350.
50. Wallace, R.K. (1970). The physiological effects of transcendental meditation. *Science,* 167, pp. 1751–1754.
51. Wallace, R.K., Benson, H., Wilson, A.F., & Garrett, M.D. (1971). Decreased blood lactate during transcendental meditation. *Federation Proceedings,* 30, p. 376.
52. Wallace, R.K., Benson, H., & Wilson, A.F. (1971). A wakeful, hypometabolic physiological state. *American Journal of Physiology,* 221, pp. 795–799.
53. Wallace, R. K. & Benson, H. (1972). The physiology of meditation. *Scientific American,* 226, pp. 84–90.
54. Wright, S.M. (1987). The use of therapeutic touch in the management of pain. *Nursing Clinics of North America,* 22, pp. 705–713.

Name: ____________________ Date: __________

ASSESS YOURSELF 9-1

Relaxing Words, Sounds, and Images

Many of the passive relaxation strategies in this chapter revolve around the use of a relaxing word, sound, or image. This self-survey is designed to help you clarify these relaxation aids. Try to come up with at least one entry for each of the three categories (words, sounds, and images). This will enhance your ability to perform the activities in this chapter.

Relaxing Words

Fill in a personally relaxing word for each category:

1. ________ human body (*relax, slow, deep,* etc.)
2. ________ interpersonal (*love, sex,* etc.)
3. ________ outdoors (*sun, water, beach,* etc.)
4. ________ vacation spot (*Bahamas, Maui,* etc.)
5. ________ other

RELAXING IMAGES

Fill in a personally warming, relaxing, or meditative image for each category:

1. ________ human body (watching breathing, muscles stretching, etc.)
2. ________ interpersonal (making love, massage, etc.)
3. ________ outdoors (floating on a raft, etc.)
4. ________ vacation spot (beach, lake, etc.)
5. ________ inanimate object (candle flame, etc.)
6. ________ other

RELAXING SOUNDS

Fill in a relaxing, warming, or meditative sound for each category:

1. ________ human body (breathing, heartbeat, etc.)
2. ________ exercise (breathing, footfalls during running, etc.)
3. ________ outdoors (rainstorm, wind, etc.)
4. ________ music (specific artist, type of music, etc.)
5. ________ object (metronome, air conditioner, etc.)
6. ________ other

Name: ______________________ Date: __________

ASSESS YOURSELF 9-2

Relaxation Assessment

At least once in the next week, try each of the relaxation strategies described in chapter 9. At the end of a week, rate each activity by using the following instrument:

1. What I liked about the activity:

____

____

____

____

2. What I disliked about the activity:

____

____

____

____

3. Potential barriers to using this activity on a regular basis:

____

____

____

____

4. Types of stressors this activity might be effective against:

____

____

____

____

CHAPTER

10

Release: Using Physical Activity to Dissipate the Effects of Stress

OUTLINE

Fight-or-Flight Revisited

The Health Benefits of Exercise and Physical Activity

Physiological Benefits

Psychological Benefits

The Effects of Physical Activity on Stress

Mild, Moderate, and Vigorous Physical Activity

The Effects of Mild Physical Activity on Stress

The Effects of Moderate Physical Activity on Stress

The Effects of Vigorous Physical Activity on Stress

Cathartic Release Activities and Stress

OBJECTIVES

By the end of the chapter students will:

- Compare and contrast release as a coping strategy with the other strategies described in Part II.
- Define and give examples of moderate and vigorous physical activity.
- Describe the physiological and psychological stress-reducing properties of physical activity and exercise.
- Analyze their personal physical activity levels.
- Understand the benefits and basic movements of mild physical activities such as systematic muscle relaxation, yoga, and massage.
- Describe the stress-countering benefits of moderate and vigorous physical exercise and cathartic physical release activities.

Watch a group of children at play. Observe the way they run and jump, roll and dive, stretch and reach. There is a simple, almost primitive quality to their physical release. When they have pent up tension and energy they run and play, hoot and holler.

Now switch gears and think about adults who release the tension and energy of their stress by pleasuring each other. Think about these lovers, intent on pleasing each other, the way they tease and tantalize, stroke and move. Their movements, without pretense and oblivious to the outside world, are also a primitive and natural response to a stressful day. Thinking of these examples we are reminded that we are all born with the ability to be physical creatures and physical activity to purge the tension and by-products of stress.

For many, the benefits of physical release need no explanation. Physical activity, whether at work, at play in sports, or in bed, seems like a natural outlet for stress and tension. These people know intuitively that they simply feel better after they have released tension through physical activity. Their minds are clear, and their muscles have that tired but relaxed feeling. They feel content and at peace with themselves. Unfortunately, many others somehow lose the ability to be physical. Somewhere along the way they disconnect from their physical selves. They become dualistic, separating their minds from their bodies and trying to think their way out of everything. They forget about the primitive ability deep within all of us to bust loose and move.

This chapter will explore the relationship between exercise, fitness, and stress management. All these activities form the basis of the fourth line of defense against stress, release, which uses active physical involvement to cope with stress. The major portion of the chapter will concentrate on exercise and fitness as they relate to stress management. The remainder will focus on the physiological and psychological benefits of physical activity.

Kids don't need to be taught how to release stress. All they need is to be allowed to.

Fight-or-Flight Revisited

If you recall, the phrase *fight-or-flight* refers to the body's preparation to confront or run away from potential threats to one's well-being. In the days of the cave person, you either fought or ran away from the saber-toothed tiger when you discovered that you both inhabited the same cave. The earliest humans were equipped with an incredible self-defense system that activated when they perceived a threat to their well-being.

We are still equipped with this ability to mobilize strength and energy to fight or flee, but we rarely have the opportunity to use this energy when confronted by the less life-threatening but just as real modern threats to our well-being. The irate boss, traffic jam, inconsiderate sales clerk, and excessively demanding professor all are capable of invoking the same intense stress response as the saber-toothed tiger. Also unchanged is our ability to deal with these threats through physical release.

When we are under stress and our bodies have mobilized energy for the fight-or-flight response, we are prepared for action. We are in a state that calls for physical release. We have the energy, the muscles are tense and ready, and the mind is alert and willing. When we act, we use the by-products of this response (blood sugars, hormones, muscle tension, and high blood pressure) constructively. If we do not act and dissipate this stress response, it begins to exact a toll. In time, as we discussed in chapter 6, the response will lead to a decreased quality of life, inefficient functioning, illness, and breakdown.

However, instead of fighting or fleeing, we can release our pent-up energy by going for a run, swim, or bike ride or by making love. We can take a brisk walk or chop some firewood. We can dance or work out on exercise equipment. We can give a massage or please ourselves through masturbation. We can constructively use up the by-products of the stress response, or they can use us up.

The Health Benefits of Exercise and Physical Activity

As illustrated in fig. 10-1, there are many physiological and psychological benefits associated with **exercise** and physical activity. Lifestyle changes such as a healthful diet and regular exercise not only benefit an individual's fitness level but also are essential for effective stress management.

exercise a formal series of movements and activities designed to work targeted muscles, muscle groups, and body systems

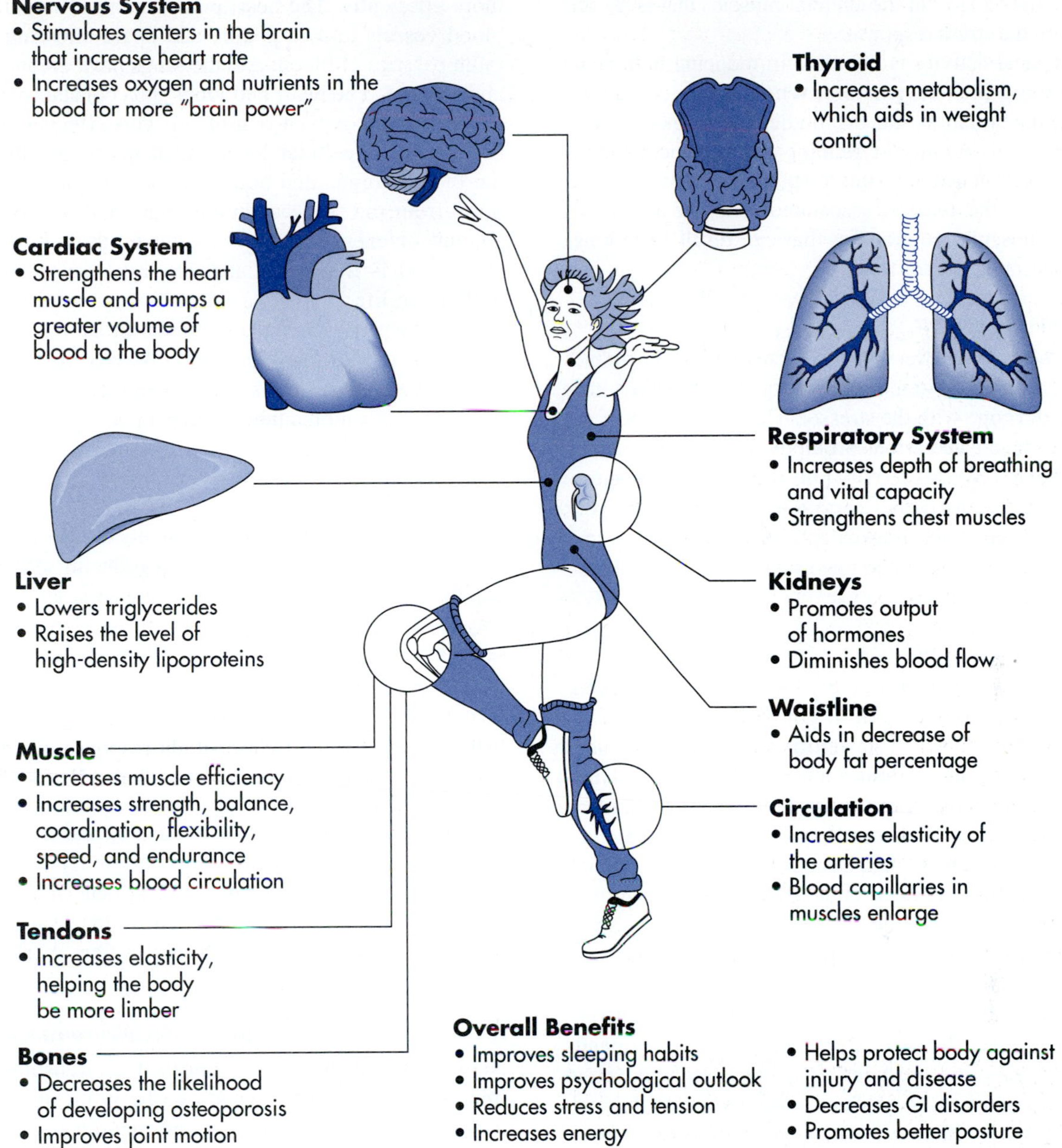

Figure 10-1
The benefits of exercise are plentiful. Exercise is a valuable way to release stress.

Physiological Benefits

There are many physiological benefits of physical activity and exercise that also have stress-reducing effects. Stretching and movement are natural reactions to the stress response that release muscle tension and use the energy produced by excess hormones in a productive way. Incorporating periods of physical activity and formal exercise into your daily routine is an excellent way to both get in shape and moderate the effects of stress.

Tension Reduction

During all forms of physical activity, muscles are contracted and relaxed. The intensity of this is determined by the level of resistance and demand put on the muscles, but in general, they are forced to perform work. Exercise, then, is an appropriate use of our skeletal muscles and does not result in chronic muscle tension. Physical activity

> **KEY TO UNDERSTANDING**
>
> Feeling tense and jumpy is the body's warning sign that it is time to get up and get moving. The best way to deal with the energy and muscle tension created by the stress response is to use it up through physical activity and exercise.

reduces the tension in the skeletal muscles that is associated with the stress response.

Physical activity is effective in reducing both acute and chronic **muscle tension.** When we are in a life-threatening situation and our bodies are primed to fight or flee, either fighting or running away reduces the intense muscle tension of this response. Likewise, action will reduce the tension associated with the low-level, chronic muscular contraction that can result from long-term, resistance-stage stress.

Hormone Utilization

When the body is stressed, it secretes various hormones into the circulation to mobilize energy to maintain homeostasis and cope with the stressor. These hormones, if not utilized, can create various problems, as was documented in chapter 6. Physical activity puts these hormones to use. Rather than allowing these hormones to wear down your immunity and place unusually high demands on your tissues, organs, and systems, you get rid of these chemicals during physical activity.

Fat/Cholesterol Utilization

During the stress response, the liver works overtime, converting its stored glycogen to glucose for fuel. In addition, it produces extra cholesterol, which normally is used to transport fats to the tissues where they are needed. Exercise helps remove the excess cholesterol produced by the liver during the stress response by triggering the production of extra high-density lipoproteins, which carry the cholesterol back to the liver, where it is broken down and secreted as **bile.**

If the body's available calories and stored glycogen reserves cannot meet the demand of the activity being performed, storage fat is broken down into glucose, which provides the needed energy. If energy demands are acute, as in the stress response, the body will turn to the protein in muscle tissue to meet its needs for fuel. This process is called **gluconeogenesis.** Exercise serves a valuable function in protecting muscle tissue from this process and ensuring that calorie needs are met by storage fat rather than lean tissue: exercise keeps muscles toned while burning extra calories. This is a benefit for those trying to lose weight as well as manage their stress.

Enhanced Cardiorespiratory Function

The heart, lungs, and circulatory system take part in all forms of exercise by pumping oxygen-rich blood to tissues and removing carbon dioxide and other wastes. It is during aerobic exercise, however, that the greatest cardiorespiratory effects are realized. The net cardiorespiratory effects of exercise are increased energy, greater endurance, increased mental alertness and acuity, improved mood, and decreased risk of cardiovascular disease.

In general, when the heart and lungs work together effectively, they transfer oxygen and carbon dioxide more efficiently. The heart pumps more efficiently; the blood vessels remain pliable and open, allowing maximum passage of blood; and the lungs have greater depth and volume. The heart and lungs thus constantly supply the body with oxygen-rich blood. This affects our functioning at the cellular level and helps us get the most out of each organ and body system. This affects everything from the way our brains think and reason to the amount of energy we have to get us through the day. Our mood is improved, and we have a more positive outlook on life.[3]

All these physiological benefits of exercise help us cope with stress more effectively. We have more energy on reserve and can think through things with a clearer brain that pays more attention to details.

Psychological Benefits

There are many psychological benefits of physical activity and exercise that also have stress-reducing effects. Engaging in physical activity and exercise is an excellent way to shift your attention off of your problems and onto something that is invigorating and fun. These periods of activity are like mini-vacations where you can get away from your problems and enjoy the sheer delights involved in using your body. There is one thing to be cautious about concerning exercise: Do not let it become a *source* of stress. To get the benefits of stress reduction from your physical activity, you must maintain a mental attitude that keeps your activities in the proper perspective. If you really want to become a competitive athlete in any sport, choose another type of physical activity to use as a stress-management technique (see Stress in Our World 10-1: "Ken and I").

Release of Neuropeptide and Amine Neurotransmitters

Neurotransmitters are chemicals that transmit nerve impulses across nerve synapses (the point at which a nervous impulse passes from one neuron to another). There are different types of neurotransmitters. **Neuropeptide neurotransmitters** are a type of neurotransmitter

muscle tension partial contractions of the skeletal muscles that are triggered during the stress response

bile a bitter, yellow-green fat emulsifier secreted by the liver

gluconeogenesis the physiological process of converting noncarbohydrate sources of energy into glucose

neurotransmitters chemicals that transmit nerve impulses across nerve synapses (the point at which a nervous impulse passes from one neuron to another)

neuropeptide neurotransmitters neurotransmitters, made from amino-acid chains produced in the brain and spinal cord

STRESS IN OUR WORLD 10-1

Ken and I

Ken is a fairly competitive guy. A frustrated high school athlete, Ken at 40 is still competing against everyone, all the time. He's so competitive, he would rather sacrifice a triple word space in a game of Scrabble than relinquish that tile to anyone.

I used to run with Ken. To me, running was a fun way to keep in shape. Being outside in all kinds of weather, listening to the sounds, and watching the horizon roll by as we ran along the path were terrific.

Then things changed. Running became a competition. We began to enter local middle-distance races. I thought we were both in it for the T-shirts. Boy, was I mistaken. Ken became a maniac. Each run had to have a purpose. We ran for either time or distance, always trying to do "better" than the last time. I began to focus less on the scenery and more on winning. It was beginning to become work.

I stopped running with Ken after a while. Actually, I stopped running for a while, period. It was no longer fun and had become a source of stress rather than a stress reliever. I feel bad about it now; it's as if I lost two friends, Ken and my running.

Has anything like this ever happened to you? Is something you truly enjoy beginning to turn into a source of stress? What did you do or can you do to prevent that from happening?

made from amino-acid chains produced in the brain and spinal cord. **Amine neurotransmitters** are a different type of neurotransmitter synthesized from amino-acid molecules and found in various regions of the brain that affect emotions among other activities. **Endorphins** are a subclass of neuropeptide neurotransmitters that act like opiates to block pain. Researchers have found that the pituitary glands of long-distance runners release extra amounts of endorphins during vigorous exercise.[16,49] **Serotonin, dopamine,** and **epinephrine** are types of amine neurotransmitters related to mood that are produced in the brain and other regions of the central nervous system.

All three act like antidepressants that elevate mood, increase energy, and create a mild euphoria. Low levels of serotonin and dopamine have been related to depression. Serotonin, dopamine, and epinephrine are also released by the body as a by-product of sustained physical activity.[16,49] These naturally occurring neurotransmitters act much like legal (available by prescription) and illegal painkillers and mood-enhancing drugs. The advantage of these substances, however, is that they are legal, you can produce them yourself through physical activity, and they have no harmful side effects.[21,28]

Enhanced Self-Esteem and Self-Image

Sticking to a fitness program requires self-discipline, hard work, delayed gratification, and self-control. These are important qualities that habitual exercisers share and that improve self-esteem and self-image. Studies have shown that exercise can improve one's self-esteem, self-reliance, and self-efficacy.[39] In a sense, exercisers are more hardy. Hardiness, as discussed in chapter 2, is related to reduced stress and a greater sense of being in control of life.

Increased Creativity and Concentration

Exercise provides a break from reality. During exercise, one can dissociate from reality, take one's mind off the task at hand, and take a "mini-vacation," as Mott[41] calls it. This break from reality also can provide an opportunity for creativity and a chance to explore options. Gondola[18] found that creative problem-solving abilities were improved by aerobic exercise. She found some improvement after just one exercise session.

Reduced Anxiety and Improved Outlook on Life

Ornstein and Sobel[42] report that exercise can also improve mood. They found that walking a mile or two, even at a mild to moderate pace, can substantially reduce an individual's anxiety level. Exercise can divert our attention away from our problems and to a more relaxing and positive focus.[44] Exercise also can serve as an outlet for relieving anger and anxiety in a positive, socially acceptable way.[49]

A key to using exercise as a stress-management technique is to incorporate a variety of different types of physical activities into your fitness plan. This gives you a variety of options as well as providing a reasonable level of fitness. For instance, you may want to play golf for relaxation even though you realize it offers very little, if any, cardiorespiratory exercise. Or you might take up running not so much because it relaxes you but because it is an efficient way to burn off those stress by-products of your fast-paced lifestyle.

THE EFFECTS OF PHYSICAL ACTIVITY ON STRESS

In the next section of this chapter we will discuss the effects of physical activity on stress. We will discuss mild,

amine neurotransmitters neurotransmitters, synthesized from amino-acid molecules, that are found in various regions of the brain that affect emotions among other activities

endorphins a subclass of neuropeptide neurotransmitters that acts like opiates to block pain

serotonin, dopamine, epinephrine amine neurotransmitters that act like antidepressants to enhance mood and trigger feelings of mild euphoria

DIVERSE PERSPECTIVES 10-1

Coffee, Chocolate, and Other Pseudostressors

Sympathomimetics, also known as pseudostressors, are chemical substances that stimulate the sympathetic nervous system. Some sympathomimetics can also activate the central nervous system. The effects of this nervous system activation include increased heart rate and blood pressure, through the release of epinephrine and epinepherine. Because these stress hormones are released as a by-product of the ingestion of sympathomimetics, they are known as "pseudo" stressors.[15] As we have mentioned countless times in this text, true stressors are things that you appraise as a threat and with which you are unable to cope. Unless your use of sympathomimetics results in such a threat-appraisal process, these substances continue to be pseudostressors.

The most common sympathomimetic is caffeine. A clinical dose of caffeine when it is prescribed as a drug or included in drug preparations is 200 mg. A five-ounce cup of coffee contains about 150 mg of caffeine and stays in the bloodstream about three hours. A lethal dose of caffeine is between 2,000 and 10,000 mg.[15]

The table lists and describes some of the more common sympathomimetic substances. Although typically not considered sympathomimetic agents, common herbal products such as MaHuang (a form of ephedra) are powerful stimulants that can cause irritability and anxiety and even trigger panic attacks. These herbs are often used in powerful and dangerous combinations and are commonly added to "weight-loss" and "energy" drinks and snacks. Because of this, they are included in the table.

Food Product	Sympathomimetic Agent	Concentration
Coffee	Caffeine	150 mg/cup
Tea	Caffeine	25–50 mg/cup
Cocoa	Caffeine	15 mg/5 oz
Soft drinks	Caffeine	30–65 mg/12 oz
Chocolate bar	Caffeine	40 mg/1 oz
Herbal teas	Guarana	Varies
	MaHuang	Varies
	Yohimbine	Varies
Energy drinks and bars	Cola	Varies
	Guarana	Varies
	MaHuang	Varies
	Ginseng	Varies
	Ginkgo biloba	Varies
Dietary aids	Ephedra	Varies
	Cola	Varies
	Guarana	Varies
	MaHuang	Varies
	Ginseng	Varies
	Ginkgo biloba	Varies
Over-the-counter drugs		
Anacin	Caffeine	32 mg/dose
Excedrin Extra	Caffeine	65 mg/dose
Midol	Caffeine	32 mg/dose
NoDoz	Caffeine	100 mg/dose
Stay Awake	Caffeine	250 mg/dose
TrimPlan Plus	Caffeine	200 mg/serving
Vivarin	Caffeine	200 mg/dose

Source: Everly, G.A. and Lating, J.M. *A clinical guide to the treatment of the human stress response.* (2nd ed.).[15]

moderate, and vigorous physical activity. Each has the ability to dissipate the muscle tension and circulating hormones that are a potentially harmful by-product of the stress response. As we mentioned in chapter 6, the muscle tension associated with the stress response is the result of partially contracted smooth, skeletal, and cardiac muscle tissue. Using physical activity to stretch, massage, and fully contract and relax muscle tissue helps us release this tension before it can continue to build, resulting in muscle pain and spasms. The hormones (sugars and salts) released during the stress response provide extra energy and increase fluid buildup and blood pressure. This can make us feel on edge and make it difficult to perform a variety of activities ranging from thinking clearly to sleeping soundly. Daily periods of physical activity can use up this energy productively, improving the efficiency of our wakeful hours and sleep.

Mild, Moderate, and Vigorous Physical Activity

One way to categorize physical activity is by the type and amount of energy they use. All types of activities, even sitting quietly or sleeping, use energy. Our bodies constantly produce and use energy. We obtain energy from the carbohydrates, fats, and protein in the food we eat. Converting these nutrients into energy occurs in the **cytoplasm** of our cells and is used to fuel all of our activities. Energy in the cells is produced through both *aerobic* **(citric acid cycle)** and *anerobic* **(glycolosis)**

cytoplasm all of the substances of the cell, other than the nucleus, combined

citric acid cycle the aerobic production of energy within cells

glycolosis the anerobic production of energy within cells processes. Carbohydrates and fat can be metabolized either aerobically or anerobically. Fats can only be utilized through aerobic energy production.

Aerobic versus Anaerobic Exercise

The amount of oxygen available to cells during physical activity and exercise influences the proportions of fat and carbohydrate that will be used for energy production. Energy needed to supply short-term, intensive bursts of activity is produced anaerobically. This type of **anaerobic exercise** is explosive, usually involves maximum effort, and lasts no longer than about ninety seconds. Power lifting and sprints (running, swimming, or cycling) are examples of this type of activity. This type of activity leaves you gasping for air because that is exactly what happens; it starves your cells of oxygen because it occurs in the absence of oxygen. Anaerobic exercise is fueled primarily by carbohydrates. This is why you do not burn fat while exercising in short, demanding bursts.[43] Activities that extend beyond four minutes of continuous moderate performance produce energy aerobically, with oxygen. Running, cycling, step aerobics, and swimming laps carried on at a comfortable pace that allows you to carry on a conversation are four examples of **aerobic exercise.** Fat is the main fuel utilized during aerobic activity along with lesser amounts of carbohydrates.[12] Combined energy production occurs with activities that are ninety seconds to four minutes in duration and produce energy through a combination of aerobic and anaerobic processes. Tennis, baseball, and touch football are examples of activities that incorporate intermittent bursts of high-intensity activity.

Adjusting the Level of Physical Activity

Most of the activities we just discussed were designed to be performed at a very mild intensity. In the next two sections of this chapter we will differentiate between moderate and vigorous physical activity and exercise. It is relatively easy to moderate the level of most forms of physical activity and exercise by changing their frequency, intensity, or time. This is also known as the acronym *FIT* (stands for *f*requency, *i*ntensity, and *t*ime). *Frequency* refers to how often a person works out. Frequency is typically measured in days. *Intensity* refers to the level of demand a workout places on the muscles, muscle groups, and body systems affected. *Time* refers to the duration of the workout. Training time is typically measured in minutes. Depending upon what your activity and exercise goals are, you can manipulate any or all of the three variables to increase or decrease the intensity of the activity. There are countless training materials available that use these three variables to help people begin formal exercise programs and systematically and safely increase their intensity to build fitness (see Stress Buster Tips: "Walk/Run Your Way to Cardiorespiratory Fitness").

Running is a good form of aerobic exercise.

The Effects of Mild Physical Activity on Stress

In the next section of this chapter we will discuss several classic stress management techniques that involve mild physical activity to release the muscle tension associated with stress. While they all share the common thread of using mild physical activity to release tension, each goes about it in a slightly different way. While you can learn and practice these activities on your own, many people find taking classes with others to be quite enjoyable.

Systematic Muscle Relaxation

As was described earlier, acute and chronic muscle tension is a common by-product of the stress response. In many cases we do not realize that we are tense until our bodies send us warning signs in the form of pain, tightness, and reduced functioning. Practicing some form of muscle relaxation or stretching on a regular basis is key in the prevention of this tension.

Systematic muscle relaxation is a technique developed by Edmund Jacobson,[23] a Chicago physician. His

anaerobic exercise explosive activity which occurs in the absence of oxygen; usually involves maximum effort and lasts no longer than 90 seconds

aerobic excercise exercise in which the amount of oxygen taken into the lungs is equal to or slightly more than that required to meet the body's energy demands

Stress Buster Tips

Walk/Run Your Way to Cardiorespiratory Fitness

Dr. Kenneth Cooper (1982) is the father of aerobic training. His "10-Week Jogging/Running Program" is a perfect illustration of how to make an activity more vigorous by manipulating its frequency, intensity, and time. By increasing these variables in the ten-week program below, you can slowly adjust to increasing levels of demand and develop higher-level cardiorespiratory fitness.

Cooper's Jogging/Running 10-Week Program

Week	Activity	Distance (miles)	Time Goal	Freq/Wk	Points/Wk
		Under 30 Years of Age			
1	walk	2.0	32:00	3	13.5
2	walk	3.0	48:00	3	21.7
3	walk/jog	2.0	26:00	4	24.9
4	walk/jog	2.0	24:00	4	28.0
5	jog	2.0	22:00	4	31.6
6*	jog	2.0	20:00	4	36.0
7	jog	2.5	25:00	4	46.0
8	jog	2.5	23:00	4	49.5
9	jog	3.0	30:00	4	56.0
10	jog	3.0	27:00	4	61.3
		30–49 Years of Age			
1	walk	2.0	34:00	3	12.2
2	walk	2.5	42:00	3	16.3
3	walk	3.0	50:00	3	20.4
4	walk/jog	2.0	25:00	4	26.4
5	walk/jog	2.0	24:00	4	28.0
6	jog	2.0	22:00	4	31.6
7†	jog	2.0	20:00	4	36.0
8	jog	2.5	26:00	4	43.7
9	jog	2.5	25:00	4	46.0
10	jog	3.0	31:00	4	53.7
11	jog	3.0	29:00	4	57.6
12	jog	3.0	27:00	4	61.3

*By the sixth week, a minimum aerobic fitness level has been reached (36 aerobic points per week), but it is suggested that a higher level of fitness be achieved. By the tenth week of the program, a total of 61 points per week is being earned, consistent with the excellent category or aerobic fitness.

†By the seventh week, a minimum aerobic fitness level has been reached (36 aerobic points per week), but it is suggested that a higher level of fitness be achieved. By the twelfth week of the program, a total of 61 points per week is being earned, consistent with the excellent category or aerobic fitness.

early work was with presurgical hospital patients. He noticed that patients awaiting surgery seemed stressed and had high levels of muscular tension, particularly in the neck and back. Jacobson felt that if he could help his patients relieve tension, it might reduce some of their suffering and facilitate their recovery. When he made patients aware of their tension and asked them to relax, it did not work; they needed more help in relaxing their muscles.

Jacobson developed systematic muscle relaxation as a technique to help patients relax their muscles before surgery to enhance their response to treatment and care. Jacobson found that with practice, patients could learn to relax their skeletal muscles whenever they wanted to. The technique not only worked in reducing skeletal muscle tension, it also had a calming effect on the mind and on the activity of internal organs. Once the perception of muscle tension was removed, the mind and the internal organs relaxed.

Jacobson also found that his technique could be used to prevent muscle tension from building up. Systematic muscle relaxation has been found to be effective in treating insomnia, nervous anxiety, depression, hypochondria, hypertension, colitis, and tension headaches.[22]

In its most basic use, systematic muscle relaxation helps people know what relaxed muscles and bodies feel like. By alternating the contraction and relaxation of muscles, students learn the difference between tension and relaxation. This can be used as a preventive approach to tension-related problems in the muscles by helping students become aware of stress before it results in muscular disorders.[34,35]

People with a history of low back pain, disc or other spinal problems, and musculoskeletal disorders should speak to their physicians before engaging in these exercises. All the exercises should be carried out as vigorously as possible to the point of feeling uncomfortable but short of pain.[35]

Instructions for Systematic Muscle Relaxation

1. Find a quiet place away from others.
2. Minimize distractions by closing the door and turning off the radio, television, and telephone.
3. Loosen any tight clothing and remove jewelry and shoes.
4. Lie on your back with your arms at your sides.
5. Let your legs assume a gentle flex, with your knees slightly bent and falling outward.
6. Your body should not need support to hold this position, but if it does, you may use a small pillow under the knees and/or the small of the back. (See fig. 10-2.)

Feet and Calves

1. Point the toes of both feet back toward your face; this is similar to removing your foot from the gas pedal (fig. 10-3).
2. Hold for a few seconds and then gradually let your feet return to their normal resting position.
3. Repeat this activity.
4. Point the toes of both feet away from your face, pushing them down toward the floor.
5. Hold for a few seconds, then gradually let your feet return to their normal resting position.
6. Repeat this activity.

Spine

1. Straighten your legs, touching your feet together, and push down on the floor with the bottoms of your legs and knees. (Be sure to take your pillow out if you have one under your knees.)
2. Hold for a few seconds and then gently let your knees pop up and your legs return to their normal resting position.
3. Repeat this activity.
4. Tense all your stomach muscles (pull them in as if you were preparing to get punched in the stomach).
5. Hold them tightly for a few seconds and then let your stomach muscles return to their normal resting position.
6. Repeat this activity.
7. Tightly clench the muscles in your buttocks and anus. If you are doing this correctly, your groin and genitals should push up.
8. Hold for a few seconds and then return to your normal resting position.
9. Repeat this activity.
10. Grasp your elbows with your hands and lift your arms over your head.
11. As you do this, tilt your head to the rear and arch your back as far as it will go (fig. 10-4).
12. Hold for a few seconds and then gently let your head fall forward and your spine straighten. Return your arms to their resting position on your abdomen.
13. Repeat this activity.

Shoulders

1. Shrug your shoulders up toward your ears; try to touch your ears with your shoulder blades (fig. 10-5).
2. Slowly let your shoulders return to their normal resting position.
3. Repeat this activity.
4. Move your arms so that your palms are pressing inward on the sides of your legs. Press as hard as you can against the sides of your legs.

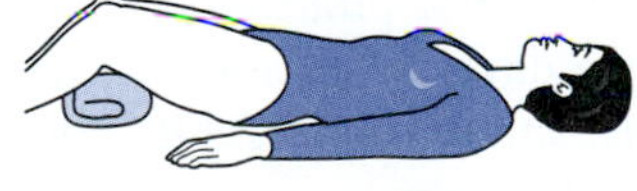

Figure 10-2
Starting position

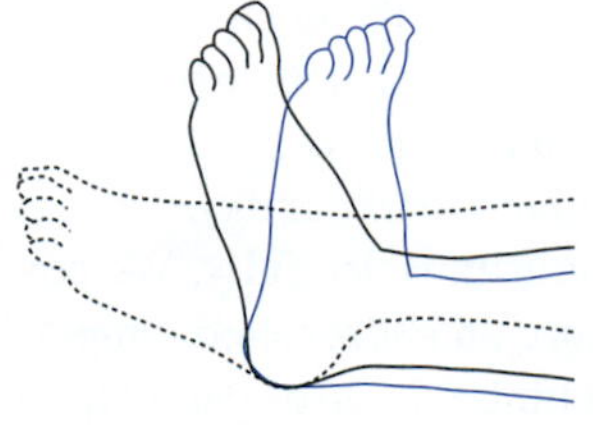

Figure 10-3
Feet/calves

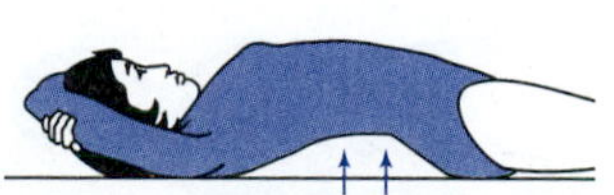

Figure 10-4
Spine

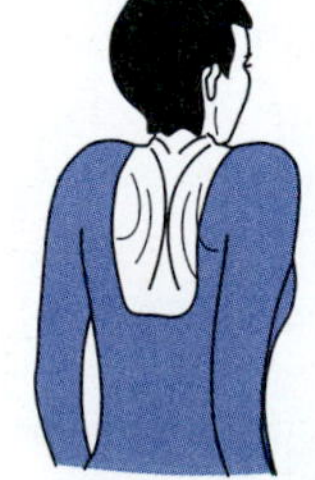

Figure 10-5
Shoulders

KEY TO UNDERSTANDING

Stretching and relaxation help prevent muscle pain, tightness, and reduced functioning.

5. Hold this for a few seconds and then let your arms return to their normal resting position.
6. Repeat this activity.

Hands and Arms

1. Clench both of your hands into tight fists (fig. 10-6).
2. Hold for a few seconds and then slowly let your hands return to their normal resting position.
3. Repeat this activity.
4. Clench both of your fists and curl your arms tightly so that your hands press up against your shoulders.
5. Hold for a few seconds and then relax and let your arms return to their normal resting position.

Head and Neck

1. Bend your head forward, trying to touch your chest with your chin. Keep your shoulders flat against the floor while you are attempting this.
2. Hold this position for a few seconds and then gently let your head fall backward to its normal resting position.
3. Repeat this activity.
4. Tilt your head backward, trying to touch your nose to the wall behind you. Keep your shoulders on the floor.
5. Hold this for a few seconds and then gently let your chin fall forward, returning your head to its normal resting position.
6. Repeat this activity.
7. Gently turn your head as far as it will go to the right side; try to touch your cheek to the floor (fig. 10-7a).

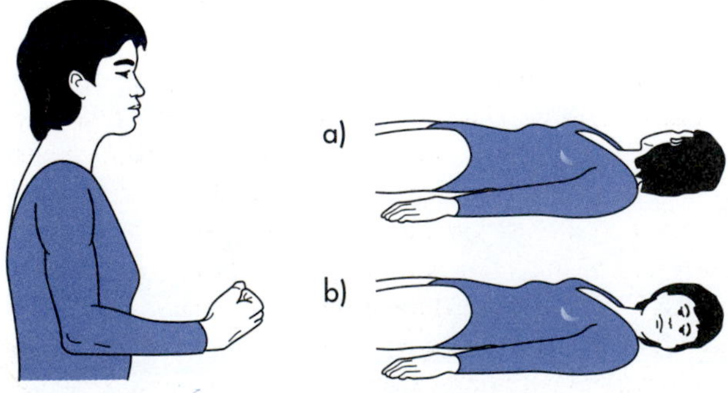

Figure 10-6
Hands and arms

Figure 10-7
Head and neck

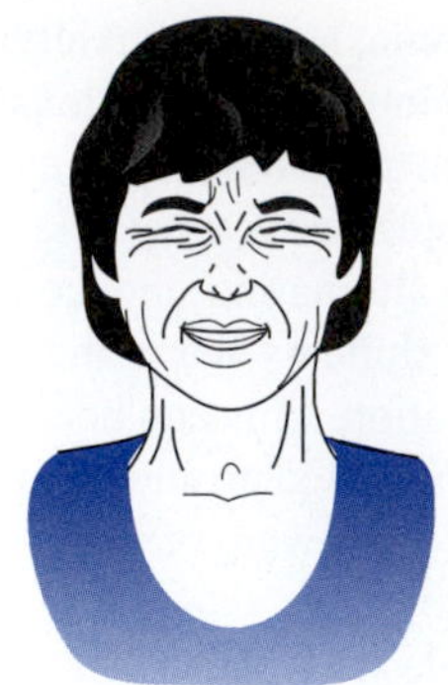

Figure 10-8
Face

8. Hold this position for a few seconds and then gently return your head to its normal resting position.
9. Repeat this activity.
10. Gently turn your head to the left side as far as it will go; try to touch your cheek to the floor (fig. 10-7b).
11. Hold this position for a few seconds and then gently return your head to its normal resting position.

Face

1. Scrunch up your face into the tightest, funniest expression you can make (fig. 10-8).
2. Hold this for a few seconds and let your face return to its normal resting position.
3. Repeat this activity.
4. Open your mouth and eyes as wide as they will go.
5. Hold this position for a few seconds and then return to your normal resting position.
6. Repeat this activity.

With practice these activities will take less time to perform. Even though they seem simple, try to perform them exactly as directed to minimize any risk of injury and maximize their effectiveness. A benefit of performing these relaxation activities is that they promote muscle awareness and connect you to the inner power of these muscles and their intended motions.

Yoga and Stretching

It is not surprising that most of us start the day with a good stretch upon awakening. It is a natural reaction to reduce the muscle tension associated with lying in one position for a prolonged period. You probably also find yourself stretching during the day when you have spent too long hunched over a desk, sitting too long at the computer terminal, or standing in one spot.

Common results of our modern sedentary lifestyle are chronically shortened muscles, tendons, and ligaments. As was discussed in chapter 6, the negative health effects of chronically shortened muscles include restricted range of motion, fatigue, pain, and spasms.

Most of us do not, as a regular part of our day, perform work that forces us to stretch our muscles fully. We perform a series of tasks that require an abbreviated range of motion. Hatha yoga and stretching exercises can help us reduce stress by reducing muscle tension and the consequent stress messages that tense muscles send to the brain.

Yoga and Static Stretching The word *yoga* is derived from the Sanskrit (the ancient literary language of India) root word meaning "to yoke or join." Yoga is an ancient Hindu ascetic philosophy that includes mental, physical, social, and spiritual components. Traditional yoga instruction involved a master teacher who passed his teachings on to his disciples through an integrated eightfold process called *asthanagayoga*.[57] The eightfold process includes:

1. Yama—rules and restraints for productive living in society, such as being truthful
2. Niyama—self-rules governing cleanliness and personal contentment
3. Asaana—physical exercises called *postures*
4. Pranayama—deep-breathing training
5. Pratihara—freeing the mind from the senses
6. Dharana—focused concentration on an object
7. Dhyana—meditation
8. Samadhi—cosmic meditation

Yoga, as initially intended, was a way of life and a way of being. As students progressed through the eight stages of training, they would liberate and control their life force, which was believed to be located in the spinal cord and vital organs.

There are several different types of yoga, each one focusing on different aspects of the asthanagayoga. *Bhakti yoga* (the path of devotion), *gyana yoga* (the path of knowledge), and *raja yoga* (the path of wisdom, self-realization, and enlightenment) are examples.[57]

Hatha is a type of yoga that employs various stretching exercises called postures. They are designed to reduce muscle tension and facilitate a relaxed state of being that is conducive to meditation. However, one does not need to practice meditation to enjoy the benefits of tension reduction that can be attained through hatha yoga exercises.[31]

The type of stretching most similar to that used in hatha yoga is static stretching. Static stretching involves passively stretching a specific muscle by putting it into a maximally stretched state and holding it for an extended period. Recommendations for the length of holding time range from six to sixty seconds. Thirty seconds is most often recommended as the optimal time to build up to.[44]

Many people interested in stretching perform hatha yoga postures without realizing they are doing so. Modern static stretching programs, designed to increase flexibility, draw many of their stretches from hatha yoga postures.[17] Our current interest in stretching has evolved in part from the desire to achieve maximum flexibility for athletic purposes. *Flexibility* can best be defined as the ability of a joint to move through its full range of motion.[51] Flexibility has long been recognized as an essential component of fitness. Some athletic activities, such as gymnastics, ballet, and diving, require maximum flexibility. Athletes in other sports can also benefit from increased flexibility because it is related to a variety of other qualities, including stride length, balance, and reaction time.[3,51]

Interest in stretching spread from the athletic community to the general public during the fitness movement of the 1980s and 1990s. People realized that having more flexible joints that could move easily and smoothly through their full range of motion was essential to healthy living.[6]

Yoga and stretching work by taking advantage of the elastic properties of muscles and connective tissue such as ligaments and the tissue that encapsulates joints. Through systematic stretching of muscles and tissue, it is possible to lengthen muscles and loosen the connective tissue. This increases a joint's range of motion. An additional advantage of stretching and yoga is the reduction of muscle tension. Through stretching, tension that has built up in immobile or braced muscles and joints is released.

KEY TO UNDERSTANDING

Increased awareness of the functioning and power of your muscles is a side benefit of systematic muscle relaxation.

Preparation for Yoga and Stretching Yoga and stretching exercises are designed to be performed slowly and gently; therefore, you should not rush. You are not trying to develop cardiovascular fitness. Never force yourself beyond the point of pain. The old maxim "no pain, no gain" does not hold true in the practice of yoga, static stretching, or any physical activity. Always stretch to the point of tension (just short of but never to the point of pain) and then hold that position. Initially, hold the stretch for a count of ten seconds. In time you will find that you can stretch farther and hold it longer. Do not rush this development. It took you a lifetime to get this tight. It will take a few months to loosen up. You may also find that because of your body type you are never able to stretch as far as others can. This is normal. A key to success is to try to stretch to your personal limit.

Do not bounce when you stretch and hold. This is called ballistic stretching. Ballistic stretching employs rapid and forceful bouncing movements designed to push resistant muscle tissue beyond its normal stretching point. These quick, forceful movements have been shown to be effective in stretching, but they can also injure your muscles, tendons, and ligaments. If the forces generated by the jerks, bounces, and pulls are greater than the tissue's ability to extend, injury may result.[51] Ballistic stretching can also be counterproductive because when you bounce, your muscles are forced to pull against themselves. The brain, sensing the bounces, sends a message to the muscles to contract rather than lengthen.[3]

KEY TO UNDERSTANDING

Stretch to your personal best.

When you are stretching and performing yoga, always breathe normally. Do not hold your breath and never lock your joints fully when extending your arms or legs. You should keep your knees and elbows slightly bent.

Beginners are advised to take an introductory class with a certified yoga instructor to learn correct body positioning.

A Simple, Full-Body Static Stretching and Hatha Yoga Routine The following routine consists of ten beginner-level stretches. It combines exercises taken from modern static stretching with asanas, or postures derived from hatha yoga. This simple routine is designed to stretch every part of the body gently. Take your time when performing the exercises and postures. Try to maintain good form and focus on the feelings associated with each activity. You may find it beneficial to practice in front of a mirror so that you can adjust your form to match the diagrams in the book. With practice you will be able to perform this routine in less than thirty minutes.

Sky Reach

This stretch is derived from the yoga asana Tadasana, or the mountain pose. The major difference is that the sky reach (fig. 10-9a) starts with your feet shoulder width apart and ends with your upraised hands also shoulder width apart. The mountain pose (fig. 10-9b) begins with your feet together and finishes with your palms touching.[1]

1. Stand with your feet shoulder width apart, hands resting at your sides.
2. Slowly reach for the sky, trying to touch the clouds (or the ceiling if you are inside).
3. As you reach, make sure to stretch your wrists, elbows, and shoulders and all your fingers. Do not raise up on your toes.
4. When you reach your maximum stretch, hold for a count of ten seconds.

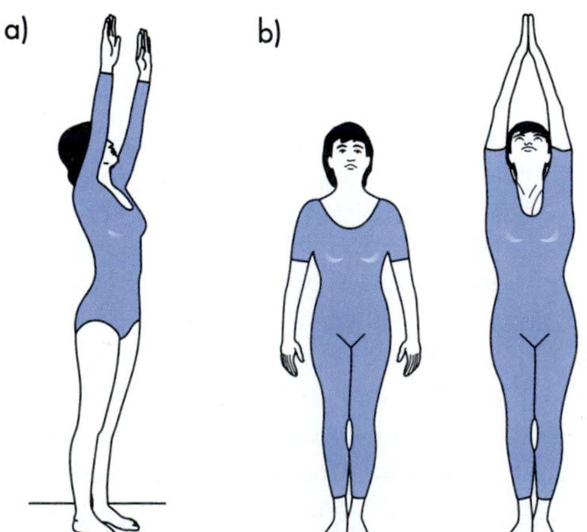

Figure 10-9
a. Sky reach; b. Mountain pose

Toe Touch

This stretch is the same as the yoga asana Uttanasana, commonly referred to as the standing forward bend. Although this exercise is designed to have you ultimately touch your toes, you will probably have to begin by aiming for your knees, then your shins, and in time your feet. Do not cheat by bending your knees too much. In time you will reach your toes. This posture will stretch your arms, hands, wrists, fingers, legs, neck, and back.

1. Stand with your feet shoulder width apart.
2. Slowly bend from the waist, trying to touch your knees with your hands.
3. Let your head fall forward, nestling close to your thighs if possible. Try to keep your neck and head loose.
4. Bend your knees slightly.
5. When you reach your maximum stretch, hold for a count of ten seconds.
6. Slowly return to the upright position.
7. Repeat this twice more, reaching for your shins and finally your toes (fig. 10-10).

Achilles Stretch

This posture is designed to stretch the Achilles tendons and calf muscles.

1. Stand facing the wall, feet shoulder width apart, arm's length away.
2. Keeping both heels on the ground, knees slightly bent, and feet flat, lean into the wall, touching it gently, using your hands and arms to balance.
3. Keep leaning into the wall until you reach your maximum stretch. You will feel pressure in your calves and Achilles tendons.
4. Hold for a count of ten seconds.
5. Repeat twice more (fig. 10-11).

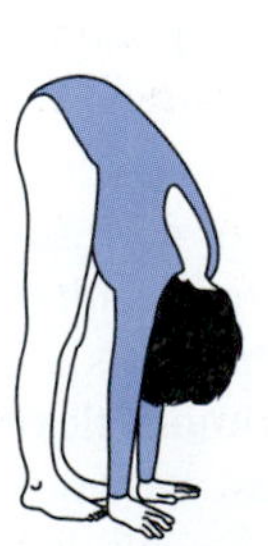

Figure 10-10
Toe touch

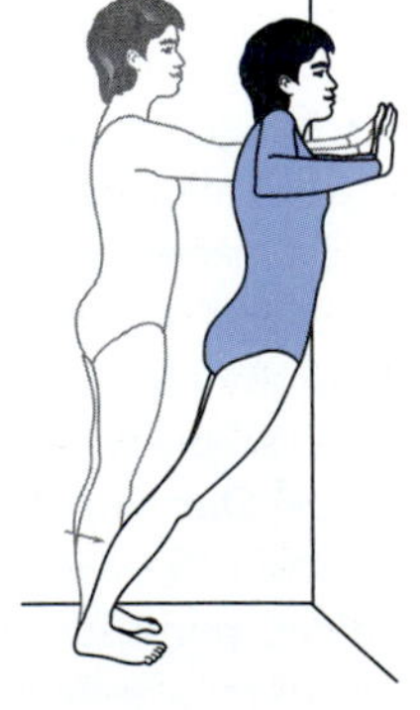

Figure 10-11
Achilles/calf stretch

Figure 10-12 **Side bends**

Caution: Side bends should not be performed by persons with back problems. A modified reach directly up to the ceiling with a slight slant would be safer. Check with your doctor before performing this stretch.

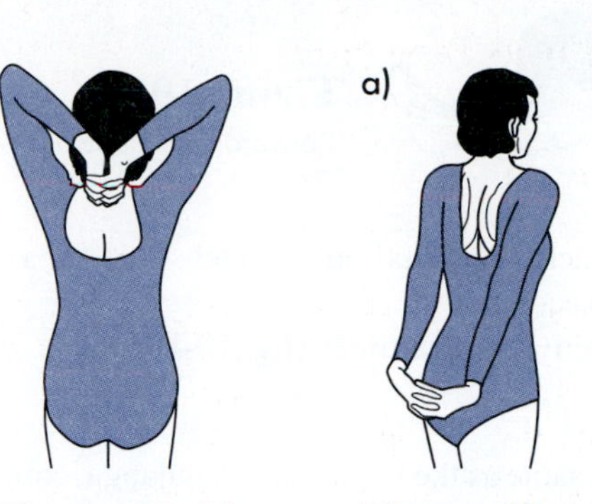

Figure 10-13

Back reach

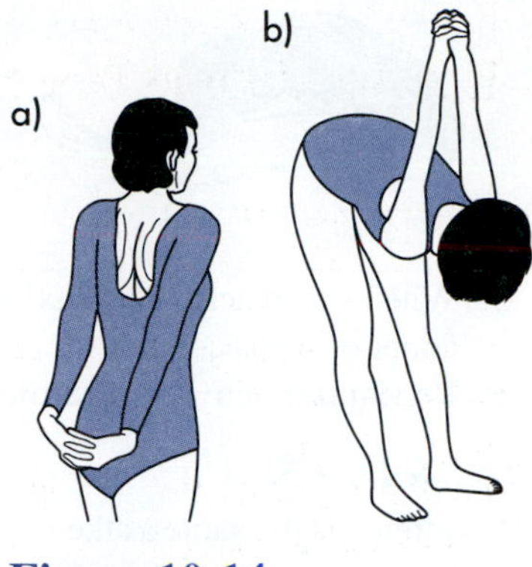

Figure 10-14

a. Shoulder roll; b. End position

Standing Side Trunk Bends

These bends are designed to stretch your hips, side abdominals, ribs, and shoulders.

1. Stand with your feet flat and shoulder width apart, arms at your sides.
2. Slowly raise your arms overhead, palms facing forward.
3. Keeping your feet flat and your hips rigid, bend as far as you can to the right.
4. Stretch your arms out, keeping your elbows slightly bent as you bend to the side.
5. Let your head follow gracefully, trying to keep your neck and head loose.
6. When you reach your maximum stretch, hold for a count of ten seconds.
7. Slowly return to the starting position.
8. Repeat this posture, stretching this time to the left side.
9. Do three stretches to each side (fig. 10-12).

Back Reach

This posture can be done either seated or standing and is designed to stretch the back, arms, and shoulders.

1. Either standing or sitting with your back straight, feet shoulder width apart, clasp your hands together and extend your arms over your head.
2. Keeping your fingers intertwined, bend from the elbows and touch the base of your neck with your fists.
3. As you are doing this, push your arms and elbows back.
4. When you reach your maximum stretch, hold for a count of ten seconds.
5. Repeat three times (fig. 10-13).

Shoulder Roll

This stretch is the same as the yoga asana Araha Chakrasana, commonly referred to as the fist over head posture. This posture is designed to stretch your shoulders, back, arms, and neck.

1. Stand straight with your feet flat and shoulder width apart.
2. Clasp your hands together into a fist behind your back (fig. 10-14a).
3. Keeping your hands clasped and feet flat, lift your arms up toward your shoulders.
4. At the same time you are doing this, bend forward from the waist as far as possible, slowly raising your hands over your head.
5. Keep your knees slightly bent when you are doing this and try to tuck your chin against your chest (fig. 10-14b).
6. When you reach your maximum stretch, hold for a count of ten seconds.
7. Repeat this exercise three times.

Forward Back Stretch

This stretch is the same as the yoga asana Paschimottasana, commonly referred to as the seated forward bend or sit and reach posture. This posture is designed to stretch your back, neck, arms, and legs. Ultimately, you will be trying to reach and hold your ankles. Do this in stages, however, aiming first for the knees, then the shins, and finally the ankles.

1. Sit on the floor with your legs stretched out in front of you, feet together, hands at your sides.
2. Keeping the backs of your legs on the ground as much as possible and your knees slightly bent, slowly bend forward, sliding your palms along the sides of your legs until you reach your knees.
3. As you reach forward, you can extend your elbows outward.
4. Try to keep your chin tucked in as close to your chest as possible for a maximum stretch.

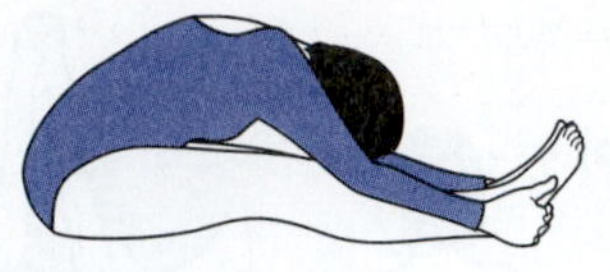

Figure 10-15
Forward back stretch

5. When you reach your maximum stretch, hold for a count of ten seconds.
6. Repeat this activity three times (fig. 10-15).

Reverse Back Stretch

This stretch is the same as the yoga asana Bhujanga, commonly known as the cobra. *Bhujanga* means "serpent" in sanskrit. If it is done properly, with your back arched and your head up, you should resemble a cobra ready to strike. This posture is designed to stretch your spine in the opposite direction. It will also stretch your arms, chest, neck, and shoulders. Ultimately, you will be fully extending your arms for maximum stretching of your spine. You will start, however, by rising to your elbows, eventually lifting them off the floor.

1. Lie on your stomach, feet together, hands to your side.
2. Bring your hands under your shoulders, palms flat on the ground, fingers pointing forward (similar to getting ready to do a push-up).
3. Slowly push your torso off the floor, arching your back.
4. Keep your forearms and elbows on the floor as you arch and let your head stretch backward, chin trying to touch the ceiling.
5. Stretch until you reach your maximum stretch and then hold for a count of ten seconds.
6. If you feel no pain, on the next repetition, try to arch farther by straightening your arms and letting your elbows come off the floor.
7. Repeat this posture three times (fig. 10-16).

Hurdler's Stretch

This stretch, also known as the one-legged seated forward bend, is a variation of the two-legged seated forward bend Paschimottanasana. This is a one-legged variation of the forward back stretch that puts additional emphasis on stretching the quadriceps (front of the thighs) and hamstrings (back of the legs), as well as the knees and groin.

1. Sit on the floor with your legs together.
2. Tuck one leg into your groin as illustrated in fig. 10-17.
3. Keep the other leg extended, knee slightly bent.

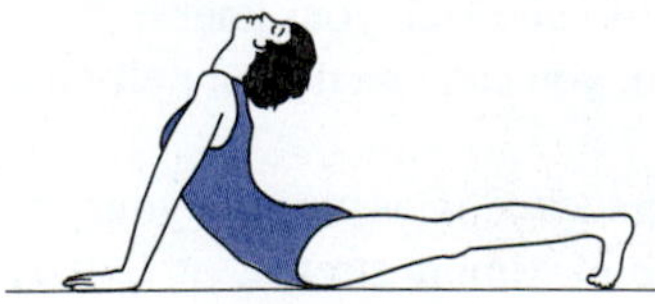

Figure 10-16
Reverse back stretch

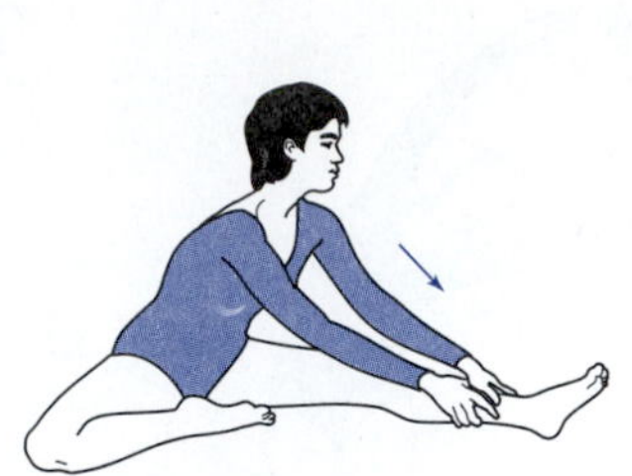

Figure 10-17
Hurdler's stretch

Figure 10-18
Groin stretch

4. Keeping the knee of the tucked leg as close to the ground as possible, tuck your chin and slowly bend your head forward toward your knee.
5. Stretch as close to your knee as possible and then hold for a count of ten seconds.
6. Do this three times and then switch to your other leg.

Groin Stretch

This stretch is the same as the yoga asana Baddha Konasana, commonly known as the butterfly pose. As the title indicates, this posture is intended to stretch the muscles of the groin.

1. Sit on the floor with your back straight, heels together, and knees bent pointing out to the side.
2. Keeping your head up, gently push down on your knees, forcing them closer to the floor.
3. Stretch until you reach your maximum stretch in the groin and then hold for a count of ten seconds.
4. Repeat this three times (fig. 10-18).

T'ai Chi Ch'uan

The purpose of this section of the chapter is not to teach you t'ai chi ch'uan; it takes years of study and practice to master this art. Rather, this section is designed to introduce the underlying concepts associated with t'ai chi ch'uan and illustrate its value as a stress-management technique.

T'ai chi ch'uan is a form of self-defense that was developed in China and dates back several thousands of years. It is a unique blend of physical movement and philosophical outlook. The physical movements of t'ai chi ch'uan (more than 100 exercises) are fluid, emphasizing the philosophical belief of flowing or harmonizing with one's opposition rather than fighting against it. T'ai chi ch'uan has adopted many of its philosophical underpinnings from **Taoism,** which emphasizes the balance of opposing forces in life.

Taoism Chinese philosophy of life and religion, founded by Lao Tzu, that emphasizes the duality of life and opposing forces

The blending of opposing forces, referred to as yin and yang, characterizes the Taoist philosophy of life.[6] Yin can be described as a negative force, and yang as a positive one. Crompton[11] uses an analogy of a battery and flashlight to describe how yin and yang can work together or against each other. When the flashlight is switched on, the electrical current flows from one pole of the battery to the other, resulting in the creation and harnessing of the energy. As with the flashlight, when we are in balance, our yin and yang are working in harmony; they serve as a source of energy and help light the way through the path of life. Taoism explores this essential duality of life and teaches us how to flow with it rather than against it. This "going with the flow" is one of the characteristics that sets t'ai chi ch'uan apart from many other forms of self-defense.

Chi is a Chinese word used to describe the life force, or subtle energy, that flows throughout the body. The Chinese believe that health involves the continual, unobstructed flow of chi. When our yin and yang are balanced, we are healthy and experience an unobstructed flow of chi. Disease and illness are not caused by pathogens per se but rather by a restriction or obstruction of the flow of chi. We are constantly surrounded by viruses, bacteria, and other disease-causing pathogens. What allows these and other invaders to enter and cause disease is a breakdown in the flow of life-giving energy. **Acupuncture** and yoga are also practices that are believed to unblock constriction of the free flow of energy.[14]

T'ai Chi Ch'uan and Stress Management T'ai chi ch'uan, also referred to as *moving meditation,* teaches people to remain calm and centered against the forces of opposition. It emphasizes conserving energy, remaining balanced, and using rather than fighting the forces of opposition. It is not a violent exercise but an exercise in maintaining balance in life.[48]

In a sense, t'ai chi ch'uan teaches people how to maintain homeostasis in the face of stressors. The mental (staying calm, not giving into fear, harmonizing with the opposition) blends with the physical (keeping a low center of gravity, maintaining balance, using your opponent's energy to conserve your own) in seeking to maintain equilibrium.[24,29]

Learning t'ai chi ch'uan involves practicing and perfecting its many different exercises. The movements of t'ai chi ch'uan are graceful and continuous and emphasize even, effortless, coordinated breathing. Seward[48] outlines six underlying concepts of t'ai chi ch'uan that illustrate some of its stress-reducing qualities:

1. Effortless, deep breathing—Breathing should be natural, and in time students learn to coordinate breathing with the specific exercises. Students get in touch with their breathing, making sure it comes from the abdomen rather than the chest.
2. Tension reduction—All exercises are performed gracefully. Students are taught to look for signs of tension that may inhibit the flow of energy.
3. A perpendicular stance—Students are taught to maintain their balance as they move from position to position, keeping the spinal column straight.
4. A low center of gravity—Keeping centered has a lot to do with maintaining a stable base, a lower center of gravity.
5. An even speed—Keep movements continuous and even flowing, conserving energy by avoiding sudden, jerky movements.
6. Mind/body integration—T'ai chi ch'uan is referred to as moving meditation because the student is instructed to concentrate on the body and visualize its movements. Students are instructed to get back to focusing on their movements when their minds stray.

These six underlying concepts illustrate how t'ai chi ch'uan blends strategies we have already discussed (deep breathing, visualization, meditation, and muscle relaxation) with a philosophy of life that is flexible and emphasizes the need to adapt to change rather than fight it.

Massage

You no doubt have experienced the "electrifying" tingling sensations, physical pleasure, and muscular relaxation associated with a good back rub or full-body massage. The relaxation benefits of massage affect not only the person being massaged but also the masseur or masseuse. Giving a massage requires slowing down and becoming fully involved in the process. The person giving the massage must clear his or her head and focus on properly stroking and kneading the skin and muscles of the receiver. The feel of warm human flesh and the knowledge that you are pleasing someone else are also rewarding and relaxing for the masseur. Massage has two major effects: It relieves muscle tension, and it stimulates circulation to the tissues and muscles. This is why you feel warm and relaxed after a massage.[7,46,51]

Massage is used in a variety of clinical and therapeutic settings. Hospitals, clinics, and other medical centers use it to help relax patients, increase circulation to injured parts of the body, and speed the healing process. Massage is especially effective in improving the circulation of bedridden patients who are unable to move freely. Lack of movement and being forced to lie in bed in the same position for extended periods put undue pressure on tissue and reduce circulation. Massage promotes circulation, which helps supply oxygen and other nutrients to all parts of the body while removing waste products.[19,30]

acupuncture the Chinese medical practice of puncturing the body with thin needles at precise points to free constricted or blocked energy centers

Massage is also used by athletes, trainers, and sports medicine specialists to prevent and treat **soft-tissue** injuries and speed the healing process. Massage is especially useful in the treatment of a **sprain,** a **strain,** and a **contusion.** Massage works by stimulating blood flow to the injured area. This increased blood flow reduces swelling, promotes healing, and reduces the likelihood of **fibrosis.**[36,46,53]

Types of Massage There are many different types of massage. Some of the more common are Swedish, shiatsu, and medical or sports massage.

- ***Swedish Massage*** Swedish massage, or total body massage, is probably the form with which most people are familiar. It is one of the most commonly used forms of massage and combines a variety of strokes that build in pressure. Swedish massage starts with light, flowing strokes called *effleurage*. These light, flowing strokes are followed by *petrissage,* a series of shorter, more pressurized squeezes and rolls. These are followed by deeper, penetrating, kneading strokes (friction), chops (tapoment), and deep vibrating movements (vibration).

  A person receiving a Swedish massage lies nude, facedown on a massage table or bed, with a towel covering the buttocks. Massage oil is usually used to minimize friction. A Swedish massage progresses up and down the spine, working the neck, shoulders, buttocks, hamstrings, and calves. These are the areas most susceptible to the buildup of tension, associated aches and pains, strained muscles, and fatigue.[8,53]

- ***Shiatsu*** Shiatsu, or acupressure massage, is similar to another healing technique—acupuncture. Both are based on the belief that stress, tension, and disease are due in part to a blocking of the body's vital energy. Acupuncture relieves the blockage of chi through stimulation of pressure points by inserting needles into them, while acupressure manipulates those pressure points through massage.

  Acupressure involves applying pressure to the pressure points for a few seconds, using the thumbs in a series of circular movements. The entire massage is shorter and simpler than a Swedish massage. Unlike Swedish massage, which is best obtained in the nude, shiatsu does not require the removal of clothes.[8,53]

- ***Medical/Sports Massage*** Medical, or sports, massage is directed at healing muscle tissue that has been damaged by injury or overexertion. Sports masseurs and masseuses are eclectic in their approach, employing a variety of strokes, pulls, and touches during the application of pressure.

  Sports massage is intended to help athletes recover from strenuous workouts by increasing the circulation of blood into specific muscles. This increased circulation helps carry nutrients to the tissue and facilitate the removal of waste products such as lactic acid. The accumulation of lactic acid in muscles is associated with fatigue and discomfort.[36,53]

  Medical massage is also intended to increase circulation to the muscle tissue. In many cases bedridden patients cannot walk or perform enough physical activity to stimulate their circulation. This can hinder their treatment and increase muscle tension and soreness. Massage can help counteract these physical conditions by reducing stress, relieving pain, and restoring a sense of emotional well-being.[47]

Preparation for Massage: A Word about Sensuality and Sexuality When it comes to massage, it is sometimes hard for us to separate our sensuality from our sexuality. The only time many of us touch others in such an intimate way is when we are being sexual. Massage is not an inherently sexual activity; however, it is sensual (see Diverse Perspectives 10-2: "Janet"). Kneading, stroking, and manipulating another person's flesh require that we be in tune with the sensation of touch. We must be acutely aware of pressure and motion when giving a massage. Also, many of the massage oils available are scented and bring into play the sense of smell. Visually, the sight of exposed flesh has the potential for arousal.

It may take time to enjoy giving and getting a massage and view them as sensual delights that do not have to lead to sexual activity. Of course, giving a massage with the intent to arouse your partner sexually is a wonderful way to initiate erotic activities if that is your intention. Practicing the ability to give and receive sensual pleasure in the absence of sexual release is wonderful training in becoming a compassionate lover.

How to Give a Massage Giving a massage is a natural behavior. Most of us massage others the way we like to be massaged. Instinctively, we believe that if it feels good to us, it will feel good to the person we are massaging. While this is true for the most part, there is more to know. Some basic instructions in massage will help you refine your technique.

In general, it is easier to give a massage if you use some form of lubricating oil. Some people prefer powder as an agent to reduce friction, and they like the dry sensations powder offers. However, most people prefer oil. Try both and decide for yourself.

soft tissue tissue other than bone

sprain a traumatic injury to the tendons, muscles, or ligaments around a joint; characterized by pain, swelling, and discoloration of the skin

strain minor muscular damage do to excessive physical effort

contusion a bruise characterized by pain, swelling, and discoloration; does not break the skin

fibrosis an abnormal condition where fibrous connective tissue spreads over smooth muscle tissue

DIVERSE PERSPECTIVES 10-2

Janet

Janet is a returning student in her thirties with two children. She raised both of her sons while working part-time selling real estate on weekends. With both boys in high school and her husband doing well in his own business, Janet felt it was time to pursue her dream, earning a bachelor's degree in psychology. As a senior, she had finished all her major courses and was taking all the fun electives she could that were somewhat related to her field. She had one semester to go.

However, Janet was uneasy because in her stress-management class the students were going to be giving each other warm-oil foot massages. The professor had explained that this was intended to be an exercise in stress relief. Janet understood this and really wanted to experience what a warm-oil foot massage was like, but she did not feel right about doing it. What would she do if she was paired up with an attractive young guy? What if she was paired up with another woman and found that she enjoyed the experience? Did that mean she was gay? Janet was filled with stress as the time got closer.

Put yourself in Janet's place. Would this affect you in a similar way? Are sensuality and sexuality that closely related? Could you separate the two? How could the stress of this activity be defused?

If you use oil, make sure it is warm or at room temperature. Nothing gets a massage off to a worse start than having someone dump cold oil on your skin. If possible, let the oil sit at room temperature or warm the container under hot water in the sink before you start. Pour the oil into your hands and rub it around and then onto the body rather than squirting it directly onto the person's skin.[24]

Make sure you have enough room to get completely around the person without having to lean on or jump over him or her. You should be able to position yourself over the person so that you can apply firm pressure during some strokes. A massage table or high bed is ideal because it allows you to stand while giving a massage. You can also kneel next to the person receiving the massage.

Additionally, a massage table has a well for the person's head to rest in, allowing him or her to lie comfortably with the face down, facilitating easy access to the neck, shoulders, and head. A professional table is not essential, however, when giving a massage. You can place a pillow under the person's head for support and have the person move his or her head gently to the side. Playing soothing background music can help a person relax.[19]

The most important thing about giving a massage is to take your time. The other person will instantly sense if you feel obligated to do this and are rushing through it. Giving a massage is an act of kindness and must be done slowly and lovingly, with no expectations for anything in return.

Massage Strokes

There are several types of strokes that can be used when giving a massage. A key element is to maintain contact with your partner, if possible, as you move from one stroke to the next. Try to have your strokes merge to form a sense of continuous motion with the muscles. Sometimes having a visual image of the muscular system can help.

Try to keep your strokes rhythmic and symmetrical. Do not worry if your strokes are not perfect; they will get better with practice. Try hard to keep your motion flowing. You will need to use your whole hand to master all the strokes. Your fingers, palm, heel, and fist all come into play.

1. Kneading—In kneading, you grasp the flesh with all four fingers of both hands and rotate your thumbs in opposite directions. Kneading works beautifully with the muscles of the arms, legs, hands, feet, and shoulders.
2. Pressing—Pressing involves pushing against the body with the heel of the hand. For extra pressure you can use your other hand to apply pressure against the hand involved in the pressing. Pressing can be used in long strokes or a circular motion and is very effective with thicker muscles such as those in the back.
3. Stroking—Stroking involves the fingertips and can be done by either pushing away from you in circles or drawing toward you. Stroking can also involve all five fingers gently drawing flesh toward you. Stroking is wonderful for the scalp, neck, and inner thighs but is also great for long continuous motion along the back, torso, arms, and legs.
4. Pulling—Pulling is very similar to stroking toward you, except it involves more pressure. In stroking your movements glide over the skin, but in pulling you actually grab hold and gently tug. You can pull with just your fingers or with your entire hand(s). Pulling is terrific for the head, hands, fingers, toes, feet, arms, and legs.
5. Lifting—In some cases actually lifting a part of the body such as the head, torso, or leg and supporting it in your hands is very relaxing. When you are lifting, your hands are cupped and are used to cradle the part being elevated.
6. Pounding—Making a fist and gently pounding a body part can release the tension that has accumulated in it. Pounding obviously is not for everyone or every body part. However, it is very effective on the back.

You can give full-body or partial massages. Sometimes just a back massage or foot massage will do the trick. Other times a full-body massage, complete with scented candles, is indicated.

KEY TO UNDERSTANDING

Take your time when giving a massage.

When giving a full-body massage, you can start anywhere. Some people start with the feet and then work up to the head and finish at the hands. Other people give the massage in the reverse order or start at the abdomen because it is the center of the body and the place where blood pools when the body is stressed. Wherever you start, remember to cover the entire body in a systematic way. Try not to jump around from feet to head to toes. Finish a part thoroughly and then move on to the next body part.

Feet

Begin the massage by having the person lie on his or her stomach. Apply the warm oil to your hands liberally and reapply it as indicated.

1. Work on each foot separately.
2. Position yourself kneeling at the person's feet. Grasp the center of the foot with both hands and knead it.
3. Work down to the toes and pull on all five toes simultaneously.
4. Still holding the toes, switch to a circular pulling motion.
5. Work on each toe individually, gently pulling and kneading in a circular motion.
6. Press the arch of the foot from toes to heel.
7. Lift the foot and rotate it gently while holding on to the middle of it.
8. Finish off the foot by pressing the ball of it back and stroke the Achilles tendon in the heel.
9. Repeat this on the other foot.

Legs

1. Straddle a leg while facing the person's head and work on the back of the leg, using long pressing strokes. Press firmly all the way up to the back of the thigh and let your hands slide gently back along the outside of the leg on their way back. Try to maintain contact with the leg throughout this stroke.
2. After a few strokes grasp the leg on the return and gently lift and pull it as your hands return back. You may have to raise your body off the table, floor, or bed to make room for the leg.
3. Repeat this on the other leg.
4. Still straddling the leg, grasp the lower leg (calf) with both hands and knead deeply with the thumbs. The calf muscle is very dense, and so you will be able to apply firm pressure.
5. Gently massage the back of the knee with mild circular kneading.
6. Repeat this on the other leg.

Buttocks

1. Work on the entire buttocks area at once.
2. Straddle the person's legs and firmly knead the buttocks with both hands.
3. After kneading the buttocks, grasp the person's hips and gently lift the hips off the floor, stretching this region.

Back

1. Either straddle the person's hips or lean over from the side and firmly massage the back, using long presses from the small of the back to the neck.
2. Push hard, using the heels of your hands as you press upward. Let your hands trail down the person's sides as they return to the small of the back.
3. After a few strokes, grasp the person's sides and gently pull and lift the back and hips as you return your hands to the starting position.

Head and Shoulders

1. Move up to the person's shoulders. Do not sit on the person's back as you do this. Lean over the person and grasp the meaty part of the shoulders on either side of the neck. This muscle, the trapezius, can be well developed in athletes and can be firmly kneaded.
2. Knead this muscle with the thumbs and the entire hand. Use a circular thumb motion.
3. Use the same motion on the rounded muscles (deltoids) at the end of the shoulder.
4. Return to the center of the back and, with the thumbs only, gently knead the base of the spine from the shoulders to the base of the skull.
5. Using both hands, knead the entire neck. You should be able to grasp the neck gently as you use your thumbs and fingers simultaneously.
6. Using your fingers, massage the entire head with gentle circular pressing strokes. You may also use your entire hands to cradle and massage the head. After asking the person to turn over, finish the massage by working on the arms, hands, torso, abdomen, and fronts of the legs.

Arms

1. Kneeling next to the person, grasp the arm closest to you and, starting at the wrist, knead toward the underarm.
2. Let your hands slide down the sides of the person's arms on their way back to the starting position.
3. After a few strokes, grasp the arm and gently lift and pull on the way back.
4. Repeat the procedure on the other arm.

Hands

1. Grasp the person's hand in both of your hands. Firmly knead the backs and fronts of the hands using your thumbs and fingers.
2. Gently pull and rotate each finger.
3. Repeat the procedure on the other hand.

Front of the Body

1. Either straddle the person's waist or lean over him or her. Using the heels of both hands simultaneously, press upward on the chest from the center outward. Be careful, especially with women, about the amount of pressure exerted.
2. When you reach the shoulders, let your hands slide to the side for their return journey.
3. After a few strokes, grasp the person's sides and lift as you pull your hands back to their starting place at the top of the stomach.
4. As an alternative to pulling or sliding down the sides, you can use long continuous finger strokes as you pull your hands back across the chest on their return journey.
5. The stomach/abdomen from the rib cage to the pubic area can be massaged using both hands simultaneously in a gentle circular stroking motion.
6. Kneel to the side of a leg and massage the front of it, using a kneading stroke from the inner thigh down. Your hands should slide to the sides and maintain contact as you gently push them back to the top of the thigh.
7. After a few strokes, lift the leg and gently pull it toward you as you knead it with both hands.
8. As an alternative, you can use a pulling stroke to bring your hands down from the inner thigh to the ankle.
9. You may also spend some time kneading the inner thigh firmly with the thumbs, as this is an area where muscle tension seems to accumulate.

Many people feel relaxed and a little sleepy after a massage. Try to let them have some quiet time to savor the results. Hopefully, they will be so appreciative, they will want to reciprocate.

See Assess Yourself 10-1, "Release Assessment," to record your personal experiences with the relaxation strategies described in this chapter.

The Effects of Moderate Physical Activity on Stress

The surgeon general's report on physical activity and health[52] recommends getting a moderate amount of physical activity each day. A moderate amount of physical activity is roughly equivalent to physical activity that uses approximately 150 calories (kcal) of energy per day, or 1,000 calories per week.

KEY TO UNDERSTANDING

An effective exercise program uses all three types of exercise and includes a variety of activities. When using exercise to reduce stress, make sure the activity does not become a source of stress.

What Is a Moderate Amount of Physical Activity?

Table 10-1 illustrates a variety of ways you can obtain a moderate amount of physical activity. Because amount of activity is a function of the duration, intensity, and frequency of an activity, the same amount of exercise can be obtained in longer sessions of moderately intense activities (such as brisk walking) as in shorter sessions of more strenuous activities (such as running).[52] Table 10-2 outlines the major benefits derived from moderate levels of physical activity. Research has shown that this level of physical activity and exercise is associated with reducing the risk of premature mortality as well as the risks of coronary heart disease, hypertension, colon cancer, and diabetes mellitus. Engaging in regular physical activity also reduces depression and anxiety, improves mood, and enhances one's ability to perform daily tasks throughout the life span.[38,39,52]

Table 10-1 Moderate Activity Guidelines

Less Vigorous, Requires More Time
Washing and waxing a car for 45–60 minutes
Washing windows or floors for 45–60 minutes
Playing volleyball for 45 minutes
Playing touch football for 30–45 minutes
Gardening for 30–45 minutes
Wheeling self in wheelchair for 30–40 minutes
Walking 1¾ miles in 35 minutes (20 min/mile)
Basketball (shooting baskets) for 30 minutes
Bicycling 5 miles in 30 minutes
Dancing fast (social) for 30 minutes
Pushing a stroller 1½ miles in 30 minutes
Raking leaves for 30 minutes
Walking 2 miles in 30 minutes (15 min/mile)
Doing water aerobics for 30 minutes
Swimming laps for 20 minutes
Playing wheelchair basketball for 20 minutes
Playing basketball for 15–20 minutes
Bicycling 4 miles in 15 minutes
Jumping rope for 15 minutes
Running 1½ miles in 15 minutes (10 min/mile)
Shoveling snow for 15 minutes
Stairwalking for 15 minutes
More Vigorous, Requires Less Time

Source: *The surgeon general's report on physical activity and health.* http://www.cdc.gov/nccdphp/sgr/ataglan.htm.[52]

Table 10-2 The Health Benefits of Regular Physical Activity

Regular physical activity that is performed on most days of the week reduces the risk of developing or dying from some of the leading causes of illness and death in the United States. Regular physical activity improves health in the following ways:

- Reduces the risk of dying prematurely.
- Reduces the risk of dying from heart disease.
- Reduces the risk of developing diabetes.
- Reduces the risk of developing high blood pressure.
- Helps reduce blood pressure in people who already have high blood pressure.
- Reduces the risk of developing colon cancer.
- Reduces feelings of depression and anxiety.
- Helps control weight.
- Helps build and maintain healthy bones, muscles, and joints.
- Helps older adults become stronger and better able to move about without falling.
- Promotes psychological well-being.

Source: *Surgeon general's report on physical activity and health.*[52]

Laughter as a Form of Moderate Physical Activity

What are the physiological effects of a good belly laugh? Is there something more to the stress-reducing effects of humor that go beyond the cognitive?

The answer is a resounding yes! It is physiologically impossible to be stressed when you are laughing. **Laughter** creates a physiological state that is incompatible with stress. Almost all the body systems are involved: The skeletal and smooth muscles contract, respiration increases in depth and rate, heart rate and blood pressure elevate, body temperature increases, and the central nervous system is activated.

The real benefit of laughter is that the levels of activity of these systems and physiological processes (breathing, pumping blood, and muscle contraction) initially are higher than they are when the body is at rest. After a good laugh, they fall below normal resting levels, resulting in the same sense of deep relaxation and contentment.[28]

A hearty belly laugh is physiologically incompatible with stress.

DIVERSE PERSPECTIVES 10-3

The Laughing Clubs of India

In 1995, in Bombay, India, Dr. Madan Kataria, a medical doctor, went public with a treatment he had been testing. He had been meeting with a group of patients and neighbors on a regular basis to explore the effects of laughter on stress. Dr. Kataria developed a laughter-inducing technique derived from yoga that not only loosened inhibitions and got them laughing but also was good for improved breathing and was associated with reducing hypertension and the effects of arthritis and migraine headaches. After seeing these results in individual patients and his small groups, Dr. Kataria was convinced that his technique could work in a group or *club* setting, thereby increasing his ability to help much larger numbers of people. He organized the first *laughing club* in Priydarshini Park, bringing people from all castes and classes together to laugh for forty minutes each day. In Dr. Kataria's laughing clubs, members meet in groups of up to fifty, and after loosening up with some stretching and breathing exercises, they cajole and egg each other on to sustain lengthy bouts of laughter. Kataria trains members to produce many different styles of laughing ranging from silly giggles to deep belly laughs. In 1998 Kataria organized a World Laughter Day at the Bombay Racetrack where more than 10,000 people gathered together to have a big laugh. Kataria's work was immortalized by director Mira Nair and producer Adam Bartos in their critically acclaimed 2000 film, *The Laughing Club of India.*

At least five major muscle groups react rhythmically when you laugh: the abdomen, neck, shoulders, diaphragm, and face. When you are finished laughing, they all are more relaxed than they were when you started. Laughter is a good tonic for muscle tension.

Laughter also is a proven pain reliever. Laughter, like physical exercise, can trigger the release of endorphins. Karren et al.[28] ask, Could there also be a "laugher's high" created by the release of these same endorphins? They think so.

Norman Cousins[10] used humor to help fight his life-threatening illness. He found that ten minutes of laughter provided up to two hours of pain-free sleep. Not only

laughter a uniquely human reaction typically in the form of a physical as well as emotional response indicating feelings of amusement, joy, or merriment

Living Constructively

Mindful Stove Cleaning

You don't have to engage in anything glamorous to use up the by-products of stress through moderate physical activity. If you have ever cleaned a stove, you know it can be a time-consuming, physically demanding job. For most people it is not fun and they go about it infrequently and without too much joy.

Kabat-Zinn[27] describes how even something as grueling as stove cleaning can be stress-reducing if approached mindfully. In his book Kabat-Zinn[27] describes how he approached the task in a playful way to see how close he could get the stove to look as if it were brand new. Each step of the process, from removing the knobs and burners and letting them soak in the sink for later through wiping the finished product off with a clean, damp sponge, is approached mindfully. That means being fully involved in the *present cleaning moment* and not thinking about yesterday's problems at work or tomorrow's packing for a weekend getaway trip.

He described the actual process of cleaning from choosing the right kind of cleanser (abrasive enough to remove the baked-on food yet not too abrasive that it would scratch the finish) to the actual circular cleaning motions and the amount of pressure applied to clean various parts of the stove. Each component of the cleaning process was approached with full attention, as if there was nothing else more important to attend to at that moment than cleaning the stove.

Lastly, Kabat-Zinn[27] describes how he was playing a funky jazz CD at the time and how his cleaning became one with the music. He describes how his motions kept pace with the rhythms of the songs and his intensity mimicked the intensity of the music. In essence, his stove cleaning became a dance, a total immersion in the here and now and a release of tension while still performing productive work.

Have you ever had a similar experience while waxing the car, moving the lawn, doing the dishes, preparing a meal? What keeps you from being more mindful of every activity you choose to engage in?

has laughter been associated with a reduction in physical pain, it has been shown to reduce psychological pain and suffering. Using "humor therapy," researchers in Sweden showed that humorous books, videotapes, and records can be used to reduce psychological pain in patients with chronic degenerative diseases.[28]

Although the short-term benefit of laughter lies mostly in its ability to induce relaxation and reduce muscle tension and pain, humor may have a long-term benefit of increasing one's ability to ward off disease and prolong life. In studies at California's Loma Linda University, laughter has been found to enhance immune-system functioning by increasing the concentration of lymphocytes, killer-cell activity, and overall level of functioning.[45]

Laughter also halts the stress response, in particular, the production of excess hormones, which are related to decreased immune functioning. These immune-enhancing effects may suggest the use of humor and laughter in preventing disease.

Humor also seems to have a beneficial effect on recovery. Norman Cousins[10] has reported for ten years on the effects of laughter and humor on several conditions, including his own serious illness. Simon[50] described the beneficial effects of humor and laughter in helping patients prepare for and cope with upcoming medical treatment.

Which Type of Moderate Physical Activity Works Best?

All forms of moderate physical activity counter the effects of stress in three ways: they fully contract and relax tense muscles; they use the energy mobilized during the stress response in a productive way; and they shift our attention away from our problems and onto something that we enjoy, providing a mini-vacation from our stress. It is important to perform these activities in a mindful way, giving them your full attention and energy (see Living Constructively box).

The thing they all have in common is that they get you moving. Unlike mild physical activities, moderate activities are designed to make you work and burn calories. The best form of moderate activity to use is the one you enjoy and are most likely to do on a regular basis. Even better is to have at least one form of activity that you can engage in despite the season or weather. Table 10-1 (moderate activity guidelines) gives you an idea of the scope of activities. Some are fun and forms of play. Others are types of labor. It really doesn't matter which ones you enjoy. Some people find lawn care or gardening very relaxing while others see them as work. Some people like getting dressed up and going ballroom dancing while others wouldn't want to come near a dance club. If you plan on engaging in these activities with others, make sure you are doing them because you really want to and not because you are trying to please these people. This is where the assertiveness you learned in chapter 8 will come in handy. If you choose your activities around the wants of others rather than your own preferences these supposedly *stress-reducing* activities will become *stressors* for you.

The Effects of Vigorous Physical Activity on Stress

Earlier in this chapter we discussed how moderate physical activity can release accumulated stress-related tension and energy. We discussed the surgeon general's recommendations for moderate physical activity involving a variety of common daily activities. Sometimes, however, we need more than moderate levels of physical activity to release the effects of stress from our bodies and minds. When moderate physical activity doesn't seem to work, we may need to increase the level of intensity to get the stress-reducing effects we desire. In this section we will turn our attention toward more vigorous release strategies.

Increasing Intensity

The simplest way to make an activity more vigorous during the time we are performing it is to increase its level of intensity. Any activity, from weight lifting to housework, can be made more vigorous by increasing its intensity. Increasing the intensity of the activity will increase its effectiveness in releasing stress.

There are several different ways to increase the intensity of any activity. Intensity can be upped by increasing the speed with which the activity is performed or by adding resistance while performing the activity. In either case, we are using overload to make the body work harder by increasing its energy demands. An activity's intensity can be systematically increased over time to improve fitness or can be altered on a specific occasion to create a more vigorous way to release stress.

As an example, imagine that you use weight lifting as a way to release stress. During your scheduled workout you just can't seem to relax and clear your mind or release the tension you feel in your neck and shoulders. One way to increase the intensity of the workout would be to increase the number of repetitions you normally perform during any exercise. If you normally perform eight repetitions of that exercise, you might try lowering the amount of weight but increasing the number of repetitions to fifteen. Or you might try lowering the weight, adding more repetitions, *and* increasing the pace of your movements. Another way to increase the intensity is to lower the amount of rest between sets of the exercise, thereby forcing your body to work faster and harder. Instead of resting one or two minutes between exercises, try resting for only forty-five seconds.

Let's use mowing the lawn as another example. If you normally take one hour to mow the lawn, try reducing the time by fifteen minutes and moving faster. Or if you have a power-assisted walking mower, turn it off and use your muscles to push it instead of just guiding it.

If you are a walker and find taking a walk the best way to release stress but it doesn't always work, try walking faster. Walk your normal distance but try to cut the time you take by 20 to 25 percent. You could also modify your walk and incorporate some gradual hills or other inclines that will increase the intensity of the walk. Another way to increase the intensity is to carry hand weights or swing your arms more vigorously to make it more of a power walk.

Cathartic Release Activities and Stress

Maximum-effort, explosive, vigorous physical activities have the ability to create a cathartic effect on stress. **Catharsis** is defined as a purification or purging that brings about spiritual renewal or physical release from tension. When you focus all of your attention and exert maximum physical effort for a short, intense burst of activity, the stress-releasing causes dramatic and immediate effects. Stress Buster Tips offers a list of ten different activities that you can do by yourself to release stress. They all share the common denominator of maximum physical effort in a short time frame.

Driving a golf ball is a good example. Think about going to a golf range and driving golf balls. You tee the ball up, focus your attention on your balance and staying loose, draw the club back up and over your shoulder, and quickly swing down and through the ball. At the moment of impact you can tell if the hit is solid and true. You can hear the sound and feel the tension flow down your neck, shoulders, and arms and out with the ball as it flies through the air. Athletes from all sports can relate to the feel (and also the sound) of a solid hit whether it is a golf ball, a tennis ball coming off the sweet spot on the racket, or a baseball coming off the fat part of the bat. In all three cases the power and tension is transmitted through the swing and out with the struck object.

Stress Buster Tips

Here are examples of ten physical activities that can exert a cathartic release of stress tension. How many more can you think of?

1. Driving golf balls at a range.
2. Hitting baseballs in a batting cage.
3. Serving tennis balls on an empty court.
4. Kicking soccer balls into an empty net.
5. Punching a heavy bag.
6. Kicking a heavy bag.
7. Having an orgasm.
8. Sprinting as fast as you can for 100 yards.
9. Skiing a very steep downhill slope fast.
10. Bench press your maximum weight for one repetition.

catharsis a cleansing or purifying effect derived from the dramatic release of stress-related tension

STRESS IN OUR WORLD 10-1

Cardio Kickboxing[20,25,26,55]

What do you get when you combine Muay Thai kickboxing, a devastatingly effective martial art from Thailand, with aerobic dancing? You get one of the biggest exercise crazes, "cardio kickboxing."

Most cardio kickboxing programs combine training routines similar to those used in boxing, American-style kickboxing, and Thai-style kickboxing with more mainstream aerobic dance workouts. Cardio kickboxing classes are not designed to make "fighters" out of the participants but to give them an overall total-body program that combines a cardiovascular workout with self-defense techniques.

Cardio kickboxing routines also provide strength-training benefits similar to those of lifting weights because of the "resistance" provided when one is punching or kicking the various bags and pads. Participants get both upper- and lower-body workouts because of the combination of punching (which primarily works the upper body) and kicking (which primarily works the lower body).

Classes typically begin with a three- to five-minute warm-up and then go directly into drills that include foot movement, bobbing and weaving, basic punches and kicks, and basic kicks and punches combined. Students then move to stations, hitting and kicking various bags to develop power, accuracy, timing, and movement. Classes usually also include one-on-one work with instructors who move around using punch mitts and hand-held bags to help students learn balance and judge distance.

Advanced classes usually involve modified sparring in which students and instructors using head gear, mouthpieces, chest protectors, and gloves simulate real action by throwing punches and kicks at each other. Although these sessions are not designed to include contact, the blows sometimes land.

Typically, the kickboxing portion of a class is followed by floor exercises, stretches, and breathing performed as part of the cool-down. The after-kickboxing exercises typically include upper abdominal crunches, lower abdominal stretches, and side lifts designed to tighten and strengthen the musculature of the abdomen.

University of Mississippi researchers found that most cardio kickboxing participants can expect to burn about 350 to 450 calories per hour; this is less than original estimates but is still a good workout. This rate of caloric consumption is roughly equivalent to an hour of brisk walking or light jogging. Participants in the study also maintained a heart rate of 75 to 85 percent of the maximum, which falls within the range of 65 to 90 percent recommended for aerobic exercise.

Cardio kickboxing provides strength training with both upper- and lower-body workouts.

Some other physical and psychological benefits of kickboxing are:

1. Tone and tighten legs and buttocks—fast
2. Increase upper- and lower-body strength
3. Release tension
4. Burn up to 700 calories an hour (based on a 150-pound person)
5. Make workouts exciting
6. Boost confidence
7. Enhance flexibility
8. Improve balance and coordination
9. Introduce basic self-defense moves

SUMMARY

In this chapter we examined ways to use physical activity to dissipate the effects of stress. The chapter started with a discussion of how everyone is born with the ability to use physical activity to release stress; however, over time many people become sedentary and less physical in their daily activities.

The chapter then moved into a discussion of the physiological and psychological benefits of exercise and physical activity. The physiological benefits included tension reduction and hormone and fat/cholesterol utilization. The psychological benefits included the release of neurotransmitters, enhanced creativity and self-esteem, and a more positive outlook on life.

The chapter continued with a discussion of mild, moderate, and vigorous physical activity, defining each and giving examples. Mild activities discussed included systematic muscle relaxation, yoga and stretching, tai chi ch'uan, and massage.

The chapter also provided a thorough explanation of the surgeon general's guidelines for moderate physical activity. Laughter was discussed as a form of moderate physical activity. The next part of the chapter examined how to use frequency, intensity, and time to increase the vigor of moderate activities.

The chapter ended with a discussion of the effects of vigorous physical activities on stress. Attention was given to cathartic activities, a special form of vigorous activity that purges tension in a dramatic fashion.

STUDY QUESTIONS

1. Describe how release works as a coping strategy.
2. What are the criteria for moderate exercise described in the surgeon general's report on physical activity and health?
3. Describe five health benefits of exercise.
4. How does vigorous physical contact work to relieve stress?
5. What are three physiological stress-reducing properties of exercise?
6. What are three psychological stress-reducing properties of exercise?

DISCOVER OUR CHANGING WORLD

The Surgeon General's Report on Physical Activity and Health

www.cdc.gov/nccdphp/sgr/sgr.htm

This is the home page for *The Surgeon General's Report on Physical Activity and Health.* This document clarifies the differences between moderate and vigorous physical activity and explains the benefits of regular physical activity for health.

Click on the Executive Summary and read the key findings of the report.

Critical Thinking Question

How do the surgeon general's recommendations regarding physical activity compare to your perceptions about how much daily exercise you always thought you needed to derive the health benefits described in the report?

ARE YOU THINKING CLEARLY?

In this chapter we discussed a variety of strategies to help you learn how to use exercise and physical activity to release stress in a healthy way. Often students complain that they do not have time to exercise. They claim they believe it is important but just can't find the time. If you find yourself saying these things regarding exercise, *stop* and ask yourself the following questions:

1. Is it *really* impossible to find three ten-minute blocks over the course of a day to set aside for exercise?
2. What am I doing that is more important than exercising in these thirty minutes?
3. What am I doing now that I don't enjoy that I can cut out of my daily routine?
4. Is it really the word *exercise* that is turning me off to exploring this health benefit?
5. What type of enjoyable physical activity can I substitute for exercise as a release strategy?
6. Even though this is hard for me, can I view it as a challenge instead of a stressor?

The answers to these questions should help you assess whether you are thinking clearly about releasing your stress through exercise and physical activity. If you are not thinking clearly, try using the Ellis and Harper's ABCDE technique to work through your illogical thoughts about release.

REFERENCES

1. Ainsworth, B.E., Haskell, W.L., & Leon, A.S. (1993). Compendium of physical activities: Classification of energy costs of human physical activities. *Medicine and Science in Sports and Exercise,* 25, pp. 25–71.
2. Anspaugh, D., Hamrick, M., & Rosato, F. (1994). *Wellness: Concepts and applications.* (2nd ed.). St. Louis: McGraw-Hill.
3. Birkel, D.A. & Edgren, L. (2002). Hatha Yoga: Improved vital capacity of college students. *Alternative Therapies,* 6(6), pp. 55–63.
4. Blair, S. (1990). Exercise and health. *Sports Science Exchange,* 3(21), pp. 1–6.
5. Blonna, R. & Levitan, J. *Healthy sexuality.* Atlanta: Wadsworth.
6. Bynner, W. (1980). *The way of life: According to Lao Tzu.* New York: Perigee Books.
7. Carpentino, L.J. (1992). *Nursing diagnosis: Application to clinical practice.* (3rd ed.). Philadelphia: Lippincott.
8. Cohen-Suib, S. (1987). *The magic of touch.* New York: Harper & Row.
9. Cooper, K. (1982). *The aerobics program for total well-being*. Toronto: Bantam.
10. Cousins, N. (1979). *Anatomy of an illness as perceived by the patient.* New York: W.W. Norton.
11. Crompton, P. (1987). *The t'ai chi workbook.* Boston: Shambhala.
12. Crowley, C., Lodge, H. (2004). Younger Next Year: a single to living like 50 until you're 80 and beyond. NY: Workman Pub.
13. Debusk, R.F., Stenestrand, U., Sheehan, M., & Haskell, W.L. (1990). Training effects of long versus short bouts of exercise in healthy adults. *American Journal of Cardiology,* 65, pp. 1010–1013.
14. Dunn, T. (1987). The practice and spirit of t'ai chi ch'uan. *Yoga Journal,* November/December.
15. Everly, G.A. & Lating, J.M. (2002). *A clinical guide to the treatment of the human stress response.* (2nd ed.). New York: Kluwer Academic/Plenum.
16. Flippin, R. (1989). Beyond endorphins: The latest research on runner's high. *American Health,* October, pp. 78–83.
17. Girdano, D.A., Everly, G.S., & Dusek, D.E. (2001). *Controlling stress and tension: A holistic approach.* (6th ed). Englewood Cliffs, NJ: Prentice-Hall.
18. Gondola, J.C. (1990). Physical fitness: Activity and rest. In Williams, B.K. & Knight, S. (Eds.). *Healthy for life.* Pacific Grove, CA: Brooks/Cole.
19. Good Arts (2003). *Sensual massage*. http:www.goodarts.com.
20. Hanlon, T. (1999). Kickboxing. *Prevention,* 51(11), p. 77.
21. Hopson, J.L. (1988). A pleasurable chemistry. *PT,* July/August, pp. 29–33.
22. Jacobson, E. (1970). *Modern treatment of tense patients.* Springfield, IL: Charles C. Thomas.
23. Jacobson, E. (1978). *You must relax.* New York: McGraw-Hill.
24. Jacobsen, B.H., et al. (1997). The effect of tai chi ch'uan training on balance, kinesthetic sense, and strength. *Perceptual and Motor Skills,* 8, pp. 27–33.
25. Jaeger, P. (1998). Kickboxing. *American Fitness,* 16(4), pp. 35–37.
26. JOPERD (1999). Cardio kickboxing benefits confirmed. *Journal of Physical Education, Recreation and Dance,* 70(18), p. 9.
27. Kabat-Zinn, J. (1994). *Wherever you go you are there.* New York: Hyperion.
28. Karren, K.J., Hafen, B.Q., Smith, N.L., Frandsen, K.J. (2002). *Mind/Body Health: The effects of attitudes, emotions, and relationships.* (2nd ed.). San Francisco, CA: Benjamin Cummings.
29. Koh, T.C. (1981). Tai chi ch'uan. *American Journal of Chinese Medicine,* 8, pp. 15–22.
30. Kozier, B., Erb, G., & Olivieri, R. (1991). *Fundamentals of nursing: Concepts, process, and practice.* (4th ed.). Redwood City, CA: Addison Wesley.
31. Luby, S. (1977). *Hatha yoga for total health.* Englewood Cliffs, NJ: Prentice-Hall.
32. Marieb, E.M. (1992). *Human anatomy and physiology.* (2nd ed.). Redwood City, CA: Benjamin Cummings.
33. McGuinan, F.J. (1983). Progressive relaxation: Origin, principles, and clinical applications. In Lehrer, P.M. & Woolfolk, R.L. (Eds.). *Principles and practice of stress management.* (2nd ed.), pp. 17–52. New York: Guilford Press.
34. McGuigan, F.J. (1991). *Calm down: A guide for stress and tension control.* Dubuque, IA: Kendall Hunt.
35. McGuigan, F.J. (1993). Progressive relaxation: Origins, principles, and clinical applications. In Lehrer, P.M. & Woolfolk, R.L. (Eds.). *Principles and practices of stress management.* (2nd ed.). New York: Guilford.
36. Mellion, M. (1994). *Sports medicine secrets.* St. Louis: Mosby.
37. Mood, D., Musker, F., & Rink, J. (1995). *Sports and recreational activities.* (11th ed.). St. Louis: McGraw-Hill.
38. Morgan, W.P. (1982). Psychological effects of exercise. *Behavioral Medicine Update,* 4, pp. 25–30.
39. Morgan, W.P. & Goldstein, S. (1982). *Exercise and mental health.* New York: Hemisphere.
40. Montoye, H.J., et al. (1988). *Living fit.* Menlo Park, CA: Benjamin Cummings.
41. Mott, P. (1990). Mental gymnastics. *Los Angeles Times,* October 1, pp. 18–19.
42. Ornstein, R. & Sobel, D. (1989). *Healthy pleasures.* Reading, MA: Addison-Wesley.
43. Pollock, M.L., Gaesser, G.A., Butcher, J.D., et al. (1998). The recommended quantity and quality of exercise for developing and maintaining cardiorespiratory and muscular fitness, and flexibility in healthy adults (American College of Sports Medicine, Position Stand). *Medicine and Science in Sports and Exercise,* 29(5), pp. 975–1010.
44. Prentice, W. (1994). *Fitness for college and life.* St. Louis: McGraw-Hill.

45. Robinson, R. (1989). He who laughs . . . lasts. *Vibrant Life,* September/October, p. 5.
46. Russel, J.K. (1994). Bodywork: The art of touch. *Nurse-Practitioner Forum,* 5(2), pp. 85–90.
47. Sayre-Adams, J. (1994). Therapeutic touch in health visiting practice. *Health Visitation,* 67(9), pp. 304–305.
48. Seward, B.L. (2002). *Managing stress: Principles and strategies for well-being.* (3rd. ed.). Boston: Jones and Bartlett.
49. Sime, W.E. (1984). Psychological benefits of exercise. *Advances,* 1, pp. 15–29.
50. Simon, J.M. (1988). Therapeutic humor: Who's fooling who? *Journal of Psychosocial Nursing and Mental Health Services,* 26(4), p. 11.
51. Smith, M., et al. (1999). Benefits of massage therapy for hospital patients: A descriptive and qualitative evaluation. *Alternative Therapies in Health and Medicine,* 5(4), pp. 64–71.
52. Surgeon General of the United States. (1999). *Surgeon general's report on physical activity and exercise.* http://www.cdc.gov/nccdphp/sgr/atagan/htm.
53. Tappan, F. (1980). *Healing massage techniques: A study of eastern and western methods.* Reston, VA: Reston.
54. Thibodeau, G. & Patton, K. (1993). *Anatomy and physiology.* (2nd ed.). St. Louis: McGraw-Hill.
55. Thiboutot, F. (1996). What a kick! Kickboxing workout classes can spice up your programming. *Fitness Management,* December, pp. 42–44.
56. U.S. Department of Agriculture. (2003). Food pyramid. Washington, DC: U.S. Department of Agriculture.
57. Werner, K. (1980). *Yoga and Indian philosophy.* Delhi, India: Motilal.

Name: ________________________ Date: __________

Assess Yourself 10-1

Release Assessment

At least once in the next week, try each of the release strategies described in chapter 10. At the end of a week, rate each activity by using the following instrument:

1. What I liked about the activity:

   ____

   ____

   ____

   ____

2. What I disliked about the activity:

   ____

   ____

   ____

   ____

3. Potential barriers to using this activity on a regular basis:

   ____

   ____

   ____

   ____

4. Types of stressors this activity might be effective against:

   ____

   ____

   ____

   ____

Name: ______________________________ Date: __________

ASSESS YOURSELF 10-2

Level of Physical Activity

Circle the number that best represents your physical activity level.

1. I engage in ______ minutes of mild physical activity daily.
   a. <10
   b. 10–20
   c. 20–30
   d. 30–40
   e. >40
2. I engage in ______ minutes of moderate physical activity daily.
   f. <10
   g. 10–20
   h. 20–30
   i. 30–40
   j. >40
3. I engage in ______ minutes of vigorous physical activity daily.
   k. <10
   l. 10–20
   m. 20–30
   n. 30–40
   o. >40
4. Most of my physical activity comes from ______ activities.
   a. formal exercise
   b. work
   c. household chores
   d. hobbies/recreational activities
   e. other______________
5. My greatest barrier to engaging in more physical activity is . . .
   a. family responsibilities
   b. work responsibilities
   c. too overbooked
   d. injury/illness
   e. don't enjoy being physical
   f. other ________
6. Three things I can do to overcome these barriers are . . .
   a. ______________________________________
   b. ______________________________________
   c. ______________________________________

Name: ______________________________ Date: ____________

ASSESS YOURSELF 10-3

Assess Your Cardiovascular Health

Steps involved in calculating your aerobic training zone:

1. Calculate your maximum heart rate (MHR):
   220 − your age = MHR (EQ)
2. Calculate your resting heart rate (RHR):
   Pulse rate upon waking in the morning
3. Identify your lower and upper training intensity (TI) levels:
   65% MHR
   90% MHR
4. Calculate your lower and upper target heart rates (THR):
   THR = (MHR − RHR) × (TI% + RHR)
   Lower THR = (MHR − RHR) × 60% + RHR
   Upper THR = (MHR − RHR) × 90% + RHR

   ____

   ____

   ____

5. As long as your heart rate during exercise falls between your lower and upper target heart rates, you are in your aerobic training zone.

   THR, target heart rate; MHR, maximum heart rate; RHR, resting heart rate; TI%, training intensity (% of maximum heart rate).

   ____

   ____

   ____

Example: 20-year-old student with a resting heart rate of 60 beats/minute.

1. 220 − 20 = 200 MHR = 200
2. 60 = RHR
3. 65% lower limit; 90% upper limit
4. (200 − 60) × .65 + 60 = 78 + 60 = 138
   (200 − 60) × .90 + 60 = 126 + 60 = 186
5. Training zone = 138 to 186 beats/minute

CHAPTER

11

Reorganize: Becoming More Stress-Resistant by Improving Your Health

OUTLINE

A Lifestyle-Based Approach to Coping
- Moving toward Optimal Functioning
- High-Level Health and Stress Management

A Two-Pronged Model for Reorganizing Our Health

Reorganizing the Environmental/ Occupational Dimension of Health
- Reorganizing the Environmental Dimension of Health
- Reorganizing the Occupational Dimension of Health

Reorganizing the Social Dimension of Health
- A Problem-Focused Approach to Reorganizing the Social Dimension
- An Emotion-Focused Approach to Reorganizing the Social Dimension

Strengthening the Spiritual Dimension of Health
- A Problem-Focused Approach to Reorganizing the Spiritual Dimension
- An Emotion-Focused Approach to Reorganizing the Spiritual Dimension

Reorganizing the Intellectual Dimension of Health
- A Problem-Focused Approach to Strengthening the Intellectual Dimension
- An Emotion-Focused Approach to Strengthening the Intellectual Dimension

Reorganizing the Emotional Dimension of Health
- A Problem-Focused Approach to Strengthening the Emotional Dimension
- An Emotion-Focused Approach to Strengthening the Emotional Dimension

Reorganizing the Physical Dimension of Health
- A Problem-Focused Approach to Strengthening the Physical Dimension
- An Emotion-Focused Approach to Strengthening the Physical Dimension

Wellness and Coping

OBJECTIVES

By the end of the chapter students will:

- List and describe the five levels of defense against stress.
- Describe how the lines of defense mesh with the six dimensions of health and wellness to provide a synergistic effect.
- Describe how reorganize works as a line of defense against stress.
- Describe the differences between problem-focused and emotion-focused approaches towards reorganizing one's health.
- Compare and contrast a problem-focused approach to strengthening the environmental dimension to an emotion-focused approach.
- Compare and contrast a problem-focused approach to strengthening the occupational dimension to an emotion-focused approach.
- Compare and contrast a problem-focused approach to strengthening the intellectual dimension to an emotion-focused approach.
- Compare and contrast a problem-focused approach to strengthening the emotional dimension to an emotion-focused approach.
- Compare and contrast a problem-focused approach to strengthening the social dimension to an emotion-focused approach.
- Compare and contrast a problem-focused approach to strengthening the spiritual dimension to an emotion-focused approach.
- Compare and contrast a problem-focused approach to strengthening the physical dimension to an emotion-focused approach.
- Compare a lifestyle-based approach to stress management to a strategy-based approach.
- Discuss the movement toward wellness and how it is related to stress management.

This final chapter on coping discusses the fifth and final R, **Reorganize.** Reorganize is based on adopting a healthier lifestyle as a defense against stress. It is a **lifestyle-based approach** rather than a **strategy-based approach** to coping with stress. It is an approach aimed at improving your overall level of health to make you more stress-resistant.

Over 20 years ago Kobassa, Maddi, and Kahn[4] found that one of the key characteristics of hardy people is their use of "hardy health practices." Examples of hardy health habits are regular exercise, good nutrition, and relaxation. These hardy health habits went hand in hand with developing a hardier, more stress-resistant personality. If you have started to use some of the Rethink, Reduce, Relax, and Release strategies discussed in chapters 7–10 to deal with individual stressors, you have already taken steps to improve your overall level of health. The strategies taught in these chapters could be considered hardy health practices and, used individually, are very effective against specific stressors. In this chapter we will concentrate on how to make these and other hardy health practices a habit, part of your daily lifestyle.

A key to understanding *Reorganize* is realizing that engaging in hardy health habits daily helps prevent certain stressors from even arising in the first place. In this sense Reorganize is *preventive* in nature. Part of this comes out of the benefits of using multiple strategies simultaneously *before* potential stressors appear rather than confronting individual stressors with specific coping strategies *after* they arise. A key to understanding this preventive effect of *Reorganize* is realizing that by linking hardy health practices and Five Rs strategies together and practicing them on a daily basis, you can generate a **synergistic** effect against stress. That is, the overall effect of practicing hardy health habits and Five Rs strategies together, on a daily basis, is greater than the sum of using them independently to either build health or cope with stress. In a sense it is a proactive, intentional, lifestyle-based approach to coping compared to a reactive, strategy-based approach to coping.

A Lifestyle-Based Approach to Coping

In a lifestyle-based approach to coping we continually move toward optimal functioning in the physical, emotional, intellectual, social, spiritual, occupational, and environmental dimensions of health by engaging in hardy health practices daily. This *intentional* health-building process is designed to both improve our overall level of functioning across the six dimensions of health *and* develop a more stress-resistant lifestyle. Making lifestyle changes such as exercising regularly and eating for health are done preventively, not as coping strategies in response to a stressor. Often these same hardy health habits *can be used* as coping strategies in response to stressors.

Exercise is a perfect example of a hardy health habit that is also one of the Release coping strategies described in chapter 10 that can be used to cope with stress. Imagine that as a hardy health habit you strive to get thirty minutes of jogging, bike-riding, or swimming in daily. You build this into your daily routine, even when on

Key to Understanding

A key to understanding *Reorganize* is realizing that engaging in hardy health habits daily helps prevent certain stressors from even arising in the first place; it is *preventive* in nature.

Key to Understanding

A key to understanding the preventive effect of *Reorganize* is realizing that by linking hardy health practices and Five Rs strategies together and practicing them on a daily basis, you can generate a **synergistic** effect against stress.

Planting and tending to a garden provides a synergistic effect against stress for many people, offering moderate to vigorous exercise, a spiritual connection with nature, and an outlet for creativity.

reorganize the fifth line of defense against stress; reorganize is based on changing the way you view your health to make it a higher priority as a defense against stress

lifestyle-based approach an approach to coping that integrates individual coping strategies with hardy health practices to form a more stress-resistant lifestyle

strategy-based approach an approach to coping that uses individual coping strategies to cope with specific stressors as the need arises

synergistic when the end result of adding two or more things together is greater than the sum of their parts

←-------High Levels of Functioning	Six Dimensions of Wellness	Low Levels of Functioning-------→
• *Enjoy good physical health* • *Strong and flexible muscular system* • *Fit cardiovascular system* • *Able to work physically* • *Able to concentrate*	**Physical Dimension**	• *Weak muscles, unable to work physically* • *Poor cardiovascular health* • *Low levels of endurance* • *Inability to focus on tasks*
• *A strong social network for support* • *Feelings of security and contentment* • *Able to form and maintain friendships* • *Able to sustain loving relationships* • *Desires intimacy*	**Social Dimension**	• *Feelings of loneliness, insecurity* • *Does not value intimacy* • *Unable to sustain friendships* • *Unable to sustain loving relationships*
• *Faith in the world and in the future* • *A sense of order in the world*	**Spiritual Dimension**	• *Feelings of despair or helplessness* • *Feelings of detachment*
• *Makes good decisions* • *Can organize thoughts clearly* • *Communicates ideas verbally and in writing* • *Is able to process information effectively*	**Intellectual Dimension**	• *Poor decision making capability* • *Cannot organize thoughts effectively* • *Poor verbal and written communication skills* • *Cannot process information effectively*
• *In touch with our emotions* • *Feelings of contentment and security* • *Able to handle potentially stressful situations appropriately* • *Feelings of optimism* • *Can co-exist with troubling emotions*	**Emotional Dimension**	• *Detached from our emotions* • *Tends to overreact to stressors* • *Tends to be pessimistic* • *Tends to always emphasize the negative* • *Cannot co-exist with troubling emotions*
• *Able to work* • *Feelings of financial security* • *Intellectually stimulated*	**Occupational/ Environmental Dimension**	• *Unable to work* • *Feelings of financial insecurity* • *Intellectually unchallenged or overburdened*

Figure 11-1
We can plot our overall wellness level on a continuum of functioning that ranges from high-level functioning to being dysfunctional, and from high levels of wellness to illness.

vacation. You do this because it helps you maintain your fitness, moderate your weight, and sleep better. Obtaining thirty minutes of daily exercise has become part of your lifestyle. Sometimes however, your thirty minutes of exercise is not enough to prevent you from getting stressed. In this case, in addition to your daily exercise, you find that when you are stressed you like to work out on the heavy punching bag in your basement. The release associated with hitting the bag for a few rounds really drains the tension right out of you. Although this is a vigorous physical workout, you are not using it in a preventive fashion as part of your daily routine, you are using it specifically as a coping strategy. Using Rethink, Reduce, Relax, and Release strategies on a daily basis actually integrates them into our hardy health practices and contributes to the synergistic effect just described. As we will discuss next, this is considered part of moving toward optimal functioning.

Moving toward Optimal Functioning

As we have just discussed, a key to controlling your stress is improving your level of functioning across all of the dimensions of health. A key to understanding this is realizing that the journey, or the "process" of moving toward **optimal functioning,** is as important as the results you achieve. As fig. 11-1 shows, the direction you are moving in is the key. We strive to gain more control of and responsibility for our health while at the same time developing the support systems we need to help us in our journey. This model also helps us appreciate the role of time. It took us years to get where we are in terms of our health and stress. It may also take us years to get well, to reorganize our lives and our daily habits to make them more health-enhancing. Enjoy the time spent doing this. Don't try to rush it. As we improve our level of functioning, we develop more reserve energy and confidence in our ability to stay well and cope with stress. Lazarus & Folkman (1984) refer to this as our perceived ability to cope. Believing in our ability to cope is crucial to being able to cope.

Be patient and forgiving in this journey towards optimal functioning. You are human, you will face setbacks.

optimal functioning functioning at the highest level possible in any dimension of health

KEY TO UNDERSTANDING

A key to understanding optimal functioning is realizing that the journey, or the "process" of moving towards it, is as important as the results you achieve.

A key to understanding this is realizing that to be human is to sometimes give in to temptation and eat or drink too much or overextend ourselves for a period of time. A big part of reorganize is *intentionally reorganizing our thoughts* and becoming more logical in our thinking about these setbacks. They are not the end of the world and engaging in them does not make us bad people. We realize that we are not perfect beings, and we allow ourselves these imperfections without excess guilt, shame, or anger. We lighten up and tell ourselves, "It's OK, there will be days when I backslide and engage in behaviors that are not conducive to high-level health. The important thing is my overall direction. I'm making progress and moving in the right direction."

High-Level Health and Stress Management

A key to understanding the stress transaction, as has been pointed out at several points, is that stress does not take place in a vacuum. During any given stress transaction, our ability to appraise a potential stressor is influenced by our general level of wellness across all six dimensions of health. The reason something stresses us has as much to do with our general level of functioning as it does with the nature of the stressor. In addition, our belief in our ability to cope with a potential stressor is also strongly influenced by our general level of health and wellness. Our hardy health practices, over time, play a big part in this (see Stress in Our World: "Coming Home from the Shore").

STRESS IN OUR WORLD 11-1

Coming Home from the Shore

To understand how your overall level of health impacts your appraisal of potential stressors, let's create two different traffic scenarios. While each scenario will end with facing the same potential stressor, traffic, each person appraises the traffic differently because of his or her overall health status.

Scenario One

Imagine that you went to the beach with your girlfriend/boyfriend for the weekend. You are in great shape; you run a few miles daily, eat a well-balanced diet, use alcohol in moderation, and get enough sleep every night. You are doing great in school and have a decent part-time job where you are liked by your fellow workers and your boss. You meditate on a regular basis and are active in a campus group that helps build houses for poor people. Your relationship with your girlfriend/boyfriend is solid, and you each are supportive of the other's well-being. You and your partner are looking for a great weekend of running on the beach, swimming, relaxing in the sun, and spending some romantic time together.

The weekend turns out even better than you planned. In fact, the two of you woke up early this morning, went for a run on the beach, and had great sex in the shower before having breakfast and leaving to return home. You are not in a rush because you have no plans for the rest of the day. You are going to take a leisurely ride home. As you get on the highway to head home, you get stuck in traffic.

Scenario Two

Imagine the same beach scenario with your girlfriend/boyfriend for the weekend. Instead of being in great shape, however, imagine that you are sadly out of shape. You haven't gotten any regular exercise (let alone running a few miles daily) in months and your diet consists of high-calorie, high-fat, high-sugar products bought in fast food restaurants. You rarely sit down for dinner with your partner. You are in jeopardy of failing a major course at school and your part-time job is very demanding. You have no time to get involved in campus or community activities and rarely think about anyone but yourself and your personal needs.

You and your partner have been fighting constantly lately, and you have been using alcohol to cope with your displeasure with the relationship. You haven't been sleeping much lately because of this and problems at school and on your job. Your relationship with your girlfriend/boyfriend is going downhill fast (as are the rest of your relationships) and s/he is rarely there to comfort and support you. You dread this weekend together but you have already paid for the room, so the two of you are going, even if you fight all weekend.

The weekend turns out even worse than you imagined. Not only do you fight for two days straight, but your partner winds up going home early with a friend because you got drunk over dinner last night and embarrassed your partner in front of friends from school you went out with. You woke up late with a hangover and rushed out of your motel to get started on your trip home. You get about ten miles from the motel and realize that you left your wallet in your room. You turn around and speed back to your room. Fortunately, the cleaning person turned your wallet into the desk clerk and nothing is missing. Now you are in even a greater rush to get home. As you get on the highway to head home, you get stuck in traffic.

Do you think you would view the potential stressor (traffic) the same in each scenario? How do the different dimensions of health influence the stress appraisal process in these two scenarios?

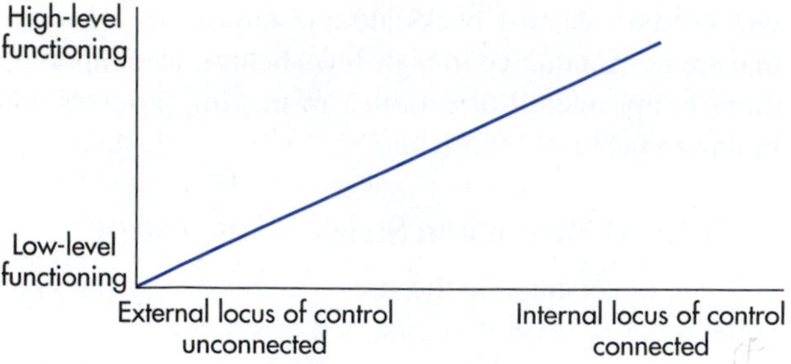

Figure 11-2

Movement in wellness is away from illness and toward optimal functioning. It also involves moving away from an external locus of control and toward connections to support systems and a spiritual life.

Figure 11-2 illustrates how our level of functioning across the dimensions of health influences our ability to cope with stressors.

As you can see, each dimension of health adds to our overall hardiness and ability to cope with stress more effectively. For example, our physical health helps us by providing the strength and energy needed to cope with potential stressors we face everyday. Our physical health also improves our intellectual functioning. High-level cardiorespiratory fitness means that our hearts and lungs process oxygen and remove waste efficiently, allowing our brains to think more clearly and process information better. This improves our thinking and decision-making abilities. High-level emotional health means we are in touch, understand, and can co-exist with our emotions. We are less likely to react inappropriately or overreact to situations because we realize that emotions ebb and flow with time. High-level social well-being ensures that we have strong relationships with others, feel loved and cared for, and have various social resources to help us in times of need. High-level spiritual well-being gives us faith in ourselves, others, and the world in general. It also helps us put our lives and problems in a more realistic, less stressful perspective. High-level environmental and occupational well-being provides safe, supportive, less stressful living and working conditions. It ensures that we have a place to seek refuge from potential stressors.

In the next section of this chapter we will examine how to develop hardy health practices for each dimension of health and build these into a set of daily habits that form the basis of a reorganized, more stress-resistant lifestyle.

A Two-Pronged Model for Reorganizing Our Health

Reorganizing implies that we are going to start organizing things differently. In a sense, reorganizing is something we do *in response* to some perceived weakness or shortcoming in our lifestyle. We realize that there are hardy healthy habits that we are not engaging in at all or that we are not putting enough effort into. For example, we might reorganize our level of physical activity because we realize that we are not active enough to derive any of the benefits associated with it. Another example might involve our level of spirituality. We can't put our finger on it but we feel some void in our lives, a sense of being disconnected or alienated. After thinking it through, we realize that we haven't really been doing anything that connects us with others in a meaningful way. Based on this we decide to join an environmental group and clean our local streams and rivers with other like-minded people.

Sometimes the best way to approach these deficiencies is to attack these problems head on and make changes in our behavior. This, if you remember from the introduction to Part II of the book at the beginning of chapter 7, is called a problem-focused approach. Other times, the best way to reorganize is to change the way we view things. Maybe things are not as bad as they appear and we don't necessarily have to change our behavior or our environment. There are also aspects of our lives that we either can't change or can't reorganize now but can get to at a later point. In these situations an emotion-focused approach to reorganizing our thoughts works best. If you recall, in an emotion-focused approach we concentrate on changing our thoughts about the situation, not the situation itself.

Throughout the rest of the chapter we will use this model and work through problem-focused and emotion-focused approaches to reorganizing the six dimensions of health. We will integrate strategies from the Five Rs, hardy healthy habits, and skills from Japanese psychology in our reorganizing.

Reorganizing the Environmental/Occupational Dimension of Health

Reorganizing the Environmental Dimension of Health

A good place to start reorganizing your health is the environmental dimension because all of our other activities designed to improve our health occur within some environmental context, whether it is our home, workplace, community, or college campus. In chapter 1 we referred to this as our immediate or **micro environment.** Sometimes we are stressed by things going on in the world at large. This is referred to as the global community or **macro environment.** In the next section of this chapter we use two examples of how to use a problem-focused

micro environment one's immediate environment, including immediate family and friends and living and working space

macro environment the world at large

and an emotion-focused coping strategy to cope with micro- and macro-environment stressors and reorganize this dimension of your health.

A Problem-Focused Approach to Reorganizing the Micro Environment

In the introduction to coping section of this book we discussed emotion-focused and problem-focused coping. Many of the problem-focused approaches to coping involve altering one's environment. If you think about the Three As of Coping strategy discussed in chapter 7, it illustrates how sometimes just altering our exposure to stressors, modifying our environment slightly, can defuse something as a stressor.

Let's use a common environmental stressor, traffic, as an example. Imagine that you have a great job that you really love. Unfortunately, you can't afford to buy a house or rent an apartment nearby, so you are forced to live in a more affordable community fifty miles away. This means that you must commute to work along a couple of different routes that are very congested during peak travel periods. You've found that commuting to work during peak traffic periods is a stressor. When you've had to go into work on a weekend or some other off-peak time period, you have found the same ride to be very pleasant and not a stressor at all. In fact, you love to drive and usually find it very relaxing.

You've tried to Rethink this stressor and see if you can view the commute differently. This hasn't worked for you. You've also tried a couple of different Relax strategies but they just don't seem to do the trick either. You also make sure that during the week you engage in hearty health practices such as getting enough sleep and eating a breakfast each morning before you leave for work. You are worried that the stress of commuting will ultimately cause enough stress that it will carry over into your job and affect your performance. This is a perfect time to employ short- and long-term reorganize strategies to change this environmentally based stressor. You decide to think logically about this and realize that it might take some time and effort to alter this stressor, but it is important enough to you to at least try to make it work.

As a short-term reorganize strategy you decide to approach your boss about developing a more flexible approach to your work schedule. Although your employer is a small business and doesn't have an official *flex hours* policy, you've noticed that most of the important meetings and activities go on between 10:00 A.M. and 5:00 P.M. during the workday. You decide to meet with him and propose that your workday start at 10:00 A.M., after the peak morning rush hours, and end at 7:00 P.M., after most of the evening rush.

As a long-term reorganize strategy you have decided to save more money, so you can afford to move into a condominium closer to work and cut your commute in half. Buying a condominium about twenty to twenty-five miles from work is not your ideal solution but it will make your commute tolerable and build equity. The equity in your condominium will help you eventually buy something even closer to work. You realize such long-range planning is not a sure thing since a lot can change over the next few years. Since you cannot control the future, you accept this and put your plan into action, fully aware that you'll have to reassess it every year and make adjustments as your life changes.

An Emotion-Focused Approach to Coping with the Macro Environment

Let's use another common macro-environmental stressor, terrorism, to illustrate how to use emotion-focused coping. Since September 11, 2001, most Americans have become more concerned about terrorism. Although America has not suffered any terrorist acts, *terrorist alerts* issued by the President of the United States and other officials have reminded us of our vulnerability. Most of the time we are able to co-exist with our fears and do not let the threat of terrorism remain a stressor for very long. What can we do, however, if these thoughts persist and the threat of terrorism becomes a chronic, macro-environmental stressor? Emotion-focused coping can help us defuse macro-environmental stressors such as terrorism by helping us change our illogical thinking about them and/or be able to co-exist with the emotions associated with them. Let's use Ellis and Harper's[2] ABCDE technique as an example. Imagine you just saw a short segment on the evening news about a suspected terrorist cell that was uncovered in a city one thousand miles away from you. After the report and for the next few hours, you find yourself tense, anxious, and fearful and realize you are in the middle of a stress response over the report. Instead of continuing to be stressed, you take out a pen and paper and use the ABCDE technique to change your illogical thinking.

A (activating event)

Watching the news report on the terrorist cell.

Bs (illogical beliefs)

"*No American* is safe anywhere in this country anymore."

"There is probably a terrorist cell in my town also."

"The government isn't doing *anything* to protect us."

"We are *all* going to be blown to bits."

Cs (consequences)

muscle tension in neck

fear and anxiety

loss of desire to go out in public

D (dispute)

"*No American* is safe anywhere in this country anymore."

"Despite this happening, most Americans are safe. There is very little terrorist activity in this country that our government doesn't know about."

"There is probably a terrorist cell in my town also."

"It is highly unlikely that there is a terrorist cell in my town. While there are cells operating in America, they are few and far between."

"The government isn't doing *anything* to protect us."

"The government is doing a lot to combat terrorism starting with better cooperation among nations involved in this fight to more aware police on the street. Every day we are learning more about how to combat terrorism."

"We are *all* going to be blown to bits."

"As horrible as it is to say, even if there was a terrorist incident, the vast majority of citizens would not be physically harmed."

E (effects)

"After disputing the illogical thoughts, you have a more realistic appraisal of the threat and start to feel better."

There are many other emotion-focused ways to cope with macro-environmental stressors. We could use Morita therapy to redirect our attention to productive work and co-exist with the strong feelings reminding ourselves that they will dissipate in time. One could also use a more problem-focused approach and take direct action to change the environment. In the case of terrorism one could learn how to prepare for a terrorist attack, join a neighborhood watch group, move to a rural area, or many other strategies. One could also join and contribute money to groups that fight terrorism. These same strategies could be used to cope with other macro-environmental stressors.

In essence, when you take steps like this to cope with micro- and macro-environmental stressors, you are also starting to reorganize this dimension of your health. This kind of coping is **proactive** and helps you assume a degree of control over your life. In addition, it has the potential to change the stressful environment for you and for others. Instead of feeling entirely helpless, you are taking concrete steps to reorganize aspects of your environment to make them more health-enhancing and to make yourself more stress-resistant.

Reorganizing the Occupational Dimension of Health

As we discussed in chapter 3, most Americans who work full-time spend close to fifty hours a week at their worksites. Reorganizing occupational well-being is vitally important since work time represents such a large part of one's day. There are many ways to reorganize your work site to make it more health-enhancing ranging from improving the physical environment in which you work to improving your communications with bosses, co-workers, and associates. A first step in reorganizing this dimension of health is assessing areas that could be strengthened. Chapter 3 offers some advice regarding assessing things such as ergonomics, lighting, etc. Some of the emotion-focused strategies we've already learned also provide insight into the nature of work and how it relates to your values, goals, and purpose in life.

A Problem-Focused Approach to Reorganizing the Occupational Dimension

A good example of using a problem-based approach to strengthening your occupational well-being is to be more proactive in monitoring your employer's compliance with NIOSH health and safety standards. As we mentioned in chapter 3, the government, through the National Institute for Occupational Safety and Health (NIOSH[6]), monitors worksite health and safety. If you feel that your workplace is not in compliance with federal standards, and your job is unionized, you might consider working through the employee union to address these short-comings. If that is not the case, you can contact NIOSH directly and report suspected violations. At the end of this chapter there is a reference for the NIOSH Web page that describes how any worker can contact them for help in investigating potentially hazardous worksite materials or practices (NIOSH[6]).

In terms of your individual workspace and work habits, be sure to take advantage of all protective devices, including noise suppression ear muffs/plugs and glare reducers, supplied by your employer to reduce potential environmental stressors. If you have any input into how your individual workspace is designed or retrofitted or into the ordering of equipment, furniture, and workstations, make recommendations for products that conform to the ergonomic guidelines discussed in chapter 3.

Another problem-oriented approach to reorganizing your occupational well-being is communicating more effectively by taking responsibility for expressing your concerns or clearing up misunderstandings *before* these potential stressors escalate into stressors. Try to use "I" language and verbal assertiveness techniques more consistently. Simply incorporating these techniques into your everyday communications with employers and co-workers reorganizes your workplace. People begin to see that you are taking responsibility for communicating clearly and that you are being more assertive in your job. Others will respond to your behavior by adapting and changing the way they relate to you. They will begin to see that they can no longer get away with partial communications or

proactive an approach to things based on acting rather than reacting to situations miscommunications and that you can no longer be taken advantage of because of your assertiveness.

An Emotion-Focused Approach to Reorganizing the Occupational Dimension

Often, there are workplace situations and relationships that you'd like to improve but are not able to change now or in the immediate future for a variety of reasons beyond your control. They might involve your salary or position, work duties, workspace, or a host of other issues. The best you can hope to do in this situation is to understand and co-exist with the emotions associated with the situations or the relationships. In a sense, if you can't improve the situations or relationships by taking action or making physical changes, you can *reorganize the way you think* and feel about them.

A good way to start doing this is to think about how important these situations and relationships really are in relation to the bigger picture of your life (your values, life goals, and daily life criteria for happiness). As we described in chapter 7, these are the key issues that connect your purpose in life with how you choose to earn a living. What you want to do is to assess how your current job situation and relationships mesh with what you value, what your purpose in life is, and whether they support or conflict with your daily life criteria for happiness. In a sense you want to assess whether or not these situations and relationships are even worth reorganizing. If they are you can employ various Rethink strategies to help you reorganize the way you think about work.

As an example of the latter let's imagine that you have been in the same job for the past ten years. You are a computer programmer for a mid-sized corporation and you just became vested in the pension program. The job is related to what you trained for. You have an Associate's Degree in computer programming from a junior college. While you still enjoy computer programming, your company has changed their business plan and has begun to outsource several key components of their operations. You don't really like this new direction. One of the functions that is now outsourced is the Help Desk. Up until last month, the Help Desk was housed in a group of offices down the hall from you. Not only did you know and like all of the workers there, it was very convenient to walk down the hall and get help if you needed it. Now you have to call and talk to people who are not on-site and not employees of your company. You are not really stressed by this, just annoyed at this inconvenience and the thought that other components of your company (including yours) might be outsourced.

The first step in taking an emotion-focused approach to this is to assess whether your job still meets your needs and is consistent with your values, goals, and criteria for happiness. You do this and find that your job is still consistent with your needs.

The next step is to assess your illogical thinking about this work situation using either a formal model such as Ellis and Harper's[2] ABCDE technique or informally jotting your thoughts down and examining them. You do this and realize that you have no illogical thoughts about what is going on at work. You realize that there are pros and cons to outsourcing and that your employer has every right to pursue this strategy. You don't feel particularly threatened about your job being outsourced.

Lastly, you realize that there is a certain element of uncertainty in all jobs and that it is normal to have strong emotions arise from time to time regarding work. You remind yourself that this is normal and when this happens you have to tell yourself, "I can co-exist with these emotions. In time, if I don't dwell on them, they will pass." You also remind yourself that you need to continue to reassess your work and how it meshes with your life and what gives it meaning and purpose.

REORGANIZING THE SOCIAL DIMENSION OF HEALTH

As we've discussed throughout the book, our social relationships provide connections to other people that add richness and depth to our lives. Family, friends, and

True friends understand and support you. They are there when you need them, and they boost, not destroy, your self-esteem.

acquaintances enrich our lives and give them meaning. Being someone's child, sibling, husband, wife, partner, lover, or friend connects us to others in unique ways. It is in relationships with others that we most fully develop our potential as people.

As we discussed in chapter 2, humans are social animals. We need interaction with others to be fully human. Our relationships with others also form the basis for social supports. Our social support networks evolve out of our connections with others. In chapter 4 we discussed how important social support networks are in helping us cope with stress. In many cases our social support networks can even prevent potential stressors from becoming actual stressors because they enable us to feel that we can cope with unanticipated problems. If we feel we can cope with things, they become challenges to face, not stressors.

A Problem-Focused Approach to Reorganizing the Social Dimension

One way to approach reorganizing our social dimension of health is to evaluate our social networks and support and take steps to shore up any weaknesses or build on the strengths that already exist. This assessment can occur on many levels. As we mentioned in chapter 4, there are many objective and subjective measures of social networks and social supports.

An example of an objective measure is to merely count the number of social relationships we have (family, friends, associates, etc.) and social organizations we belong to. If you recall from chapter 4, this kind of assessment will give us a measure of our social embeddedness, the level and complexity of our social connectedness to others. More subjective measures of our social health, our relationship quality, and enacted social support describe the types of support we receive from others and their effectiveness. This kind of assessment can be used as an ongoing part of reorganizing our social dimension.

As an example of the former, imagine that you are the single parent of a one-year-old child. You have managed to take a year off, living on your savings, to take care of your newborn. You now want to reenter the workforce and you are concerned about the cost and shortage of child-care facilities in your area that take children who are not yet toilet trained. As part of your planning you examine your social support network and think about who might be able to provide the kind of child care you need and can afford. You think about family, friends, and neighbors. You call friends who returned to work and ask them who they use for child care. You speak to your minister about the child-care center at your church as well as his contacts in the community. He mentions that he knows a woman, a mother of a one-year old who lives nearby and who is looking to stay home and supplement her income by caring for one additional child. Your minister vouches for the woman's credentials and integrity. You call her and find that she is the answer to your needs. You hire her and after a couple of months she turns out to be a new friend as well as your child-care resource person. Your child-care concerns are removed and your social network is strengthened at the same time.

An Emotion-Focused Approach to Reorganizing the Social Dimension

In chapter 4 we discussed that how in addition to being a coping resource our social support network can also be a source of stress. Social embeddedness and social support require an investment of time and energy. In some cases we find that the time and energy we must invest in building social support is either not worth it or it becomes a source of stress, often stretching us beyond optimal stimulation and into stressful demand. A key to understanding social support is realizing that the same people and groups that support us often also stir up strong emotions within us. Learning to co-exist with these negative emotions that accompany social commitments is important.

Let's use family commitments as an example. Imagine that you grew up in a cultural environment where family was very important. As a child you were very close to all of your aunts, uncles, cousins, and even second cousins. Your parents felt it was very important to keep the family close, so most of your socializing was with family and revolved around family events ranging from christenings, to birthdays, to even major holidays. You also remember the family helping each other out through minor and major crises ranging from losing a job to putting a new roof on your grandfather's house.

The older you got, the less interested you were in attending all of the family occasions where your presence was expected. You really preferred to spend more time with your friends. This caused a lot of problems with your parents and was a major source of tension and arguments within your family. This became less of a problem for you when you went away to college. The distance from home, cost, and academic workload made it next to impossible to attend most of the family functions. Now that college is almost over and you will be returning home soon, you are getting anxious about having to deal with this again.

Once again you need to assess what is really important in your life. Do you share your parents' and culture's values regarding family and family responsibilities? Do the benefits of staying as closely connected to your extended family equal what you feel you have to give up to maintain them? Are you thinking logically about these responsibilities and expectations?

After much analysis you decide that you really do not want to spend as much time with your family as they expect of you. You realize that this is going to cause bad feelings in the family, especially with your parents, and you accept this. You've decided that you don't want to divorce yourself from the family and like the safety net they

KEY TO UNDERSTANDING

A key to understanding social support is realizing that the same people and groups that support us often also stir up strong emotions within us. Learning to co-exist with these negative emotions that accompany social commitments is important.

Helping others by engaging in meaningful work is a great way to increase your spirituality.

provide. On the other hand, you simply don't want to spend every weekend attending some family function or another. This makes you a little anxious and guilty, but you decide that you can coexist with these feelings. You realize that in time you will feel even less anxious and guilty for spending less time with the family and that their emotions will also diminish and they will become a little more accepting of your lifestyle choice. You also realize that if that doesn't happen you can also handle that and co-exist with whatever feelings that provokes.

STRENGTHENING THE SPIRITUAL DIMENSION OF HEALTH

As we mentioned in chapters 1 and 4, the key element in spirituality is a sense of interconnectedness with something beyond the self. Spirituality could be religious in nature or secular, or both. If one's spirituality is religious in nature, the interconnectedness one feels is with a source of divine power or God. If one's spirituality is secular in nature, the interconnectedness is with other living things, nature, the universe, etc. It is not unusual for people to feel both, a belief in a divine power and a sense of interconnectedness with other living things, nature, etc.

A Problem-Focused Approach to Reorganizing the Spiritual Dimension

If you are religious, your religion connects you to a faith community through your church, temple, mosque, or other place of worship. This becomes the hub of your spirituality and the base for your faith. It is a place of worship, a meeting place, a community center. It is the place where you commune with like-minded others to discuss and work on issues of fellowship. Often churches, temples, mosques, and other places of worship serve as the base for a variety of community services. Many of these religious sanctuaries serve as distribution centers for food and clothing for the needy, meeting sites for help groups such as Alcoholics Anonymous, and refuges for the less fortunate until they can get back on their feet. This provides an excellent opportunity to reorganize your spiritual health through a problem-focused approach.

For example, let's imagine that you are feeling a little alienated and that you have lost a little of your faith in life and in your fellow humans. You've witnessed war, terrorist attacks, and the gulf between the very rich and the very poor get larger. You've begun to question how humans can be so mean and care so little about each other. Your priest, minister, imam, or rabbi's sermons seem a little shallow and you are questioning your faith.

One way to cope with this and at the same time strengthen your spiritual well-being is to take action and use your faith community's outreach programs to serve others. This is an excellent example of co-existing with the troubling doubts and emotions you have regarding your faith while engaging in the productive work of serving others. Rather than intellectually trying to analyze your thoughts and feelings about losing your faith, you shift your attention away from this and focus it on helping others. You start to volunteer one afternoon a week to go into the community and spend an evening with a member of the congregation who is homebound and cannot prepare their own meals or clean their house. You find the actual work of preparing meals, cleaning, and caring for another human being enlightening. You enjoy feeling connected to another person in a meaningful way. This person is so grateful for your company and help that you decide to spend an additional afternoon and occasional Saturday there. When you come home from these sessions, you realize that your doubts about your faith are fewer and less intense.

An Emotion-Focused Approach to Reorganizing the Spiritual Dimension

Although Naikan self-reflection is not considered a spiritual activity per se, it is an excellent tool to help you become aware of your interconnectedness to others in your life and to help become more grateful for the role they've played in your life. Although Naikan self-reflection isn't intended for use in examining troubling thoughts and emotions, the insights gained by reflecting on the three questions that are central to its practice often shed light on these and help defuse them as stressors.

For example, imagine that you are upset with your nineteen-year-old son. It seems sometimes that he no longer shares your values and that he is beginning to resemble the narcissistic, self-absorbed upper-middle-class children of your community more than you and your husband. You decide to use him as the focus of Naikan self-reflection and perform this for three different periods of your life together: from ages 0–8, 9–15, and 16 to the present. You answer the three questions diligently: 1. What have I done for . . . , 2. What has . . . done for me? And 3. What problems have I caused . . . ?

After many hours of self-reflection, you realize that while your son has changed lately and sometimes does seem to be someone other than your own child, for the most part he still embodies most of the values you and your husband instilled in him. Further, it makes you realize that what he is going through is a normal part of development, one that you went through yourself. In a sense, he is part of the cycle of life that involves growth and separation. You walk away from the Naikan self-reflection with a new appreciation for your son and all of the parents who are part of this cycle of life and the perpetuation of the culture and the species. You not only see the interconnectedness between you and them, you feel at peace playing your part in it. This results in a reorganization of your thinking about your relationship with your son and opens the door for a new approach to dealing with him and appreciating the connection you have with him.

Reorganizing the Intellectual Dimension of Health

The fact that you are a college student means that you've already taken a step toward improving your intellectual dimension. Intellectual functioning is the ability to think and process information clearly and accurately. On countless occasions this book has emphasized the importance of logical thinking in the stress transaction. Logical thinking revolves around our ability to be objective and see through all the media noise, mixed messages, and misinformation that not only contribute to our stress but also to our overall quality of life. Being able to distinguish fact from fiction depends on the extent of our knowledge as well as the way we use it. Reorganizing the intellectual dimension requires that we develop a commitment to thinking clearly and using reason and logic to guide us. It needs to be a conscious decision and commitment that extends beyond the self to include others who give your life meaning (partners, family, friends etc.). It means that you gently try to get others to use their reason and logic when dealing with you. Not only are you changed, you become a *change agent* for a more reasoned, intelligent life.

Key to Understanding

Commitment and action are the key to successful change.

Key to Understanding

Your chances of success are greater if you get involved with volunteer work that you enjoy.

A Problem-Focused Approach to Strengthening the Intellectual Dimension

A big component of strengthening the intellectual dimension is keeping up with the literature in your area of interest. The research, information, technology, and resources associated with a discipline, job, profession, or career seem to change on a daily basis. Knowledge of this research, information, technology, and resources gives you power and control in your life. Keeping pace with what you need to know to remain current in your interest area requires that you use your time and resources wisely. An excellent strategy for strengthening your intellectual dimension is to join, and take an active role in, professional organizations related to your discipline or area of interest. They can help you in many different ways.

For example, imagine you are just starting out in your career. You are in your senior year in college and are an education major. You are feeling overwhelmed at the thought of finding a job and keeping current in your area of interest, teaching science at the middle school level. You realize that although you will be student teaching

Although graduation day may be the culmination of formal academic training, it is only the beginning of lifelong learning.

DIVERSE PERSPECTIVES 11-1

Finding Your Personal Walden Pond

A long time ago, Henry David Thoreau wrote about his need to seek a place away from the crowds, in a more natural environment, to explore the meaning of his life and the trappings of the civilized world. He wasn't renouncing society, merely stepping back from it to get a better look at his life.

Similarly, in our fast-paced culture, we need to get off the fast track to find the spiritual element in our lives. By doing this we can return to our daily responsibilities and commitments renewed and refreshed. Although vacations are meant to do this, they've unfortunately become a source of stress for many people. We cram so much into our vacations and often visit places that provide more rather than less stimulation that many times we feel we need a vacation to recuperate from our vacation!

Thoreau's pilgrimages to Walden Pond were his attempts to seek out a more natural place to slow down, be among the elements of nature, and sort through the trials and tribulations of his life in civilized society.

Colin Fletcher, in *The Complete Walker,* talks about his need to escape from the travails of everyday life by hiking and backpacking for a few days or weeks at a time. He describes how this recharges his batteries. The time away with no phones, TV, radio, or newspaper gives him time to pause and think without interference from media noise. His trips also renew his sense of wonder and awe of the natural world. In addition, he now appreciates coming home to clean sheets and a hot bath, simple things that people take for granted.

In most cultures and religions, there are times and places—in daily life—for contemplation. The Japanese have gardens replete with miniature bonsai trees. Oases in a crowded society, these gardens offer sanctuary from the hurried pace of industrialized society. Moslems set aside several times every day to turn toward their holy city, Mecca, and pray to Allah. Buddhist monks live in monasteries high in the mountains, where, removed from the busyness of the world, they can contemplate the meaning of existence. Catholic priests and nuns have seminaries and communities where long hours are spent in quiet contemplation of the spiritual world, far removed from the hustle and bustle of everyday life. Native Americans seek the sanctuary of special places—mountains, deserts, canyons—to retreat into a vision quest for inner peace.

Wherever we find our Walden, we must make the time to visit it often. We must find time to disconnect from our busy lives so that we may reconnect with something greater than ourselves.

this semester and have gone to a seminar about finding your first teaching job, you really are very insecure about the whole job search process and starting out in your career. You are not really sure you want to stay in this area after graduation and don't know anything about teaching opportunities for science teachers elsewhere.

An excellent way to strengthen your intellectual dimension would be to join the state and national chapters of your educational association. Your advisor at college should be able to give you their names and addresses. Most professional organizations have greatly reduced membership dues for students and also have student committees. These organizations all feature newsletters, journals, and other special publications that provide an ongoing source of information about your area of interest. Reading this material is an excellent way to stay current with the new developments in your field. Membership also entitles you to use their job bank or other job-related service to find entry-level and other teaching jobs. Many teaching and other professional jobs are not advertised in newspapers. In addition to joining and being a passive recipient of the services these organizations offer, you could also take a more active role, joining committees and holding positions. This type of active involvement provides another form of hands-on learning and networking that also strengthens your intellectual abilities. Working in committees will give you opportunities to apply what you've learned in the classroom to real-world situations.

An Emotion-Focused Approach to Strengthening the Intellectual Dimension

Improving your intellectual health often requires *Reorganizing* the way you think about learning and making the transition from being a passive recipient of knowledge to an active seeker of it on a lifelong basis. Since you're in college and have made it this far, you've gotten a good start in this process. Completing your college degree and, in the process, getting a broad liberal arts background is the next step. Finishing school can do more than provide you with the skills and information necessary to find work in your chosen field. It can change your perspective on learning and the importance of becoming a lifelong learner. It can lay the foundation for an appreciation of learning that extends well beyond the college years. To build on this foundation, however, and view learning as a lifelong journey, we often have to reorganize our thoughts about what this actually entails. For example, imagine that you have graduated from college and accepted a job somewhere. You move out of your house and are living on your own. Initially you miss college life,

Living Constructively

Life at the ToDo Institute

Throughout this book we have discussed the components of living constructively. Living constructively revolves around the Morita principle of accepting that feelings cannot be controlled and need not stand in the way of leading a productive life. Rather than *working on* trying to control or eliminate troubling feelings, living constructively teaches us that it is better to accept them and spend our valuable time doing what gives our life meaning and purpose. Co-existing with troubling feelings while performing meaningful work becomes easier with practice, as we learn how to shift our attention away from ourselves and onto others, the world around us, and the work that needs to get done. Naikan practice helps us make this shift by teaching us how to reflect on our lives and the support we have received from others and the world around us. Reflecting on the support of others helps us develop grace and gratitude as our attention moves from ourselves to others and how important they have been in our achievements.

Nowhere in America is the application of living constructively more clearly illustrated than at the ToDo Institute in Vermont. Taking a course at the Institute provides an intimate glimpse into the real-world application of living constructively because ToDo is not only a school, it is a home.

The Institute's directors and their two daughters live in the downstairs part of the rambling Vermont farmhouse while students share living quarters on the third floor. The middle floor comprises of the kitchen, dining area, living room, library, and deck. Adjacent to this space is the ToDo Institute's professional office where their newsletter, *Thirty Thousand Days,* is produced. Students and family share the middle floor where daily activities such as cooking, eating, and cleaning co-exist with teaching and learning. Indeed, some of the most memorable lessons in living constructively occur over communal meal preparation, daily meditation sessions, and doing chores with the kids.

The ToDo lifestyle is a peaceful one, lived in consort with nature and respect for the natural resources and the beauty of the Vermont countryside. Everything that can be is recycled. Students are instructed where to put glass, metal, plastic, and paper-based recyclables. Food scraps are composted. Students are urged to use water sparingly (even though it is in abundance) by turning off water when not necessary (e.g., when brushing teeth) and limiting showering to once daily. A morning and evening showering schedule is informally agreed upon to ease congestion for nine students sharing one bathroom. Everyone (students, instructors, kids, and guests) performs one hour of *meaningful household work* such as cleaning the house, pruning trees, planting gardens, weeding, stacking wood, or the author's favorite, picking raspberries at a local patch. Everyone is expected to help in preparing the three meals a day eaten communally. Sign-up sheets are posted and everyone is encouraged to experiment with different recipes. All meals are vegan and supplies are bought fresh daily. Clean up is also communal as everyone clears the table and helps wash and put away the dishes. Television viewing is limited to an occasional movie or educational show.

Courses at the ToDo Institute are taught by the directors and outside instructors from around North America. Courses in Naikan and Morita Therapy are generally from one to two weeks in duration. A typical day consists of the following schedule:

7:00–7:30 A.M.	Morning Meditation
8:00–9:00 A.M.	Breakfast
9:00–12:00 A.M.	Group Instruction
12:00–1:00 P.M.	Lunch
1:30–4:30 P.M.	Individual 1/2 hour individual sessions with instructor
4:30–5:30 P.M.	household work (3 people on dinner preparation)
6:00–7:00 P.M.	dinner*
7:00–10:00 P.M.	homework or evening session or entertainment**
>10:00 P.M.	quiet time and sleep

Taking a course at the ToDo Institute is an immersion in living constructively. It is evident from the moment that you set foot in the house and meet the directors and their children that these are special people and that this is a special place. It is a living laboratory dedicated to demonstrating the application of Morita, Naikan, and Zen Buddhist principles in a real family and a real center of learning. It is probably the most peaceful place the author has ever been, filled with love, learning, and caring. It is a glimpse into the potential that lies within all of us to live lives that are peaceful and gentle, filled with purpose and lived with vigor. It is not a stress-free life but one filled with more challenge than stress, more optimism than pessimism, more joy than despair.

*when the author attended a 10-day summer course, dinner one evening was a picnic at a local town festival in Middlebury, Vermont, and another evening was a picnic on the shores of Lake Champlain

**entertainment one evening consisted of a communal music fest (students were encouraged to play piano, guitar, or various percussion instruments available at ToDo) living in the dorms, going to football games, etc., but you tell yourself, "This is normal and I've got to stop living in the past and get on with my life." After a while, your life begins to fall into a rhythm that involves work, rest, socializing and recreating, household duties, etc. Eventually you think of *the college life* less and less and move on. At times however you feel that something is missing. The sameness of your life begins to wear on you and you finally realize that part of what you liked about college was the change and the exposure to new ideas and new information. You realize that a big part of what you miss is the richness of the intellectual life of college. You decide to explore ways to reestablish your intellectual life.

One of the best ways to be a lifelong learner is to use continuing education programs to learn more about things that appeal to you. Unlike formal school-based learning which is driven by a *curriculum,* lifelong learning is driven by whatever interests you and peaks your curiosity. If you take the time to explore the courses offered at your local community or university continuing education programs, you'll be amazed at their diversity and richness. As an added bonus, noncredit, continuing education courses have no tests, grades, or attendance policies to worry about. They are also excellent places to meet new friends and partners who share your interests and passions.

Most communities offer continuing education courses through either the municipal government or the Board of Education. Many programs are run as a cooperative venture between these two organizations and local colleges or universities. Consequently, you can find continuing education courses by calling your town hall, board of education office, or college/university Office of Continuing Education. Whichever organization manages the program usually has a printed or online course catalog similar to the one you worked with as an undergraduate.

Start with a course that is fun and has always been something you wanted to learn more about but never had the time while in college. Your author has taken courses in scuba diving, pottery, gourmet cooking, wine tasting, and tennis, just to name a few. Costs vary but generally are much less than tuition for credit-bearing college courses. Local municipalities try to keep costs to a minimum to encourage more people to sign up.

Once you have taken a few adult, continuing education courses, you find that your whole mindset towards learning shifts. Learning becomes *fun* again. Freed from the worries of tests, grades, forced reading assignments, and attendance policies, you begin to get the sense of what a lifelong approach to learning entails. When this happens your perception of what learning is all about shifts. It is no longer something associated with school, a career, a required course. It is really a tool for satisfying and stimulating your *curiosity* about life. One of the healthiest outcomes of reorganizing this dimension is regaining your intellectual curiosity. This is a priceless commodity that can help you maintain a vibrancy that can stay with you throughout your adult and older adult years. Of course there are many other roads to lifelong learning. Stressbusters Tips: "Tips for Lifelong Learning" provides some other avenues for becoming a lifelong learner.

Key to Understanding

Knowing as much as you can about a potential stressor can reduce the stress associated with it.

Stress Buster Tips

Ten Tips for Becoming a Lifelong Learner

Becoming a lifelong learner requires that you reorganize what you think learning is all about. Here are some tips that will get you started.

1. *Keep reminding yourself that your education is never finished.* Learning is a life-long process.
2. *Read anything and everything.* Join a book club. Subscribe to magazines, newspapers, online news services. Go to the library. These all provide a smorgasbord of reading opportunities.
3. *Keep an open mind.* Read, watch, and listen to different opinions and sides of an argument. Try to think about an Issue from opposing viewpoints just to understand it better. You don't have to agree with opposing views to appreciate their intellectual value.
4. *Seek the viewpoints of your elders and young people.* Their views represent a different space and time than yours that has intrinsic value.
5. *Travel.* Expose yourself to the ideas and lifestyles of people and cultures that are different than your own. These could be across the state or across the globe.
6. *Listen to talk radio when driving.* Try to locate stations and hosts that represent differing political positions on issues. This is an easy and interesting way to expose yourself to new information. Listen to both public and commercial talk radio.
7. *Take continuing education courses for fun.* Want to learn how to scuba dive, make pottery, cook ? These and countless other fun courses await you.
8. *Join and become active in civic and professional groups.* Attending meetings and conferences sponsored by these groups exposes you to new ideas and information that keeps your mind active.
9. *Create.* Write, paint, sing, sculpt, or build something. Use your creative talents. Everyone has some creative outlet. Don't worry about being good at it, just do it.
10. *Question.* Never stop asking the why, how, what, or where of things. The answers to these questions are what give life meaning.

Reorganizing the Emotional Dimension of Health

While the intellectual dimension of health addresses the cognitive aspects of our minds, the emotional domain is concerned with understanding our feelings and how we deal with them. Reorganizing the emotional dimension involves becoming more emotionally hardy, or developing emotional toughness. This doesn't mean being insensitive or denying your feelings. In fact, it is just the opposite. It involves being acutely aware of what one is experiencing and accepting the reality of those emotions. Mental toughness is learning how to co-exist with troubling emotions while being productive.

Too many people live under the delusion that emotional health is an either-or phenomenon; one is either happy or sad, or emotionally well or emotionally ill. As should be obvious to you by now, nothing could be farther from the truth. During any given twenty-four-hour period we experience a wide range of emotions. As we've learned from Morita therapy, no one knows where these emotions come from or *why* you feel the way you do from one moment to the next. In fact, Moritists argue, understanding the origin of our emotions isn't even necessary for learning how to co-exist with them. The twin goals of reorganizing your emotional well-being are (1) becoming more mindful of your emotions and (2) learning how to co-exist with them.

A Problem-Focused Approach to Strengthening the Emotional Dimension

In chapter 2 we examined the relationship between psychological factors, emotional styles, and stress. We learned how negative emotions such as anger, hostility, and pessimism are related to increased stress levels and illness and how positive emotions such as happiness, commitment, challenge, optimism, and a sense of humor are related to improved health status. In this section, we'll examine how to use mindfulness and co-existing with negative emotions to deal with a common example.

Imagine you are a college senior majoring in business management. One of the courses you must take in order to graduate is a course in public speaking. The course is designed to teach you how to speak in front of small and large groups. The idea is to prepare you for real-world tasks such as running meetings and presenting proposals to corporate clients. This class is very troubling to you. You've always disliked speaking out and presenting to groups. You much prefer to be part of a working group than the leader. You find yourself getting anxious even thinking about this class. You start to question, "Why do I always get anxious over these things? I'll never be relaxed and enjoy giving these presentations. I should switch majors."

This is a perfect example to demonstrate the use of mindfulness and co-existing with negative emotions. There are a few steps involved in doing this.

1. The first thing you need to do is become more mindful of these anxious feelings when they arise. In fact, you should pay close attention to exactly how that anxiety feels and make note of them in the following nonjudgmental manner: "Isn't this interesting. I am getting anxious again. I notice that when I feel this way my neck muscles start to tighten, my hands get clammy, and I start to breathe more rapidly and in a shallow fashion. When I am not feeling this way I seem to breathe deeper and more slowly."
2. The second thing you need to do is accept these feelings. Tell yourself: "I am definitely feeling anxious. I'd rather not feel this way but I guess it is normal to feel like this if I have to do something I don't like to do or am uncomfortable with."
3. The third step is telling yourself that you can co-exist with these feelings and still be productive. Here is an example: "I really envy people who find it easy to give presentations. It is hard for me to stand in front of a group feeling the way I do. I'll have to prepare harder and just accept the discomfort."
4. The fourth step is being completely prepared whenever you are asked to present. Make sure you know your subject inside and out. Use practice rehearsal in a mirror or in front of a couple of friends. Use audiovisual aids and other props to take the focus off yourself and give yourself a break while presenting.
5. Use simple relaxation techniques just before you get in front of the group. Do some diaphragmatic breathing and muscle relaxation (especially in the face, neck, and upper body).
6. Remind yourself that you can give a productive presentation despite being anxious.

In time, becoming more mindful of your troubling feelings and practicing co-existing with them will become part of your daily routine. This will probably not eliminate the troubling feelings but will reinforce your ability to be productive despite them and will help you become more mentally tough.

An Emotion-Focused Approach to Strengthening the Emotional Dimension

In emotion-focused approaches to reorganizing the emotional dimension, you are actually trying to eliminate or reduce troubling emotions. As we've seen in chapter 7, this is often done by changing the illogical, irrational, or pessimistic thoughts that are associated with the feelings. This approach is based on the premise that you can modify or eliminate troubling emotions by dealing with the thoughts that they revolve around. In addition, by learning to think more logically about a stressor, you reduce the likelihood that troubling emotions associated with it will arise in the first place.

We can use the same example that we used in our problem-focused approach to demonstrate this. An emotion-focused approach to the anxiety and other troubling emotions associated with giving presentations could start with the illogical beliefs surrounding one's perceived ability to cope with the stressors. If you identify the negative, illogical self-talk associated with giving presentations in the future when you are called upon to give them you will perceive them differently. If you can perceive them as a challenge or more positively, they will no longer trigger troubling emotions.

Lets actually work through Ellis and Harper's ABCDE Model[2] using the presentation as our example.

A (activating event)

Having to give a ten-minute presentation to the class on a business topic of my choice.

Bs (illogical beliefs)

"Why do I hate these presentations so much?"

"I'll never be able to last ten minutes in front of the class."

"I'll just die if I make a mistake."

"I should quit this major."

"The professor is just trying to torture us with this stuff. Doesn't he realize how much students hate this stuff?"

Cs (consequences)

muscle tension in neck

fear and anxiety

sweaty palms

shallow, irregular breathing

D (dispute)

"Why do I hate these presentations so much?"

"It really is silly of me to waste my time trying to figure out why I am feeling this. I should just accept it."

"I'll never be able to last ten minutes in front of the class."

"Of course I'll last. I might be a nervous wreck and uncomfortable, but I can stand up there and speak for ten minutes about something of my choosing."

"I'll just die if I make a mistake."

"Such drama. I might not feel too great, but I am not going to die up there."

"I should quit this major."

"I really like this major. Quitting over one class is silly."

"The professor is just trying to torture us with this stuff. Doesn't he realize how much students hate this stuff?"

"I am sure the professor is doing this exactly because most people are uncomfortable speaking in front of groups. He is just trying to make us better students and future businessmen and women."

E (effects)

After disputing the illogical thoughts, you have a more realistic appraisal of the threat and start to feel better.

The key to emotion-focused approaches to improving emotional well-being is using them consistently and keep reminding yourself that it is normal to experience troubling emotions. Becoming more mindful of them and accepting them set the stage for being able to co-exist with them and do what needs to be done.

Reorganizing the Physical Dimension of Health

As we learned in chapter 10, there are many psychological and physiological stress-reducing benefits associated with physical activity, exercise, and fitness. A key to reorganizing the physical dimension is realizing that many of these benefits take a couple of months to take effect. Many people start an exercise program with the best intentions but try to do too much too soon and often wind up with sprains, strains, and other injuries. A more reasonable approach is starting slowly and working physical activity and exercise into your daily routine. Similarly, people often try to make radical changes in their eating behavior either drastically reducing the number of calories their bodies are used to or attempting some fad diet that loses its appeal shortly thereafter because it is not varied or interesting enough to maintain on a long-term basis.

Making physical activity, exercise, and healthy eating part of one's daily lifestyle is easier for some than for others. For many of you, reorganizing this dimension of your health is easy to do because you grew up in households where physical activity was a part of daily life. Many of you grew up on farms where your daily chores and activities involved vigorous physical activity. Hard work and physical activity are part of your cultural heritage. Others grew up in households where parents and siblings were athletic and involved in sports. Following in those footsteps, you have lived the athletic life for many years and are used to vigorous physical activity. Still others grew up in households where outdoor activities ranging from hiking and camping to swimming, hunting, and ice skating were woven into the fabric of your family's leisure and recreation time. For all of you, reorganizing the physical dimension involves merely continuing or fine-tuning what you are already doing.

Others however have no such role models or history to draw from and have to create their own plan for reorganizing their physical well-being. Those of you starting from the beginning need to be careful about setting clear goals and reorganizing the way you think about physical activity, exercise, and healthy eating.

A Problem-Focused Approach to Strengthening the Physical Dimension

Many people fail in their attempts at incorporating physical activity and exercise into their lives because they don't have a four-season plan. They start out in the summer, for instance, with a daily outdoor physical activity, such as swimming, and when autumn rolls around and the pool closes, they have nothing to take its place: no backup plan. They become very inactive during the autumn and winter months, falling grossly out of shape, and then must start all over again when springtime rolls around. The extra weight they put on over this dormant period makes getting in shape even more difficult. The older they get, the longer it takes to get back into shape. All this contributes to a negative perception of the entire process and an appraisal of physical activity and getting into shape as stressors.

This is a destructive cycle for several reasons. First, it stops the momentum of moving toward optimal functioning. Instead of progressing to a higher activity level and greater fitness, it's always an uphill battle just to get back to the starting point. Second, it wreaks havoc on weight control, since one's metabolic rate fluctuates from the reduced energy expenditure (and possible greater calorie consumption) of the autumn and winter months to the increased expenditure of the summer. From a psychological perspective, moving indoors and being less physically active may contribute to seasonal affective disorder (SAD) if a person is predisposed to it. SAD sufferers are victims of winter depression. The short, gray days of winter that begin in October and end in March can make them feel depressed and sluggish and lose interest in life. Deprived of both physical activity and sunshine, a person sinks deeper into inactivity and depression. A key to understanding reorganizing the physical dimension is making physical activity such a priority that you don't allow yourself to fall out of shape once you attain a certain level of fitness. Developing a four-season physical activity plan is what one needs to do this.

Here is an example of how to develop a four-season physical activity plan to ensure that you continue your daily level of exercise despite the weather.

1. Start by identifying physical activities that are fun (or potentially fun) things you can do in each of the four seasons. Look at some of the moderate and vigorous physical activities identified by the Surgeon General in chapter 10. If nothing there appeals to you, research activities that are available through your local YM or YWCA, town recreation programs, private gyms, and continuing education courses.
2. Pick at least one activity for each season. Having more than one activity will make it even less likely that you will get bored and stop your physical activity. This will also give you the opportunity to cross-train as we discussed in chapter 10. You may be able to pursue outdoor activities all year long if you live in a temperate climate.
3. Try to have at least one indoor activity and one outdoor activity that you enjoy in each season. For instance, in the summer you might walk and garden outdoors and do aerobic dance indoors. In the

Stress Buster Tips

Finding an Inexpensive Place to Work Out

Finding an affordable place to swim or work out during the winter months can be a real challenge. The cost of joining a gym is one of the major reasons cited by students for failing to exercise over the winter. The following tips will help you find a place that meets your budget.

1. Make use of public spaces. Some of the healthiest activities, like walking, running, cycling, and skating, don't require gym memberships at all. Once you've invested in a bicycle or skates and any necessary safety equipment, or a good pair of running or walking shoes, all you need to do is head out the door. Check out your local parks for suitable trails, make use of the track at your public high school, or just go for a walk along a safe local road.
2. Join your college or university's recreation center. Joining most college and university recreation centers costs about half as much as joining a private gym. Most college and university recreation memberships include access to a weight room, cardiovascular equipment, and a pool. Many offer free or inexpensive courses in everything from yoga to spinning.
3. Join a Young Men's or Young Women's Christian or Hebrew Association (YM/YWCA or YM/YWHA). Most of these organizations have comprehensive fitness facilities and offer three-month memberships that will get you through the coldest winter months. Often they have reduced rates for students.
4. Inquire about your health insurance benefits. Many health insurers (especially health maintenance organizations) offer discounts or rebates for members at specific health clubs as an inducement to exercise.
5. Inquire about scholarships at all the previously mentioned organizations. Often they have need-based discounts for low-income students.

Cross-country skiing is an excellent winter choice of a fitness activity.

winter you could cross-country ski or snowshoe outdoors and play racquetball or lift weights indoors. By having both indoor and outdoor outlets for your physical activity, you will be less likely to go without it for too long.

4. Plan ahead and prepare for the seasonal transitions. For instance, if you really love to swim and want to swim indoors all year, start to investigate the availability of indoor pools during the *summer* months. Identify a pool you can afford to join and enroll during the waning days of summer. By doing this during the summer, when you can still swim outdoors, you can continue to exercise and ensure a seamless transition to indoor swimming during the colder months.
5. Don't be put off by the cold. There is a whole new generation of lightweight and waterproof cold-weather garments that allow you to enjoy being outdoors throughout the year. The sheer stark beauty of outdoor winter activities can be a revelation for people who previously did not venture out in the winter.

Remember to start out slowly and get clearance from your doctor if you have any pre-existing health problems that might be contraindications to some activities.

Stress Buster Tips

Reorganize Your Eating by Making Healthier Food Choices

It is very likely that you can improve your dietary health and reduce the risk of developing heart disease and cancer by implementing the following practices.

Eat More High-Fiber Foods

- Eat whole-grain breads, cereals, and crackers.
- Eat more vegetables and fruits—raw and cooked.
- Try other high-fiber foods, such as oat bran, barley, brown rice, and wild rice.

Eat Less Sugar

- Avoid regular soft drinks. One twelve-ounce can has nine teaspoons of sugar!
- Choose fresh fruit or fruit canned in natural juice or water.
- If desired, use sweeteners that don't have any calories, such as saccharine or aspartame, instead of sugar.

Use Less Salt

- Avoid adding salt to food at the table.
- Eat fewer high-salt foods, such as canned soups, ham, sauerkraut, hot dogs, pickles, and foods that taste salty.

Eat Less Fat

- Eat smaller servings of meat. Eat fish, poultry, or vegetarian entrees more often.
- Avoid fried foods. Avoid adding fat when cooking.
- Eat fewer high-fat foods, such as cold cuts, bacon, sausage, hot dogs, butter, margarine, nuts, salad dressing, lard, and solid shortening.
- Drink skim or low-fat milk.

InfoLinks

www.nal.usda.gov/fnic

Source: From Payne, W. & Hahn, D. (2002). *Understanding your health.* St. Louis: McGraw-Hill.[7]

An Emotion-Focused Approach to Strengthening the Physical Dimension

Negative emotions about physical activity, exercise, and healthy eating often contribute to their discontinuance. Activity and eating patterns are among the hardest habits to change and are often accompanied by a pessimistic or cynical attitude. Because of its focus on pessimistic thinking, Seligman's ABCDE model[8] is an excellent reorganizing strategy to use when you find yourself lapsing into illogical, negative thinking about your ability to be more active and eat healthier. If you remember from chapter 7, the key elements of his illogical beliefs revolve around pessimism (permanence, pervasiveness, and personalization).

Imagine you have been trying to change the way you eat to conform to a new healthy eating plan. Your husband and child are giving you a lot of grief about your new healthy food choices, ways of cooking, and portion sizes. You've been doing this for a month now and you really don't notice any big weight loss or change in your energy level. You are about ready to give up eating this way and go back to your meat-and-potatoes, dessert-every-night old way of eating. Instead, you decide to try to work through your thinking using Seligman's model before you throw in the towel. Here is what you come up with:

A (adversity)

Doubts about being able to stick to eating according to the new Food Pyramid.

Bs (illogical beliefs)

"I'll *never* be able to get used to this diet" (permanence)

"I can't do *anything* right." (pervasiveness)

"I really shouldn't expect the kids and my husband to eat this way. It is *my fault* that they are mad. They need their sweets." (personalization)

"How come *every time* I try something new I fall flat on my face?" (pervasiveness)

"I'll *never* learn how to eat right?"(permanence)

Cs (consequences)

pessimism

sense of failure

sense of lack of control

muscle tension in lower back

D (dispute)

"I'll *never* be able to get used to this diet" (permanence)

"I need to give these changes more time. I'll reevaluate them after three months."

"I can't do *anything* right." (pervasiveness)

"I'm really not doing anything wrong. I am following the recommendations perfectly."

"I really shouldn't expect the kids and my husband to eat this way. It is *my fault* that they are mad. They need their sweets." (personalization)

"It is not my fault that they do not like eating this way. It will take time for them to adjust. I care about them and limiting unhealthy foods is a good thing for me to do."

"How come *every time* I try something new I fall flat on my face?" (pervasiveness)

"I don't fall flat on my face every time. I've tried lots of new things and I and the family have loved them. This one might take more time or they may never like eating this way more than their old, unhealthy way."

"I'll *never* learn how to eat right?"(permanence)

"I already know how to eat right. My problem is not giving it enough time to see the effects."

Distraction (not needed)

E (energization)

feeling renewed sense of hope and control

feeling less pessimistic

KEY TO UNDERSTANDING

A key to understanding reorganizing the physical dimension is realizing that many of the benefits associated with increasing physical activity and exercise and eating for health take a couple of months to take effect.

Working on the pessimistic thoughts that accompany our thinking can help us think more positively, gain confidence in our ability to change, and help us cope with doubts and fears associated with any long-term lifestyle change, not just those associated with physical activity and healthy eating.

WELLNESS AND COPING

By adopting this long-range focus, we prevent a certain amount of stress from ever cropping up because we now view life differently and plan accordingly. We take into account both the six dimensions of wellness and the five Rs when planning our lives and making decisions.

We wouldn't think, for instance, of going away for a vacation without planning some kind of physical exercise or recreation. We know that to be healthy and to cope with the demands of any particular day, whether on vacation or not, we need time and opportunity for exercise.

We wouldn't seriously consider a job change that demanded so much of our time that we'd have to give up the hours we now allot to exercise or to relationships and activities that help keep us spiritually, emotionally, environmentally, and intellectually healthy. We become very protective of our time, with whom we share it, and how we spend it. We know that a commitment to wellness and stress management means we need time to spend on preventive and restorative activities.

We think twice about entering into relationships with people whose values conflict seriously with ours. We realize that our support system is crucial for coping, and we are careful about becoming too intimate with people who don't support or mock our efforts.

In other words, as we approach wellness, we begin to examine our commitments and the demands placed on our lives in the context of their relationship to all five dimensions of health and their effects on these domains. In a sense, what happens is that our values change. Health and stress management become core values. They become things that are no longer an afterthought. They earn priority status as we consider the options and choices our lives present. We have changed. We are moving toward wellness.

SUMMARY

This chapter discussed *Reorganize,* the final R of the author's five Rs of coping with stress model. As we mentioned in the beginning of the chapter, *Reorganize* is based on a *lifestyle-based approach* rather than a *strategy-based approach* to coping with stress. *Reorganize,* as a level of coping, involves a commitment to a healthier lifestyle. By reorganizing your environmental/occupational, social, spiritual, intellectual, emotional, and physical well-being you are both improving your overall level of health and increasing your coping resources. *Reorganizing* involves engaging in hardy health habits daily to prevent stressors from even arising in the first place. *Reorganize* is *preventive* in nature, using multiple strategies simultaneously *before* potential stressors appear rather than confronting individual stressors with specific coping strategies *after* they arise. Finally, by linking hardy health practices and Five Rs strategies together and practicing them on a daily basis, you can generate a synergistic effect against stress.

Throughout the book we've discussed how high-level health assists us in coping with stress. In this chapter we examined ways to incorporate strategies from the book to improve all the dimensions of health. We organized these strategies around a two-pronged model for reorganizing our health. The approach uses both problem-focused and emotion-focused approaches to strengthening your overall level of health. Problem-focused approaches attack stressors head on and revolve around making changes to our environment, the actual stressor, or our behavior. Emotion-focused strategies change the way we view the world in general and stressors in particular. The remaining parts of the chapter explain how to strengthen each of the dimensions of health using both problem-focused and emotion-focused strategies drawn from chapters 7 through 10.

STUDY QUESTIONS

1. What are the five levels of defense against stress and how do they work?
2. How do the lines of defense mesh with the six dimensions of health and wellness to provide a synergistic effect against stress?
3. How does reorganize work as a line of defense against stress?
4. What are the major differences between problem-focused and emotion-focused approaches towards reorganizing one's health?
5. Using any dimension as an example, compare and contrast a problem-focused approach to strengthening it with an emotion-focused approach.
6. How does a lifestyle-based approach to stress management differ from a strategy-based approach?
7. How is wellness related to stress management?

DISCOVER OUR CHANGING WORLD: NIOSH AND YOUR HEALTH

The National Institute for Safety and Occupational Health (NIOSH) has a mechanism in place for employees, employee representatives, and employers to request a health hazard evaluation (HHE) whenever they suspect that they may be exposed to a dangerous worksite condition or product.[6] A typical HHE involves studying a workplace such as a particular department in a factory, industrial plant, or other worksite. The study is done by NIOSH to find out whether there is a health hazard to employees caused by exposure to hazardous materials (chemical or biological contaminants) in the workplace. NIOSH also evaluates other potentially hazardous working conditions, such as exposure to heat, noise, radiation, or musculoskeletal stresses.

1. Go to the NIOSH website and read about the HHE process http://www.cdc.gov/niosh/hhe/
2. Have you or anyone in your family been exposed to suspected harmful worksite materials or conditions?
3. Have you or your representatives requested a NIOSH HHE investigation? What were the results of the investigation?
4. If you didn't request a HHE, explain why you didn't carry out this step.

ARE YOU THINKING CLEARLY?

In this chapter we discussed ways to reorganize your lifestyle that will increase your wellness and reduce your stress. We've examined several ideas for integrating strategies from chapters 7 through 10 into your lifestyle. Now that you have the blueprint, what is holding you back from implementing it? When confronted with such a question, students typically respond with a variety of reasons, excuses, and barriers. If you find yourself doing this, *stop* and answer the following questions as honestly as you can:

1. What are the consequences of not reorganizing your lifestyle?
2. How effective is your current lifestyle in coping with stress?

3. Have you developed a better plan for managing stress?
4. Do you really believe that managing stress is important at this point in your life?
5. Are you willing to suffer the consequences of dealing with stress in a hit-or-miss fashion?

The answers to these questions should help guide you as you consider ways to apply the information in this chapter to your life. Only you can decide if the information in this chapter is important enough for you to start reorganizing your life. Only you can decide if this is the right time to start reorganizing your life. These questions should help you think more clearly about this. If they do not, try using the Ellis and Harper's ABCDE technique[2] to work through your illogical thoughts about Reorganize.

References

1. Anderson, L. & Krech, G. (2005). *Residential Certification Course in Japanese Therapy.* ToDo Institute: Monkton, VT.
2. Ellis, A. & Harper, R. (1979). *A new guide to rational living.* Englewood Cliffs, NJ: Prentice-Hall.
3. Fletcher, C. (1972). *The complete walker.* New York: Knopf.
4. Kobassa, S., Maddi, S., & Kahn, S. (1982). Hardiness and health; a prospective study. *Journal of Personality and Social Psychology,* 42(1), pp. 168–77.
5. Lazarus, R.S. & Folkman, S. (1985). *Stress appraisal and coping.* New York: Springer Publishing.
6. NIOSH. (2003). *Health hazard evaluation.* http://www.cdc.gov/niosh/hhe/.
7. Payne, W. & Hahn, D. (2005). *Understanding your health.* 8th Ed. St. Louis: McGraw-Hill.
8. Seligman, M.E.P. (1998). *Learned optimism: How to change your mind and your life.* New York: Simon & Shuster.
9. Thoreau, H.D. (1854). *Walden.* Boston: Houghton.

Name: ______________________________ Date: ____________

ASSESS YOURSELF 11-1

Social and Spiritual Health Begins at Home

Although you should have a perspective on the world and the global things that stress you, you probably will have the greatest ability to affect stressful events that are closest to you. The following five tips can help you in this process.

1. Identify issues and situations in your community that either create stress or reduce the quality of your life.

____

____

____

____

2. Involve your family if you can. Can you work as a family on any of the issues identified in tip 1?

____

____

____

____

3. Identify community resources that you and your family can use in your work and that can link you with other people.

____

____

____

____

4. Call or meet with the director of social services, recreation, or health and welfare of your town or city. This person is responsible for coordinating all social services in your area.
5. Volunteer for the kind of activities you enjoy. Do not let your volunteer activities become a source of stress.

Name: ______________________ Date: __________

Assess Yourself 11-2

Reorganizing Your Health

As we mentioned in this chapter, by combining hardy health habits with the individual Five Rs strategies you can achieve a synergistic effect in your efforts to manage stress by strengthening your health. The following activity will help you accomplish this goal.

1. Go back to chapter 1 and review the results of your Wellness test. Describe your lifestyle's strengths and weaknesses.

2. Describe how you would apply a problem, or emotion-focused approach to strengthening one aspect of your environmental health.

3. Describe how you would apply a problem- or emotion-focused approach to strengthening one aspect of your occupational health.

4. Describe how you would apply a problem- or emotion-focused approach to strengthening one aspect of your spiritual health.

5. Describe how you would apply a problem- or emotion-focused approach to strengthening one aspect of your social health.

6. Describe how you would apply a problem- or emotion-focused approach to strengthening one aspect of your intellectual health.

ASSESS YOURSELF 11-2 (cont'd)

7. Describe how you would apply a problem- or emotion-focused approach to strengthening one aspect of your emotional health.

____

____

____

____

8. Describe how you would apply a problem- or emotion-focused approach to strengthening one aspect of your physical health.

____

____

____

____

PART

III

Stress: A Developmental Perspective

This, the third and final section of the text, will examine stress through a developmental perspective rather than devoting individual chapters to specific stressors as most textbooks do. The chapters in this part will use Erikson's eight stages of development as a rough guide to the tasks normally associated with psychosocial development.

In a sense, one might consider Erikson's tasks as *potential stressors* since mastery of them involves trial and error, success or failure over a variety of situations and experiences. As we evolve as individuals, we bring with us all the skills and competencies established by working through the tasks associated with the previous stages. A key to understanding the significance of these tasks, as far as stress is concerned, is realizing that mastery or failure with regard to these tasks feeds into our perceived ability to cope with future tasks. The potential stressors of future stages therefore are appraised in light of the strength of our perceived coping resources that were developed in the past. In other words, a person's ability to cope is developmental in nature.

As we experience success with various coping strategies, we begin to have faith in the ability of these strategies to help us deal with potential stressors. We begin to trust our own ability to handle things, and our overall perceived capacity to cope is enhanced. We feel confident in our ability to cope regardless of the type of potential stressor and the factors that surround it. Children's coping is more problem-specific. As they grow, children adopt a more generic emotion-focused basis of coping which builds on their earlier problem-focused approach.

This final section of the book will examine the key tasks associated with normal development and the potential for stress that is associated with those tasks. We will also examine common experiences that we go through in mastering the developmental tasks. Each chapter in this section will use boxes, keys to understanding, and other aids to illustrate the application of the Five Rs of coping (Rethink, Reduce, Relax, Release, Reorganize) to common stressors associated with each developmental stage.

CHAPTER

12

Childhood and Adolescent Stress

OUTLINE

OBJECTIVES

By the end of the chapter students will:

- Understand the developmental nature of personality and stress.
- Describe how coping with stress also is a developmental process.
- Describe Erikson's major developmental tasks for the first four stages of life (childhood, early childhood, late childhood, and school age).
- Understand how the developmental tasks could be perceived as either stressors or challenges.
- Understand how the five Rs of coping could be employed to reduce childhood stress.
- Describe Erikson's major developmental task of adolescence.
- Describe the influence of puberty on adolescent stress.
- Differentiate between reproductive readiness and psychosocial readiness.
- Describe the influence of school on adolescent stress.
- Describe how to cope with adolescent stress by using the five Rs model.

As we discussed in the introduction to Part III, in this chapter we will begin examining stress in a developmental perspective by using Erikson's eight-stage development model.[10] That model proposes that psychosocial development occurs in response to a series of developmental "tasks." In this chapter we will view Erikson's developmental tasks for childhood and adolescence as potential stressors, since mastery of them involves trial and error and success and failure in a variety of situations and experiences.

Erikson's Stages of Child Development

If you remember from chapter 2, Eric Erikson,[10] was a psychotherapist who studied with Freud. He constructed a model of personality development that was similar to Freud's in that he also viewed personality development as a result of a struggle between opposing forces. These forces present themselves in a series of eight stages that occur throughout our lives. Erikson's theory differs from Freud's because of their differing views on the nature of the opposing forces. Erikson viewed development as a conflict between opposing *psychosocial* forces and qualities where Freud viewed it as a conflict between the id, ego, and the superego. According to Erikson, healthy personality development results from accomplishing the developmental tasks required for each stage. Inadequate task resolution results in thwarted development in that particular area.

In this chapter we will begin examining stress in a developmental perspective using Erikson's eight-stage development model.[10] The eight stages of development outlined by Erikson are presented in Table 12-1. This chapter focuses on the first five stages in Erikson's model. We will examine the tasks associated with childhood and adolescence in the context of their ability to be potential stressors, since mastery of them involves trial and error and success and failure in a variety of situations and experiences.

Infancy: Birth to 18 Months

The major task of infancy according to Erikson,[10] is the development of a **sense of trust** (see Table 12-1). That trust wins out over mistrust is central to continued healthy psychological development in all people.

Infancy is a time of total dependence. Infants rely entirely on caregivers—whether they are mothers, fathers, other family members, or legal guardians—to provide for all their survival needs. One can easily see that our ability to trust in the world as a safe place and in ourselves as deserving, worthwhile beings is entirely dependent on others.

sense of trust a feeling of comfort, hope, and faith that infants develop in response to having their basic needs (food, cleanliness, safety, physical contact) met

Table 12-1 Erikson's Stages of Development

Age	Stage of Development	Task/Area of Resolution	Concepts/Basic Attitudes
Birth–18 months	Infancy	Trust versus mistrust	Ability to trust others and a sense of one's own trustworthiness; a sense of hope **or** withdrawal and estrangement
18 months–3 years	Early childhood	Autonomy versus shame and doubt	Self-control without loss of self-esteem; ability to cooperate and to express oneself **or** compulsive self-restraint or compliance; defiance, willfulness
3–5 years	Late childhood	Initiative versus guilt	Realistic sense of purpose; some ability to evaluate one's own behavior **or** self-denial and self-restriction
6–12 years	School age	Industry versus inferiority	Realization of competence, perseverance **or** feeling that one will never be "any good," withdrawal from school and peers
12–20 years	Adolescence	Identity versus role confusion	Coherent sense of self; plans to actualize one's abilities **or** feelings of confusion, indecisiveness, possibly antisocial behavior
18–25 years	Young adulthood	Intimacy versus isolation	Capacity for love as mutual devotion; commitment to work and relationships **or** impersonal relationships, prejudice
25–65 years	Adulthood	Generativity versus stagnation	Creativity, productivity, concern for others **or** self-indulgence, impoverishment of self
65 years to death	Old age	Integrity versus despair	Acceptance of the worth and uniqueness of one's life **or** sense of loss, contempt for others

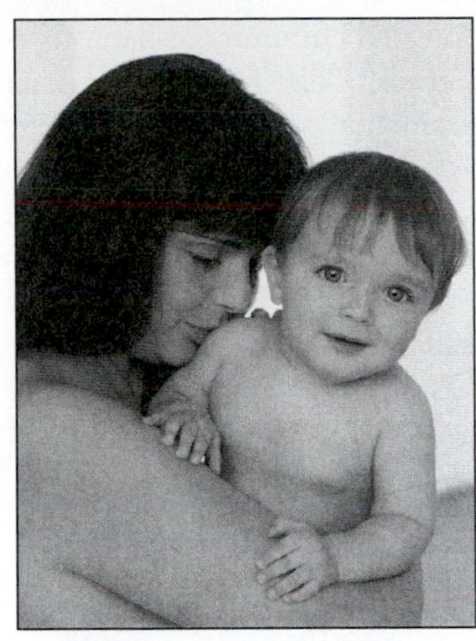

Children need nurturing from parents or a caregiver to develop a sense of trust in the world and themselves.

Children are naturally inquisitive. If they are left alone in a protected environment, they will explore endlessly.

KEY TO UNDERSTANDING

Mastery of developmental tasks feeds into one's perceived ability to cope with stress.

Infants have basic needs that must be met. They must be fed when they are hungry, changed when they are wet or soiled, and hugged when they need nurturance. To develop as healthy humans, we must have these needs met in a timely, caring fashion. If they are met consistently, and with positive nurturing emotions, we begin to believe that the world is a safe, worthwhile place. We begin to feel that we are worthwhile creatures in a safe world. We also begin to believe that others are worthy of our trust. We begin to believe that others will be there for us when we need them.

If these basic needs are not met consistently and correctly, we do not fully develop this sense of trust in ourselves and others. If, by the end of this stage, as we get ready to move on to other developmental tasks, a healthy sense of trust has not been fully established, we do not bring trust to this next level of growth. We become emotionally disadvantaged in a sense, handicapped by the lack of development of the foundation of the personality, a sense of trust.

Early Childhood: 18 to 36 Months

The major task of early childhood is the development of a **sense of autonomy.**[10] In this stage children begin to develop self-control and self-esteem. Children learn how to express themselves and begin to cooperate with others. Empowered by their newfound mobility, children walk about exploring the environment and mastering simple tasks that give them some degree of control and freedom.

Children need freedom within limits to explore the world and begin to act independently. With this mobility and freedom, children put themselves at risk for varying types of harm, ranging from the assorted bumps and bruises to poisoning, abduction, and sexual abuse. Although this is scary, a key to understanding this stage is that without being given a certain amount of freedom to take chances and explore the world, children run the risk of not developing the self-esteem and self-control that will be critical in their progress through childhood and life.

KEY TO UNDERSTANDING

Coping with stress is a developmental process.

For most children and their parents, the early childhood years are a pure delight. Many landmark events take place during this period which allow the child to master the key developmental tasks of this stage.

Learning to walk is a major developmental task that usually occurs during this stage. Children who are helped with but not overly protected from the bumps and falls that are a normal part of learning to walk develop a sense of control over their environment. They learn about

sense of autonomy a feeling of freedom and independence that children develop along with self-esteem and self-control as they are allowed to explore their environment and master simple tasks like toilet training

KEY TO UNDERSTANDING

Developing self-esteem and self-control requires mobility and freedom to suffer from life's bumps and bruises.

the literal "bumps and bruises" that are a normal part of achieving anything meaningful in life. Children who are overly protected and shielded from even the most minor stumble have a harder time becoming autonomous.

When children can walk around independently, they need to be able to explore their environment. They need to have both hazard-free environments and the freedom to explore them autonomously to develop a sense of self-control and self-esteem. Children whose exploratory play is restricted or unsafe face a retarded development of autonomy. They may even become fearful of being alone or taking a risk at later points in their life.

Toilet training is another example of an event whose mastery is essential for the completion of the developmental tasks of this stage as well as the building of a solid foundation of stress-coping skills. The toilet-training process is empowering for children. Along with mastery of bowel control, children gain a measure of self-control, self-esteem, and independence.

If toilet training is handled skillfully by parents or caregivers and is not rushed, children develop a sense of pride in accomplishing something very important to them. If toilet training is rushed or children are punished or criticized too harshly for the inevitable "mistakes" and soiled underpants, they can pass through this stage without developing those all-important feelings of self-control and self-esteem.[15]

The skills that are essential for the development of autonomy are critical for coping with stress. If someone grows up without fully developing a sense of autonomy, this will have an impact later in life on that person's perceived ability to cope with potential stressors and on the stress-appraisal process in general.

Late Childhood: 3 to 5 Years

In this stage of development, children continue to gain freedom and begin to be exposed to a variety of people and experiences as they further explore their environment. The major task for this stage is the development of **initiative.** Children's actions are more purposeful as they evaluate their competencies and initiate behaviors that are consistent with this. Children's likes and dislikes are more firmly established, and their behavior is more purposeful to further this.

Children at this age struggle with their overwhelming preoccupation with the self as they are increasingly exposed to other youngsters in a variety of play and social situations. These situations force children to share, take turns, and accommodate others. This socialization is a vital and necessary developmental step which prepares children for the kinds of social interactions necessary for future success in school.

This is also a potentially stressful time as children need to satisfy their **egocentric** needs while learning to live in an increasingly social world. Caregivers also can be stretched to their limits as they try to provide opportunities for children to grow. On the one hand, children need the freedom and space to initiate and take responsibility for their behavior; on the other hand, they need limits on their freedom.

Children who are given unlimited freedom may be stressed simply because they don't have the cognitive or moral development to act rationally and logically when given too many choices. They are unable to decide, or they make choices that are based on unrealistic perceptions or expectations. Children who are not allowed to make independent decisions and initiate actions will never develop the ability to act purposefully and will not learn to trust their own abilities. They also will never experience the pain of failure, a great learning tool. Children need to learn that some choices are bad choices and that not all of their desires are always achievable.

Children learn to tolerate frustration by being put into situations that require them to decide, act, and sometimes experience defeat or failure. If these failures are handled properly, caregivers can turn them into valuable learning experiences that can promote initiative and self-confidence through a realistic perception of one's abilities.

School Age: 6 to 12 Years

The next stage we will cover in this chapter is the school age which lasts from about age 6 to age 12. The main developmental task of this stage is the development of **industry.**[10] Children develop perseverance and a sense of competence. They learn about the necessity of working hard and sticking to the things they initiate.

School greatly affects children's lives. Their day changes dramatically. For some, whose lives were relatively unstructured until this point, this can represent a radical departure. For others, with preschool or recreational-activities experience that introduced them to structured experiences at an earlier age, the school day is not such a new and unusual experience.

initiative a trait characterized by taking responsibility for acting in a more purposeful manner; behaving in ways that are consistent with one's likes and dislikes

egocentric feeling as if you and your needs are the central focus of everything and everyone

industry a sense of diligence or productivity in one's work or activities

An elementary school classroom should be a place of cooperation and working together to achieve goals.

The Challenge of School

School also puts children in a situation where the main caregiver and disciplinarian is no longer a parent or someone they have grown up with but is, rather, a teacher. Some children have never been separated from the primary caregiver up to this point and have a very hard time separating and getting used to school. Children who have been in preschool or day care because both parents work may not find the adjustment that difficult. In fact, children who have experienced preschool or have been in day-care centers where there are opportunities to interact with other children and adults may have an easier time separating from their parents and adjusting to kindergarten and elementary school.

Besides the generic differences between school, home, and child-care facilities, school introduces children to a formalized world of learning with strict rules, regulations, and work expectations. This is a time when formal competition begins. Children begin to compete for grades, athletic achievement, social connectedness, and attention. It is a competition that, in our society, never ends. How students cope with this is contingent on their success in working through the previous developmental stages and on the strategies they learned in the past.

Besides the competition, students begin to be categorized. For many this categorization has already begun in preschool. In many communities readiness for kindergarten is assessed by preschool teachers as well as by formal entrance tests. Rarely is this labeling overt, but students learn (often from older siblings) what the A, B, or C group stands for or what reading level 1, 2, or 3 means. Although intended to help students progress at their own pace and work in an appropriate class level, labels sometimes follow students through a school system, providing an easy categorization for future reference.

Schools provide an unlimited opportunity for the development of industry and competence. They provide a rich milieu of academic, social, athletic, and recreational experiences and situations in which students can grow. Children can test their limits. They can experience a variety of things that challenge them and push them on to higher levels. In a safe, protected environment, children can grow not just as students but into competent, whole persons.

School as a Potential Stressor

Schools, as we've hinted, can also be stressful. Eliss[6] identified the following sources of school stress: overemphasis on academic acceleration, competition, evaluation, and test-based accountability. Eliss cautions that the term *overemphasize* is important. Academic acceleration is important and beneficial for some students. Not all students are able to deal with being "pushed" academically and may need more time and less taxing coursework in order to grow. Overemphasizing competition rather than self-improvement can also be stressful. Finally, an overemphasis on evaluation, especially test-based evaluation, can add extra stress to the school experience.

Helms and Gable,[12] found that interactions with teachers and peers were often sources of stress for children. In addition, academic achievement and academic self-concept were cited as school stressors. Communicating with, being acknowledged by, and being accepted by teachers and peers could be a source of stress, especially for students with a low academic self-concept. Perceiving oneself as being "not smart" or "below average" could be a source of stress, especially in overly competitive school settings. Murphy and Della-Cortes[17] found that pressure to conform and live up to the expectations of others at school was a significant source of stress for children.

Children who are not ready or prepared for school can suffer their first bitter taste of failure. If they are not prepared for this by having worked their way through the previous developmental issues, the effects can be devastating and long-lasting. Some of these students fall behind early and never catch up. Many just give up on school, feeling they can't succeed.

Many children find the social aspects of school very stressful. They are not ready to share anything, let alone the spotlight! Or they are different and the target of taunts and abuse. In time most find their niche and a good friend or two who can help them get through this.

COPING WITH PARENTING CHILDREN USING THE FIVE RS

Helping children learn to cope with stress isn't always easy. Even in the best circumstances children have a short attention span, can be irrational and make absolutely no sense, and can test the wisdom and patience of King Solomon. Parents, caregivers, and friends must approach helping

STRESS IN OUR WORLD 12-1

Reducing Childhood Stress by Not Rushing Children through Childhood

Parents and caregivers can reduce childhood stress by not rushing children into becoming young adults too quickly. In a classic work written over twenty years ago, psychologist David Elkind[7] coined the term *hurried child* to describe children who are rushed through childhood. These children were pushed too hard and too fast and were not allowed to "be children." Hurried children are kids who are not allowed to be kids. They are pushed into competitive academic, athletic, and social situations before they are developmentally ready for them. (See Diverse Perspectives 12-1, "Greg: An Overscheduled Child")

Elkind[7] warns that children need lots of unstructured time for free, noncompetitive play. Often, in an attempt to help their kids get a head start on the competition, parents push their children too much, rush them into experiences too soon, and generally "hurry" them along through their childhood. In many cases, children are pushed because of their parents' narcissistic desires to make their kids geniuses.[9]

Elkind[8] warns that children are not merely adults in small bodies capable of understanding and handling the pressures and responsibilities grown-ups can. He argues that children need to be protected from some of the pressures and decisions adults face. Exposing children to all the facts about the tough issues that adults face, such as money problems, divorce, and other relationship issues, is not always the best way to handle these problems. Exposing kids to these things does not toughen them up and prepare them for the hard road life often gives us. Kids are not ready developmentally for this exposure. They often blame themselves and worry over problems they have no responsibility for or control over. In a sense, this shielding and protecting is a reduce strategy because it cuts back on the volume of potential stressors kids face. (See Assess Yourself 12-1, "Unfinished Sentences—Childhood.")

DIVERSE PERSPECTIVES 12-1

Greg: An Overscheduled Child

Greg is a nice kid. He has very highly developed social skills. He's polite in front of adults, has excellent manners, and is very verbal. Unfortunately, he's also a nervous wreck at times. His life is so scheduled that he needs his own appointment book to keep track of his commitments. Besides attending the local public school's fourth grade, Greg is enrolled in his temple's Hebrew classes on Tuesday night. He's on the local club soccer team. They practice on Fridays and have games on Sundays, but sometimes they schedule extra practices or have makeup games on other nights. He plays Little League baseball also, with games on varying evenings and on Saturdays. Sometimes Little League practices are scheduled on Tuesday or Friday night. When this happens, Greg finds himself scurrying from one place to another, gulping a burger down in between. He's also in the Cub Scouts. They meet on Wednesday evenings at 7:00 P.M. If he has a game on Wednesday, he'll sometimes leave early or rush right out immediately after the game.

He drives his Little League coach nuts. During team meetings and games, Greg is constantly fidgeting. He seems unfocused and unable to sit still and pay attention to instructions. It seems he wants to do two things at once. The coach constantly has to remind Greg to slow down. He rushes through everything.

Do you know Greg?

children with compassion, kindness, tolerance, and, above all, a sense of humor. If something doesn't work, try something else. If you try something and it seems like the wrong time to bring it up, don't. Come back later and try again. Don't become a source of stress or get stressed trying to help children learn how to cope with their stress.

The best way for parents and caregivers to teach children to cope with stress using the Five Rs is to use a combination approach that includes (1) being a role model by using the Five Rs yourself and (2) teaching children how to use the Five Rs in different circumstances.

Being a role model involves a commitment to understanding and action. Reading this and other books will provide caregivers with the basic information and tools they need to put the Five Rs into practice in their own homes. If parents and caregivers must act, using the Five Rs themselves will create a home atmosphere and lifestyle for their families that is stress-resistant. Children growing up in this kind of environment learn by observation and role modeling of appropriate stress-management activities.

The next component of helping children cope with stress is teaching them how to use the Five Rs at appropriate times.

KEY TO UNDERSTANDING

Hurried children are kids who are not allowed to be kids.

Teaching Your Child to Rethink

It is very difficult for most children to think logically and rationally. The best way to teach them how to do this is to role model rational thinking. Share your disputes with your children when you use the ABCDE model to work through your own illogical beliefs about your stressors (see chapter 7). Limit this sharing to stressors that do not involve issues that could create more stress for your children. Certain world events or personal issues that you can manage as an adult may be too stressful for your children to think about logically.

The other thing you can do is point out your children's illogical beliefs when you hear them. Be sure to use nonjudgmental language when doing this. Try pointing out more logical beliefs as an option they might consider. For instance, saying "You might consider. . . ." or "Have you ever thought about that issue this way . . ." is preferable to telling children how they "should" or "must" view situations.

Teaching Your Child to Reduce

Talking to children in advance about potentially stressful situations helps them learn about anticipatory stress. This, if you remember from chapter 7, is the basis of the triple As of coping technique. This is an excellent technique because it is easy to learn and helps children understand that they can manage their stress by understanding the different kinds of stressors in their lives. The triple As technique helps them cope with current stressors and can also be used to reduce the likelihood of having the same problem occur in the future.

Most parents and caregivers know their children's limits and can anticipate conditions and situations that will become stressful if they are allowed to occur. Adults need to discuss these situations clearly and simply with their children before they are allowed to occur. Working with children to limit their level of demand will help them perform the things they enjoy at peak efficiency without those things becoming stressors due to overstimulation (see the Stress Curve in chapter 8).

Teaching children how to assert themselves and "say no" will help them avoid being stressed because it will teach them how to say no to things they do not want to do (see chapter 7).

Teaching Your Child to Relax

Teaching children relaxation techniques is easiest if the techniques are simple and don't require much time to learn and perform. Diaphragmatic breathing is a simple yet effective technique for children (see chapter 9). It also is the basis for all other relaxation techniques children will learn in the future. They can perform it anywhere, and it will help them settle down. The calming response, described in chapter 9, is another simple yet effective technique that employs all the key relaxation components of breathing, muscle relaxation, visualization, and logical thinking. Children enjoy this technique because it allows them to use their imaginations in developing their calming, warming scenes and dialogues.

Teaching Your Child to Release

These strategies are easy to incorporate into the average child's repertoire of coping techniques. Kids love to run around and play. The average child's game of tag, for instance, provides an excellent method for purging stress tension. Many children find karate and other martial arts that employ punching and kicking fun ways to purge stress (see chapter 10). Be careful if you decide to use formal martial arts training to help reduce your children's stress. Many martial arts schools are very competitive and can become a source of stress for a child.

Teaching Your Child to Reorganize

Help children reorganize their lives by creating family lifestyles that are stress-reducing (see Stress Buster Tips: "Things Parents Can Do to Teach Their Children about Stress"). If your daily schedule is hectic and you run around half crazed and stressed out all the time, it will be very difficult for your children to develop a lifestyle that helps them manage stress (fig. 12-1). Create family stress-reduction times and activities. A good way to start is to develop healthy, four-season physical activity plans that provide opportunities for you and your children to get outdoors and walk, run, hike, swim, and release tension together (see chapter 10).

Erikson's Stage of Adolescence Development

Erikson's[10] fifth stage of development is adolescence. As we discussed earlier in the chapter, the adolescence period extends from approximately 12–20 years of age. The major task of adolescence is to establish a sense of identity and avoid role confusion. Adolescents seek answers to the question, "Who am I?". If all of the previous tasks associated with prior stages of development have not been resolved successfully, trying to answer this question can result in a severe **identity crisis,** a state of confusion about what one believes is the correct role for themselves versus what others expect of them. This often leads to trouble making decisions about diverse issues ranging from career choices to sexual orientation. Those who enter adolescence having mastered the tasks of previous

identity crisis a state of confusion about what one believes is the correct role for themselves versus what others expect of them

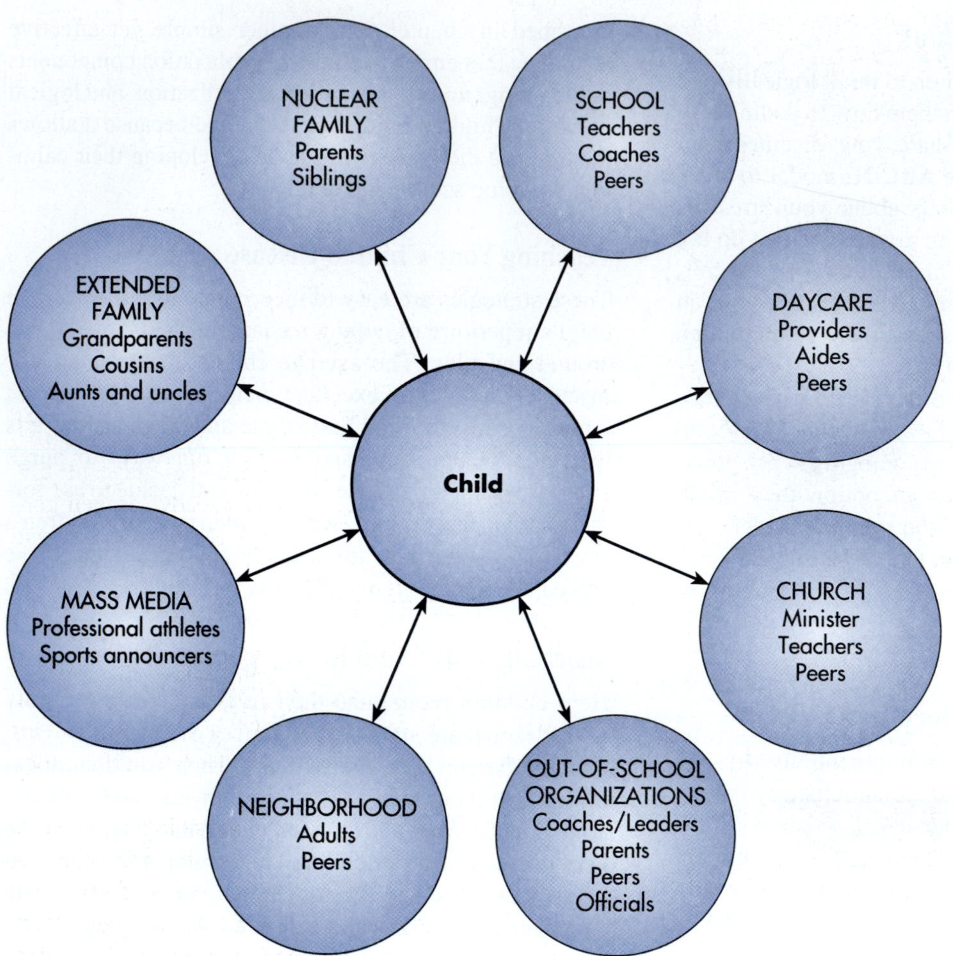

Figure 12-1
Kids can sometimes feel as if they are being pushed and pulled in too many different directions by too many different forces at the same time.

Stress Buster Tips

Things Parents Can Do to Teach Their Children about Stress

- Give your children permission to relax.
- Remember that children are not short adults, and so learning these skills should not be a "graded project."
- Share with your child the value of using relaxation to be creative. This will be easier if you believe it and practice it yourself.
- Allow for "solo" time for your child during the day.
- Occasionally monitor your child's daily schedule.
- Parental guilt is a needless worry.
- Try to not compare your family to another family (for example, the Cleavers).
- Validate your child's feelings of fear and exultation.
- Use age-appropriate metaphors in teaching skills to younger children.
- Pace your child's breathing in assisting in the calming after a crisis.
- Be a good role model.

Modified from Yaeger Group. *Managing parental stress in the eighties.*[20]

stages of development will solve their identity crisis and leave this stage with a strong sense of who they are.

Adolescence is a period in our development that begins as we leave childhood and ends as we enter young adulthood. Adolescence is often viewed as the teenage years but can begin a couple of years earlier and end a couple of years later, depending on the individual. The major task associated with adolescence is the development of self-identity.[8] Discovering who they are and accepting this while at the same time feeling pulled in a hundred different directions can be very stressful for most adolescents. It can also be a time of great excitement and joy as adolescents literally move from childhood to adulthood. During adolescence, bodies as well as minds change and grow. Adolescents outgrow not only their old clothes but often their old ideas and sometimes their old friends as they struggle to come to grips with who they are and where they are going.

Usually the media report only the problems and failures associated with adolescence. We hear about teenage

adolescence the developmental period between the end of childhood and the beginning of young adulthood

Exciting sports such as rock climbing can help build self-esteem and confidence through mastery of a very demanding task.

drug and alcohol misuse, AIDS, teen pregnancy, satanic cults, and defiant behavior. Movies often glorify adolescent rebelliousness and juvenile delinquency instead of praising teens' competence.

However, as Michael Carrera,[4] a respected adolescent sexuality expert, notes, most teenagers go through this period without major problems and emerge into young adulthood strong, competent, and whole. Adolescence is when most young men and women develop their "psychosocial readiness" for young adulthood. They develop the knowledge and skills necessary to move into young adulthood. On top of all of this, their bodies are changing from children to adults. Puberty is a time of profound physiological change as our bodies mature.

In the next part of this chapter, we will examine some of the types of experiences that confront adolescents and

KEY TO UNDERSTANDING

A key to surviving adolescence is to keep focused on one's goals while trying out new things and taking chances.

KEY TO UNDERSTANDING

Most adolescents, although "reproductively ready," are not "psychosocially ready" for sexual intercourse.

discuss how for some these are perceived as stressors, while for others they are seen as challenges.

Puberty

Puberty is a biological term used to describe the physiological transition from childhood to adulthood. A myriad of physiological events characterize this stage of life. Adolescents become "reproductively ready" as their genitals and reproductive systems grow to full adult size and sex hormones begin coursing through their bloodstreams, sending messages to their brains that they have arrived sexually (fig. 12-2). For most adolescents, however, psychosocial readiness for sexual activity with another person takes a while to catch up to **reproductive readiness.** They often find themselves in a state of confusion as their bodies send messages about sex to their brains that they may not be ready to handle.

They are "ready" in a purely physiological sense to do what nature intended them to do: mate with others of our species. In our culture, however, many, if not most, adolescents are not ready in a psychosocial sense to carry out these sexual urges with others. This is a key to understanding adolescent sexuality. It creates a disparity between being ready for intercourse in a physiological sense and being ready in terms of social skills and emotional readiness. Many factors, ranging from parental attitudes to cultural traditions, contribute to this disparity.

Most parents view adolescent intercourse with disfavor and, regardless of their own sexual lifestyles, tend to be less permissive about their children's premarital sexual activity.[15] American culture in general views adolescent sexual intercourse as a problem that will lead only to negative outcomes (unintended pregnancy, sexually transmitted diseases such as AIDS, sexual abuse, etc.) instead of viewing it as a symbolic event in the transition from childhood to young adulthood.

Besides having a moral tradition which views adolescent sexuality and independence with disfavor, American culture, like those of many industrialized societies, prolongs adolescent and young adult dependency. To succeed, adolescents in most cases need to further their education.

puberty a biological term used to describe a variety of bodily changes associated with physical maturation from childhood to adulthood

reproductive readiness the state of complete adult physiological maturation

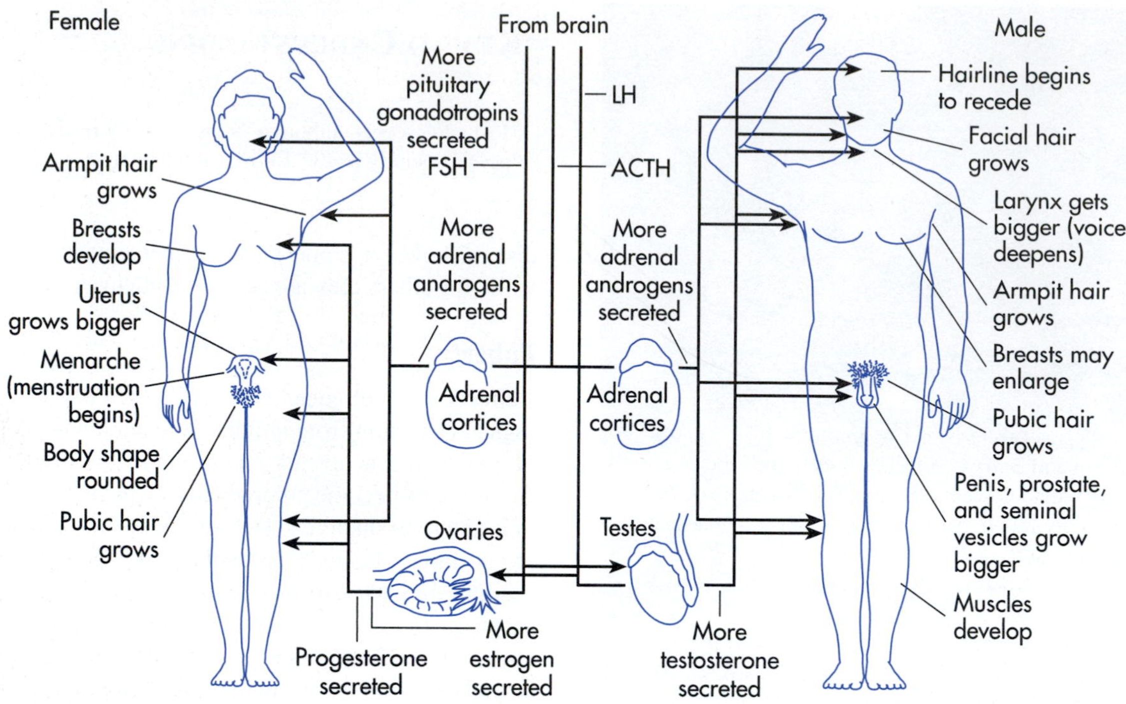

Figure 12-2

Puberty is a time of many changes when adolescents' bodies move from being childlike to being fully adult.

For most of them, this means remaining indebted to their parents and pursuing additional training and education while either living at home or remaining financially obligated to their parents.

In a sense what this does is delay the transition from childhood to adulthood, delaying with it adult privileges such as sexual experimentation. In other cultures adolescents are encouraged to begin to separate from their parents, and in many cultures this separation is institutionalized in a formal rite of passage (see Diverse Perspectives 12-2: "Rites of Passage").

Puberty, Sex, and Stress

It's easy to see why their emerging sexuality can be a major source of stress for adolescents. Adults often try to protect adolescents from this stress by trying to avoid altogether the subject of sex. Maybe (they believe) if we don't talk about it, it will disappear. Many people try to rechannel adolescent sexual energy into other pursuits. Maybe (they feel) if we keep them busy enough with schoolwork, sports, and cultural pursuits, it will take their minds off sex.

Unfortunately, this isn't the case. There are strong biological and, some would argue, evolutionary forces driving adolescent sexual interest. To deny that this exists or to try to rechannel it without first acknowledging it and explaining its power to young people is unethical and doomed to fail.

A key to understanding this is to realize that it is one thing for a society to honestly admit to young people that sex is a powerful force in their young lives and that as a culture America would prefer adolescents to redirect (if possible) that sexual energy into other pursuits. It is another thing to deny its existence or, worse, not even mention it, hoping it will go away, or to trivialize sexual urges by advising that when you feel horny, "take a cold shower."

The mixed messages adolescents receive about sex can be a real source of stress. Their bodies are telling them "yes, yes, yes," but adult society is telling them "no, no, no." Media (music stars, television, movies, etc.) which target adolescents say to them that it is okay and a normal part of teenage rebelliousness to give in to and even glorify their sexual urges, yet parents want them to wait and to fear the power of sex.

This is a hard dilemma to work through, even in a culture that is open about sex and incorporates sex education into the curricula of elementary schools. For American adolescents, many of whom lack the most rudimentary

KEY TO UNDERSTANDING

A key for parents in handling adolescent sexuality is to admit its power and explain why it's important to channel it appropriately.

DIVERSE PERSPECTIVES 12-2

Rites of Passage

Marriage rituals usually contain sexual motifs, as do adolescent rituals or initiation rites that remove individuals from the status of child and place them in the status category closer to adulthood. For girls, these ceremonies often occur near the time of the first menstruation and sometimes signify that they are ready to begin sexual activity or to be married. For boys, there is rarely any physical marker for these rites, but in many societies the penis is physically altered during initiation.

Schlegel and Barry (1979, 1980) examined the distribution of adolescent ceremonies in a sample of 192 societies. They found that 80 societies had no adolescent initiation ceremonies; 17 had ceremonies for boys only, 39 had rites for girls only, and 46 had ceremonies for both genders. Larger societies with intensive agriculture and more complex forms of social organization tend not to have ceremonies for either gender. The fact that American culture lacks a formal initiation rite for boys and girls thus agrees with the findings of Schlegel and Barry. Schlegel and Barry (1980) see initiation ceremonies as ritualized communication about gender status and suggest that such rituals occur in societies where gender plays an important role in the organization of social life.

Most food-collecting societies have a division of labor based on gender: men hunt and women gather. Thirty-four of the 45 food-collecting societies in the Schlegel and Barry sample perform initiation ceremonies for at least one gender. Two have rites for boys only, 20 have rites for girls only, and 12 perform rituals for both genders. The content of the rituals in the 32 societies that have rites for girls indicates that most of these societies ceremonially emphasize a girl's first menstrual flow. Schlegel and Barry suggest two reasons for this concern. First, many of these societies believe that if a man or his weapons come into contact with menstrual blood his ability to hunt will be destroyed. The initiation ceremony notifies the new woman that she must observe menstrual taboos to avoid risking the band's meat supply. Another possibility is that these rather small groups virtually celebrate evidence that a woman is capable of bearing children, which ensures the continued existence of the group.

sexual knowledge, working through these conflicting sexual messages and urges can be overwhelmingly stressful.

It can be very helpful for adolescents to be able to talk about these conflicting messages and feelings with older people who have worked through them. Although parents, older siblings, teachers, and coaches often fulfill this role, any older person who has worked through these conflicts can help.

Adolescents need to feel that there is someone who will listen to them. Talking things out can help relieve stress.

Chronic Depression and Suicide

With the myriad of changes going on both physiologically and psychosocially during this period, life for adolescents and their caregivers can be an emotional roller coaster. The same hormones (and a variety of others) that influence sexual desire also contribute to rapidly shifting emotional states.

Adolescents need to know that these things are normal and that they will survive them. They need to feel that there is someone with whom they can discuss anything that is on their minds, no matter how bizarre they think it is. They need to believe that they are not alone with their problems.

They also need to know that it is normal to get depressed at times. Short-term depression (less than two months) that is related to a loss or disappointment is common during adolescence. **Chronic depression,** however,

chronic depression depression that lasts most of the day, more days than not, and persists for more than two years (one year in children and adolescents)

STRESS IN OUR WORLD 12-2

Growing Up Straight: Rich

Rich's adolescence was a fairly tumultuous experience for a straight lower-middle-class young man growing up in urban America. Rich's parents were high school graduates who worked in factories as piecework tailors. Although both were very loving and attentive parents, neither was skilled at communicating openly with Rich about the issues he'd face as an adolescent. Indeed, neither even knew about the key developmental aspects of puberty and adolescence, let alone felt comfortable talking to Rich about these issues. Consequently, Rich's adolescence was a kind of hit-or-miss, trial-and-error experience for which he was totally unprepared.

Rich remembers experiencing such things as wet dreams, his first "true" love, masturbation, his first ejaculation, and how puzzled he was trying to figure out how male and female genitalia came together during sexual intercourse.

Rich desperately wanted to talk to his mom or dad about some of the things he was going through but remembers feeling as if these issues were off limits simply because they were never discussed. He remembers agonizing about his first ejaculation, feeling as if perhaps he had injured himself or something had gone wrong because all of a sudden there was this liquid coming out of the end of his penis. Rich had to be content with asking his friends or older brother about some of these things. He knew, based on the responses he received, that some of the answers were not the right ones.

Rich also remembers reading the "girlie" magazines his father hid in the closet. Rich hoped to get some answers from them. He somehow knew that these also weren't what he was looking for.

The only comforting thing about Rich's adolescence was that he didn't go through it alone. Mike, his closest friend, had almost the exact experiences. At least he had Mike to bounce things off. He also felt normal because he was "just one of the guys." They were all going through the same things and shared a common attraction to girls and other "manly" pursuits, such as football, basketball, and fixing cars.

It took Rich several years to get over much of the guilt and shame he had about his sexual feelings and behavior during adolescence. He spent the better part of his twenties looking for the answers to unresolved questions and issues from his adolescence.

Growing Up Gay: Paul

Paul, like Rich, had a very tumultuous adolescence. The only son of immigrant parents, Paul had very little preparation for what he'd experience during puberty and adolescence. (As adults, Paul and Rich met and discussed the similarities they had in going through that troubling time.) Like Rich, Paul had a tremendous amount of curiosity and guilt about his sexual desires. A Roman Catholic, Paul dutifully recited the Hail Mary after he masturbated. He was confused about masturbation, confused by his church's teachings and by his own feelings. He also felt he had no one to talk to about it. Once, during confession, he did try to talk to the priest. He was told to ignore his sexual feelings and pray when he had the urge to masturbate.

Paul had one major difference from Rich. Paul was gay. Going through adolescence as a gay young man was doubly troubling for Paul. Paul never felt any sexual desire toward females. He played along when his friends talked about "getting laid" and carrying on with girls in general. Inside, however, Paul was very troubled because he really felt attracted to some of the boys in his class. Paul agonized all through his adolescence as he tried to figure out who or what he was. He tried dating girls but found it unsatisfactory. Paul suspected he was gay but didn't want to admit it. He felt he had no one whom he could trust, no one in whom to confide, no one with whom to explore this facet of himself.

Paul coped with this by suppressing most of his sexual feelings. He'd deny that they existed and spend most of his time immersed in studying. It wasn't until he entered college as a pre-med student that he finally gave in to his urges to explore this part of himself. Later, in medical school and in a steady relationship with another male student, Paul was able to work through some of the pain and confusion of his adolescence.

is a serious condition that significantly reduces the quality of a person's life. Chronic depression can make you feel constantly fatigued and uninterested in eating or cause you to overeat, feel hopeless, have low self-esteem, and lose interest in life.[1]

Chronic depression is also a risk factor for suicide. Suicide is the second leading cause of death in the United States among people age 15 to 24. The reasons for suicide are many and varied. Basically, young people take their lives because they feel that there is no other way out. There are several risk factors for suicide which contribute to this sense of hopelessness.[19]

Sometimes they have suffered a loss that has deeply hurt them (divorce, death of loved one). In other cases they feel they simply can't keep pace with the pressures in their lives or have failed and let someone down.

In any case, a key to understanding suicide is realizing that it is a permanent solution to a temporary problem that in most cases can be worked out. Adolescents need to know that feeling sad and depressed is a normal part of adolescence but that if it persists for more than two months, they need to get help. They need to know that even if they can't approach their parents or caregiver, there is someone out there who can help. All adolescents

Stress Buster Tips

Suicide's Warning Signs and How to Help Someone Contemplating Suicide

Usually a person considering suicide says or does something that should serve as a warning signal; 75 percent of suicide victims give verbal or behavioral clues to what they are planning. The most obvious clue is a previous attempt. Other clues are dramatic changes for no apparent reason in familiar routines of eating or sexual activity. Among young people, the most common indications are the following:

- Increased moodiness, seeming down or sad
- Feelings of worthlessness or discouragement
- A withdrawal from friends, family, and normal activities
- Changes in eating and sleeping habits
- Specific suicide threats
- School compositions revealing a preoccupation with death
- Persistent boredom
- A decline in the quality of schoolwork
- Violent, hostile, or rebellious behavior
- Running away
- Breaking off of friendships
- Increased drug and alcohol use
- A failed love relationship
- Unusual neglect of personal appearance
- Difficulty concentrating
- A radical personality change
- Complaints about physical symptoms, such as headache or fatigue

If someone you know has talked about suicide, behaved unpredictably, or suddenly emerged from a severe depression into a calm, settled state of mind, do not rule out the possibility that he or she may attempt suicide.

- Encourage your friend to talk. Ask concerned questions. Listen attentively. Show that you take the person's feelings seriously and truly care.
- Do not offer trite reassurances or list reasons to go on living.
- Do not analyze the person's motives or try to shock or challenge him or her.
- Suggest solutions or alternatives to problems. Make plans.
- Encourage positive action, such as getting away for a while to gain a better perspective on a problem.
- Do not be afraid to ask whether your friend has considered suicide. The opportunity to talk about thoughts of suicide may be an enormous relief and—contrary to a long-standing myth—will not fix the idea of suicide more firmly in a person's mind.
- Do not think that people who talk about killing themselves never carry out their threat. Most individuals who commit suicide give definite indications of their intent to die.

Source: From Hales, D. (1993). *An Invitation to Health.* Reprinted with permission of Wadsworth Publishing, a division of International Thomson Publishing.[9]

KEY TO UNDERSTANDING

Suicide is a permanent solution to a temporary problem.

need to know the warning signs of suicide so that, if need be, they can help themselves.

Adolescents also need to know how to help a friend they think is contemplating suicide. Stress Buster Tips describes guidelines for helping a friend who you think is contemplating suicide.

School and Stress

The primary task of adolescence is coming to terms with oneself, finding out who one really is and what one really cares about. It is a time of struggling with being an individual, the person one really is, and at the same time wanting to fit in, to be what society wants one to be.

The arena in which this task is played out to a great extent is school. As adolescents move through middle school and high school and into college, the classroom, the schoolyard, and playing fields can exert a great deal of pressure.

Developing a sense of self and self-esteem occurs, in part, by succeeding in one's interests, pursuits, and friendships. Feeling competent is a big part of developing self-esteem. An adolescent's competence is severely tested in school. A key to understanding the influence of school as a potential stressor is to view it as the place where academic, social, and athletic pressures to succeed come to a head.

Prior success in elementary school in classwork, making friends, and youth sports makes the transition to middle and high school easier simply because it represents a continuation of prior patterns of success. Despite past success, however, the adolescent school experience is vastly different.

The physical environment of most middle and high schools is very different. Physically, everything is larger. Buildings, hallways, and even the chairs and desks are larger and intimidating. The mix of students is different. Typically, students from several elementary schools funnel into a middle school. Similarly, a community may have more than one middle school channeling students to a high school. Some high schools are regional, serving students from different communities.

KEY TO UNDERSTANDING

School is a powerful potential stressor because it is where academic, athletic, and social pressure to succeed all come to a head.

DIVERSE PERSPECTIVES 12-3

Expeditionary Learning

Expeditionary learning is an alternative K–12 school curriculum built on ten design principles derived from Outward Bound. Since 1941, Outward Bound has been providing alternative learning experiences through its wilderness-based programs. The principles of expeditionary learning connect the spirit and philosophy of Outward Bound with alternatives in teaching, learning, and the culture of schools. The ten principles of expeditionary learning are:

1. *The Primacy of Self-Discovery.* Learning happens best when people discover their abilities, values, passions, and responsibilities in situations that offer adventure, challenge, and the unexpected.
2. *Having Wonderful Ideas.* Students learn through situations that provide something important to think about, time to experiment, and time to make sense of what is observed.
3. *The Responsibility for Learning.* Learning is both a personal and a social activity and occurs when both children and adults become increasingly responsible for directing their own personal and collective learning.
4. *Empathy and Caring.* Learning is fostered best in communities where students' and teachers' ideas are respected and where there is mutual trust.
5. *Success and Failure.* Students build the confidence and capacity to take risks and meet increasingly difficult challenges by having opportunities to learn from their successes as well as their failures and to persevere when things are difficult.
6. *Collaboration and Competition.* Students learn best when they are encouraged to compete not against each other but with their own personal best and with rigorous standards of excellence.
7. *Diversity and Inclusion.* Both diversity and inclusion increase the richness of ideas, creative power, problem-solving ability, and respect for others.
8. *The Natural World.* Students learn to become stewards of the earth and of future generations by developing a direct relationship with the natural world.
9. *Solitude and Reflection.* Students need time alone to explore their own thoughts, make their own connections, and create their own ideas if they are to share those ideas with others.
10. *Service and Compassion.* Students lives are strengthened by acts of consequential service to others.

To find out more about how expeditionary learning programs work in creating an alternative environment for children and adolescents, go to http://www.elob.org/ index.html.

School: the idyllic haven for adolescents or the epicenter of their stress?

Essentially, these differences make middle and high schools mixing pots where there are a lot of new, unfamiliar faces and places to which to become accustomed. Instead of the familiar, intimate elementary school serving kids from the neighborhood they've been around for the last few years, adolescents are in unfamiliar territory with unfamiliar faces. Couple this with the dramatic physiological changes occurring in their bodies as a result of puberty and add the social, academic, and athletic pressures that are part of school and you get a sense of how much potential stress adolescents face.

Social Pressures

Adolescence is a time of developing a personal style of one's own. Most adolescents go through several styles as they explore new and different interests, friends, and experiences, adding to those parts of their personalities that have evolved up to this point.

Pop culture idols and media that pander to adolescents start the trends that set broad standards for dress, language, and other lifestyle choices. Friends create additional pressure to conform to their expectations concerning these standards for dress, language, and behavior. Adolescents are caught in the middle as they try to be true to themselves and follow their own instincts while being bombarded by their family, their peers, and the media.

Adolescents who possess high self-esteem because it was nurtured and developed throughout their childhood have an easier time sorting out the conflicting messages of adolescence. They may, in fact, relish this task and view it as a challenge. Their decision-making skills, self-confidence, and trust enable them to be true to their values despite pressure from others. One of the strengths

Teenagers need to feel that they can do something right. Reward them for a job well done, whether it is changing the oil or getting an A on a test.

KEY TO UNDERSTANDING

A key to helping adolescents develop confidence and build self-esteem is to assist them in finding something they are good at.

these adolescents possess is a greater sense of control over their lives. Compas et al.[5] found that a sense of control is related to an increased ability to cope with stress and that it affects how adolescents cope. A key to helping adolescents develop confidence and build self-esteem is to assist them in finding something they are good at and reward them for a job well done.

Adolescents with a sense of control are still being bombarded with the zillion new ideas, experiences, situations, and temptations that are part of their life. They are just more in control of their emotions and are able to sort through potential stressors a little easier, make better choices, and feel better about whatever decisions they make in relation to this pressure than are adolescents who don't have a strong foundation of self-esteem on which to build.

In a sense, these adolescents are struggling with issues that are part of normal acculturation into mainstream society. They are not rebelling against society per se but, rather, are struggling with the conflicting messages and urges, restrictions, and pressures that are part of the transition from childhood to adulthood in American society.

Adolescents who don't have high levels of self-esteem because of deficiencies in their childhood development will struggle more with peer, media, and parental pressure. Unsure of themselves and their abilities and fearful of failure or rejection, they will struggle with decisions and make inappropriate choices and decisions. Many of them feel disenfranchised, with no vested interest in the future. Unlike their peers who are working through the process of becoming a part of mainstream American culture and look forward to the future and the role they will play in it, disenfranchised youth have no such vision. They will latch on to peers and even go as far as joining gangs to gain the approval and self-esteem they crave and need. A key to understanding the lore of youth gangs is to understand that they are filling a void in the lives of adolescents with low self-esteem and self-control.

Planning for the Future

The last aspect of adolescence that contributes to the development of self-identity is planning for the future. Formulating plans for the future is a normal part of adolescent development that can be either a challenge or a major source of stress. As we've seen in this chapter, it isn't always easy for adolescents to know who they are and understand what they believe in and value. This is especially true when they are bombarded with other people's opinions about who they "should" be and what they "should" do with their lives. It seems that everyone has an opinion about what adolescents should do with their future.

Parents and caregivers, often acting in what they feel are the best interests of their children, try to steer them in one direction. "Go to college," they say, or "You can't get a good job without a college degree." Others might say,

KEY TO UNDERSTANDING

A key to understanding gangs is to realize that they fill a void in the lives of their members.

"Get a job and earn some money" or "Join the service and grow up a little."

Friends try to pressure adolescents to follow their lead. "Come on," they tell them, "go to this college. It's the hot school this year." Or they might say, "School is for chumps. You can make more money in a week dealing drugs than you would in your first year out of college." Other friends, with no plans for the future, encourage them to "kick back, get high, and let things work themselves out."

The media tell them which jobs are hot and which are not. The evening news goes on and on about how job prospects for this year's crop of college graduates are the worst in a decade.

Adding to all these confusing messages is an adolescent sense of time urgency. Parents, friends, guidance counselors, and a host of others rush adolescents to make critical decisions that will affect their lives for years to come. In some cases, the need to make decisions quickly is real. Certain courses must be taken as prerequisites for more advanced studies. Application deadlines must be adhered to for college admission, scholarships, enrollment in the armed forces, and the like. Some choices will mean missed opportunities elsewhere. Pursuing certain tracks in high school, such as "college prep" or "business and secretarial," may make it difficult or impossible to take certain courses or pursue other interests later.

In other cases, however, decisions don't have to be made right away. Some issues, such as going to college, choosing the "right career," and deciding "what you want to be" can be delayed or postponed until a later date. Most adolescents are unsure of what they really want to do in terms of school, work, or a career.

In some cases postponing decisions about going to college or getting other forms of schooling is the best answer. Many adolescents opt for joining the armed forces and taking a couple of years to decide about their career plans. In many cases the armed forces can prepare them for civilian jobs by providing valuable training and experience. Other adolescents may decide to seek employment right out of high school, preferring to work as they sort through what they ultimately want to do with their lives.

All these decisions about the future are potentially stressful if an adolescent feels unable to cope with them. (See Assess Yourself 12-2, "Unfinished Sentences—Adolescence.")

Coping with Parenting Adolescents Using the Five Rs

Helping adolescents learn to cope with stress isn't always easy. Even in the best circumstances, adolescents, like children, often have short attention spans and can be irrational and make absolutely no sense. Timing is very important. Try talking with them when it is convenient for *them,* not for you. Schedule an appointment with them to talk about stress. Talk about coping when the opportunity presents itself. Don't become a source of stress or get stressed trying to help adolescents learn how to cope.

The best way for parents and caregivers to teach adolescents about coping with stress is to use the Five Rs in a combination approach. This should include being a role model through the use of the Five Rs and teaching adolescents how they can use the Five Rs in different stressful circumstances.

Teaching Adolescents to Rethink

It is often difficult for adolescents to think logically and rationally because of all the factors we previously described. Being a role model for rational thinking will continue to be your best strategy, as it was with helping children. Share your disputes with your adolescents when you use the ABCDE model to work through your own illogical beliefs about your stressors. Unlike young children, adolescents can handle a wide range of stressors. You may find that you can share certain world events or personal issues with adolescents that you might not have shared with younger children.

One of the best ways to help adolescents rethink potential stressors is to be a source of accurate, up-to-date information. You can do this in many ways. If you know your adolescent is struggling with an issue (abstinence vs. having intercourse, for example) you can provide information about becoming sexually active. Try to provide information that speaks to both sides of the question (advantages vs. disadvantages). You can do this directly by obtaining the material and giving it to your adolescent (or directing them where to find it) or indirectly. Some parents find indirect methods, like leaving material or books out on the coffee table for the adolescent to see, is less threatening to both parent and child. Both direct and indirect methods show the adolescent that you are an approachable parent who wants to help.

You can continue to point out illogical beliefs when you hear them from adolescents. As when speaking with younger children, be sure to use nonjudgmental language. Try pointing out more logical beliefs as an option they might consider. For instance, saying, "You might consider . . ." or "Have you ever thought about that issue this way . . ." is preferable to telling adolescents how they should or "must" view situations. Words like *should* and *must* are red flags for most adolescents, who generally do not like being told what to do.

Teaching Adolescents to Reduce

Talking to adolescents about identifying potential stressors in advance of their occurrence is particularly important since adolescents have a greater degree of control over their world than children do. The triple As of coping is an excellent technique for adolescents because it is easy to learn and helps them cope with stressors they can identify and control. The triple As technique helps them

Living Constructively

Teaching Adolescents How to Co-Exist with Their Feelings

One of the greatest gifts you can give adolescents is the gift of normalcy. Adolescents are constantly asking the question, "Is it normal to feel this way?" The question could be in response to a hundred different stimuli ranging from falling in love to deciding on a vocation. A major strength of the constructive living skill, co-existing with your feelings, is its adaptability.

Instructions

1. When confronted by an adolescent with questions regarding feeling normal, use the opportunity as a teachable moment to introduce or reinforce this constructive living skill.
2. Explain to the adolescent that all feelings are normal and acceptable.
3. Explain to the adolescent that feelings (both pleasant and unpleasant ones) come and go, and are often beyond our control. Since they are beyond our control, there is no need to feel guilty or bad about them. Everyone (use yourself as an example) occasionally has feelings that they are ashamed or embarrassed or confused about.
4. Ask the adolescent to think about times when s/he was experiencing pleasant or exhilarating feelings and wished that they would never end (like in a dream). What happened to those feelings? Did they last forever or did they pass, even though you wished they would not?
5. Describe how the same principle holds true with negative, unpleasant feelings. If you leave them alone and do not dwell on them, they too will disappear.
6. Tell the adolescent that shifting their attention off of the feelings and on to something they enjoy doing or needs doing will help the feelings disappear.
7. Give them examples of solo (exercise, listen to music, dance, paint a picture, etc.) or group (go to a movie with friends, play Frisbee, go surfing, etc.) activities they can use to shift their attention.
8. Have them list three solo and three group activities they could easily shift their attention to when co-existing with painful, uncomfortable feelings.

cope with current stressors and can also be used to reduce the likelihood that the same problem will occur in the future.

Adolescents also need to understand that limiting their level of demand will help them perform the things they enjoy at peak efficiency without those things becoming stressors due to overstimulation.

The DESC model can be particularly helpful in teaching adolescents how to assert themselves. It will help them learn how to communicate their needs and wants more effectively and minimize the stress associated with miscommunication.

Music and natural sounds can be very healing and have a natural appeal for adolescents.

Teaching Adolescents to Relax

Teaching adolescents to relax is similar to working with children. Focus on techniques that are simple and don't require much time to learn and perform. Diaphragmatic breathing is a simple yet effective technique for adolescents, is the basis for all other relaxation techniques they may want to learn, and they can perform it anywhere. The calming response is another simple yet effective technique that employs all the key relaxation components.

Teaching Adolescents to Release

There are many opportunities to incorporate release techniques into the average adolescent's repertoire of coping skills. Most high schools offer extensive interscholastic and intramural sports that serve as excellent release strategies. Once again, martial arts that employ punching and kicking are fun ways to purge stress.

Teaching Adolescents to Reorganize

Help adolescents reorganize their lives by creating lifestyles that are stress-reducing. Continue to create family stress-reduction time and activities that revolve around four-season physical activity plans. Help your adolescents develop similar lifestyles with their friends. Encourage them to invite their friends to participate in some activities.

DIVERSE PERSPECTIVES 12-4

Drumming Circles for Children and Teenagers

A drumming circle is a facilitator-led hands-on rhythm experience. Participants sit in a circle with a drum or other percussion instrument of their choice. Extra percussion instruments sit in the center of the circle. Participants can exchange their drums for instruments such as wooden blocks, maracas, washboard-type scrapers, etc. The facilitator leads the members of the circle in playing the drums and hand percussion instruments. The participants communicate with each other by answering the facilitator's beat with a rhythm of their own. The *conversation* continues as the other participants add their *voices* to the group rhythms. Participants are asked to become a part of the rhythm of the group without dominating other participant's individual beat. In a sense, every member plays his or her rhythm between and in response to the other participants. After several minutes the rhythms and beats usually mesh into a heart-thumping, mesmerizing release of tension and act of communion. One does not need drumming or musical experience to play in a drumming circle. Arthur Hill, a pioneer in American drumming circles, claims that humans have always used drums and percussion to communicate and release tensions. Hill[13] describes how Rhythmaculture has evolved through an intimate relationship of people of all cultures, the earth they live on, and the animals they live with.

A drumming circle is an excellent stress management strategy for children and adolescents because it is a healthy form of physical release of tension, creates social support, offers a number of proven health benefits, and, best of all, is fun. Studies clearly show that group drumming circles provide the following health benefits:

- Relieves stress-related tension
- Helps hyperactive people relax
- Provides exercise
- Supports fine motor skills
- Decreases depression
- Boosts immune system response
- Reduces feelings of loneliness
- Increases white blood cells
- Increases quality of life
- Increases creativity
- Provides a fun experience
- Helps focus the mind
- Boosts self-confidence
- Boosts intellectual stimulation
- Fosters feeling of belonging
- Creates positive peer identification
- Fosters community and cooperation
- Creates team synergy (Bittman et al.,[3] Bittman et al.,[2] Hill,[13] Silverman[18])

Group drumming stimulates creative expression that unites our bodies, minds, and spirits. A drum circles allow children and adolescents to share their rhythmical spirit and create the power of unity through music. In the drumming circle experience children and adolescents are allowed to express their individual rhythmical spirits without fear of criticism. They also learn basic universal principles found in culturally specific drum circles. Drumming is a natural way to provide young people with a safe outlet to creatively channel and release the pent-up emotions and frustrations that accompany the process of growing up.

SUMMARY

In this chapter we explored developmental stressors from birth through adolescence. We examined these years using Erikson's model to explain the tasks normally associated with growth and development.

Erikson's tasks in themselves can be perceived as either stressors or challenges, depending on how children and adolescents perceive them. The developmental tasks were presented as building blocks not only for healthy psychosocial development but also for coping with stress. If children and adolescents work through the stages and master the developmental tasks, they develop a sense of competence. This competence builds self-efficacy and feeds into their perceived ability to cope with life's stresses. As you recall, our belief in our ability to cope with situations factors into our perception of them as stressors or challenges.

If children and adolescents do not master the tasks associated with the various stages of development, they will have a harder time coping with life's stresses because their repertoire of psychosocial skills and strengths will be limited or incomplete. They may be unable to use certain coping strategies because they lack adequate development of certain personality constructs, such as self-esteem.

We started the chapter by examining the primary task of infancy: developing trust versus mistrust. We described how trust evolves as a result of nurturing, bonding, and meeting children's most primary needs for love, nurturance, and sustenance.

The chapter described how the major task of early childhood, the development of autonomy versus shame and doubt, is contingent on providing opportunities for children to develop self-control and self-esteem. The handling of issues such as toilet training was covered.

The chapter continued with an exploration of late childhood and school age. The primary task of these stages, building initiative and industriousness, was covered, with special emphasis placed on the role of outside influences (such as school, friends, and the media). We talked about outside influences because this is the time when children have opportunities to stretch themselves and grow outside the confines of the family.

In the second half of the chapter, three major factors—puberty, school, and planning for the future—were presented as issues which influence the development of a coherent sense of self for adolescents. All three have a great impact on an adolescent's search for self. A short description of Erikson's major developmental task for adolescence—the development of a coherent sense of self—was presented. Developing a sense of one's identity can be a major source of stress for adolescents who feel caught between trusting their own instincts and the demands of parents and the pressure from peers and media images.

The chapter continued with a description of the difference between puberty and adolescence. Specific physiological changes associated with puberty were discussed in detail. In particular, the emergence of "reproductive readiness," the point of full maturation of the male and female reproductive systems, was discussed, with an emphasis on its role as a potential stressor. A discussion of the differences between physiological and psychosocial readiness was presented. The author described how these two states of readiness rarely coincide for American youth and how this is can be a source of stress.

The chapter ended with a look at planning for the future and the role of planning in shaping adolescent identity.

STUDY QUESTIONS

1. List and describe Erikson's eight stages of development.
2. Describe the major developmental task for each of Erikson's stages.
3. Explain how these tasks could be perceived as either stressors or challenges.
4. Describe the developmental nature of coping with stress.
5. How does failure to master a developmental task relate to stress?
6. Explain two Rethink strategies that could be used in coping with childhood stress.
7. Describe how Rethink can be employed with "irrational" children.
8. Describe three Reduce strategies for coping with childhood stress.
9. Describe three Relax strategies that could be used in coping with childhood stress.
10. Describe the role of safety in using the Release strategy with children.
11. Describe how the final R, Reorganize, relates to coping with childhood stress.
12. Describe Erikson's major developmental task for adolescence.
13. Define adolescence and puberty. Explain the differences.
14. How can one be reproductively ready but not psychosocially ready?
15. List and describe three potential adolescent stresses associated with school.
16. Describe two adolescent coping strategies associated with Rethink, Reduce, Relax, and Release.
17. How can the final R, Reorganize, be used to cope with adolescent stress in the absence of more specific strategies?

DISCOVER OUR CHANGING WORLD

Living at Peace

http://www.livingatpeace.com/index.html

Living At Peace is an organization that provides experiential workshops that give both adults and children tools and techniques to realize and overcome self-limiting beliefs. Living At Peace empowers and influences people to live life with a positive mindset by developing greater self-awareness. Living At Peace works to create a world where adults and children feel unconditional love for themselves and others.

Critical Thinking Question

How can participating in a drum circle help foster greater tolerance of each other and promote peace at the level of the individual?

ARE YOU THINKING CLEARLY?

Often we are stressed when we feel pressure to do something that we are not comfortable with because it conflicts with our values. Sometimes we agree to do these things even though they don't feel right and we really don't want to do them. The next time you are being pressured to do something you do not want to do, *stop* and ask yourself the following questions:

1. Am I doing this because I really want to or because I am letting myself be pressured into it?
2. Are the rewards for doing this greater than the stress I am feeling and will continue to feel?
3. How will I feel about myself when this is over?
4. How does doing this relate to my values about this act?
5. Are these people really my friends if they continue to pressure me to do this?

If you think you are being illogical when answering these questions, use the ABCDE model from chapter 7 to work through your beliefs about the situation.

References

1. American Psychiatric Association (2000). *Diagnostic and statistical manual.* (4th ed.). Text Revising. Washington, DC: APA Press.
2. Bittman, B., Berk, L., Felten, D., Westengard, J., Simonton, O., Pappas, J., & Ninehouser, M. (2001). Composite Effects of Group Drumming Music Therapy on Modulation of Neuroendocrine-Immune Parameters in Normal Subjects. *Alternative Therapies in Health and Medicine,* 7, pp. 38–47.
3. Bittman, B., M.D., Bruhn, K.T., Stevens, C., M.S.W., M.T.-B.C., Westengard, J., & Umbach, P.O., M.A. (2003). Recreational music-making: A cost-effective group interdisciplinary strategy for reducing burnout and improving mood states in long-term care workers. *Advances in Mind-Body Medicine,* 19, No. 3/4.
4. Carrera, M. (1981). *Sex: The facts, the acts, and your feelings*. New York: Crown.
5. Compas, B., Banez, G.A., Makcarne, V., & Worsham, N. (1991). Perceived control and coping with stress: A developmental perspective. *Journal of Social Issues,* 47(4), pp. 23–35.
6. Eliss, M. (1988). Schools as a source of stress to children: An analysis of causal and administrative influences. *Journal of School Psychology,* 27(1), pp. 383–407.
7. Elkind, D. (1981). *The hurried child.* Reading, MA: Addison-Wesley.
8. Elkind, D. (1987). The child yesterday, today, and tomorrow. *Young Children,* 42(4), pp. 6–11.
9. Elkind, D. (1991). Instrumental narcissism parents. *Bulletin of the Menninger Clinic,* 55(3), pp. 299–307.
10. Erikson, E. (1978). *Childhood and society.* (2d ed.). New York: W.W. Norton.
11. Hales, D. (1993). *An Invitation to Health.* Wadsworth Publishing.
12. Helms, B.J. & Gable, R.K. (1990). Assessing and dealing with school-related stress in grades 3–12 students. Paper presented at Annual Meeting of the American Educational Research Association, Boston, April 1990.
13. Hill, A. (1998). *Drum Circle Spirit: Facilitating Human Potential through Rhythm.* Incline Village, Nevada: White Cliffs Media.
14. Living at Peace. http://www.livingatpeace.com/index.html
15. Masters, V., Johnson, W., & Kolodny, R. (1992). *Human sexuality.* (4th ed.). New York: HarperCollins.
16. Miller, A. (1991). Do gangs deserve a rap? Marketing using youth gang image. *Newsweek,* 118, p. 55.
17. Murphy, L. & Della-Cortes, S. (1990). School related stress and the special child. *Special Parent/Special Child,* 6(1), pp. 15–20.
18. Silverman, S. (2005). Drumming Circles. http://www.livingatpeace.com/for Children.html#dc
19. USDHHS. (1991). Attempted suicide among high school students: United States, 1990. *MMWR,* 40(37), pp. 35–37.
20. Yaeger Group. (1990). *Managing parental stress in the eighties*. USDHHS (1993a). Position Papers from the Third National Injury Control Conference. Washington, DC: U.S. Government Printing Office.

Name: ______________________________ Date: ____________

ASSESS YOURSELF 12-1

Unfinished Sentences—Childhood

Completing unfinished sentences is a helpful way to assess the impact of something that occurred in the past and continues to exert an influence on the way you feel today. Unfinished sentences provide some structure for helping you think about the past. They also allow you to begin to control some of the emotions associated with the events captured in the sentences.

INSTRUCTIONS

Finish each of the sentences using the blank lines provided.

Use additional paper if necessary.

Restrict your memories to your childhood years (birth to age 12)

1. The three major stressors of my childhood were ______________________________
2. One particularly stressful event for me was ______________________________
3. I still feel guilty about ______________________________
4. I'm still angry about ______________________________
5. I'm still confused about ______________________________
6. The pace of my childhood life was ______________________________
7. As a child I coped with stress by ______________________________
8. My parent(s)/guardian coped with stress by ______________________________
9. My parent(s)/guardian told me the following about coping with stress: ______________________________
10. As far as stress is concerned, my brothers and sisters ______________________________
11. The person who coped with stress most effectively was ______________________________
12. The greatest strength I had as a kid for dealing with stress was ______________________________
13. The most positive coping experience I remember was ______________________________

Name: ______________________________ Date: ______________

Assess Yourself 12-2

Unfinished Sentences—Adolescence

The following unfinished sentences were designed to help you remember significant issues related to your stress as an adolescent. Completing them can help you understand your current stress level and coping style.

Instructions

Finish each sentence using the blank lines provided.

Use additional paper if necessary.

Restrict your memories to your adolescent years (early to middle teens).

1. The most stressful thing about adolescence is ______________________________
2. The three major stressors of my adolescence were ______________________________
3. A particularly stressful event for me was ______________________________
4. I still feel guilty about ______________________________
5. I still feel angry about ______________________________
6. I'm still confused about ______________________________
7. The pace of my adolescence was ______________________________
8. As an adolescent I coped with stress by ______________________________
9. My parent(s)/guardian coped with stress by ______________________________
10. My parent(s)/guardian told me the following about stress and coping ______________________________
11. As far as stress is concerned, my brothers and sisters ______________________________
12. As far as stress is concerned, my friends ______________________________
13. The person who coped with stress most effectively was ______________________________
14. The greatest strength I had as an adolescent for coping with stress was ______________________________
15. The most positive coping experience I remember was ______________________________
16. A coping strategy that's evolved from my adolescence is ______________________________

CHAPTER

13

Young Adulthood: Relationships, College, and Other Challenges

OUTLINE

The Challenges of Young Adulthood

Friendship and Intimate Relationships
- Forming Friendships
- What Is Intimacy?
- Forming Intimate Relationships
- Dating and Breaking Up
- Love
- College Sexual Standards
- Living Arrangements of College Students

Intimacy, Sexuality, and Stress
- Sexual Victimization
- Sexual Harassment in College
- Sexually Transmitted Diseases

College, Work, and Stress
- Academics and Stress
- Financial and Career-Related Stressors

Coping with the Stress of Young Adulthood by Using the Five Rs
- Rethink Strategies
- Reduce Strategies
- Relax Strategies
- Release Strategies
- Reorganize Strategies

OBJECTIVES

By the end of the chapter students will:

- Describe Erikson's major developmental task for young adulthood.
- Discuss the importance of friendship.
- Define intimacy and describe how it develops.
- Describe how sexual victimization affects intimacy and stress.
- Explain how drinking and drug use are related to sexual victimization.
- Describe ways to reduce risks for sexual victimization.
- Explain how sexually transmitted diseases affect intimacy and stress.
- Describe how the pyramid of risk works for STDs.
- Describe how to reduce risks for STDs.
- Define love according to Sternberg.
- Compare and contrast friendship, intimacy, and love.
- Describe some of the stresses associated with academic and other work.
- Explain how to cope with the stress of young adulthood by using the Five Rs.

The Challenges of Young Adulthood

Young adulthood begins with the transition from adolescence. In a sense, adolescence is like a launching pad for a mission into adulthood. Adolescence is a time for figuring out who we are and what we want and need out of life. It is also a time for planning and preparing. These plans are actually set into motion during the early part of young adulthood. This is an exciting time of life, when we meet new friends, explore intimate and loving relationships, and test the waters for work and career possibilities. The end of young adulthood is a time for reassessment of commitments, focusing on those that have the most meaning for you.

If you are reading this book, your plans probably included attending college. For many college students this is the first time they live apart from their parents and a time of unparalleled freedom. Students who have mastered the developmental tasks of childhood and adolescence enter this period of their lives ready and eager to sample all that life has to offer. You set out on your journey through college: setting up residence in a dormitory or apartment, choosing courses, deciding on a major, getting involved in organizations and clubs, and meeting new people.

For others, their plans included joining the armed forces. For these young adults their lives involve an entirely different set of expectations and experiences. Still others have decided to hit the road and explore new people and places before deciding upon a major commitment to a school, job, or career.

While these three paths are entirely different and will result in being exposed to different places, people, and experiences, their common thread is taking action and launching the mission planned in adolescence. The same developmental tasks await all three. The primary task we face as young adults, according to Erikson,[20] is to develop intimacy. We begin to move away from our adolescent focus on ourselves and are ready to begin exploring mutually satisfying relationships. This stage emphasizes commitment in both our intimate relationships and our work.

This can also be a time of great stress. The same tasks that are perceived as challenges for some are viewed as stressors by others. Not everyone is equally prepared for the freedom, the work, and the tasks of young adulthood. Many have yet to work through some of the key developmental tasks of earlier periods in their lives and are unable to handle the pressures of young adulthood. Many lack work and study skills. Others have limited resources for managing pressures. All these factors, along with many others, enter into our perceived ability to cope with the normal developmental tasks of this period. If we feel unable to cope or are unsure of our ability to cope, these daily challenges will be perceived as stressors.

This chapter examines some of the key stressors that normally accompany this developmental period. Most of them are associated with interpersonal issues related to intimacy, academic issues, and work.

Friendship and Intimate Relationships

The major developmental task of young adulthood is forming committed, intimate, loving relationships. In most cases our friendships form the basis of our intimate relationships. Intimacy grows out of friendships as people become more trusting and comfortable with each other.

Forming Friendships

Pals, buddies, chums, comrades, sisters, brothers, amigos, and amigas are the names we give to our friends. Joel Block,[4] in his book *Friendship,* contends that humans are "wired" with a basic desire for contact with others. Our friendships, Block feels, are what make us whole. Friends enrich our existence and bond with us to form a conspiracy against the world: We like one another, understand one another, share interests, and have similar lifestyles or problems in life.[4]

What draws friends together? Many friendships grow from shared interests and experiences. These similarities provide the initial attraction. If the initial attraction is strong enough, it provides the basis for the friends to spend further time together. As the friendship progresses, the friends share more time and experiences, reinforcing their commonality, deepening their bonds, and enriching their lives.

Friendship is a unique bond. Although it is fraught with entanglements similar to those that characterize romantic relationships—competition, jealousy, and betrayal—it offers what Block calls "psychological space." Friendships are more open-ended than relationships with family members, mates, or lovers. Unlike in these more intimate relationships, in friendships friends live separate lives that allow time away from entanglements. Consequently, the relationship has a greater tolerance for growth and change. In many cases when we do not see our friends for days, weeks, or months, we pick up where we left off, renewed and eager to share where we've been or what we've done. In a sense, true friendships are timeless.

With our friends we are most truly ourselves. "A friend is one who knows you as you are, understands where you've been, accepts who you've become, and still invites you to grow."[4] Sometimes our true friendships are so unforced and seem so natural that we take them for granted. We assume they'll always be there, and we start to neglect our friends. Stress Buster Tips: "Maintaining Friendships" offers some excellent tips for maintaining friendships.

Stress Buster Tips

Maintaining Friendships

Like all relationships, friendships require attention and work to survive. Here are some behaviors that can keep you close to those you care about most:

- Be willing to open up. The more you share, the deeper the bond between you and your friend will become.
- Be sensitive to your friend's feelings. Keep in mind that, like you, your friend has unique needs, desires, and dreams.
- Express appreciation. Be generous with your compliments. Let your friends know you recognize their kindnesses.
- See friends clearly. Admitting their faults need not reduce your respect for them.
- Know that friends will disappoint you from time to time. They, too, are only human.
- Talk about your friendship. Evaluate the relationship periodically. If you have any gripes or frustrations, air them.

What Is Intimacy?

Intimacy is an often misunderstood phenomenon. Many people equate intimacy with sexual activity and love, yet they are three separate entities. One can be intimate and sexual with another person but not love him or her. One also can be intimate with, but not sexually involved with, another person. Finally, one can be sexual with another person but neither love nor be intimate with that person. So what *is* intimacy?

Intimacy is the process of gradually sharing one's innermost feelings with another. The word *intimacy* comes from the Latin word for "within." Intimacy involves risk; sharing one's innermost feelings involves making oneself vulnerable, which requires trust and takes time. More than a sexual or physical act, intimacy is an act of faith. Intimacy is sharing your true self with another because you feel you can entrust them with this information. A key to understanding intimacy, however, is realizing that all intimate relationships take time to develop.

Most young adults learn this through trial and error as they pass through this stage in their development. People have multiple types of relationships that exist simultaneously; we are intimate with some people, friends with others, and loving toward others. Some of these relationships have a sexual component and some do not. The foundation for deeper, committed, intimate relationships is the healthy self-esteem and identity that one has developed by successfully working through the previous developmental tasks. Without this it is hard to trust another person and open up to them.

Intimate relationships can be a source of great comfort and enjoyment.

Forming Intimate Relationships

We live in a culture that expects instant intimacy. Our lives are fast-paced and mobile with drive-in services for everything: call waiting, cellular telephones, faxed lunch menus, express checkout counters, and computerized dating services. People move around and relocate every seven years on the average, leaving old friends and expecting to make new ones quickly to fill this void. Television soap operas play out several entire romantic encounters in one thirty-minute segment. People expect that their own intimate relationships will develop as quickly. As we've just discovered, however, real intimacy takes time to develop. For intimacy to grow, people must share and then step back to assess how the other person handles the situation.

With intimate friends we share not only our thoughts and feelings but also our experiences. Intimacy often springs from the shared experiences of friendship. We develop a camaraderie between ourselves and another person when we experience difficult, challenging, or enjoyable times together. A special bond develops between us.

KEY TO UNDERSTANDING

Intimacy develops gradually over time and can take many forms. While sexual relationships can be intimate, intimacy does not require sex.

intimacy the process of gradually sharing one's innermost feelings with another person; the word *intimacy* comes from the Latin word for "within"

Females in our culture have been raised to be intimate with their friends. It is sometimes hard for males to become intimate with their male friends.

In time, if the other person treats our intimate revelations with caring, confidentiality, and respect, and if that person in turn reveals his or her own innermost feelings, intimacy will grow between us. If this does not happen and the other person violates our trust or does not respect our feelings, our desire for intimacy wanes. In some cases this can make us leery about wanting to develop new intimate relationships (see Assess Yourself 13-1, "IQ Test," for a tool for measuring a person's capacity for intimacy).

Another key to understanding intimacy is that it does not necessarily include sexual relations. Many of us have intimate relationships with people to whom we are not sexually attracted. This can be confusing as we try to sort through the feelings we have for that person. Are we looking for a sexual relationship, or is it intimacy we desire? Should we have sex with someone with whom we are not intimate? Should intimacy grow out of sexuality? We may think we should have sexual feelings for someone with whom we share our deepest feelings, yet we may not be ready for that special kind of commitment.

Intimate relationships can form between members of the same gender or opposite genders. Traditionally, women have enjoyed same-gender intimate relationships more frequently than men have. Women typically share intimate information with female confidants much more than men share with men. Most men perceive intimate sharing of any feelings with another man as unmanly or feminine and therefore to be avoided. Men are socialized to keep their feelings to themselves, much to the detriment of their mental and emotional well-being.[51]

Intimacy knows no racial or ethnic boundaries. If allowed to develop, intimate relationships and love can flourish between people of different races and cultures. Indeed, the racial and cultural differences often are what attract us to each other in the first place (see Diverse Perspectives 13-1, "Robert and Monica").

Attraction and intimacy are not bound by race or color. Often what first attracts lovers is the uniqueness of their differences.

Dating and Breaking Up

Every society has some rituals or norms for pairing and courtship. Although the "rules" for dating and courtship vary from culture (and subculture) to culture, every society has traditions that it passes along from one generation to the next. Adults who came of age in the late 1960s and early 1970s in the United States vividly remember the differences between the rigid rules of the 1950s and those of the more liberated 1960s. Before the cultural revolution of the 1960s, a young woman would not even consider asking a man out for a date. Men were expected to ask women out, pay for the evening's activities, and be responsible for picking up and dropping off their dates. Women were expected to wait for men to call them, even if a woman was interested and wanted to initiate contact. The popular media played out these and other traditional dating scenarios, and mothers and fathers passed them on to their daughters and sons. Everyone was assumed to be heterosexual, and sex was not part of the evening's activities.

The face of dating today is dramatically different. Dating behavior allows more freedom. A woman can initiate a date, pick up her date, and pay for things herself. Straight, gay, and bisexual men and women have their own clubs, organizations, and dating services that make

DIVERSE PERSPECTIVES 13-1

Robert and Monica

Robert and Monica have been lovers for about a year. Both are juniors attending a large, urban Midwestern university. They started going out as freshmen and last year stopped dating other people. Robert is white, Protestant, and from a middle-class farming family in Wisconsin. Monica is black, Baptist, and from a middle-class business family (her father and mother are accountants) in Baltimore.

"I'll have to admit," Rob says "that when I first saw her [Monica], it was her blackness that attracted me. Growing up on a farm in Wisconsin, I'd never really met any black girls in school. Monica is dark, so unlike me, that I found myself staring at her in freshman English class, getting aroused."

"He was aroused all right," says Monica. "I could tell from across the lecture hall that Rob was having a hard time concealing his interest in me. My friend Clarissa was the first to notice, elbowing me to look at that 'crazy white boy over there staring at us.' Boy, was he hot! With those beautiful blue eyes, white skin, and bulging farm-boy muscles popping out from all over, I felt my knees getting a little weak as I found myself staring back."

"I remember that first lecture," Rob interjects, cutting Monica off with a smile and a gentle touch of her knee. "All through the class I fantasized about what Monica would look like naked, her black skin against my pale, white body. As a matter of fact, I missed most of the notes because I was paying more attention to her than to the professor." Rob laughs and continues, "It worked out all right, though, because I went up to her after class and asked her for her notes. We started talking and made plans to see each other later on that evening. That was our first date and the start of our three-year relationship."

"It was weird," Monica continues. "The last thing I needed or wanted was a white guy messing up my life. My mom and dad, although not racist, wanted me to meet someone 'of my own kind' and warned me about all these lily-white farm boys who had never seen any black women before. I really wasn't interested in meeting a white guy and explaining things to my parents, but I must admit, when I saw Rob staring at me, I also kind of lost track of what the professor was lecturing about. Later on in our relationship, Rob and I had a good laugh when we each confided about what was going on in our minds during class that day and how we ever passed freshman English."

"It's funny," says Rob, "although the thing that first attracted me to Monica was the difference between us, as our intimacy and love grew, I found her more similar to me than different. The color thing that everyone still makes such a big deal about kind of vanished in my mind. What's really funny is that I tend to like the things that most people associate with black people and African-American culture. I love rap music; she hates it and can listen to classical for hours. I like cities; she prefers the quiet and solitude of the mountains. I'm liberal; she's conservative politically and questions the value of federal entitlement programs."

Do you know a Robert and Monica?

finding a partner easier and safer. In the past, bars and clubs for gay and lesbian women were disguised and subject to harassment from bullies and the police. Today they are more accepted and open, with directories available to identify various facilities, particularly in urban areas.

Although the rituals and rules of dating change over time, the purpose of dating hasn't changed much. Dating is a mechanism for developing intimate relationships. Intimate relationships, in turn, influence both sexual behavior and living patterns.

Romantic relationships end for a variety of different reasons. Some breakups occur simply because students are just too busy with academics and other college-related commitments to put the time and effort into building and maintaining intimate relationships. Others find that being at college and apart from their partners gives them time and space to reevaluate their relationships. This often leads to the realization that it is time to move on. Others simply find someone new who excites them and with whom they want to get involved. Families often exert pressure to breakup because they find faults in partners of their children. Whatever the reason, for at least one of the partners, the relationship wasn't working and the decision was made to end it.

Just as relationships can start and evolve in healthy ways, they can also be ended in a nondestructive fashion. This is easiest when the feelings are mutual and both parties realize that the relationship is not working and want to end it. In this case both people walk away on their own terms and with the fewest regrets. This can still be stressful and painful, however, as people often blame themselves when relationships don't work out. Having a partner break up with you when you didn't feel there was anything wrong with the relationship can be a different story. When this happens, feelings can run the gamut from sadness and depression to anger and rage directed at the former partner. Stress Buster Tips: "Dealing with Unhealthy Behaviors after Ending a Relationship" provides some guidelines for dealing with unhealthy reactions to breaking up.

Stress Buster Tips

Dealing with Unhealthy Behaviors after Ending a Relationship

1. It is common to experience sadness, anger, and other feelings following the breakup of an intimate relationship.
2. It is also common to behave in ways that are atypical for you, such as not wanting to go out with friends for a while, wanting to be alone more than usual, etc.
3. Though the above behaviors can be expected following a breakup, the following ones can become increasingly problematic if they persist:
   - Sleeping too much or too little
   - Using drugs and alcohol excessively
   - Inability to eat
   - Inability to concentrate on work
   - Inability to study
   - Wanting to drop classes
   - Wanting to drop out of school
   - Driving recklessly
   - Making harassing phone calls to the ex-partner
   - Following the ex-partner around
   - Harassing any new partner
   - Being violent toward the old partner or his/her property
   - Wanting to commit murder or suicide.
4. If you are engaging in these kinds of behaviors following your breakup, you need to get some help from a counselor or therapist immediately.
5. Failing to do so could result in serious consequences ranging from attempting suicide to getting arrested for harassment.

Love

What is love? There are many kinds of love, such as the love parents have for their child, the love of God, and the love you may have for your pet. Erich Fromm, in his classic work *The Art of Loving,* defines mature love between two adults as "a union under the condition of preserving one's integrity, and one's individuality, in which lovers become one yet remain two."[26] A key to understanding Fromm's conceptualization of mature love is realizing the role of respect in loving relationships. Fromm believed that self-respect and respect for one's lover are essential ingredients for love. Although Fromm refers to this type of love as mature love and refers to "adult" lovers, adolescents and young adults are capable of forming love relationships built on the same respect.[26]

More recently, Sternberg[50] developed a triangular theory of love to characterize the relationship that exists between two adults. According to Sternberg, there are three facets to adult love, or what Fromm would characterize as mature love: passion, intimacy, and decision/commitment. Passion involves romance, physical attraction, and sexual desire. Intimacy refers to the desire for bonding, sharing, warmth, and emotional closeness. Decision or commitment is the conscious decision to love another person and remain committed to that person despite the inevitable problems that arise in any relationship. Decision or commitment might be viewed as the rational or cognitive aspect of love, while passion and intimacy could be viewed as the motivational and emotional components, respectively.

KEY TO UNDERSTANDING

Respect is central to mature love.

According to Sternberg, when all three components of love exist in equal proportion, the partners have consummate love. Ideally, both partners have consummate love at the same time. More typically, however, one or both of the lovers lack one or more of the three components (fig. 13-1).

Friendship is a state characterized by intimacy alone. There is no passion, nor is there any decision or commitment.

Companionate love, which often is characteristic of couples who have been together for many years, has everything but passion.

In **empty love,** the partners are committed to each other but the fires of passion and the deep personal warmth of intimacy have long been extinguished.

Infatuation is immature love. It is shallow in that there is neither an intimate bond nor a long-term commitment between the partners.

Romantic love is characterized by passion and intimacy. It is intense and overwhelming but not longstanding and committed.

Similar in nature is **fatuous love,** in which partners are passionate and have a commitment. The rapidity and

friendship characterized by intimacy but is without passion and commitment

companionate love involves intimacy and commitment but lacks passion

empty love involves commitment without passion and intimacy

infatuation characterized by passion without intimacy and commitment

romantic love involves passion and intimacy but not commitment

fatuous love passionate and committed but not intimate

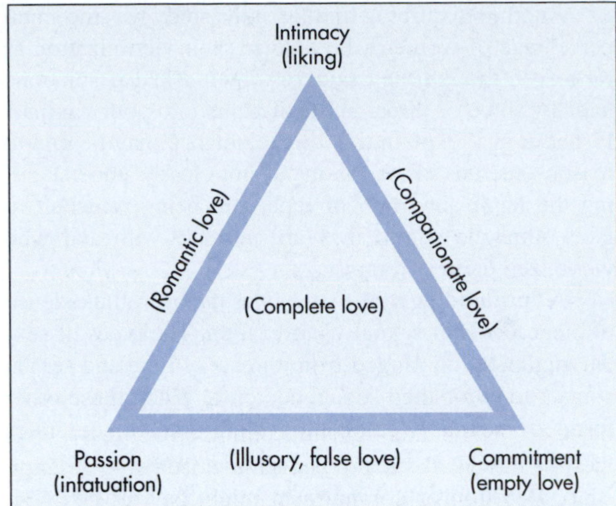

Sternberg's theory allows us to depict a couple's compatability–how well their feelings match. The closer the match, the more satisfying the partners' relationship.

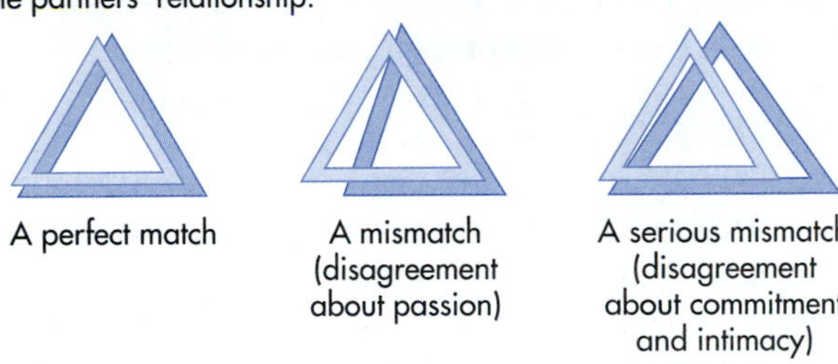

Figure 13-1

Sternberg's triangular theory of love.[50]

intensity of this commitment, however, are usually shortsighted and based on an unrealistic perception of the true nature of the partner.

Sternberg[50] believes that passion and intimacy develop early and intensely in relationships and level off as a relationship matures. Decision and commitment, however, take more time to develop but intensify as the relationship matures and endures. A key to understanding Sternberg's model is realizing that although equality of all three components characterizes consummate love, each can occur in varying degrees for each partner at any stage of the relationship. Figure 13-1 characterizes what this may look like when mismatches between lovers occur. Sternberg developed a scale to help one determine the nature and type of one's loving relationship (see Assess Yourself 13-2, "Sternberg's Love Scale").

Consummate love involves loving another person for who he or she really is, not for who we want him or her to be. Sternberg believes that consummate love grows out of self-love. In other words, before one can love another, one must love oneself. Self-love grows out of self-esteem and self-control, issues that arise during childhood (see chapter 12). Consummate love involves sacrifice, caring, and sharing, qualities that result from working through developmental tasks related to the self.

KEY TO UNDERSTANDING

Each component of love can exist in varying amounts for each partner at various stages of the relationship.

College Sexual Standards

Research on college sexual mores has found three standards of behavior: traditional, sexually moderate, and sexually liberal or permissive.

1. Traditional students believe that intercourse should occur only when the partners are in love and committed to marry. Heavy petting and other forms of sexual expression are allowed, but intercourse is accepted only when marriage plans are clearly established.
2. Sexually moderate students believe that intercourse is acceptable if the couple love each other. The couple need not commit to marriage or even discuss it.
3. Sexually permissive students believe that intercourse is a logical outcome of friendship and intimacy. They do not think being in love and planning to marry are prerequisites for intercourse.[42]

Evidence suggests increasing levels of sexual activity among college students over the last two decades, and women seem to be catching up to men in terms of number of partners, level of sexual activity, and types of sexual activities.[36] A study of college students found that the total number of sex partners for both the previous year and the total lifetime, has increased for both college men and college women.[45] The average number of total sexual partners for college women was 5.6, and men reported an average of 11.2 partners. Similar percentages of male and female college students were found for the following behaviors: vaginal intercourse (68 percent for men and women), masturbation (men 78 percent, women 71 percent), performing oral sex (60 percent of men, 68 percent of women), receiving oral sex (64 percent of men, 71 percent of women), anal intercourse (6 percent of men, 10 percent of women), and using pornography (58 percent of men, 37 percent of women).[42]

Living Arrangements of College Students

Living arrangements of college students vary, determined by the type of campus and student (residential or commuter), personal finances, and relationship status (single, married, cohabiting). At most universities, the majority of residential undergraduates are single and live in either dormitories or apartments. Whereas married undergraduate students were the exception years ago, today many students are both married and older, some with young children. Consequently, more colleges are finding the need to include day-care facilities on campus. According to the U.S. Census Bureau, about 6.3 million people in the United States cohabited in 1998. Among them, approximately half were under 25 years of age. No accurate numbers have been forthcoming regarding the actual number of college students who cohabit. Cohabitation is distinguished from having roommates of the opposite gender by the nature of the sexual interaction between cohabitors. Cohabitors are lovers who live together but are not married. Cohabitors describe their relationships as intimate and affectionate but not necessarily as leading to marriage.[54]

Intimacy, Sexuality, and Stress

As we have discussed, developing intimacy is the primary task of young adulthood. Besides the normal challenges we just discussed, there are many threats to intimacy and sexuality that young adults face. The next part of this chapter will focus on three of the major threats: sexual victimization, sexual harassment, and sexually transmitted diseases.

Sexual Victimization

Sexual victimization occurs when a person is coerced, deprived of free choice, and forced to endure, observe, or comply with sexual acts. Sexual victimization can take many forms. We will focus on two: rape and sexual harassment. The commonality in both is the element of power and victimhood.

Rape

A major form of sexual victimization is rape. The term **rape** includes all forms of nonconsensual physical sexual activity directed against women, men, and children. Rape encompasses all victims, regardless of their sexual orientation. Rape includes date rape (also known as acquaintance rape), stranger rape, marital rape, gang rape, and statutory rape. More than 95 percent of all rapes are committed by men against women or other men. Male rape usually is committed by men against other men but does occur rarely with women as the perpetrators.[8]

Date rape is a form of rape defined as forced sexual intercourse by a dating partner and is considered the most common and least reported form of rape.[8]

The National College Women Sexual Victimization Study (NCWSV) is the most comprehensive analysis of the sexual victimization of college women.

The most startling finding of the NCWSV study was the overall high incidence of sexual victimization and attempted sexual victimization among college women. Overall, 2.8 percent of the sample had experienced either a completed rape (1.7 percent) or an attempted rape (1.1 percent) incident. The overall incidence of rape was 35.3 rapes per 1,000 women which correlates to an estimated 350 rapes per year among 10,000 college women in any university.[24]

Another disturbing finding of the study was the small percentage of women who defined their victimization as rape even though they said yes when asked if someone had "by force or threat put their penis into your vagina." Fisher et al.[24] explain that this reluctance may be due to reasons such as embarrassment, not clearly understanding the legal definition of rape, and being reluctant to label someone whom they are intimate with and who victimized them as a rapist.[24]

A third finding of the study was the overall incidence of other forms of sexual victimization. The types of sexual victimization ranged from threats of rape and sexual contact to completed sexual coercion. When these other forms of sexual victimization were studied, the rates varied from 9.5 to 66.4 cases per 1,000 women.

A fourth finding was the relationship of the perpetrator to the victim. For both completed and attempted rape, nine of ten women knew the perpetrator. The relationships most often cited were a boyfriend, ex-boyfriend, classmate, friend, acquaintance, and coworker.

Date Rape Risk Factors

The NCWSV study found that the vast majority of the rapes occurred after midnight, on campus in the victim's residence, at other living quarters on campus, or at a fraternity house. Living on campus and frequently drinking to get drunk were two other key risk factors that were positively associated with rape.[24]

Fisher et al.[25] found that college women were at a greater risk for rape and other forms of sexual assault than were women in the general population or in a comparable age group. This is due, in part, to the nature of the college environment, where large concentrations of young women come into contact with young men in a variety of public and private settings at various times on and off college campuses. Men and women on college campuses also engage in higher levels of drinking than the general population.

Drinking and Date Rape Many college students use alcohol and other drugs to cope with college stressors and reduce inhibitions related to dating and sex. Despite the overall decline in drinking among all adults in the United States over the last two decades, drinking on college campuses has not shown a corresponding drop-off. Drinking by college students often revolves around its social nature. College women perceive drinking as a way of being around others and seeking acceptance from peers.[29]

rape sexual activity directed at a person without that person's consent; includes date/acquaintance rape, stranger rape, marital rape, gang rape, and statutory rape

date rape a form of rape defined as forced sexual intercourse imposed by an acquaintance or dating partner; also known as acquaintance rape

Alcohol is consumed more for social than for personal reasons.[37] Students reported using alcohol more for the purpose of meeting members of the other sex than for personal reasons, although alcohol did make them feel better about themselves (see Assess Yourself 13-3, "How Do You Drink?" to determine your personal use of alcohol).[37]

Among college students, alcohol is often consumed in large quantities for the express purpose of getting drunk. Weschler et al.[57] coined the term **binge drinking** to describe this pattern of alcohol consumption. Binge drinking is defined operationally as "having five or more drinks in a row, at least once during the previous two week period."[57] The most important risk factors for binge drinking were living in a fraternity or sorority house, engaging in drinking games, and living a "party-centered" lifestyle.[57]

Weschler et al.[57] found that binge drinking is associated with the following consequences: unplanned and unsafe sexual activity, physical and sexual assault, other criminal violations, physical injury, interpersonal problems, and poor academic performance. Binge drinkers were more likely than non-binge drinkers and abstainers to engage in unplanned sexual activity, not use protection when having sex, get hurt or injured, damage property, argue with friends, miss classes, get behind in schoolwork, and do something they later regretted (see Stress in Our World 13-1: "Robin: Party Animal"). Frequent binge drinkers were ten times more likely than nonbingers to have unplanned and unprotected sex, get into trouble with campus police, and get injured or damage property. When asked to evaluate the seriousness of their binging and its repercussions, under 1 percent of binge drinkers designated themselves as problem drinkers.[57,58]

In a follow up study, Weschler et al.[56] found that 1 percent of students living in residence halls or fraternity and sorority houses were victims of alcohol-related sexual assault and/or rape. About 20 percent of students experienced alcohol-related threats and/or attempted sexual contacts.

STRESS IN OUR WORLD 13-1

Robin: Party Animal

Robin is in big trouble. She is a second-semester sophomore at a large southern school and is on academic probation. Robin is a party animal. She just squeaked by in her freshman year by dropping two classes and getting the lowest possible GPA.

As a freshman Robin went wild. She is the daughter of very conservative parents, and her life before college was very strictly regulated. She had curfews, could date only certain guys, and was not allowed to be on her own much. Once at school and living away from home for the first time, she broke all the rules. She stayed out late, cut class, dated anyone who turned her on, got drunk frequently, and generally carried on as if there were no tomorrow. She paid little attention to her studies, cut class frequently, and, when she did show up, was often hung over.

This year she is rushing a sorority and is spending less time on her studies. Her sorority sisters warned her about flunking out, but Robin blew them off as being "alarmists." Now on academic probation, Robin must begin to make some major lifestyle changes if she is to survive.

Do you know a Robin? How do you feel about students who go wild? Is Robin's behavior typical? Ethical?

Other Date Rape Drugs Many other drugs, used alone or with alcohol, have been implicated in the sexual victimization of women. Marijuana, cocaine, gamma hydroxybutyrate (GHB), benzodiazepines, ketamine, barbiturates, chloral hydrate, methaqualone, heroin, morphine, and LSD and other hallucinogens have all been implicated in sexual victimization.[32] When combined with alcohol, which they often are, these drugs cause reduction of inhibitions, weakness, memory loss, and blackout. Sexual victimization perpetrators use these incapacitating effects to take advantage of their targets.[32]

Rohypnol and GHB in particular have been dubbed "date rape" drugs because of their association with sexual assault and rape. Rohypnol is a tasteless, odorless, clear drug available in powder form. It mixes easily in liquids and is virtually undetectable when mixed in alcoholic beverages, which is the delivery method preferred by date rape perpetrators. When swallowed, it takes effect in fifteen to twenty minutes, and its effects last for more than twelve hours. Victims experience a slowing of psychomotor performance, muscle relaxation, sleepiness, and/or amnesia. Rohypnol leaves the body after seventy-two hours and is undetectable after that time.[40] GHB, also known as Cherry Meth, Liquid X, Organic Quaalude, and fantasy (to name a few), is similar in its nature and effects to Rohypnol. It is also a tasteless, odorless, clear depressant drug. It is available in powder or liquid form and easily mixes in alcoholic beverages, where it is undetectable.

Both drugs, besides having the classic depressant drug characteristics of slowing central nervous system functioning, can cause memory loss and loss of consciousness. Because of this, women who have been assaulted and raped while under the influence of these drugs are unable to resist the perpetrator or recall any of the details of the incident. The assailant mixes the drug into the drink of the unsuspecting woman, allows it to take effect, takes advantage of her, and denies any knowledge of the event if the woman realizes or suspects what has happened (see Stress Buster Tips: "Reducing Risks

binge drinking having five or more drinks in a row at least once during the previous two-week period

Stress Buster Tips

Reducing Risks for Date Rape

The following are specific strategies for women to reduce their risks for date rape:

1. Arrange for your first date to be in a public place or as part of a larger group.
2. Arrange your own transportation or go with friends.
3. In the earliest stages of the relationship, suggest paying for things yourself. This will derail any notion on the part of your date that you owe him something. It also will give you an opportunity to assess his views about women.
4. Pay attention to your date's attitudes and behavior. Is he controlling? Does he want to make all the decisions?
5. Avoid using alcohol and other drugs if you don't want to become involved in intimate sexual activities.
6. Do not accept *any* drinks from another person. Pour your own drink or drink only from sealed bottles.
7. Don't send mixed messages or anything that can be perceived as "teasing." If kissing is acceptable but you don't want to go any farther, state this clearly: "I'd like to hug and kiss, but I don't want to let things go any farther than this."
8. If things begin to get out of control, resist. Use more and more emphatic verbal resistance: "I said *no*!" If this doesn't work, use physical force: punch, slap, kick. Push him away, stand up, open the door, and ask him to stop or leave. If this doesn't work, say, "This is rape. I'm calling the police."
9. Run away. If he persists, escape. Get away. Go to a public place and call the police.

for Date Rape"). Because both drugs pass through the victims' systems within seventy-two hours, the victims typically do not have the opportunity to get tested for the drugs.[40,41]

Sexual Harassment in College

The second form of sexual victimization is sexual harassment. Sexual harassment has two facets: unwanted sexual attention or advances and a hostile environment (work or school) where the person faces daily stress and oppression because of the unwanted sexual attention.[19] As was noted in chapter 3, sexual harassment consists of unwelcome sexual advances, requests for sexual favors, and other verbal or physical conduct of a sexual nature.

Over the last decade, many colleges have instituted sexual harassment policies in response to the concerns of students, faculty members, and administrators. Most sexual harassment in college is between male professors and female students. Although the reverse can happen (a female professor harassing a male student), it is much less common. Between 15 and 50 percent of undergraduate college women and 10 to 20 percent of college men report having been the victim of sexual harassment by a professor.[3]

Sexually Transmitted Diseases

The last major threat to intimacy and sexuality discussed in this chapter is sexually transmitted disease. Sexually transmitted diseases (STDs), also known as sexually transmitted infections (STIs), are infections that are almost always contracted through sexual contact. Although STDs theoretically can be transmitted by any form of sexual contact, vaginal and anal intercourse are much more *efficient* modes of transmission than is oral-genital sexual contact. Some STDs, such as HIV and hepatitis B, also are transmitted by contaminated blood through needle sharing associated with injectable drug use.[21]

More than 65 million people in the United States are currently infected with an incurable sexually transmitted disease, and each year an additional 15 million people develop new cases of one or more of the twenty-five diseases categorized as STDs.

A Pyramid of Risk for STDs/HIV

Blonna and Levitan[6] proposed a new way to evaluate STD/HIV risk by linking the relationship between community and personal risks and placing it within a pyramid. Figure 13-2 illustrates this pyramid of risk.

The foundation of the pyramid is made up of demographic variables that influence STD/HIV risk and are

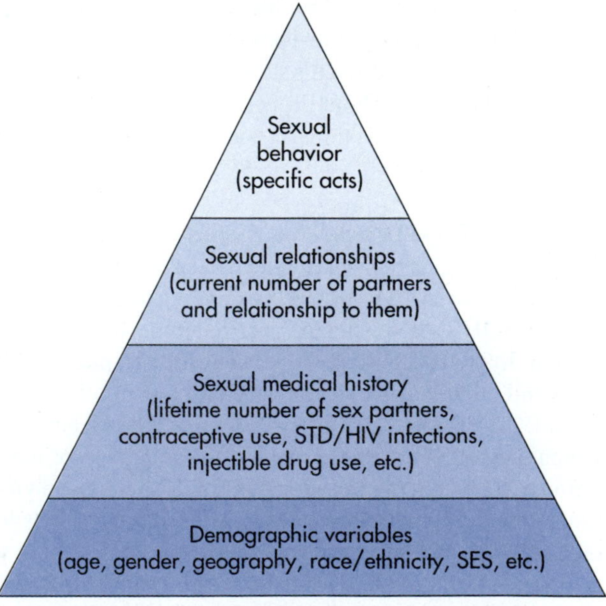

Figure 13-2
Pyramid of risk for STDs.[6]

generally beyond one's individual control. The next level of risk revolves around the sexual and medical history of ourselves and our partners. Because these risks are part of a person's past, they also cannot be changed. They are the history that each person brings to any sexual encounter. The third level of risk represents a person's current sexual lifestyle, the number and quality of that person's relationships. The last level of risk is the one most educators focus on: personal sexual behavior. Although the four levels of factors influence STD/HIV risk independently, the interaction of levels can have a synergistic effect that can increase or reduce personal risk dramatically.

Demographic Variables and the Distribution of STDs/HIV

Seven major **demographic variables** that contribute to STD/HIV risk are age, gender, sexual orientation, community levels of injectable drug users (IDUs), geography, socioeconomic status (SES), and race and ethnicity.

Age There are more cases of STDs distributed among people age 15 to 25 than there are in any other age group. Because more cases exist in this age group, the risk of acquiring an infection is greater if someone has sex with persons in this age category compared with another category (for example, the 55-plus age group, which has the lowest STD rate). The risk is associated with the likelihood that someone will interact sexually with a member of this subpopulation. Sexually active teenagers have the highest rates of infection for almost all STDs.[16,17]

Gender The risk for STDs/HIV is different for men and women. Biological gender is a risk factor related to the genetic, anatomic, and physiological differences between men and women. Women face a greater risk than men for both acquiring a sexually transmitted disease and developing complications for several reasons.

Heterosexual women are receptive sexually—vaginally, orally, and anally. This greatly increases their risks for an initial infection.[44] Once infected with most STDs, heterosexual women tend to be asymptomatic more often than heterosexual men. Most heterosexual men notice the initial symptoms of infection, whereas about half of women are asymptomatic.[38]

Because of the asymptomatic nature of STDs in women, more women than men do not seek treatment during the initial stages of infection. This delayed access to treatment results in progression of the disease and a greater likelihood of developing complications. For example, about 15 percent of women develop complications associated with gonorrhea or chlamydia versus less than 1 percent of men.[38]

Menstruation also plays a role in facilitating the movement of pathogens from the lower reproductive tract (below the cervix) to the upper parts, facilitating the development of complications.[49]

Sexual Orientation Risks for STDs are affected by a person's sexual orientation. Gay and bisexual men and heterosexual women share the risk of being receptive sexually. In addition, certain diseases, such as HIV and hepatitis B, exist at endemic levels in the gay community. These diseases are incurable and capable of causing death.[1,2]

Heterosexual men are at less risk than heterosexual women and gay men because they usually are the insertive sexual partners and develop external symptoms. This facilitates early detection, prompt treatment, and reduced complications. Also, female-to-male transmission of STDs is more difficult because heterosexual men are not receptive sexually and vaginal fluids are less likely to transmit infection than is contaminated semen.[21]

Of the four groups, lesbian women have the lowest rates of infection. Gay women tend to have fewer sexual partners over the course of a lifetime and do not engage in vaginal or anal intercourse.[33]

IDU The risk for STD/HIV is becoming increasingly related to the prevalence of injectable drug users (IDUs) in a community. Drug use is associated with increased STD/HIV risk in two ways:

1. Psychoactive drugs impair users' ability to make good decisions about engaging in safer sex behaviors and choosing sex partners carefully.
2. Injectable drug use often involves needle sharing between users. This facilitates the transmission of bloodborne infections such as HIV and hepatitis B if one of the users is infected.[23]

Urban/Rural and Geographical Differences The incidence of STDs, including HIV, is much higher in urban areas than in rural or suburban locations (see fig. 13-3).[17] This contributes to a disproportionately high personal risk despite individual behavior.[26] The rate of acquisition of STDs among core inner-city urban populations can be as much as 300 times higher than that in the rest of the population.[46]

Socioeconomic Status SES can either facilitate or hinder access to preventive and interventive STD health care. People of lower SES tend to lack enabling factors related to prevention and treatment of STDs, such as health care insurance and access to treatment services. Poverty and lower SES are also related to higher levels of injectable drug use.[43]

Race and Ethnicity African Americans and Hispanics continue to have the highest rates of STD infection in the United States. Rates for almost all STDs are substantially

demographic variables population-based factors such as age, gender, sexual orientation, socioeconomic status (SES), and race and ethnicity

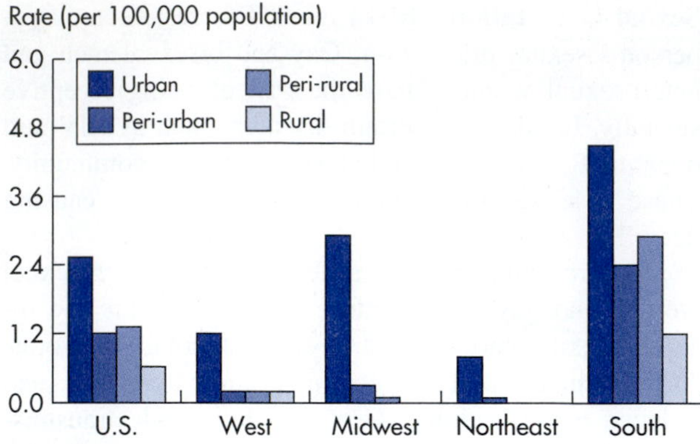

Figure 13-3

Primary and secondary syphilis rates by urban and rural locations.[17]

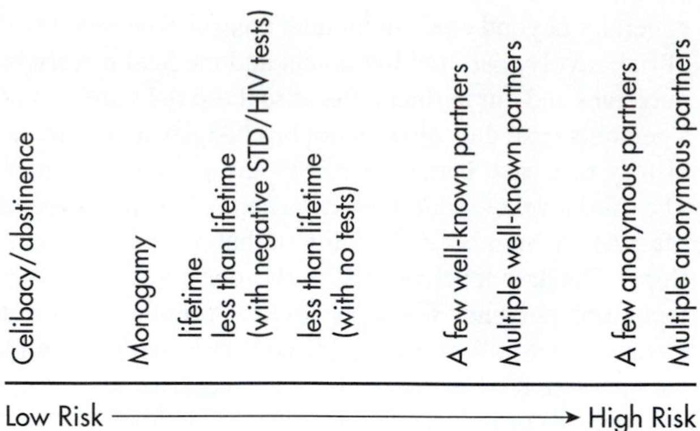

Figure 13-4

A continuum of risk for sexual relationships.[6]

higher for these groups than for whites. Risks for certain STDs, such as gonorrhea and syphilis, are as much as thirty times higher for African Americans than for whites.[15] Part of that disparity is attributed to the higher use of public health clinics by African Americans than by whites. Public clinics tend to have more complete reporting of STDs than do private health care providers.[15] Racial and ethnic differences in STD risk may also be due to the unequal distribution of SES among minority populations attending public health clinics in inner cities. When studies are conducted that control for SES factors, racial differences in disease rates drop significantly.[39]

Sexual Medical History

Sexual medical history is a level of risk that cannot be controlled because it occurred in the past. However, it can greatly influence the current level of risk for STDs. The sexual medical factors most associated with current risk for STDs are:

1. Lifetime number of sexual partners. In general, the greater the number, the higher the risk.
2. Contraceptive use. People who have used barrier contraceptives such as condoms have the lowest rates of infection.
3. History of IDU. Persons with a history of IDU have an increased incidence of infection with bloodborne diseases, particularly HIV and hepatitis B.[1,23]
4. Prior STD history. Persons who have been infected with STDs in the past are more likely to become infected again than are those who have never been infected.[14]

Sexual Lifestyle

Sexual lifestyle refers to the connections between people rather than the specific behaviors in which they engage. In general, the risk for STDs/HIV decreases as sexual lifestyles move away from multiple, anonymous sexual encounters and toward monogamous (with an uninfected partner), trusting partnerships. STD/HIV sexual lifestyle risks are specifically related to the overall numbers of partners and the quality of the relationship, including trust, understanding, and knowledge of one's partner.[6] Figure 13-4 shows the continuum of risks for sexual lifestyles.

The highest risks are associated with a lack of exclusivity and familiarity and having many partners. This sexual lifestyle combines multiple partners with anonymous sexual encounters and is associated with the highest risk of STD infection.[35]

Sexual Behavior

At the top of the pyramid of risk is sexual behavior. In general, as illustrated in fig. 13-5, the risks increase as sexual behaviors incorporate unprotected penetration and ejaculation. The lower-risk behaviors are nonpenetrative and do not involve any exchange of bodily fluids. As we move along the continuum of risk, the behaviors include the use of barrier protection against infectious agents. The highest-risk behavior is receptive anal penetration including ejaculation, which entails unprotected ejaculation of semen into the delicate, nonlubricated tissue of the rectum. This allows direct access of infectious STD agents to the bloodstream. Theoretically, as fig. 13-5 illustrates, the risk for STDs is greater for receptive partners in all sexual activities.[6]

Using the Pyramid to Reduce Risks

A comprehensive plan to reduce STD risk can't focus on just one level of risk factors and ignore the others. All the levels of risk must be assessed, and the results must be used to develop a plan based on their interaction. For example, even if people are rather conservative in their behavior, if they live and interact sexually in a high-incidence area, engaging in any sexual activity carries a higher risk of becoming infected. This demographic influence may make their risk-reduction measures much different from those of people who live in a lower-risk rural area.

The same dynamic can hold true for sexual medical history. People with sex partners who have high-risk

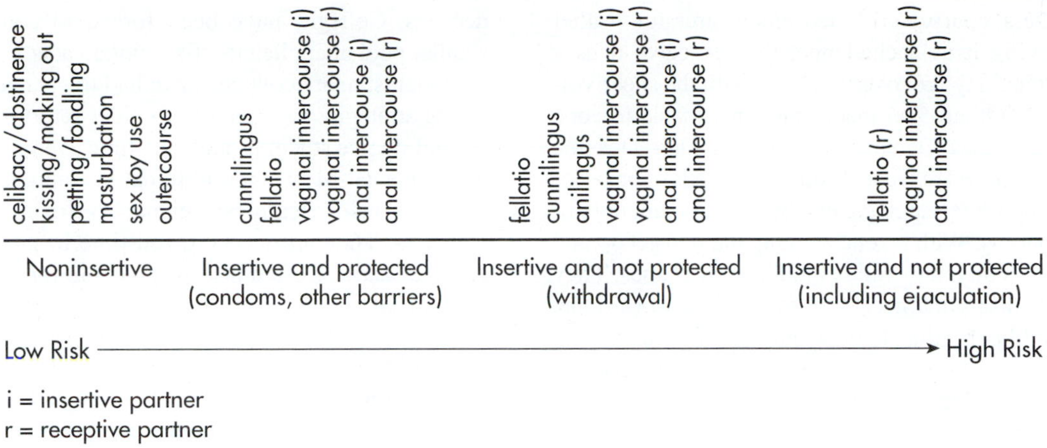

Figure 13-5

A continuum of risk for sexual behaviors.[6]

histories (used injectable drugs and might be HIV-positive, for instance) might choose to engage in sexual behaviors that are much different from those of people whose sex partners have low-risk histories. Although reducing risks this way takes a little more thought, it also respects individuality.

Although sexual victimization, sexual harassment, and sexually transmitted diseases pose real threats to developing intimacy, with knowledge and understanding, they can be turned into challenges that can be overcome.

College, Work, and Stress

The second major developmental task of early adulthood is making a commitment to work. For most college students, this work is their schoolwork. However, many students are employed at least part-time and have some sense of commitment to a paying job in addition to their schoolwork.

Academics and Stress

College-level academic work can be very demanding. For some students, this represents a real change from their work in high school. In most cases, college classes require much more reading and written work. Each class might require that students read hundreds of pages of text a week, write at least one major research paper, take three examinations in a semester, and always be prepared to discuss the current topic in class.

In addition, many colleges emphasize communication skills and require students to present their work to their classmates and participate in classroom discussions. Debates, group discussions, and role playing are common parts of most classes.

The workload can be difficult to manage under the best of circumstances as, for example, when students are full-time, live on campus, and do not have to work. When students must commute, work part- or full-time, and raise families, they have difficulties finding the time to prepare for their classes.

Commuter students and evening students also may have difficulty fitting in and developing the kinds of support systems available to full-time residential students. Commuters and part-time evening students often do not have the luxury of spending their free time on campus, making friends, joining clubs, and getting involved in extracurricular activities. They also frequently have a more difficult time accessing some of the college's resources, ranging from advisement and career counseling to the use of equipment which may not be as readily available in the evening. Because of this, commuters and part-time evening students sometimes feel estranged from their schools. Many colleges are acknowledging the special needs of these and other non-traditional students and developing special services to meet their needs. These services include extending into the evening the hours of key college personnel such as advisers, registration staff, and counselors. Many colleges have special commuter or evening-student organizations, complete with privileges to vote in the school's elections.

Not only are college classes more demanding than high school classes, college students are much more independent. Students are expected to keep track of assignments and test dates by reading the class syllabus. Attendance usually is not as closely watched as in high school, and students must be self-motivated to attend class. Absent students are held accountable for all information presented in class.

To survive, students must be focused, self-motivated, and able to work autonomously. Some students perceive the rigors of academia as a challenge. They are focused and are motivated to do well. They perceive coursework as a true test of their abilities and respond favorably to its demands. They relish the freedom and view their autonomy positively.

For others, coursework is extremely stressful. Rather than perceiving it as a challenge, they perceive it as a stressor. Some may feel overwhelmed with the sheer volume of work. Others feel inadequate and unable to cope with the intellectual demands of college. They lack the study skills required to wade through hundreds of pages of text and compose research papers. Still others cannot handle the autonomy. With no one nagging them to get up and go to class or study, they fall behind in their classes. They lack the self-discipline necessary to get their work done. They prefer to party than to delay any gratification.

As a result of these and other factors, most college students have difficulty maintaining the same high grade-point averages they had in high school. Many who don't plan on continuing their education beyond the bachelor's degree have difficulty staying motivated and studying hard for each class to maintain the highest possible grade-point average. This is very unlike their high school days, when each grade was important and could make the difference between being accepted into the college of their choice and not being accepted anywhere.

Some students cut corners in one class to concentrate on another. Others try to figure out what it takes to get a good grade and focus on mastering those assignments and tasks rather than on learning the subject matter. Still others lower their sights and are willing to accept lower grades in order to cope with college's increased academic demands.

Most students, however, try to get the highest grade possible and find grades a significant source of stress. In analyzing several years' worth of students' self-reported stress logs, the author has found that grades are consistently among the top five student stressors.[5] This holds true for both the students who are trying to achieve the highest grade-point average possible and the ones who are willing to sacrifice a high grade in one class to do better in another (see Assess Yourself 13-4, "Values Clarification").

Financial and Career-Related Stressors

College students face many different types of work-related stressors. College was much different twenty or more years ago when the parents of this generation's college students were in school. Freshman were young, came right out of high school, and were full-time day students. Average tuition was much lower, and most students worked only during the summer to help defray costs incurred during the academic year. The government helped reduce college costs by providing easily obtainable grants and low interest loans for almost everyone. Students who could not afford tuition were almost always able to borrow what they needed or work part-time to help pay their way.

Changing demographic and economic trends have decreased the numbers of traditional freshman applicants. The post–baby boom generation of college-age students is smaller than the college-age population in recent decades. Colleges have been forced to compete for a smaller pool of applicants. To maintain adequate numbers of students, many colleges have had to change their marketing strategies to reach out to older returning students, second-degree students, and part-time evening and weekend students. Most nontraditional students do not work part-time just to earn pocket money for miscellaneous expenses. They are working full-time to pay for tuition and fees and are often also responsible for raising families as well.

Paying for College

Add to tuition and fees the cost of room and board, books, computers, and expense money and you can understand how difficult it is for the average parents to save enough to fully fund their child's college education. Most are forced to tap into the equity in their homes if they are fortunate enough to own a house. Others pay the expenses through an elaborate mixture of cash, savings, various types of loans, scholarships, and grants. Most traditional students find themselves working, as do their nontraditional peers, to help defray these costs.

College tuition, room and board, and fees have soared over the past thirty years. As we mentioned in chapter 8, thirty years ago the average annual tuition and fees at private and public four-year colleges were about $7,500 and $1,750, respectively. In the 2004–2005 academic year, the average tuition and fees for four-year private colleges were $20,082 (up 6 percent from 2003–2004) and $5,132 (up 10.5 percent from 2003–2004) at four-year public institutions (College Board[10]). The average total charges (tuition, fees, room and board) for four-year private institutions were $27,516 ($1,459 more than 2003–2004's $26,057—a 5.6 percent increase) and for four-year public institutions were $11,354 ($824 more than 2003–2004's $10,530—a 7.8 percent increase) (College Board[11]).

Student Debt

As we mentioned in chapter 8, more than half of all college graduates owe between $10,000 and $40,000 in student loans. The average debt load has increased significantly in just a couple of years. In 2002, the average debt was $17,000. In 2005 that figure is expected to jump to $20,000, an increase of $3,000.

While costs continue to escalate, so does financial aid in the form of grants and loans. As we discussed in chapter 8, about 60 percent of college students receive some form of financial aid. The bulk of this money (about 70 percent) is in the form of loans that are not subsidized by the federal government. This was not the case in the 1960s, 70s and 80s, when most loans given as financial aid were offered at lower rates than those available commercially because the federal government subsidized them.

The remaining financial aid (about 30 percent) comes from a combination of subsidized government loans and grants. About half of those receiving financial help obtain grant aid. In 2002–2003 grant aid averaged almost $2,000 per student in two-year public colleges, over $2,400 at public four-year colleges, and about $7,300 at private four-year colleges.[12]

Even though more students receive financial aid now than ever before, they still finish college with debt loads much higher than those of their parents a generation ago. While most students can manage this higher level of debt, especially those who graduate, many are left with a heavy debt load that they can't repay. This is particularly true for students who do not complete their degrees and lower income students.

More and more students are not only concerned about their ability to repay their college debts once they graduate, they are using cost as a key criterion for choosing a college. Many students are opting for public colleges and two-year institutions to further their education because costs at those institutions are much lower than those at private two- and four-year schools. Many prestigious private colleges are experiencing a dramatic drop in enrollments due to a combination of fewer available applicants and escalating college costs.[51]

As we mentioned in chapter 8, credit card use is playing a larger and larger role in student debt. Credit card solicitation and use on campus was unheard of thirty years ago. The overwhelming majority of colleges not only permit credit card companies to solicit on campus, they allow credit card vendors to give away free *t*-shirts and other perks and use low introductory teaser rates to get students to sign up. Colleges themselves promote student use of credit cards with bookstores, alumni associations, and other groups leading the way. The easy availability of credit cards, escalating costs, and unsophisticated young consumers is a combination that often results in high student credit card debt.

As we mentioned in chapter 8, an unfortunate consequence of heavy student debt loads is students continuing to work in jobs that might be financially lucrative but do not provide the entry point into the career of their choice that they studied for while attending college (see Stress in Our World 13-2: "Darrah: Still Tending Bar at 26").

Working during College

As the previous section and "Darrah" illustrate and as a result of this change in the nature of work and college over the last twenty years, work-related stress has taken on a new meaning for students. Students not only are stressed about future work and career decisions, they are under a tremendous amount of pressure to perform their current jobs and survive economically.

For many, this means having to work twenty to forty hours a week and taking a full-time course load. They are caught in a bind: if they work fewer hours they cannot cover their expenses and have to borrow more (mortgaging their futures), whereas if they cut back on their coursework and drop below 12 credits they lose their full-time student status. Loss of full-time student status usually means loss of eligibility for most financial aid programs, loss of eligibility to reside in on-campus housing, and loss of other privileges.

The result is that many of them are stretched too thin with little free time to take advantage of the extracurricular activities and cultural events that make up a big part of the college experience. Working students often find themselves choosing courses for convenience more than for content. They will take any 8:00 A.M. course available, followed by another one at 9:30 A.M. (and often a third one at 12:30) so they can condense their coursework into the shortest possible window regardless of the nature of

STRESS IN OUR WORLD 13-2

Darrah: Still Tending Bar at 26

Darrah was a student in the author's Stress Management class. She was single, 26 years old, and an Elementary Education Major. Here is her story.

"I was thinking about what you were talking about in class the other day because it is my life story. I am going to graduate in a couple of months. All I have left is this class and my student teaching. I am doing really well in my student teaching assignment. I'm working in a small elementary school in a rural area and I love it. The kids are so cute and I really love them. My supervising teacher really likes my work and she recommended to the Board that they hire me for an upcoming vacancy next fall. I talked to the Superintendent of Schools and he said they are not going to even advertise the position, it is mine for the asking. I told him I have to sleep on it. I think he was kind of shocked at first but then he said, 'Of course, I'll talk to you next week.' I should be real excited about this but I spent the whole weekend crying. I'm in debt to the tune of about $30,000. I know it is hard to believe but things just got crazy with me the past couple of years. I've had to work to support myself since my parents got divorced and my mom died. Between the rent and the car and school, I just kept charging things and charging things. The bottom line is that I have to keep bartending until I can at least get my credit rating back to a decent level. The job sucks but the money is great. I'd love to take that job but the school district is small and pretty poor. They would pay me about half of what I can earn now in salary and tips. About half of my income is cash under the table. Oh well, maybe next year."

KEY TO UNDERSTANDING

Sometimes we need to take a step backward in order to move forward in life.

the courses themselves (as long as they fit within their graduation requirements). From their last class it is a mad dash across campus to get to their cars and race off to their jobs in order to pay their tuition.

Many fear that if they lose their jobs they will have to drop out of school. Many would like to spend more time on campus and get involved in activities or simply study but can't because they have to work and return home to care for children, spouses, or aging parents.

Preparing for Graduation and Career

As college begins to wind down, many students find themselves having to make decisions regarding accepting lower-paying, entry-level jobs in the career field for which they have been preparing. These students, who have worked their way through college, find, as Darrah (see Stress in Our World 13-2) did, that they often can earn more in their current jobs (sometimes even if they are part-time) than they can starting out at the bottom in their chosen disciplines. As we've mentioned, debt and other economic considerations exert tremendous pressure on them. Many find the prospect of not being able to pay off student loans and credit card debt quickly and having to carry it over a long period unacceptable. As we've mentioned, others simply can't afford to take a cut in pay and still be able to meet their living expenses.

A common response to this for many students is moving back into their parent's home. While this might solve their financial problems, it sets the stage for other kinds of problems. For parents and students alike, the idea of adult children returning to the family home is a mixed blessing. Under the best of circumstances, both parties slowly readjust to their loss of freedom and peacefully co-exist as they establish new rules and guidelines for living together. In other cases both sides battle continuously as they are unable to get past their emotions, talk things through, and reexamine their relationship.

Many students have unrealistic expectations of their earning power or ability to advance in their chosen professions. They find that the reality of the marketplace dictates what they can earn and how quickly they can advance. In areas where competition for certain kinds of jobs is intense, students must weigh the benefits of relocating to other areas where the job market might be better and the prospects of higher pay and more rapid advancement is more realistic.

Another issue that graduating students must face is the prospect of losing their health coverage if this has been provided by their parent's job. In most cases such coverage ends with graduation or soon thereafter. Parents or graduating students can pay continuation of coverage for eighteen months at additional cost if they can afford it. In the current economy, many new jobs offer employment without benefits (health insurance, paid vacation, etc.). Jobs that offer benefits have waiting periods that range from a couple of weeks to a few months. Faced with this scenario, many students choose to keep their current jobs with benefits (if they have them) rather than start in their chosen disciplines.

Coping with the Stress of Young Adulthood by Using the Five Rs

Rethink Strategies

Thinking rationally can be very difficult when one is faced with the stressors of young adulthood. For the first time in their lives, many young adults are on their own, juggling the forming of intimate relationships and the assumption of new responsibilities while managing academic coursework and the demands of a job and maintaining living quarters.

Ellis and Harper's[20] and Seligman's[48] ABCDE models are excellent tools to help young adults sort through their thinking regarding relationships, work, and school. These tools help identify illogical beliefs and aid in the process of thinking more logically.

College life exposes young adults to a myriad of new ideas and behaviors. Working through and trying to understand and assimilate some of these ideas while holding on to and reaffirming deeply held beliefs can be both stressful and challenging. Values-clarification activities, such as those described in chapter 7 can help assess how core values match up to these new ideas and behaviors. These activities can help young adults rethink everything from beliefs about intimacy and sexuality to values regarding grades or the choice of a major.

Reduce Strategies

Young adults face countless daily demands on their time. Attending class, studying, meeting new people, exercising, keeping in touch with old friends and family members, earning spending money, and joining clubs and organizations are just a few examples of the activities that compete for their time. Sometimes these and other demands can become potential stressors.

The triple As of coping discussed in chapter 8 is an excellent technique that can help a person manage the stressors that feel like they have taken control. This, combined with the DESC model of verbal assertiveness, also discussed in chapter 8, can be used to become more assertive and reduce stress.

Finally, good time-management skills will help young adults free up time so that they can meet the demands of forming intimate relationships, attend to academic demands, and earn extra money. The ACT model in chapter 8 provides everything needed to take control of time.

Relax Strategies

Relaxation techniques will help you cope with stressors by putting your body in a state that is incompatible with stress. This will stop the stress response and recharge your adaptation energy. This will slow your body down and cancel the harmful effects of the stress response.

Chapter 9 provides both passive and active techniques to help you relax. Try identifying one of each so that you have two relaxation techniques that work in contrasting ways to rid your body and mind of stress. Check with your college or university's recreation center or student services to see if they offer courses in these relaxation techniques; most offer courses in aerobics, martial arts, t'ai chi ch'uan, yoga, and other popular forms of relaxation to help students and faculty learn how to relax. Taking breaks from your work and relaxing help you manage academic stress.

Make a habit of taking frequent relaxation breaks when studying or writing. Get up, stretch, go for a walk around your room or dorm floor, or, better yet, go outside. Take a five-minute break about every forty-five minutes. Take twenty minutes after you finish studying to relax fully before continuing with your day. Also try to build relaxation time into your work schedule. If you have morning and afternoon coffee breaks, use them wisely. Take time out to do stretching, deep breathing, and visualization. Get up from your desk and take a walk around the dorm floor. Use your lunch hour to take a walk, exercise, or relax rather than eat a heavy meal. Get away from your phone and desk. Try to break the habit of eating at your desk.

Release Strategies

Engaging in moderate and vigorous physical activity is an excellent way to purge the tension associated with young adult stress. Having an orgasm and using nonsexual outlets such as sports and vigorous physical exercise are excellent ways to use up the energy that the body mobilizes in response to relationship-related stress.

Exercise vigorously before and afterward if you plan to spend several hours working. As a preparation for studying, vigorous physical activity will help loosen tense muscles and circulate oxygen-rich blood throughout your brain. When you are done studying, exercise will help rid your body of accumulated tension. Exercise helps clear your mind after several hours of focusing on a specific topic, whether it is at work or studying. Exercise also relaxes you and helps you sleep well, replenishing the energy you expended throughout the day.

Take advantage of any exercise or recreational programs your place of employment offers during lunchtime. If it does not, try to start a lunchtime aerobics program. Find out if your place of business has showers or locker rooms. At the least you can walk at lunchtime (stair walking can be very intense).

Your college is an excellent resource for recreational programs and exercise facilities. Most colleges have intramural athletic programs and have gymnasium hours for students who do not compete in varsity athletics. These programs offer an opportunity to play a friendly game of basketball, volleyball, and many other sports without the need to commit to an organized team. Most colleges also offer classes in aerobic exercise, weight training, and swimming and have nonclass open hours scheduled for the pool, the weight room, and workout rooms.

Reorganize Strategies

As we have mentioned throughout this book, wellness means having a high level of functioning across the physical, mental, emotional, spiritual, social, and environmental/occupational dimensions of health. Young adulthood is an excellent time to start incorporating strategies of reorganization into your routine to build a more stress-resistant lifestyle.

Physical Wellness

The greater your physical well-being is, the more efficiently you can meet the challenges of this demanding stage of life. High levels of fitness will give you greater energy, increased strength, more endurance, and greater flexibility. All these facets of fitness can help you meet the demands of work and relationships and keep you energized, thinking clearly, and performing efficiently. Try incorporating some of the ideas in chapter 10 into your daily lifestyle. Getting thirty minutes of physical activity daily would be a good goal for next semester.

Emotional and Spiritual Wellness

Understanding your emotions and controlling them instead of allowing them to control you is a hallmark of mentally healthy adults. The rethink strategies in chapter 7 will help you understand and control your emotions by examining them logically. Seligman's ABCDE model is particularly helpful in doing this.[48]

When these techniques don't work, however, you may need to turn to others for help. Find out about the counseling services available at your college or university. Often these services are available on campus through the counseling center. Sometimes they are available through off-campus professionals whose services are available to you as part of your student fees.

Don't overlook your campus's faith communities as a source of emotional and spiritual help. Often the ministers, rabbis, and priests associated with campus religious groups are certified counselors who are more than willing to help you in a time of need.

Most colleges and universities also offer opportunities to enhance your spirituality through service work within the community. This, whether it is through community organizations such as food pantries or national environmental groups such as the Sierra Club, offers opportunities to get connected to something beyond yourself. Take advantage of these opportunities.

Living Constructively

Looking Back at College Using Naikan Self-Reflection

As we've mentioned throughout this book, Naikan self-reflection is an excellent tool for increasing awareness, changing our perspective about our lives, and developing grace and gratitude. This can be an invaluable tool for helping young adults look back on their college years and the people who enriched their lives and academic growth.

Instructions:

1. The focus of this Naikan self-reflection is your college years and the people who helped you along the way. Divide your college years into three stages: the year before you began college, the first year of college, and the remaining years (however long the span is).
2. For each time frame answer the following three Naikan questions:
   a. What did other people do to help guide, nurture, and support me?
   b. What did I do for other people during this time to help guide, nurture, and support them?
   c. What problems or difficulties did I cause others during this time?
3. Examine the results of your self-reflection, focusing on how others enriched and shaped your college life and enabled you to graduate or get to where you now are.
4. Send a Mindful Thank You note to some of these people. Make sure you are specific in thanking them for the different ways they helped you in your college life.

Intellectual Wellness

High-level intellectual functioning is essential to college success. Utilizing the specific study skills you have mastered up until this point is essential. Most colleges run study skills courses through the office of academic support if you've never mastered them. These courses will teach you skills such as reading more effectively, outlining, writing papers, and improving your memory, to name a few.

Learn how to use technology to improve your mental skills. Mastering a simple word-processing computer program will save you countless hours in rewriting papers and other assignments. Learn how to perform computerized information searches to save time. Learn the locations and operation of your college's fax machines. These machines can move information at the speed of a telephone call when you need information quickly.

Social Wellness

Having a strong social support system both on campus and at home can provide valuable resources in coping with young adult stress. Maintain old social networks and develop new ones. Join a study group or form one with your friends. Include your professors in your social networks. Visit your professors during their office hours to let them know you care about their classes. Ask them to clarify any unresolved class issues before they turn into problems.

Make sure your family understands the rigors of your class assignments. Try to arrange things at home so that you have the time and personal space to devote to your studies. Let your family members know what you need from them to be able to get your coursework done. Simply having friends and family nearby for play is a valuable resource for temporarily putting your worries aside.

Environmental Wellness

Your campus is your microenvironment. If you are a residential student, you will spend twenty-four hours a day there. If you are a commuter, you will spend anywhere from two to twelve hours a day on campus. Do whatever you can to enhance the campus environment. Take the time to discard your trash properly, recycle, park properly, and minimize noise and other forms of pollution. Know your campus's rules and regulations. Be a good campus citizen and report violations to the campus police and other authorities. Make sure to attend to your personal safety and follow recommendations for traveling across campus at different times during the day and evening.

SUMMARY

This chapter examined the stress associated with Erikson's major developmental tasks of young adulthood: forming intimate relationships and committing oneself to work. It discussed how these issues are merely potential stressors until we perceive them differently. Some people are more prepared than others to handle the demands and confusion associated with developing relationships and focusing on school, a job, and a career.

The chapter examined intimacy and discussed how it is often confused with love and sexual relations while, in fact, these three are related yet different. Stress often arises from the strong emotions evoked in trying to understand these confusing relationships. Forming intimate relationships is often stressful because it forces us to confront our long-held beliefs and values.

For many students, living independently for the first time in their lives creates an opportunity to explore intimate relationships. Dealing with roommates, making new friends, and developing romantic relationships all provide potentially challenging or stressful situations. The chapter examined this transition, including the factors that influence the way we interpret these opportunities to develop intimacy.

The chapter then described some of the major threats to building intimacy: sexual victimization, sexual harassment, and sexually transmitted diseases. It explored each in detail as well as the role alcohol and other drugs play in these threats.

The second major developmental task of young adulthood is committing to one's work. Two major sources of work for young college students are academic coursework and part- or full-time employment.

The chapter compared the academic rigors of college with those of high school. The differences can be perceived either as challenges or as stressors. Issues such as the nature of college classes, autonomy, the time requirements of academic work, and outside demands on students' time were examined as factors that influence the perception of academic work as stressful.

Finally, the chapter examined work-related stress, exploring current and future work-related issues and analyzing some of the factors that contribute to the perception of work as a stressor or challenge. The role of employment for college students has changed in the last twenty years. Many students must work to cover the costs of their education. For some, their part-time jobs become lucrative options, often rivaling entry-level salaries for their professions. For all working students balancing the requirements of work with those of school becomes a juggling act that may be perceived as stressful.

The chapter ended with a discussion of how to incorporate strategies from all Five Rs to build a comprehensive stress-management plan for young adulthood.

STUDY QUESTIONS

1. Describe Erikson's major developmental task of young adulthood.
2. Why does intimacy take time to develop?
3. Define rape and give examples of three types of sexual activities considered "nonconsensual" by the police.
4. Describe the level of sexual victimization of college women reported by Fisher et al.[24]
5. How is drinking related to the sexual victimization of college women?
6. How are "date rape" drugs related to the sexual victimization of college women?
7. Describe three ways to reduce the risk for date rape.
8. Describe Blonna's pyramid of risk for sexually transmitted disease.[5]
9. How would you evaluate your current STD risk using Blonna's model?
10. Develop a personal STD risk-reduction plan using Blonna's model.
11. How does Sternberg[50] define consummate love?
12. Describe two other types of love that are lacking components necessary for consummate love.
13. Describe some of the variables involved in appraising college academic work as stressful.
14. How does the escalating cost of attending college relate to stress?
15. How does your personal budget relate to your stress?
16. Develop a personal stress-reduction plan using at least one strategy for each of the Five Rs.

DISCOVER OUR CHANGING WORLD: CHASE UNDERSTANDING STUDENT CREDIT

Understanding Student Credit

http://creditcardsatchase.com/portal/site/marketing/index.jsp?pgTitle=pg_studentcredit&se

This is the Chase Manhattan Bank's Web page devoted to student credit. Although it is a commercial site, it provides an excellent overview of credit for students and their parents.

Click on the "Credit 101" link and read about credit: what it is and how it works.

Critical Thinking Question

Why is it beneficial for a college student to establish a good credit history regardless of the type and overall amount of credit used? Describe two relatively inexpensive ways to establish a good credit history.

ARE YOU THINKING CLEARLY?

It is very easy to think illogically about debt. Credit card and loan companies emphasize tantalizingly low introductory rates, ease of application, and seemingly affordable monthly payments as ways to entice young adults to use credit freely. To assess your thinking about credit and ability to manage debt, answer the following questions:

1. Do I know the real cost (annual percentage rate, late fees, charges for late payments, how interest accrues) of credit?

2. Do I have a written budget based on my current cash flow?
3. Do I know the consequences of a bad credit history?
4. What is my debt tolerance (feelings about ongoing debt)?
5. What will my total debt be (loans for school plus other debt from car loans and credit cards) after leaving college?
6. How much will I have to earn to live the lifestyle I want and be able to manage this level of debt?
7. Can I realistically find a job and earn the income identified in item 6 when I graduate?

If you have trouble assessing whether your answers to these questions are logical and rational, use one of the ABCDE models described in chapter 7 to work through your beliefs about your answers.

REFERENCES

1. Alter, M. & Margolis, H. (1990). The emergence of hepatitis B as a sexually transmitted disease. *Medical Clinics of North America,* 6, pp. 1529–1541.
2. American Medical Association, Council on Scientific Affairs. (1996). Health care needs of gay men and lesbians in the United States. *Journal of American Medical Association,* 275, pp. 1354–1359.
3. Benson, D. & Thompson, G. (1991). Sexual harassment on a university campus: The confluence of authority relations, sexual interest, and gender stratification. *Social Problems,* 29(3), pp. 236–251.
4. Block, J.D. (1980). *Friendship: How to give it, how to get it.* New York: Macmillan.
5. Blonna, R. (1994). Unpublished manuscript.
6. Blonna, R. & Levitan, J. (2005). *Healthy sexuality.* Atlanta: Wadsworth.
7. Blumstein, P. & Schwartz, P. (1983). *American couples.* New York: McGraw-Hill.
8. Cate, R.M. & Lloyd, S.A. (1992). *Courtship.* Newbury Park, CA: Sage.
9. Cates, W., et al. (1999). Estimates of the incidence and prevalence of sexually transmitted diseases in the United States. *Sexually Transmitted Diseases,* 26(suppl), pp. S2–S7.
10. College Board. (2005). *Trends in College Pricing 2005–2006.* Report #050341686. Washington DC: The College Board.
11. College Board. (2004). *Trends in College Pricing 2004–2005.* Report #040341319. Washington DC: The College Board.
12. College Board. (2003). *College costs: Keep rising prices in perspective.* http://www.collegeboard.com/article/0,1120,6-29-0-4494,00.html?orig=sec.
13. College Board. (1998). *Increases in college tuition and fees average four percent: Student financial aid at a record high.* http://www.collegeboard.org/press/cost98/htm/98100/.htm.
14. Darrow, W.W., Barrett, D., McPhil, K.J., & Young, A. (1981). The gay report on sexually transmitted diseases. *American Journal of Public Health,* 71(9), pp. 1004–1011.
15. Division of STD Prevention. (2000). *Tracking the hidden epidemics: Trends in STDs in the United States 2000.* Atlanta: Centers for Disease Control and Prevention, U.S. Public Health Service.
16. Division of STD Prevention. (2001). *Sexually transmitted disease surveillance report 2000.* Atlanta: Centers for Disease Control and Prevention, U.S. Public Health Service.
17. Division of STD Prevention. (2002). *Sexually transmitted disease surveillance report 2001.* Atlanta: Centers for Disease Control and Prevention, U.S. Public Health Service.
18. Donelan, K., Blendon, R.J., Hill, C.A., et al. (1996). Whatever happened to the health insurance crisis in the United States? Voices from a national survey. *Journal of the American Medical Association,* 276, pp. 1346–1350.
19. Equal Employment Opportunity Commission. (2003). Sexual harassment charges EEOC and Fair Employment Practices Agencies (FEPA) Combined: FY 1002–FY 2001. http://www.eeoc.gov/stats/harass.html.
20. Ellis, A. & Harper, R. (1975). *A guide to rational living.* North Hollywood, CA: Melvin Powers.
21. Eng, T.R. & Butler, W.T. (Eds.). (1997). *The hidden epidemic: Confronting STDs.* Washington, DC: Academy Press, Institute of Medicine.
22. Erikson, E. (1978). *Childhood and society.* (2nd ed.). New York City: WW Norton.
23. Finelli, L., Budd. J., & Spitalny, K. (1993). Early syphilis: Relationships to sex, drugs, and changes in high-risk behavior from 1987–1990. *Sexually Transmitted Diseases,* 2, pp. 89–95.
24. Fisher, B.S., Cullen, F.T., & Turner, M.G. (2000). *The sexual victimization of college women.* Washington DC: U.S. Department of Justice.
25. Fisher, B., Koss, M.P., Gidycz, C.A., & Wisnewski, N. (1987). The scope of rape: Incidence and prevalence of sexual aggression and victimization in a national sample of higher education students. *Journal of Counseling and Clinical Psychology,* 55, pp. 162–170.
26. Fromn, E. (1956). *The art of loving.* New York: Harper & Row.
27. Gallo, E. (2003). Strategies and trends. *Journal of Financial Planning,* 16(6), p. 26.
28. Garnett, G.P. & Anderson, R.M. (1996). Core-group transmission of STDs. *Sexually Transmitted Diseases,* 20(4), pp. 181–191.
29. Gleason, N.A. (1994). College women and alcohol: A relational perspective. *Journal of American College Health,* 42(6), pp. 279–289.
30. Hales, D. (1991). *An Invitation to Health.* Pacific Grove, CA: Wadsworth.
31. Hayes, R.J., Schulz, K.F., & Plummer, F.A. (1995). The co-factor effect of genital ulcers on the per-exposure risk of HIV transmission in Sub-Saharan Africa. *Journal of Tropical and Medical Hygiene,* 98, pp. 1–8.
32. Higher Education Center. (2003). *Sexual assault: Alcohol and other drugs.* http://www. Edc.org/hec/pubs/factsheets/fact_sheet1.html.

33. Kennedy, M.B., Scarlett, M.I., Duer, A.C., & Chu, S.Y. (1995). Assessing HIV risk among women who have sex with women: Scientific and communication issues. *Journal of the American Medical Women's Association,* 50, pp. 103–107.
34. Kim, J.J. (2003). College grads, student loans, and job hunting. *Wall Street Journal,* September 2, p. D2.
35. Laumann, E.O., Gagnon, J.H., Michael, R.Y., & Michaels, S. (1994). *The social organization of sexuality: Sexual practices in the United States.* Chicago: University of Chicago Press.
36. Masters, W., Johnson, V., & Kolodny, R. (1992). *Human sexuality.* New York: HarperCollins.
37. Montgomery, R., Benedicto, J., & Haemmerlie, F. (1993). Personal vs. social motivations of undergraduates for using alcohol. *Psychological Reports,* 73(3), pp. 960–962.
38. Morse, S., Moreland, A., & Thompson, S. (1990). *Sexually transmitted diseases.* New York: Gower Medical.
39. Navarro, N. (1990). Race or class: Mortality differentials in the United States. *Lancet,* 336, pp. 1238–1240.
40. Office of National Drug Control Policy. (2002a). Rohypnol. http://www.whitehousedrugpolicy.gov/publications/factsht/rohypnol/index.html.
41. Office of National Drug Control Policy. (2002b). Gamma Hydrobutyrate (GHB). http://www.whitehousedrugpolicy.gov/publications/factsh/tgamma/index.html.
42. Person, E.S. (1989). Women—*Sex and sexuality.* Chicago: University of Chicago Press.
43. Potterat, J.J., Rothenberg, R., Woodhouse, D.E., Muth, J.B., Pratts, C.I., & Fogle, J.S. (1985). Gonorrhea as a social disease. *Sexually Transmitted Diseases,* 1, pp. 25–32.
44. Quinn, T. & Cates, W. (1993). Epidemiology of STDs in the 1990s. In Quinn, T. (Ed.). *Sexually transmitted diseases,* pp. 20–35. New York: Raven Press.
45. Reinisch, J.M. (1992). *The Kinsey Institute new report on sex.* New York: St. Martin's Press.
46. Rice, R.J., Roberts, P.L., & Handsfield, H.H. (1991). Sociodemographic distribution of gonorrhea incidence: Implications for prevention and behavioral research. *American Journal of Public Health,* 10, pp. 1253–1257.
47. Rosenberg, M.J. & Gollub, E.L. (1992). Commentary: Methods women can use that may prevent sexually transmitted disease, including HIV. *American Journal of Public Health,* 82(11), pp. 1473–1478.
48. Seligman, M. (1998). *Learned optimism.* New York: Knopf.
49. Smeltzer, S. & Whipple, B. (1991). Women and HIV: Image. *Journal of Nursing,* 4, pp. 249–256.
50. Sternberg, R.J. (1988). *The triangle of love: Intimacy, passions, commitment.* New York: Basic Books.
51. Stoffel, J. (1991). College economics 101. *Fidelity Focus,* Summer, pp. 15–18.
52. Task Force of the National Advisory Council on Alcohol Abuse and Alcoholism. (2002). *A call to action: Changing the culture of drinking at U.S. colleges.* NIH Publication no. 02-5010. Washington, DC: National Institute on Alcohol Abuse and Alcoholism.
53. Thompson, C. (1993). The male role stereotype. In Cyrus, V. (Ed.). *Experiencing Race, class, and gender in the United States,* pp. 146–148. Mountain View, CA: Mayfield.
54. U.S. Census. (2001). Washington, DC: *U.S. Department of Commerce News,* U.S. Census Public Information Office, June 29.
55. Wasserheit, J. (1988). Epidemiological synergy. *Sexually Transmitted Diseases,* 2, pp. 61–77.
56. Weschler, H., Eun, L.J., Kuo, M., Sebring, M., Nelson, T.F., & Lee, H. (2002). Trends in college binge drinking during a period of increased prevention efforts: Findings from four Harvard School of Public Health college alcohol study surveys: 1993–2001. *Journal of American College Health,* 50(5), pp. 203–217.
57. Weschler, H., Davenport, A., Dowdell, G., Moeykens, B., & Castillo, S. (1994a). Health and behavioral consequences of binge drinking in college. *JAMA,* 272(21), pp. 1672–1677.
58. Weschler, H., Isaac, N., Grodstein, F., & Sellers, D. (1994b). Continuation and initiation of alcohol use from the first to the second year of college. *Journal of Studies of Alcohol,* 55(1), pp. 41–45.

Name: ______________________ Date: __________

Assess Yourself 13-1

Sternberg's Love Scale

The blanks represent the person with whom you are in a relationship. Rate each statement on a 1-to-9 scale where 1 equals "not at all," 5 equals "moderately," and 9 equals "extremely." Use intermediate points on the scale to indicate intermediate feelings.

1. I am actively supportive of ______________________'s well-being.
2. I have a warm relationship with ______________________.
3. I am able to count on ______________________ in times of need.
4. ______________________ is able to count on me in times of need.
5. I am willing to share myself and my possessions with ______________________.
6. I receive considerable emotional support from ______________________.
7. I give considerable emotional support to ______________________.
8. I communicate well with ______________________.
9. I value ______________________ greatly in my life.
10. I feel close to ______________________.
11. I have a comfortable relationship with ______________________.
12. I feel that I really understand ______________________.
13. I feel that ______________________ really understands me.
14. I feel that I can really trust ______________________.
15. I share deeply personal information about myself with ______________________.
16. Just seeing ______________________ excites me.
17. I find myself thinking about ______________________ frequently during the day.
18. My relationship with ______________________ is very romantic.
19. I find ______________________ to be very personally attractive.
20. I idealize ______________________.
21. I cannot imagine another person making me as happy as ______________________ does.
22. I would rather be with ______________________ than anyone else.
23. There is nothing more important to me than my relationship with ______________________.
24. I especially like physical contact with ______________________.
25. There is something almost "magical" about my relationship with ______________________.
26. I adore ______________________.
27. I cannot imagine life without ______________________.
28. My relationship with ______________________ is passionate.
29. When I see romantic movies and read romantic books, I think of ______________________.
30. I fantasize about ______________________.
31. I know that I care about ______________________.
32. I am committed to maintaining my relationship with ______________________.
33. Because of my relationship with ______________________, I would not let other people come between us.
34. I have confidence in the stability of my relationship with ______________________.
35. I could not let anything get in the way of my commitment to ______________________.
36. I expect my love for ______________________ to last for the rest of my life.
37. I will always feel a strong responsibility for ______________________.
38. I view my commitment to ______________________ as a solid one.
39. I cannot imagine ending my relationship with ______________________.
40. I am certain of my love for ______________________.

ASSESS YOURSELF 13-1 (cont'd)

41. I view my relationship with ________________________________ as permanent.
42. I view my relationship with ________________________________ as a good decision.
43. I feel a sense of reponsibility toward ________________________________.
44. I plan to continue my relationship with ________________________________.
45. Even when ____________________ is hard to deal with, I remain commited to our relationship.

Average____________

Items 1 to 15 are for measuring the intimacy component; 16 to 30, for the passion component; and 31 to 45, for the decision/commitment component. To obtain your score, add your rating for each of the component subscales in the space below and divide the total by 15. This will give you an average rating for each component. Compare your scores for each component with your partner's. The closer your scores are, the more compatible you are.

From Sternberg, R.J. (1988). *The triangle of love.* New York: Basic Books, Inc.[48]

Name: ______________________ Date: __________

Assess Yourself 13-2

How Do You Drink?

Answer the following questions in terms of your personal alcohol use. Record your number of yes and no responses in the totals spaces at the end of each of the columns.

	Yes	No
1. Do you drink more often than you did a year ago?	____	____
2. Do you drink more heavily than you did a year ago?	____	____
3. Do you drink to get drunk?	____	____
4. Do you drink to cope with stress?	____	____
5. Do you go drinking to meet people?	____	____
6. Do you drink to feel accepted by others?	____	____
7. In the last two weeks have you had five drinks in a row at one sitting?	____	____
8. Have you had five or more drinks at one sitting more than three times in the past month?	____	____
9. Following one or more episodes of drinking this year have you:		
– Had a hangover?	____	____
– Missed class?	____	____
– Done something you regretted?	____	____
– Forgotten where you were?	____	____
– Argued with friends?	____	____
– Gotten in trouble with campus police?	____	____
– Gotten injured or hurt?	____	____
– Gotten into a fight?	____	____
– Had unplanned sex?	____	____
– Not used protection during sex?	____	____
Totals	____	____

Scoring

Tally your yes answers. If you had two or more yes answers, you may be exhibiting a pattern of unacceptable alcohol use and should consider exploring this with someone associated with your college's counseling center.

Name: ______________________ Date: __________

ASSESS YOURSELF 13-3

Values Clarification

Place the twenty statements concerning school/work/career on the following continuum:

1	2	3	4	5
Strongly agree	**Agree**	**Uncertain**	**Disagree**	**Strongly disagree**

1. I must finish school in four years or less.
2. I would feel guilty about taking fewer credits per semester.
3. I could accept getting a lower grade in one class to reduce my workload and academic stress from my other classes.
4. I feel guilty about taking difficult courses pass/fail.
5. I must put the same amount of effort into all my classes.
6. Grades are not as important as enjoying school and life.
7. Grades really don't matter to me.
8. I like to space out my classes so that I don't feel rushed.
9. I don't like to waste time between classes.
10. I'm not going to sacrifice my lifestyle just for school.
11. I can't cut back on my work hours at all.
12. I'll take fewer classes rather than cut back on my work hours.
13. Schoolwork is not as important as my job.
14. Working so that I can buy things and have extra spending money is more important than taking a full load of courses.
15. Students are supposed to be stressed.
16. Money is the most important factor in my career choice.
17. I couldn't take a pay cut to work in my profession.
18. I'd never make it up if I took a pay cut to work in my profession.
19. Doing something I like is more important than my salary.
20. I could do without certain luxuries for a while in order to break into the job of my choice.

Examine each of your responses in light of the information presented so far concerning the role of school, work, and career. Is your current lifestyle/academic style consistent with your values?

CHAPTER

14

Stress in Adulthood and Older Adulthood

OUTLINE

Erikson's Last Two Stages

The Meaning of Work

- A Multidisciplinary Look at Work
- The Six Dimensions of Work
- Understanding Erikson's Major Developmental Task of Adulthood Using the Six Dimensions of Work

Work as a Potential Stressor

- The Culture of Work
- Changing Work Status
- Changes in Financial Status
- Changes in Daily Activities
- Retirement

The Meaning of Community and Living Environment

- Non–Age-Restricted Housing
- Age-Restricted Housing
- Other Types of Living Environments

Relationships in Adulthood and Older Adulthood

- Singlehood
- Stress Associated with Being Single
- Cohabitation
- Stress Associated with Cohabitation
- Marriage and Long-Term Gay and Lesbian Relationships
- Stress Associated with Marriage and Long-Term Gay and Lesbian Relationships
- Divorce
- Stress Associated with Divorce

Aging and Changing Health Status

- Healthy Aging and Premature Disability and Death
- Changing Health Status as a Source of Stress
- Thinking about Our Own Mortality
- Widowhood
- Loss, Grief, and Bereavement Stress

Coping with Adulthood and Older Adulthood Stress Using the Five Rs

- Rethink Strategies
- Reduce Strategies
- Relax Strategies
- Release Strategies
- Reorganize Strategies

OBJECTIVES

By the end of the chapter students will:

- Know the major tasks associated with Erikson's adult and older adult stages of development.
- Know the major sources of stress associated with these stages.
- Be able to describe the meaning of work from a variety of perspectives.
- Understand the relationship between the meaning of work and the way it contributes to stress.
- Describe some of the typical changes associated with retirement.
- Describe a variety of living environments associated with adulthood and older adulthood.
- Compare and contrast a variety of relationships in adulthood and older adulthood.
- Describe common stressors associated with a variety of adult and older adult relationships.
- Describe the health changes and risks associated with aging.
- Discuss how lifestyle is related to health in adulthood and older adulthood.
- Define death anxiety and describe how various groups react to it.
- Understand how to develop a stress-management plan related to adulthood and older adulthood by employing the Five Rs of coping.

ERIKSON'S LAST TWO STAGES

In this chapter we will examine Erikson's[15] final two stages of development: adulthood and older adulthood. The major task associated with adulthood is generativity versus stagnation. The major developmental task of older adulthood is maintaining integrity in the face of despair.[15] According to Erikson, the struggle between generativity and stagnation is one of striving to be productive, creative, and nurturing versus self-indulgent and impoverished. In older adulthood maintaining integrity in the face of despair involves looking back on our lives and accomplishments and accepting their worth and uniqueness despite a growing awareness of our mortality and the nearness of death.

Adulthood involves building and solidifying relationships and becoming gainfully employed and productive in our work. It is a time when many people choose to enter committed relationships, raise families, and focus on taking care of personal and family needs. It is also a time when we are most likely to make our mark and leave a legacy as individuals.

For people who have mastered the earlier developmental tasks, adulthood is also a time of wanting to give back, to help out, to ensure the continuity of life and happiness. It is a time of hard work and then enjoying the fruits of one's labors. For those who have not mastered prior developmental tasks, it is a time of continued self-indulgence and self-centeredness. It is a time of total freedom to focus on the self with no limits and no moral obligations to anyone or anything else.

Older adulthood is a time of looking back and taking stock of where we've been, what we've accomplished, and whom we have touched. If we have mastered the tasks associated with adulthood, we look back at our lives with a sense of integrity, of a job well done. The process of verifying our lives and finding meaning in them often involves reminiscing with family, friends, and others. In a way, these people bear witness to our life and our integrity and help give us strength to look to the future without despair. We can get a sense of what this is like by doing Assess Yourself 14-1, "My Epitaph."

Many older adults also continue to look to the future. Confident in their integrity, they look for continued opportunities for generativity until the final days of their lives. Now, freed from any of the responsibilities of adulthood, they take on new roles, such as grandparents, mentors, and community volunteers.

KEY TO UNDERSTANDING

The elderly need to relive the past in order to assess the meaning of their lives.

There are many potential challenges and stressors during these final two stages of development. This chapter will focus on the main sources of stress and challenge in the adult and older adult years: work, relationships, community, health, and death.

THE MEANING OF WORK

Work means different things to different people. This is particularly true in adulthood and older adulthood when most people settle into a job or profession and set about the business of earning a living. As we'll examine in this next section, the meaning of work varies slightly according to who is defining and studying it. For example, economists view work differently than artists or psychologists. Each looks at work through a different lens. Later in this section we'll take a cross-cultural look at work to discuss the common threads of working that cut across disciplines and cultures.

A Multidisciplinary Look at Work

Work represents more than just economic viability. Economists tend to define work as merely the opportunity to make money. Working is a means for obtaining money which can be used to secure goods and services and lead a productive life.[19,56]

Psychologists view work as an outlet for expressing oneself. Through personally meaningful work, we satisfy needs and wants, create, share, and have a vehicle for exploring who we truly are.[19]

Sociologists view work as an arena in which we interact with others. In this arena we play a variety of roles and become involved in many different kinds of relationships. Through engaging in these roles and

Many Americans define who they are by the work they perform.

exploring these relationships, we reach our full potential as social creatures. We need others to self-actualize fully, and it is only in relationship with others that this can occur.[19]

Political scientists view the workplace as a battlefield where inherent power struggles between workers and their employers are played out. While economists view long-term profit as the guiding force behind the majority of business decisions, political scientists view the quest for power as the major determinant in human relations in the workplace.[19] Feminists extend the political argument by pointing to "privileged social position" as a major factor in the meaning of work. They cite phenomena such as the **"glass ceiling"** (a metaphor for the supposedly available but limited ascension in the corporate world available to women) in corporations as barriers to those who do not have this privileged social status due to race, gender, or socioeconomic background.[19]

The Six Dimensions of Work

A hallmark for understanding the meaning of work in adulthood was the Meaning of Work (MOW) study.[41] In 1987 the Meaning of Work International Research Team conducted a multinational study of work in eight industrialized nations (United States, Belgium, Britain, Japan, the Netherlands, West Germany, the former Yugoslavia, and Israel). The MOW team found that the meaning of work is determined by the choices and experiences of individual workers and the organizational and environmental context in which they work and live. The MOW team also identified six major dimensions from which work derives its meaning for people: work centrality, economic orientation, intrinsic orientation, interpersonal relations, the entitlement norm, and the obligation norm.[41] These dimensions individually and collectively affect the ways individual workers derive meaning from their work.

Work Centrality

Work centrality refers to the central and fundamental role of work in the life of most individuals in industrialized nations. Work centrality can be measured, which allows researchers to assess the general importance working has in a person's life at any given time.

Absolute work centrality refers to a person's belief in or valuing of work as a life role. *Relative* work centrality refers to the importance of work compared with other aspects of one's life, such as leisure time, family, community, and religion. Studies have found that for most workers in industrialized nations, work is considered more important than leisure time, religion, and community, second only to family.[52] *High* work centrality has been found to be positively related to job satisfaction, commitment to work, and deriving a sense of purpose and contentment from work.[52]

Economic Orientation

Economic orientation refers to the belief that people work mainly for and are motivated by the extrinsic rewards associated with paid labor: salary, fringe benefits, and the like. The MOW study found economic orientation to be the single most valued dimension of work.[41] Not surprisingly, subjects who were labeled as having an "acute inclination to instrumental or economic values" viewed work primarily as a vehicle for providing income.[52] Additional studies have shown that other variables, such as the intrinsic or expressive benefits of work, are rated more important by workers but economic orientation is always a major criterion associated with the meaning of work.[52]

Intrinsic Orientation

Intrinsic orientation refers to the aspects of work that satisfy a worker's internal and expressive needs. The intrinsic orientation of work refers to variables such as creativity, autonomy, interest, variety, and challenge. The intrinsic orientation of a job has to do with its ability to provide workers with a vehicle for exploring and expressing themselves. Some people equate intrinsic orientation with job centrality because of their close relationship. In the MOW study,[41] intrinsic orientation was found to be the greatest predictor of work centrality in the United States, Germany, Israel, and Japan, demonstrating an almost universal perception of the relationship of the two. For many people, it seems, work offers the most important opportunity for self-expression.[41]

Interpersonal Relations

As we discussed in chapter 4, humans are social creatures. Human interaction is essential for healthy functioning. For many people, the workplace is the primary vehicle for interacting with others. Work provides a sense of purpose through engagement in collective activity.[19] For many people, the workplace has replaced the community and the family as the locus of collective activity. The workplace has become the hub of both worksite and offsite activities.

glass ceiling a metaphor for the supposedly available but limited ascension in the corporate world available to women

work centrality the central and fundamental role of work in the life of most individuals in industrialized nations

economic orientation the belief that people work mainly for and are motivated by the intrinsic rewards associated with paid labor: salary, fringe benefits, and so on

intrinsic orientation the aspects of work that satisfy a worker's internal and expressive needs, such as creativity, autonomy, interest, variety, and challenge

KEY TO UNDERSTANDING

Work, even in the best of times, creates a multitude of potential stressors.

KEY TO UNDERSTANDING

Work means different things to different people. It is not unusual for the meaning of work to change as we move through different phases of our lives.

Entitlement

Citizens of industrialized societies generally perceive work as an entitlement in a free society. Work underlies both the rights and the responsibilities of citizens. People are expected to work, and in turn they expect to have the opportunity to be gainfully employed. This is one of the most basic covenants in a free society. While workers understand that job opportunities will vary in relation to the overall economy and sectors within economies, they maintain an overall belief that every able-bodied worker is entitled to a job.[41]

Obligation

The flip side of entitlement is obligation, the belief in the societal norm that everyone has the responsibility to contribute to the overall good of society through working. This obligation stems from both internal personal standards (work ethic) and external community standards (being a responsible member of society). One's obligation to work goes hand in hand with the belief that every citizen is entitled to work in a free society.[41,52]

Understanding Erikson's Major Developmental Task of Adulthood Using the Six Dimensions of Work

The dimensions of work from the MOW study[41] provide a helpful framework for understanding the role of work in achieving Erikson's major task of adulthood: generativity versus stagnation. Everyone will not use work in the same fashion to meet this task. How people use work to master this task will vary depending on how they perceive these dimensions.

Those who view work as absolutely central to their lives will also evaluate generativity versus stagnation in terms of what they have achieved at work. Their lives will revolve around work, and the meaning of their existence as adults will be based on their occupation. Many will forgo marriage, children, and the establishment of deep community roots to achieve this because of their absolute centrist position.

Others with a more relative work centrality may view their accomplishments at work in the context of their families and community ties. They will evaluate their generativity in terms of what they have accomplished at work in relation to their happiness and success in these other aspects of their lives.

Some people view generativity in terms of monetary success. They have an "economic orientation" toward work and consider the most important aspect of employment to be maximizing earnings and advancement in one's career.

Those with an intrinsic orientation toward work may assess their generativity in terms of their ability to create and express themselves through their work. If their work provided ample opportunities for self-expression and creativity and they took advantage of that and were able to produce in those areas, they would feel that their adult years were meaningful and that they hadn't stagnated.

People with an interpersonal orientation towards work find meaning in their work and lives if their jobs have provided opportunities to meet others and develop meaningful friendships and relationships at work. Their generativity would be more centered in their interpersonal relations than in monetary or intrinsic achievements.

Finally, those who view work as an entitlement and an obligation may feel satisfied that they have made a contribution by the fact that they were willing and able to hold down a job and were contributing members of society.

As we'll see in the next section of this chapter, the same dimensions factor into the way we view ourselves and our work as we make the transition into older adulthood and begin thinking about our legacy.

WORK AS A POTENTIAL STRESSOR

A key to understanding work as a potential stressor is to realize that even in the best of times, it creates a multitude of situations and scenarios that are potentially stressful. In the best of times, finding a job that is satisfying and productive, performing well in it, growing with it, establishing friendships and collegiality, earning the rewards and perks that are part of it, and then retiring from it constitute a difficult task. In the best of times, work can be hard, competitive, inflexible, demanding, confusing, ironic, and demeaning. It also, however, can be challenging, rewarding, enabling, satisfying, heroic, even noble.

In tough economic times, when the global economy and marketplace are changing the way America and companies do business and view work and workers, work can be extremely stressful. Not only do we have to cope with the normal demands involved in working, we have to worry about things that our parents took for granted, such as companies standing by their employees in tough times,

Retirement after a lifelong job of hard manual labor is often eagerly anticipated.

rising salaries, enhanced benefits over time, a guaranteed job for life if they performed well, retirement benefits they could bank on, and a solvent Social Security system to supplement their retirement.

The Culture of Work

Americans use work, more than any other variable, to define who they are. Americans live to work. Ask Americans who they are and you're likely to get a dissertation concerning their work. Americans define themselves by their vocations. We're teachers, doctors, mechanics, computer programmers, housewives, firefighters, and so on.

People from other cultures work to live. Other cultures view work as a means to an end, not merely an end in itself. People work so that they can enjoy the fruits of their labor. In most European countries, people "go on holiday" for a minimum of four weeks in the summer. The pace of work is more relaxed, and the emphasis on work is less in the big picture of their lives. To top it off, productivity remains high, in some cases higher than that of the United States. West Germany, for example, before its merger with East Germany enjoyed a standard of living second to none while its workers toiled fewer hours on the job than Americans did.[34]

Changing Work Status

Because Americans define themselves so much by their work, changes in work status can be particularly threatening and therefore stressful. The shifting American economy has triggered many changes in work status during the young, mid, and older adulthood periods. These changes range from new definitions of workplace and work time to new conceptualizations of what it means to be a mother and father.

Changing Work Status in Young and Mid-Adulthood

Some of these changes are related to work time and space. For example, rising oil and transportation costs have fueled the rise in people **telecommuting:** working from home using the Internet and other technological advances. This shift has given the work *workplace* a new meaning. One's workplace can now be a home office augmented by fax, e-mail, teleconferencing, and other high-tech tools.

The concept of work time has also changed. Most of the parents of telecommuters reported to the office or factory on Monday through Friday morning and punched **time clocks** to show they came into work on time. Their children come to work virtually, often on a 24/7 basis, and work when they find it most convenient. Job sharing is becoming increasingly more common as more and more men and women take advantage of more flexible policies regarding work hours. In job sharing, two people working part-time hours share one full-time position. Unlike part-time jobs of the past which were usually lower status positions, job sharing usually involves maintaining the same work status and tasks but working half the time.

Work roles have also changed. It is becoming more and more common for husbands and wives to shift roles according to job status. More flexible gender roles have prompted couples to reassess their parenting responsibilities and make who has the better job the prime criterion for who works full-time. This has led to an increase in the number of "stay-at-home" dads, fathers who have put their careers on hold (or abandoned them) to stay at home to raise their children while their wives (with the better jobs) have gone back to work after having their children.

All of the above changes could be viewed as either challenges or potential stressors. To some, they represent new options and opportunities and are not viewed as threats. They are viewed as challenges that open new doors. To others, they represent the unknown, a new way of doing something that forces them to change. People with this perception of changing work status will be threatened by these and other changes and therefore will be stressed by them.

Changing Work Status in Older Adulthood

Older adulthood is typically accompanied by a change in work status as many people look forward to cutting back on their work hours and responsibilities. Older adulthood is a time for people to reappraise the meaning of work in their lives. In older adulthood most but not all workers retire. People's attitudes toward retirement differ according to the nature of the work in which they have been employed. People with rewarding jobs typically are not happy to see them end. These jobs have been a source of

telecommuting the practice of working for a business from a location other than the main place of business, such as a home or satellite office, through heavy use of modern communications technology

time clock machines that keep track of the time of arrival to and departure from work for hourly employees gratification, pleasure, and in many cases financial reward. Those who have viewed work as a lifetime of drudgery often eagerly look forward to the day when they can quit. Blue-collar workers tend to desire retirement, while professionals and self-employed people may not.[6]

The reappraisal of the meaning of work and decisions about working are influenced not only by our success in achieving the major task of young adulthood but also by our level of wellness across the six dimensions of health and our financial status. The reappraisal is also influenced by the type of career or job we are in, whether we are self-employed, and the flexibility our employment offers. For instance, a 65-year-old self-employed professional in good health with an excellent social support system has the ability practically to define the parameters of his or her work in older adulthood. That person can work fewer days or hours, take on fewer clients or assignments, take more vacation time, and so on. In contrast, a 62-year-old assembly-line worker with chronic health problems and limited social support is in an entirely different situation. This person may seek early retirement because of failing health, job dissatisfaction, and the inability to modify his or her work schedule, overall hours, and vacation time. Parnes and Sommers[46] found that higher levels of education, being married to a working wife, and having good physical and psychological health were related to men in their seventies and eighties continuing to work and shun retirement.

Changes in Financial Status

Working part-time or retiring in adulthood and older adulthood often results in a diminished income. Feeling financially secure is a major reason cited for both early retirement and enjoyment of being retired.[6] Financial security can temper the loss of full-time worker status because people can see, and live off, the fruits of their labor. Financial security allows people to maintain the lifestyles they are accustomed to or, in many cases, improve the quality of their lives because of their newfound freedom. In a sense, it is a measure of the mastery of the major task of young adulthood (generativity) and is part of the process of maintaining integrity in the face of despair (the major task of older adulthood).

Not all adults and older adults, however, have the financial security to meet all their needs. Lack of financial security factors can work in exactly the opposite way. Those who are not financially secure may view their working lives as a failure or look back on their careers and ask where things went wrong. Their identities, self-image, and integrity may be a bit tarnished if they feel that they did not live up to their earning potential or were not rewarded commensurately for their worth as workers. Lack of financial security may also influence an older adult's perceived ability to cope with retirement and the loss of a full-time income.

Lack of financial security can be a major stressor as the cost of living continues to escalate. Those on fixed incomes may find that increases in the cost of basic necessities such as housing, food, and medical coverage outpace their savings and retirement income. Lack of financial security can also cut into one's ability to enjoy travel, recreation, and other pleasures.

Changes in Daily Activities

One's day-to-day schedule can change dramatically when one shifts to part-time work or full retirement depending on the nature of one's previous work and schedule. Those retiring from a full-time job with traditional, fixed work hours now face the prospect of a day that begins and ends when they want it to. They no longer have to set an alarm, fight rush hour traffic, and get to work at a specific time, only to reverse the process at the end of the workday. It takes time to adjust to this newfound freedom after years of regimentation to a full-time work schedule. Those leaving more flexible jobs in which they owned their own businesses, set their own schedules, worked off hours, or worked out of their homes or from their cars will find less change in their daily schedules.

Regardless of the type of schedule one had when working full-time, part-time and retired people have a lot more free time to use any way they desire. Many factors have an impact on how this time is spent and whether it is enjoyed. Factors such as disposable income, health status, hobbies and recreational pursuits, and interest in community service are just a few that can be used to illustrate how this time is spent.

A key to understanding this is to examine the lifestyle people lead while still working full time. This usually is indicative of how they will spend their time when they cut back their hours or retire. People with various interests outside of work, such as hobbies, sports, and community service, have a myriad of activities to pursue. Chances are, their days will be as full as, if not fuller than, the days they spent working full-time. People whose lives revolve around work or who have few outside interests will face a much tougher time adjusting to retirement or part-time work.

Another thing that changes besides one's daily schedule is the nature and extent of one's interactions with others. For people who had an interpersonal orientation, work was their primary source of social interaction.[52] Their workday provided multiple opportunities for various levels of interaction with coworkers, colleagues, and the general public. For them, work meant being with other people as much as it meant a source of income. Becoming a part-time worker or retiring can bring an end to this. In a best-case scenario, the interpersonal aspects of work are replaced with increased time spent with family, friends, and neighbors pursuing hobbies, recreational activities, and community service. In a worst-case scenario,

Living Constructively

Looking Back at Our Work Using Naikan Self-Reflection

As we've mentioned throughout this book, Naikan self-reflection is an excellent tool for increasing awareness, changing our perspective about our lives, and developing grace and gratitude. This can be an invaluable tool for helping older adults look back on their life's work and the people who enriched their lives.

Instructions:

1. The focus of this Naikan self-reflection is your work and the people who helped you along the way. Divide your adult life's work into three stages: the first ten years, the next fifteen years, and the remaining years after that.
2. For each time frame answer the following three Naikan questions:
   a. What did other people I worked with during this time do to help guide, nurture, and support me?
   b. What did I do for other people I worked with during this time to help guide, nurture, and support them?
   c. What problems or difficulties did I cause others who worked with me during this time?
3. Examine the results of your self-reflection, focusing on how others enriched and shaped your work life and enabled you to get to where you are.
4. Send a Mindful Thank You note to some of these people. Make sure you are specific in thanking them for the different ways they helped you in your work.

Retirement provides people with many opportunities to pursue old interests and explore new ones.

particularly for widowed or divorced people, leaving full-time employment often brings endless hours of aloneness in a quiet house or apartment with no one for companionship.

KEY TO UNDERSTANDING

A key to understanding work stress, whether in adulthood or older adulthood, is realizing that because work means different things to different people depending on their orientation to it, potential work stressors will be appraised differently across individuals and within individuals over time.

Retirement

Retirement is very difficult to define. Most people view it as a complete withdrawal from the workforce. This definition is inadequate, however, because many people continue to work part-time, sometimes out of necessity to earn an income and often because of a need to feel productive and maintain personal identity and status. This is particularly true for workers with absolute or high work centrality. These workers have the greatest need to maintain some connection to their work. This also holds true for workers with an intrinsic orientation to work. Since their work often revolves around a central life interest and a strong identification with their jobs or professions, it is particularly difficult for them to make the transition to retirement.[39] The best way to view retirement is as a complex process leading to withdrawal from a full-time occupation.[6] It is a process that begins with thinking about retirement. Retirement involves tremendous change in everything from one's self-perception to one's daily schedule and interactions with other people. As the MOW study[41] demonstrated, Americans (like Israelis, Germans, and Japanese) define themselves by their work. Americans have high centrality and an intrinsic orientation toward work. Consequently, when faced with retirement, they have to redefine themselves.

Part of this redefining has to do with simple things such as how we spend our time. Regardless of the type of work performed, when people spend ten, twenty, thirty, or more years getting up, going off to an office or factory, and putting in eight or more hours on the job, it becomes a routine that defines their day, week, month, and year. This is much more of a factor for people who have worked in traditional jobs for employers. People who have been self-employed or worked part-time or as consultants are more accustomed to nontraditional hours and work arrangements.[52]

Another part of redefining ourselves has to do with changing our perception of ourselves. For some older adults the change is minimal. For instance, for older adults with an intrinsic orientation to work, transitioning to part-time work or retirement may not interfere with their ability to engage in the same activities they performed as full-time employees. Artists, writers, photographers, and professors, to name a few, can still paint, write, shoot pictures, and teach either part-time for a salary or at their leisure for no pay (assuming they are financially able). Because their intrinsic orientation to the activities they are passionate about doesn't change as their work status changes, their perception of themselves is only minimally affected.[35]

For others with work centrality or an economic or interpersonal orientation to work, their perceptions of themselves are more rooted in their work status. They develop identities as businessmen and businesswomen, supervisors, foremen and forewomen, breadwinners, high earners, deal closers, members of a team, union members, bowling team members, and so on. Changes in their work status usually result in changes in their self-perception because it is so tied to the job.[41]

Even though many continue to work part-time, older adults are perceived by others as moving from the ranks of the working to those of the nonworking, from the employed to the unemployed. They are often regarded as unproductive in economic terms and are lumped with children as the "dependent" population.[57] This is an interesting characterization, considering the fact that this generation of retirees is the best educated, the best fed and housed, and the healthiest there has ever been.[57] Many have led, and continue to lead in retirement, creative, satisfying, productive lives.

THE MEANING OF COMMUNITY AND LIVING ENVIRONMENT

Most adults and older adults live in **age-integrated communities** where people of all ages live together. The majority of older Americans remain in the same houses they have lived in for most of their lives. This is due in part to the perception that a home represents more than just a place to live. For most Americans, home is the center of an environment that includes friends, family, community resources, and a history rich with memories. Most adult Americans develop ties to the community through child-rearing activities, religious affiliation, membership in clubs and organizations, connections with neighbors, and a sense of familiarity and belongingness. As with work, communities mean different things to different people. The way people view the meaning of community will influence their perception of possible changes in residence (see Stress in Our World 14-1, "Yvanna").

Non–Age-Restricted Housing

The overwhelming majority of adult and older adult Americans live in non–age-restricted housing. These communities have no age restrictions and people of all ages are free to rent, buy, and sell property. Most adults live and raise their families in such communities. About 7.7 million Americans age 55 and older also live in non–age-restricted housing though their homes tend to be older (43 percent built before 1950) than those owned by younger people.[14, 29]

Age-Restricted Housing

While the norm for most adults and older adults is staying in the family home for their adult lives, that trend may be changing. An amendment to the 1988 Fair Housing Act made it legal for builders to exclude younger residents from properties intended for those age 55 and older. The American Housing Survey (2001) found that 1.8 million older adults live in "conventional" (detached single family homes and condominiums and apartments) structures in age-restricted housing.[14] Among those living in **age-restricted housing,** 1.1 million lived in multifamily housing and the remaining 700,000 lived in single family homes.

Although age-restricted housing represents only 2 percent of the overall housing market, it represents 14 percent of the over-55 market. People in this market are much more likely than are past generations to spend more for their retirement homes than they spent for the homes of their early adult years.[17] In addition to spending more money, the older adults of the 2000s want to stay close to their homes of origin and purchase homes that make it easier to have a more active lifestyle than that of their counterparts from past generations and peers who live in non–age-restricted communities.[17] Over 75 percent

age-integrated communities communities where people of all ages live together

age-restricted housing housing restricted by age for older adults

STRESS IN OUR WORLD 14-1

Yvanna

Yvanna is 70 years old and has been retired for five years from her job as a factory worker in the meat-packing industry. A small, trim woman with bright blue eyes and a quick smile, she has raised six children in the same small brick row house in a major Midwestern city where she's lived for the last forty years. All her children have moved away except for her youngest son, who serves in the navy and lives at home between his tours of duty. Yvanna is in good health but is occasionally bothered by arthritis in her hands and fingers.

Stephen, Yvanna's husband of fifty years, recently died of lung cancer. She misses him terribly and feels all alone in their empty house. Many of her neighbors have moved away or died, and the neighborhood is undergoing a period of transition as old residents die or move away and new ones move in and renovate the aging structures. Last week, Mrs. Olson, an elderly woman across the street and Yvanna's favorite neighbor, broke her hip on the ice in front of the house and moved into a nursing home. Money is not too big of a deal as Yvanna's house is paid for and she has a pension as well as survivor's benefits from her husband's job.

Marie, Yvanna's oldest daughter, has offered to let Yvanna move in with her family. Marie lives in North Carolina in a large suburban home with a guest room and plenty of space. Her three children would love to have their granny live with them, and the idea is fine with Marie's husband, George. George travels extensively and wouldn't mind having his mother-in-law around to keep his wife company.

Yvanna is feeling very confused. She'd really like to see more of her daughter and grandchildren but isn't sure she wants to give up her freedom. She likes her house and the neighborhood. It's home to her. She knows the area and its residents, and she has a lot of friends and acquaintances around the city. She likes being able to get by without a car, walking to the market and other stores. She feels safe here and likes the urban environment. She really has no desire to relocate anywhere, least of all to a suburban area where she'd be lost without a car and totally dependent on her daughter to get around. She thinks she'll get over her husband's death more easily if she stays where she is, but the uncertainty is causing her a lot of stress.

of newer over-55 communities are **active adult communities** that feature clubhouses, fitness facilities, pools, recreation directors, walking trails, and golf courses.

In addition to these recreational features, most new homes in age-restricted over-55 communities have features such as low-maintenance exteriors, maintenance-free grounds care, high-speed Internet and cable television access, high-efficiency heating and central air conditioning, upscale kitchen and bath appliances and designs, two full bathrooms, and other amenities. Many are equipped with low-step entries, walk-through showers and tubs, handrails, and other features to accommodate owners with mild physical limitations.

Other Types of Living Environments

Independent living facilities, or congregate care facilities, are apartments designed for older adults who are physically well but dislike the responsibilities associated with maintaining a single-family home or even an apartment and are looking for a more communal environment. These facilities offer several forms of congregate services, including meals, housekeeping, transportation, organized group activities, and common area facilities and group-oriented services. Like apartment dwellers, residents pay rent and do not own their apartments.

Another type of living environment tailored to older adults are **assisted living facilities.** Besides providing housing, these facilities typically offer care and support services to older adults who need assistance in daily activities because of increasing frailty or health conditions such as Alzheimer's disease. The overall level of health of these people is not at the stage that requires nursing home care. Assisted living facilities typically contain individual "apartments" for residents that range from simple studio apartment-type quarters to "suites" which have one or two bedrooms as well as a sitting room. The amenities in the living facilities usually include accommodations that make dressing and bathing easier (walk-in tubs, handrails, etc.) for older adults. The facilities as a whole have communal dining and recreation areas and amenities such as fitness centers, computer labs, libraries,

active adult communities age-restricted communities (age 55 or older) that feature clubhouses, fitness facilities, pools, recreation directors, walking trails, and golf courses

independent living facilities age-restricted apartments that typically offer several forms of congregate services, including meals, housekeeping, transportation, organized group activities, and other common area facilities and group-oriented services

assisted living facilities age-restricted communities that provide housing and support services to older adults who need assistance in daily activities because of increasing frailty or health conditions such as Alzheimer's disease

Retirement can be a time to take advantage of the recreational facilities available in many communities.

and a host of other options. Transportation to shopping and other areas is usually provided. In most cases, residents are able to maintain personal automobiles.[25] Costs vary tremendously depending on the level of amenities, the geographic location, and other factors. At the end of 1999 it was estimated that there were approximately 585,000 of these units in the United States.[25]

Skilled nursing facilities, also known as nursing homes, provide the highest level of care among the housing alternatives for older adults. Approximately 5 percent of the adult population over 65 years old resides in a nursing home. The typical nursing home resident is very old, female, widowed or divorced, financially disadvantaged, and without children. Nursing homes are regulated by state and federal government standards and may be nonprofit or for-profit institutions. The types of facilities vary according to a person's ability to pay. Nursing home care is extremely expensive (the average cost is $25,000 a year), and only a small portion of that cost is covered by private medical insurance and Medicare (2 percent and 1 percent, respectively). Not all types of facilities accept residents who must rely on government subsidies to pay for their care. Typically, average nursing home residents must deplete their life savings to pay for care. Government subsidies for nursing home care take over when the elderly are no longer able to pay.[6] In 1999 there were approximately 1.9 million nursing home beds available to older Americans.

Skilled nursing facilities play a vital role in the lives of elderly people who need constant supervision and medical care.

Continuing care retirement communities (CCRCs) combine a spectrum of living environments and services. These communities integrate older adults of varying levels of health and combine independent living, assisted living, and skilled nursing care in one facility. They are designed to provide residents with continuity of care as they move from being able to live independently to requiring nursing home care.

RELATIONSHIPS IN ADULTHOOD AND OLDER ADULTHOOD

The second major task of adulthood is the continuation, deepening, and ending of the committed relationships that began in young adulthood. For adults and older adults who choose to remain single, relationships with

skilled nursing facilities formerly known as nursing homes, a type of age-restricted living environment that provides the highest level of care and is equipped to handle seniors with acute or intensive medical care needs and offers posthospitalization and rehabilitation therapy

continuing care retirement communities (CCRCs) communities that integrate older adults of varying levels of health and combine independent living, assisted living, and skilled nursing care facilities friends and lovers from young adulthood continue to evolve and new ones form. Some choose to cohabit, while the large majority prefer to live alone. For most Americans, however, relationships in adulthood and older adulthood usually involve a commitment to marriage and family. Older adulthood is characterized by the changing nature of relationships and family life as partners age, children grow up and move out, and grandchildren are born. For many people this is a period marked by divorce or the death of a spouse or lover.

Over the last thirty years, an increasing percentage of Americans have been choosing to remain single. Among the reasons for remaining single are voluntary delays in getting married, changes in sexual standards, increased financial independence for women, changing economic times, changing concepts of marriage, and the desire to remain single permanently.[6]

Singlehood

The U.S. Census Bureau found that the median age at first marriage in 1970 was 20.8 years for women and 23.2 years for men. By 2000, those ages had risen to 25.1 years and 26.8 years for men and women, respectively.[53] After the 1970s, as the median age of first marriage was increasing, the divorce rate also increased. Both of these demographic shifts have altered the composition of the nonmarried population. Overall, never married and divorced men and women now make up a larger share of the population than they did in 1970, while the proportion currently married has declined (fig. 14-1).

The decision to remain single for life is usually made by men and women between the ages of 25 and 30.[48] Regardless of the reasons, those who choose to remain single for life report that they are quite happy. Contrary to popular belief, most singles are not lonely and, in fact, develop alternative social patterns based on friendships and nonmarital love relationships.

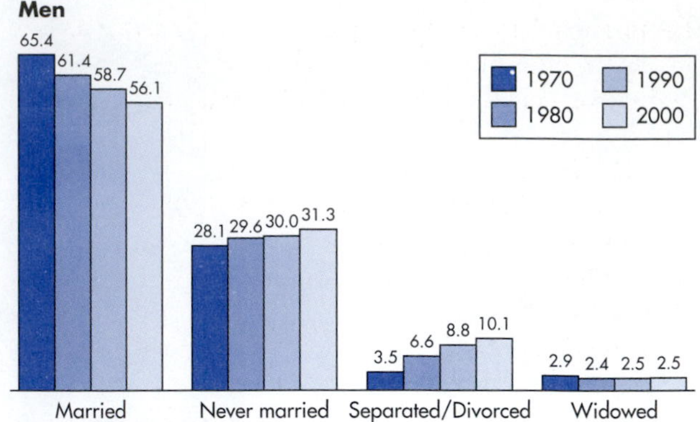

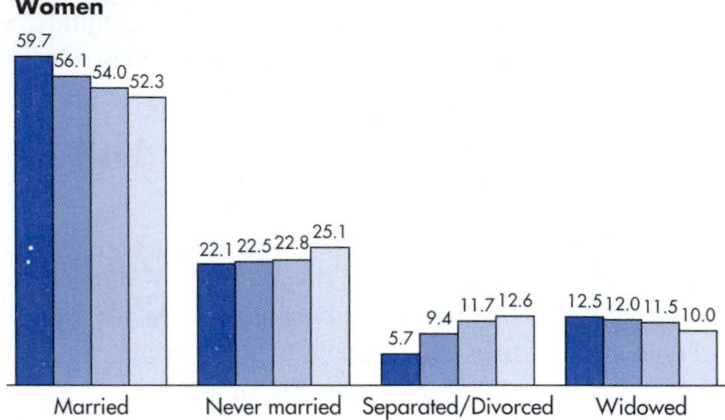

Figure 14-1

Although in 2000 more American men and women were never married, separated, or divorced, marriage by far continues to be the predominant lifestyle for adults.

> **KEY TO UNDERSTANDING**
>
> America is a "couples-oriented" culture which puts an inordinate amount of stress on single people to get married.

Stress Associated with Being Single

In many cases the stress associated with being single has more to do with the attitudes and reactions of others than with the single person's own perceptions. Cavanaugh[6] reports that the two most stressful issues for single people are how to handle dating and others' expectations that they will marry.

Some of the potentially stressful dating issues that crop up are how to deal with role expectations, how to handle sexual involvement, how to date without getting too serious too fast, and how to initiate close friendships without coming on too strong.[6]

A key to understanding singles stress is realizing that America is a "couples-oriented" society that puts a premium on adults interacting socially as part of a heterosexual couple. Most Americans assume that everyone expects to get married some day. This puts an inordinate amount of pressure on single people, especially when friends and associates are always trying to "fix them up." Singles typically find themselves at times having to defend their position. Singles also tend to be ostracized from old friendships as their friends marry and raise families. Gay single people face similar pressures to settle down in a relationship, often having to defend their single lifestyles to family and friends.

Cohabitation

Cohabitation is defined as the relationship between two members of the opposite gender who live together but are

> **cohabitation** a shared living arrangement between two unmarried romantic partners

not married. Unmarried couples who live together are not much different from married couples. They share, argue, and make decisions about money, sex, and household labor.

The reasons for living together but not marrying are many and varied, but generally there are three forms of cohabitation: casual or temporary involvement, preparation or testing for marriage, and a substitution for or alternative to marriage.[40]

Cohabiting households, or households with unmarried partners, grew substantially after the 1970s. In 2000, there were 3.8 million households that were classified as unmarried-partner households, representing 3.7 percent of all households in the United States. These numbers represent more than 3 million unmarried couples (6 million individuals). This count may underrepresent the true incidence since only heads of household are counted by the census and respondents may be reluctant to classify themselves as cohabitors in a personal interview.[53] Over 6 million people in America cohabit. The age breakdown for cohabitors is as follows:

	Gender	
Age	**Men (%)**	**Women (%)**
15–24-year-olds	15	22
25–34-year-olds	39	37
35–44-year-olds	22	23
45 and over	24	18

The majority of cohabiting relationships are short-lived, and the partners either separate or marry.[53]

Stress Associated with Cohabitation

The stresses associated with cohabitation are similar to those experienced by married individuals and generally revolve around four issues: unrealistic expectations, communication problems, money, and sex.

Cohabitors may experience a unique type of stress associated with others' perceptions and expectations of their relationship. Disapproval from parents is a common problem among cohabitors. Some parents think it's morally wrong to cohabit. Other parents expect those living together to be taking the first step toward marriage, an assumption that is not always valid.

Another type of stress is lack of recognition of the bond by law. Cohabitors often have a difficult time concerning property ownership and rights of survivorship involving the death of one of the parties. Unless the couple has an up-to-date will, the survivor has no clearly established property rights. These are similar stressors for gay couples; their situation is like that of cohabitors except that they are of the same gender.

For most Americans, marriage is something they believe in.

Marriage and Long-Term Gay and Lesbian Relationships

While Americans have been delaying marriage and the overall percentage of men and women who marry has dropped since 1970, as fig. 14-1 illustrates, the vast majority of Americans marry.

Unquestionably, most Americans want to marry although they are postponing it longer than in the past. Although an integral part of most cultures, marriage takes on many forms and assumes many different purposes throughout the world. In America, most people take the following issues for granted concerning marriage: a legal bond, permanence, heterosexuality, sexual exclusivity, emotional exclusivity, and monogamy.[8]

Also, most Americans expect more from marriage than do those in many other cultures. A key to understanding this is to realize that historically marriages were intended to provide a stable economic unit in which to raise children. Today most Americans expect marriage to fulfill their social, emotional, financial, and sexual needs.[8]

What people find when they do marry is that many of these expectations are unrealistic and cannot be fully realized. This can lead to frustration, disillusionment, separation, and divorce. What they also find is that marriage is hard work. Even under the best of circumstances and with a good match in a partner, successful marriage requires continual assessment, communication, commitment, willingness to change, and hard work (see Assess Yourself 14-2, "Relationship Contract").

The large majority of research regarding relationships relates to married heterosexuals. Comparatively

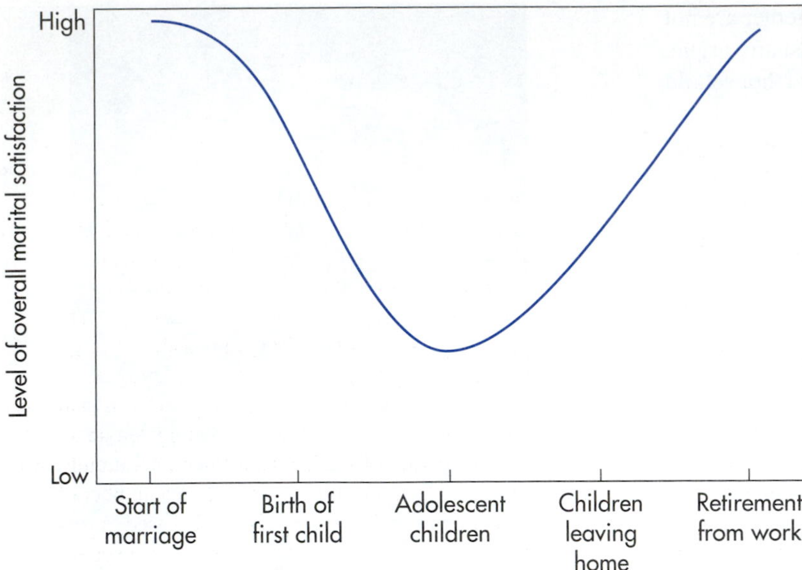

Figure 14-2
The Berry and Williams scale[3] shows marital satisfaction across adulthood. However, not all couples show a significant decline in satisfaction.

little has been written regarding long-term gay and lesbian relationships. In a prospective study of sixty-five gay and forty-seven lesbian long-term relationships, Kurdak[33] found that the length of the relationship was a predictor of satisfaction. Gay and lesbian subjects in relationships longer than eight years reported greater satisfaction than did subjects in relationships of shorter length. Kurdak[33] also found that lesbian couples reported higher levels of relationship satisfaction than gays did. Lippman[36] found that as homosexuals aged, those in close, committed relationships, were the happiest. Variables related to happiness in relationships, such as commitment, companionship, intimacy, and fulfillment of needs, were the same for homosexual and heterosexual couples.

The stereotypical picture of old age for gay men and women is that of unhappiness, loneliness, and aloneness. In actuality it is quite the opposite. As a rule homosexual men and women may be better prepared for the demands and challenges of old age than are many traditional heterosexual couples. Traditional heterosexual marriages are much more likely, because of stereotypical male and female gender roles, to be built on dependency. In traditional heterosexual relationships, husbands rely on wives for certain activities (cooking, cleaning, child care, etc.) and wives are more dependent on husbands for others (wage earning, long-term financial security, heavy household work, etc.). Gay and lesbian relationships are, out of necessity, more egalitarian. Each partner has been socialized to be self-reliant since there are no social norms for gay male or female relationship roles. The absence of hard and fast gender role stereotypes forces homosexual men and women to communicate more effectively and be more flexible and creative in meeting relationship needs.[32] Masters and Johnson[40] found gay men and women more willing to communicate, experiment, and be attentive to detail in their sexual behavior.

The Developmental Course of Marriage

Berry and Williams[3] have proposed a developmental model of marriage across adulthood (fig. 14-2).

In the early, honeymoon phase, marriage is at its most intense. The partners spend considerable time together, talking, sharing interests and leisure, establishing their roles within the relationship, arguing and making up. As the honeymoon phase begins to wind down, the couple settles into a routine. The intensity of the honeymoon phase diminishes and, along with that, marital satisfaction. A big reason for this is the birth of children. Children result in decreased time available for the spouses and the relationship.

Marital happiness reaches rock bottom during the midlife phase of the relationship, which also coincides with adolescence in the couple's children. A myriad of problems ranging from financial considerations to coping with teenagers to changing roles for husband and wife contribute to this (see Diverse Perspectives 14-1, "Midlife Crisis or Middle-Age Myth?").

Happiness begins to rebound with the sending off of adult children. Along with children moving out, there is a freeing up of time and money. The couple finds they have the time, money, and privacy to reestablish the things in their relationship that provide pleasure as well as to investigate new things together.

Marital happiness continues to rise in the later adult years and carries over into retirement. Depending on a number of factors, ranging from health to retirement income, the couple continues to enjoy their freedom and in some cases relationships with their children's families and their grandchildren.[6]

Table 14-1 presents a well-known and frequently cited theory of the stages of family life cycle.[12]

Duvall's stage 8, the postparental years, generally coincides with late adulthood and old age. Many events

DIVERSE PERSPECTIVES 14-1

Midlife Crisis or Middle-Age Myth?

You've heard the story. Happy, successful 45-year-old businessman quits his job, leaves his wife and kids, and runs off to Tahiti with his 25-year-old secretary. Or maybe its the 40-year-old mother of two facing the "empty nest" who jumps into her convertible with her 20-year-old former tennis instructor and heads west into the sunset in a torrid blaze of passionate sex.

These and other "midlife crises" that have been popularized by the print and film media make for interesting stories and pose a romantic solution to many of life's more difficult issues that confront us when we hit "middle age." In real life, however, relatively few people experience such catastrophic, turn-everything-upside-down changes. New information, fueled by long-term research on aging, is showing that middle age is the very best time of life. It is a developmental stage unlike most others, for it is not particularly tied to changes in the body such as those of early childhood, adolescence, and old age. Midlife is characterized more by psychological adaptations and is very "reality-based."

By midlife many of the stressful questions that faced us as young adults are answered: Will anyone ever love me? Will this marriage work out? Will I ever find a job? What kind of lifestyle can I afford to lead? By midlife most people have found love. If they are married, they are more likely to stay married (the overwhelming number of divorces occur within the first six to eight years of marriage). They have settled into a job and have a pretty good idea of where they are headed (most professionals who are going to "make it" have done so by this time). They have a good sense of their earning capacity and therefore can gauge the kind of lifestyle they can look forward to.

Whereas the myth of midlife is that this is a period characterized by unrest, discomfort, dissatisfaction, and upheaval, the reality is that this is a very comfortable, satisfying time. It is a time to enjoy the rewards of ten to twenty years of scuffling. It's a time to not have to push as hard at work, a time to enjoy getting off a little early to watch your kid's Little League game. It's a time to focus on vacations and social get-togethers, to take a class in painting, or to improve your backhand. It's a time to lighten up a little.

Midlife is a period of gradual adjustment, not tumultuous change. It gradually unfolds and is based on a number of adjustments to reality. For most people it is based in reality, not fantasy. Those most likely to experience a true crisis (about 5 percent) are people who, for the most part, have experienced similar crises in all the developmental stages of their lives. Their lives are based on unrealistic (therefore unrealized) notions and expectations. One of the major criticisms of earlier "studies" of midlife is that they were based on small numbers of case studies of atypical populations (mostly affluent, professional, and white). In the recent, cross-sectional studies of more representative samples of Americans, researchers have found that the average person's midlife adjustment is based on reality. Gradually, people adjust their expectations to fit the reality of their lives. By the time they settle into midlife, they have learned to make the best of what they have and are not constantly longing for (and thereby tempted by) things that realistically are beyond their reach.

From Gallagher, W. (1993). *The Atlantic,* 271(5), pp. 51–63;[18] Harris, P. & Lyon, D. (1990). *Reader's Digest,* 136(818), p. 108;[24] Forrest, D. (1992). *Canadian Business,* 65(9), pp. 96–100.[16]

Table 14-1 Duvall's Family Life Cycle

Stage 1.	Establishment (newly married, childless)
Stage 2.	New parents (infant to 3 years)
Stage 3.	Preschool family (oldest child 3 to 6 years, possibly younger siblings)
Stage 4.	School-age family (oldest child 6 to 12 years, possibly younger siblings)
Stage 5.	Family with adolescent (oldest child 13 to 19 years, possibly younger siblings)
Stage 6.	Family with young adult (oldest child 20, until first child leaves home)
Stage 7.	Family as launching center (from departure of first child to departure of last child)
Stage 8.	Postparental family (after all children have left home)

From Cart, C.S. (1994). *The Relatives of Aging.* (4th ed.). Needham Heights: Mass. Allyn & Bacon.

blend during this time, such as menopause and other physiological changes of aging, retirement, older children leaving the nest, and the emergence of grandchildren, just to name a few. Although often characterized negatively as a time of loss and failed health, this stage is also a very dynamic period in which new freedom, psychological and social stability, and wisdom can be a springboard to increased happiness for couples.

Most older couples today have grown old together. The average couple can expect at least fifteen years after the last child leaves. This is quite different from the situation at the turn of the century, when half of all marriages were affected by the death of one of the spouses before the last child left the house.[29]

In a long-term study of seventeen happily married couples, Weishaus and Field[58] found that the most significant factor related to marital satisfaction was their ability to adapt to change and "roll with the punches." These couples had the ability to adapt to changing circumstances that might normally be interpreted as stressful and potentially damaging to the relationship. A serious illness, for instance, might be viewed as an opportunity for increased caring and closeness rather than anger and alienation.

In one of the most extensive, long-term prospective studies of male homosexuals to date, McWhirter and Mattison[42] followed 156 gay couples for over twenty years. Subjects were gay couples who had been together for approximately nine years before enrolling in the study. McWhirter and Mattison found that gay relationships, like their heterosexual counterparts, went through a series of stages. Stage one, the "blending stage," occurred in the first year of the relationship. As with heterosexual couples, this year was characterized by the highest levels of sexual activity, strong love and passion, and a blending of personal interests. Stage two, the "nesting stage," occurred during years 2 and 3 and emphasized building the relationship and starting a home together. Ambivalence, problems, and doubts about the relationship were most likely to begin to surface at this stage. Stage three, the "maintaining stage," was characterized by a decline in the passion and frequency of sexual activity and an emphasis on conflict resolution and reassertion of some of the individuality subverted during the initial stages of the relationship. Stage four, the "building stage," occupied years 6 through 10 and was marked by increased personal productivity and independence but also an enhanced collaboration and developing sense of trust and dependability between partners. Stage five, from years 11 to 20, was labeled the "releasing stage." This stage was characterized by the merging of money and other assets and beginning to take each other for granted. Sexual activity dropped off noticeably in this stage. The final stage, "renewing," extended beyond twenty years together and was marked by personal security and a restored sense of partnership based on remembering shared experiences and good times together.

Stress Associated with Marriage and Long-Term Gay and Lesbian Relationships

As we've touched upon, there are many potential sources of stress over the lifetime of a marriage, ranging from the loss of initial sexual passion to economic instability in retirement. There are six major sources of relationship stress: unrealistic expectations, communication problems, money, sex, care of children, and care of elderly parents.

Unrealistic Expectations

Many relationships are doomed from the start because they are based on a set of unrealistic expectations that can never be fulfilled. As we found in chapter 13, many unrealistic expectations in relationships are due to an immature or romantic perception of relationships. A key to understanding this is realizing that romantic love, unlike consummate love, is based on unrealistic perceptions of never-ending bliss, sexual passion, happiness, lack of arguing, and beauty. The harsh reality is that bliss turns to boredom and aggravation, passion turns to comfort, happiness will give way to periods of sadness, arguments will sometimes be necessary to work out problems, and your spouse is not very attractive at 6:00 A.M. before he shaves or she fixes her hair.

Communication Problems

Communication problems can sabotage any relationship. They are usually related to the inability to talk about problems or misunderstandings in the relationship. Sometimes they have their root in a lack of assertiveness where one partner is unable to stand up for himself or herself or where both are unable to do that. Communication problems can also arise when partners are unable to express positive and constructive thoughts and feelings (see Stress Buster Tips: "Fighting Fairly"). Many people are raised in an environment where communication seems to revolve around problems and the expression of negative emotions.

Stress Buster Tips

Fighting Fairly

- Start your sentences with *I,* not *you.* Instead of attacking with a statement such as "You're jealous and immature," say "I feel hurt when you quiz me about my old relationships."
- Make sure you are arguing about the right issue. Are you angry simply because your partner is never on time or because you do not seem to be the top priority?
- Do not embarrass each other by fighting in front of others.
- Even if you are alone, do not attack each other so viciously that one of you is backed into a corner.
- Avoid generalizations such as "You always interrupt me."
- Be fair. Whenever there is a cheap shot, one of you should stop the fighting by crying "Foul!"
- Focus on the issue at hand.
- Think before you open your mouth. Taking a few deep breaths will give you a chance to weigh your words.
- Learn to listen. Rather than thinking about what you will say next, tune in to your partner's words, gestures, or expression.
- If you cannot come to terms on a particular issue, agree to disagree or to keep talking about your differences in the future.

From Hales, D. (2001). *An Invitation to Health.* Pacific Grove, CA: Wadsworth.[23]

Relationships can whither from a lack of expression of caring, tenderness, compassion, and recognition of worth.

Money Problems

Money, or, more significantly, what money means to each partner, is a major source of stress in long-term relationships. Unless the partners have similar feelings about money, money can be a chronic source of stress in the relationship. For instance, if one partner views money as relatively unimportant and only a means to obtaining material goods necessary for survival and the other perceives money as being very important and a ticket to a better life, higher status, and possession of greater luxury, this couple is in trouble. Their core values concerning money are completely opposite.

The perception of credit is another example. One person may view credit as a fundamental economic necessity and have no problem with having outstanding balances on credit cards and personal loans and home-equity lines. The other may not even be comfortable with a mortgage or a car loan and may prefer to delay all purchases until they can be paid for in cash.

Gender-role stereotyping can also be a source of money stress if one partner has traditional expectations about gender roles concerning work and money and the other does not.

Sexual Problems

Sexual problems can spring from the first two problems in long-term relationships: unrealistic expectations and poor communication. Unrealistic expectations about sex within the marriage can lead to dissatisfaction. Further, if one is unable or unwilling to communicate about sexual concerns and problems, they invariably worsen and become a source of stress within the relationship.

Sexual incompatibility is a major source of stress and a factor in the dissolution of relationships. Research indicates that many couples who cohabit in preparation for marriage do so in an effort to gauge sexual compatibility before entering into marital relationships.[40]

Sexual activity changes once people leave the single life and either cohabit or marry. It no longer is as frantic or segmented from the rest of their lives as it was when the partners lived separately. While sexual pleasure is not sacrificed, sex becomes more integrated into the ebb and flow of the couple's life. It is balanced with other needs and responsibilities, which is an important developmental task in this stage of the relationship.[40] Those who cannot adjust to this change become sexually dissatisfied and may turn to extramarital sex, counseling, or divorce.

The frequency of sexual intercourse declines as relationships age (Table 14-2). Peak sexual activity occurs within the first year of marriage and then begins to drop off. The average frequency for marital coitus is two to three times a week for couples in their twenties and thirties, a frequency that gradually declines with increasing age.[8]

Table 14-2 Frequency of Marital Intercourse

	Number of Couples Surveyed	Mean Frequency of Intercourse per Month
First year	12	14.8
Second year	10	12.2
Third year	19	11.9
Fourth year	7	9.0
Fifth year	18	9.7
Sixth year	8	6.3

From Masters, et al. *Human sexuality.* (4th ed.). Published by Allyn and Bacon, Boston, MA. Copyright © 1992 by Pearson Education. Reprint by permission of the publisher.

Married couples who have fun and are spontaneous can keep sex in their relationship.

The frequency of sexual relations is highly correlated with marital satisfaction. Blumstein and Schwartz[4] found that nine of ten married couples who were having sex three or more times a week reported satisfaction with their relationships. On the other hand, only 50 percent of couples having sex one to four times a month were satisfied with their relationships. Physiologically, sex doesn't necessarily get better or worse as we age, it just gets different. Most men and women experience very little change during their thirties and early forties. Women begin to experience noticeable changes in sexual response associated with menopause. About 25 percent of women go through menopause before age 45, 50 percent from 45 to 50, and the remaining 25 percent after age 50.[29]

Changes in sexual physiology are less noticeable among most men in their forties and fifties. Although sperm production slows down after forty, it continues into the eighties and nineties. Similarly, though male sexual hormone levels decline gradually after age 55, most men have no noticeable drop-off in sexual desire. About 5 percent of men over sixty experience a syndrome called the *climacteric,* which produces symptoms similar in nature to those of menopause.[40]

Essentially, the physiological changes associated with aging result in a gradual slowing down of sexual response: It takes longer to become fully aroused. There is also a slight lessening of the intensity of sexual response; the contractions associated with orgasm are slightly less intense. These changes, however, are more than offset by increased comfort about sexuality, no fear of pregnancy, familiarity with one's partner, and the drawing out of the sex act.

Care of Children

Children can be a major source of sexual stress for adults. Whether the partners are married or cohabiting, straight or gay, children change the couple's established patterns of interaction. Parenthood contributes to adult stress in several different ways. Parenting requires a tremendous amount of time at every stage of child development. Children decrease, by up to half, the amount of time partners have for shared activities.[6] The demands children impose on their parents cut into the time parents have for themselves individually and for their spouse or lover.

The specific demands change, but the time requirement remains. Newborns require constant supervision. Even when parents are sleeping, they sleep lightly, ready to react to their children's cries for help in the night. Young children need help with everything from getting washed and dressed to cutting the food on their plates. Older children need parents to spend time helping them with everything from doing their homework to getting them safely to and from friends' houses. Parents of adolescents spend countless hours car-pooling their kids all over the place, while parents of older teens stay up to all hours of the night waiting for their teenager's safe return of themselves and the family car.

Besides the stress associated with the sheer time demands of children, children's needs (time and otherwise) are unpredictable. From early-morning feedings of babies, to car-pooling children, to waiting for an adolescent to return home from a date, parents must bear unpredictable demands on their time, temperament, and sexual desire.

Care of Elderly Parents

The last stress associated with marriage, although it can happen to all adults, is care of aging parents. Daughters are over three times more likely than sons to be the primary caretaker of elderly parents.[6] In many cases, care involves making the decision whether to take the aging parent in to live with the middle-aged child, who may have a family. It's a particularly hard choice because after living apart for many years both the child and the parent would prefer to remain alone.

Cavanaugh cites two main sources of stress concerning caring for aging parents: Adult children often have a hard time coping with their parents' deteriorating state of mental functioning, and many adult children find the caring role confining. In many cases caring for a parent occurs after years of raising their own children. If caring for a parent severely restricts their newfound freedom, middle-age children can become very resentful. This can be even more stressful for single children used to years of total freedom and mobility.

Homosexual men and women may be better prepared for dealing with relationship stressors such as the death of their partner and retirement because of better planning throughout the relationship. Many homosexuals have planned for their own financial support and have consciously developed supportive social networks. They also may be more prepared to cope with hardship, having lived a life of adversity as a member of a stigmatized group.[9] This combination of attitude, social and financial resources, and self-reliance may help gay men and women cope with the demands of aging. Berger[2] found that older homosexual men match or exceed the general population in measures of life satisfaction.

Divorce

Not all marriages progress completely through the Berry and Williams phases (fig. 14-2).[3] More than half of all first marriages end in divorce.[8] Although raw numbers are misleading when interpreting divorce statistics, the divorce rate (which examines both numbers of divorces and numbers of marriages), has been on the rise over the last twenty years, reaching a high of 5.3 divorces per 1,000 residents in 1981 and declining to a rate of 4.0 per 1,000 in 2001.[54]

Most people marry with the hope that the relationship will last forever. Divorce therefore often represents a loss of this hope. This often accompanies the loss of economic status (particularly for low- and middle-income women), lifestyle, and the security of familiarity, friends, and sometimes children.[8]

A key to understanding the psychological effects of divorce is to compare it to the grieving process of those who have experienced the death of a loved one. There is initial shock ("This can't be happening to me"), followed by disorganization ("Everything feels like it's turned upside down"). Volatile emotions and guilt ("It's my fault") usually follow. Loneliness also often accompanies

KEY TO UNDERSTANDING

The grieving associated with divorce is similar to that of those experiencing the death of a loved one.

divorce. Finally, after several months to a year, these feelings are replaced by a sense of relief and acceptance.[8]

This grieving process leads to a healing, a cleansing of wounds which allows the divorced person to move on with his or her life and start over. If, after several months to a year, the divorced person hasn't gotten over the divorce and begun to accept what has happened, counseling and psychotherapy may be needed.[8]

Stress Associated with Divorce

Coping with divorce entails a grieving process, which is stressful. The intensity and duration of this stress, however, vary and in most cases are less stressful than remaining in the marriage. This is especially so in childless marriages in which both spouses return to work and the kind of lifestyle that preceded the marriage. Many states have adopted no-fault divorce statutes that facilitate separation and property division. In these divorces alimony is rarely granted, especially if both spouses have nearly equal wealth and earning potential.

In divorces involving children, issues such as custody, child care, and child support can be formidable stressors. Even under the most amicable no-fault divorces involving joint custody, the task of raising children can be daunting for divorced parents. Two households now have to be maintained, sometimes (especially if there are very young children involved) still on one income. Women, especially of low and middle income, usually wind up having a reduced standard of living and lifestyle after divorce, while men seem to fare better. In traditional relationships the father's job provided the bulk of income for the family, and newly divorced mothers are either just entering the workforce or returning to lower-paying jobs than their husbands have while trying to maintain the same standard of living for themselves and their children.

Under optimal circumstances, a fair and equitable amount of child support and alimony minimizes the stress associated with this adjustment and allows the woman to provide for the needs of the family. Alimony laws in most states were revised after the 1979 *Orr v. Orr* Supreme Court case, which essentially ended the practice of specifying the gender of the spouse. Until that time, most states had language in their alimony statutes that automatically assigned payment to wives but disallowed money for husbands. From that point on, alimony laws were based on need rather than gender.[59] Most current alimony legislation is designed to protect the "economically dependent spouse" until that person is able to secure gainful employment. Alimony awards take into account such factors as financial needs and resources, age and physical condition, factors contributing to the breakup, duration of the marriage, contributions to the marriage (financial and otherwise), standard of living established during the marriage, the ability to pay, and the length of time necessary to obtain the training and education necessary for suitable employment.[10]

In less than optimal situations, fathers fail to pay child support and alimony, creating stress for the former wife and children, who wonder where the money will come from to meet expenses. Lengthy and frequent litigation can provide further stress.

Besides financial stress, divorce involving children creates a whole new dimension of stress associated with relationships between the children and the spouse who is no longer present. Visitation, decision making about a variety of child-rearing issues, and parents' new partners are just a few of the many potential stressors that exist.

In many cases, remarriage involves a merging of families, where children and family members of one spouse blend with those of the other to form a new, "blended" family. Adjusting to step-parents and half-siblings can be either a formidable challenge or a stressor for children. Blended families pose a unique challenge as they combine all the usual components of family life and child rearing with the merging of two family units, each with its own history, lifestyle, habits, and patterns of interaction. It takes time for each family to adjust and adapt to the new living situation. Parents and children have to decide how to merge preexisting patterns and expectations of family life with new standards for their new family. Much of the success of this process will depend on the interpersonal skills and resources each family brings to the new relationship and their desire to work things out as they create a new unit.

AGING AND CHANGING HEALTH STATUS

While the media decry the state of health in America, subjecting adults to a string of bad news interrupted by commercials for everything from laxatives, to medications, to enhanced sexual response, the actual health status of Americans is far from dismal. In his annual report to the nation, *Health, United States, 2002,* the secretary for health and human services, Tommy G. Thompson, reported that America's health has changed dramatically for the better. Much of this change can be attributed to the lifestyle changes made by average Americans.[55]

In 2000, American men and women enjoyed the longest life expectancy in U.S. history: almost seventy-seven years. Life expectancy for men was seventy-four years, and for women it was almost eighty years. Men and women who reach age 65 now can expect to live to ages 81 and 84, respectively. A century ago life expectancy was forty-eight years for men and fifty-one years for women. The gap in life expectancy for blacks and whites narrowed by a full year during the 1990s (down from a seven-year difference to six years). Infant mortality (the number of deaths before the first birthday) hit a record low of 6.9 deaths per 1,000 live births in 2000, down from 7.1 the year before and down 75 percent

Table 14-3 Chronic Health Problems Causing Limited Activity in Men and Women Age 65 Plus

Rank	Men (65+ years of age)	Women (65+ years of age)
1	Diseases of the heart	Arthritis
2	Arthritis	Diseases of the heart
3	High blood pressure	High blood pressure
4	Emphysema	Diabetes
5	Arteriosclerosis	Orthopedic impairment—lower back
6	Visual impairment	Visual impairment
7	Diabetes	Arteriosclerosis
8	Orthopedic impairment—lower extremity	Orthopedic impairment—lower extremity
9	Cerebrovascular disease	Other musculoskeletal disorders
10	Paralysis	Cerebrovascular disease
11	Other musculoskeletal disorders	Paralysis
12	Orthopedic impairment—lower back	Cancer

From Payne, W. & Hahn, D. (2002). *Understanding your health*. St. Louis: McGraw-Hill.[47]

since 1950. Infectious disease rates have declined. The incidence of syphilis is at the lowest rate since reporting began in 1941 (down to 2.2 cases per 100,000 people). Many public health experts have reported that AIDS, a major killer in the 1980s, is at its lowest rates in a decade and that AIDS deaths have plummeted since the introduction of many new antiviral drugs in the 1990s. Fewer Americans smoke now than at any time in the last fifty years. In 1965, about 40 percent of all Americans smoked. In 2000, only 23 percent of the population smoked.

While it is clear that too many Americans still smoke and that a large proportion of us are overweight and don't exercise enough, the rates of major killers such as cancer, cardiovascular diseases, stroke, and unintentional injuries have declined markedly in the last decade.[55]

Table 14-4 Ten Leading Causes of Death in the United States

Heart disease: 699,697
Cancer: 553,251
Stroke: 163,601
Chronic lower respiratory disease: 123,974
Accidents: 97,707
Diabetes: 71,252
Pneumonia/influenza: 62,123
Alzheimer's disease: 53,679
Nephritis, nephrotic syndrome, and nephrosis: 39,661
Septicemia: 32,275

Source: *National Vital Statistics Report*.[54]

Healthy Aging and Premature Disability and Death

Aging is a highly variable and little understood phenomenon. While no one knows why we age, we do know a lot about how to delay the effects of the aging process and the chronic diseases that diminish the quality of our lives and lead to premature disability and death. Most of the chronic diseases and leading causes of death listed in Tables 14-3 and 14-4 are directly related to lifestyle. Throughout this book we have discussed reorganize as a way to create a healthy lifestyle. Besides improving your day-to-day quality of life, reorganize strategies are the foundation of living a longer, healthier life. The benefits of daily physical activity, sensible eating, strong social support systems, lifelong learning, and a host of other reorganize strategies are the basis of healthy aging.

Changing Health Status as a Source of Stress

Poor health is cited as a reason for early (forced) retirement and for perceiving retirement as stressful.[6] Failing health can be a source of stress in itself as it can quash retirees' plans for travel, entertainment, and relaxation. Poor health can also contribute to stress by draining income to pay for health care. Logue[37] found that minorities and less-educated whites suffer disproportionately from long-term disability. Additionally, lower socioeconomic status is related to a higher level of long-term disability and a decreased quality of life in old age and retirement. Minorities and less-educated whites also are disproportionately represented at the lower end of the socioeconomic scale.[37]

Thinking about Our Own Mortality

We all must die. As cold and cruel as those four words sound, they are nevertheless true. The meaning of death varies for people. For some, it is a source of great anxiety, while others are less fearful and more accepting of it. Some of the variables that seem to be related to fear of death are pain, body malfunction, humiliation, rejection, nonbeing, punishment, interruption of goals, and negative impact on survivors.[6] In a sense what these variables represent are threats to our well-being, to continuing life as we know it and enjoy it.

Studies differ about the influence of gender on death anxiety. Some research indicates that women score higher than men on measures of death anxiety. Other studies do not support this.[6] In studies that found differences between the way men and women perceived death, researchers found that the women tended to view death more emotionally while men looked at it in more cognitive terms. Although this seems to indicate that because women view death more emotionally, they would have a harder time accepting it, Kalish[27] found that the opposite is true. Although women become more emotionally aroused by the prospect of their own death, they also demonstrate higher levels of acceptance of their demise than men do.

Findings concerning racial differences in death anxiety are mixed. Bengston, Cuellar, and Rage[1] found no significant differences in death anxiety among African Americans, Mexican Americans and whites. Myers, Wass, and Murphey,[45] however, found that elderly African Americans had a higher death anxiety than white subjects. Bengston, Cuellar, and Rage[1] also found that although there were no differences concerning death anxiety, of the three groups studied, African Americans were most likely to expect to live a longer life.

Some of the differences in death anxiety between blacks and whites can be attributed to the influence of religion, social support, and kinship ties.[30] African Americans were found to have more extensive kinship ties with nuclear and extended families and greater levels of social support than whites. As we discussed in chapter 4, a high level of social support is related to physical and mental health and improved outcomes in treating illnesses.

Social support and kinship networks are so strong within the African-American community that they have been recognized by gerontologists, social service providers, and government officials as major resources available to the black elderly. Gratton and Wilson[20] warn that the strength of the African American community in meeting the needs of their elderly should not be used as an excuse to cut funding for programs that target this population.

The black church has long been a source of strength in African-American communities. Religion and church involvement are major threads binding black families and the African-American community together and are sources of strength in troubled times. In many African-American communities, life revolves around church activities. The church is a rallying point for everything from political activism to social support. Indeed, even in urban America, the church is much more of a focal point for African Americans than for whites.

This relationship to the church is especially important in aging. There has been much research documenting the relationship between religion and lowered death anxiety. There are multiple dimensions to religion, such as belief in an afterlife, prayer, church attendance, and participation in fellowship activities. Some research suggests that church attendance and participation are related to lower death anxiety while belief in an afterlife is not.[27]

Religion and church attendance provide a forum for the practice of faith and spirituality. As was discussed in chapter 4, one's social and spiritual life are significantly related to reduced stress and increased health. Faith and spirituality are also related to death anxiety. Faith and spirituality provide help in understanding the meaning of one's life and the inevitability of death. Faith and spirituality also assist people in understanding, coping with, and bouncing back from personal crises and loss. Reed,[50] in studying 300 terminally ill patients, found spirituality and faith positively related to low death fear, positive death perspectives, and better emotional adjustment. Little is known about the relationship between the more secular ways of defining spirituality discussed in chapter 4 and death anxiety.

Age is another demographic variable that is related to the way we view death. Even though the elderly think about death more than does any other age group, they generally are less fearful and more accepting of it.[6] Kalish[28] provides several explanations for this: They have completed the most important tasks in their lives and therefore don't feel they haven't had the time to accomplish the things they need to do; they have suffered from more chronic diseases, realize they are unlikely to improve, and thus view death with some relief; they have already lost many of their friends and loved ones; and they have already spent a great amount of time thinking about death.

Widowhood

Widowhood can occur at any time during a marriage but is much more likely to occur later in life. Widowhood is more common for women; over half of all women over 65 are widows, while just 15 percent of men at that age are widowers. This is due primarily to two reasons: Men have shorter life expectancies than women, and women tend to marry men older than themselves.[5] Consequently, most American married women can expect to live for ten to twelve years as a widow if they choose not to remarry.[6]

Widowhood can be stressful in a number of ways besides the ending of a partnership. Our society does not have very well-defined social roles for widowed people (see Diverse Perspectives 14-2, "Lopata's Widows"). Widowed people therefore are very often left alone by family and friends who don't know how to respond to them. Widowed individuals also may feel awkward as single people trying to fit into their previously coupled world.[6]

Men are generally older when they become widowed. Many people feel that men are more stressed by the death of their wives than women are by the loss of their

DIVERSE PERSPECTIVES 14-2

Lopata's Widows

Not all women find widowhood equally stressful or stressful at all. Lopata[38] (1973, 1975), in studying over 300 widows in Chicago, found six different behavior patterns that women employed following the deaths of their husbands:

1. "Liberated wives" were able to grieve the loss of their spouse and move on to live full, productive lives.
2. "Merry widows" went on to live lives that were fun filled and involved dating and enjoying various forms of entertainment.
3. "Working widows" continued on in their careers or took on a new job.
4. "Widows' widows" continued to live alone, were independent, and primarily enjoyed the company of other widows.
5. "Traditional widows" moved in with their children and took an active role in the lives of their grandchildren.
6. "Grieving widows" were not able to work through their loss and willingly isolated themselves from others.

Source: Lopata, H.Z. (1973). *Widowhood in an American City.*[38]

husbands. Cavanaugh[6] speculates that this may be due to several issues: the way men are raised, the fact that a wife is usually a man's only close confidant, the difficulty most men have in living alone since often they can't cook or clean, and the tendency of most men to be more socially isolated than women.

Loss, Grief, and Bereavement Stress

Researchers have long noticed an association between human loss, grief bereavement, and illness. For over 2,000 years physicians and philosophers have recognized that the strong emotions that follow loss are the precursors to physical and mental illness.[22] **Bereavement** is a form of depression with anxiety and is a common reaction to the loss of a loved one. Loss of a loved one is significantly related to increased stress and illness.

In studies involving patients with a variety of diseases ranging from cancer to respiratory and cardiovascular disease, a common thread was the loss of a loved one. This loss lead to feelings of helplessness, hopelessness, and a sense of emptiness in one's life.[22]

Cohen and Syme[7] studied 4,500 adults over age 45 who lost a spouse to premature death. Their study became known as the "broken heart" study because they found that nearly 40 percent of the surviving spouses died of heart problems during the six months after the death of their spouses. This percentage of deaths steadily dropped after this time and returned to that of the control group after five years. Other studies have confirmed these findings and have indicated that one of the factors that return the risk of death to a normal rate is remarriage of the surviving spouse.[22]

Grief and Stress

Grief is the nearly universal pattern of physical and emotional responses to bereavement separation and loss. Grief is a natural process, essential to healing from the pain of loss as well as coming to terms with terminal illness. Kubler-Ross[31] identified six stages of grief:

1. Denial–disbelieving that the loss has occurred
2. Anger–strong displeasure over the loss, which could be directed at anyone or anything
3. Bargaining–trying to bargain with God or oneself ("I'll change and be like . . .") to reverse the loss
4. Depression–intense sorrow over the loss
5. Acceptance–accepting the inevitable
6. Hope–faith in the future

One must work through each of the stages of grief in order to heal after a loss. The grieving process cannot be rushed. The average amount of time it takes to grieve after a loss ranges from eighteen to twenty-four months, but the process can last for years.[22] A key to understanding grief is realizing that people vary in the amount of time they need to recover fully from the loss of a loved one. Trying to rush the grieving process can result in not thoroughly working through the individual stages. Stress Buster Tips: Easing the Grieving Process can help you ease the pain associated with grieving.

In a study of grief and loss among those in nontraditional relationships (extramarital affairs, cohabitation, and homosexual relationships), Doka[11] found that the normal stages of grief are compounded by the nontraditional nature of the relationships studied. In homosexual and other relationships, conflicting needs compound the healing process of grief. A need to declare and demonstrate one's sorrow and affection for the loved one is tempered by a need to maintain secrecy and fear of disclosure of the relationship. The need for social support and to grieve with the other mourners is countered by a sense of social isolation.

Among homosexual couples who are out and are not maintaining a secret relationship, these compounding factors are minimized. Quam and Whitford[49] found that being active in the gay community helps gay couples

bereavement a form of depression with anxiety that is a common reaction to the loss of a loved one

grief the nearly universal pattern of physical and emotional responses to bereavement

Stress Buster Tips

Easing the Grieving Process

Realizing that there is no single guaranteed formula for helping the bereaved, friends and caregivers can help by doing some or all of the following:

- Make few demands on the bereaved; allow him or her to grieve.
- Help with the household tasks.
- Recognize that the bereaved person may vent anguish and anger and that some if it may be directed at you.
- Recognize that the bereaved person has painful and difficult tasks to complete; mourning cannot be rushed or avoided.
- Do not be afraid to talk about the deceased person; this lets the bereaved know that you care for the deceased.
- Express your own genuine feelings of sadness but avoid pity. Speak from the heart.
- Reassure the bereaved person that the intensity of his or her emotion is very natural.
- Advise the bereaved to get additional help if you suspect continuing major emotional or physical distress.
- Keep in regular contact with the bereaved; let him or her know that you continue to care.

From Payne, W. & Hahn, D. (2002). *Understanding your health.* St. Louis: McGraw-Hill.[47]

KEY TO UNDERSTANDING

People vary in the amount of time they need to grieve over the loss of loved ones.

develop social support networks that enable them to cope more effectively with a variety of issues associated with grief and, for that matter, with aging.

Funerals and memorial services provide a valuable step in the griving process, offering the bereaved some time to mourn their loss within the safety and security of their social network. They also provide survivors with a chance to celebrate the life of their decreased loved one. For an example, see Stress in Our World 14-2.

Material Losses

The loss that leads to disease doesn't always have to be the loss of a person or a relationship. Depression and disease may follow the loss of a career, self-respect, economic security, or a treasured possession.[44] Possessions (one's home in particular), especially for the elderly, are often viewed as extensions of oneself or as a personal record of memories, accomplishments, and experiences. Loss of possessions can result in a loss or destruction of identity. This can be observed in the elderly, who, because of illness or death of a spouse, lose their home and their wealth and are forced to move in with children or into a nursing home.

Grief evokes feelings of profound loss.

COPING WITH ADULTHOOD AND OLDER ADULTHOOD STRESS USING THE FIVE RS

Rethink Strategies

One major advantage of using rethink strategies in adulthood and older adulthood is the benefit of life experience. When we are younger and have limited life experience, much of our rethinking is based on hypothetical models of what "might be." We don't have an experiential base from which to draw. Ellis and Harper's[13] and Seligman's[51] ABCDE models are valuable tools that can help adults and older adults examine their illogical beliefs and irrational thoughts about potential work stressors.

We can use the threat of reorganization as an example. Companies and organizations reorganize all the time. They do it for greater efficiency, for greater profits, and to

STRESS IN OUR WORLD 14-2

A Eulogy: Celebrating a Life while Mourning a Death
Eulogy for the Memorial Service of Marie Riedel (1915–2003)
Reverend John L. Tipton 8/16/03
Connecticut Farms Church, Union NJ

It has been said that you know someone more by what they choose to do than by what they have to do. We all have to work. Sometimes we choose our work with intentionality and what we do becomes a reflection of our interests and perhaps even our personality. But often we fall into work situations making a choice because we have to earn a living only to discover later that we may not like it but we have to do it.

In this sense, what we choose to do gives us more insight than what we have to do.

Marie was a quilter. It was her pastime and her recreation. It is a deliberate and exacting craft to quilt. A pattern is envisioned. Fabric is chosen and cut into squares and each is stitched to another. Batting is added. The fabric is put into place and the quilting begins. The running stitch draws the backing fabric together with the batting and intricate squares of color.

It is this stitch, the running stitch, that is exact and deliberately made. It outlines the colorful squares fixing the pattern to the batting. Tiny stitches are carefully sewn. It requires patience. It isn't a craft for those of us who rush, but for those of us who find contentment in small things as those small things give way to larger things—say squares of fabric to a quilt or minutes to a lifetime.

Marie was a quilter. She had the marked capacity for contentment. She wasn't agitated and she didn't aggravate. She seemed at peace with what life brought her. She found peace in her own living. She spoke softly. I, for one, can't imagine her shouting (though perhaps she did when her girls were young). But I can't imagine it. She seemed content, had patience enough to listen, wasn't as concerned (as some of us others are) of getting our own opinions out there.

Marie was a quilter. And, as each stitch contributed to the whole quilt, so she understood that each action and every deed done contributes to a whole life. And when enough stitches are made we see a pattern—of generosity, of doing for others. It was driving the kids to swimming at 6:00 A.M. It was involvement with the Brownies and Girl Scouts. And meals cooked. And church on Sundays.

It was evenings with Bill after the girls went to bed. It was Christmases and the first days of school and lunches packed and laundry done. It was Women's Association meetings. And when enough stitches are made, we see a pattern—of generosity, of doing for others. But the pattern is unique. Underlying the pattern is a batting of independence.

She'd do things for herself and on her own. She didn't want to be a burden, she'd tell us. And when she defined her daughters as wonderful, she'd quietly remark with regret (or perhaps disappointment) that they'd had to take care of her in some way because of her illness. She'd apologize to the nurses at the hospital for having to attend to her. Yet this was her own doing too. As a quilt draws admiration and wonderment at the work done, Marie seemed to draw gratitude and grace from us.

The wonderful thing about people who quilt is that they spend so much time and energy on something to give away. What real quilter hordes each quilt for themselves? But rather, crib quilts are given to newborns and large quilts are given as wedding presents and quilts are pulled out of cedar chests and laid upon the bed awaiting a visitor who'd stay the night. They warm us and delight our eyes—these carefully constructed pieces of fabric and love. And who should know this fabric of love quilted by Marie but those who were her heart's delight—her family. So there are memories of Marie watching her grandsons play sports or visiting with her family in Pittsburgh or loving enough to include her sons-in-law. There were phone calls, always short, and to the point, but inquiring, "how were things going?" "How are things doing?"

But there are fine stitches in a quilt. There is a moment when the last stitch is made and the quilt is done. The diagnosis of pancreatic cancer was a jarring to us as well as its prognosis of months remaining, not years.

I do not know what Marie did with that knowledge of that prognosis. She didn't talk about it. Perhaps she thought that if she did, she'd appear needy, something she didn't want to be. But I think for Marie, 88 years old, looking back on a life she'd found contentment in, a life of faith and grace, a life of quiet presence, of daughters well married and on their own. For Marie, this is how the remaining stitches are to be made. Not with a sense of resignation or depression, but of a pattern coming to completion, as all things must, a moment when the work is done and it is all finished.

And yet there is a greater quilter than Marie or any of us. There is the one who takes all our lives and stitches them together into his quilt of purpose. What we are and what we have done is not lost, but God receives Marie and ultimately us to himself and we find ourselves in his presence. Quilted together by love into an amazing pattern of color and fabric, of works, and faith,

Marie finds her place in this heavenly quilt this day.

Amen

remain competitive in the marketplace. If you have never been through the process of reorganization, you really don't know what to expect. Chances are, you think and fear the worst. It will be harder for you to think logically and rationally about this potential stressor than it will be for someone who has survived three corporate reorganizations and managed to ascend to a better job. The latter worker's experience is a valuable intellectual resource that comes into play during the primary appraisal process. Life experience can also be a big help in learning how to use rethink strategies to cope with relationship stress as well as work stress. Being able to dispute illogical beliefs about our partners, children, and parents requires that we be able to think rationally and clearly about them. Experience can help us do this. We can use the lessons we learned from the past regarding relationship stressors to help us assess our illogical beliefs about potential stressors involving our current relationships.

Finally, Ellis and Harper's[13] and Seligman's[51] ABCDE models can be extremely helpful when we are examining our beliefs about our changing health and future mortality. Understanding that our health to a certain extent is in our own hands and taking responsibility for this often involves examining illogical beliefs.

Values clarification and goal setting (see chapter 7) can also help us examine our work and relationships and how they fit with what is central to who we are as people. These techniques will help us regain a sense of perspective in our lives when we tend to blow things out of proportion. Values clarification and goal setting can also help us examine our attitudes and values relating to our health. These techniques will help us put our health in perspective.

Reduce Strategies

Adulthood and older adulthood offer unique opportunities to incorporate reduce strategies into our lives. Most adults and older adults are in better financial and work positions than they were at any other point in their lives. They actually have the luxury to cut back on their responsibilities if they want to. The Living Simply Network (see chapter 8) is a wonderful resource for adults and older adults who can afford to reduce the amount of work in their lives or rethink the focus of their work. Many people in these stages of life are able to devote time to pursuits that they simply did not have much time or money to pursue in the earlier phases of their lives when they were consumed with earning a living, raising a family, and making their mark in their careers or in life. Read about downscaling in chapter 8 and think about areas where you can start to cut back stressors and demands in your life. If you are not in a position financially to cut back on work demands, focus on other aspects of your life that are more amenable to cutting back. Try to free up some time to pursue things you have always wanted to explore but have never had the time to do. They don't have to be expensive. Take the "Things I Love to Do" inventory in chapter 8 to help you identify simple, inexpensive things that are fun to do but for some reason have fallen out of your life.

Relax Strategies

Ideally, adulthood and older adulthood represent a continuation of the relaxation techniques that were mastered and used earlier in life. If they do not, it is not too late to try out some of the strategies described in chapter 9. Adulthood and older adulthood offer greater opportunities to relax for most people. Relaxation activities can help slow the aging process as you conserve vital energy and replenish energy supplies lost to everyday activities. Depending on your health status and level of fitness, you may choose activities from chapter 9.

Take advantage of this. Start to take twenty- to thirty-minute daily stress breaks if you haven't already begun to do so. Pick one of the strategies from chapter 9 and put it on your A list (see the section on time management in chapter 8) as something that must get done daily.

Chances are that you have more free time and disposable income now than you did when you were younger. If you can afford it, pamper yourself a little more. Try to surround yourself with things that relax you and slow you down a little. Bring flowers to work for your desk. Take a bubble bath more often. Light fragrant candles for the dinner table. Start to slow down a little and enjoy your life more. Try pampering yourself with a weekly massage. You've worked hard all of your life, so reward yourself.

At the very least, learn the calming response and diaphragmatic breathing (see chapter 9) and practice them daily. Neither takes much time to learn and should help you develop a more relaxed lifestyle.

Release Strategies

Take advantage of any newfound time and freedom in your adult and older adulthood years by investing it in your sexual relationship with your partner. Set up romantic dates with your significant other. Spend a Saturday morning in bed. Take your time and read the paper, have a snack, take a bubble bath, give each other a massage, or make love with the windows open and the sounds of nature streaming in through the window. While sexual response changes with age, it is still possible to enjoy sexual release until death. If you find yourself buying into ageist myths that portray adults and older adults in nonsexual ways, seek professional help to work through these perceptual blocks.

If you have a hard time "releasing," spend the time to fix this problem. Maybe you need professional help to work through relationship problems (both sexual and generic) that have you stuck and are keeping you from enjoying life.

Develop a four-season physical activity and fitness plan. Reread chapter 10 for ideas about how to incorporate some physical activity into each day. It will help you cope with the pressures from work or retirement and your relationship while enhancing your overall health.

Invest in a heavy punching bag and hang it in your basement, garage, or extra room. Use it to release pent-up anger and stress. Maybe this will help you unblock the barriers that stand in your way of releasing.

Reorganize Strategies

It is never too late to reorganize your life and begin to develop a more healthy, stress-resistant lifestyle. Reread chapter 11 to find out how to incorporate strategies from the book to develop high-level environmental/occupational, social, spiritual, physical, intellectual, and emotional health. Rather than viewing this stage as the beginning of the end of your life as you knew it (work, family, community), why not view it as the beginning of a new life?

Intellectually you can begin to learn about the things you always were interested in and curious about but never had the time and money to pursue. Join a group. Take an adult school course. Take a course online. Start to explore those things today.

If you have had some emotional issues that you have not been able to understand and resolve, why not start to work on them now? Find a counselor you can talk to and start to understand and take control of your emotions. Local community mental health centers, churches, and area colleges are good places to find reasonably priced counseling services.

It's never too late to get physical. The single greatest thing you can do for your health at this or any other point is to begin to get at least thirty minutes of physical activity every day. This will help you lose weight, give you more energy, increase your resistance to illness, improve your sexual functioning, and enhance your self-esteem.

Combine your interests and physical activity by expanding your social network. Join a hiking club, a canoeing group, or a bird-watching organization. Get some exercise and meet some new people. Look for ways to expand your social networks by getting involved with people who like to do the things you like to do. Most over-55 communities revolve around a "clubhouse" that is the focal point for integrating physical and social activities.

If you get involved in groups that are committed to preserving the environment, you can contribute to improving your environmental well-being. Start to pay attention to your use of nonrenewable resources and start to recycle. You have the time now to start paying attention to these things.

Finally, adulthood and older adulthood, as we've discussed, are a time when most of us begin to pay more attention to our mortality and spirituality. Working through the last developmental tasks involves assessing our lives and coming to terms with our successes and shortcomings. An excellent way to do this is to renew our spiritual commitment, whether it is through religious participation or secular involvement in groups and activities that connect us with something beyond ourselves. Adulthood and older adulthood is a time when we can afford to be more altruistic and serve others. In doing this we serve ourselves and make more sense of our lives and the great unknown that we all face as we approach the end of our existence on this earth.

SUMMARY

This final chapter took us through Erikson's remaining stages: adulthood and older adulthood. The chapter began with a review of the potential stressors associated with Erikson's major tasks of adulthood and older adulthood (generativity versus stagnation and integrity versus despair, respectively).

The next part of the chapter discussed the meaning of work and the way it related to stress during adulthood and older adulthood. Citing data from recent studies, the chapter showed how the meaning of work varies among individuals over the course of their lifetimes. For some people work is central to their lives and, in essence, defines who they are. For others, work is viewed as a means to an end, a way to earn a living and buy the things that give their lives meaning. Because the meaning of work varies among individuals, work-related stress also varies. Work-related stressors are not universal and are related to what work means to people. The same can be said about retirement stress. What work means to us also plays a major role in how we perceive retirement (the cessation of work).

The chapter then examined the meaning and changing nature of community. It examined a variety of different living situations ranging from non–age-restricted communities to assisted living facilities. It also examined how living environments change as we age and our interests and needs change. Once again, the chapter showed how stress related to living environments varies according to how adults and older adults view their living situations and what their perceptions are of any changes in their living environments.

The next part of the chapter focused on how relationships change through adulthood and older adulthood. It described how, for most Americans, adulthood and older adulthood are times for relationship strengthening and deepening of commitments made earlier in relationships. It demystified the notion of midlife crises and showed that for most Americans midlife is a time of happiness and prosperity and a time to enjoy the fruits of their labor.

The chapter then moved into a discussion of the changing nature of health in aging. It described the relationship between aging, healthy living, and normal physiological changes associated with getting older. The chapter discussed how health can become a stressor as illness changes the way we view ourselves and our potential.

Finally, the chapter showed how to apply the Five Rs of coping to stressors associated with adulthood and older adulthood.

STUDY QUESTIONS

1. Describe the major tasks associated with Erikson's adult stage of development.
2. Describe the major tasks associated with Erikson's older adult stage of development.
3. Compare and contrast the developmental tasks associated with adulthood and those of older adulthood.
4. What are the major sources of stress associated with these stages?
5. List and describe the six different meanings of work orientation.
6. Pick one meaning of work orientation and describe how it is related to stress.
7. How does a person's potential work stress relate to the meaning that person derives from work?
8. List and describe three changes associated with retirement.
9. Describe the fastest growing segment of the housing market for adults and older adults.
10. What are the major demographic trends in America related to singlehood, cohabitation, and marriage?
11. Describe three of the most common stressors associated with marriage.
12. How does relationship stress vary over a person's life?
13. Write a stress-management plan employing the Five Rs of coping for adulthood and older adulthood.
14. What is the relationship between lifestyle and healthy aging?
15. Describe Kubler-Ross's stages of death and dying.

DISCOVER OUR CHANGING WORLD

The Healthy Aging Campaign

http://www.healthyaging.net/

This is the home page for the Healthy Aging Campaign, a non-profit group dedicated to promoting health and wellness across the life span. Click on a few of the links to get an idea of the scope of its services.

When you are finished exploring the site, click on the "Tip of the Week" link and read it.

Critical Thinking Question

How can you apply the advice given in this week's Tip of the Week to your own lifestyle at the present moment? How might this application differ twenty years from now?

ARE YOU THINKING CLEARLY?

In this chapter we discussed how work and relationships change throughout adulthood and older adulthood. Change can be looked at as a positive adaptation to evolving circumstances of it can be seen as a threat to what is known and comfortable. A key factor in understanding how we will view these changes in adulthood and older adulthood is how we view change now.

Your answers to the following questions will help you assess whether or not you are thinking clearly about change?

1. Do I tend to view change as a threat to my present life situation?
2. Once I finish college, get a good job, and settle into a solid relationship will I be "home free" and not have to worry about change?
3. How do I feel about the following statement; "the only constant in life is change"?
4. Am I prepared with a "plan B" for anticipated changes in my work and relationships?
5. Can I effectively co-exist with the strong emotions and uncertainty that accompany change?

If you answer them honestly, the information you gather from this mini-assessment will help you understand your appraisal of change. In general, the more you view change as a threat, the more stressed you will be by work and relationships because responsibilities, circumstances and opportunities that present change crop up constantly throughout our lives. They don't stop in adulthood or older adulthood, they just differ from those that occur during the earlier stages in life.

REFERENCES

1. Bengston, V.L., Cuellar, J.B., & Raga, P.K. (1977). Stratum contrasts and similarities in attitudes toward death. *Journal of Gerontology,* 30, pp. 688–695.
2. Berger, R. (1982). *Gay and gray.* Urbana: University of Illinois Press.
3. Berry, R.E. & Williams, W. (1987). Assessing the relationship between quality of life and marital and income satisfaction: A path analytic approach. *Journal of Marriage and the Family,* 49, pp. 107–116.
4. Blumstein, P. & Schwartz, P. (1983). *American couples.* New York: Morrow.
5. Cain, B. (1982). Plight of the gray divorcee. *New York Times Magazine,* December 19, pp. 89–94.
6. Cavanaugh, J.C. (1993). *Adult development and aging.* Belmont, CA: Wadsworth.
7. Cohen, S. & Syme, S.L. (1985). *Social support and health.* Orlando, FL: Academic Press.
8. Crooks, R. & Baur, K. (1993). *Our sexuality.* (4th ed.). Redwood City, CA: Benjamin Cummings.
9. Dawson, K. (1982). Serving the older gay community. *SIECUS Report,* 11, pp. 5–6.
10. Diggs, D.V. (1995). *Recent trends in alimony and child support.* Interbit Computer Group. http://www.interbit.com/ksc/alimony.htm.
11. Doka, K.J. (1987). Silent sorrow: Grief and loss of significant others. *Death Studies,* 11(8), pp. 455–469.
12. Cart, C.S. (1994). *The Relatives of Aging.* (4th ed.). Needham Heights, Mass: Allyn & Bacon.
13. Ellis, A. & Harper, R. (1975). *A guide to rational living.* Englewood Cliffs, NJ: Prentice-Hall.
14. Emrack, P. (2002). Age-restricted communities. *Housing Economics,* 50(8), pp. 6–13.
15. Erikson, E. (1986). *Childhood and society.* New York: W.W. Norton.
16. Forrest, D. (1992). Now for something completely different: Success and midlife crisis. *Canadian Business,* 65(9), pp. 96–100.
17. Franklin, M.B. (2003). The appeal of active adult communities. *Kiplingers,* 57(7), p. 83.
18. Gallagher, W. (1993). Midlife myths. *Atlantic Monthly,* 271(5), pp. 51–63.
19. Gilla, F. (1999). The meaning of work: Lessons from sociology, psychology, and political theory. *Journal of Socio-Economics,* 28(6), pp. 729–744.
20. Gratton, B. & Wilson, V. (1989). Family support systems and the minority elderly: A cautionary analysis. *Journal of Gerontological Social Work,* 13(1–2), pp. 91–93.
21. Haynes, M. (2003). Survey highlights keys to facilitate aging in place. *Professional Builder,* 68(3), pp. 34–35.
22. Hafen, B.Q., Frandsen, K.J., Karren, K.J., & Hooker, K.R. (1992). *The health effects of attitudes, emotions, and relationships.* Provo, UT: EMS Associates.
23. Hales, D. (2001). *An Invitation to Health.* Pacific Grove, CA: Wadsworth.
24. Harris, P. & Lyon, D. (1990). Midlife crisis: A myth? *Reader's Digest,* 136(818), p. 108.
25. Hess, R.C., Liang, Y., & Conner, P. (2001). A maturing seniors housing market. *Real Estate Finance,* 17(4), pp. 29–31.
26. Jamal, M. & Baba, V.V. (1992). Shiftwork and department-type related to job stress, work attitudes, and behavioral intentions: A study of nurses. *Journal of Organizational Behavior,* 13(5), pp. 449–464.
27. Kalish, R.A. (1985). The social context of death and dying. In Binstock, R.H. & Shanas, E. (Eds). *Handbook of aging and the social sciences,* (2nd ed.), pp. 149–170. New York: Van Nostrand.
28. Kalish, R.A. (1987). Death and dying. In Silverman, P. (Ed.). *The elderly as modern pioneers,* pp. 320–334. Bloomington: Indiana University Press.
29. Kart, S.C. (1994). *The realities of aging: An introduction to gerontology.* Boston: Allyn & Bacon.
30. Krause, N. & Wray, L. (1991). Psychosocial correlates of health and illness among minority elders. *Generations,* 15(4), pp. 25–30.
31. Kubler-Ross, E. (1969). *On death and dying.* New York: Macmillan.
32. Kurdak, L. (1993). The allocation of household labor in gay, lesbian, and heterosexual married couples. *Journal of Social Issues,* 49(3), pp. 127–139.
33. Kurdak, L. (1989). Relationship quality of gay and lesbian cohabiting couples. *Journal of Homosexuality,* 15(3–4), pp. 93–118.
34. Lawday, D. (1991). Letter from a productive lover of leisure. *US News and World Report,* 111(6), pp. 6–8.
35. Lazarus, R.S. (1999). *Stress and emotion: A new synthesis.* New York: Springer.
36. Lipman, A. (1986). Homosexual relationships. *Generations,* 10(4), pp. 51–54.
37. Logue, B. (1990). Race differences in long-term disability: Middle-aged and older American Indians, blacks, and whites in Oklahoma. *Social Sciences Journal,* 27(3), pp. 253–272.
38. Lopata, H.Z. (1973). *Widowhood in an American city.* Cambridge, MA: Schenkman.
39. Marcellini, F. & Sensoli, C. (1997). Preparation for retirement: Problems and suggestions. *Educational Gerontology,* 23(4), pp. 377–381.
40. Masters, et al. *Human sexuality.* (4th ed.). Published by Allyn and Bacon, Boston, MA. Copyright © 1992 by Pearson Education.
41. Meaning of Work—International Research Team. (1987). *The meaning of work—An international view.* London: Academic Press.
42. McWhirter, D. & Mattison, A. (1984). *The male couple.* Englewood Cliffs, NJ: Prentice-Hall.
43. Morrison, E. & Price, M.U. (1974). *Values in sexuality: A new approach to sex education.* New York: Hart.
44. Murrell, S.A., Himmelfarb, S., & Phifer, J.E. (1988). Effects of bereavement/loss and pre-event status on subsequent physical health in older adults. *International Journal of Aging/Human Development,* 13(2), pp. 89–107.

45. Myers, J.E., Wass, H., & Murphey, M. (1980). Ethnic differences in death anxiety among the elderly. *Death Education,* 4, pp. 237–244.
46. Parnes, H.S. & Sommers, D.G. (1994). Shunning retirement: Work experience of men in their seventies and early eighties. *Journal of Gerontology,* 49(3), pp. 117–124.
47. Payne, W. & Hahn, D. (2002). *Understanding your health.* St Louis: McGraw-Hill.
48. Phillis, D.E. & Stein, P.J. (1983). Sink or swing? The lifestyles of single adults. In Allegeir, E.R. & McCormick, N.B. (Eds.). *Changing boundaries: Gender roles and sexual behavior.* Palo Alto, CA: Mayfield.
49. Quam, J.K. & Whitford, G.S. (1992). Adaptation and age-related expectations of elder gay and lesbian adults. *The Gerontologist,* 32(3), pp. 367–374.
50. Reed, P.G. (1987). Spirituality and well-being in terminally ill hospitalized adults. *Research in Nursing and Health,* 10, pp. 335–344.
51. Seligman, M. (1998). *Learned optimism: How to change your life.* New York: Free Press.
52. Snir, R. & Harpaz, I. (2002). Work-leisure relations: Leisure orientation and the meaning of work. *Journal of Leisure Research,* 34(2), pp. 173–203.
53. United States Bureau of the Census. (2001). *Current population survey 1970–2000: Living arrangements.* Washington, DC: U.S. Government Printing Office.
54. National Center for Health Statistics. (2001). *U.S. National vital statistics report,* vol. 51, no. 5. Washington, DC: U.S. Government Printing Office.
55. U.S. Department of Health and Human Services. (2002). *Annual report to the nation: Health.* Washington, DC: U.S. Government Printing Office.
56. Wagner, C.G. (2002). The new meaning of work. *Futurist,* 36(5), pp. 1–4.
57. Warburton, J. & Rosenman, L. (1995). The meaning of retirement: Why retirement gets bad press. *Social Alternatives,* 14(2), pp. 4–6.
58. Weishaus, S. & Field, D. (1988). A half century of marriage: Continuity or change? *Journal of Marriage and the Family,* 50, pp. 763–774.
59. *West legal dictionary.* (1989). http://www.wld.com/weal/walimony.htm.

Name: ________________________________ Date: ____________

ASSESS YOURSELF 14-1

My Epitaph

Purpose

Sometimes contemplating death helps one gain perspective on life. What is life all about? What difference would it make if you were not alive? This strategy has us look at the meaning of our lives in a simple but challenging way.

Procedure

The teacher says, "Have any of you ever been to old graveyards and read some of the inscriptions on the tombstones? For example:

"Here lies Mary Smith. She had more love to give than was ever wanted."

"Sara Miller, A Woman of Valor."

"Ezra Jones lived as he died. Out of debt, out of sight, and out of sorts."

What would you want engraved on your own tombstone? What would be an accurate description of you and your life in a few short words?

____

____

____

____

____

____

Note

Every student has the right to pass in this exercise. Death can be frightening, and some students are superstitious enough to believe that if you talk about your own death, it will happen. Be sensitive to this.

Sometimes students may be given time to consult *Bartlett's Quotations* or old yearbooks to choose appropriate statements for their epitaphs.

The teacher can help by having an epitaph of his or her own ready to read. The teacher must be willing to put his or her own values on the line if he or she expects the students to learn to do so.

From Morrison, E. & Price, M.U. (1974). *Values in sexuality: A new approach to sex education.* New York: Hart.[43]

Name: ______________________________ Date: ____________

ASSESS YOURSELF 14-2

Relationship Contract

If you could plan the perfect relationship, what would it be? Answer the following questions with your partner to compare your ideas of the perfect relationship.

Name:
Should the wife take on the husband's last name, the husband take on the wife's name, both take a hyphenated name, both take a new name, or both keep their own names?
If there are children, what will their surname be?

Birth Control:
What kind?
Whose responsibility?

Household Duties:
Who does what?

Leisure Time:
Should evenings and weekends be spent together?
Who decides what to do?
Should vacations be spent together?
With children?
Separately?

Living Arrangements:
Where will you live?
What kind of privacy do you want?
Shared bedroom?
Do you want to live with others?
What will you and your partner do if you want to live in different places because of jobs or for any other reason?

Money:
Will both partners be wage earners?
If so, will you pool your income?
Each keep own salary?
Share equally the cost of living expenses and keep the remainder for yourselves?

Sexual Rights:
Commitment to monogamy?
Who initiates sex?
Is either partner free not to respond?

Children:
How many?
When?
Adopt?
Who will take primary responsibility for raising the children?
Will one partner have to quit a job?

Other Relationships:
Are you and your partner free to have relationships with other people?
With those of the same sex?
With those of the opposite sex?
What is to be the extent of these relationships?
Do you include each other in these relationships?

From Morrison, E. & Price, M.U. (1974). *Values in sexuality: A new approach to sex education.* New York: Hart.[43]

Epilogue

Coping with Stress in a Changing World

After all these years of thinking, writing, and teaching about stress, I'm convinced that stress management isn't about learning how to meditate or thinking about warming scenes and positive thoughts, although those techniques and many others are very useful in reducing stress. The secret to coping with stress in a changing world is contained in two words: *challenge* and *lifestyle.*

Challenge is significant because stress management begins with our perception, an attitude that we develop about our lives and the world we live in, and evolves each and every day as we live our lives in consort with this view. It's a perception of life founded on the belief that each day brings change and the challenges that are inherent in change. When we feel challenged, we feel confident, strong, optimistic, and energized.

Lifestyle is significant because coping with stress in a changing world revolves around a style of living that is always moving forward toward optimal functioning, "being the best that we can be." Whether we achieve optimal functioning isn't everything. Although we've seen how high levels of well-being across the six dimensions of health can assist us in coping with stress, this isn't the only reason we strive for optimal functioning. The journey, the quest for optimal functioning, is equally important. It is living a life that is disciplined yet joyful, hardworking yet playful and full of healthy pleasures. Setting goals that challenge us across all six dimensions of well-being keeps us on our toes, invigorated and focused. We don't dread change; we embrace it and assess how we can use it to help us meet our goals.

When students ask for one piece of advice in helping them cope with the stress in their lives, I tell them, "I can't give you one piece of advice, but here are several tips for coping with stress in a changing world."

1. Have some fun each and every day. You deserve it. Life is hard. Allow yourself the luxury of some fun. Make time to have some fun each day. Start to drop activities and people who weigh you down and kill your fun.
2. Lighten up. As Metcalf said, "Learn how to take yourself lightly and your work seriously." You are not the center of the universe. The sun would still shine tomorrow if you no longer existed.
3. Stop, think, and count to ten when you feel you are going to explode from stress.
4. Don't do anything rash or make any major decisions when you are stressed. Often these decisions made under duress will come back to stress you more than help you.
5. Smile more. It's hard to be stressed when you smile.
6. Be kind to others. It's amazing how your expressions of kindness can work wonders in reducing your stress.
7. Forgive more. It's so easy to screw up in life. Give people a break before you lash out at them and raise your own stress level.
8. Slow down. Rushing to get everything you want out of life now usually reduces the quality of experiences rather than enhancing experiences. You can realize all your hopes and dreams if you spread them out over a lifetime. There is time for life.
9. Hug more. It's hard to be stressed when you are hugging another living thing—a loved one, a pet. We all need hugs!
10. Get physical. Getting some exercise every day will help you release tension and other stress by-products as well as increase your overall health.
11. Take a chance on love. I cannot think of anything that has helped me cope with stress more than the love of my wife, my children, my parents, and my friends. Their caring and my commitment to them have been a source of strength and inspiration through my most troubled times. Do not give up on love even if your initial attempts have failed.

Coping with stress in a changing world requires active participation in your life. You control your destiny. You chart your course through your life's journey. I wish you well on your journey. Enjoy the trip!

Glossary

absurdity a sense of amusement at the silliness and irony of a situation

ACT model an approach to time management based on prioritizing tasks to be accomplished in a given time period

ACTH the abbreviation for adrenocorticotropic hormone, a powerful hormone produced in the adrenal cortex (the outer part) that is indicative of the resistance phase of Selye's General Adaptation Syndrome

active adult communities age-restricted communities (age 55 or older) that feature clubhouses, fitness facilities, pools, recreation directors, walking trails, and golf courses

active listening listening with understanding and feedback

actual stressor a stimulus that does cause stress

acupuncture the Chinese medical practice of puncturing the body with thin needles at precise points to free constricted or blocked energy centers

acute stress disorder a disorder characterized by the rapid development of anxiety, dissociation, and other symptoms following within a month after experiencing an extremely traumatic stressor

acute stress response a short-duration but high intensity response triggered by a highly threatening (often life-threatening) stressor that is often referred to as the *fight-or-flight response*

adaptation energy the body's finite energy reserves available for coping with stressors

adolescence the developmental period between the end of childhood and the beginning of young adulthood

adrenal cortex the outer shell of the adrenal gland

adrenal medulla the inner core of the adrenal gland

aerobic excercise exercise in which the amount of oxygen taken into the lungs is equal to or slightly more than that required to meet the body's energy demands

affirmative action a part of the 1964 Civil Rights Act which was designed to ensure that all groups had equal access to work and advancement within a job

age-integrated communities communities where people at all ages live together

age-restricted housing housing restricted by age for older adults

aggressiveness understanding your wants and needs and pursuing them at the expense of others, with little or no regard to how this affects the rights of others

alarm the first phase of GAS, in which the body mobilizes energy to meet the demands of stressors

alpha waves slow, low-amplitude brain waves associated with a wakeful, resting state

ambient lighting background lighting that encompasses the surrounding space in a room

amine neurotransmitters neurotransmitters, synthesized from amino-acid molecules, that are found in various regions of the brain that affect emotions among other activities

amino acids organic chemical compounds that are the building blocks of protein

anaerobic exercise explosive activity which occurs in the absence of oxygen; usually involves maximum effort and lasts no longer than 90 seconds

anger a strong feeling of displeasure targeted at anything

anxiety a vague, uneasy feeling of nonspecific or unknown origin

arrhythmias irregular heart rhythms

arteriosclerosis a general term used to refer to a number of degenerative changes in the arteries that lead to decreased elasticity and blood flow

assertiveness understanding your wants and needs and pursuing them without infringing on the wants and needs of others

assisted living facilities age-restricted communities that provide housing and support services to older adults who need assistance in daily activities because of increasing frailty or health conditions such as Alzheimer's disease

associational connecting together individual sensory inputs

atherosclerosis the buildup of plaques on the inner walls of arteries

autonomic nervous system the part of the peripheral nervous system that is automatic and involuntary

belief system a collection of values, attitudes, and beliefs about the world and interactions between people

benign/positive appraisal the assessment of encounters with people and situations that are perceived favorably by us

bereavement a form of depression with anxiety that is a common reaction to the loss of a loved one

bile a bitter, yellow-green fat emulsifier secreted by the liver

binge drinking having five or more drinks in a row at least once during the previous two-week period

biofeedback a technique for evaluating the effects of stress on the body by using instruments that monitor body functions, such as temperature, muscle tension, brain wave activity, and perspiration

blood pressure the pressure created against the walls of blood vessels in response to the beating of the heart and the pumping of blood

body language a term used to describe the intentional and unintentional messages we send through our posture, gestures, physical appearance, and even silence

bracing a state of chronic muscle tension

breath meditation a form of focused meditation where the focal point is one's breathing

budget a system for allocating net income to meet actual expenses

cadence the beat, time, or measure of rhythmical motion or activity

carpal tunnel syndrome a painful disorder of the wrist and hand caused by the compression of the nerve running through the wrist

Category One Stressors stressors that are forseeable and can be controlled; you know about them in advance and can do something about them

Category Three Stressors stressors that are neither foreseeable nor controllable; these are the ones that catch you completely off guard

Category Two Stressors stressors that are foreseeable but cannot be controlled; you see them coming but cannot do anything about them

catharsis a cleansing or purifying effect derived from the dramatic release of stress-related tension

central nervous system the part of the nervous system consisting of the brain and the spinal cord

challenge appraisal an anticipatory evaluation of a situation that focuses on positive things that can result from it; during challenge appraisal a person looks at a situation for its growth potential or for what might be gained from it

chronic depression depression that lasts most of the day, more days than not, and persists for more than two years (one year in children and adolescents)

chronic stress response an adaptive response to a nonlife-threatening or low-threat stressor associated with the resistance phase of Selye's General Adaptation Syndrome

cognitive reappraisal the process of reevaluating a potential stressor using information synthesized from the primary and secondary appraisals

cohabitation a shared living arrangement between two unmarried romantic partners

companionate love involves intimacy and commitment but lacks passion

continuing care retirement communities (CCRCs) communities that integrate older adults of varying levels of health and combine independent living, assisted living, and skilled nursing care facilities

contusion a bruise characterized by pain, swelling, and discoloration; does not break the skin

core values our most deeply held beliefs about the things that are central to who we are as people

corticoids adrenal cortical hormones

cytoplasm all of the substances of the cell, other than the nucleus, combined

date rape a form of rape defined as forced sexual intercourse imposed by an acquaintance or dating partner; also known as acquaintance rape

decibel a unit for measuring the relative loudness of sounds

decoding the use of knowledge, memory, language, context, and personal history and experience to interpret a message

demand a positive or negative condition or activity or stimulus that forces the body to use energy

demographic variables population-based factors such as age, gender, sexual orientation, socioeconomic status (SES), and race and ethnicity

diaphragmatic breathing a deep breathing technique that uses the diaphragm to assist in completely filling the lungs from the bottom up

discrimination to make a difference in treatment or favor on a basis other than individual merit

distress any negative demand that is capable of triggering the GAS

downscaling voluntarily cutting back on one's lifestyle so one can afford to do what he or she really wants to do

downsizing cutting back on the number of employees and divisions, departments, and programs within an organization

dyspareunia genital pain associated with sexual intercourse

economic insecurity one's mistrust in the strength of the economy

economic orientation the belief that people work mainly for and are motivated by the intrinsic rewards associated with paid labor: salary, fringe benefits, and so on

economic uncertainty how people feel about the economy in general and their personal job security

egocentric feeling as if you and your needs are the central focus of everything and everyone

emotional arousal another way of saying feeling threatened or harmed using Lazarus and Folkman's threat appraisal model

emotion-focused coping coping that focuses on changing the way one views potential stressors in order to defuse their threat

emotions a feeling or state of mind, and the thoughts and physical reactions associated with it

empty love involves commitment without passion and intimacy

enacted social support the outcomes associated with the support that is rendered

encoding the selection of signs, symbols, emotions, and words to transmit a message

endorphins a subclass of neuropeptide neurotransmitters that acts like opiates to block pain

endothelium squamous tissue that lines the walls of the heart, blood vessels, and lymphatic vessels

entrepreneurs one who organizes, owns, manages, and assumes the risks of a business

epidemiology the study of the distribution and determinants of diseases/conditions in populations

ergonomics an applied science concerned with designing and arranging things people use so that the people and things interact most efficiently and safely; also known as human engineering

eustress any positive demand that is capable of triggering the GAS

exchange rate the rate at which new outdoor air replaces old indoor air through natural or man-made ventilation

exercise a formal series of movements and activities designed to work targeted muscles, muscle groups, and body systems

exhaustion the third phase of GAS, in which a body part or system breaks down as a result of the energy demands of chronic stressors

explanatory style the way in which a person views the world and explains his or her misfortune

faith the belief in something that cannot be proven empirically

family relationships social relationships based on either a connection through blood or a civil bond

fatuous love passionate and committed but not intimate

Feng shui a Chinese practice in which a structure or geographical site is chosen or configured so as to harmonize with the spiritual forces that inhabit it

fibrosis an abnormal condition where fibrous connective tissue spreads over smooth muscle tissue

fight-or-flight the state of physiological readiness for action created by the body during the alarm phase

focused meditation a type of meditation that uses focal point (an object, word/phrase, sound, breathing etc.) to direct one's attention to

formal mindfulness a type of mindfulness meditation training implemented over an eight-week period and designed to have people practice for 45 minutes a day

friendship characterized by intimacy but is without passion and commitment

General Adaptation Syndrome (GAS) the three-phase stress response identified by Selye, involving three phases: alarm, resistance, and exhaustion

glare an uncomfortably bright reflection of light onto a viewing surface

glass ceiling a metaphor for the supposedly available but limited ascension in the corporate world available to women

gluconeogenesis the physiological process of converting noncarbohydrate sources of energy into glucose

goal an end toward which we direct our effort

grief the nearly universal pattern of physical and emotional responses to bereavement

hardy personality a stress-resistant personality characterized by commitment, control, and ability to accept change

harm/loss appraisal an actual assessment of situations that have already occurred; the evaluation of what harm or losses have occurred as a result of the potential stressor

hassles irritating, frustrating, and/or distressing demands (such as traffic jams, arguments, bad weather, etc.) that characterize everyday transactions with the environment

high-contrast lighting conditions lighting that creates extreme differences in the foreground and background light

holistic related to the whole rather than to its individual parts

homeostasis a state of relative stability in the body's internal environment, sustained by natural adaptive responses

homeostats thermostat-like mechanisms that regulate a variety of anatomic functions

homophobia the irrational fear and hatred of homosexuality in ourselves and others

hormonal releasing factors chemicals secreted by the hypothalamus that trigger the pituitary to release specific hormones

hormones powerful chemicals that control a host of bodily functions ranging from growth to the metabolic rate

hostility anger that is directed at someone

humor a quality or sense of silliness, absurdity, or amusement

hyperimmunity an exaggerated autoimmune response, meaning that the body literally turns on itself, perceiving itself as an antigen

hypertension another name for high blood pressure, meaning elevated blood pressure that consistently exceeds 140/90 mmHg

hypometabolic state a restful waking state characterized by decreased metabolic rate and respiration

hypothalamus an area of the brain located directly underneath the thalamus at the end of the brain stem that receives messages from the thalamus and works in consort with the nervous and endocrine systems, sending nerve and hormonal messages to the tissues, organs, and body systems involved in the stress response

identity crisis a state of confusion about what one believes is the correct role for themselves versus what others expect of them

immunosuppressive effect anything that slows down or interferes with the correct immune response

independent living facilities age-restricted apartments that typically offer several forms of congregate services, including meals, housekeeping, transportation, organized group activities, and other common area facilities and group-oriented services

individual relationships the social connections we have with significant individuals and groups

industry a sense of diligence or productivity in one's work or activities

infatuation characterized by passion without intimacy and commitment

informal mindfulness the application of mindful behavior into daily experience

initiating skills encoding techniques you can employ to begin to express yourself and to start a dialogue

initiative a trait characterized by taking responsibility for acting in a more purposeful manner; behaving in ways that are consistent with one's likes and dislikes

intelligence the capacity to understand, know, or mentally grasp

intercessory prayer a type of prayer done for someone else; praying for another

interpersonal events that go on between two or more individuals

intimacy the process of gradually sharing one's innermost feelings with another person; the word *intimacy* comes from the Latin word for "within"

intrapersonal events that go on within an individual

intrapersonal conflict problems arising because of conflicts within a person, such as an assault on a person's values

intrinsic orientation the aspects of work that satisfy a worker's internal and expressive needs, such as creativity, autonomy, interest, variety, and challenge

irrelevant appraisal the assessment of potential stressors that have no relevance to us

job insecurity the way people feel about the stability of their job, including the perceived likelihood of actually keeping one's job and personal satisfaction with that job

laughter a uniquely human reaction typically in the form of a physical as well as emotional response indicating feelings of amusement, joy, or merriment

life events life-changing experiences that use energy and can cause stress

lifestyle-based approach an approach to coping that integrates individual coping strategies with hardy health practices to form a more stress-resistant lifestyle

loneliness an unpleasant feeling that occurs when one's network of social relationships is significantly deficient in quality or quantity; it can happen when one is alone or with other people

luminance the level of brightness in an area as measured in candles per square meter, also called nits

macro environment the world at large

major depressive episode a period of depressed mood or loss of pleasure that lasts at least two weeks

mandala a Hindu or Buddhist graphic symbol of the universe in its ideal form depicting the transformation of a universe of suffering into one of joy

manic states distinct periods when a person's predominant mood is elevated, expansive, or irritable and is accompanied by other manic symptoms

mantra a special word or phrase used by those practicing transcendental meditation that has added personal spiritual significance for the individual

meditation the process by which we go about deepening our attention and awareness by refining them and putting them to greater practical use in our lives

meditative effect a slowing or lowering of metabolic functions (breathing, heart rate, blood pressure, and brain wave activity)

micro environment one's immediate environment, including immediate family and friends and living and working space

migraine headache a type of headache caused by the constriction followed by rapid expansion of the carotid arteries in the neck

milieu interieur the body's internal environment

mirroring repeating the initiator's exact words while mimicking his or her exact body language

mood a state of mind dominated by a particular emotion or set of emotions

morphological concerned with the structure and function of an organism

mortality the number of deaths associated with a condition in a year

motor relating to nerve impulses going out to muscles

motor area the part of the cerebral cortex that controls nerve impulses going out to muscles

multitasking the practice of attending to more than one thing or activity at the same time

muscle tension partial contractions of the skeletal muscles that are triggered during the stress response

neuropeptide neurotransmitters neurotransmitters, made from amino-acid chains produced in the brain and spinal cord

neurotransmitters chemicals that transmit nerve impulses across nerve synapses (the point at which a nervous impulse passes from one neuron to another)

noise a sound that is undesired or that interferes with one's ability to hear

nonassertiveness failing to pursue your needs and wants while allowing others to meet theirs, often at your expense

object meditation a form of focused meditation that uses an object such as a candle, a hanging crystal, or a mandala as the focal point

open meditation a type of meditation, also referred to as nonfocused or mindful meditation, that does not employ a focal point but instead directs one's full attention to the experience of existing in the present moment

open-ended statements statements that can't be answered with a simple yes/no answer

optimism a generally positive interpretation of life and events

optimal functioning functioning at the highest level possible in any dimension of health

orgasmic disorders sexual dysfunctions related to the orgasm phase of the sexual response cycle

outsourcing taking components of an organization (such as payroll, information technology, etc.) out and subcontracting them to independent contractors often working in other states or countries

panic attack discrete periods of intense fear and discomfort that come on suddenly, without warning, and reach their peak within 10 minutes

panic disorder a condition in which a person suffers from frequent panic attacks

paraphrasing repeating back your version of the initiator's message

parasympathetic nervous system the part of the autonomic nervous system responsible for turning off the autonomic system

passive mental state a state achieved by allowing your mind to slow down and, as thoughts and emotions arise and enter consciousness, accepting them for what they are and then allowing them to pass

passive listening one-way listening that provides no feedback

perceived noisiness a subjective assessment of noise that combines the decibel level and the context in which a noise occurs

perceived social support the subjective rating of the satisfaction, adequacy, and availability of supportive relationships

perception the subjective way in which information is regarded and interpreted

peripheral nervous system all other nerves emanating from the spinal cord

peristaltic action contracting and relaxing of the smooth muscles of the digestive system that pushes partially digested food along the gastrointestinal tract

person factors a person's commitments and beliefs, such as ideals, values, and faith; formerly referred to as *personality factors*

personality our unique collection of thoughts, attitudes, values, beliefs, perceptions, and behaviors that define who we are as people

perspective a person's relative mental picture, or point of view, in regard to a particular situation or event

pessimism a generally negative interpretation of life and events

physiological pertaining to the functions of the human body and the body systems

pituitary gland a pea-sized endocrine gland nestled in a bony shell at the base of the brain; often referred to as "the master gland" because of its role in secreting a variety of hormones that orchestrate several complex physiological functions from growth to ovulation

plaques accumulations of fat and cholesterol on the endothelium

post traumatic stress disorder (PTSD) a form of acute stress disorder that persists for more than one month

potential stressors stimuli that may cause a stress response

prayer an address (as a petition) to God or a god in word or thought

prejudice a preconceived judgment or opinion about someone or something

primary appraisal the part of the initial appraisal of the potential stressor that answers the question: "Is it a threat to me?"

primary stressor the original stressor that triggers the stress response

proactive an approach to things based on acting rather than reacting to situations

problem-focused coping coping that focuses on changing either the environment related to the potential stressor, or doing something to change the way the potential stressor affects the person; rather than changing the way the potential stressor is viewed, one finds different ways of managing it

procrastination a tendency to put tasks off until later

prodrome a group of symptoms occurring before the onset of illness

psychogenic psychosomatic illnesses without a causative germ

psychological pertaining to the functions of the human mind; includes thoughts, feelings, memories, sensations, and associations

psychoneuroimmunology the emerging field that studies the effects of stressful emotions on immune functioning

psychosomatic the interaction of the mind and body in the disease process

puberty a biological term used to describe a variety of bodily changes associated with physical maturation from childhood to adulthood

racial profiling the practice of singling out individuals as potential suspects based only on their race

rape sexual activity directed at a person without that person's consent; includes date/acquaintance rape, stranger rape, marital rape, gang rape, and statutory rape

readjustments the body's physiological adaptations to life events

reduce the second level of defense against stress; revolves around finding one's optimal level of stimulation by cutting back on the overall volume of stressors in one's life

reflected light the illumination that bounces or bends off another object and then enters a person's field of vision

relationship quality the subjective assessment of the quality of the support one receives from his/her social networks

relaxation response a popular form of focused meditation developed by Herbert Benson of Harvard University that incorporates the key elements of transcendental meditation (TM)

relaxed state a state of being characterized by the decrease of key physiological processes such as muscle tension, heart rate, breathing rate, and blood pressure; it is also accompanied by a passive mental state

religion an organized system of worship and belief that includes faith and spirituality

religiosity a formal measure of the level of religious practice that includes attendance at services, participation in church-related activities, etc.

reorganization changing the structure of the units within an organization; this affects whom they report to and how they work together or independently

reorganize the fifth line of defense against stress; reorganize is based on changing the way you view your health to make it a higher priority as a defense against stress

repetitive motion injuries injuries to the soft tissues as a result of performing ergonomically incorrect tasks over and over, day in and day out

reproductive readiness the state of complete adult physiological maturation

resistance the second phase of GAS, in which the body attempts to maintain homeostasis in the face of chronic stressors

responding skills verbal or nonverbal feedback skills used to respond to an initiator of a dialogue that involve reacting to the initiator's message

rethink changing the way we think about the world and potential stressors

reticular activating system (RAS) a collection of neurons running through the three regions of the brain stem that is responsible for sending messages between the higher parts of the brain (which control thoughts and awareness) to the lower parts (responsible for the activities of organs, muscles, and glands)

road rage a stress reaction characterized by feelings of extreme impatience, anxiety, and intense anger while driving a vehicle

romantic love involves passion and intimacy but not commitment

rotating shifts work hour blocks that change or rotate on a regular basis; for example, switching from working days to working nights every two weeks

satellite values values that are less important to us and more open to compromise and change

scale of living an arbitrary measure of personal affluence and comfort in terms of income, possessions, and achievements

seasonal pattern specifier a shift from manic to depressive states that is influenced by the change in seasons, and concurrent weather and daylight changes; formerly called *seasonal affective disorder (SAD)*

secondary appraisal the part of the initial appraisal of the potential stressor that answers the question: " Can I cope with this?"

secondary stressor our illogical thoughts about the primary stressor that keep the response alive long after the initial event has passed

secondhand noise noise generated by others that invades your personal environment

secular something that is not overtly or specifically religious in nature

self-talk a person's inner dialogue

sense of autonomy a feeling of freedom and independence that children develop along with self-esteem and self-control as they are allowed to explore their environment and master simple tasks like toilet training

sense of trust a feeling of comfort, hope, and faith that infants develop in response to having their basic needs (food, cleanliness, safety, physical contact) met

sensory relating to nerve messages coming into the brain

sensory area the part of the cerebral cortex that controls nerve messages coming into the brain from the senses

serotonin, dopamine, epinephrine amine neurotransmitters that act like antidepressants to enhance mood and trigger feelings of mild euphoria

sexual arousal disorders sexual dysfunctions related to the arousal phase of the sexual response cycle

sexual desire disorders sexual disfunctions that relate to the desire phase of the sexual response cycle

sexual harassment any unwelcome sexual advances or requests for sexual favors, and other verbal or physical conduct of a sexual nature

situation factors originally called *factors in the stimulus configuration,* or *stimulus factors,* situation factors include the potential stressor (originally called the stimulus) novelty, predictability, event uncertainty, imminence, duration, and temporal uncertainty

skilled nursing facilities formerly known as nursing homes, a type of age-restricted living environment that provides the highest level of care and is equipped to handle seniors with acute or intensive medical care needs and offers posthospitalization and rehabilitation therapy

social embeddedness the number, stability, and complexity of connections individuals have to others in their social environments

social network an interrelated chain, system, or group of relationships composed of membership in both formal and informal groups and organizations

social relationships are our human connections with other individuals and groups. Social relationships can take many forms such as casual (associates at work), intimate (close friends), and sexual (lover, spouse)

social support the emotional (comforting, congratulating, loving, etc.), informational (spiritual guidance, personal and professional advice, role modeling, skill building, job referrals, etc.), and tangible (money, housing, etc.) resources people derive from their social relationships

soft tissue tissue other than bone

somatic nervous system the part of the peripheral nervous system under our voluntary control

somatogenic psychosomatic illness that involves a causative germ

sound meditation a form of focused meditation where the focal point used is man-made or natural sounds

spasms sudden, involuntary muscle twitches that range in severity from mild to very painful

specific anxiety disorder a type of anxiety disorder linked to an identifiable object, event, or situation

spirituality a sense of interconnectedness with something or someone beyond the self

sprain a traumatic injury to the tendons, muscles, or ligaments around a joint; characterized by pain, swelling, and discoloration of the skin

stereotype a standardized mental picture of members of a particular group that represents an oversimplified opinion, prejudiced attitude, or uncritical judgment

stimulation the state of being aroused, excited, energized, or forced to react in some way

strain minor muscular damage due to excessive physical effort; the wear and tear on body parts and systems as they fight to maintain homeostasis in response to stressors

strategy-based approach an approach to coping that uses individual coping strategies to cope with specific stressors as the need arises

stress a holistic transaction between an individual and a potential stressor resulting in a stress response

stress appraisal an assessment of a potential stressor that appraises it as a threat resulting in the initiation of a stress response

sympathetic nervous system the part of the autonomic nervous system that is responsible for activating the organs that maintain homeostasis

synergistic when the end result of adding two or more things together is greater than the sum of their parts

systematic muscle relaxation starting from one extremity (hands or feet) and systematically contracting and releasing all of the major muscle groups in the body

t'ai chi ch'uan a form of self defense originating in China, which blends physical movements with philosophical outlook

Taoism Chinese philosophy of life and religion, founded by Lao Tzu, that emphasizes the duality of life and opposing forces

telecommuting the practice of working for a business from a location other than the main place of business, such as a home or satellite office, through heavy use of modern communications technology

temperament a long-standing predisposition to a certain emotional state

tension partial shortening of a muscle

thalamus a hidden region of the brain often referred to as the gateway to the cerebral cortex, which serves as a relay center for all inputs to the cerebral cortex; plays a key role in mediating all sensations, motor activities, cortical arousal, and memory

threat the perception of harm

threat appraisal an anticipatory evaluation of harm or loss that has not yet occurred; during threat appraisal a person anticipates that something bad (threatening) will happen

time clock machines that keep track of the time of arrival to and departure from work for hourly employees

time management the process of systematically allocating one's time to maximize one's use and enjoyment of it

transaction an exchange involving two or more parties or events, which reciprocally affect one another during the process of the exchange

transcendental meditation (TM) a type of focused meditation popularized by Maharishi Mahesh Yogi from India

Type A personality a stress-prone personality characterized by aggressive, competitive, and hostile attitudes and behavior

Type B personality a personality type that is easygoing and noncompetitive and doesn't get angry or hostile easily

Type C personality a personality type also known as the helpless/hopeless personality because of the prominence of these emotions

uplifts happy, satisfying experiences (such as hearing your favorite song on the radio, eating your favorite food, taking a day off work, etc.) that characterize everyday transactions with the environment

vaginismus recurrent or persistent involuntary contraction of the perineal muscles surrounding the outer third of the vagina

values personal beliefs, morals, ethics, and/or ideals

ventilation the process of mixing outdoor air with indoor air through natural or artificial means

venture capital money available from private individuals and firms that specialize in lending capital to business ventures often deemed too risky by other financial institutions

weak links susceptible body parts or systems that break down under the wear and tear of chronic stressors

wellness a state of optimal health across six dimensions: physical, social, intellectual, emotional, spiritual, and environmental/occupational

word/phrase meditation a form of focused meditation where the focal point used is a word or a phrase

work centrality the central and fundamental role of work in the life of most individuals in industrialized nations

yoga an ancient Hindu ascetic philosophy that includes mental, physical, social, and spiritual components. The word *yoga* is derived from the Sanskrit (the ancient literary language of India) root word meaning "to yoke or join"

CREDITS

Text and Line Art Credits

CHAPTER 1
Assess Yourself 1-1.

From *Understanding Your Health,* 7th Ed., by Wayne A. Payne & Dale B. Hahn, copyright © 2002 by The McGraw-Hill Companies, Inc. Reprinted by permission.

Living Constructively: Basic Naikan Meditation.

Adapted from Krech, G. (2002). Naikan; Gratitude, Grace, and the Japanese Art of Self-Reflection: Berkeley CA: Stone Bridge Press. Used with permission.

CHAPTER 2
Figure 2-1.

MASLOW, ABRAHAM H.; FRAGER, ROBERT D. (EDITOR); FADIMAN, JAMES (EDITOR), MOTIVATION AND PERSONALITY, 3rd Edition, © 1987. Adapted by permission of Pearson Education, Inc., Upper Saddle River, NJ.

Figure 2-3.

From *Harditraining* by D.M. Khoshaba and S.R. Maddi, 1999. Newport Beach, CA: The Hardiness Institute. Reprinted by permission.

Table 2-3.

From *Stress Management and Wellness* 2nd edition by SCHAFER. © 1992. Reprinted with Permission of Wadsworth, a division of Thomson Learning: www.thomsonrights.com. Fax 800 730-2214.

CHAPTER 4
Assess Yourself 4-1 and 4-2.

Excerpt adapted from *Journal of Psychosomatic Research,* 11, T.H. Holmes and R.H. Rahe, "Social Readjustment Rating Scale," 1967 with permission from Elsevier Science.

Diverse Perspectives 4.2.

Adapted from *Myths & Assumptions about LGB People,* The Texas Woman's University Counseling Center. Used with permission.

CHAPTER 5
Living Constructively: Mistaken Attention.

Adapted from Krech, G. (2005) *Life is a Matter of Attention.* Audio Program. Middlebury, VT: ToDo Institute. Used with Permission.

CHAPTER 6
Assess Yourself 6-1.

From *Understanding Your Health,* 7th Ed., by Wayne A. Payne & Dale B. Hahn, copyright © 2002 by The McGraw-Hill Companies, Inc. Reprinted by permission.

CHAPTER 7
Stress Buster Tips: Absurdity Library and Photo Funnies.

Both from From *Lighten Up: Survival Skills for People Under Pressure,* by C.W. Metcalf and R. Felible. Copyright © 1992 by C.W. Metcalf and Roma Felible. Reprinted by permission of Perseus Books publishers, a member of Perseus Books, L.L.C.

Stress Buster Tips: Establishing Your Daily Life Criteria.

Adapted from Anderson, L., & Krech, G., (1996). *A Finger Pointing to the Moon.* Middlebury, VT: ToDo Institute. Used with Permission.

Living Constructively: Changing Your Perspective by Paying Attention.

Adapted from Krech, G. (2005). "Working with Your Attention." *Distance Learning Course: Exercises and Daily Journal.* Middlebury, VT: ToDo Institute. Used with Permission.

Stress Buster Tips: Close Up.

Adapted from Anderson, L., & Krech, G., (1996). *A Finger Pointing to the Moon.* Middlebury, VT: ToDo Institute. Used with Permission.

Assess Yourself 7-1.

From *Values Clarification: A Handbook of Practical Strategies for Teachers and Students,* by Sidney B. Simon, Leland W. Howe and Howard Kirshenbaum, 1994, Values Press, Hadley MA 01035. Reprinted by permission.

Assess Yourself 7-6, 7-7.

Both from *Lighten Up: Survival Skills for People Under Pressure,* by C.W. Metcalf and R. Felible. Copyright © 1992 by C.W. Metcalf and Roma Felible. Reprinted by permission of Perseus Books publishers, a member of Perseus Books, L.L.C.

CHAPTER 8
Stress Buster Tips: A 12-Step Guide for Junkaholics.

From "Clutter's Last Stand" by D. Aslet, Health, October 1994. Reprinted with Permission from Health, © 1994.

Stress Buster Tips: "Open Ended Statements for Keeping People Talking."

From *Conversationally Speaking* by A. Garner, copyright © 1980 by The McGraw-Hill Companies, Inc. Reprinted by permission.

Assess Yourself 8-5.

From *Understanding Your Health,* 7th Ed., by Wayne A. Payne & Dale B. Hahn, copyright © 2002 by The McGraw-Hill Companies, Inc. Reprinted by permission.

Living Constructively: Thirty Thousand Days.

Adapted from Anderson, L., & Krech, G. Resource Materials; Residential Certification Program in Japanese Psychology. Middlebury, VT: ToDo Institute. Used with permission.

CHAPTER 9
Living Constructively: Letting Go Mindfully.

Adapted from Anderson, L., and Krech, G. (2003). Resource Materials; Working With Your Attention: Distance Leraning Program. Middlebury, VT: ToDo Institute. Used with permission.

CHAPTER 10
Stress Buster Tips: "Jogging/Running 10 Week Program."

From THE AEROBICS PROGRAM FOR TOTAL WELL BEING by Kenneth H. Cooper, M.D., M.P.H., copyright © 1982 by Kenneth

H. Cooper. Used by permission of Bantam Books, a division of Random House, Inc.

CHAPTER 11
Stress Buster Tips: Reorganize your energy by making healthier food choices.

From *Understanding Your Health,* 7th Ed., by Wayne A. Payne & Dale B. Hahn, copyright © 2002 by The McGraw-Hill Companies, Inc. Reprinted by permission.

Living Constructively: Life at the To-Do Institute.

Adapted from Anderson, L., and Krech, G. (2005). Residential Certification Course in Japanese Therapy. Monkton, VT: ToDo Institute, Used with permission.

CHAPTER 12
Diverse Perspectives 12-2.

From Masters Et Al, *Human Sexuality,* 4e. Published by Allyn and Bacon, Boston, MA. Copyright © 1992 by Pearson Education. Reprinted by permission of the publisher.

Table 12-1.

"Figure of Erickson's Stages of Personality Development", from *CHILDHOOD AND SOCIETY* by Erik H. Erickson. Copyright 1950 © 1963 by W.W. Norton & Company, Inc., renewed © 1978, 1991 by Erik H. Erikson. Reprinted by permission of W.W. Norton & Company, Inc.

CHAPTER 13
Asses Yourself 13-2.

"Sternberg's Love Scale" from *The Triangle of Love* by Robert J. Sternberg, 1988 Basic Books, Inc. Reprinted by permission of the author.

Figures 13-2, 13-4, 13-5.

From Healthy Sexuality (with InfoTrac) 1st edition by BLONNA/LEVITAN. © 2005. Reprinted with permission of Brooks/Cole, a division of Thomson Learning: www.thomsonrights.com. Fax 800 730-2214.

CHAPTER 14
Table 14-1.

From Cary S. Kart, *The Realities of Aging: An Introduction to Gerontology 4e.* Published by Allyn and Bacon, Boston, MA. Copyright © 1994 by Pearson Education. Adapted by permission of the publisher.

Table 14-2.

From Masters Et Al, *Human Sexuality,* 4e. Published by Allyn and Bacon, Boston, MA. Copyright © 1992 by Pearson Education. Reprinted by permission of the publisher.

Table 14-3.

From *Understanding Your Health,* 7th Ed., by Wayne A. Payne & Dale B. Hahn, copyright © 2002 by The McGraw-Hill Companies, Inc. Reprinted by permission.

Stress Buster Tips: Easing the Grieving Process.

From *Understanding Your Health,* 7th Ed., by Wayne A. Payne & Dale B. Hahn, copyright © 2002 by The McGraw-Hill Companies, Inc. Reprinted by permission.

Stress Buster Tips: Fighting Fairly.

From *An Invitation to Health* (Non-Info Trac Version) 9th edition by HALES. © 2001. Reprinted with permission of Brooks/Cole, a division of Thomson Learning: www.thomsonrights.com. Fax 800 730-2214.

Photo Credits

Page 4: © Steve Cole/Getty Images; **34**: © Digital Vision/Getty Images; **49**: The McGraw-Hill Companies, Inc./Gary He, photographer; **64**: © M. Freeman/PhotoLink/Photodisc/Getty Images; **66**: © Creatas/PunchStock; **69**: © Arthur S. Aubry/Getty Images; **75**: © Royalty-Free/Corbis; **78**: © Getty Images; **88**: © Ryan McVay/Getty Images; **92**: AP Photo/Jerry Torrens; **96**: © Jack Star/PhotoLink/Getty Images; **101**: © Thinkstock; 107: © Royalty-Free/Corbis; **124**: © Ryan McVay/Getty Images; **141**: © PhotoLink/Photodisc/Getty Images; **158**: © Mel Curtis/Getty Images; **183**: © Ryan McVay/Getty Images; **210**: © Neil Beer/Photodisc/Getty Images; **214**: © Rim Light/Photodisc/Getty Images; **260**: © Ryan McVay/Getty Images; **265**: © Photodisc; **278**: © Monica Lau/Getty Images; **281**: © Digital Vision; **289**: © C. Borland/PhotoLink/Getty Images; **295**: © Jacobs Stock Photography/Getty Images; **297**: © Brand X Pictures/PunchStock; **298**: © Greg Kuchik/Getty Images; **305**: © PhotoLink/Getty Images; **317**: (Left) © Digital Vision/Getty Images; **319**: © Stockbyte/PunchStock; **323**: © Royalty-Free/Corbis; **325**: © Steve Smith/Getty Images; **328**: © Masterfile Royalty Free; **329**: Comstock Images; **331, 339**: © Ryan McVay/Getty Images; **340**: (Left to right) © Steve Mason/Getty Images, © Ryan McVay/Getty Images; **363**: © David Hiller/Getty Images; **366**: © Royalty-Free/Corbis; **368**: © Ryan McVay/Getty Images; **371**: (top) © Keith Brofsky/Photodisc/Getty Images, (bottom) Photodisc/Getty Images; **377**: © Photodisc/Getty Images; **383**: © Keith Brofsky/Photodisc/Getty Images

INDEX

Page numbers in **bold** type indicate definitions. Page numbers in *italic* type indicate figures or tables.

A

B

D

E

F

L

M

P

Q

R

S

T

U

V

W

Y